A New
Reference
Grammar
of Modern
Spanish

A New Reference Grammar of Modern *Spanish*

J O H N   B U T T   &
C A R M E N   B E N J A M I N

THIRD EDITION

McGraw-Hill

*A Division of The **McGraw·Hill** Companies*

McGraw-Hill

A Division of The McGraw·Hill Companies

Library of Congress Cataloging-in-Publication Data

Butt, John, 1943–
  A new reference grammar of modern Spanish / John Butt & Carmen Benjamin. – 3rd ed.
    p. cm.
  Includes bibliographical references (p.) and index.
  ISBN 0-658-00873-0
  1. Spanish language–Grammar. I. Benjamin, Carmen. II. Title.

PC4112.B88 2000
468.2'421–dc21
                                               99-047014

This edition first published 2000 by McGraw-Hill,
A Division of The McGraw-Hill Companies
4255 West Touhy Avenue, Lincolnwood (Chicago), Illinois 60712–1975, U.S.A.

Copyright © 2000, 1994, 1988 John Butt and Carmen Benjamin

Originally published by Edward Arnold, a member of the Hodder Headline Group.

6 7 8 9 10

International Standard Book Number: 0–658–00873–0

Printed in Malta

Contents

Preface to the third edition

This reference grammar offers a comprehensive description of the syntax and morphology of the plain written and spoken Spanish of Spain and Latin America at the close of the twentieth century.

Spanish is the main language of twenty-one countries,[1] and it will have more native speakers than English by the year 2000 (English will have more non-native speakers). This vast extension inevitably ensures that the language is a good deal less unified than French, German or even English, the latter more or less standardized according to either American or British norms.

This diversity has become more noticeable since the 1950s. Until the 1960s, the criteria of internationally correct Spanish were dictated by the *Real Academia Española*, and its decisions were more or less observed by literate persons everywhere. But the Academy has lost prestige, and even in Spain its most solemn decrees are hardly taken seriously – witness the fate of the spelling reforms laid out in the *Nuevas normas de prosodia y ortografía* of 1959, which were supposed to be applied in all Spanish-speaking countries and, some forty years later, are still wholly or partly ignored by publishers and literate persons. The question of what is 'correct' Spanish is therefore nowadays really decided, as in all living languages, by the more or less conscious consensus of native speakers of Spanish; but international agreement about grammar and vocabulary is obviously difficult to achieve between so many independent, far-flung and sometimes mutually hostile countries.

At the same time, the prestige of the various varieties of Latin-American Spanish has risen sharply, thanks to the international success of Latin-American literature, so the day is now long past when one could claim that the only Spanish worthy of serious study and imitation is the standard language of Spain, based on the Castilian dialect of the North and Centre, and nowadays spoken by less than eight per cent of the Spanish-speaking world. However, now that this European model has lost ground, it has not been replaced by any one national variety of Spanish to which other countries and regions defer. This situation will last in the foreseeable future.

This does not mean that Spanish is no longer one language: provided slang and popular local expressions are avoided, anyone who speaks one variety well

---

[1] Argentina, Bolivia, Chile, Colombia, Costa Rica, Cuba, the Dominican Republic, Ecuador, Equatorial Guinea (on the African Atlantic coast between Gabon and Cameroon), Guatemala, Honduras, Mexico, Nicaragua, Panama, Paraguay, Peru, Puerto Rico, El Salvador, Spain, Uruguay and Venezuela.

can travel the Spanish-speaking world with far fewer problems of communication than Englishmen, Americans or Australians meet in many parts of the English-speaking world. But at the level of detail at which textbooks like this must work, there are regional and national variations of vocabulary and, to a much lesser extent, syntax, that make it difficult to lay down the law about 'correct' or even preferred Spanish usage. These differences not only separate European from 'Latin-American' Spanish. Strictly speaking, the latter does not exist: Mexican, Cuban, Colombian, Peruvian, Argentine and all the other national varieties differ from one another, above all and often quite markedly in colloquial and popular vocabulary, and Mexican and Argentine Spanish, for example, differ as much from one another as does the Spanish of Spain from Argentine Spanish or Cuban from Bolivian.

This problem of diversity becomes more serious beyond the intermediary stage. It disheartens foreign students to find that the fifth edition of *Collins Spanish–English English–Spanish* dictionary, in its definition of the noun *chiva*, which in Spain means 'she-goat' or 'kid' (of a goat), also gives fifteen different regional Latin-American definitions, including 'goatee', 'bus', 'car', 'blanket', 'bedclothes', 'naughty girl', 'mannish woman', 'immoral woman', 'knapsack', 'tantrum', 'junk', 'tall story', 'informer' and 'alert' (but the average native Spanish-speaker will know only a few of these meanings). The dimensions of the problem become clearer when one reads such headlines in a popular Peruvian daily as *Choros chupan tres palos a Cristal* ('Thieves steal three million *soles* from Crystal Brewery') or *Lorchos datean que los afilaron tres años* ('Peruvians claim they were trained for three years'), language that mystifies Mexicans as much as Spaniards. The lack of universal norms also poses a dilemma for fair-minded grammarians who are obliged to give foreign students some guidance about which forms they should imitate. Should foreign students imitate the widespread Latin-American construction *es con ella que quiero hablar* ('it's her that I want to talk to') when Spaniards insist on *es con ella **con la** que quiero hablar*? And can one claim that *dentro de* is the only valid translation of 'inside' when a writer as famous as Borges uses *adentro de* even in literary prose, a form considered totally incorrect in Spain?

To get round the problem, and at the same time to do justice to the variety of Spanish, we have tried to illustrate as many grammatical points as possible with both Spanish and Latin-American examples. At the same time we try to report as faithfully as possible which forms are acceptable or otherwise to educated Spaniards, and where no comment is made readers can assume that the Latin-American examples are also perfectly good instances of Peninsular Spanish. We hope that this method will give readers sense of authentic, living Spanish and also do justice to the plurality of the language. What we cannot guarantee, however, is that our Peninsular examples always also represent current usage in every part of Latin America. Some of our unattributed examples will amuse or puzzle Latin Americans, and it is doubtful whether any book could provide all the Latin-American alternatives to a typically Spanish phrase.

With rare exceptions, examples come from texts published since the 1960s, most of them from the 1980s and 1990s. Problems of space have obliged us to omit historical considerations. We also concentrate on syntactic and morphological questions: lexical issues such as word formation (except diminutive and other affective suffixes) are barely discussed, mainly because of lack of space, but also because teaching foreigners how to coin new words encourages badly-formed vocabulary. Questions of pronunciation have also been omitted as numerous guides to the sound system of Spanish are already available.

We assume that readers have a native knowledge of English and explanations have been shortened by reference to English wherever the languages seem to coincide. Since interference from French and occasionally Italian and Portuguese is a constant problem for teachers of Spanish, sporadic mention of these languages is made in order to emphasize some peculiarity of Spanish.

The term 'Latin-American' is used throughout in preference to the more accurate 'Spanish-American': the latter can be as annoying to Spanish-speaking Latin Americans as 'British-American' would no doubt be to most citizens of the USA.

In the third edition we have made numerous small alterations in the interest of clarity, brevity and precision, and we have added new material, especially on tenses, connectors and on the use of *se de matización*, i.e. *se* used to alter the meaning of common verbs like *ir, caer, llegar, morir, salir, volver*, etc. However, we have tried as far as possible to leave the section numbers unchanged so that readers of the second edition will adapt quickly to this new one.

Acknowledgements

We have availed ourselves of the labours of Andrés Bello, María Moliner, Ramsey and Spaulding and of other eminent grammarians and lexicographers, especially Manuel Seco: one disregards the recommendations of his *Diccionario de dudas y dificultades de la lengua española* at one's peril. Of the works mentioned in the bibliography we are particularly indebted to E. García (1975) and C. E. Kany (Chicago, 1945, reprinted and translated into Spanish). Three other works often supplied information, explanations and insights: R. Quirk et al. (1972), A. Judge and F. G. Healey (1983) and the first edition of A. E. Hammer (1971), perusal of which originally inspired the present work.

A very large number of Spanish-speakers from many countries have helped us and we cannot name them all: those who gave us most assistance are thanked in the prefaces to previous editions. This new edition is especially indebted to Nick Cowan, who generously read the manuscript and proofs, to Roger Wright, Hugh Attwooll, and above all to George DeMello of the University of Iowa, whose personal communications and numerous published statistical analyses of the syntax of spontaneous spoken Spanish have clarified many points. Antonia Moreira Rodríguez has once again made many valuable suggestions. We are nevertheless acutely aware that a book of this nature must contain mistakes, omissions and inaccuracies for which we alone are responsible.

John Butt and Carmen Benjamin
King's College London
London, 2000

Conventions, spelling and abbreviations

El mujer: a preceding asterisk marks a form that is not Spanish. It is occasionally also used for forms that may be heard but are very aberrant.

A preceding uninverted question mark *–?se puso detrás mío, ?se los dije–* shows that a form is doubtful or disputed and not accepted by all speakers.

'Colloquial' describes forms that are accepted in spontaneous educated speech but are usually avoided in formal speech or writing.

'Familiar' describes forms that are commonly heard in spontaneous speech but should be avoided or used with caution by foreign learners.

'Popular' describes commonly heard forms that may be stigmatized by some speakers as uneducated.

Forms separated by / are alternatives, either alternatives that have different meanings but use the same construction, e.g. *yo sé/él sabe* 'I know'/'he knows', or alternative ways of saying the same thing, e.g. *antes de que/antes que* 'before'. Words in round brackets may be optionally deleted with no or only slight effect on meaning or style, e.g. *con tal (de) que* 'provided that'.

Except where indicated, all examples represent usage worthy of imitation by foreigners, and the Latin-American quotations are also good European Spanish unless we state otherwise. Words that represent the speech of fictional characters are marked 'dialogue' to show that they reflect spoken usage and to avoid their language being attributed to their author.

The spelling of Spanish words observes the Academy's rules laid down in the *Nuevas normas de prosodia y ortografía* of 1959, although we follow general usage where this is clearly at odds with the Academy's prescriptions. In the cases of the word *sólo/solo* 'only'/'alone' and of the demonstrative pronouns *éste/este, ése/ese, aquél/aquel*, modern written usage usually deliberately flouts the Academy's current rules (which say that the accent is optional) and we show both forms. The spellings *México, mexicano* are used throughout for *Méjico, mejicano* on the grounds that Mexicans prefer them, as does the prestigious Spanish daily *El País*.

English spelling is British, but American alternatives are regularly shown except in the case of 'preterit', where the British form 'preterite' is used throughout. In some constantly occurring cases, like 'col(o)ur', 'neighbo(u)r', 'judg(e)ment', readers who use US spelling can mentally delete the bracketed letter.

Spanish regularly omits subject pronouns and does not systematically mark sex, number or person in its object pronouns. Thus in the absence of contextual clues, *se lo daba* means 'I gave it to her/him/them/you', 'he/she gave it to him/ her/them/you', 'you (*usted*) gave it to him/her/them/you', '(s)he gave it to himself/herself', and so on. One cannot show all the possibilities all the time, but the temptation to translate such sentences always using masculine English pronouns is misleading and possibly shows sexual bias. For this reason we often use the unsightly form '(s)he' in the translations, or arbitrarily put 'she' rather than 'he', if only to recall that native speakers of Spanish do not automatically conjure up a mental picture of a man on hearing the verb *tosió* '(s)he/you/it coughed'.

The following abbreviations are used:

Esbozo	Real Academia de la Lengua, *Esbozo de una nueva gramática de la lengua española* (Madrid, 1973)
lit.	'literally', 'literal translation'
Nuevas normas	*Nuevas normas de prosodia y ortografía. Nuevo texto definitivo* (Madrid, 1959)
Lat. Am.	Latin America(n)

1

Gender of nouns

1.1 General

All nouns in Spanish are either masculine or feminine in gender, except for one or two nouns of undecided gender. There are, however, some neuter pronouns: see Chapter 7. Discussion of the gender of Spanish nouns is made clearer by dividing nouns into two groups:

(a) Nouns referring to humans, to domesticated animals, and a few wild animals,: see section 1.2.

(b) Nouns referring to inanimate things or to plants, or to animals not included in group **(a)**: see sections 1.3 and 1.4.

The gender of the nouns in group **(a)** almost always depends on the sex of the person or animal in question. With very few exceptions, the masculine noun is also used in the plural to refer to a mixed group of males and females: *los padres* = 'fathers' and also 'parents', *los hermanos* = 'brothers' and also 'brothers and sisters', *los gatos* = 'tom-cats' and 'cats' in general.

The gender of nouns in group **(b)** has nothing to do with sex and is strictly speaking arbitrary: the Latin *arbor* 'tree' was feminine, its Spanish descendant *árbol* is masculine. The gender of these nouns is a property of the word, not of what the word refers to, so one should memorize each noun with an accompanying article: *la mesa* 'table', **un libro** 'book'.

1.2 Nouns referring to human beings and domesticated animals (and a few wild animals)

Nouns referring to male human beings or to male domesticated animals and to the male of a few well-known wild animals such as wolves, lions, tigers, elephants, bears and foxes, are almost always masculine, and those referring to females are feminine.

The gender of these nouns is more biological in Spanish than in French, where the masculine nouns *le professeur* or *le docteur* can refer to a woman and *une recrue* (fem.) 'recruit' can be a man, or in Italian where a policeman may be *la guardia*. (Forms like *la recluta*, *la centinela* used to be applied to men in Golden-Age Spanish, but one now says *el recluta* for a male recruit, *la recluta* for a female.) However, a few Spanish nouns of fixed gender, e.g. *la víctima*, *la celebridad*, may refer to both males and females: see 1.2.11 for a selection.

1.2.1 Special forms for male and female

Some nouns have special forms for the male and female which must be learnt separately. The following list is not exhaustive:

> *el abad/la abadesa* abbot/abbess
> *el actor/la actriz* actor/actress
> *el barón/la baronesa* baron/baroness
> *el caballo/la yegua* stallion/mare
> *el macho/la cabra** billy-goat/nanny-goat
> *el carnero/la oveja** ram/ewe (sheep)
> *el conde/la condesa* count/countess
> *el duque/la duquesa* duke/duchess
> *el emperador/la emperatriz* emperor/empress
> *el gallo/la gallina** cockerel/hen (or chicken)
> *el héroe/la heroína* hero/heroine (or heroin)
> *el jabalí/la jabalina* wild boar/wild sow
> *el marido/la mujer* husband/wife (or woman)
> *el padre/la madre* father/mother
> *el príncipe/la princesa* prince/princess
> *el rey/la reina* king/queen
> *el sacerdote/la sacerdotisa* priest/female priest
> *el toro/la vaca** bull/cow
> *el yerno/la nuera* son/daughter-in-law (*la yerna* is heard in parts of Lat. Am.)
> *el varón* (or *el macho*)/*la hembra* male/female

Notes

(i) Asterisks mark a feminine form which is also used for the species in general. Normally the masculine is the generic form: *los caballos* = 'horses'.
(ii) In Lat. Am. one should use *la esposa* for 'wife'. but *mujer* means both 'woman' and 'wife' in Spain.
(iii) *El varón* = 'human male' and *el macho* = 'male of an animal'.

1.2.2 Feminine of nouns ending in -o

The great majority of nouns referring to human beings or to the animals included in this group make their feminine in *-a*:

> *el abuelo/la abuela* grandfather/grandmother
> *el amigo/la amiga* friend
> *el candidato/la candidata* candidate
> *el ganso/la gansa* gander/goose
> *el gato/la gata* cat
> *el hermano/la hermana* brother/sister
> *el novio/la novia* boyfriend/girlfriend
> *el oso/la osa* bear/she-bear
> *el perro/la perra* dog/bitch
> *el tío/la tía* uncle/aunt

Some words denoting professions or activities are invariable, the sex of the person referred to being shown by an article or adjective:

> *el/la modelo* model; *modelos francesas* 'female French models'
> *el/la piloto* pilot/racing driver
> *el/la reo* accused (in court)
> *el/la soldado* soldier; *una soldado israelí* 'an Israeli woman soldier'
> *el/la soprano* soprano
> *el/la testigo* witness (*la testiga* is popular Spanish)

Others, like *el médico/la médica* 'doctor', are controversial. See 1.2.7.

1.2.3 Feminine of nouns ending in *-or*, *-ón*, *-ín*, *-és*

These add *-a* when they refer to a female:

el asesor/la asesora adviser/consultant
el anfitrión/la anfitriona host/hostess
el bailarín/la bailarina dancer
el burgués/la burguesa bourgeois
el campeón/la campeona champion

el doctor/la doctora doctor
el león/la leona lion/lioness
el profesor/la profesora teacher
el programador/la programadora programmer

Notes

(i) Adjectives (which in Spanish can almost always double as nouns) ending in -és make their feminine in -a: *el francés/la francesa* 'Frenchman'/'Frenchwoman'. The only important exception is *cortés/descortés* 'courteous'/ 'discourteous' (masc. and fem. singular; the plural is *(des)corteses*). Adjectives are discussed in detail in Chapter 4.

(ii) *El/la peatón* 'pedestrian' seems to be the only invariable noun ending in -ón: *la peatón recibió graves heridas* (*La Voz de Galicia*, Spain, confirmed by native informants), 'the female pedestrian received severe injuries'.

1.2.4 Nouns ending in *-a*

These are invariable:

el/la artista artist
el/la astronauta astronaut
el/la atleta athlete
el/la colega colleague/workmate

el/la guía guide (*la guía* also 'guidebook')
el/la socialista socialist

However, *el modisto* 'fashion designer' is well-established in everyday Peninsular usage: *todo las separa, los lazos de sangre, el destino, e incluso los modistos* (*El Mundo*, Spain) 'everything stands between them, blood ties, fate and even fashion designers'. Seco (1998), 299 and *El País* recommend *el modista* 'fashion designer', *la modista* 'dressmaker'/'woman fashion designer'.

1.2.5 Feminine of nouns ending in *-nte*

The majority are invariable:

el/la adolescente adolescent
el/la agente police officer/agent
el/la amante lover

el/la cantante singer
el/la representante representative

But a few feminine forms in *-nta* are in standard use (at least in Spain; they may be unacceptable in parts of Latin America):

el acompañante/la acompañanta companion/escort
el asistente/la asistenta batman (military)/daily help (or cleaner)
el cliente/la clienta customer (some speakers prefer *la cliente*)
el comediante/la comedianta* actor/'actress'
el dependiente/la dependienta shop assistant/(US) 'sales clerk'
el pariente/la parienta relative
el principiante/la principianta beginner (young Peninsular informants preferred *la principiante*)
el sirviente/la sirvienta servant

(*These words tend to be derogatory in Peninsular usage, particularly the feminine: *¡qué comediante/a eres!* 'what an act you put on!' Polite forms are *actor cómico/actriz cómica* 'comic actor'.)

Note

The following also occur, the invariable form being more formal: *el/la asistente social* 'social worker' (also *la asistenta social*), *el/la presidente* 'president' (also *la presidenta*, which Seco, 1998, 354, recommends). Forms like **la estudianta* for *la estudiante* are considered substandard. A few popular nouns/adjectives form a feminine in *-nta*: *el golfante/la golfanta* 'lout'/'good-for-nothing', *el atorrante/la atorranta* (Lat. Am.) 'tramp'/'slacker' (US) 'bum', *dominanta* 'bossy'/'pushy' (applied to women).

1.2.6 Feminine of other nouns ending in -e or in a consonant

Apart from those already mentioned in the preceding section, these are mostly invariable:

el/la alférez subaltern	*el/la joven* young man/woman
el/la enlace union representative/ (British) shop steward	*el/la rehén* hostage
el/la intérprete interpreter	*el/la mártir* martyr
el/la líder (political) leader	*el/la tigre* (or *la tigresa*) tiger

But *el huésped/la huéspeda* 'guest' (also *la huésped*), *el monje/la monja* 'monk'/ 'nun', *el sastre/la sastra* 'tailor'. For *la jefa* see 1.2.7.

1.2.7 Feminine of nouns referring to professions

Until the last third of the twentieth century feminine forms of professional or educational titles had pejorative or comic overtones or denoted the wife of the male, cf. *el bachiller* (someone who has passed the equivalent of the baccalaureat or pre-university examination), *la bachillera* 'bluestocking' (i.e. a woman sneered at for being too intellectual), *el sargento/la sargenta* 'sergeant'/'battleaxe' (i.e. a fierce woman), *el general/la generala* 'general'/'the general's wife'.

In parts of the Spanish-speaking world, especially in Spain, a lingering stigma still attaches to the feminine form of words referring to professionals, so formal language tends to show respect by using the masculine form with a feminine article, e.g. *el/la abogado* 'lawyer'/'legal counsel' (*la abogada*, originally 'intercessionary saint', is, however, now widespread for a woman lawyer).

In the case of the following words, the masculine form (preceded by *la* or *una*) may be used to show respect. The bracketed forms are gaining ground but may be avoided:

El/la catedrático 'professor'[1] (*la catedrática*); *el/la juez*: *El País* insists on *la juez*. In Spain *la jueza* may still mean 'the judge's wife' in rural usage. ***El/la médico*** doctor. *La médica* is spreading and is considered normal in much of Latin America, cf. *una médica blanca sudafricana* (*Granma*, Cuba) 'a white South-African female doctor', but it is thought disrespectful by many speakers of European Spanish. *Doctora* is, however, normal as a form of address.

El/la miembro 'member' (of clubs); also *el socio/la socia* (the old use in slang of *la socia* for 'prostitute' seems now to have disappeared). ***El/la ministro*** 'minister' is common, but *la ministra* is increasingly acceptable. Both ***la primer ministro*** and

---

[1] *El catedrático* = 'professor' in the European sense, i.e. someone who occupies a university chair or *cátedra* and is often, but not always, head of the department. US 'professor' = *profesor universitario*.

la primera ministra are used for a woman prime minister. The former is more common, although *El País* and Manuel Seco both recommend *la primera ministra*. In much of Latin America **la jefa** is an accepted feminine of *el/la jefe* 'boss', but it may sound disrespectful or too colloquial in Spain. Compare also *Maruja había sido . . . jefe de relaciones públicas* (G. García Márquez, Colombia) 'Maruja had been . . . head of public relations.'

Other nouns in -*o* may be regular: *el arquitecto/la arquitecta* 'architect', *el biólogo/la bióloga* 'biologist', *el filósofo/la filósofa* 'philosopher', *el letrado/la letrada* 'counsel'/'legal representative', *el político/la política* 'politician', *el sociólogo/la socióloga* 'sociologist', etc. Nevertheless, forms like *la arquitecto, la filósofo, la letrado* 'legal counsel' may be preferred in Spain and are common in respectful language.

The feminine form is often used when the woman referred to is not present: *¿qué tal te llevas con la nueva jefa?* 'how are you getting on with your new woman boss?', but *me han dicho que usted es la jefe del departamento* 'they tell me that you are the head of the department'; *ha llegado otra clienta* 'another woman customer has come', but in her presence *atiende a esta cliente* 'serve this customer'.

1.2.8 Nouns referring to mixed groups of males and females

With rare exceptions (some noted at 1.2), the masculine plural denotes either a group of males, or of males and females. In fact the masculine plural is usually assumed, out of context, to refer to both sexes, which is confusing for English speakers: *¿tienes hermanos?* is taken to mean 'have you got any brothers or sisters?'; 'have you got any brothers?' would be said *¿cuántos hermanos tienes?* *Hoy vienen los padres de los niños* = 'the children's parents are coming today'. 'The children's fathers are coming' would have to be clarified by *vienen los padres de los niños – los padres solos* (= 'the fathers on their own'):

los hijos children/sons	*los perros* dogs/male dogs
los ingleses the English/Englishmen	*los reyes* the king and the queen/
los niños children/little boys	kings and queens/kings
los profesores teachers/male teachers	

Feminine nouns refer only to females, so the masculine noun is obligatory in sentences like *no tengo más amigos que mujeres* 'the only friends I have are women' or *todos los profesores son mujeres* 'all the teachers are women'. **No tengo más amigas que mujeres* means 'the only female friends I have are women'!

Care must be taken with words like *uno, otro*. If a woman from Madrid says *todos los madrileños me caen gordos* 'all Madrid people get on my nerves' one could reply *¡pero tú eres uno de ellos!* 'but you're one of them!', but not * *. . . una de ellos*, since *madrileños* includes both males and females.[2] Compare also *Ana es una de las profesoras* 'Ana is one of the women teachers' and *Ana es uno de los profesores* 'Ana is one of the teachers (who include men as well). However, this principle is not applied consistently. In sentences like the following use of the feminine noun does not necessarily exclude males: *María es la mejor profesora del instituto* 'Maria's the best teacher in the school (may or may not include males), *Emilia Pardo Bazán*

---

[2] *Pero ¡tú también eres madrileña!* 'But you're from Madrid too!' avoids the problem.

es la mejor intérprete de la vida rural de toda la literatura española del siglo XIX 'Emilia Pardo Bazán is the best interpreter of rural life in the whole of 19th-century Spanish literature.'

Ambiguity must be removed in sentences like *Emilia Pardo Bazán es la mayor novelista **femenina** española del siglo pasado* 'Emilia Pardo Bazán is the greatest Spanish woman novelist of the last century'; *la mayor novelista española* could be read either as 'the greatest novelist' or as 'the greatest woman novelist'. However, context usually makes the issue clear.

In some cases usage seems uncertain. A woman might say either *unos están a favor y otros en contra. Yo soy de **las** que están a favor* or *. . . de **los** que están a favor* 'some are for, others are against. I'm one of those who are for it.'

1.2.9 Gender of inanimate nouns when applied to humans

Feminine nouns applied to male humans may acquire masculine gender:

***una** bala perdida*	stray bullet	***un** bala perdida*	ne'er-do-well/waster
la cámara	camera	*el cámara*	cameraman
la piel	skin	*el piel roja*	redskin
la primera clase	first class	*un primera clase*	someone first-class
la superventa	top sale	*el superventa*	top seller (male)
la trompeta	trumpet	*el trompeta*	trumpet-player
etc.			

The reverse case is better avoided: *la que toca la trompeta* 'the woman playing the trumpet', not *la trompeta*, which is the instrument.

1.2.10 Gender of names applied across sex boundaries

A female's name applied to a male acquires masculine gender: *tú eres **un** Margaret Thatcher* 'you're a Margaret Thatcher' (said to a man of his right-wing political ideas). But men's names usually remain masculine: *María, tú eres **un** Hitler con faldas* 'Maria, you're a female Hitler' (lit. 'Hitler with skirts').

1.2.11 Nouns of invariable gender applied to either sex

Some common words applied to human beings do not change their gender. One says *el bebé está enfermo* 'the baby is ill', whatever its sex:[3]

el ángel angel		*el genio* genius
la calamidad calamity		*el ligue* 'date'/casual boy or girlfriend
la celebridad celebrity		*la persona* person
el desastre disaster		*el personaje* character (in novels, etc.)
el esperpento 'fright'/weird-looking person		*(eres) un sol* you're wonderful/an angel
la estrella star (TV, etc.)		*la víctima* victim

and a few other masculine nouns referring to women, most involving sexual innuendo or comparisons with objects, cf. *el pendón* 'trollop' (lit. 'pennant'), *el marimacho* 'tomboy', etc.

Note

The titles *Alteza* 'Highness', *Excelencia*, *Ilustrísima* 'Grace' (title of bishops) and *Majestad* 'Majesty'

---

[3] *Bebé* used to be considered a Gallicism in Spain but it is now often heard for the more common *niño/niña*.

are feminine, but the person addressed keeps his/her gender: *Su Majestad estará cansado* (to the king), 'Your Majesty must be tired'.

1.3 Nouns referring to animals not included under 1.2.1–1.2.11

Animals not included in the preceding sections – i.e. most wild animals – are treated as inanimates. The noun is of fixed, arbitrary gender:

la araña spider	*el castor* beaver	*el puma* puma
la ardilla squirrel	*la marsopa* porpoise	*la rana* frog
la ballena whale	*la nutria* otter	*el sapo* toad
el canguro[4] kangaroo	*el panda* panda	*el tejón* badger

If sex must be distinguished, the male is denoted by adding *macho* 'male' and the female by adding *hembra* 'female': *la ardilla macho* 'male squirrel', *el cangrejo hembra* 'female crab', etc. Agreement of adjectives in good Spanish is with the noun, not with the animal: *la rana macho está muerta* 'the male frog is dead', *el ratón hembra es blanco* 'the female mouse is white' Neither *macho* nor *hembra* agrees in gender or number: *las cebras macho* 'male zebras', *los gavilanes hembra* 'female sparrowhawks'.

Note

Familiar language and popular journalism tend to give such nouns biological gender: *el/la gorila* 'he-gorilla' and 'she-gorilla' (properly invariably **el** *gorila*), *el/la jirafa* 'giraffe' (**la** *jirafa* is properly invariably feminine).

1.4 Gender of nouns referring to inanimates

The gender of nouns referring to lifeless things (and to plants) must be learnt for each noun. The gender is arbitrary and cannot be predicted from the meaning of the word. It also has no sexual implications and occasionally varies from place to place or century to century (e.g. Golden-Age *la puente*, modern *el puente* 'bridge').

There are few infallible rules, and only those are quoted which in our view do not encourage false generalizations. The other Romance languages are uncertain guides to the gender of Spanish nouns: innumerable subtle differences exist to confuse learners, cf. *un oasis*, French *une oasis*, *el límite*, French *la limite*, *el calor*, French *la chaleur*, *el paisaje*, Portuguese *a paisagem*, *la flor*, Italian *il fiore*.

1.4.1 Masculine by meaning

Many nouns acquire the gender of an underlying or implied noun (metonymic gender). The following are typical:
(a) Rivers (*el río*): *el Amazonas* 'the Amazon', *el Jarama*, *el Manzanares*, *el Plata* 'the River Plate', *el Sena* 'the Seine', *el Támesis* 'the Thames', *el Volga*. Locally some rivers may be feminine, but outsiders rarely know this and the masculine is always correct.

---

[4] *La canguro* is used in Spain to mean 'childminder'.

(b) Mountains, oceans, seas and lakes (*el monte, el océano, el mar, el lago*): *el Etna, el Everest, el Himalaya* (singular), *el Pacífico, el Caribe* 'Caribbean', *el Windermere*.

(c) The names of cars, boats and aircraft (*el coche, el barco, el avión*): *un Fiesta, un Mercedes, el caza* 'fighter plane', *el Queen Elisabeth, el Marie Celeste, un DC10, un Mig 21*. But small boats (*la barca*) are usually feminine. Light aircraft are usually feminine because of the underlying noun *la avioneta: una Cessna*.

(d) Months and days of the week (*los meses y los días de la semana*): *enero/abril pasado, el lunes, el viernes*.

(e) Wines (*el vino*): *el Borgoña* 'Burgundy', *el champaña/el champán* 'champagne',[5] *el Chianti, un Rioja*.

(f) Pictures (*el cuadro*) by named artists: *un Constable, un Leonardo, un Rembrandt, un Riley*.

(g) Sports teams (*el equipo*): *el Barça* 'Barcelona FC' (pronounced [bársa]), *el Betis* one of Seville's soccer teams, *el España, el Bilbao*, etc.

(h) All infinitives and all words referred to for grammatical or typographical purposes: *el fumar* 'smoking', *el escupir* 'spitting',

El "cama" no se lee	You can't read the word 'bed'
No viene la señal, el "siga" que él esperaba	The signal doesn't come, the 'go on' that
(E. Poniatowska, Mexico)	he was expecting

(i) Any adverb, interjection or other genderless word used as a noun: *el más allá* 'the Beyond', *un algo* 'a "something"'', *tiene un no sabe uno qué que gusta* (L. Rafael Sánchez, Puerto Rico, dialogue) 'she's got something nice about her'.

(j) Numbers (*el número*): *un seis, un 5, la Generación del 98* the 'Generation of '98', *el dos por ciento* 'two per cent'.

(k) Musical notes: *el fa, el la* (underlying noun unclear).

(l) Colours (US 'colors') (*el color*): *el azul* 'blue', *el ocre* 'ochre'; *se amplía el naranja del horizonte* 'the orange of the horizon is spreading' (A. Gala, Spain), . . . *sus uñas de un discretísimo rosa pálido* (M. Benedetti, Uruguay) '. . . her nails, coloured a very discreet pale pink'.

(m) Certain trees (*el árbol*) whose fruit is feminine, e.g.

el almendro: la almendra almond	*el guindo: la guinda* morello cherry
el avellano: la avellana hazel	*el mandarino: la mandarina* tangerine
el castaño: la castaña chestnut	*el manzano: la manzana* apple
el cerezo: la cereza cherry	*el naranjo: la naranja* orange
el ciruelo: la ciruela plum	*el nogal: la nuez* walnut (or simply 'nut')
el granado: la granada pomegranate	*el papayo: la papaya* papaya
el guayabo: la guayaba guava	*el peral: la pera* pear

Some fruits are masculine: *el limón* 'lemon', *el aguacate* 'avocado' (*la palta* in southern Latin America), *el melón* 'melon', *el albaricoque* 'apricot', *el higo* 'fig', etc. 'A banana' is *una banana* for many Latin Americans, but *el plátano* in Spain and parts of Lat. Am. The latter also means 'plane-tree' in Spain, so banana tree is *plátano bananero*.

---

[5] Often *la champaña* in Latin America. In Spain *el champán* is most common in spoken language, or *el cava*, which strictly speaking refers only to home-produced brands.

1.4.2 Masculine by form

(a) Nouns ending in *-o*: *el eco* 'echo', *el tiro* 'shot'. Exceptions:

la dínamo dynamo (also *el dínamo*)
la foto photo
la Gestapo the Gestapo
la libido libido
la magneto magneto (masc. in Latin America)
la mano hand (diminutive *la manita* (Spain), *la manito* (Lat. Am.))
la moto motorbike
la nao ship (archaic)
la polio polio
la porno porn(ography), i.e. *la pornografía*

La radio 'radio' is feminine in Spain and in the Southern Cone, but in Mexico, Cuba and Central America and sporadically in northern parts of South America it is masculine: *el radio*. In some places *el radio* is 'radio set' and *la radio* is 'radio station'. *El radio* also everywhere means 'radius', 'radium' and 'radiogram'. In Gabriel García Márquez's *Noticia de un secuestro* (Colombia, 1996) *el radio* and *la radio* appear with about equal frequency.
(b) Words ending in *-aje, -or, -án, -ambre* or a stressed vowel:

el equipaje luggage	*el valor* value	*Canadá* (masc.) Canada
el paisaje landscape	*el mazapán* marzipan	*el sofá* sofa/couch
el amor love	*el refrán* proverb	*el champú* shampoo
el calor heat	*el calambre* spasm/twinge	*el tisú* tissue (Kleenex)
el color colo(u)r	*el enjambre* swarm	*el rubí* ruby

But *la labor* 'labour', *la flor*, 'flower'. *El hambre* 'hunger' is also feminine: see 3.1.2 for explanation of the masculine article. The forms *la calor* and *la color* for *el calor* 'heat' and *el color* 'colo(u)r' are heard in dialect and rural speech in Spain and in parts of Latin America. *La televisor* for *el televisor* 'television set' and one or two other unusual genders are also found in local Latin-American dialects.

1.4.3 Common masculine nouns ending in *-a*

Foreign learners make many mistakes by assuming that nouns ending in *-a* must be feminine. Many nouns ending in *-ma*, and several other nouns ending in *-a* are masculine.
(a) Masculine nouns ending in *-a*, including some nouns referring to animals (for masculine nouns ending in *-ma* see list **(b)**)

el aleluya alleluia (*la aleluya* is 'doggerel'/'jingle')
el alerta alert (*el alerta rojo* 'red alert'; *la alerta* is spreading)
el bocata familiar Peninsular for 'sandwich' (*bocadillo*)
el busca bleeper/pager/electronic locating device
el caza fighter plane
el cometa comet (*la cometa* = 'kite', the toy)
el día day
el escucha listening device/ electronic 'bug'
el extra extra, extra payment
el gorila gorilla
el guardarropa wardrobe (all such compounds are masculine)
el insecticida insecticide (and thus all chemicals ending in *icida*)
el mañana the morrow/tomorrow (*la mañana* = 'morning')

el mapa map
el mediodía noon
el nirvana Nirvana
el panda panda
el planeta planet
el puma puma/cougar/mountain lion
el telesilla ski-lift
el tequila tequila (the drink. *La tequila* is also heard)
el tranvía tram
el vodka vodka
el yoga yoga

(b) Masculine nouns ending in *-ma*
These words are masculine, in most cases because the Greek words that they are derived from are neuter.

el anagrama anagram
el anatema anathema
el aroma aroma
el cisma schism
el clima climate
el coma coma (*la coma* = 'comma')
el crisma holy oil (but *te rompo la crisma* 'I'll knock your block off')
el crucigrama crossword puzzle
el diagrama diagram
el dilema dilemma
el diploma diploma
el dogma dogma
el drama drama
el eccema/el eczema eczema
el emblema emblem
el enigma enigma
el esquema scheme
el estigma stigma
el fantasma ghost
el fonema phoneme

el holograma hologram
el lema slogan/watchword
el magma magma
el miasma miasma
el panorama panorama
el pijama pyjamas/(US 'pajamas') (*la pijama* or *la piyama* in Latin America. Not Greek)
el plasma plasma
el poema poem
el prisma prism
el problema problem
el programa program(me)
el radiograma radiogram
el reúma rheumatism (less commonly *el reuma*)
el síntoma symptom
el sistema system
el telegrama telegram
el tema theme/topic/subject
el trauma trauma

and most other scientific or technical words ending in *-ma*. But *la estratagema* 'stratagem', *el asma* 'asthma' (see 3.1.2 for masculine article) and *la flema* 'phlegm' are feminine even though they are neuter in Greek. *La amalgama* 'amalgam' (Medieval Latin) is also feminine. For feminine words ending in *-ma* see 1.4.6.

Note

A few of these words are feminine in popular speech, dialects and pre-nineteenth-century texts, especially *problema, clima, miasma* and *fantasma,* cf. *pobre fantasma soñadora* in Lorca's *El maleficio de la mariposa.*

1.4.4 Feminine by meaning

The following are feminine, usually because of an underlying noun:

(a) Companies (*la compañía, la firma*): *la IBM, la Seat, la Hertz, la Volkswagen, la Ford.*
(b) Letters of the alphabet (*la letra*): *una b, una c, una h, la delta, la omega. El delta* 'river delta' is masculine.

(c) Islands (*la isla*): *las Azores, las Baleares, las Antillas* 'West Indies', *las Canarias,* etc.

(d) Roads (*la carretera* 'road' or *la autopista* 'motorway'/US 'freeway'): *la N11, la M4.*

1.4.5 Feminine by form

Nouns ending in *-eza, -ción, -ía, -sión, -dad, -tad, -tud, -umbre, -ie, -nza, -cia, -sis, - itis:*

la pereza laziness	*la superficie* surface
la acción action	*la esperanza* hope
la tontería foolishness (but *el día* 'day')	*la presencia* presence
la versión version	*la crisis* crisis
la verdad truth	*la tesis* thesis
la libertad freedom	*la bronquitis* bronchitis
la virtud virtue	*la diagnosis* diagnosis
la muchedumbre crowd	*la diálisis* dialysis
la servidumbre servitude	*la parálisis* paralysis
la serie series	etc.

But the following are masculine:

el análisis analysis	*el éxtasis* ecstasy
el apocalipsis apocalypse	*el paréntesis* parenthesis/bracket
el énfasis emphasis/pomposity of style	

1.4.6 Common feminine nouns ending in *-ma*

The majority of nouns ending in *-ma* are masculine (see 1.4.3), but many are feminine. The following are common examples (asterisked forms require the masculine article for reasons explained at 3.1.2, despite the fact that they are feminine nouns):

la alarma alarm	*la forma* shape
*el alma** soul	*la gama* selection/range
la amalgama amalgam	*la goma* rubber
*el arma** weapon	*la lágrima* tear (i.e. teardrop)
*el asma** asthma	*la lima* file (for nails, wood)/lime (fruit)
la broma joke	*la llama* flame/llama
la calma calm	*la loma* hillock
la cama bed	*la máxima* maxim
la cima summit	*la merma* decrease
la crema cream	*la norma* norm
la Cuaresma Lent	*la palma* palm
la chusma rabble	*la paloma* dove
la diadema diadem/tiara	*la pantomima* pantomime
la doma breaking-in/taming (= *la domadura*)	*la pamema* unnecessary fuss
la dracma drachma	*la prima* female cousin; bonus/prize
la enzima enzyme	*la quema* burning
la escama scale (fish)	*la rama* branch
la esgrima fencing (with swords)	*la rima* rhyme
la/el esperma sperm	*la sima* chasm/abyss
la estima esteem	*la suma* sum
la estratagema stratagem	*la toma* taking
la firma firm/signature	*la yema* egg yolk/fingertip
la flema phlegm	

1.4.7 Gender of countries, provinces, regions

Countries, provinces or regions ending in unstressed *-a* are feminine, e.g.

la España/Francia/Argentina de hoy	Spain/France/Argentina today
la conservadora Gran Bretaña	conservative Britain
la Alemania que yo conocía	the Germany I knew

The rest are masculine: (*el*) *Perú*, (*el*) *Paraguay*, (*el*) *Canadá; Aragón, Devon, Tennessee* (all masculine). Some place names include the definite article and may exceptionally be feminine, cf. *las Hurdes* (near Salamanca, Spain). For use of the article with countries and place names, see 3.2.17.

Note

Such constructions as *todo Colombia lo sabe* 'all Colombia knows it' are nevertheless normal and correct, especially with the adjectives *todo, medio, mismo*, etc., probably because the underlying noun is *pueblo* 'people'. Cf. *todo Piura está muerta* (M. Vargas Llosa, Peru, dialogue) 'the whole of Piura is dead'. Compare the following, which refers to a place, not to the people: *toda Argentina está inundada de obras mías* (M. Vargas Llosa, Peru) 'the whole of Argentina is full of books of mine'.

1.4.8 Gender of cities, towns and villages

Cities ending in unstressed *-a* are usually feminine, the rest are masculine:

la Barcelona de ayer	the Barcelona of yesterday
la Roma de Horacio	Horace's Rome
el Moscú turístico	the tourist's Moscow
. . . la exaltación demagógica de un imaginario Buenos Aires de cuchilleros (J. L. Borges, Argentina)	. . . the demagogic celebration of an imaginary Buenos Aires (full) of knifemen

But there are exceptions like *Nueva York*, but note *Nueva York está lleno de ventanas* (I. Aldecoa, Spain) 'New York is full of windows', *la antigua Cartago, Nueva Orleans, vieja Delhi, fétida Delhi* (Octavio Paz, Mexico) 'old Delhi, fetid Delhi', and spontaneous language often make cities feminine because of the influence of the underlying noun *la ciudad* 'city': *Bogotá, antes de ser remodelada* (Colombian press, in *Variedades*, 20) 'Bogota, before it was refashioned'. Some cities include the definite article (written with a capital letter) in their name: *El Cairo, La Habana* 'Havana', *La Haya* 'The Hague'.

Villages are usually masculine even when they end in *-a*, because of underlying *el pueblo* 'village'.

For the construction *todo Barcelona habla de ello* 'all Barcelona's talking about it' see the note to 1.4.7.

1.4.9 Gender of compound nouns

Compound nouns consisting of a verb plus a noun (frequent) are masculine:

el cazamariposas butterfly net	*el paraguas* umbrella
el cuentarrevoluciones rev-counter	*el sacacorchos* corkscrew
el lanzallamas flame-thrower	*el saltamontes* grasshopper

Compound nouns consisting of two nouns have the gender of the first noun: *el año luz* 'light year', *un perro guía* 'guide dog', *un coche bomba* 'car bomb', *la mujer objeto* 'woman viewed as an object'. The gender of other compound nouns should be learnt separately.

1.4.10 Gender of foreign words

A large number of foreign, especially English words, are in daily use, but they are often used in ways that differ subtly from the source language. Words that refer to human beings will be feminine or masculine according to the gender of the person referred to: *los yuppies, el recordman* 'record-holder' (probably borrowed from French), but *la nanny*.

Foreign words referring to inanimates may be feminine if the word closely resembles a familiar feminine Spanish word in form or meaning or, occasionally, because they are feminine in the original language:

la beautiful people the rich set, jet-set (because of *la gente?*)
la chance chance (Lat. Am. only, sometimes masc.)
la élite élite (usually pronounced as three syllables)
la Guinness because of *la cerveza* 'beer'
la hi-fi because of *la alta fidelidad*
la Web the Web (cf. *la telaraña* 'spider's web')
la Kneset the Knesset (Israeli parliament), because of *las Cortes?*
la NASA because of *la agencia*
la opus in music (cf. *la obra*), but *El Opus* = Opus Dei
la pizza
la roulotte caravan
la sauna sauna (masc. in Argentina)
la suite suite (all senses)

At the time of writing (1999), *el Internet* is the more common gender, and often the word is used without the article, especially after prepositions.

But if a word is un-Spanish in spelling or ending, or is not clearly associated with a feminine Spanish word, it will be masculine. The great majority of foreign-looking words are therefore masculine, even though some of them are feminine in their original language:

el affaire affair (love or political; fem. in French)
el after-shave
el airbag (pronounced [ayrßá])
el best-seller
los boxes pits (in motor racing, more correctly *el taller*)
el boom financial boom
el chalet (British) detached house, i.e. a house built on its own land
el chándal tracksuit
el Christmas Christmas card
el diskette floppy disk; also *el disquete*
el echarpe (light) scarf (fem. in French; pronounced as a Spanish word)
el eslogan/los eslóganes advertising slogan/catch-phrase
el escalextric 'spaghetti junction'
el fax
el footing jogging (from French)
el gel de baño bath gel
el hardware (colloquially *el hard*; the Academy prefers *el soporte físico*)
el iceberg iceberg (pronounced, in Spain, as [iθeßér])
el jazz
el karaoke
el lifting face-lift
el módem
el performance performance (of a machine)
el poster

el pub (in Spain, a fashionable bar with music)
el puenting bungee jumping
el quark cf. *el neutrón, el protón* and *el electrón*, but *las partículas subatómicas*
el ranking
el slip men's underpants/(US 'shorts')
el software (colloquially *el soft*; the Academy prefers *el soporte lógico*)
el (e)spray aerosol
el standing rank/prestige
el vodka vodka
el yoga yoga

The formation of the plural of foreign words is discussed at 2.1.5. There is wide variation between the various Hispanic countries as to the source and number of recent loanwords, so no universally valid list can be drawn up.

1.4.11 Gender of abbreviations

This is determined by the gender of the main noun:

la ONU UN
la OTAN NATO
las FF.AA. (*Fuerzas Armadas*) Armed Forces
la UVI (*Unidad de Vigilancia Intensiva*) Intensive Care Unit
el FBI
la CIA
el OVNI (*objeto volante no identificado*) UFO

If the gender of the underlying noun is unknown the abbreviation is masculine unless there is a good reason otherwise: *el* (or *la*) *KGB, el IRA* 'the IRA (Irish Republican Army)' (*la ira* = 'anger'); but *la RAF, la USAF* (**las** *fuerzas aéreas* 'air force'), etc. Note, however, *la ETA*, the Basque separatist organization.

1.4.12 Gender acquired from underlying noun (metonymic gender)

Many of the examples in previous sections illustrate cases of a noun acquiring the gender of another that has been deleted. This accounts for many apparent gender anomalies. Compare:

el Avenida = *el Cine Avenida, la avenida* = 'avenue'
una EBRO = *una camioneta EBRO* 'an EBRO light truck'
la Modelo = *la Cárcel Modelo* 'Model Jail'
Radio Nacional de España, la número uno (RNE, 11–1–92, *la emisora* 'broadcasting
    station' omitted) 'National Radio of Spain, the number one (station)'
la setenta y tres = *la habitación número setenta y tres* 'room seventy-three'

1.4.13 Doubtful genders

There are a few words of doubtful gender, one of the oddest being *el azúcar* 'sugar' which is masculine, despite the fact that a following adjective may be of either gender: *azúcar moreno/morena* 'brown sugar'. In the following list the more common gender comes first (Peninsular usage, and probably elsewhere as well):

el acne or *el acné* acne, both genders valid
el calor heat (*la calor* is rustic)
la cochambre dirt
el color colo(u)r (*la color* is rustic)
la dote dowry/gifts (*tiene dotes* 'he's gifted')
la/el duermevela snooze/nap/light sleep

los herpes herpes
el hojaldre puff pastry (Latin America *la hojaldra*)
el/la interrogante question (both genders are used)
el/la lente lens (but *las lentillas* = 'contact lenses')
el/la linde boundary
la/el pelambre thick hair/mop of hair
la pringue fat/grease/sticky dirt (*esto está pringoso* 'this is sticky')
la sartén (see 1.4.15)
el/la testuz forehead (of animals)
la tilde the sign over an *ñ*
el/la tizne soot/black smear or stain
la/el tortícolis stiff neck
el trípode tripod

Pre-twentieth-century texts may contain now obsolete genders, e.g. *la puente* 'bridge', *la fin* 'end', *la análisis* 'analysis', etc.

1.4.14 Gender of *mar*, 'sea'

Masculine, except in poetry, the speech of sailors and fishermen, in weather forecasts and in nautical terms (*la pleamar/la bajamar* 'high/low tide', *la mar llana/picada* 'calm/choppy sea', *hacerse a la mar* 'to put to sea', *en alta mar* 'on the high seas', etc.) and whenever the word is used as a colloquial intensifier: *la mar de tonto* 'absolutely stupid', *la mar de gente* '"heaps" of people'.

1.4.15 Some Latin-American genders

Some words are given different genders in provincial Spain and/or some parts of Latin America. Examples current in educated usage and writing in some (but not all) Latin-American countries are:

el bombillo (Sp. *la bombilla*) light bulb
el llamado (*la llamada*) call
el protesto (*la protesta*) protest
el sartén (Sp. *la sartén*) frying-pan; also masc. in Bilbao
el vuelto (*la vuelta*) change (money)

There are surely many other examples, locally more or less accepted in educated speech.

1.4.16 Words with two genders

A number of common words have meanings differentiated solely by their gender. Well-known examples are:

busca (m.) bleeper/pager (f.) search
cometa (m.) comet (f.) kite (toy)
coma (m.) coma (f.) comma
consonante (m.) rhyming word (f.) consonant
cólera (m.) cholera (f.) wrath/anger
corte (m.) cut (f.) the Court/'Madrid'
capital (m.) capital (money) (f.) capital (city)
cura (m.) priest (f.) cure
delta (m.) river delta (f.) delta (Greek letter)
doblez (m.) fold/crease (f.) duplicity
editorial (m.) editorial (f.) publishing house
escucha (m.) electronic 'bug' (f.) listening/monitoring
final (m.) end (f.) final (race, in sports)

frente (m.) front (military) (f.) forehead
guardia (m.) policeman (f.) guard
génesis (m.) genesis (= birth) (f.) Genesis (Bible)
mañana (m.) tomorrow/morrow (f.) morning
margen (m.) margin (f.) riverbank
moral (m.) mulberry tree (f.) morals/morale
orden (m.) order (opposite of disorder) (f.) command or religious order
ordenanza (m.) messenger/orderly (f.) decree/ordinance
parte (m.) official bulletin (f.) part
pendiente (m.) earring (f.) slope
pez (m.) fish (f.) pitch (i.e. tar)
policía (m.) policeman (f.) police force
radio (m.) radius/radium/spoke (f.) radio
terminal (m.) terminal (computers, electrical) (f.) terminus/terminal
vocal (m.) member of a board (f.) vowel

Notes

(i) *Arte* 'art' is usually masculine in the singular, but feminine in the plural: *el arte español* 'Spanish art', *las bellas artes* 'fine arts'. But note set phrase *el arte poética* "Ars Poetica"/'treatise on poetry'. However, Seco (1998), 60, notes that a phrase like *esta nueva arte* 'this new art-form' is not incorrect, and that **los** *artes de pesca* 'fishing gear' (of a trawler) is standard usage, although *las artes* is also used: . . . *temiendo que un lobo marino o un delfín se hubiera introducido en las artes* (*El País*, Uruguay) '. . . fearing that a seal (Spain *la foca*) or dolphin had got into the tackle'.
(ii) For the gender of *radio* 'radio' see 1.4.2a.

2

Plural of nouns

2.1 Formation of the plural of nouns

2.1.1 Summary of rules

The vast majority of Spanish nouns form their plurals in one of the following three ways:

Method	Main types of nouns	Examples
Add -s	Ending in an unstressed vowel Many foreign words ending in a consonant	*la casa>las casas* *el chalet>los chalets* *el show>los shows*
Add -es	Spanish (not foreign) nouns ending in a consonant other than -s Nouns ending in a stressed vowel + -s Many nouns ending a stressed vowel	*la flor>las flores* *el inglés>los ingleses* *el tabú>los tabúes*
No change	Nouns already ending with an unstressed vowel + s Families (people or things) Some foreign nouns	*la crisis>las crisis* *el virus>los virus* *los Blanco, los Ford* *el CD-ROM>los CD-Rom*

2.1.2 Plural in -s

(a) Nouns ending in an unstressed vowel:

la cama	*las camas*	bed
la serie	*las series*	series
el huevo	*los huevos*	egg
la tribu	*las tribus*	tribe

(b) Nouns ending in stressed -*e*, including words of one syllable ending in -*e*:

el café	*los cafés*	coffee/café
el pie	*los pies*	foot/feet
el clisé	*los clisés*	cliché/photographic plate
el té	*los tés*	tea

(c) Nouns of more than one syllable ending with a stressed -*o* (rare):

el dominó	*los dominós*	domino(es)
el buró	*los burós*	(roll-top) desk

(d) Many foreign words ending in a consonant, e.g. *el club>los clubs*. See 2.1.5.

2.1.3 Plural in -es

(a) Native (or nativized) nouns ending in a consonant other than *-s*:

el bar	*los bares*	bar (i.e. 'café')
el avión	*los aviones*	aeroplane/airplane
el color	*los colores*	colo(u)r
la verdad	*las verdades*	truth
el rey	*los reyes*	king
la vez	*las veces*	time (as in 'three times')

Note

If -es is added to a final z, the z becomes c: *el matiz/los matices* 'shade' (of colour/'nuance'), *la paz/las paces* 'peace', *la voz/las voces* 'voice'. For words ending in -g (rare) or -c see 2.1.5.

(b) Nouns ending in a stressed vowel plus *-s*:

el autobús	*los autobuses*	bus
el francés	*los franceses*	Frenchman
el dios	*los dioses*	god
el mes	*los meses*	month
el país	*los países*	country
la tos	*las toses*	cough

Exception: *el mentís>los mentís* 'denial' (literary style).

(c) Nouns ending in stressed *-i, -u* or *-a*:

The following plural forms are considered correct in formal or written language:

el bisturí	*los bisturíes*	scalpel
el maniquí	*los maniquíes*	tailor's dummy, model
el rubí	*los rubíes*	ruby
el zulú	*los zulúes*	Zulu
el tabú	*los tabúes*	taboo
el ombú	*los ombúes*	ombu tree (Lat. Am.)
el jacarandá	*los jacarandaes*	jacaranda tree

No intento siquiera poner el punto sobre las íes (A. Gala, Spain) 'I'm not even trying to dot the i's'.

There are several important exceptions: *papá/papás* 'father'/'dad', *mamá/mamás* 'mother'/'mum'/'mom', *sofá/sofás* (illiterate **sofases*) 'sofa'/'couch', *el menú/los menús* 'menu', *el tisú/los tisús* '(paper) tissues'.

However, all words of this kind usually simply add *-s* in spontaneous speech: *los colibrís* 'humming-birds', *los iranís* 'Iranians' (properly *los iraníes*), *los jabalís* (properly *jabalíes*) 'wild boars', *los jacarandás, los rubís, los tabús, los zahorís* 'clairvoyants'/'water diviners'. A literary plural form of a truly popular word, e.g. *la gachí/las gachís* 'woman' (Spanish slang) would sound ridiculous. The Latin-American words *el ají* 'chilli/chilli sauce', and *el maní* 'peanut' (Spain *el cacahuete*) often form the plurals *los ajises, los manises* in speech, although *ajíes, maníes* are used in writing.

Notes

(i) If, when *-es* is added, the stress naturally falls on the last syllable but one, any accent written in the singular disappears: *el alacrán/los alacranes* 'scorpion', *el irlandés/los irlandeses* 'Irishman', *la nación/las naciones* 'nation', *el/la rehén/los/las rehenes* 'hostage'.

This does not apply to words that end in *-í* or *-ú*: *el pakistaní/los pakistaníes* (or *el paquistaní/los paquistaníes*) 'Pakistani', *el tabú/los tabúes* 'taboo'. These are discussed above at 2.1.3c.

(ii) Words ending in *-en* (but not *-én*!) require an accent in the plural to preserve the position of the stress. Since they are frequently misspelt, the following commonly seen forms should be noted:

> *el carmen/los cármenes* 'villa with a garden' (in Andalusia), *el crimen/los crímenes* 'crime', *el germen/los gérmenes* 'germ', *la imagen/las imágenes* 'image', *el lumen/los lúmenes* 'lumen' (in physics), *el/la margen/los/las márgenes* 'margin' (masc.)/'river-bank' (fem.), *el origen/los orígenes* 'origin', *la virgen/las vírgenes* 'virgin'.

This also affects the nativized word *el mitin/los mítines* 'political meeting' (the ordinary type of meeting, e.g. family, business, is *una reunión*. A 'reunion' is *un reencuentro*).

(iii) When an accent written on *í* or *ú* shows that these vowels are pronounced separately and do not form a diphthong, the accent is retained in the plural after the addition of *-es*: *el baúl/los baúles* 'trunk'/'chest', *el laúd/los laúdes* 'lute', *el país/los países* 'country', *la raíz/las raíces* 'root'.

2.1.4 No change in the plural

(a) Words ending in an unstressed vowel plus *s*:

el/los análisis	analysis	*el/los lunes*	Monday (similarly all weekdays)
el/los atlas	atlas	*el/los mecenas*	patron of the arts
el/los campus	campus	*el/los paréntesis*	bracket
la/las crisis	crisis	*la/las tesis*	thesis
la/las dosis	dose	*el/los virus*	virus

In words of one syllable the vowel is always stressed, so the plural ends in *-es*, e.g. *el mes/los meses*; see 2.1.3b.

(b) Words ending in *-x*, e.g. *el/los dúplex* (US) 'duplex apartment' (i.e. a flat on two floors, 'split-level apartment'), *el/los fénix* 'phoenix', *el/los Kleenex* 'Kleenex' (the usual generic word in Spain for 'tissue'), *el/los fax* 'fax': *no bajamos de tres o cuatro fax por día* (interview in *Cambio16*, Spain) 'we don't send less than three or four faxes a day'. The plural *los faxes* is also heard.

(c) Latin words ending in *-t* (at least in careful language) and a few other foreign words:

> *los altos déficit presupuestarios* (*El País*) 'high budgetary deficits'
> *el CD-ROM/los CD-ROM*
> *el láser disc/los láser disc*

Likewise *los superávit* 'budgetary surpluses', *los accésit* 'second prizes', *el quórum/los quórum*. But in everyday usage Latin words in *-um* usually form their plural in *-ums*, *el memorándum/los memorándums*, *el referéndum/los referéndums*, *el ultimátum/los ultimátums*, *el currículum vitae/los currículums vitae*. *El País* prefers the plurals *memorandos, referendos, ultimatos* and *currículos*, though common usage says *-ums*. The corresponding singular forms *el memorando, el referendo, el ultimato* are Academy recommendations that the public has not accepted. *El currículo* 'curriculum' has recently spread in Spain (and possibly also elsewhere).

In spontaneous speech all Latin words may be treated like other foreign words (see 2.1.5). Spanish speakers do not try to impress by using Latin plurals, cf. our (incorrect) 'referenda' for 'referendums'. Most other foreign words add -s. See 2.1.5.

(d) Words ending in a consonant plus -s: *los bíceps, los fórceps.*

2.1.5 Plural of foreign words ending in a consonant

The universal tendency is to treat them all as English words and add -s, whatever language they come from (although a few foreign words do not add -s; see 2.1.4c). This produces words that end in two consonants, which goes against the spirit of the Spanish language and irritates the grammarians. As a result some foreign words have recommended written plurals in -es and everyday spoken plurals in -s, e.g. *los cócteles/los cóctels* 'cocktail', *los córneres/los córners* 'corner' (in soccer), *los fraques/los fracs* 'dress-coat' / 'tails'.[1]

As a rule, if a word ends in *b, c, f, g, k, m, p, t, v,* or *w,* or in any two or more consonants, it is almost certainly a foreign word and will make its plural in -s unless it ends with a *s, sh* or *ch* sound, cf. *el kibutz* 'kibbutz', *el flash, el lunch, el sketch,* in which case it will probably be invariable in spontaneous speech. Well-informed speakers may use foreign plurals like *los flashes, los kibutzim, los sketches.* Some common examples:

> *el barman/los barmans* barman (the most usual colloquial plural in Spain)
> *el boicot/los boicots* boycott
> *el complot/los complots* (political) plot
> *el coñac/los coñacs* cognac
> *el chalet/los chalets* detached house
> *el esnob/los esnobs* 'snob' / 'trendy' (can be applied to things)
> *el gay/los gays* gay (i.e. homosexual)
> *el hit/los hits* hit parade
> *el hobby/los hobbys* hobby / hobbies
> *el iceberg/los icebergs* iceberg
> *el kart /los karts* go-kart
> *el módem/los módems* modem

Notes

(i) *El sandwich* (made with sliced bread, and therefore different from *el bocadillo,* made from a roll, in familiar Peninsular language *el bocata*), makes the plural *los sandwiches* in educated usage, but *los sandwich* is usually heard. It is usually pronounced [sángwich]. The Academy's preferred word for sandwich, *el emparedado,* has never been accepted. A common Latin-American form is *sangüiche,* which is more pronounceable.

(ii) Some modern loanwords are treated as Spanish words. This happens most readily when the word ends in *-l, -n* or *-r: el bar/los bares* 'bar', *el dólar/los dólares* 'dollar', *el electrón/los electrones* 'electron', *el escáner/los escáneres* 'scanner'/'scanning' (also *el scanner/los scanners*), *los espaguetis* 'spaghetti' (also *los espagueti*), *el gol/los goles* 'goal' (in sport), *el hotel/los hoteles* 'hotel'.

(iii) 'Academy' plurals like *el gong/los gongues* 'gong', *el zigzag/los zigzagues* 'zigzag', etc. are not used; -s alone is added. However, *el film(e)/los filmes* is not uncommon and is recommended by *El País* (the everyday word is *la película*), and *el club/los clubes* 'club' is normal in Latin America for the

---

[1] Grammarians often recommend Hispanized forms of foreign words, e.g. *güisqui* for *whisky,* *yip* for *jeep, yóquey* or *yoqui* for *jockey,* etc. Since such forms suggest ignorance of foreign languages, people tend to avoid them.

common Peninsular *los clubs* (*El País* prefers *los clubes* but it is rare in Peninsular speech). *Los álbumes* is generally preferred in writing and also in educated speech, to *los álbums* 'albums'. *Los eslóganes* is commonly heard, as well as *los eslogans* '(publicity) slogan'.

(iv) Some writers and editors occasionally treat foreign words ending in a consonant like Latin words (see 2.1.4c), so forms like *los hit, los láser* are seen; *El País* recommends *los laser*. Zero plural forms are often given to foreign words in spontaneous speech.

2.1.6 Proper names

If a proper name refers to a collective entity such as a family, it has no plural form: *los Franco, los Mallol, los Pérez; en casa de los Riba hay una niña que amaré toda la vida* (E. Poniatowska, Mexico, dialogue) 'in the Ribas' house there's a girl whom I'll love for the whole of my life'. A group of individuals who merely happen to have the same name will be pluralized according to the usual rules, although names in *-és* and *-z* are almost always invariable:

Este pueblo está lleno de Morenos,	This village is full of Morenos,
Blancos y Péreces/Pérez	Blancos and Perezes
Los de la Torre me han invitado	The de la Torres have invited
a su barbacoa	me to their barbecue
no todos los Juan Pérez del mundo	not all the Juan Perezes in the world
(J. Donoso, Chile)	

Notes

(i) The same principle also applies to objects that form families: *los Ford* 'Ford cars', *los Chevrolet, los Simca*.

(ii) Royal houses are considered to be successive individuals: *los Borbones* 'the Bourbons', *los Habsburgos*.

2.1.7 Compound nouns

(a) Those (the most common) consisting of a verb plus a plural noun do not change in the plural:

el/los abrelatas tin-opener
el cumpleaños/los cumpleaños birthday
el elevalunas automatic window-opener (in a car)
el/los guardaespaldas bodyguard
el/los lanzamisiles missile-launcher
el/los limpiabotas shoeshine
el/los portaaviones aircraft carrier
la/las quitanieves snowplough/(US 'snowplow'). Seco, 1998, 378, gives the
    gender as feminine
la/las tragaperras gaming machine/'one-armed bandit'/(Brit.) 'fruit machine'
    Masculine gender is also used

(b) There is a growing class of compounds consisting of two juxtaposed nouns. Normally only the first noun is pluralized. The following forms have been noted from various written sources:

el año luz/los años luz light year
el arco iris/los arcos iris rainbow
el coche cama/los coches cama sleeping car
la ciudad satélite/las ciudades satélite dormitory suburb
el hombre rana/los hombres rana frogman
la hora punta/las horas punta rush hour (lit. 'point hour')

la mujer objeto/las mujeres objeto woman-as-object
el perro policía/los perros policía police dog

But always *el país miembro/los países miembros* 'member country', *la tierra virgen/las tierras vírgenes* 'virgin land'. Pluralization of the second noun robs it of its adjectival force: *los hombres ranas* sounds like 'men who are frogs'; compare *las ediciones pirata* 'pirate editions' and *los editores piratas* 'pirate publishers', *los niños modelo* 'model children', *los niños modelos* 'child models'.

As the examples show, in Spanish the qualifying or adjectival noun comes second: *un hombre rana* is a man with some of the characteristics of a frog, not vice-versa. A very rare exception is *la ciencia ficción* 'science fiction', which is a direct borrowing from English.

(c) The following compound nouns are invariable in the plural:

	los sin casa	the homeless
el/la sinvergüenza	*los/las sinvergüenza*	scoundrel, good-for-nothing
el hazmerreír	*los hazmerreír*	laughing-stock
el vivalavirgen	*los vivalavirgen*	fun-lover/laid-back/someone who couldn't give a damn

(d) Other compound nouns are treated as single words with regular plurals:

el altavoz/los altavoces loudspeaker (Lat. Am. *el altoparlante*)
la bocacalle/las bocacalles side street
el correveidile/los correveidiles tell-tale
los dimes y diretes gossip
el hidalgo/los hidalgos nobleman (the old plural was *hijosdalgo*)
el parabién/los parabienes congratulations
el pésame/los pésames condolences
el quehacer/los quehaceres task
el rapapolvo/los rapapolvos telling-off/dressing down
el sordomudo/los sordomudos deaf-mute
el tentempié/los tentempiés snack
el todoterreno/los todoterrenos four-wheel-drive vehicle
el vaivén/los vaivenes ups-and-downs/swaying motion

2.1.8 Irregular plurals

(a) Three common nouns shift their stress in the plural:

el carácter	*los caracteres*	character (*los carácteres* is not Spanish!)
el espécimen	*los especímenes*	specimen
el régimen	*los regímenes*	regime

(b) *El lord* (British) 'lord' has the plural *los lores*: *la Cámara de los Lores* 'the House of Lords'. The scholarly word *el hipérbaton* 'hyperbaton' usually forms the plural *los hipérbatos*.

2.2 Syntax and semantics of plural nouns

2.2.1 Mass nouns and count nouns in Spanish and English

A count noun refers to countable items, 'egg' – 'two eggs'. Mass or uncountable nouns denote non-countable items: 'justice', 'bread', but not *'two justices', *'two breads'). In both English and Spanish, mass or uncountable nouns can often be pluralized to mean different varieties of the thing in question: 'her fear'/'her fears', 'my love'/'my loves', 'I love French wine'/'I love French wines', 'the water of Finland'/'the waters of Finland'. This device is far more frequent in Spanish than in English, and idiomatic translation of the resulting plural noun may require thought, e.g.:

Para nosotros existen dos urgencias (interview in *Cambio16*, Spain)	For us there are two urgent issues (lit. 'urgencies')
Ejercía diversas soberbias (J. L. Borges, Argentina)	He practised (US 'practiced') various kinds of arrogance
La Sociedad argentina reclama mayor transparencia en las conductas de los hombres políticos (*La Nación*, Argentina)	Argentinian society demands greater openness in the behaviour of politicians

A number of Spanish nouns can be pluralized in this way whereas their English translation cannot. Examples:

la amistad	friendship	*las amistades*	friends
la atención	attention	*las atenciones*	acts of kindness
la bondad	goodness	*las bondades*	good acts
la carne	meat	*las carnes*	fleshy parts
la crueldad	cruelty	*las crueldades*	cruel acts
la gente	people	*las gentes*	peoples/people
la información	information	*las informaciones*	news items
el negocio	business	*los negocios*	business affairs
el pan	bread	*los panes*	loaves of bread
el progreso	progress	*los progresos*	advances
la tostada	toast	*las tostadas*	slices of toast
la tristeza	sadness	*las tristezas*	sorrows
el trueno	thunder	*los truenos*	thunderclaps

2.2.2 Nouns denoting symmetrical objects

As in English, these nouns are usually invariably plural:

los auriculares earphones
las gafas glasses (Lat. Am. *los anteojos*)
los gemelos binoculars/cufflinks/twins

las pinzas tweezers
las tijeras scissors

But usage is uncertain in some cases, with a colloquial tendency towards the singular. The more usual form (in Spain) comes first:

los alicates/el alicate pliers/pincer
los calzoncillos/un calzoncillo men's underpants/(US 'shorts')
la nariz/las narices nose (the plural is colloquial)
el pantalón/los pantalones trousers/(US 'pants': sing. and plur. equally common in Spanish)

Note

Las escaleras/la escalera 'stairs', singular if it means a 'ladder'.

2.2.3 Nouns always plural in Spanish

As happens in English, some nouns or phrases are normally found only in the plural. The following list is by no means exhaustive:

las afueras outskirts
los alrededores surroundings

buenas tardes good afternoon
las cosquillas tickling

los altos (Lat. Am.) upstairs flat/apartment	*las ganas* urge/desire
los bajos (Lat. Am.) downstairs flat/apartment	*(tener muchas) ínfulas* to be conceited
los bártulos (colloquial) belongings/'gear'	*los prismáticos* binoculars
los bienes goods, provisions	*las tinieblas* darkness
buenos días good morning	*los víveres* provisions/supplies
buenas noches good night (greeting or goodbye)	*las vacaciones* holiday/vacation

2.2.4 Singular for objects of which a person has only one

The English sentence 'they cut their knees' is ambiguous: one knee or both? Spanish normally clarifies the issue by using the singular if only one each is implied or if only one thing is possessed:

Les cortaron la cabeza	They cut off their heads
Se quitaron el sombrero	They took off their hats
Todos tenían novia	All had girlfriends (one each)
tres israelíes con pasaporte alemán	three Israelis with German
(*Cambio16*, Spain)	passports
La cara de Antonio no refleja el mismo	Antonio's face doesn't reflect the
entusiasmo. Ni la de sus cuñados tampoco	same enthusiasm. Nor do those
(Carmen Rico-Godoy, Spain)	(lit. 'nor that of') of his brothers
	and sisters-in-law

This rule is sometimes ignored in Latin-American speech: *nos hemos mojado las cabezas* (Bolivia, quoted Kany, 26) 'we've wet our heads', *lo hacían para que no les viéramos las caras* (L. Spota, dialogue, Mexico) 'they did it so we wouldn't see their faces'. Note that the plural can sometimes remove ambiguity, as in *los extranjeros felicitaban al maquinista por su gran pericia para lograr el descarrilamiento en el lugar preciso donde sus vidas corrieran peligro* (*La Época*, Chile, from a satirical article about Chilean trains) 'the foreigners congratulated the engine-driver for his great skill in managing to bring about a derailment exactly at the spot where their lives would be at risk', where the singular *su vida* might be taken to refer only to the train-driver.

The rule is often ignored in Spain with articles of clothing and possessions: *quítense el sombrero/los sombreros* 'take off your hats', *podéis dejar la chaqueta/las chaquetas aquí* 'you can leave your jackets here'.

2.2.5 Singular for plural

Singular nouns may sometimes be used to represent large numbers after words like *mucho, tanto*, etc., often, but not exclusively, with an ironic tone:

También había mucha estudiante con vaqueros	There were also a lot of female
y camiseta (J. Marías, Spain)	students in jeans and T-shirts
Se emocionó de ver tanto libro junto	He was moved to see so many
(L. Sepúlveda, Chile)	books together
. . . porque también la juventud era inferior	. . . because young people were
y allí había mucho alumno	also inferior and there were a
(A. Bryce Echenique, Peru)	lot of students there

2.3 Number agreement rules

This section covers various aspects of number agreement, mainly with nouns. For further remarks on the agreement of adjectives see 4.7. For the agreement of possessive adjectives, see 8.3.2. For agreement with *cuyo* see 35.7. For tense agreement see 16.16.

2.3.1 Number agreement with collective nouns

(a) Adjectives that modify a collective noun (one that refers to a group of persons or things) are singular and the verb is in the singular when it immediately follows the collective noun. As the following translations show, such nouns may be treated as plurals in English – especially in spoken British English, cf.

El gobierno considera . . .	The government consider(s)
La gente dice . . .	People say . . .
La tripulación está a su disposición	The crew is/are at your disposal
La mayoría dice que sí	The majority say yes

(b) If the collective noun is linked to a plural noun (usually by *de*), the safest option is to make the adjective or verb plural: *un grupo de vecinos airados* 'a group of angry neighbours', *una mayoría de españoles creen que* . . . 'a majority of Spaniards think that . . . '. The singular is, in fact, quite common in such constructions, but use of the plural will prevent beginners uttering nonsense like **un grupo de mujeres embarazado* * 'a pregnant group of women' for *un grupo de mujeres embarazadas* 'a group of pregnant women'. Examples:

Un mínimo de 13 presos habían sido asistidos de heridas (El País, Spain)	A minimum of 13 prisoners had been treated for injuries
El resto de mis bienes es ya vuestro (A. Gala, Spain)	The rest of my goods are yours now
La gran mayoría de los chilenos quiere resolver sus problemas concretos (Pres. Eduardo Frei in *La Época*, Chile)	The great majority of Chileans want to solve their specific problems
La masa de los creyentes no era menos compleja que sus creencias (O. Paz, Mexico)	The mass of believers were no less complex than their beliefs

Notes

(i) The question of agreement with collective nouns in constructions like *una mayoría de personas* (collective + *de* + plural noun) is controversial. Seco (1998), 126, advocates the plural, but the style book of *El País* recommends the singular wherever possible.

Native speakers will sometimes hesitate over agreement with collective nouns: *una pareja amiga que se llama/llaman Mario y Ana* 'a couple who are friends of ours and are called Mario and Ana'.

When the collective noun is separated from the verb by intervening words, plural agreement is very common: *una muchedumbre entró en el Palacio Real, pero al encontrarse con las tropas, huyeron* 'a crowd entered the Royal Palace, but on encountering the troops, they fled'.

(ii) For constructions like *esa gente son unos desgraciados, el comité son unos mentirosos*, see 2.3.3.

2.3.2 Plural noun after *tipo de*, etc.

After *tipo de* and similar phrases, countable nouns are often made plural:

¿Por qué hacen los hombres este tipo de cosas? (C. Rico-Godoy, Spain)	Why do men do this kind of thing?
Ya que ese tipo de rostros es frecuente en los países sudamericanos (E. Sábato, Argentina)	Since that type of face is frequent in South American countries

2.3.3 *Esto son lentejas, todo son problemas*, etc.

When *ser* (and occasionally a few other verbs like *volverse*) has a singular subject and a plural noun for its predicate, the verb agrees in number with the predicate, a construction unfamiliar to English speakers and difficult to analyse according to the traditional rules of grammar. This most commonly occurs after neuter pronouns like *lo que . . .* 'what . . . ', *todo* 'everything . . . ', *esto* 'this . . . ', etc.

A similar phenomenon is found in French and German, which say 'it are lies': *ce sont des mensonges, es sind Lügen*:

El escrito eran sus 'condiciones' (*Cambio16*, Spain)	The document was his 'conditions'
Esa gente son unos ladrones	Those people are thieves
Lo demás fueron un par de detalles burocráticos (A. Bryce Echenique, Peru)	The rest was a couple of bureaucratic details
Su morada más común son las ruinas (J. L. Borges, Argentina)	Their most usual dwelling-place is (in) ruins
Lo importante en sus relatos no eran las personas sino los lugares (P. Armando Fernández, Cuba)	The important thing in his stories wasn't people but places

However, the following examples show that this rule is not rigidly applied in Latin America:

*Lo único que no falta **es** cigarrillos* (M. Vargas Llosa, Peru, for *son cigarrillos*)	The only thing that isn't lacking is cigarettes
Lo primero que vi fue policías (A. Bryce Echenique, Peru)	The first thing I saw was policemen
Lo que mejor se ve es las casas de enfrente (M. Puig, Argentina, dialogue)	What you can see best is the houses opposite

Note

For this rule to be applied, the predicate must literally refer to a series of different things. In the following example Maria is only one person: *María es en realidad muchas personas diferentes* 'Maria is really a lot of different people'.

2.3.4 Agreement with nouns linked by y, o and phrases meaning 'as well as'

(a) Nouns linked by *y* require plural agreement unless they are felt to form a single concept. Compare *su padre y su madre estaban preocupados* 'his father and his mother were worried' and *un atolondrado ir y venir* 'a mad coming and going'. Further examples:

Su modestia y dulzura me encantaba (or *encantaban*)	Her modesty and gentleness charmed me
El derrumbe del socialismo y la desaparición de la URSS causó el mayor daño en el orden económico (speech by Fidel Castro; *causaron* equally possible)	The collapse of socialism and the disappearance of the Soviet Union caused the greatest damage in the economic sphere

Note

As in any language, a speaker may start an utterance with a single noun and then add further nouns as an afterthought. In this case the rules of agreement will not be applied: *por supuesto que podemos pensar que en el juicio de Lope pesaba la rivalidad, el sentimiento, y la cercanía* (E. Sábato, Argentina, interview; *pesaban* equally possible) 'obviously we can assume that rivalry, emotion and closeness to the events played their part in Lope's judgement'.[2]

(b) With *o* agreement is optional, but the singular stresses the idea of 'one or the other' more than the plural: *viene(n) Mario o Antonia* 'Mario or Antonia is/are coming'. Singular agreement is usual when the nouns represent a single idea: *la depresión o tristeza que afecta(n)* . . . 'the depression or sadness that affect(s) . . . '.

(c) Agreement after phrases that mean 'as well as', 'likewise', etc., seems to be optional, although the plural is more common: *tanto Mario como María pensaba(n) que* . . . 'both Mario and Maria thought that . . . '

---

[2] The seventeenth-century playwright Lope de Vega allegedly said that *Don Quixote* was the worst book he had ever read.

3

Articles

Use of the definite article *el/la/los/las* is discussed in section 3.2. The indefinite article *un/una/unos/unas* is discussed in section 3.3. *Unos/unas* is discussed at 3.4. For the use of the definite article to replace a possessive adjective, e.g. *se ha roto el brazo* 'he's broken his arm', *me dejé la cartera en casa* 'I left my wallet/(US 'bill-fold') at home', see 8.3.4. For the definite article in superlatives see 5.3. For the 'neuter article' *lo* see 7.2.

3.1 Forms of the definite article

3.1.1 Masculine and feminine definite articles

	Masculine	Feminine
Singular	*el*	*la*
Plural	*los*	*las*

La is always written in full in modern Spanish: compare Spanish *la artista* 'woman artist' with Italian *l'artista* and French *l'artiste*. The *-a* is not elided in pronunciation before words beginning with a vowel other than *a*: *la emisora* 'radio station' is pronounced [laemisóra], **not** [lemisóra].

3.1.2 Use of *el* and *un* before certain feminine nouns

El and *un* are used immediately before singular feminine nouns beginning with stressed *a-* or *ha-*, but all the adjectives and pronouns that modify these nouns must remain in the feminine form. This rule is not broken in modern Spanish, although it may not be applied in pre-nineteenth-century texts and in some dialects. Common examples:

el/un abra mountain pass (Lat. Am.; Spain *el puerto*)
el África de hoy Africa today
el/un aguila eagle
el/un alba dawn (poetic)
el/un alma soul
el/un alza rise/increase
el/un ancla anchor
el/un área area
el/un arma weapon
el/un arpa harp
el Asia de hoy Asia today
el asma asthma
el/un aula lecture-room
el/un haba bean
el/un habla language/speech
el/un hacha axe/US 'ax'
el/un hada fairy
el/un hambre hunger
el hampa the criminal underworld
el/un haya beech-tree

Compare the following words which do not begin with a stressed *a*:

la/una amnistía amnesty	*la/una apertura* opening	*la/una arroba* at-sign (@)
la/una armonía harmony	*la/una ardilla* squirrel	*la/una hamaca* hammock

Exceptions:

la a, la hache a, h (letters of the alphabet)	*la Ángela, la Ana* and other
la aya children's governess	women's names
La Haya the Hague	*la árabe* Arab woman
la/una haz surface/face	*la ácrata* anarchist woman

Notes

(i) As was stated, the noun remains feminine, so the plural is always with *las/unas: las águilas* 'eagles', *las hachas* 'axes'. The feminine article must also be used if any word intervenes between the article and the noun: *una peligrosa arma* 'a dangerous weapon', *la misma área* 'the same area'.

(ii) The rule applies only to nouns, not to adjectives: ***una** amplia estancia con libros y cuadros* (F. Umbral, Spain) 'a wide room with books and paintings', ***una** amplia panorámica de una playa montevideana* (M. Benedetti, Uruguay) 'a broad view of a Montevideo beach', *una alta mujer silenciosa* (J. L. Borges, Argentina) 'a tall, silent woman'.

(iii) This rule should apply to those feminine compound nouns whose first element would have begun with a stressed *a* had it stood alone: *el aguamarina* 'aquamarine', *el aguanieve* 'sleet', *un ave-maría* 'an Ave Maria'.

(iv) Masculine agreement is a bad error: one must say *un aula oscura* 'a dark lecture hall', *el habla popular hispanoamericana* 'popular Spanish-American speech', *se lo va a agradecer con **toda** el alma* (M. Puig, Argentina, dialogue) 'he'll thank him with all his heart (lit. 'soul')' etc., not **un aula oscuro, *el habla popular hispanoamericano, *todo el alma* . . . , etc.

However, mistakes like *?habrá que encontrar otro aula* 'we'll have to find another lecture-room' (for *otra aula*) or . . . *a raiz **del** último alza del petróleo* (ABC, Spain, quoted by Seco, 1998, 176, properly *la última alza*) ' . . . following the latest rise in oil prices' are extremely common, and constructions like *?tengo un hambre bárbaro* 'I'm starving hungry' or *?tengo mucho hambre* 'I'm very hungry' pass unnoticed in relaxed speech on both continents. They are not allowed in formal language.

(v) *Alguna* 'some' and *ninguna* 'no' are pronounced 'algún', 'ningún', in spontaneous speech before such nouns and this sometimes appears in writing; but all the authorities insist on *alguna, ninguna* in written language. *Este* 'this', *ese* and *aquel* 'that' are also very common in speech before such nouns and some speakers find the normal feminine forms pedantic. But grammarians and editors everywhere insist on *esta área* 'this area', *esta agua* 'that water', etc.

(vi) The use in written Spanish of the masculine article *un* before these nouns is a more recent innovation, and forms like *una alma* for *un alma* 'a soul' are often found in pre-modern texts.

3.1.3 *Del* and *al*

De plus *el* is shortened to *del* 'of the'. *A* plus *el* is shortened to *al* 'to the'. *De él* 'of him' and *a él* 'to him' are not abbreviated in modern Spanish. The abbreviated forms are not used (at least in writing) if the article is part of a proper name:

la primera página de El Comercio	page one of *El Comercio*
Viajaron a El Cairo	They journeyed to Cairo
el autor de El intruso	the author of *The Intruder*
. . . *en el último número de El*	. . . in the latest number of *The*
Vocero Cristiano (J. J. Arreola, Mexico)	*Christian Spokesman*

3.2 Uses and omission of the definite article

3.2.1 General remarks on the use of the definite article

Article usage is especially difficult to define, and usage of the definite article notoriously so: why *does* one say *en la práctica* 'in practice' but *en teoría* 'in theory'? Article usage also varies in detail from region to region in the Spanish-speaking world, so the following remarks must be supplemented by careful study of good writing and educated speech. The following pages should make it clear to readers who know French that although use of the Spanish definite article resembles French usage, the definite article in Spanish is in fact less used than its modern French counterpart, and is apparently less used than fifty years ago.

3.2.2 The French and Spanish definite articles

The following summary of the main differences may be useful.

French	Spanish
Usual with unqualified names of countries, provinces, continents: *l' Espagne est un beau pays, L'Amérique*, etc.	Not used (with occasional exceptions – see 3.2.17): *España es un hermoso país, América*, etc.
Often used when addressing people: *salut les gars!, oui, monsieur le Président*	Not used: *¡hola muchachos!, sí, señor Presidente*
Used without preposition with numerous time words: *le soir* 'in the evening', *le matin* 'in the morning', *le lendemain* 'the next day'	Preposition often required: *por la tarde, por la mañana, al día siguiente*, but *el año pasado*, 'last year', etc.
Not used in time expression of the type *il est huit heures*	Used: *son **las** ocho*
Used with generic nouns: *le vin est mauvais pour la foie* 'wine's bad for the liver', *l'amour est aveugle* 'love is blind'	Very similar, but not identical (see 3.2.6–3.2.10): *el vino es malo para **el** hígado, **el** amor es ciego*
Used instead of possessives with parts of body, clothing, mental faculties: *il ferme les yeux, il a perdu la mémoire*, etc.	Same, but more extensive: *cierra **los** ojos, ha perdido **la** memoria*; also *te he aparcado **el** coche* 'I've parked your car', etc. See 8.3.4
Double article in superlatives when adjective follows noun: *le livre **le** plus intéressant*	Only one article, *el libro más interesante*. See 5.3
Used with superlative adverbs: *c'est lui qui chante **le** mieux*	Not used: *él es quien mejor canta*; see 5.4
De used before partitive nouns (i.e. to express 'some'): *il boit **de** l'eau, il y avait **de** la neige*	No article or preposition in partitive constructions: *bebe agua, había nieve* (except occasionally before demonstratives; see 3.2.8 note ii)

3.2.3 A useful generalization about the Spanish definite article

With two important exceptions, if the definite article is used in English it is also used in Spanish:

la caída del gobierno	**the** fall of **the** government
Es difícil definir el uso del artículo definido	It is difficult to define **the** use of **the** definite article

Exceptions:

(a) Ordinal numbers with kings, popes, etc.: *Fernando séptimo* 'Ferdinand **the** Seventh', *Carlos quinto* 'Charles **the** Fifth'.

(b) A number of set phrases in Spanish take no article whereas their English equivalent usually does. They must be learnt separately:

a corto/largo plazo in **the** short/long run	*a voluntad de* at the discretion of
a gusto de to the liking of	*de plantilla* on the payroll/staff
cuesta abajo down (the) hill	*en alta mar* on the high seas
cuesta arriba up (the) hill	*en dicho mes* in the said month
hacia oriente, etc. towards the east	*en manos de* at/in the hands of
(*hacia el este*, etc.)	*en nombre de* in the name of
a título de in the capacity of	

This applies only to set adverbial phrases: compare *en las manos de Julia* 'in Julia's hands'. Note also *a fuerza de* 'by dint of', and *a la fuerza/por fuerza* 'by force'.

3.2.4 Definite article with more than one noun

If two or more nouns appear together, each has its own article if they are individually particularized or are felt to indicate different things (see 3.2.7 for further remarks on lists of nouns). In this respect Spanish differs sharply from English, which omits the second determiner (definite and indefinite articles, possessives or demonstrative adjectives) in phrases like 'the sun and moon', 'a dog and cat', 'my brother and sister', 'those men and women'. Spanish says *el sol y la luna, un perro y un gato, mi hermano y mi hermana, esos hombres y esas mujeres*. ?*Un gato y perro* suggests a cross between a dog and a cat and **mis hermano y hermana* 'my brother and sister' is definitely not Spanish:

el padre y la madre	the father and mother
entre el hotel y la playa	between the hotel and (the) beach
Ayuda a mantener el país en el subdesarrollo, es decir la pobreza, la desigualdad y la dependencia (M. Vargas Llosa, Peru)	It helps to keep the country in a state of underdevelopment – i.e. poverty, inequality and dependence
El desorden callejero y las piedras son contrarios a la democracia (E. Frei in *Época*, Chile)	Street disorders and stones are contrary to democracy

But if the nouns are felt to form a single complex idea or are felt to be aspects of the same thing (often the case when they are joined by *o* 'or'), all but the first article may be omitted, especially in writing:

el misterio o enigma del origen . . . (O. Paz, Mexico)	the mystery or enigma of the origin . . .
El procedimiento y consecuencias son semejantes (M. Vargas Llosa, Peru)	The procedure and consequences are similar

. . . *renunciando a contar con **los** laboratorios, equipos, bibliotecas, aulas, sistemas audiovisuales indispensables para cumplir con su trabajo . . .* (M. Vargas Llosa, Peru)	. . . by giving up the laboratories, equipment, libraries, lecture-rooms, audio-visual systems indispensable for it to do its work. . .

Notes

(i) Nouns may constitute similar things in one context and not in another. One says *voy a comprarme **un** libro y **una** revista* 'I'm going to buy a book and a magazine' (two different things), but *los libros y (las) revistas están en el estante de arriba* 'the books and magazines are on the top shelf' (books and magazines both seen as members of the set 'publications').

(ii) If a single article is possible but the first noun in a list is feminine and the second masculine, good style requires that the article should nevertheless appear before both. One could say *las aulas y **los** equipos* 'lecture-rooms and equipment' or *los equipos y aulas* but preferably not *las aulas y equipos*. But this is often disregarded, cf. *las liebres, las perdices y faisanes, los cacé esta mañana* (M.Vargas Llosa, Peru, dialogue) 'I shot the hares, partridges and pheasants this morning' (*el faisán* = 'pheasant').

(iii) In pairs of animate nouns of different sex both require the article: *el toro y la vaca* 'the bull and (the) cow', *el abuelo y la abuela* 'grandfather and grandmother', never **el toro y vaca,* **el abuelo y abuela.*

3.2.5 Omission of articles in proverbs

Articles, definite and indefinite, are often omitted in proverbs and in statements that are meant to sound proverbial:

Gato escaldado del agua fría huye	A scalded cat runs from cold water
Virtudes y defectos van unidos	Virtues and defects go together
Oveja que bala, bocado que pierde	A bleating sheep misses a nibble (i.e. you miss out if you talk too much)
Turista que se enoja, no regresa (Luis Spota, Mexico, dialogue. The verb *enfadarse* is more usual than *enojarse* in Spain)	An angry tourist doesn't come back

3.2.6 Definite article with generic nouns

With the exceptions noted at 3.2.10, the definite article is required before generic nouns, i.e. nouns that refer to something in general. These are typically:

(a) Abstract nouns referring to a concept in general:

la democracia	democracy
el catolicismo español	Spanish Catholicism
La sociedad cubana reclama . . .	Cuban society demands . . .
Mi relato será fiel a la realidad (J. L. Borges, Argentina)	My story will be true to reality
*El debate conceptual sobre **la** cultura, **los** derechos y **la** autonomía indígena* . . . (*La Reforma*, Mexico)	The conceptual debate about culture, rights and native (i.e. Amerindian) autonomy . . .

Colo(u)r nouns are members of this class and require the article: *el azul* 'blue', *el negro* 'black', *el amarillo es un color que no me gusta* 'yellow is a colour I don't like'. A sentence like *¿te gusta el rojo?* is therefore ambiguous: 'do you like the red **one**' or 'do you like red?'. Illnesses are also treated as abstract nouns: *la tuberculosis* 'tuberculosis', *el SIDA* 'AIDS', *la diabetes* 'diabetes', *el sarampión* 'measles'.

(b) Substances in general:

El salvado es bueno para la digestión	Bran is good for the digestion
El acero inoxidable es carísimo	Stainless steel is extremely expensive
La sangre no tiene precio	Blood has no price

(c) Countable nouns which refer to all the members of their class:

Los *belgas beben mucha cerveza*	Belgians (in general) drink a lot of beer
A las 15:00 **los** *automovilistas debían*	At 3 p.m. car-drivers had to make
contentarse con escuchar la radio	do with listening to their radios
(*La Nación*, Argentina; refers to all the	
drivers present at the time)	
El tigre es un animal peligroso	The tiger is a dangerous animal
El periodista escribe para el olvido	Journalists (lit. 'the journalist') write for
(J. L. Borges, Argentina, dialogue)	oblivion

Notes

(i) These rules are especially binding when the noun is the subject of a verb. The article cannot be omitted in the following sentences (but see 3.2.7. for the omission of the article from lists of two or more generic nouns):

no me gusta **la** *manzanilla*	I don't like camomile
el *azúcar es malo para los dientes*	sugar is bad for the teeth

But when the generic noun is the object of a verb or is preceded by a preposition, the definite article is sometimes omitted. See 3.2.10 for examples. See 3.2.8 note **(i)** and 3.4.2 for sentences like *expertos americanos dicen* . . . 'American experts say' in which the noun may in fact be partitive, i.e. it does not really apply to every member of the class it denotes.

(ii) Sentences like *me gusta el vino, me gustan las cerezas* are therefore ambiguous out of context: 'I like the wine/the cherries' or 'I like wine/cherries'. In practice context or intonation makes the meaning clear, or a demonstrative – *este vino* 'this wine', *estas cerezas* 'these cherries' – can be used for the first meaning.

(iii) Use of a singular count noun with a generic meaning is more frequent and less literary in Spanish than in English, where it may sound old-fashioned, e.g. *el español, cuando está de vacaciones, come mucho marisco* 'Spaniards, when they're on holiday, eat a lot of shellfish' (rather than 'the Spaniard, when on holiday, eats . . . ').

3.2.7 Omission of the article in lists

When two or more generic nouns follow one another, all the articles may be omitted, especially (but not exclusively) in literary style. One must say *esto podrá interesar a* **los** *jóvenes* 'this may interest the young' (i.e. 'young people'), but in both languages one could omit the bracketed items in *esto podrá interesar a (los) jóvenes y (a los) viejos* 'this may interest (the) young and (the) old'. Compare also *Darwin descubrió la idea* **del** *orden* 'Darwin discovered the idea of order' and *Darwin descubrió las ideas de orden y estructura* 'Darwin discovered the ideas of order and structure.' Further examples:

Ingleses y alemanes, en cuyos idiomas no	Englishmen and Germans, in whose
existe la ñ, encuentran cierta dificultad en	languages ñ does not exist, find it
pronunciarla (instead of *Los ingleses y*	somewhat difficult to pronounce
los alemanes)	

Debilidad y falta de autoridad no son garantía de seriedad negociadora de la contraparte (*El Tiempo*, Colombia)	Weakness and lack of authority are no guarantee of seriousness in negotiating on the part of the opposite party
Tanta tripulación como oficialía se habían convertido en sus amigos (S. Galindo, Mexico)	Both crew and officers had become his friends

3.2.8 Omission of article before partitive nouns

The article is not used before nouns that refer not to the whole but only to part of something ('partitive' nouns), i.e.

(a) before partitive mass (uncountable) nouns, i.e. nouns that refer only to a part of the whole:

Quiero cerveza	I want (some) beer
Eso necesita valor	That needs courage
No hay agua	There isn't any water/There's no water
Dame paciencia	Give me patience

The difference between generic and non-generic mass nouns is, however, not always obvious, as in the sentence *como carne* 'I eat meat', where *carne* apparently refers to meat in general. See 3.2.10 for further comments on the subject.

(b) Before partitive count nouns, i.e. countable nouns that in English could normally be preceded by 'some':

No se te olvide traer clavos	Don't forget to bring (some) nails
Incluso nos dieron flores	They even gave us (some) flowers
Llevan armas	They're carrying weapons

Notes

(i) Unqualified partitive nouns rarely appear in front of the verb of which they are the subject: *caían bombas por todas partes* (not **bombas caían por todas partes*) 'bombs were falling everywhere', *salían malas hierbas entre las flores* 'weeds were emerging among the flowers', *ahora pasan taxis* 'there are some taxis going past now'.

However, partitive nouns modified by an adjective or by some expression like *como ése/ese* 'like that one' may appear in front of the verb of which they are the subject, but see 3.4.2 for the omission of *unos/unas*: *cosas como ésas/esas sólo/solo te pasan a ti* (example from M. Moliner) 'things like that only happen to you', *hombres como él no se encuentran a menudo* 'one doesn't often find men like him'. For *expertos americanos dicen que . . .* 'American experts say that' see 3.4.2.

(ii) French and Italian regularly use *de* or *di* before partitive nouns: *il a **des** roses rouges/ha **delle** rose rosse* = *tiene rosas rojas* '(s)he's got some red roses'. De is not used in this way in Spanish, but it may occasionally appear before a demonstrative adjective to make it clear that 'some of' rather than 'all of' is meant. Compare *tráenos **de** ese vino tan bueno que nos serviste ayer* 'bring us **some of** that really good wine you served us yesterday', and *tráenos ese vino tan bueno que nos serviste ayer* 'bring us that really good wine you served us yesterday'.

3.2.9 Definite article required before nouns restricted by a qualifier

As in English, a noun that does not require the definite article when it stands alone usually requires it when it is qualified by a following word or phrase. Compare:

Estamos hablando de religión	We're talking (about) religion
Está hecho de oro	It's made of gold

and

*Estamos hablando de **la** religión de*	We're talking about the religion
los antiguos persas	of the ancient Persians
*Está hecho **del** oro que trajeron de las Indias*	It's made from the gold they brought
	from the Indies

This rule must be understood to override any of the rules of article omission that follow. However, a qualifier does not always make a noun specific: the resulting noun phrase may still be generic in its own right:

Está hecho de oro macizo	It's made of solid gold
Estamos hablando de religión antigua	We're talking about ancient religion
No hablo con traidores de su patria	I don't talk to traitors to their own
	country

3.2.10 Apparent exceptions to the rules outlined in 3.2.6

The general rule given at 3.2.6 – that generic nouns require the definite article – has exceptions. In the sentence *yo como carne* 'I eat meat', *carne* seems to be generic: it refers to all meat and should apparently require the definite article. Such exceptions usually arise because the noun does not really refer to the whole of its class but only to a part, although this may not always be obvious. This is especially true of nouns which (a) follow prepositions or (b) are the object of certain kinds of verb:

(a) Omission after prepositions
Nouns following prepositions very often really only denote a part or an aspect of the thing they refer to. If this is the case, they take no definite article:

Le gusta salir con ingleses	(S)he likes going out with English people
(one or a few at a time, not the	
whole species)	
El Ministerio de Justicia	The Ministry of Justice
(local, not universal justice)	
Ella siempre acaba hablando de sexo	She always ends up talking about sex
(S. Puértolas, Spain, dialogue)	
. . . las polémicas sobre diálogos regionales	. . . arguments about regional dialogues
con la guerrilla (El Tiempo, Colombia)	with the guerrilla forces

For further details about omission after the preposition *de*, see 3.2.11.
(b) After certain verbs, e.g. of consuming, desiring, producing, nouns which at first sight seem generic may on examination be seen to be partitive:

Los lagartos comen moscas	Lizards eat flies (one or two at a time)
Escribo novelas de ciencia ficción	I write science-fiction novels
Claro que uso jabón	Of course I use soap
Queremos paz	We want peace

But if the verb really affects the whole of its object in general – usually the case with verbs of human emotion like 'love', 'hate', 'admire', 'criticize', 'censure', 'reject', etc. – then the article is required:

*Odio **las** novelas de ciencia ficción*	I hate science-fiction novels
*Me encanta **el** helado de vainilla*	I love vanilla ice cream
*Hay que combatir **el** terrorismo*	Terrorism must be fought

(c) Omission in adverbial phrases

The article is not used in numerous adverbial phrases involving a preposition plus a noun:

*la confusión **por antonomasia***	confusion personified/par excellence
a cántaros	in pitcherfuls
por avión	by plane
en tren/coche	by train/car
Estamos aquí de observadores	We're here as observers
De niña yo sólo/solo hablaba catalán	As a little girl I only spoke Catalan

Note

Omission or retention of the article with abstract and mass nouns after a preposition often depends on the point of view of the speaker. One can say either *publicó tres artículos sobre poesía* 'he published three articles on poetry' or ... *sobre la poesía* 'on Poetry'. The latter implies the universal concept 'Poetry'; the former implies 'aspects of poetry'. The difference is slight and the strong modern tendency is to avoid using the article; but in some cases the article is more likely, as in *una conferencia sobre **la** Libertad* 'a lecture on Freedom'.

3.2.11 The definite article after *de*

When two nouns are joined by *de* to express what is effectively a new concept, the article is not used before the second noun. Compare *la rueda **del** coche* 'the wheel of/from the car', and *una rueda **de** coche* 'a car wheel':

la carne de la vaca	the meat of the cow
la carne de vaca	beef
los sombreros de las mujeres	the women's hats
los sombreros de mujer	women's hats
el dolor de muelas	toothache
un crimen de pasión	a crime of passion
lecciones de contabilidad	lessons in accountancy
... *la tristeza de flor de cementerio que dan*	... the cemetery-flower sadness that
los lirios (M. Puig, Argentina, dialogue)	irises give off (lit 'give')

Such combinations are often denoted in English by compound nouns: *la noche de la fiesta* 'the night of the party', *noche de fiesta* 'party night'.

Note

Latin-American language, particularly the press, uses *de* constructions without the article that are rejected in Peninsular Spanish, cf. *el problema **de** orden público* es cada día más grave (*El Tiempo*, Colombia; Spain *el problema **del** orden público*). This may be due to the influence of English compounds like 'the public order problem'.

3.2.12 Use of the definite article after *haber* ('there is'/'there are')

Spanish does not normally allow the definite article to appear after *haber*: *hay agua* 'there's water', *hubo una tormenta* 'there was a storm', but *está el cartero* 'there's the postman'/ 'the postman's arrived'. See 30.2.1 note **(iii)**.

3.2.13 Omission of the definite articles in book, film and other titles

At the beginning of titles of works of literature or art the definite article is often suppressed before nouns that are not felt to be unique entities (for the non-use of capital letters in book titles, see 39.3.2d):

Política y estado bajo el régimen de Franco	*Politics and the State under the Franco Regime*
Casa de campo, de José Donoso	*The Country House*, by José Donoso
Selección de poemas	*Selected Poems*

But with unique entities or proper names the article is retained:

La casa verde, de Mario Vargas Llosa	*The Green House*, by Mario Vargas Llosa
La Iglesia en España ayer y mañana	*The Church in Spain Yesterday and Tomorrow*

3.2.14 Omission in headlines

In Spain the grammar of headlines is fairly normal with respect to article omission, but in Latin America headlines follow English practice in omitting articles (for the word order of these Latin-American headlines see 37.5.1, note **(iii)**):

Ingleses toman Islas Georgias luego de combate de 2 horas (*La Prensa*, Peru)	British[1] take Georgias after two-hour battle
Causa de deslizamiento verán expertos (idem)	Experts to investigate cause of landslide
Afirma divorcios producen temblor (*Última Hora*, Dominican Republic, quoted in *Variedades* 20)	'Divorces cause Earthquakes' Claim

3.2.15 The definite article with names of unique entities

Use of the definite article with unique entities more or less corresponds to English practice, e.g. *la Casa Blanca* 'the White House', *el Atlántico* 'the Atlantic', *el Pacífico* 'the Pacific', *la Virgen* 'the Virgin', *el Camino de Santiago* 'the Milky Way' (lit. 'St James's Way'), *la estratosfera* 'the stratosphere', *la Luna* 'the Moon', *el Sol* 'the Sun'; but, as in English, no article with the names of planets: *Marte* 'Mars', *Júpiter* 'Jupiter', *Venus* 'Venus'. For the article with names of languages and countries, see 3.2.16 and 3.2.17.

Unlike English, Spanish also uses the definite article with mountains, volcanoes, heaven and hell: *el Infierno* 'hell', *el Cielo/el Paraíso* 'heaven'/'paradise', *el Everest*, *el Mont Blanc*.

As in English, the definite article is not used with personal names as opposed to epithets, titles or nicknames: *Dios* 'God', *Cristo* 'Christ' (very rarely *el Cristo*), *Jesucristo* 'Jesus Christ', *Satanás* 'Satan', but *el Salvador* 'the Saviour', *la Inmaculada* 'the Blessed Virgin', *'el Che'* 'Che Guevara'. For the article before ordinary personal names see 3.2.21.

3.2.16 Definite article with names of languages

Usage is capricious and departures from the following rules may occur:

(a) no article after *en*, or, usually, after *saber, aprender, hablar*:

en español, en inglés	in Spanish, in English
Sé quechua	I know Quechua
Aprendo alemán, habla griego	I'm learning German, he speaks Greek

---

[1] The distinction between 'English' and 'British' is not widely understood, especially in Latin America.

But when the verb is modified by an adverb the article is used: *habla correctamente **el** francés* 'he speaks French fluently', *hablaba bien el italiano* (J. L. Borges, Argentina). This also applies to the following section.

(b) Optional article after *entender* 'understand', *escribir* 'write', *estudiar* 'study':

Entiendo (el) inglés	I understand English
Escribe (el) italiano	He writes Italian

(c) After *de* meaning 'from' and after other prepositions, the article is used:

traducir del español al francés	to translate from Spanish to French
una palabra del griego	a word from Greek
Comparado con el ruso, el español parece poco complicado	Compared with Russian, Spanish seems uncomplicated

(d) After *de* meaning 'of', the article is used only if the whole language is meant: *curso de español* 'Spanish course' (really only 'aspects of Spanish'), but *dificultades del español* 'difficulties of Spanish' (in general), *las sutilezas del japonés* 'the subtleties of Japanese'.

(e) After *traducir* 'translate', *dominar* 'master', *chapurrear* 'speak badly', *destrozar* 'murder' and other verbs and prepositions not discussed above, the article is used: *domina perfectamente el portugués* 'he's a complete master of Portuguese', *chapurrea el inglés* 'he speaks broken English'.

(f) If the language is the subject of a verb it requires the article:

El francés es difícil	French is difficult
El español es una lengua hermosa	Spanish is a beautiful language

(g) If the language is qualified by a following word or phrase, the article is required:

el español de Colombia	the Spanish of Colombia
el inglés que se habla en Tennessee	the English spoken in Tennessee

3.2.17 Definite article with names of countries

This is a difficult problem since spoken usage varies and is out of line with the most modern written styles. *El País* (*Libro de estilo* 8.28) orders its journalists to write all countries without the article except *la India, el Reino Unido* 'the United Kingdom' and *los Países Bajos* 'the Low Countries'. One even sees *en Reino Unido* in advertisements.

Spoken language tends to make more use of the article than written, especially journalistic styles. The rules of everyday spoken language seem to be:

(a) Obligatory: *la India, El Salvador* (capital *E* because the *El* is part of the name), *el Reino Unido* 'the United Kingdom', *La República Dominicana*.

(b) Usual: *el Camerún* Cameroon, *el Líbano* Lebanon, *la China, el Oriente Medio* 'The Middle East', *el Senegal, el Sudán, la Somalia, el Yemen*.

(c) Optional: *(la) Arabia Saudita, (la) Argentina* (article always used in Argentina), *(el) Brasil, (el) Canadá, (el) Ecuador, (las) Filipinas* 'the Philippines', *(el) Irak, (el) Irán, (el) Japón, (el) Nepal, (el) Pakistán, (el) Paraguay, (el) Perú, (el) Tibet, (el) Uruguay, (el) Vietnam*.

The article is frequently heard with these nouns in everyday speech, probably more so in Latin America than in Spain. Other countries do not take the article:

tres años en Australia/Egipto/Noruega/Europa Oriental/África del Sur 'three years in Australia/Egypt/Norway/Eastern Europe/South Africa'.

Notes

(i) 'The United States' is either *los Estados Unidos* (plural agreement) or, much more usual, *Estados Unidos* (singular agreement, no article), the only form allowed in *El País* (Spain). *Gran Bretaña* 'Great Britain' does not take the article, but *el Reino Unido* 'the United Kingdom' does.

(ii) In older texts, particularly in solemn diplomatic language, names of countries occasionally appear with the article: *la Francia, la Inglaterra*, etc.

(iii) All place names require the article when they are qualified or restricted by a following adjective, phrase or clause, unless the qualifier is part of an official name: *la España contemporánea* 'contemporary Spain', *la Suecia que yo conocía* 'the Sweden I knew', but *en Australia Occidental* 'in Western Australia', *en Irlanda del Norte* 'in Northern Ireland'.

(iv) Names of some well-known regions, as opposed to countries, tend to be variable: *(la) Europa Central, (la) América del Sur*.

3.2.18 Definite article with provinces, regions, cities and towns

Some place names include the article as an inseparable feature:

Los Ángeles	*La Haya* The Hague	*la Plata*
El Cairo	*la Mancha*	*la Rioja*
La Coruña	*La Meca* Mecca	
El Havre	*La Paz*	

Otherwise the article is not used, unless 3.2.9 applies, as in *el Buenos Aires de hoy* 'Buenos Aires today', *la Roma de Cicerón* 'Cicero's Rome', etc.

Note

The article is usually written with a capital letter only in the case of cities (Seco 1998, 177). This is the practice recommended by *El País* (Spain).

3.2.19 Definite article before names of streets, roads, squares, etc.

The definite article is used before roads, squares, avenues, lanes, alleys and similar places:

*Vive en **la** plaza/**la** calle de la Independencia*	He lives in Independence square/street
*la Embajada de los EE.UU., en **la** avenida*	the US Embassy on Wilson Avenue
Wilson (Caretas, Peru)	

3.2.20 Definite articles with days of the week, months and years

(a) The definite article appears with days of the week, but it does not appear when the day is the predicate of *ser* 'to be':

Llegan el martes	They're arriving on Tuesday
cerrado los viernes	closed on Friday(s)
Los domingos las calles están casi vacías	On Sundays the streets are nearly empty
(M. Benedetti, Uruguay, dialogue)	
Odio los lunes	I hate Mondays
El miércoles es cuando habrá menos	Wednesday's the day there'll be least
a partir del domingo	after Sunday

But

*Hoy **es** lunes*	Today is Monday
Trabajo de lunes a jueves	I work **from** Monday to Thursday

Note, however, that if *ser* means 'to happen' the article is used: *fue el jueves por la tarde* 'it was/happened on Thursday afternoon'.

When the day of the week is preceded by *de*, when it means 'of', the article is used: *ocurrió en la noche del viernes* 'it happened on Friday night.'

The article is not used in dates: *miércoles 23 de marzo de 1943* 'Wednesday 23 March 1943'.

(b) The definite article is not used with the names of months, but it is used with the words *mes* 'month', *año* 'year', *mañana* 'morning', *tarde* 'afternoon'/'evening', *noche* 'night', and *madrugada* 'dawn', except in phrases like *a finales de mes* 'at the end of the month', *a principios de año* 'at the beginning of the year':

Se casan en enero	They're getting married in January
Empezarás el mes que viene	You start next month
El año próximo iremos a Cuba	We'll go to Cuba next year
¿Dónde estaba usted la mañana/tarde	Where were you on Monday morning/
/noche/la madrugada del lunes?	afternoon/night/on Monday at dawn?

3.2.21 Definite article with personal names

The definite article occasionally appears before the surname of very famous women: *la Loren, la Callas, la Pardo Bazán, . . . tengo que estar en Nueva York para el funeral de la Garbo* (Terenci Moix, Spain, dialogue) ' . . . I have to be in New York for Greta Garbo's funeral'. But it is not used in this way before men's surnames, except occasionally in law courts to refer to the accused.

Use of the article before first names, e.g. *la María, la Josefa, el Mario*, is considered substandard, regional or typical of courtroom language or police reports, unless the name is qualified, as in *la simpática Inés* 'the kindly Inés'.

The definite article usually appears before nicknames: *el Che nunca fue derrotado* '"Che" (Guevara) was never defeated' (*Cuba Internacional*, Cuba),[2] *detuvieron a Ramón Pérez 'el Duque'* 'they arrested Ramón Perez "the Duke"' (in Spain virtually all notorious criminals are referred to by nicknames).

In some places, e.g. Chile and Catalonia, use of the article before first names is quite common even in educated speech,[3] but it is generally best avoided by foreign learners since it may sound condescending or imply notoriety. Students of Portuguese should not use the article in Spanish: *o António quer um café = Antonio quiere un café*.

3.2.22 Definite article with sports teams

The masculine article is used before sports teams: *el Granada* 'Granada FC', *el Manchester United, el Argentina*.

3.2.23 Definite article before nouns of family relationship

Abuelo/abuela takes the article: *entré a dar un beso a la abuela* 'I went in to give grandmother a kiss', *el abuelo comía en silencio* 'grandfather was eating in silence',

---

[2] But a few lines above in the same article *Che nunca fue derrotado*, no doubt because the revolutionary hero's nickname 'Che' is sometimes felt to be a proper name.

[3] The survey by DeMello (1992, 3) of spoken usage in eleven major Hispanic cities reveals Santiago, Chile, to be the place where the construction is most common, and overwhelmingly more so with women's names.

la abuelita llamó a un sacerdote (A. Mastretta, Mexico, dialogue) 'grandmother called a priest'.

Tío/tía 'uncle'/'aunt' also take the article *di un beso a la tía* 'I gave auntie a kiss'. But if the person is named the article is not used by everyone: *le di un beso a tía Julia* 'I kissed aunt Julia' (this rule is no longer observed universally, but children in Madrid were until quite recently sometimes rebuked for saying *a la tía Julia*). Latin-American usage also seems to be uncertain, although it overwhelmingly favours use of the article:

La tía Julia y el escribidor	*Aunt Julia and the Scriptwriter*
(title of novel by M. Vargas Llosa, Peru)	
La tía Verónica era una niña de ojos profundos	Aunt Veronica was a girl with deep eyes
y labios delgados (A. Mastretta, Mexico)	and thin lips

In rural areas *tío/tía* may be used before the first names of local worthies: *el tío José/la tía Paca* 'old José'/'old Paca'. With *papá, mamá* use of the article may also sound uneducated to some speakers if the noun stands alone: *dale un beso a papá* 'give daddy a kiss'.

3.2.24 Definite article with personal titles

The definite article is used before the title of a person being talked about: *el señor Moreira, el profesor Smith, el general Rodríguez, el presidente Belaúnde, el doctor Fleming, el padre Blanco* 'Father Blanco'. It is also used to refer to a couple: *los señores de Barral* 'Mr and Mrs Barral'. It is not used if the person is directly addressed: *pase usted, señor Sender/señor Presidente/padre Blanco* 'come in, Mr Sender/Mr President/Father Blanco'.

The definite article is not, however, used before *don, doña, fray, san, santa, sor* or before foreign titles like *míster, monsieur, Herr*: *don Miguel, fray Bentos, santa Teresa, sor Juana, míster Smith*, etc.

Notes

(i) *Don/doña* are used before the first names of older persons of respected social status and on envelopes (less now than formerly): *señor don Miguel Ramírez, doña Josefa, don Miguel.*
(ii) For the military forms of address *mi general* 'General', *mi coronel* 'Colonel' see 8.3.3.

3.2.25 Definite article in apposition

The definite article is usually absent in apposition when the following phrase is non-restrictive – i.e. it does not limit the meaning of the previous phrase:

Madrid, capital de España	Madrid, the capital of Spain
Lázaro Conesal, propietario del hotel	Lázaro Conesal, the owner of the hotel
(V. Montalbán, Spain)	
Buenos Aires, ciudad que no me atrae	Buenos Aires, a city that doesn't
(J. L. Borges, Argentina, dialogue)	attract me
Ahora, a buscar un digno sustituto de	Now let's start looking for a worthy
Pedro, tarea nada fácil (J. J. Arreola,	substitute for Pedro, no easy task
Mexico, dialogue)	

But it is retained:

(a) if the following phrase is restrictive, i.e. it is used to remove a possible confusion of identity: *Miró, **el** autor* 'Miró the author' (not the painter); *Córdoba, **la** ciudad argentina* 'Cordoba, the Argentine city' (not the one in Spain);

(b) if the following phrase is a comparative or superlative: *Cervantes, **el** mayor novelista español* 'Cervantes, the greatest Spanish novelist', *Joaquín, el **más** listo de los dos* 'Joaquin, the cleverer of the two', *Alma Pondal, la mejor novelista ama de casa* (M. Vázquez Montalbán, Spain) 'Alma Pondal, the best of the "housewife" novelists.'

(c) if the apposition is qualified by a following word or phrase:

*Javier Marcos, **el** arquitecto que diseñó las dos fuentes*	Javier Marcos, the architect who designed the two fountains

3.2.26 Definite article with numbered nouns

Unlike English, nouns identified by a number take the article:

*Vivo en **el** piso* (Lat. Am. *el apartamento/ el departamento*) *38*	I live in apartment 38
Vive en la calle Serrano, en el 23/en el 23 de la calle Serrano/(but *vive en Serrano 23*)	He lives at 23 Serrano Street
*una disposición **del** artículo 277 de la Constitución*	a provision in Art. 277 of the Constitution
*unas fotos **del** 93*	some photos from 1993
el diez por ciento	ten per cent

3.2.27 Definite article in phrases denoting place

The following require the definite article in Spanish:

*a/en/de **la** cama* to/in/from bed	*en el escenario* on stage
a/en/de la iglesia to/in/from church	*en la televisión* on television
al/en el/del cielo/infierno to/in/from heaven/hell	*en el espacio* in space
al/en el/del hospital to/in/from hospital/	*en el mar* at sea, on/in the sea
en la cárcel/en la iglesia/en el colegio/ en el trabajo in prison/at school/at work	*debajo de la tierra* (but *bajo tierra*) underground

Notes

(i) *A/en/de casa* 'at/in/from home' are often expressed by *a/en/de **la** casa* in Latin America.
(ii) Many speakers differentiate *en cama* 'in bed ill' and *en la cama* 'in bed resting', but the distinction is not universal.

3.2.28 Definite article after the verb *jugar*

Jugar requires the article in Spain: *jugar a la pelota* 'to play ball/with a ball', *jugar al ajedrez* 'to play chess', *jugar a las cartas* 'to play cards', *jugar al escondite* 'to play hide and seek'. It often appears without the article in Lat. Am.: *mi padre no juega golf y mi madre no juega bridch* (L. Otero, Cuba, dialogue; the usual spelling is *bridge*) 'my father doesn't play golf and my mother doesn't play bridge', *jugar tenis con él era como un consejo de ministros* (G. García Márquez, Colombia, dialogue) 'playing tennis with him was like (being at) a Cabinet Meeting'. But compare *ya sea fumando una pipa o jugando **al** ajedrez* (M. Puig, Argentina, dialogue) 'either smoking a pipe or playing chess'.

3.2.29 Definite article with personal pronouns

The definite article is required after first- and second-person plural pronouns in phrases like the following: *ustedes **los** uruguayos* 'you Uruguayans', *nosotros **los*** *pobres* 'we poor people', *vosotras **las** españolas* 'you Spanish women'. It is also used when the pronoun is not present:

***Los** ingleses siempre ocultáis vuestras emociones*	You English always hide your emotions
***Las** mujeres de los mineros siempre estamos en vilo pensando en los hombres* (A. López Salinas, Spain, dialogue)	We miners' wives are always on tenterhooks thinking about the men

3.2.30 Colloquial use of *la de*

In familiar language, *la de* may mean 'lots of':

. . . con la de números de abogado que vienen en la guía . . .	. . . with all the dozens of lawyers' numbers there are in the directory . . .
. . . la de veces que han dicho eso	. . . the number of times they've said that!
. . . la de lágrimas que solté (L. Sepúlveda, Chile, dialogue)	. . . the amount of tears I shed . . .

3.3 The indefinite article

3.3.1 Forms of the indefinite article

	Masculine	Feminine
Singular	*un*	*una*
Plural	*unos*	*unas*

Un is used before feminine nouns beginning with a stressed *a*, e.g. *un arma*. See 3.1.2.

3.3.2 Use of the indefinite article: general

In general terms, use of the indefinite article in Spanish corresponds to the use of 'a'/'an' in English, but there are two important differences:

(a) it is not used before singular countable nouns in certain contexts described below at 3.3.6–12, e.g. *tengo coche* 'I've got a car', *Mario es ingeniero* 'Mario's an engineer', *lo abrió sin llave* 'he opened it without a key', *es mentira* 'it's a lie';
(b) it can appear in the plural: ***unos** pantalones* 'a pair of trousers', *han organizado **unas** manifestaciones* 'they've organized demonstrations', *son **unos** genios incomprendidos* 'they're misunderstood geniuses'.

3.3.3 The indefinite article in French and Spanish

Use of the indefinite article corresponds quite closely in French and Spanish, but Spanish almost never uses partitive *de*; cf. *tengo vino* and *j'ai **du** vin* 'I've got some wine' (see 3.2.8 note **(ii)** for discussion), and French has no plural form of *un/une*, cf. Spanish ***unos** guantes* 'some gloves', French ***des** gants*. Neither language uses the indefinite article before professions: *je suis professeur, soy profesor* 'I'm a teacher'. Unlike French, Spanish regularly avoids the article in sentences of the type *tiene secretaria* 'he's got a secretary', c.f. *il a **une** secrétaire*. See 3.3.8.

3.3.4 Indefinite article before more than one noun

When more than one noun occurs in a sequence, the indefinite article is necessary before each noun (**un hombre y mujer* would be a cross between a man and a woman!):

Entraron **un** hombre y **una** mujer	A man and (a) woman entered
Compré una máquina de escribir y una papelera para mi despacho	I bought a typewriter and (a) wastepaper basket for my office

However, omission is necessary when the nouns refer to the same thing or to different aspects of the same thing:

una actriz y cantante	an actress and singer (same woman)
un cuchillo y abrelatas	a combined knife and tin-opener
Este libro está escrito con una maestría y delicadeza insólitas	This novel is written with unusual skill and delicacy

3.3.5 Omission before singular nouns: general

Un/una is often omitted before singular count nouns. This happens whenever the generic or universal features of the noun are being stressed. Compare *Pepe tiene secretaria* 'Pepe's got a secretary' (like most bosses) and *Pepe tiene **una** secretaria que habla chino* 'Pepe's got a Chinese-speaking secretary' (unlike most bosses), or *no salgas con él, tiene mujer* 'don't go out with him, he's got a wife' (i.e. he's married) and *no salgas con él, tiene una mujer en cada puerto* 'don't go out with him – he's got a woman in every port'.

3.3.6 Not used before professions, occupations, social status, sex

This is a common case of the phenomenon described in 3.3.7: *un/una* are not used before nouns which describe profession, occupation or social status, and are often omitted before nouns denoting sex. In this case the noun can be thought of as a sort of adjective that simply allocates the noun to a general type:

Soy piloto/Son buzos	I'm a pilot/They're divers
Es soltero/Es casada (compare está casada 'she's married'; see 29.4.1a for further details)	He's a bachelor/She's a married woman
Se hizo detective	He became a detective
Veo que es usted (una) mujer de buen gusto	I see you're a woman of good taste
. . . y aunque Alejandra era mujer . . . (E. Sábato, Argentina)	. . . and although Alejandra was a woman . . .

But nouns denoting personal qualities rather than membership of a profession or other group require the article: compare *es negrero* 'he is a slave-trader' and *es un negrero* 'he's a "slave-driver"' (i.e. makes you work too hard), *es carnicero* 'he's a butcher' (by trade); *es un carnicero* 'he's a butcher' (i.e. murderous); *es Supermán* 'he is Superman', *es un supermán* 'he's a superman', *el sargento se decía: 'No es un ladrón. Es un loco'* (M. Vargas Llosa, Peru) 'the sergeant said to himself "he's no thief. He's a madman."'

Notes

(i) The article is retained if it means 'one of . . .': *—¿Quién es ese que ha saludado? —Es **un** profesor* 'Who was that who said hullo?' 'He's one of the teachers.'

(ii) If a noun of the type discussed above is qualified, it usually becomes particularized (non-generic) and therefore requires the article. Compare *es actor* 'he's an actor' and *es un actor que nunca encuentra trabajo* 'he's an actor who never finds work', *me han dicho que usted es un hombre que se ha quedado solo* (A. Bryce Echenique, dialogue, Peru) 'they tell me that you are a man who has found himself alone'. But the resulting noun phrase may still be a recognized profession or a generic type, so no article will be used: *soy profesor de español*. See 3.3.9 for discussion.

3.3.7 Omission of the indefinite article with *ser* and nouns not included in 3.3.6

Omission of the indefinite article after *ser* is frequent **(a)** in certain common phrases, **(b)** in literary style. A rare English counterpart is the optional omission of 'a' with 'part': 'this is (a) part of our heritage' *esto es (una) parte de nuestro patrimonio*. Omission is more common in negative sentences and apparently more frequent in Peninsular Spanish than in Latin-American.

(a) In the following phrases omission seems to be optional, and it produces a slightly more literary style:

Es (una) coincidencia	It's a coincidence
Es (una) cuestión de dinero	It's a question of money
Es (una) víctima de las circunstancias	(S)he's a victim of circumstances

However, no clear rule can be formulated since the article is retained in other similar common phrases:

Es una lata (colloquial)	It's a nuisance
Es una pena	It's a pity
Es un problema	It's a problem
Es un desastre	It/(S)he's a disaster
Ha sido un éxito	It was a success

Omission may occur after the negative verb even though it is not usual after the positive verb:

No es molestia/problema	It's no bother/problem
No es exageración	It's no exaggeration
No es desventaja	It's not a disadvantage

(b) In other cases, omission often, but not always, produces a literary effect. In the following examples # indicates a deleted article:

La codorniz es # ave tiernísima (M. Delibes, Spain)	The quail is an extremely tender bird (to eat)
Es # mar de veras (M. Vargas Llosa, Peruvian dialogue)	It's (a) real sea
¡Ésta/Esta es # cuestión que a ustedes no les importa! (J. Ibargüengoitia, Mexico, dialogue)	This is an affair that has nothing to do with you!

In all the above examples the appropriate gender of *un* or *una* could have been used at the points marked, but the original texts omit the article.

Notes

(i) If the following noun is not generic but merely implies the possession of certain qualities, *un/una* is used: *el hombre es **un** lobo para el hombre* 'man is a wolf to man' (but not a member of the wolf species), *Mercedes es **un** terremoto* 'Mercedes is an earthquake' (i.e. a hell-raiser).

(ii) In formal literary styles, omission of *un/una* is normal in definitions when the subject comes first: *novela es toda obra de ficción que* . . . 'a novel is any work of fiction that . . .'.

(iii) Omission of the indefinite article before a qualified noun tends to produce an archaic or heavily literary effect (or it makes the sentence sound like stage-instructions), as in *entra una señora con sombrero verde con plumas de avestruz* 'a lady with a green hat with ostrich feathers enters', where **un** *sombrero verde* would nowadays be much more normal. Similarly, where Unamuno wrote, in the early twentieth century, *era un viejecillo [. . .] con levitón de largos bolsillos* 'he was a little old man . . . with a large frock-coat with deep pockets', a modern writer might prefer **un** *levitón*. Purists occasionally complain about this increasing use of the indefinite article, which they attribute to English or French influence.

3.3.8 Omission of *un/una* after other verbs

Spanish does not use *un/una* after a number of verbs such as *tener* 'have', *comprar* 'buy', *sacar* 'take' or 'draw out' (with cinema tickets, etc. = 'buy' or 'book'), *buscar* 'look for', *llevar* 'wear', when their object is a certain type of noun. These nouns refer to things of which one would normally have, use or be carrying only one at a time: umbrella, pen, spoon, nanny, valet, cook, hat, etc.

Pepe ya tiene secretaria	Pepe's got a secretary now
¿Tenías idea de lo que serías capaz de hacer?	Did you have any idea of what you'd be able to do?
Ya he sacado entrada	I've already got a ticket
Vamos a buscarle novia	Let's look for a girlfriend for him
Siempre lleva anillo	He always wears a ring
Barcelona tiene puerto y parque y tranvía y metro y autobús y cine (L. Goytisolo, Spain)	Barcelona has a port, park, tramway, metro, buses and cinema(s)
Hubo quien se ofendió y sacó pistola (M. Vargas Llosa, Peru)	There was one person who took offence/(US 'offense') and pulled a gun

The indefinite article is used if the particular identity of the object is relevant:

*Llevaba **una** falda blanca*	She was wearing a white skirt
Tenía [. . .] una carita de chico pecoso . . . (F. Umbral, Spain)	She had a cute face like a freckled boy's

Use of *un/una* with unqualified nouns may therefore hint at some suppressed comment: *tiene un coche/una casa . . .* 'you should see his car/house. . .'. This may sound insinuating, especially if applied to some word referring to a human being, e.g. *marido* 'husband', *novio* 'boyfriend', *novia* 'girlfriend'.

Note

If it would be normal to have more than one of the things denoted, or if the idea of 'one' is relevant, the article must be used: *¿tienes **un** hermano?* (not **¿tienes hermano?*) 'do you have a brother?', *¿tienes un dólar?* 'have you got a dollar?', *¿has comprado una novela?* 'have you bought a novel?', *tiene un novio en Burgos y otro en Huelva* 'she's got one boyfriend in Burgos and another in Huelva'.

3.3.9 Retention of indefinite article before qualified nouns

As soon as nouns are qualified (restricted) by a clause, phrase or adjective they become specific and the article is obligatory: *tengo padre* 'I've got a father' but *tengo **un** padre que es inaguantable* 'I've got an unbearable father', *era un hombre de costumbres cuidadosas* (A. Mastretta, Mexico) 'he was a man of prudent customs'. But if the resulting noun phrase is still generic the article may still be omitted: *tú eres (un) hombre respetable* 'you're a respectable man', *es pastor protestante* 'he's a Protestant minister', *el doctor Urdino es hombre serio, además de buen gerente, y* *persona curtida en asuntos económicos* (*El Tiempo*, Colombia) 'Doctor Urdino is a serious man as well as a good manager, and a person well-versed in economic matters.'

Note

This rule about the use of **unos** before qualified nouns also applies in the plural: *es* **un** *ejemplo/son* **unos** *ejemplos que hemos encontrado en tu novela* 'it's an example/they're examples we found in your novel, *en seguida me llené de* **unos** *celos juveniles hacia él* (F. Umbral, Spain) 'I was immediately filled with juvenile jealousy towards him', *nos convidó* **unas** *galletas de agua con queso fresco* (M. Vargas Llosa, Peru; in Spain *convidó* **a**) 'he offered us some water-biscuits (US 'crackers') with cheese'.

3.3.10 Omission of indefinite article in apposition

The indefinite article is not normally used in appositive phrases in written language:

El Español de hoy, lengua en ebullición	Spanish Today, A Language in Ferment (book title)
Estuvimos quince días en Acapulco, lugar que nunca olvidaré	We spent a fortnight in Acapulco, a place I'll never forget
a orillas del Huisne, arroyo de apariencia tranquila ... (J. L. Borges, Argentina)	on the banks of the Huisne, a seemingly tranquil stream ...

But in informal language, or if the noun in apposition is qualified by an adjective or clause, the article may optionally be retained:

... el Coronel Gaddafi de Libia, **un** *ardiente admirador del ayatollah Jomeini* (*Cambio16*, Spain)	... Colonel Gaddafi of Libya, a fervent admirer of Ayatollah Khomeini

3.3.11 Indefinite article to distinguish nouns from adjectives

Many Spanish nouns are indistinguishable in form from adjectives: use of *un/una* indicates that the noun is meant:

Juan es cobarde	John is cowardly
Juan es un cobarde	John is a coward
Papá es (un) fascista	Father is a fascist
Soy extranjero/un extranjero	I'm foreign/I'm a foreigner

Papá es fascista implies 'he's a committed Fascist', whereas *papá es* **un** *fascista* suggests 'he acts like a fascist'. The indefinite article is also used in the plural to retain the distinction: *son desgraciados* 'they're unhappy', *son* **unos** *desgraciados* 'they're wretches' (there is a change of meaning: *un desgraciado* 'a wretch', 'a "creep"').

3.3.12 Omission after *como, a modo/manera de, por, sin, con*

(a) The indefinite article is not used after *a manera de, a modo de* and after *como* when it means 'in the capacity of' or 'by way of':

a manera de prólogo	by way of a prologue
a modo de bastón	as/like a walking stick
como ejemplo	as an example
Utilicé mi zapato como martillo	I used my shoe as a hammer
Vino como ayudante	He came as an assistant

(b) It is not used after *por* when it means 'instead of', 'in place of' or 'for' in phrases like *por respuesta le dio un beso* 'she gave him a kiss as a reply', *por toda comida me dieron un plato de arroz* 'for a meal they gave me a plate of rice' (i.e. 'all I got for a meal was . . . ').

(c) It is not usually used after *sin* without:

No lo vas a poder cortar sin cuchillo/No vas a poder cortarlo sin cuchillo	You won't be able to cut it without a knife
Ha venido sin camisa	He's come without a shirt on
un gato sin cola	a cat without a tail

But if the idea of 'one' is stressed, or, in most cases, if the noun is qualified by an adjective or clause, the article is required:

sin una peseta	without a (single) peseta
	sin un amigo a quien contar sus problemas
without a friend to tell his problems to	

(d) It is not used after *con* when it means 'wearing', 'equipped with' and in many other adverbial phrases:

Siempre va con abrigo	He always wears an overcoat
una casa con jardin	a house with a garden
La Esfinge [. . .] es un león echado en la tierra y con cabeza de hombre (J. L. Borges, Argentina)	The Sphinx is a lion stretched out on the ground, with a man's head
Lo escribí con lápiz	I wrote it with a pencil

3.3.13 Omission in exclamations, after *qué*, and before *tal, medio, cierto, otro*

The following constructions differ from English:

¡Extraña coincidencia!	What a strange coincidence!
¡qué cantidad!/¡qué ruido!/¡qué pena!	What a quantity/noise/pity!
¿Cómo ha podido hacer tal/semejante cosa? (colloquially *una cosa así; un tal* = 'a certain')	How could he have done such a thing?
media pinta/medio kilo	half a pint/kilo
cierta mujer/otra cerveza	a certain woman/another beer

See 9.7 for *cierto* and 9.13 for *otro*.

3.4 *Unos/unas*

Despite the fact that it derives from the Latin word for 'one', the Spanish indefinite article can nevertheless be used in the plural with a variety of meanings. (For a comparison of *algunos* and *unos*, which may sometimes both mean 'some', see 9.4.2. For the pronoun *uno* see 9.3 note **(iv)** and 28.7.1).

3.4.1 Uses of *unos/unas*

(a) before numbers, = 'approximately':

El terremoto duró unos 25 segundos	The earthquake lasted some twenty-five seconds
. . . y unos cinco minutos después se detuvo (G. García Márquez, Colombia)	. . . and about five minutes later it stopped

(b) before plural nouns, = 'some' or 'a few'

Tomamos unas cervezas	We had some beers
Todavía tenía unos restos de fe	He still had some vestiges of faith
Sonreí . . . pero fue peor: unos dientes	I smiled, but it was worse: a set of
amarillos aparecieron	yellow teeth appeared (or 'some
(C. Rico-Godoy, Spain)	yellow teeth appeared')
En unas horas vuelve a su casa	You'll be going back home in
(G. García Márquez, Colombia, dialogue.	a couple of hours'
In Spain, usually *dentro de unas horas*	
in this type of sentence)	

When used thus it may simply moderate the force of a following noun. It can therefore add a modest note:

Mira estas fotos – son unas vistas	Look at these photos – they're a couple
tomadas en Guadalajara	of shots taken in Guadalajara
Se sintió viejo, triste, inútil, y con unos deseos	He felt old, sad, useless, and with an
de llorar tan urgentes que no pudo hablar	urge to weep that was so urgent that
más (G. García Márquez, Colombia)	he could speak no more

But sometimes use of *unos* makes little difference:

El pacifismo debería traducirse en unos	Pacifism ought to be translated into
comportamientos políticos que no tuviesen	(a set of) patterns of political
ninguna indulgencia con los violentos	behaviour which show no indulgence
(*La Vanguardia*, *unos* deletable)	towards the violent

(c) Before nouns that only appear in the plural, *unos* shows that only one is meant. If the noun denotes a symmetrical object like trousers, binoculars, scissors, *unos/unas* means 'a pair of':

Me caí por unas escaleras/por una escalera	I fell down some/a flight of stairs
Voy a tomarme unas vacaciones	I'm going to have a holiday/vacation
unos pantalones/unas gafas/unas	a pair of trousers(US
cortinas a rayas	'pants')/glasses/curtains
Se quedó mirándolo con unos ojos azules	He stood looking at him with totally
totalmente idos (M. Vargas Llosa, Peru)	vacant blue eyes (i.e. a pair of eyes)

(d) Use of *unos/unas* may show that the plural noun following is not being used generically:

Son payasos	They're (circus) clowns
Son unos payasos	They're (acting like) clowns
Son zorros	They're foxes (species)
Son unos zorros	They're really cunning/like foxes

(e) *Unos/unas* may be needed to show that the following noun is a noun and not an adjective or noun used as an adjective. See 3.3.11 for examples.

3.4.2 Omission of *unos/unas*

There is a growing tendency in written Spanish, especially in journalism, to avoid the use of *unos* (and of *algunos*) in sentences of the kind *expertos americanos afirman que . . .* 'American experts claim that . . . '. The omission is no doubt a journalistic ruse to hide the fact that only one or two experts were really consulted. Spoken Spanish requires *los* if the meaning is 'all American experts', *algunos* if the meaning is 'some' and *unos* if 'a few' is intended.

In other cases omission produces a literary effect: *eléctricas letras verdes intermitentes anunciaron la salida del vuelo* (M. Vázquez Montalbán, Spain) 'flashing green electric lights announced the departure of the flight', where **unas** *letras verdes eléctricas e intermitentes* . . . would have been more usual.

4

Adjectives

4.1 General

(a) Spanish adjectives agree with nouns and pronouns in number and, if possible, in gender. Adjectives therefore have either two forms, e.g. *natural/naturales*, or four forms: *bueno/buena/buenos/buenas*. A few unusual adjectives, e.g. *macho* 'male', *violeta* 'violet', are invariable in form. They are discussed at 4.2.3.

(b) The positioning of adjectives is a subtle problem, the difference between *un problema difícil* and *un difícil problema* 'a difficult problem' or *una nube lejana* and *una lejana nube* 'a distant cloud' being virtually untranslatable in English. See section 4.11

(c) It is necessary to distinguish 'descriptive' and 'attributive'[1] adjectives. Descriptive adjectives can be thought of as replacements of a relative clause: *un libro aburrido* 'a boring book' is the same as *un libro que es aburrido* 'a book that is boring'. Attributive adjectives usually replace *de* + a noun: *un programa televisivo* = *un programa de televisión* ' TV program(me)'. Descriptive adjectives are discussed at 4.12.

(d) As in other Romance languages, adjectives in Spanish become nouns if an article, demonstrative, numeral or some other qualifier is added: *viejo/el viejo* 'old'/'the old man' or 'the old one', *enfermo/estos enfermos* 'ill'/'sick'/'these ill/sick people', *joven/estos jóvenes* 'young'/'these young people', etc. In this respect the difference between adjectives and nouns in Spanish is not very clear, especially in view of the fact that nouns can occasionally be used like adjectives, as in *ella es más mujer que Ana* 'she's more (of a) woman than Ana' (or 'more feminine'). Such adjectival use of nouns is discussed at 4.10.

However, although adjectives can serve as nouns, adjectives are nevertheless formed in unpredictable ways *from* nouns: *automóvil>automovilístico*, *legislación> legislativo*, *montaña>montañoso*, *leche>lácteo* 'milk', etc.

(e) Some adjectives can be used with object pronouns and the verb *ser*: *me es importante* 'it's important to me', *nos es imprescindible* 'he's indispensable to us', *estas materias primas le son muy necesarias* 'these raw materials are very necessary for him/you'; but most cannot. See 11.9 (Pronouns) for discussion.

(f) Adjectival participles ending in *-ante*, *-iente*, e.g. *vinculante* 'binding', *preocupante* 'worrying', are discussed under participles at 19.4.

(g) The gerund in *-ndo* is a verbal form in Spanish and must not therefore be used

---

[1] This is the term used in *Collins Spanish–English/English–Spanish Dictionary*. Judge and Healey (1983) use the term 'relational'.

as an adjective: *una muñeca que anda* 'a walking doll', **not** *una muñeca andando* 'a doll **walking**'. For two exceptions to this rule, see 4.4. For a discussion of the gerund see Chapter 20.

(h) The invariable masculine singular form of a few adjectives is used as an adverb, e.g. *los teléfonos están* **fatal** 'the phones are in a dreadful state'. See 31.3.3 for discussion.

4.2 Forms of adjectives

Spanish adjectives are of three types:

> **Type 1** adjectives agree in number and gender with the noun or pronoun.
> **Type 2** adjectives agree in number but not gender.
> **Type 3** adjectives are invariable in form (not very numerous).

4.2.1 Type 1 adjectives (agree in number and gender)

These include adjectives whose masculine singular ends in: *-o* (with the rare exceptions noted at 4.2.3), *-án*, *-és* (except *cortés* 'courteous' and *descortés* 'discourteous', which are type 2), *-ín* (usually a diminutive suffix – but see note **iii**), *-ón* (usually an augmentative suffix, but see note **iii**), *-or* (with the dozen or so exceptions listed in note **i**), *-ote* and *-ete*. Also type 1 are *español*, *andaluz* and *gandul/gandula/gandules/gandulas* (colloquial Peninsular Spanish 'slacker'/'layabout'), which are unusual in that they end in a consonant other than *-és* and nevertheless have a feminine in *-a*.

The feminine of type 1 adjectives is formed thus:

(a) if the masculine singular ends in a vowel, change the vowel to *-a*: *colombiano>colombiana*.[2]

(b) If the masculine singular ends in a consonant, add *-a*: *pillín>pillina* 'mischievous', *embellecedor>embellecedora* 'beautifying'/'aesthetically enhancing', etc. By the normal rules of spelling (explained at 39.2.1), any accent on the final vowel of the masculine is dropped, e.g. *mandón > mandona* 'bossy'.

The plural of type 1 adjectives is formed thus:

(a) Add *-s* to a vowel: *colombiano>colombianos, colombiana>colombianas*.

(b) Add *-es* to a consonant to form the masculine plural, *pillín>pillines*, and add *-as* to the masculine singular to form the feminine plural: *pillín>pillinas*. By the normal rules of spelling, a final *-z* is changed to *c* before *e*, and any accent on the final vowel of the masculine singular disappears, as in *inglés > ingleses/inglesa/inglesas* 'English'.

Examples:

Singular masc. and fem.	Plural masc. and fem.	
bueno/buena	*buenos/buenas*	good
alemán/alemana	*alemanes/alemanas*	German
aragonés/aragonesa	*aragoneses/aragonesas*	Aragonese
saltarín/saltarina	*saltarines/saltarina*	restless, fidgety

---

[2] Adjectives in Spanish are almost always written with a lower-case letter. See 39.3.1 for occasional exceptions.

mandón/mandona	*mandones/mandonas*	bossy
hablador/habladora	*habladores/habladoras*	talkative
regordete/regordeta	*regordetes/regordetas*	plump
español/española	*españoles/españolas*	Spanish
andaluz/andaluza	*andaluces/andaluzas*	Andalusian

Notes

(i) Eleven adjectives that end in *-or* and have a comparative meaning are type 2, i.e. they have no separate feminine form. These are (singular/plural):

anterior/anteriores	previous
exterior/exteriores	outer
inferior/inferiores	lower/inferior
interior/interiores	inner/interior
mayor/mayores	greater/older
mejor/mejores	better
menor/menores	minor/smaller/younger
peor/peores	worse
posterior/posteriores	later/subsequent
superior§/superiores	upper/superior
ulterior/ulteriores	later/further

§Exception: *la madre superiora* 'mother superior'.

(ii) *Cortés* 'courteous' and *descortés* 'discourteous' are type 2 adjectives, i.e. they have no feminine form. *Montés* 'wild' (i.e. not domesticated) is also usually type 2: *el gato montés* 'wild/untamed cat', *la cabra montés* 'wild goat', *hierbas monteses* 'mountain herbs'. These are the only adjectives ending in *-és* that have no separate feminine form.

(iii) One or two adjectives ending in *-ín* or *-ón* are type 2: *marrón* 'brown',[3] *afín* 'related'/'similar': *una camisa marrón*, 'a brown shirt', *ideas afines* 'related ideas'.

4.2.2 Type 2 adjectives (no separate feminine form)

No difference between masculine and feminine. This class includes (with the exceptions noted above): **(a)** all adjectives whose masculine singular ends in a consonant except those ending in *ín*, *-án*, *-ón* or *-és*, which are type 1; **(b)** adjectives ending in *-a*, *-e*, *-ú*, *-í*.

The plural is formed: **(a)** if the adjective ends in a consonant or *-í* or *-ú*, by adding *-es*, *-z* is written *c* before *e*; **(b)** in all other cases, by adding *-s*:

azteca/ aztecas Aztec	*hindú/hindúes* Hindu/	*feroz/feroces* ferocious
suicida/ suicidas suicidal	Indian (see 4.8.1 note iii)	*ruin/ruines* despicable
grande/ grandes big/great	*cortés/corteses* courteous	(it does not end in *-ín*)
farsante/ farsantes	*gris/grises* grey/(US 'gray')	*inútil/inútiles* useless
fraud/'pseudo'	*feliz/felices* happy	
iraní/iraníes Iranian		

Notes

(i) Adjectives ending in *-í* often make their plural in *-ís* in spontaneous speech, e.g. *iranís* 'Iranians', although *iraníes* is the standard written form. Some words, e.g. *maorí/maoríes* or *maorís* 'Maori' are

---

[3] There is no single word for 'brown' in Peninsular Spanish. *Marrón* is chiefly used for artificial things like shoes, although it is nowadays also used of eyes. *Castaño* is used for hair and eyes: *pelo castaño, ojos castaños*. 'Brown skin' is *piel morena*. 'Brown earth' is *tierra parda* or *tierra rojiza*. *Café* (no agreement) is used for 'brown' in many parts of Latin America.

uncertain, but at the present stage of the language, *-íes* is still felt to be the correct plural in formal styles of most adjectives ending in *-í*.

(ii) If a diminutive or augmentative suffix is added to one of these adjectives, it then becomes type 1: *mayor* 'large'/'older' > *mayorcito/mayorcita* 'grown-up', *grande* 'big' > *grandote/grandota* 'extremely large', *vulgar* 'vulgar' > *vulgarzote/vulgarzota* 'pretty disgusting'/'pretty vulgar'.

(iii) *Dominante* forms a popular feminine *dominanta* 'bossy'/'domineering'. A few other popular or slang forms in *-nta* occur, e.g. *atorrante/atorranta* (Lat. Am.) 'lazy'/'loafer', but in general adjectives ending in *-nte* are not marked for gender, whereas some nouns ending in *-nte* are. See 1.2.5 and 19.4 for further discussion.

4.2.3 Type 3 adjectives (marked for neither number nor gender)

Example: *una rata macho* 'male rat', *unas ratas macho* 'male rats'. Adjectives in this group, which also includes a number of colo(u)r adjectives discussed at 4.2.4, are presumably invariable in form because they are felt to be nouns rather than adjectives. (See also 2.1.7b for discussion of the plural of compound nouns like *perros policía* 'police dogs', *hombres rana* 'frogmen'.)

Other common examples are *alerta** 'alert' (*estamos alerta* 'we're alert'), *los puntos clave* 'the key issue(s)', *encinta* (literary), 'pregnant' (Seco recommends the plural *encintas*), *estándar* 'standard', *extra** 'extra', *hembra* 'female' (see 1.3), *esnob* 'snobbish' or, in Spain, often 'flashy'/'trendy'; *modelo* 'model', *monstruo* 'monster', *sport* (*los coches sport* 'sports cars'), *tabú** 'taboo', *ultra** 'extreme right-wing'.

Notes

(i) This group is unstable, and the words asterisked often agree in the plural: *los problemas claves, los pagos extras, los temas tabúes, nuestra obligación es vivir constantemente alertas* (M. Vargas Llosa, Peru) 'our obligation is to live constantly alert'.

(ii) Although they look like nouns, *maestro, virgen, perro* and *gigante* agree like normal adjectives: *llaves maestras* 'master keys', *tierras vírgenes* 'virgin territories', *¡qué vida más perra!* 'what a rotten life!', *berenjenas gigantes* 'giant aubergines'/(US 'eggplants'). *Gigante* has a feminine ending, *giganta*, used only when it is applied to people.

(iii) *Varón* 'male' (of humans) is type 2: *niños varones* 'male children'.

(iv) Pluralization of the adjectival word restores its full function as a noun. Compare *niños modelo* 'model children' and *niños modelos* 'child models'. See 2.1.7b for discussion.

(v) A similar phenomenon is found in French, cf. *des chemises marron* 'brown shirts', but French words like *violète, extra, tabou, modèle, rose* have separate plural forms.

4.2.4 Invariable adjectives of colo(u)r

The more usual adjectives – *negro* 'black', *rojo* 'red', *azul* 'blue'– are ordinary Type 1 or Type 2 adjectives. However, any suitable noun, preceded by *color, de color* or *color de*, can be used: *ojos color (de) humo* 'smoke-colo(u)red eyes', *color barquillo* 'wafer-colo(u)red'. The phrase with *color* is sometimes dropped and the noun is then used like a type 3 adjective, i.e. it does not agree in number and gender: *tres botones naranja/rosa/malva/violeta/esmeralda* 'three orange/pink/mauve/ violet/emerald buttons', *corbatas salmón* 'salmon ties', *cintas fresa* 'strawberry colo(u)r ribbons'. Other nouns so used are:

añil indigo	*cereza* cherry	*oro* gold (*dorado* =
azafrán saffron	*chocolate* chocolate brown	golden)
beige beige	*escarlata* scarlet	*paja* straw-colo(u)red
azur azure	*grana* dark red	*sepia* sepia
café coffee-colo(u)red/brown	*granate* garnet/dark red	*turquesa* turquoise
carmesí crimson	*lila* lilac	

Notes

(i) Colloquially, and in the work of some writers, especially Latin American, *naranja, rosa, malva, violeta* and a few others may be pluralized: *flores malvas* 'mauve flowers', *los jacarandás se pusieron violetas* (E. Sábato, Argentina) 'the jacarandas turned violet', *las uñas violetas* 'violet finger-nails' (C. Barral, Spain), . . . *los ojos violetas eran de Mary* (C. Fuentes, Mexico) '. . . the violet eyes were Mary's'. But this seems to be avoided in careful language, especially in Spain: *sus ojos violeta parpadean* (J. Marsé, Spain) 'her violet eyes are blinking', *pliegos de papel llegados de Europa, azules, malva, rosa, verdes* (F. Umbral, Spain) 'folds of paper from Europe, blue, mauve, pink, green', *rayos ultravioleta* (*El País*, Spain) 'ultraviolet rays', *la muchacha de ojos violeta* (C. Fuentes, Mexico) 'the girl with violet eyes'. *Carmesí* 'crimson' is pluralized like a regular Type 2 adjective.
(ii) It is very unusual to find such adjectives before a noun, except in poetry: *como sonreía la rosa mañana* . . . (Antonio Machado, Spain, written before 1910) 'as pink dawn was smiling . . .'.
(iii) *Color* or *de color* is, in practice, usually inserted before such words in everyday language: *una bicicleta color naranja* 'an orange bicycle', *zapatos (de) color mostaza* 'mustard-colo(u)r shoes', *eran ambas prendas de color salmón* (J. Marías, Spain) 'both were articles of salmon colo(u)r', *la pantalla de moaré color geranio* (J. Aldecoa, Spain) 'the geranium-colo(u)red moiré lampshade', *esto se está poniendo color de hormiga* (M. Vargas Llosa, Peru; the phrase is also used in Spain) 'this is getting ant-colo(u)red' (i.e. 'this is starting to look ugly/sinister').
(iv) *Beige* is pronounced *beis* in Spain and Seco and *El País* recommend the latter spelling.

4.3 Compound colo(u)r adjectives

All compound colo(u)r adjectives of the type 'dark blue', 'light green', 'signal red' are invariable in form (in this respect Spanish resembles French, e.g. *des yeux bleu clair*):

hojas verde oscuro	dark green leaves
calcetines rojo claro	pale/light red socks
una masa gris castaño	a grey(US 'gray')-brown mass
[Mis ojos] son azul pálido (E. Poniatowska, Mexico)	My eyes are pale blue

Notes

(i) Well-established compound adjectives of this kind may be used on their own, but new or unusual formations may require the addition of *de color*, e.g. *una mancha **de color** rojo apagado* 'a dull red stain/patch', not ?*una mancha rojo apagado*.
(ii) There are special words for some common mixed colo(u)rs: *verdirrojo* 'red-green', *verdiblanco* 'greenish white', *verdinegro* 'very dark green', *blanquiazul* 'bluish white', *blanquinegro* 'black and white', *blanquirrojo* 'red and white'. These agree like normal adjectives: *verdinegros/verdinegras*, etc.

4.4 *Hirviendo* and *ardiendo*

Gerunds cannot be used as adjectives in Spanish: one cannot say **un objeto volando* for 'a flying object' (*un objeto volante* or *un objeto que vuela/volaba*, etc.). See 20.3 for a more detailed discussion. There are two exceptions, *hirviendo* 'boiling' and *ardiendo* 'burning' which, despite having the form of gerunds, can be used as adjectives:

Tráeme agua hirviendo	Bring me some boiling water
Tienes la frente ardiendo	Your forehead is burning
Yo más bien soy un carbón ardiendo (i.e. sexually	
excited; M. Vargas Llosa, Peru, dialogue)	I'm more like a burning coal

Chorreando 'dripping wet' may be another exception in *llevo la ropa chorreando* 'my clothes are dripping wet'. *Hirviendo, ardiendo* and *chorreando* are invariable in form, take no suffixes and cannot appear before a noun.

4.5 Adjectives formed from two words

Some compound adjectives are made into single words and behave like any adjective: *muchachas pelirrojas* 'red-haired girls' (from *pelo* 'hair' and *rojo* 'red'), *cuernos puntiagudos* 'sharp-pointed horns' (from *punta* 'point' and *agudo* 'sharp').

In compound adjectives joined by a hyphen, only the second word agrees with the noun: *movimientos político-militares* 'political-military movements', *teorías histórico-críticas* 'historical-critical theories'. Such examples excepted, use of a hyphen to join words is very rare in Spanish; cf. *contrarrevolucionario* 'counter-revolutionary', *latinoamericano* 'Latin-American'. See 39.4.6 for details about the use of the hyphen.

4.6 Short forms of some adjectives

A number of common adjectives lose their final syllable in certain circumstances.

(a) The singular of *grande* is shortened to *gran* before any noun: *un **gran** momento* 'a great moment', *una **gran** comida* 'a great meal'. The *-de* is occasionally retained in formal literary styles before words beginning with a vowel. This archaism is rare in modern writing, but cf. *¿busca un nuevo grande amor para escapar de su hastío?* (J. César Chaves, Spain, referring to the poet Antonio Machado) 'is he seeking a new great love to escape from the monotony of his life?', . . . *y con un grande alboroto de pitos y timbales daban a conocer los nuevos inventos* (G. García Márquez, Colombia) '. . . and with a great din of whistles and kettledrums they announced the latest inventions'.

Grande is not shortened if *más* or *menos* precede: *el más grande pintor del mundo* 'the greatest painter in the world' (*el mayor pintor* is better), *la más grande ofensiva de terrorismo dinamitero de la historia del país* (G. García Márquez, Colombia) 'the biggest terrorist bombing campaign in the country's history'.

(b) The following lose their final vowel when placed before a singular **masculine** noun or combination of adjective and masculine noun:

alguno: **algún** *remoto día* some remote day	*postrero*: *tu **postrer** día* (archaic) your last day
bueno: *un **buen** cocinero* a good cook	*primero*: *mi **primer** amor* my first love
malo: *un **mal** ingeniero* a bad engineer	*tercero*: *el **tercer** candidato* the third
ninguno: *en **ningún** momento* at no moment	candidate

Notes

(i) The full form must be used if any conjunction or adverb separates the adjective from the noun or noun phrase: *esta **grande** pero costosa victoria* 'this great but costly victory', *un **bueno** aunque agrio vino* 'a good though sour wine'.

(ii) Popular speech, especially Latin American, sometimes uses short forms of adjectives before feminine nouns as well. This is also occasionally seen in several good Spanish writers of the first half of the twentieth century, but it is nowadays avoided: *la primera mujer* 'the first woman', not **la primer mujer, buena parte de* 'a good part of', not **buen parte de*.

(iii) *Alguna* and *ninguna* are pronounced 'algún' and 'ningún' in spontaneous speech before feminine nouns beginning with a stressed *a-* or *ha-*, but all the authorities recommend use of the forms
alguna, ninguna in this context in written language. See 3.1.2, 9.4 and 23.5.5 for details.
(iv) For *cualquiera* see 9.8.
(v) *Santo* 'saint' is shortened to *san* before the names of all male saints except those beginning
with *Do-* or *To-*: *san Juan, san Blas, santo Tomás, Santo Domingo*. It is not shortened when it means
'holy': *el santo Padre* 'the Holy Father', *todo el santo día* 'the whole day through', *el Santo Oficio* 'the
Holy Office' (i.e. the Inquisition).
(vi) For the short forms of *tanto* and *cuánto* (*tan* and *cuán*) see 9.16 and 24.6.

4.7 Agreement of adjectives

Some questions of number agreement of adjectives are also discussed under 2.3,
particularly agreement with collective nouns (2.3.1). For the agreement of adjectives with titles like *Alteza* 'Highness', *Excelencia* 'Excellency' see 1.2.11.

4.7.1 Agreement of adjectives that follow the noun

(a) One or more masculine nouns require a masculine adjective: *un elefante
asiático* 'an Asian elephant', *platos combinados* 'set courses'/'meals on a plate',[4]
cien mil pesos mexicanos, '100,000 Mexican pesos', *mi padre es inglés* 'my father's
English'.

One or more feminine nouns require a feminine adjective: *la Grecia antigua*
'ancient Greece', *mil pesetas españolas* '1000 Spanish pesetas', *mi madre es inglesa*
'my mother's English'.

Two or more nouns of different gender require a masculine plural adjective:

profesores y profesoras ingleses	English men and women teachers
puentes y casas decrépitos	derelict bridges and houses

Notes

(i) Seco (1998), 124, notes the possibility of singular agreement with two or more nouns denoting a single complex idea, e.g. *talento y habilidad extremada* 'extreme talent and skill' for *talento y
habilidad extremados*.
(ii) 'White irises and roses' should therefore be *lirios y rosas blancos*, but a plural adjective is occasionally given the gender of the last noun even though it qualifies all the nouns. *Adornado con lirios
y rosas blancas* (M. Vargas Llosa, Peru) may mean 'adorned with irises and white roses', although it
could mean '. . . with white irises and roses', the *blancas* being explained by the awkwardness of
following a feminine noun by a masculine adjective. Spanish is, however, more tolerant than French
of a masculine adjective following a feminine noun. French rejects constructions like *des hommes
et des femmes gros* = *hombres y mujeres gordos* 'fat men and women'.

(b) If several adjectives follow a plural noun and each adjective refers to only one
individual item, the adjective will be singular: *los presidentes venezolano y peruano*
'the Peruvian president and the Venezuelan president'. *Los presidentes vene-
zolanos y peruanos* means 'the presidents of Venezuela and (the presidents of)
Peru'.

---

[4] Usually incomprehensibly translated 'combined plates' on Spanish menus. It means
several different items served foreign-style on one plate, e.g. eggs, bacon and chips (US
'fries').

Note

Adjectives may sometimes function as adverbs, in which case they are invariably masculine singular in form: *María habla muy claro* 'Maria speaks very clearly'. See 31.3.3 for further discussion.

4.7.2 Agreement with nouns joined by *o* or *ni*

(a) With the conjunction *o* agreement is optional. Plural agreement emphasizes the fact that the *o* is not exclusive (i.e. either one or the other or possibly both) and it indicates that the adjective refers to both nouns:

Buscaban una tienda o un restaurante abiertos (*abiertos* clearly refers to both)	They were looking for an open shop or (an open) restaurant
Buscaban la mujer o el hombre capaces de asumir el cargo (for the absence of personal *a* see 22.2)	They were looking for the woman or man capable of taking on the job

Singular agreement emphasizes exclusivity: ***puede*** *venir Mario o su hermano, pero no los dos* 'Mario or his brother can come, but not both.'
(b) With *ni* 'nor' a plural verb is usual: *ni Mario ni Juan* ***eran*** *tontos* 'neither Mario nor Juan was stupid'.

4.7.3 Agreement with collective nouns

An adjective that modifies a collective noun is singular:

La organización de profesores se dio por vencida	The teachers' association gave up/ admitted defeat

However, if words that refer to the people belonging to the collection intervene between the collective noun and the adjective or verb, the latter are usually in the plural. Compare: *sólo/solo una minoría* ***es*** *culta* 'only a minority are/is educated', and *sólo/solo una minoría de los empleados* ***son cultos/es culta*** 'only a minority of the employees are/is educated'. For further details on agreement with collective nouns, including *minoría, parte, resto, mitad* and similar words, see 2.3.1.

4.7.4 Agreement of pre-posed adjectives

When an adjective precedes two or more nouns and qualifies them all, it usually agrees only with the first, thus avoiding the awkward combination of a plural adjective with a singular noun or a masculine adjective with a feminine noun (e.g. to avoid the peculiar *?frescos rosas* below):

con exagerada cortesía y deferencia	with exaggerated courtesy and deference
su habitual *sabiduría y tolerancia* (E. Sábato, Argentina, interview)	his usual wisdom and tolerance
esas frescas rosas y claveles (J. L. Borges, Argentina)	those fresh roses and carnations

The plural may avoid ambiguities: *sus amados hijo y nieto* 'his beloved son and grandson' (different people, both beloved), *pobres Mario y Jean Pierre* (A. Bryce Echenique, Peru, dialogue) 'poor Mario and Jean Pierre' (both poor).

Note

French does not allow this construction. Compare *una profunda inspiración y reflexión* and *une inspiration et une réflexion profondes* 'deep inspiration and reflection'.

4.7.5 'Neuter' agreement

An adjective that refers to no noun in particular is masculine singular in form:

Es absurdo hacerlo sin ayuda	It's absurd to do it without help
Es peligroso, pero lo haré	It's dangerous, but I'll do it
Fantástico . . . la cantidad de dinero que gasta en tabaco	Fantastic . . . the amount of money he spends on tobacco
La miseria no tiene nada de sano y placentero (M. Vargas Llosa, Peru)	Extreme poverty has nothing healthy or agreeable about it

Notes

(i) Neuter agreement is sometimes found even where a noun is present: *tampoco es bueno demasiada natación* (L. Goytisolo, Spain, dialogue) 'too much swimming isn't good either'. Here the adjective does not qualify the noun *natación* but the general idea of *demasiada natación. Buena* would also be correct. This phenomenon is quite common in everyday speech when the noun is not specified (i.e. not accompanied by a definite article, a demonstrative adjective, a numeral or some other specifier), e.g. *mucha comida así no es bueno* (or *buena*) *para la salud de nadie* (but always *esa comida no es buena* 'that food's not good') 'a lot of that sort of food isn't good for anyone's health'.
(ii) For adjectives with the article *lo* (*lo bueno, lo grande,* etc.) see 7.2.

4.8 Formation of adjectives of place

4.8.1 Adjectives from countries and regions

These are formed unpredictably. The following are noteworthy (for the use of the definite article with the names of countries, see 3.2.17):

Alemania: alemán
América: americano often 'Latin-American'; see note i
Argelia: argelino Algeria, Algerian
(la) Argentina: argentino
Austria: austriaco or *austríaco*
Bélgica: belga
Bolivia: boliviano
(el) Brasil: brasileño
(el) Canadá: canadiense
Canarias: canario
Castilla: castellano Castile/Castilian; see note (ii)
Cataluña: catalán
Chile: chileno
(la) China: chino
Colombia: colombiano
Costa Rica: costarriqueño, costarricense
Dinamarca: danés Danish
Ecuador: ecuatoriano
Egipto: egipcio (not **egipciano*)
Escocia: escocés Scottish
Estados Unidos: estadounidense: see note (i)
Europa: europeo
Francia: francés
Gales: galés Wales/Welsh
Galicia: gallego
Gibraltar: gibraltareño
Gran Bretaña: británico

Grecia: griego
Guatemala: guatemalteco
Holanda: holandés
Honduras: hondureño
Hungría: húngaro
Inglaterra: inglés, often used for 'British'
Irlanda: irlandés
(el) Japón: japonés
la India: indio; see note (iii) for *hindú*
Marruecos: marroquí Moroccan (*moro* is pejorative)
Méjico/México: mejicano/mexicano; see note (iv)
Nicaragua: nicaragüense
Panamá: panameño
(el) Paraguay: paraguayo
(el) Perú: peruano
Polonia: polaco Polish
Portugal: portugués
Puerto Rico: puertorriqueño/ portorriqueño (the former is now almost universal)
El Salvador: salvadoreño
Rusia: ruso
Suecia: sueco Swedish
Suiza: suizo
(el) Uruguay: uruguayo
Vascongadas, el País Vasco; vasco; see note (v)
Venezuela: venezolano

Notes

(i) The adjective from *América Latina* or *Latinoamérica* is *latinoamericano*. Spanish-speaking Latin Americans dislike terms like *hispanoamericano* or 'Spanish-American' for the same reason that US citizens would not like to be called 'British Americans'. However, *Latinoamérica* includes countries where other Latin-based languages are spoken – e.g. Brazil, Haiti, Martinique, French Guiana – so 'Latin-American' is linguistically misleading.

In Latin America *norteamericano* is taken to mean our 'American' and is more common than *estadounidense* (in Mexico and in some nearby republics *estadunidense*), which is used in news-papers but is rare in speech. *Americano* is assumed to mean *latinoamericano*, but in Spain it usually means the same as our 'American', although it can also mean 'Latin-American' in an appropriate context. For agreement with *Estados Unidos*, see 3.2.17.

The adjective from *América del sur* or *Sudamérica* (or *Suramérica*) 'South America' – which does not include Central America, Mexico or the Caribbean – is **sud**americano. Seco (1998), 421, is non-committal about the forms *Suramérica*, *suramericano* which he says are generally thought 'less acceptable' in Spain than the forms with *sud-*, but *El País* (*Libro de estilo*, 1998) prefers the prefix *sur-*, e.g. *Suráfrica*, *suroeste* 'South-West', *sureste* 'South-East', etc., and it is now so common every-where that it must be considered correct.

(ii) *Castellano* is the Castilian language, i.e. the language described in this book, strictly speaking the dialect of Castile which became the majority language of Spain: *el castellano* now means the same as *el español*, 'the Spanish language'. Now that Spain has several official languages, Catalans, Basques and Galicians sometimes object to *el castellano* being called *el español*. The same objection is also heard from some Latin Americans.

(iii) In Latin America the word *indio* is always assumed to mean Amerindian, so *hindú* is used there – but less often in Spain – for Asian Indian, although it properly means the Hindu religion: *los empleados **hindús** del raj británico* (C. Fuentes, Mexico, dialogue), 'the Indian employees under the British Raj' (*hindús* is colloquial for *hindúes*: see 2.1.3c). In Spain, *indiano* denotes a 'colonial' who had made a fortune in Latin America and returned home.

(iv) Mexicans always write *México/mexicano*, even though they are pronounced *Méjico, mejicano*. The *x* is a tribute to the Mexica or 'Aztecs', as their neighbo(u)rs called them. *El País* (Spain) always prints *México, mexicano*, but Manuel Seco objects because it tempts Spanish newsreaders to pro-nounce them [méksiko], [meksikáno]. The spellings *Méjico, mejicano* are not unusual outside Mex-ico. A few other Mexican place names are similarly affected, e.g. Oaxaca, Xalapa (or Jalapa). See 39.1.5 for further remarks on the pronunciation of *x*.

(v) The Basque words *Euskadi* 'Basque Country', *euskalduna* 'Basque'/'Basque-speaker', *euskara* or *euskera* 'the Basque language' are commonly seen in Spanish newspapers.

4.8.2 Adjectives from towns

There is no general rule for forming adjectives from the names of towns, and some places pride themselves on obscure forms, e.g. *Huelva – onubense*. Some of the more common are:

Álava: alavés
Alcalá: complutense see note (i)
Ávila: abulense
Badajoz: pacense
Barcelona: barcelonés
Bilbao: bilbaíno
Bogotá: bogotano
Buenos Aires: porteño/ bonaerense: see note (ii)
Burgos: burgalés
Cádiz: gaditano
Caracas: caraqueño
Córdoba: cordobés

La Coruña: coruñés
Florencia: florentino
Granada: granadino
La Habana: habanero
Lima: limeño
Londres: londinense (note spelling)
Lugo: lucense
Madrid: madrileño
Málaga: malagueño
Moscú: moscovita
Murcia: murciano
Nápoles: napolitano
Nueva York: neo-

yorquino/neoyorkino
Oviedo: ovetense
Pamplona: pamplonés/ pamplonica invariable
París: parisiense: see note (iii)
La Paz: paceño/pacense
Quito: quiteño
Río de Janeiro: carioca (after a local Indian tribe)
Roma: romano
Salamanca: salmantino/ salamanqués
San Sebastián: donostiarra a Basque word

Santander: santanderino	*Segovia: segoviano*	*Valladolid: vallisoletano*
Santiago: santiaguino	*Sevilla: sevillano*	*Zaragoza: zaragozano*
(Chile), *santiagués*	*Toledo: toledano*	
(Spain)	*Valencia: valenciano*	

Notes

(i) *La complutense* is the ancient university of Alcalá, but it is now sited in Madrid.
(ii) *Bonaerense* refers to the Province of Buenos Aires.
(iii) *El País* censures the use of *parisién* and *parisino*, but they are heard colloquially.

4.9 Intensive forms of the adjective

4.9.1 The suffix *-ísimo*: meaning and formation

The suffix *-ísimo* can be added to many adjectives. It intensifies the original meaning – *Ana es riquísima* 'Ana is extremely rich' (from *rico*) – and it should be used sparingly. It cannot be added to all adjectives, and there are irregularities. This suffix is sometimes misnamed a 'superlative' suffix, but it cannot be used in comparisons and is best thought of simply as an intensifier. *-ísimo* is added after removing any final vowel: *grande/grandísimo, guapa/guapísima*. The following spelling changes occur:

(a) adjectives ending in *-co/-ca* and *-go/-ga* require a silent *u* to keep the hard sound of the *c* or *g*: *rico/riquísimo* 'rich', *vago/vaguísimo* 'vague' / 'lazy';
(b) adjectives ending in -z change the z to c: *feliz/felicísimo* 'happy', *feroz/ferocísimo* 'ferocious';
(c) for adjectives ending in two vowels, see 4.9.2;
(d) adjectives ending in *-ble* change this ending to *-bil*: *amable/amabilísimo* 'friendly', *posible/posibilísimo. Endeble/endeblísimo* 'feeble' is a rare exception.

4.9.2 Adjectives which do not take *-ísimo*

The following adjectives do not take the suffix *-ísimo*:

(a) Those ending in *-í, -uo, -io*, or *-eo* if not stressed on the *e*: e.g. *baladí* 'trivial', *arduo* 'arduous', *espontáneo* 'spontaneous', *rubio* 'blond', *tardío* 'late'. Exceptions: *agrio/agrísimo* 'sour', *amplio/amplísimo* 'wide' / 'extensive', *frío/friísimo* 'cold', *limpio/ limpísimo* 'clean', *ordinario/ordinarísimo* 'ordinary' / 'vulgar', *pío/piísimo* 'pious', *sucio/sucísimo* 'dirty', *vacío/vaciísimo* 'empty'.
(b) Words stressed on the antepenultimate syllable (*esdrújulas*) ending in *-ico, -fero, -geno, -voro, político* 'political', *mamífero* 'mammal(ian)', *homogéneo* 'homogeneous', *carnívoro* 'carnivorous'.
(c) Diminutives and comparatives: *bonito* 'pretty', *grandote* 'enormous', *menor* 'smaller' / 'younger'. *Mayorcísimo* 'very old' is often heard, e.g. *es mayorcísimo* 'he's very old'.
(d) Compound adjectives, e.g. *patizambo* 'knock-kneed', *ojituerto* 'one-eyed'.
(e) Many adjectives of more than three syllables ending in *-ble*: *inexplicable, incontestable* 'unquestionable', *desmontable* 'collapsible'. There are exceptions, though some are uncommon: *agradable/agradabilísimo* 'agreeable', *apacible/apacibilísimo*, 'mild', *miserable/miserabilísimo* 'wretched', *venerable/venerabilísimo* 'venerable'.
(f) Those whose meaning cannot be further intensified: *fantástico, ideal, infinito*,

inmortal 'immortal', *total*, etc. Exceptions: *mismo/mismísimo* 'very' (*la mismísima persona* 'the very same person'), *singular/singularísimo* 'singular'.

(g) Time and number adjectives: *anual* 'annual', *diario* 'daily', *nocturno* 'night-time', *semanal* 'weekly', *quinto* 'fifth', *último* 'last', *vigésimo* 'twentieth', etc. Exception: *primer/ primerísimo* 'first'/'very first of all'.

(h) *Hirviendo* 'boiling' and *ardiendo* 'burning'.

(i) Technical and scientific adjectives and most adjectives ending in -*ista*, e.g. *decimal*, *termonuclear* 'thermo-nuclear', *transformacional* 'transformational', *comunista* 'Communist', *nacionalista* 'nationalist', etc.

4.9.3 Irregular intensive forms

(a) The following are best learned as separate words:

antiguo: antiquísimo ancient	*lejos: lejísimos* far (adverb)
cursi: cursilísimo affected/pseudo-refined	*mayor: máximo* supreme/greatest
	menor: mínimo slightest/least
inferior: ínfimo (literary) inferior/least/lowest	*mejor: óptimo* superb (literary)
	peor: pésimo bad/dreadful
joven: jovencísimo young	*superior: supremo* superior/supreme

Note

Augmentative forms ending in -*ón* insert a *c*: *guapetón* 'handsome'/'good-looking' > *guapetoncísimo*, *juguetón* 'playful' > *juguetoncísimo*, but they are rarely used.

(b) The following forms are occasionally found in older texts and or in flowery written styles, e.g. formal speeches:

		Literary form	Current form
amigo	friendly/keen	*amícisimo*	*amiguísimo*
áspero	harsh	*aspérrimo*	*asperísimo*
benévolo	charitable	*benevolentísimo*	none
célebre	famous	*celebérrimo*	none
cruel	cruel	*crudelísimo*	*cruelísimo*
difícil	difficult	*dificílimo*	*dificilísimo*
fácil	easy	*facílimo*	*facilísimo*
fértil	fertile	*ubérrimo*	*fertilísimo*
fiel	faithful	*fidelísimo*	*fidelísimo*
frío	cold	*frigidísimo*	*friísimo*
íntegro	whole/entire	*integérrimo*	*integrísimo*
libre	free	*libérrimo*	*librísimo* (familiar)
magnífico	magnificent	*magnificentísimo*	none
mísero	wretched (archaic)	*misérrimo*	none?
munífico	munificent	*munificentísimo*	none
pobre	poor	*paupérrimo*	*pobrísimo*
sabio	wise	*sapientísimo*	none
sagrado	sacred	*sacratísimo*	none

(c) The old rule whereby the diphthongs *ue* and *ie* are simplified to *o* or *e* when -*ísimo* is added is nowadays usually ignored, although *novísimo* 'very recent' must be distinguished from *nuevísimo* 'very new'. Bracketed forms are literary:

bueno	*buenísimo*	*(bonísimo)*	good
cierto	*ciertísimo*	*(certísimo)*	certain
diestro	*diestrísimo*	*(destrísimo)*	skilled
fuerte	*fuertísimo*	*(fortísimo)*	strong
reciente	*recientísimo*	*(recentísimo)*	recent
tierno	*tiernísimo*	*(ternísimo)*	tender

The diphthong in some words has never suffered modification, e.g. *viejo/viejísimo* 'old', *cuerdo/cuerdísimo* 'sane'.

4.10 Use of nouns as adjectives

Nouns may occasionally be used adjectivally:

*Tienes que ser más **persona decente***	You've got to be more of a decent person
*Este libro es menos **novela** que el otro*	This book is less of a novel than the other
*Es más **bailarina** que **actriz***	She's more a dancer than an actress
*Su reacción es puro **teatro***	His reaction is pure theatre

Such nouns do not agree in number or gender with the word they modify, and when they are modified by words like *más, menos, tan* they are not accompanied by a definite or indefinite article. See 3.3.11 for the indefinite article to distinguish nouns from adjectives, e.g. *es imbécil* and *es un imbécil*. See 24.4.4 for nouns and adjectives modified by *qué*: *¡qué bandido eres!*, what a villain you are!; *¡qué guapa estás!* 'wow, you look great!'

4.11 Position of adjectives in relation to nouns

4.11.1 General

For the position of *alguno, ninguno, cualquiera, mismo*, possessive adjectives, etc., consult these words in the index. For the position of ordinal number-adjectives, e.g. *primero* 'first', *sexto* 'sixth', see 10.12.3.

It is hardly true to say that the adjective 'normally' follows the noun in Spanish. Adjective position is much more flexible than in English and a good deal more flexible than in French, but the underlying rules are difficult to formulate. Many factors of convention, sound and above all style and meaning combine to determine whether, for example, one says *un lejano ruido* or *un ruido lejano* 'a distant noise'. Moreover there seem to be as yet unresearched differences between Peninsular and American Spanish, the latter apparently allowing some preposed constructions unacceptable in Spain. The basic rule for all adjectives other than ordinal numbers seems to be:

(a) Restrictive adjectives follow the noun.
(b) Non-restrictive adjectives may precede or follow the noun. Some always precede the noun.

Restrictive adjectives narrow the scope of the noun that precedes them: *vino espumoso* 'sparkling wine' denotes a restricted type of wine; *odio las novelas históricas* 'I hate historical novels' refers only to those novels which are historical. Non-restrictive adjectives typically refer to the whole of the entity denoted by the noun: *las aburridas conferencias del decano* 'the dean's boring lectures', *la poco apetitosa cocina británica* 'unappetizing British cooking' are both generalizations that attribute a quality to every member or aspect of the class of things denoted by the noun. Unfortunately the distinction between restrictive and non-restrictive adjectives is not always clear, and the decision about where to put the adjective often relies on a feel for the language rare among non-natives.

As a useful, though not absolutely foolproof guide to whether an adjective is restrictive, native speakers of English may apply the following test: if an English adjective sounds correct when spoken with a heavy stress (or, more accurately, with falling intonation) – 'I don't like **sour** apples, but I do like **sweet** apples' – then it is almost certainly restrictive and its Spanish equivalent will follow the noun: *no me gustan las manzanas **agrias**, pero sí me gustan las manzanas **dulces***. If an English adjective sounds wrong if it is stressed it is probably non-restrictive and its Spanish counterpart may well precede the noun. Thus if one stresses 'beautiful' in 'the beautiful sun of Spain', the phrase suggests that there is another Spanish sun that is not beautiful: the absurdity of this strongly suggests that the Spanish adjective precedes the noun: *el hermoso sol de España*. Ordinal number adjectives do not follow this rule, cf. *está en el quinto capítulo, no en el cuarto* 'it's in the **fifth** chapter, not in the **fourth**'. See 10.12.3.

4.11.2 Examples of restrictive (post-posed) adjectives

The following adjectives are restrictive and therefore always follow the noun:

(a) Those that create a new type or sub-set of the thing described by the noun:

el pan integral wholemeal bread
el papel secante blotting paper
los cazas computerizados computerized fighter aircraft

las teorías freudianas Freudian theories
la tracción delantera front-wheel drive

All the other examples in this section are in fact instances of this type of adjective, which can be thought of as a transformed clause: *la poesía romántica = aquella poesía que es romántica, las manzanas verdes = aquellas manzanas que están verdes*.
(b) Those used for purposes of contrast, whether explicit or implied:

Tráigame una cuchara limpia, no una sucia
Tengo un boli verde y otro azul
Adoro los ojos azules
No queremos agua salada

Bring me a clean spoon, not a dirty one
I have a green ballpoint pen and a blue one
I adore blue eyes
We don't want salty water

(c) Scientific or technical adjectives used to define or specify a noun (as is almost always the case):

la gramática transformativa transformational grammar
la crítica estructuralista structuralist criticism

el laboratorio lingüístico language laboratory
el correo electrónico e-mail ('emilio' is a new colloquialism for an e-mail in Spain)

Only the most far-fetched styles would use such adjectives poetically or as epithets, though some, e.g. *unilateral, microscópico, (p)sicoanalítico, materialista*, might conceivably be used as value judg(e)ments (see 4.11.3).
(d) Attributive adjectives. These express the origin, substance, contents or purpose of a noun. Their use is discussed at 4.12.

la nave espacial space ship	*el material bélico* war material
el túnel ferroviario railway tunnel	(= *material de guerra*)
la guerra nuclear nuclear war	

(e) Adjectives of nationality, which are almost always restrictive:

el clima argentino	the Argentinian climate
la paella valenciana	paella Valencia-style
los monumentos mayas	the Mayan monuments

Note

Adjectives of nationality may occasionally be used as epithets (because they express allegedly typical qualities. See 4.11.4 for a discussion of epithets): *mi española impulsividad me hace escribir estas líneas* (reader's letter in *Cambio16*, Spain) 'my Spanish impulsiveness makes me write these lines', *su británica reserva* 'her/his British reserve'.

4.11.3 Pre-posed (non-restrictive) adjectives indicating impression, reaction, subjective evaluation

The most common reason for putting an adjective before the noun is to emphasize its emotional content, e.g. *una **tremenda** tragedia* 'a tremendous tragedy', *un **gran** poeta* 'a great poet', *el **inquietante** problema del efecto invernadero* 'the worrying problem of the greenhouse effect'. These adjectives are non-restrictive in context because the speaker wishes to eliminate any allusion to another tragedy, poet or problem: no contrast with other nouns is suggested since, in the foregoing quotation, no allusion is made to a non-worrying greenhouse effect. Native speakers often report that such adjectives are in some way 'emphatic', but this is misleading since in the English translation the adjective is definitely not stressed, as explained at 4.11.1.

Such pre-posed adjectives may describe the speaker's impression, assessment or evaluation of a thing, or its appearance. They can include a vast range of adjectives indicating shape, distance, size, colo(u)r, texture, passage of time, praise, blame or subjective appraisal of any kind. Emotional language, e.g. literary, solemn or poetic styles, journalism and advertising, particularly favo(u)r pre-posed adjectives:

*las **magníficas** ruinas de Machu Picchu*	the magnificent ruins at/of Macchu Picchu
*¡No voy a permitir que a tu hija la envenenes con las ideas de tu **enferma** cabeza!* (L. Esquivel, Mexico)	I'm not going to let you poison your daughter with the ideas of your diseased brain!
*un profesor, dueño de una **amplísima** cultura* (S. Pitol, Mexico, dialogue)	a teacher, a highly educated man
*¡**Sensacional** oferta de verano!*	Sensational Summer Offer!

Sometimes the difference of meaning between post-posed and pre-posed adjectives can be significant, as in *el poético lenguaje de Lorca* 'the poetic language of Lorca' (aesthetic judg(e)ment) and *el lenguaje poético de Lorca* 'the language of Lorca's poetry' (factual), or *las decimonónicas actitudes del ministro* 'the nineteenth-century attitudes of the minister' (value judg(e)ment) and *la novela decimonónica* 'the nineteenth-century novel' (factual). But very often a pre-posed adjective is merely more poetic or dramatic, a post-posed one more matter-of-fact. The following examples will help to train the ear. In every case the adjective or adjectival phrase in bold letters could have followed the noun or noun-phrase:

*el **casi olvidado** nombre de James MacPherson* (J. L. Borges, Argentina)	the almost forgotten name of James MacPherson
*Hay barcos anclados en **permanente** contacto con los aviones nocturnos* (G. García Márquez, Colombia, dialogue)	There are boats anchored at sea in permanent contact with the night aircraft
*Si usted me hace **serenas** preguntas, tendrá **serenas** respuestas* (interview in *Gente*, Argentina)	If you ask me calm questions, you'll get calm answers
*La revolución significó para mí una **justa** redistribución de la riqueza* (M. Vargas Llosa, Peru)	The revolution meant for me a just redistribution of wealth
*una guirnalda de **blancas** flores* (L. Goytisolo, Spain)	a wreath of white flowers
*La pera es de **fácil** digestión* (cookery book, Spain)	Pears are easily digested
*el **creciente** costo de la tierra urbana*	The rising cost of land within the cities

Notes

(i) Adjective position is arbitrarily fixed in many set phrases: *Alto Egipto* 'Upper Egypt', *el Sumo Pontífice* 'the Pope', *Baja California* 'Lower California' (cf. *América Central, los Estados Unidos, la China Popular*, 'People's China', etc.), *altos hornos* 'blast furnaces', *en alta mar* 'on the high seas', *Dios Todopoderoso* 'Almighty God', *sentido común* 'common sense', *gramática parda* 'smartness'/'cunning', etc.

(ii) If an adjective is qualified by an adverb it usually follows the noun in ordinary styles: *esta noticia altamente reveladora* 'this highly revealing news item', *una chica frígidamente agresiva*, 'a frigidly aggressive girl', *con tres amigos igualmente roñosos* 'with three equally stingy friends'. Compare *anuncian una útil linterna* (not *linterna útil*) 'they are advertising a useful torch' and *anuncian una linterna muy útil* 'they are advertising a very useful torch'.

With *más* and *menos* either position is possible: *el más popular presentador de la TV italiana* (*Cambio 16*, Spain) 'the most popular presenter on Italian TV', or *el presentador más popular de la TV española*.

Constructions like *la altamente reveladora noticia* 'the highly revealing news item', *la siempre inquieta juventud* 'ever restless youth', *esa siempre sorprendente inteligencia de los perros* (S. Galindo, Mexico) 'that ever-surprising intelligence of dogs', *las ya de por sí interesantes confesiones del autor* 'the in themselves interesting confessions of the author', *la sorprendente y para Julián desconocida noticia*) J. Aldecoa, Spain) 'the surprising and – for Julian – unknown news' are, however, found in literary style and can be explained in terms of contrast between restrictive and non-restrictive adjectives.

(iii) Nouns with two or more adjectives: the restrictive adjective follows, the non-restrictive normally precedes: *los blancos ejércitos angélicos* 'the white armies of the angels', *una elegante camisa blanca* 'an elegant white shirt', *una siniestra cruz gamada* 'a sinister swastika', *una enorme cúpula blanca* 'an enormous white dome'.

4.11.4 Other uses of pre-posed non-restrictive adjectives

The following types of non-restrictive adjectives are also pre-posed:

(a) Epithets, i.e. adjectives used to describe qualities typically associated with the noun. These are infrequent in everyday or scientific or technical language, except in set phrases, but they are very common in literary, poetic or other types of emotive or affective language:

mi distinguido colega	my distinguished colleague
el peligroso tigre asiático	the dangerous Asian tiger

un valiente torero	a brave bullfighter
los volubles dioses romanos	the fickle Roman gods

Epithets describe predictable or typical qualities: one can say *un enorme elefante* 'an enormous elephant' but only *un elefante cojo* 'a lame elephant' since lameness is not typical of elephants and bigness is; *mi leal amigo* 'my loyal friend' but only *mi amigo vegetariano* 'my vegetarian friend'; *un difícil problema* or *un problema difícil* 'a difficult problem', but only *un problema (p)sicológico*, since problems are not typically psychological.

(b) Adjectives that unambiguously refer to every one of the items denoted by a plural noun: *tuvo que parar en boxes para cambiar sus **deterioradas** ruedas* (*El País,* Spain) 'he had to stop in the pits to change his worn tyres (US 'tires')' (*ruedas deterioradas* might imply that only some of his tyres were worn):

muchas gracias por las magníficas rosas (*rosas magníficas* suggests that some of the roses were not magnificent)	many thanks for the magnificent roses
Sus evasivas respuestas empezaban a irritarme	His/Her evasive replies were starting to irritate me
las simpáticas peticiones de nuestros oyentes	our listeners' kind requests

For this reason, adjectives applied to unique entities are likely to be pre-posed, unless they apply only to an aspect or part of the thing:

Se veía el imponente Everest	One could see imposing Mount Everest
el izquierdista Frente Farabundo Martí	the left-wing Farabundo Martí Front
tu alarmante edad . . . (you have only one age)	your alarming age . . .

But

Existe un Unamuno político y comprometido, y otro contemplativo	There is a political, committed Unamuno, and another, contemplative one

(c) Intensifiers, hyperboles and swear words – which are extreme examples of adjectives used emotively and often stripped of all real meaning:

mi negra suerte	my rotten luck
¡esta maldita máquina de escribir!	this damned typewriter!
Valiente soldado eres tú	A great soldier you are (I don't think . . .)
tu dichosa familia	your blessed family
estas condenadas hormigas	these damned ants
cien cochinas/piojosas pesetas (vulgar)	100 lousy pesetas

4.11.5 Position of adjectives with compound nouns

Choice of position here depends on whether the noun phrase is felt to be a compound word (i.e. a new concept) or merely a loose conjunction of words. Thus *las flores de España* 'the flowers of Spain' is not a compound, so one says *las flores **silvestres** de España* 'the wild flowers of Spain' not **las flores de España silvestres*. But *una casa de muñecas* 'a doll's house' is a compound and is inseparable: *una casa de muñecas **barata*** 'a cheap dolls' house', not **una casa barata de muñecas*. Only long familiarity with Spanish provides a certain guide as to what is or is not a compound noun. Some noun phrases are uncertain: one can say *una bicicleta **amarilla** de hombre* or *una bicicleta de hombre **amarilla*** 'a yellow man's bicycle' (the Spanish is unambiguous!). Further examples:

un cochecito de niño verde	a green pram/baby carriage
un médico de cabecera simpático	a nice family doctor
un libro lleno de curiosas referencias de	a book full of curious references of a
índole personal (J. L. Borges, Argentina)	personal nature

4.11.6 Position of *bueno, malo, grande, pequeño*

The general rule applies: when they are clearly restrictive, they follow the noun. When used restrictively, they usually indicate objective qualities. When they precede the noun they usually express a subjective evaluation (which is usually the case, but see note (iv) for the special case of *pequeño*).

(a) Objective qualities

Tengo un abrigo bueno para los fines de	I've got a good coat for weekends, and a
semana, y uno regular para los laborables	so-so one for weekdays
Oscar Wilde dijo que no hay libros buenos o	Oscar Wilde said there are no good or bad
malos sino libros bien o mal escritos	books, only well or badly written books
(J. L. Borges, Argentina, contrast)	
Ponlo debajo del árbol grande	Put it under the big tree
Trae la llave grande	Bring the big key/spanner
Era un hombre grande	He was a big man
mi hermana mayor/menor	my elder/younger sister

(b) Subjective qualities

un buen carpintero	a good carpenter
un gran éxito	a great success
un gran ruido/poeta/embustero	a great noise/poet/fraud
los grandes narcotraficantes	the major drug dealers
un pequeño problema (see note (iv))	a slight problem
el mayor poeta mexicano	the greatest Mexican poet
ni la menor impresión de insinceridad	not even the slightest impression of
insincerity	

Notes

(i) With *hombre* and *mujer*, *bueno* tends to mean 'good' after the noun and 'harmless' before: *un buen hombre* means 'a harmless/simple man'. *Malo* is weaker before the noun, e.g. *pasamos un mal rato* 'we had a bad time'. *Mala mujer* may be a euphemism for prostitute.

(ii) There are many set expressions: *lo hizo de buena gana* 'he did it willingly', *oro de buena ley* 'pure gold', *en buen lío te has metido* 'you're in a fine mess', *a mí siempre me pone buena cara* 'he always makes an effort to be nice with me', *¡qué mala pata!* 'what bad luck', etc.

(iii) *Grande* is pre-posed when it means 'great', but it may mean 'big' in either position.

(iv) *Un pequeño problema* is normal since 'problem' is an abstract noun. However, *una pequeña casa* is not usual for 'a little house', which is *una casita*. For discussion of this phenomenon see 38.2.

4.11.7 Position of *nuevo* and *viejo*

The usual explanation is that these are pre-posed when they mean 'another' and 'previous'/'long-standing' respectively, but in practice it is doubtful whether the distinction is always clear-cut: *tenemos un nuevo presidente/un presidente nuevo* 'we've got a new president', *nuevos progresos técnicos* 'new (i.e. more) technological developments', *un viejo amigo* 'an old friend' (i.e. long-standing, not necessarily old in years). *Nuevo* is usually post-posed when it means 'brand-new' as is *viejo* when it means 'not new': *un coche nuevo* 'a brand-new car', *un coche viejo* 'an old car'. But *viejo* may be pre-posed when it means 'not young': *un viejo americano* 'an old American'. This distinction is overridden for purposes of contrast: *prefiero el coche nuevo al viejo* 'I prefer our new (i.e. 'latest') car to the old (i.e. 'previous') one'.

4.11.8 Adjectives whose meaning varies according to position

The following are some common cases of changes of meaning determined by adjective position, but in many cases the distinction is not rigid and a good dictionary should be consulted for further information:

	After noun	Before noun
antiguo	ancient	former or ancient
medio	average	half
pobre	poor (= not rich)	miserable/wretched
puro	pure/clean	sheer
raro	strange/rare	rare
rico	rich	delicious
simple	simple-minded	simple (= mere)
triste	sad	wretched
valiente	courageous	'great' (ironic)
varios	assorted/various	several

Note

For *mismo* see 9.11, *propio* 9.14, *sólo/solo* 9.15.

4.11.9 Adjectives that occur only in front of the noun

The following phrases contain adjectives that normally occur only in front of a noun:

*Lo haré en **ambos** casos*	I'll do it in both cases
*las **llamadas** democracias*	the so-called 'democracies'
*la **mera** mención del asunto*	the mere mention of the topic
*Llevaba **mucho** dinero*	He was carrying a lot of money
*Busquemos **otro** médico*	Let's look for another doctor
*Me dejó en **pleno** centro*	He left me right in the town centre (US 'center', 'downtown')
*el **presunto** culpable*	the allegedly guilty person
***pocas** veces*	rarely
***poca** paciencia*	little patience
*el **pretendido** autor*	the alleged/supposed author
*un **sedicente** budista*	a self-styled Buddhist
*Trajeron **sendos** paquetes* (literary)	They brought a parcel each
*ante **tamaña** tontería*	in the face of such a great act of stupidity
*No puedo comer **tanta** cantidad*	I can't eat such a quantity

4.12 Attributive adjectives

'Attributive' adjectives are adjectives that replace *de* plus a noun: *la vida familiar* is another way of saying *la vida de familia* 'family life'. Spanish readily forms attributive adjectives from nouns cf. *mañana* 'morning' > **matinal** (*la televisión matinal* 'breakfast TV'), *impuesto* 'tax' > **impositivo** (*política impositiva* 'taxation policy'), *migración* 'migration' > **migratorio** (*el problema migratorio* 'the migration problem'). Many new attributive adjectives have been coined in recent decades probably because the combination noun + adjective more effectively translates English compound nouns of the type 'computer virus' (*virus informático*), 'film text' (*texto fílmico*). Some of these formations are short-lived or are rejected as journalese by educated speakers.

There is no fixed rule for forming adjectives from nouns and Latin-American coinages may differ from Peninsular inventions. In a few cases, e.g. *viento* > *eólico* 'wind' (*la energía eólica* 'wind energy', derived from *Eolo* 'Aeolus', the Roman god of the winds), the adjective is derived from a completely different root. The following are taken from various printed sources, mostly journalistic:

de + **noun**	**Attributive adjective**
problemas de presupuesto	*problemas presupuestarios* budget problems (Latin America *presupuestales*)
estancia en la cárcel	*estancia carcelaria* prison term
carestía del petróleo	*carestía petrolera* high oil prices
programa de televisión	*programa televisivo* television program(me)
política de energía	*política energética* energy policy
programa de informaciones	*programa informativo* information program(me)
industria de automóviles	*industria automovilística* car industry
crisis de la banca	*crisis bancaria* bank crisis
esfuerzo de defensa	*esfuerzo defensivo* defence (US 'defense') effort
defectos del oído	*defectos auditivos* hearing defects
industria de hoteles	*industria hotelera* hotel industry
sindicato de pilotos	*sindicato piloteril* pilots' union

Note

In both languages an adjective may be descriptive or attributive according to context: compare 'theatrical equipment' (attributive) and 'theatrical (i.e. histrionic) behavio(u)r' (descriptive). Such pairs seem to be more common in Spanish and this may confuse English speakers, who tend to misinterpret a phrase like *calidad constructiva* as meaning 'constructive quality' when it in fact means 'quality of construction'. Further examples:

lenguaje shakespeariano	Shakespearean language/the language of Shakespeare
una cantidad masiva	a massive quantity
los medios masivos	the mass media
un gesto hospitalario	a hospitable gesture
un centro hospitalario	a hospital centre (US 'center')
literatura fantástica	fantastic literature/literature of fantasy
política defensiva	defence (US 'defense') policy
actitud defensiva	defensive attitude
poesía amorosa	love poetry
una sonrisa amorosa	a loving smile
la contracción productiva	decline in output
una reunión productiva	a productive/constructive meeting

4.13 Translating the English prefix 'un-'

The Spanish prefix *in-* is much less common than the English 'un-' and English speakers should resist the temptation to invent imaginary words like **ineconómico* from 'uneconomical' (*poco económico*). The two languages often coincide:

inimaginable 'unimaginable', *insobornable* 'unbribable', *intocable* 'untouchable', *irreal* 'unreal'

But often a solution with *poco, no* or *sin* must be found:

poco profesional unprofessional
poco caritativo uncharitable
poco atractivo unattractive
poco apetitoso unappetizing
poco amistoso unfriendly
poco elegante inelegant
poco favorable unfavo(u)rable
poco práctico impractical (not **impráctico*)

poco inteligente unintelligent
no usado/sin usar unused
no autorizado/sin autorizar unauthorized
sin principios unprincipled
sin probar untried
sin comprender uncomprehending
sin convencer unconvinced

The above list shows that *poco*, like the French *peu*, negates an adjective: *poco deseable* means 'undesirable', not 'a little desirable'. A preceding indefinite article restores the meaning 'little': *un poco cansado* 'a little tired'/'slightly tired'.

5

Comparison of adjectives and adverbs

Comparison in Spanish is not particularly complicated, but English-speaking students are often hindered by interference from French, which encourages misuse of the article in the superlative and failure to use *tanto como* 'as . . . as' in comparisons of equality (cf. French *aussi . . . que*). Foreigners also tend to overlook the difference between *más de* and *más que*, and often fail to use *más/menos . . . del que* or *más/menos . . . de lo que* before clauses, verb phrases or neuter adjectives. French speakers must remember to use *yo* and *tú* after comparisons: *es más rubia que yo/tú = elle est plus blonde que **moi/toi*** 'she's blonder than me/you', never * . . . *que mí/ti*.

5.1 Regular comparison

With the exception of the six adjectives and adverbs listed at 5.2, all adjectives and adverbs form the comparative with *más . . . que* 'more . . . than' or *menos . . . que* 'less . . . than':

Los limones son más agrios que las cerezas	Lemons are more bitter than cherries
Tú andas más despacio que yo	You walk slower/more slowly than me
Tiene un traje menos/más de moda	She's got a less/more fashionable suit
más vale solos que mal acompañados	better alone than in bad company
(M. Vargas Llosa, Peru, dialogue)	

Notes

(i) For the difference between *más **que**/menos **que*** and *más **de**/menos **de*** see 5.5.

(ii) Before clauses, verb phrases and 'neuter' adjectives and participles, *más/menos **de lo que*** or the appropriate gender and number of *más/menos **del que*** are required, as in *es **más** joven **de lo que** parece* '(s)he's younger than (s)he looks'. See 5.6 for discussion.

(iii) The comparative of adverbs and, in some circumstances, of adjectives, is not distinguishable by form from the superlative. See 5.3.2 for discussion.

(iv) *Más* and *menos* need not be repeated: *él es más/menos inteligente y emprendedor que su hermano* 'he's more/less intelligent and enterprising than his brother', *me pareció el lugar más refinado y elegante del mundo* (M. Vargas Llosa, Peru, dialogue) 'it seemed to me the most refined and elegant place in the world'.

(v) '. . . than ever . . .' is translated *que nunca* (but not **que jamás*): *¡estás más joven que nunca!* 'you're younger than ever!' This use of *nunca* and of other negative words used with a positive meaning, is discussed at 23.4.

(vi) The verb *llevar*, which has numerous functions (see the Index), is used in personal comparisons involving age or height: *me lleva dos años/dos centímetros* '(s)he's two years older/two centimetres (US 'centimeters') taller than me'.

5.2 Irregular comparative forms

There are six adjectives and adverbs that have irregular comparative forms:

		Singular	**Plural**	
bueno/bien	good/well	*mejor*	*mejores*	better
malo/mal	bad/badly	*peor*	*peores*	worse
pequeño	small	*menor* (or *más pequeño*)	*menores*	smaller
grande	big	*mayor* (or *más grande*)	*mayores*	bigger/greater
poco	little	*menos*	(invariable)	less
mucho	much	*más*	(invariable)	more

Estas manzanas son mejores que ésas/esas	These apples are better than those
El mundo es peor que yo (E. Mendoza, Spain)	The world is worse than me/than I

When these words are used as adverbs only the singular form is used.

Sus hermanas hablan mejor que ella (adverb)	Her sisters speak better than she does
Aquí estamos mejor (adverb)	It's better for us here/We're better off here

Notes

(i) The uses of *mayor* and *menor* are discussed at 5.8 and 5.9.

(ii) *Más bueno, más malo* are used of moral qualities though *mejor/peor* are more usual: *a mí no me gusta pegar a los niños . . . pero es que éste es el más malo de todos* (E. Arenas, Spain, dialogue) 'I don't like hitting children, but this one's the worst of all', *tu papá es el más bueno de todos, más bueno que el mío* (M. Puig, Argentina, dialogue) 'your father's the nicest of all, nicer than mine', *es más bueno que el pan* (set phrase) 'he has a heart of gold' (lit. 'he is more good than bread').

(iii) Use of *más* or *menos* with these comparative forms, e.g. **más mejor*, is substandard and comparable to incorrect English forms like ***'more better', ***'less worse'.

5.3 Superlative of adjectives

See 5.4 for the superlative of adverbs. See 16.14.5 for the use of the subjunctive after superlative expressions.

5.3.1 Superlative of adjectives formed with *el más/menos*

In statements of the type 'the nearest station', 'the smallest tree', the superlative of adjectives (but not of adverbs) is formed with *el/la/los/las/más* 'the most' or *el/la/los/las menos* 'the least'. However, in certain cases, listed at 5.3.2, the definite article is not used.

. . . una infernal espiral de sangre y muertes que nos ha convertido en el país más inseguro y violento del mundo, con la más alta tasa de homicidios (editorial, *El Tiempo*, Colombia)	. . . an infernal spiral of blood and deaths that has turned us into the most unsafe and violent country in the world, with the highest murder rate

Notes

(i) Students of French must avoid repeating the article: *l'exemple le plus intéressant* = *el ejemplo más interesante* or *el más interesante ejemplo*. **El ejemplo **el** más interesante* is not Spanish.
(ii) Translation of sentences like 'the best restaurant **in** Madrid' usually require *de* not *en*: i.e. *el mejor restaurante de Madrid*. See 34.7 note (i) for discussion.

5.3.2 Superlative of adjectives formed without the definite article

The definite article is not used in superlative constructions in the following cases:

(a) When a possessive adjective precedes *más* or *menos*:

mi más leal amigo/mi amigo más leal	My most loyal friend
. . . pero mi capa más profunda se entristeció	But the deepest layer in me (lit. 'my
(E. Sábato, Argentina)	deepest layer') was saddened

Compare the French *mon ami **le** plus loyal*.
(b) After *ponerse* (and other verbs of becoming) and *quedar(se)*:

María se pone más nerviosa	Maria gets most nervous
Queda mejor así	It's best/better like that

Such sentences could also be understood as comparatives. The issue could be clarified by recasting the sentence using *ser*: *María es la que se pone más nerviosa, éste/este es el que queda mejor*.
(c) In relative clauses and after nominalizers, i.e. after *el/la/los/las que, quien, aquel que*, etc., meaning 'the one(s) who/which':

el curso que es menos interesante es . . .	the course that's least interesting is . . .
la que es más abordable . . .	the girl/woman who's most approachable . . .
los que son más laboriosos . . .	the ones who are most hard-working . . .
quienes tienen mejores notas son . . .	the ones with the best marks are . . .

(d) When the superlative does not involve comparison with another noun (this includes cases in which something is compared with itself):

El idealismo siempre es más fácil cuando uno es joven	Idealism is always easiest (or 'easier') when one's young
Los domingos es cuando la lluvia es más deprimente	It's on Sundays that the rain is most depressing
Aquí es donde el Rin es más romántico (the Rhine compared with itself)	The Rhine is at its most romantic here

Compare the following where true comparison with another noun is involved:

*El amor sin celos es **el** más noble* (compared with other loves)	Love without jealousy is the noblest
*Las pizzas con anchoas son **las** mejores*	Pizzas with anchovies are (the) best

(e) In the construction *qué . . . más* 'what a . . . !':

Qué hombre más cabeza dura . . . (M. Puig, Argentina, dialogue)	What an obstinate man!
¡Qué respuesta más cínica!	What a cynical answer!

5.4 Superlative of adverbs (including *más* and *menos*)

The definite article cannot be used to form the superlative of an adverb. Students of French must remember not to use the article: compare *c'est Richard qui danse le mieux* and *Ricardo es el que mejor baila*. Examples:

De las tres la que canta mejor es Ana	Of the three girls, Ana sings best
Cuando más llueve es en verano	It's in summer that it rains most (or 'more')
¿Sabes qué es lo que más cansa? (M. Puig, Argentina, dialogue)	Do you know what's most tiring?
Era el cuento que mejor nos permitía pelear (A. Bryce Echenique, Peru)	It was the short story that allowed us to quarrel most (lit. 'best'; i.e. 'short stories provoked our greatest quarrels')
. . . el ser que más lo amaba y al que más amaba (G. García Márquez, Colombia)	. . . the person who loved him most and whom he loved most
El patrón fue uno de los que más peces capturó durante los 40 minutos que se dedicaron a la pesca (*Granma*, Cuba)	The skipper was one of those who caught most fish during the forty minutes dedicated to fishing

Note

The difference between *el que más me gusta* and *el que me gusta más* 'the one I like more/most' is one of emphasis, the former being stronger and therefore more likely to carry a superlative meaning. Note that with the verb *gustar*, *más* must be used, not *mejor*; contrast English 'I like this one best/most'.

5.5 *Más/menos* **que** or *más/menos* **de?**

The difference is crucial: *más* **de** is used before numbers or quantities:

*Mi abuelo tiene más **de** cien años*	My grandfather is more than 100 years old
Son más de las tres y media	It's past 3.30
Estaba seguro de que no aguantarías quieta durante más de 6 meses (A. Mastretta, Mexico, dialogue)	I was sure you wouldn't stay still for more than six months

Compare the following examples in which the expression following *más* or *menos* is not a quantity:

*Este restaurante es más caro **que** antes*	This restaurant is dearer than before
*Cansa más el viaje **que** el empleo*	The travelling is more tiring than the job
Le escriben de Italia más que a nosotros (M Puig, Argentina, dialogue)	They write to him from Italy more than they do to us

Notes

(i) Care must be taken not to confuse this construction with *no . . . más que . . .* meaning 'only': *no he traído más que mil* (= *sólo/solo he traído mil*) 'I've **only** brought 1,000', *no he traído más de mil* 'I haven't brought **more than** 1,000', *las clases de pintura no eran más que una manera más entretenida de pasar el tiempo* (G. García Márquez, Colombia) 'the art classes were only a more entertaining way of killing time'.

(ii) In the following examples *que* must be used, even though a number follows: *tiene más fuerzas que tres hombres juntos* 'he's stronger than three men together', *habla más que siete* '(s)he never stops talking' (lit. '(s)he talks more than seven people'). The reason is that there is no comparison with an actual number: the comparison is with the *strength of* three men, *the talking* done by seven people. Spanish thus avoids an ambiguity that affects English:

*Comió **más** que tres personas*	He ate more than three people (would eat)
*Comió (a) **más de** tres personas*	He ate more than three people (cannibalism)

5.6 Comparison of quantity with clauses, verb phrases and neuter adjectives/participles

Más que cannot be used before verb phrases or past participles. *Más/menos* **de** must be used, but this phrase can only appear in front of noun phrases: **es más inteligente de crees* is clearly not Spanish for 'she's more intelligent than you think'. The appropriate form of *del que* must therefore be used to convert the verb phrase into a noun phrase: *es más inteligente* **de lo que** *crees*.

(a) If a comparison of quantity is made with a clause containing a noun or pronoun, **del que** must be used and must agree in number and gender with the noun or pronoun:

Has traído menos aceite **del que** *necesitamos*	You've brought less **oil** than we need
Han venido más **de las que** *se matricularon para el curso*	More **girls/women** have come than registered for the course
La conozco desde hace aún más años **de los que** *lleva fuera de España* (J. Marías, Spain, dialogue)	I've known her for even more years than she has been out of Spain
Habían llegado al país más novedades **de las que** *Diego Sauri hubiera podido imaginar* (A. Mastretta, Mexico)	More novelties had arrived in the country than Diego Sauri could have imagined

(b) If the comparison is made with a verb phrase, a participle or an adjective, *de lo que* must be used (the neuter form, which is required when no gendered noun or pronoun is referred to):

El viento me vuelve mucho más loca **de lo que** *mi marido y ex maridos dicen que estoy* (Carmen Rico-Godoy, Spain)	The wind drives me much crazier than my husband and ex-husbands say I am
No se haga el estúpido más **de lo que** *es* (M. Vargas Llosa, Peru, dialogue; Spain *no se haga más estúpido de lo que es*)	Don't try to be more stupid than you are
más impresionante **de lo** *esperado* (= *de lo que se esperaba*)	more impressive than was hoped
. . . o si la noche era cálida y menos húmeda **de lo** *habitual* (E. Mendoza, Spain)	. . . or if the night was warm and less humid than usual

Notes

(i) This construction often seems unnecessary to English speakers, but it is required in Spanish because *más/menos de* can only precede noun phrases, and because *más que* before a verb or adjective usually means 'rather than' or 'instead of': *gasta más que gana* 'he spends more (i.e. 'rather') than earns'.

(ii) Constructions on the lines of **eres más inteligente que pareces* have been attested in good writers in the past, and a few informants thought they might occur in spontaneous speech. Most informants condemned them as badly formed.

(iii) Use of *del que/de lo que* is apparently not always obligatory in Latin America: *había hecho más* **que** *lo posible para que Ángela Vicario se muriera en vida* (G. García Márquez, Colombia. Spain *más* **de lo** *posible*) 'she had done more than was possible so that Angela Vicario would have no life at all' (lit. 'die while alive').

(iv) Comparison between two non-neuter adjective requires *que*: *más azul que verde* 'more blue than red', *más muertos que vivos* 'more dead than alive'.

(v) French is free of the problems raised by *del/de lo que*, but, unlike Spanish, it uses a redundant negative in comparisons with a clause: *il en sait plus qu'il n'avoue* = *él sabe más* **de** *lo que admite* 'he knows more than he admits'.

5.7 *Más* as a colloquial intensifier

Más is often used as an intensifier in familiar speech on both continents, without any comparative meaning:

Es que eres más tonto . . .	Heavens, you're stupid . . .
Está más borracho . . .	Is he *drunk*!

Note

For the standard construction *qué vida más triste* 'what a sad life!', *¡qué hombre más guapo!* 'what an attractive man!', see 5.3.2 section (e). *Más* is used before plural nouns, e.g. *tengo más amigos que tú* 'I've got more friends than you', and before quantities: *tiene más dinero que yo* 'he's got more money than me.'

5.8 Uses of *mayor*

Mayor, which means both 'greater' and 'bigger', is used as follows:

(a) In the same way as *más grande* 'bigger' in comparisons involving physical objects, although it is not normally used of small things like pins, insects, etc., and its use for physical comparisons is more characteristic of written language:

Esta aula es más grande/mayor que la otra	This lecture-room is bigger than the other
Mallorca es la más grande/la mayor de las Baleares	Majorca is the biggest of the Balearic Islands

One can never say **lo mayor*: *lo más grande lo ponemos abajo* 'let's put the biggest things underneath'.

(b) To translate 'older' or 'oldest' when applied to people:

Mi hermano es mayor que el tuyo	My brother is older than yours
mi hermano mayor	my elder brother
Tienes dieciséis años pero pareces mayor	You're sixteen but you look older
Es ya mayor que su hermana mayor . . . en realidad mayor de lo que fue nunca Teresa (J. Marías, Spain, dialogue)	She's already (looking) older than her elder sister . . . actually older-looking than Teresa ever was

Mayor is also a euphemism for *viejo*: *una señora mayor* 'an elderly lady'.

(c) *Mayor* is used to mean 'greater' or 'greatest': *su mayor éxito* 'his greatest success', *el mayor criminal del mundo* 'the greatest criminal in the world', *el mayor peligro* 'the greatest danger', *su mayor preocupación/alegría* 'his/her greatest worry/joy'.

(d) Before nouns denoting sizes, intensity, frequency, power or quantity, *mayor* or *más* can be used, with *mayor* considered more elegant: *mayor/más anchura* 'greater width', *mayor/más intensidad*, *mayor/más fuerza* 'greater strength', *mayor/más potencia* 'more power', *mayor/más frecuencia* 'greater frequency', *mayor/más peso* 'more weight'. Further examples:

Más acentuado será el sabor del ajo, cuanta mayor cantidad lleve	The greater the quantity it contains, the more pronounced the garlic flavour will be
La sociedad argentina reclama mayor transparencia en las conductas de los hombres políticos (La Nación, Argentina)	Argentine society demands greater openness in the behaviour of politicians
Deseo recibir mayor información	I would like to receive more information
Tiene mayor contenido vitamínico	It has a greater vitamin content

In all the examples under **(d)** *más* is possible and much more usual in relaxed styles, though less elegant.

(e) Before *número* or words and phrases indicating number, *mayor* is obligatory: *en mayor número de casos* 'in a greater number of cases', *mayor índice de mortalidad infantil* 'a higher rate of infantile mortality', *mayor incidencia de accidentes de tráfico* 'a higher rate of traffic accidents', *la mayor parte de las víctimas* 'the majority of the victims'.

(f) Set phrases: *mayor de edad* 'of age', *hacerse mayor* 'to get old', *ganado mayor* 'live-stock' (horses, cows, mules only), *calle mayor* 'high street', etc.

(g) *Más grande* can be used as a superlative: *el más grande/mayor pensador moderno* 'the greatest modern thinker', but not in pejorative statements: *el mayor granuja del país* 'the biggest rogue in the country'.

5.9 Uses of *menor*

Menos is used before plural nouns – *tengo menos amigos que tú* 'I've got fewer friends than you' – and before quantities: *tiene menos dinero que yo* 'he's got less money than me'.

Menor is not used to mean 'smaller' (as the opposite of 'bigger'): *esta habitación es más pequeña que ésa/esa* not **menor que ésa/esa; ella es más pequeña de tamaño/más baja* 'she's smaller in size', not **menor de tamaño*. However, it can be used for dimensions where English would allow 'less': *el área es menor de lo que parece* 'the area is less/smaller than it looks'. Note also *mi hermano menor/pequeño* 'my younger brother' but *mi hermano es más joven/pequeño que yo* 'my brother is younger than me'. Also *el más pequeño de la familia* 'the youngest in the family', not **el menor de la familia*.

*Lo menor is also impossible: *lo más pequeño* 'what's smallest'/'the smallest things'.

Menor is used in the same contexts as *mayor* in (b), (c), (d) and (e) in the previous section. Examples:

Diego es tres años menor que Martita y cuatro que Sergio (C. Rico-Godoy, Spain)	Diego is three years younger than Martita and four younger than Sergio
Virginia era unos meses menor que yo (A. Mastretta, Mexico, dialogue)	Virginia was a few months younger than me
Usted no tendrá la menor dificultad (or *mínima* or *más pequeña*)	You won't have the slightest difficulty
El riesgo de un enfrentamiento es cada vez menor	The risk of a confrontation is declining

Common set phrases: *menor de edad* 'under age', *apto para menores* 'suitable for minors/young people'.

5.10 *Mucho más, mucho menos, poco más,* etc.

Before *más, menos, mayor* and *menor*, when these four words qualify a noun, *mucho* and *poco* are adjectives and must agree in number and gender with the following noun – a point that English speakers are prone to forget: *tienen muchos menos hijos que tú* 'they have far fewer children than you'. See 9.12b note (i) for a discussion.

5.11 'The more . . . the more . . .'/'the less . . . the less . . .'

Cuanto más . . . más . . . , cuanto menos . . . menos . . . are the standard formulas (no accent on *cuanto*):

Cuantos/as más, mejor	The more the better

Cuanto menos lo pienses de antemano,
    menos te va a doler
	The less you think about it beforehand, the
	    less it'll hurt

Cuanto mayor sea la distancia de una
    galaxia a la Tierra, más deprisa se aleja
    (*Abc*, Spain)
	The greater the distance between a galaxy
	    and the Earth, the faster it recedes

Cuanto más pensaba más me afligía . . . (J. Cortázar, Argentina, dialogue)	The more I thought, the more upset I got . . .

The use of *mientras* in this construction sounds popular or substandard in Spain but is normal in Latin America. Use of *contra* or *entre* for *cuanto* is typical of everyday speech in many parts of Latin America (*contra* is heard in Spain, but it is stigmatized), but they are avoided in formal writing:

Mientras más pienses en ella, más tuya la
    harás (C. Fuentes, Mexico, dialogue)
	The more you think of her, the more you
	    will make her yours

. . . la cabeza gacha, entre menos me vea,
    mejor (E. Poniatowska, Mexico,
    dialogue)
	. . . with my head bowed, the less he sees of
	    me the better

Aquí, contra menos somos, peor avenidos
    estamos (M. Delibes, Spain, illiterate,
    rural dialogue)
	Here, the less of us there are the worse we
	    get on

Notes

(i) 'all the more . . . ', 'not so much . . . but that . . . ' may be translated by *tanto . . . cuanto*: *no es tanto que entre dos personas no haya secretos porque así lo deciden cuanto que no es posible dejar de contar* (J. Marías, Spain) 'it's not so much that there are no secrets between two people because they decide it should be this way, but that it's not possible to avoid telling'.
(ii) *como para* (or simply *para*) is used after *bastante* and *lo suficiente*, as in *bastantes problemas de violencia tiene el país como para que ahora la Fiscalía se dedique a actividades proselitistas* (*El Tiempo*, Colombia) 'the country has enough problems with violence without the Public Prosecution Office now getting involved in proselytizing activities'.

5.12 'More and more . . .', 'less and less . . .'

Cada vez más/menos are the standard translations:

Está cada vez más delgado	He's getting thinner and thinner
Hace cada vez menos calor	The weather's getting less and less hot

5.13 Superlative time expressions

A neuter construction may be required:

Lo más tarde que cenamos es a las ocho	We have dinner/supper at eight at the latest
Lo antes/más temprano que puedo salir de *casa es a la una*	The earliest I can leave house is at one
Levántense lo más temprano posible	Get up as early as you can

5.14 Miscellaneous translations of English comparatives and superlatives

Todos le interesaban, el párroco no el que menos	All the men interested her, not least the parish priest
Ninguno trabaja mucho, y tú menos que todos	None of them works much, and you least of all
lo menos que podrías hacer . . .	the least you could do
Estoy agradecidísimo/muy agradecido	I'm most/extremely grateful
De los dos, este libro es el que más se lee	Of the two, this book is read more/the most
En esas circunstancias la gastronomía es lo de menos (M. Vázquez Montalbán, Spain)	In those circumstances gastronomy is the least important part of it
Dale cuanto dinero puedas/Dale todo el dinero que puedas	Give him as much money as you can
la mejor solución posible	the best possible solution
el segundo mejor/peor	the second best/worst
Sabe sacar el mejor partido de todo	He knows how to make the most of everything
Tan duquesa es como mi padre	She's as much a duchess as I am . . . (ironic: lit. 'she's as much a duchess as my father is')

5.15 Comparisons of equality

5.15.1 *Tan como, tanto como*

The formula is *tan . . . como* or *tanto . . . como* 'as . . . as', not *tanto . . . que*, which can only mean 'so much that': *se rió tanto que por poco revienta* 'he laughed so much he nearly burst'. *Tan* is used before adjectives, adverbs and nouns; *tanto* is used before *como* itself or when nothing follows:

No soy tan joven como tú	I'm not as young as you
Usted lo sabe tan bien como yo (M. Vargas Llosa, Peru, dialogue)	You know as well as I do
No eres tan hombre como él	You're not as much of a man as he is
No hablo tanto como tú	I don't talk as much as you

5.15.2 *Igual que, lo mismo que, tal como*

These are used to express equality. *Igual que* is used after verbs, not *igual a* (for which see 5.15.3):

Escribe igual que/lo mismo que tú (not **igual como, *lo mismo como*)	She writes the same way as you
Me trató igual que siempre (G. García Márquez, Colombia)	She treated me the same as always
Lo hice tal como me lo dijiste	I did it just as you told me to/exactly as you told me

Notes

(i) Comparison of equality with verb phrases can also be expressed by the formula *del mismo modo que/de la misma manera que/de igual modo que/de igual manera que*: *argüía de la misma manera que muchos filósofos de la época* 'he argued in the same way as many philosophers of the day'.
(ii) *Diferente, distinto*: *es diferente del que tú tienes* 'it's different to/from the one you have', *esta silla es diferente de la otra* 'this chair's different to/from the other', *es diferente/distinto a ti* 'he's different

to/from you'. The construction *diferente a* is found in Latin America and is heard in Spain, although Seco (1998), 164, says it is uncommon in educated Peninsular usage.

5.15.3 *Igual* or *igualmente?*

Igualmente means 'equally', but *igual* (as well as being an adjective meaning 'equal') is an invariable adverb in its own right meaning 'the same'. Compare *otros problemas igualmente difíciles* 'other equally difficult problems' and *una bata que le caía igual que hecha a medida* (L. Goytisolo, Spain) 'a housecoat which fitted her exactly as if it had been made to measure'. Further examples:

Cuando te conozcan sabrán apreciarte igual que yo (L. Otero, Cuba, dialogue)	When they get to know you they'll value you the same way as I do
En eso ustedes son igual a las mujeres (M. Puig, Argentina, dialogue. Also *igual que . . .*)	You're the same as women in that respect
Es igual que tú (also *igual a ti*)/*Es lo mismo que tú*	She's the same as you
Tú eres igualmente delgado/Tú eres igual de delgado	You're just as slim
Lo hace igual de bien que tú	She does it as well as you

Note

In Spain, *igual* very often functions colloquially as an adverb meaning 'maybe' (i.e. meaning *quizá*, *tal vez* or *a lo mejor*, discussed at 16.3.2): *yo no sé lo que me espera hoy. Igual llego tarde* (C. Rico-Godoy, Spain, dialogue) 'I don't know what's in store for me today. Maybe I'll get back late.' This is familiar style, rejected by some as 'common' and probably confined to Spain. Latin Americans may interpret *igual* as meaning 'anyway'/'all the same', e.g. *también mi estómago se mueve pero igual estoy contento* (M. Benedetti, Uruguay, dialogue) 'my stomach's churning too, but I'm happy all the same'.

6

Demonstrative adjectives and pronouns

Spanish demonstrative adjectives and demonstrative pronouns are identical in form: *este* means 'this' or 'this one' (masculine), *esas* and *aquellas* mean 'those' or 'those ones' (feminine). The ambiguities that rarely arise can be removed by writing the pronouns with an accent. See 6.3 for discussion. Spanish differs from French, German and English in having two words for 'that', depending on the distance in time or space between the speaker and the object referred to. The demonstratives have neuter forms, *esto, eso* and *aquello*, which are discussed separately in Chapter 7.

6.1 Forms of demonstratives adjectives and pronouns

	this	**that (near)**	**that (far)**
masculine	*este*	*ese*	*aquel*
feminine	*esta*	*esa*	*aquella*
(neuter	*esto*	*eso*	*aquello* (see Ch. 7)
	these	**those (near)**	**those (far)**
masculine	*estos*	*esos*	*aquellos*
feminine	*estas*	*esas*	*aquellas*

Notes

(i) See 6.3 for when to write these with an accent.
(ii) The masculine singular forms do not end in -o!
(iii) *Esta*, *esa* and *aquella* should be used before feminine nouns beginning with stressed *a-* or *ha-*: *esta agua* 'this water', *esa aula* 'that lecture-hall', *aquella haya* 'that beech-tree over there'. This is the opinion of Seco (1998, articles on *aquel, ese* and *este*) and of the Academy's *Esbozo* . . . 2.6.2d, and is also the practice of well-edited texts everywhere; but forms like *este arma* 'this weapon', *este área* 'this area' are very common in spontaneous speech and sometimes appear in informal written styles.
(iv) In Latin America *este*, and in Spain *esto*, are used and abused like the English 'er . . .' to fill pauses while the speaker is thinking.
(v) When two or more nouns are involved, the demonstratives are repeated unless the nouns refer to the same thing: *este hombre y esta mujer* 'this man and (this) woman', but *este poeta y filósofo* 'this poet and philosopher' (same man).

6.2 Position of demonstrative adjectives

Normally before the noun: *esta miel* 'this honey', *ese árbol* 'that tree', *aquellas regiones* 'those regions'. In spoken language they may appear after the noun, in which case they strongly imply that the thing referred to has been mentioned before or is very familiar. In many cases this implies irritation, exasperation or an ironic tone, and the construction should be used with caution. Compare *esa mujer* 'that woman' (neutral tone) and *la mujer esa* 'that woman . . . ' (sarcastic or weary tone). However, the construction may simply indicate a reference to a well-known topic, as in *¿quiere la bata esta? Se va a enfriar* (C. Martín Gaite, Spain, dialogue) 'do you want this dressing-gown/(US 'bathrobe')? You'll get cold' (refers to an article familiar to both). Further examples:

Pero con la agencia esa que ha montado, se está forrando el riñón (A. Buero Vallejo, Spain, dialogue)	But with that agency he's set up, he's simply raking it in
En seguida dejé de tener importancia para la gente aquella (F. Umbral, Spain, dialogue)	I immediately ceased to have any importance for those people
Se ganaron mi afecto incondicional desde la tarde aquella en que me ayudaron a llenar los formularios de ingreso a la seguridad social (A. Bryce Echenique, Peru)	They gained my unconditional affection after that afternoon when they helped me fill in my Social Security application forms

The definite article is obligatory if a demonstrative adjective follows the noun: *la gente aquella*. The demonstrative in this case remains an adjective even though it follows the noun, so it is not written with an accent.

6.3 When does one write *este, ese, aquel* with an accent?

The present confusing situation can be summarized thus:

(a) According to the Academy and to Seco (1998), 55, 200, 206, the accent is virtually never necessary on these words, so the best advice to learners is: when in doubt leave it out. Omission of the accent looks much less illiterate than incorrect use of it.

(b) The neuter pronouns, *esto, eso* and *aquello* are **never** written with an accent.

However, the Academy's ruling **(a)** is very controversial. The old (pre-1959) rules of spelling required that the demonstrative pronouns should always be distinguished from demonstrative adjectives by adding an accent, but even in carefully edited texts printed before that date many inconsistencies appear. The Academy's revised spelling rules, the *Nuevas normas* of 1959, state that the accent is now required only to remove ambiguities of the sort found in *esta protesta* 'this protest' and *ésta protesta* 'this woman is protesting', *esa compra* 'that purchase' and *ésa compra* 'that woman is buying', or *ese español* 'that Spaniard' and *ése español* 'that Spanish one'. Since such ambiguities almost never appear in written Spanish (because context makes the meaning clear), the accent can in practice be omitted: both the Academy and Manuel Seco now consider sentences like *esta es mía* 'this one's mine', *un libro como ese* 'a book like that one' to be correct.

Nevertheless, most publishing houses, newspaper editors, the more cautious grammarians and ordinary citizens everywhere reject this reform and stick to the old rule: the Madrid daily *El País*, for example, orders its journalists always to write the accent on the pronouns. Foreign students must therefore choose between following the Academy and thereby offending the eye of educated Spanish-speakers, or trying systematically to distinguish demonstrative adjectives from pronouns, which is not always easy.

In this book we show both possibilities, e.g. *un libro como ése/ese* 'a book like that one', although we omit the accent in a few cases where we cannot decide whether the demonstrative is an adjective or a pronoun.

There is one important inconsistency in printed usage. It has always been the practice in modern times even before 1959 and among the most conservative writers to omit the accent from demonstrative pronouns that are the antecedent of a relative clause or act as nominalizers (*aquel que, este de*, etc.); the reason for this is not entirely clear. As a result we write *esta novela es mejor que **aquella** en que* . . . 'this novel is better than that in which . . .', *este/ese que* . . . 'this/that one that . . .', **aquel** *de ayer* . . . 'the one from yesterday . . .', etc. This practice is encouraged by Seco (1998), articles on *aquel, ese, este*.

Examples of demonstrative pronouns:

Dame otro cuchillo – éste/este no corta	Give me another knife – this one doesn't cut
Ése/Ese sí que es inteligente	Now that one – he really is intelligent
Antonio salía cada vez más de casa, circunstancia ésta/esta que a su madre no le pasaba inadvertida (note position of demonstrative pronoun in apposition)	Antonio left the house more and more, this being a circumstance which did not pass unnoticed by his mother
Aquéllas/aquellas/ésas/esas eran las condiciones en que teníamos que trabajar	Those were the conditions in which we had to work
*. . . su proximidad o lejanía respecto de la persona que habla o de **aquella** a quien se habla* (Academy 1928 edition, *Gramática* 39; accent omitted from *aquella* followed by relative pronoun)	. . . one's closeness or distance in relation to the person speaking or to whom one is speaking

Note

Use of demonstratives to refer to someone present is humorous or insulting: *pregúntaselo a éste/este* 'ask this one here' (e.g. pointing to her husband), *¡éstos/estos fuera!* 'get this lot out!'

6.4 Use of este, ese and *aquel*

(a) *Este* refers to things near to or associated with the speaker and is equivalent to 'this': *este libro* 'this book', *estos arbustos* 'these bushes', *esta catástrofe* 'this catastrophe (that has just happened)', *estas circunstancias* 'these circumstances (that have just arisen)'.

(b) As far as physical distance is concerned, *ese* means 'that': *ese libro* 'that book', *esos árboles* 'those trees'. It can refer to objects at any distance from the speaker and can therefore in practice always replace *aquel* when space rather than time is involved, although *aquel* cannot always replace *ese* since it cannot be used for things close to the hearer or speaker.

(c) As far as physical distance is concerned, *aquel* resembles the old English 'yonder' and adds a nuance of spatial distance which is rarely obligatory but is nevertheless elegant and instinctively applied by most native speakers. As far as distance in time is concerned, it refers to something in the more remote past: *en aquella época* 'at that (distant) time' and may be obligatory. It is discussed in detail at 6.4.1.

éste/este de aquí	this one here
ése/ese de ahí[1]	that one just there
aquél/aquel de allí	that one over there
no ése/ese sino aquel/aquél	Not that one, but that one over there
Alcánzame ese/aquel libro rojo	Pass me that red book
Prefiero ese que tú tienes	I prefer that one (masc.) that you've got
¿Cómo se llama aquella/esa estrella?	What's that star (up there) called?
¿Quién se acuerda ya de aquellas tardes	Who can still remember those evenings
sin televisión? (not *esas* for remote time)	without television?

6.4.1 *Aquel* or *ese*?

Aquel may be yielding ground to *ese*: some grammarians complain about a tendency to use *ese* where *aquel* is more elegant. As a result, learners will probably do well when in doubt to translate 'that' as *ese*: it is virtually always correct, although *aquel* is obligatory in certain phrases referring to the more distant past. The nuance of *aquel*, which implies greater spatial or emotional distance, is, however, instinctively used by the immense majority of Spaniards and Latin Americans.

(a) As far as spatial distance is concerned, *aquel* implies greater distance and is usual but not absolutely necessary:

—¿Quién plantó ese árbol?	'Who planted that tree?'
—¿Ése/Ese? —No, **aquél/aquel**	'That one?' 'No, the one behind'
No esa torre sino **aquélla/aquella**	Not that tower but the one further away

Even in these cases some phrase like *ése/ese de detrás* or *ése/ese de más allá* could have been used.

(b) It is optionally but usually used to indicate something at some distance from the speaker. The difference between *ese libro* and *aquel libro* is about the same as between 'that book' and 'that book over there':

Tráeme aquella/esa taza	Bring me that cup (from over there)
¿Ves aquella/esa montaña?	Can you see that mountain?

(c) As far as time is concerned, *aquel* indicates the distant past. Once an event in the past has been mentioned, *ese* can be used in subsequent references to it:

¿Te acuerdas del 39? Pues en aquella (or *esa*) *época yo vivía en Bilbao* (*esa* is possible here because the year is specified)	Do you remember '39? Well, at that time I was living in Bilbao
Debe de haber andado ya por los sesenta años cuando se embarcó con aquel horror de mujer (S. Pitol, Mexico, dialogue; *ese horror* would imply that he is still involved with her)	He must have been getting on for sixty when he fell in with (lit. 'set sail with') that frightful woman

---

[1] See 31.6.1 for the difference between *ahí* and *allí*.

In some set phrases *aquel* is obligatory:

¡Qué noche aquélla/aquella!	What a night that was!
¡Qué tiempos aquéllos/aquellos!	What times they were!

Further examples of *ese* and *aquel*:

Era como uno de esos payasos de circo que dan miedo a los niños (*aquellos* would be possible only if such clowns no longer existed)	He was like one of those circus clowns who frighten the children
¿Te acuerdas de aquel escritorio que el abuelo quemó cuando tenías cinco años? (*aquel* appropriate for something no longer in existence)	Do you remember that desk that grandfather burnt when you were five?
. . . la luna ya como de invierno, con su halo violeta de medusa y aquellas estrellas como un hielo hecho añicos (L. Goytisolo, Spain) (*aquellas* appropriate for a childhood memory)	. . . the moon like a winter moon now, with its violet halo like a jellyfish's, and those stars like shattered ice

Notes

(i) In writing, *aquel que* (no written accent) replaces *el que* if the latter is followed by a relative pronoun. See 6.5c and 35.13 for more examples.

(ii) *Aquel* should not be used in conjunction with a historic present because of the absurdity of simultaneously stressing the remoteness and the immediacy of an action; i.e. not **en aquel año Cervantes escribe el Quijote* 'in that year Cervantes wrote *Don Quixote*' but either *en **este** año Cervantes **escribe** el Quijote*, or *en **aquel** año Cervantes **escribió** el Quijote*.

6.4.2 'The former, the latter'

Since *aquél/aquel* denotes something remote and *éste/este* something close, they conveniently translate 'former' and 'latter':

La Universidad de México . . . no favorece ni los estudios ni la amistad. La ausencia de disciplina y normas de selección impide ***aquéllos****; la plétora indiscriminada de una población de doscientos mil estudiantes dificulta* ***ésta*** (C. Fuentes, Mexico, dialogue)	Mexico University . . . encourages neither study nor friendship. The lack of discipline and admission qualifications prevents the former; the undifferentiated mass of a student population of 200,000 hinders the latter

6.5 Translation problems involving demonstratives

(a) 'The . . . which/who', 'those . . . who', etc.

El que or *quien* are the usual equivalents; *aquel que* (usually written without an accent) is used in formal language: *que se ponga de pie la que ha dicho eso* 'stand up the girl who said that', etc. See Chapter 36 (Nominalizers) for discussion.

(b) 'Those of them', 'those of you', etc. *Aquellos de* is frowned on, except perhaps before *ustedes* or *vosotros*:

Los que aplaudieron ayer	Those of them who applauded yesterday
Los nicaragüenses que sabemos la verdad	Those of us Nicaraguans who know the truth
Aquellos de (entre) ustedes que afirman eso	Those of you who claim that
Los que no hayan firmado el formulario	Those (of them/you) who haven't signed the form

(**los de ellos* or **aquellos de ellos* in this context are not Spanish)

(c) 'The one in which', 'those where', etc.

Aquel que, written without an accent in this construction, is a literary replacement for *el que* when a preposition governs a relative pronoun. One writes *la habitación era más cómoda que **aquella** en **que** había dormido antes* 'the room was more comfortable than the one he had slept in before'. The spoken language usually prefers to repeat the noun: *la habitación era más cómoda que la habitación en la que/donde había dormido antes*; **la en que* is not possible. See 6.5c and 35.13 for details.

(d) 'This/that is why . . .', 'this/that is where', 'this/that's who', 'this/that was when', etc. Translation of these phrases may involve the problem of 'cleft' sentences, e.g.: *fue por eso por lo que pagó demasiado* (Lat. Am. *fue por eso que pagó . . .*) 'that was why he paid too much'. See 36.2 for a detailed discussion of cleft sentences.

7

____

Neuter article and neuter pronouns

7.1 Neuter gender: general

Nouns in Classical Latin could have one of three genders: masculine, feminine or neuter. Most neuter nouns came to be confused with masculine nouns in everyday spoken Latin, and nowadays all traces of the neuter have vanished from the Spanish noun system.

However, a few neuter pronouns and an article survived in Spanish and remain as important features of the modern language. These forms are the 'neuter article' *lo*, the neuter third-person pronoun *ello* and its object form *lo*,[1] the neuter relative pronouns *lo que*, and *lo cual*, the neuter nominalizers *lo que* and *lo de*, and the neuter demonstrative pronouns *esto*, *eso* and *aquello*.

Neuter pronouns are necessary in Spanish to refer to concepts, ideas or statements (e.g. a preceding remark or sentence) that have no gender. Masculine and feminine articles and pronouns can refer only to nouns, present or implied, and nouns can be only masculine or feminine. Examples should make this clear:

No quiero hablar de aquél/aquel/aquélla/ aquella[2]	I don't want to talk about **that one** (i.e. some masculine or feminine noun)
No quiero hablar de aquello	I don't want to talk about **that**
No me gusta ése/ese/ésa/esa[2]	I don't like **that one** (French *celui-là/celle-là*)
No me gusta eso	I don't like **that** (*cela*)
los nuevos/las nuevas	the new ones (masc.)/the new ones (fem.)
lo nuevo	what is new

For *lo que*, *lo cual* as relative pronouns (meaning 'which . . .'), see 35.6. For *lo que* and *lo de* as nominalizers (i.e. 'the thing that/of . . .') see 36.1.5 and 36.1.3. For the humorous *la que . . .* for *lo que . . .* see 36.1.4 note (iii). For the colloquial *la de* meaning 'the quantity of . . .' see 3.2.30. For the neuter pronouns *todo* 'everything', *algo* 'something', *mucho* 'a lot' and *poco* 'a little' see Chapter 9.

7.2 The 'neuter article' *lo*

7.2.1 *Lo* with masculine singular adjectives or with adverbs

A masculine singular adjective, or an adverb preceded by *lo*, becomes a sort of abstract noun, usually a rough equivalent of an English adjective + 'thing', although in many cases translation requires ingenuity:

____

[1] But *lo* can also be a masculine object pronoun. See Chapter 11.
[2] For the optional accent on these pronouns see 6.3.

(a) with adjectives:

Lo importante es que diga la verdad	The important thing is for him to tell the truth
Eso es lo increíble de todo eso	That's the incredible thing about all that
Lo bueno de tu casa es que tiene mucha luz	The good thing about your house is that it's full of light
Lo mío es confundir (Unamuno)	My style is to confuse
Lo monótono es la felicidad (C. Solórzano, Mexico, dialogue)	Monotony is happiness (or perhaps 'happiness is things not changing')
Papá se ha enterado de lo nuestro	Father has found out about us
Felicitas había sido una estudiante dócil y estudiado lo justo (S. Puértolas, Spain)	Felicitas had been a docile student and studied just as much as was necessary
Lo mío ha sido por lo menos igual de duro que lo de ustedes (G. García Márquez, Colombia, dialogue)	What happened to me was at least as hard as what happened to you
a pesar de lo antes dicho	despite what was said earlier
en lo alto de la colina	on the top of the hill

The adjective can be preceded by an adverb:

lo nunca visto en Estados Unidos	what has never been seen before in the USA
Lo verdaderamente increíble es que yo te haya encontrado (S. Puértolas, Spain, dialogue)	The really incredible thing is the fact that I've found you
Los expertos están de acuerdo: lo más pequeño que existe y lo más grande (todo el cosmos) están íntimamente ligados (El País, Spain)	Experts agree: the smallest existing things and the biggest things (the whole of the cosmos) are intimately linked

Note

In sentences with *ser* the verb agrees with the predicate: *lo mejor de la película **son** los actores* 'the best thing in the film is (lit. 'are') the actors'. In other words, when *lo* + adjective occurs in this type of sentence, the order of the subject and predicate can be reversed without changing the meaning: *los actores son lo mejor de la película*. This topic is discussed more fully at 2.3.3.

(b) with adverbs or adverbial phrases:

Hazlo lo más rápidamente que puedas	Do it as quickly as you can
Cuélgalo lo más arriba que puedas	Hang it as high/as far up as you can
lo más atrás posible	as far back as possible
Lo antes que puedo salir de casa es a las seis	The earliest I can leave home is at six
Todo lo demás no es cierto	Everything else is untrue
Baja lo de allí arriba	Take down everything from up there

Notes

(i) Other Romance languages lack this device: the French words *le plus tragique* can mean both 'the most tragic thing' and 'the most tragic one'; the Italian *il bello e il brutto* can mean 'beauty and ugliness' or 'the beautiful one and the ugly one'.

(ii) For the choice between the indicative and the subjunctive in constructions with *lo* + adjective + *es que*, e.g. *lo curioso es que* . . . see 16.6.3.

(iii) *Lo* is occasionally found with a noun used adjectivally: *pues sí, Diego, ya sabes lo desastre que soy* (C. Rico-Godoy, Spain, dialogue) 'well yes, Diego, you know what a disaster I am', *ya te salió lo mujer* (A. Mastretta, Mexico, dialogue) 'here goes the woman in you' (lit. 'the woman in you came out').

(iv) When *bastante* and *suficiente* occur in phrases of the kind 'clever enough to . . .', 'he did it well enough to . . .' they are preceded by *lo* and followed by *para*. The *lo* survives even if *para* and what follows are deleted. *Como* may optionally precede the *para*: *el cuello de su gabardina estaba lo bastante abierto para permitirme contemplar el collar de perlas* (J. Marías, Spain) 'the collar of her raincoat was open enough to let me see her pearl necklace', *ya tenía lo suficiente para aquellos paseos* (S. Galindo, Mexico) 'he already had enough (money) for those excursions', *no la conozco lo suficiente (como) para invitarla* 'I don't know her well enough to invite her'.

7.2.2 *Lo* plus adjectives or adverbs translating 'how', etc.

Lo with an adjective or adverb often translates the English 'how' or some similar word + an adjective or adverb: when used thus the adjective must agree with the noun. This construction often occurs after verbs of perception ('see', 'realize', 'understand', 'know') and after verbs of liking or disliking:

(a) with adjectives and nouns used adjectivally:

No me había dado cuenta de lo guapa que era	I hadn't realized how attractive she was
Me irritan por lo tontos que son	I find them irritating because of their silliness
¿No se ha fijado en lo delgada que se ha quedado? (A. Buero Vallejo, Spain, dialogue)	Haven't you noticed how thin she's become?
Lo que resulta increíble es lo modernos y antiguos que son al mismo tiempo (A. Bryce Echenique, Peru)	What's incredible is how modern and ancient they are at the same time
La idea de que voy a casarme no llega a ser todo lo grata que me resultaba viéndola a distancia (J. J. Arreola, Mexico, dialogue)	The idea that I'm going to get married isn't turning out to be as agreeable as it was to me when I saw it at a distance
Tal vez no haya salido todo lo buena que yo creía (M. Puig, Argentina, dialogue)	Perhaps she hasn't turned out to be as good as I thought

(b) with adverbs and adverbial phrases:

Yo llegué confiando en lo bien que lo iba a pasar	I arrived sure of what a good time I was going to have
Haga que hablen de usted por lo bien que habla inglés (Newspaper advertisement, Spain)	Get them talking about you because you speak English so well
Si vieras lo mal que patina	If you could (only) see how badly she skates
Hay que ver lo tarde que es	I can't believe how late it is (lit. 'you have to see how late it is')

Notes

(i) A common colloquial construction is *con lo* + adjective. Translation varies with context: *pobre Ana, con lo enferma que está* 'Poor Anna, and her being so ill', *tú, con lo inteligente que eres, a ver si lo puedes abrir* 'you're so intelligent, let's see if you can open it', *. . . con lo metementodo que es* '. . . since (s)he's such a nosy-parker.'

(ii) *De* + *lo* + comparative adjective is also found in familiar speech as an intensifying phrase: *viene de lo más arregladita* 'she's coming all dressed up', *es de lo más religioso* 'he's incredibly religious', *tomaban su cerveza de lo más tranquilos* (M. Vargas Llosa, Peru, dialogue) 'they were drinking their beer really quietly', *hice un pudín de pan. Mi marido me dijo que estaba de lo más bueno* (A. Arrufat, Cuba, dialogue) 'I made a bread pudding. My husband said it was absolutely delicious.'

(iii) In expressions of cause *por* or *de* can be used before *lo* + adjective: *no pudo pasar por lo gorda que estaba/no pudo pasar de (lo) gorda que estaba* 'she couldn't get through since she was so fat'.

7.3 *Ello*

This is a neuter third-person pronoun. It is invariable in form and can be used to translate 'it' when this pronoun does not refer to any specific noun. Compare *en cuanto al régimen militar, prefiero no hablar de él* 'as for the military regime, I prefer not to talk about it' (*régimen* is masculine singular) and *todo fue tremendamente violento, y prefiero no hablar de* **ello** 'it was all tremendously embarrassing, and I prefer not to talk about it' (neuter).

Ello can be used as a subject pronoun or it can be combined with a preposition, but it cannot be used as a direct object pronoun: *lo* is its direct object form. When it is the subject of a verb (cf. the example from Borges), it normally requires translation by 'this'. This use as a subject is rather literary: *esto* comes more readily in speech:

No te preocupes por ello, que no se me olvida (see 33.4.4b for this use of *que*)	Don't worry about it – I haven't forgotten it
Por ello ya no se fía de nadie	Because of that she doesn't trust anybody any more
Las cosas que no importan no se entienden porque no se pone uno a ello (C. Martín Gaite, Spain)	Things that don't matter aren't understood because we don't apply our minds to it (i.e. to understanding them)
Habitó un siglo en la Ciudad de los Inmortales. Cuando la derribaron, aconsejó la fundación de otra. Ello no debe sorprendernos . . . (J. L. Borges, Argentina)	He dwelt for a century in the City of the Immortals. When they demolished it, he recommended the foundation of another. This (fact) should not surprise us . . .

7.4 *Lo* as a neuter pronoun

7.4.1 General uses

Lo is the direct object pronoun corresponding to *ello* (for *lo* meaning 'him' or 'it' referring to masculine nouns, see Chapter 12). *Lo* as a neuter pronoun does not refer to any specific noun, but to an idea, clause or sentence, to some unspecified thing that has no gender, or to something not mentioned before:

¿Lo hacemos o no?	Shall we do it or not?
¿No sabíais que estaba prohibido? No, no lo sabíamos	Didn't you know it was forbidden? No, we didn't (know it)
Soy incapaz de hacer eso porque mi orgullo de trabajadora femenina me lo impide (C. Martín Gaite, Spain)	I'm incapable of doing that because my pride as a woman worker prevents me
El ministro lo tiene difícil (*Cambio16*, Spain)	The minister is in a difficult situation
Se lo están poniendo mal	They're making things difficult for him/her

Notes

(i) *Lo* is used to echo or resume the predicate of *ser*, *estar* and *parecer*, and the object of *haber* 'there is/are'. In other words, Spanish does not like to leave these verbs isolated, as English does in a sentence like 'I can stand being tired, but I'd rather not **be**' *puedo aguantar el estar cansado, pero preferiría no estarlo.* Compare also *¿habrá en la tierra algo sagrado y algo que no* **lo** *sea?* (J. L. Borges, Argentina) 'is there anything sacred on earth, and anything that isn't?', *¿tolera estar solo, o tolera la necesidad que tenga su cónyuge de estarlo?* (quiz on marriage in *ABC*, Spain) 'can you stand being alone, or can you stand your partner's need to be?', *a mí me gustan los ricos que lo son hasta sus últimas consecuencias* (M. Vázquez Montalbán, Spain) 'I like rich people who take it (i.e. being rich) to its ultimate consequences', *ya nadie la llamaba Clarita, como* **lo** *habían hecho siempre sus difuntos padres y marido* (M. Puig, Argentina, dialogue) 'by now nobody called her Clarita, as her late parents and husband had done'.

Resumptive *lo* is often omitted in Latin-American speech and sometimes in Latin-American writing. See 30.2.2 for more details about the resumptive pronoun with *haber* 'there is/are'.

(ii) *Lo* is sometimes used redundantly before *todo* to make the latter more specific in meaning. Compare *Miguel lo sabe todo* 'Miguel knows it all/all about it' and *Miguel sabe todo* 'Miguel knows everything'.
(iii) For Latin-American *?se los dije* 'I said it to them' see 11.13.2.
(iv) *La* is used in a few colloquial set phrases where we would expect *lo*. This seems to be more frequent in Latin America than in Spain: *la vamos a pasar muy rico* (S. Galindo, Mexico, dialogue: Spain *lo vamos a pasar*) 'we're going to have a great time', *si los matan la pagarán también ustedes, la pagarán sus familias* (G. García Márquez, Colombia, dialogue. Spain *lo pagarán*), 'if they kill them you'll pay for it too, your families will pay', *te la estás jugando* 'you're taking a big risk', *se la está pegando con su primo* '(s)he's cheating on him with her/his/your cousin', *te la vas a ganar* 'you're asking for trouble'.

7.4.2 *Vérselas, arreglárselas, habérselas, etc.*

The feminine plural *las* is used in a few idiomatic, colloquial set phrases where we would expect *lo*. Some of these phrases have unexpected meanings. The most common are:

agenciárselas to wangle something/to acquire by 'fiddling'
apañárselas* to manage/to cope
arreglárselas to find a way to do something
cantárselas to tell someone a few home truths
dárselas de to fancy oneself as
echárselas de to fancy oneself as
entendérselas con to have it out with someone

habérselas con to be faced with/to have it out with
ingeniárselas para to fix things so that . . .
prometérselas muy felices* to have high hopes
traérselas* to be difficult/treacherous
vérselas y deseárselas* to be difficult
vérselas con to have it out with/to have a showdown with

All are in use on both continents except those marked with an asterisk, which seem to be confined to Spain:

Si haces eso te las vas a tener que haber conmigo or *te las vas a tener que ver conmigo*
If you do that you're going to have to have it out/face up to me

Él se las echa/se las da de ligón (colloquial, Spain)
He fancies himself as a great womanizer/as a great hit with the ladies

Eso me pasó por dármelas de genio (García Márquez, Colombia, dialogue)
That happened to me because I figured I was a genius

—Arréglatelas como puedas —me dijo, llorando (A. Bryce Echenique, Peru, dialogue)
'You manage as best you can', she said, weeping (i.e. 'I don't care what you do')

Tenía que ingeniárselas para mantener ocupados a sus guardianes (G. García Márquez, Colombia)
She had to fix things in order to keep her guards occupied

Por eso te digo que ella también se las trae (C. Rico-Godoy, Spain)
That's why I'm telling you that she's also not to be trusted

La Policía se las ve y se las desea para controlarlos (*Cambio16*, Spain)
The police have a hard time controlling them

7.5 Neuter demonstrative pronouns

These take the invariable forms *esto*, *eso* and *aquello*. Since they cannot be confused with demonstrative adjectives they **never** have a written accent – a fact that learners and native speakers constantly forget. They refer to no noun in particular (cf. Fr. *ceci, cela*).

The difference between *esto* 'this', *eso* 'that' and *aquello* 'that' (distant) reflects the difference between *este, ese* and *aquel*, discussed at 6.4:

¿Quién ha hecho esto?	Who did this?
—*Quisiera llamar a cobro revertido. —De eso nada*	'I'd like to make a transfer charge call.' 'No way/Out of the question'
Había comprendido cómo todo aquello jamás tuvo nada que ver con el humor ni con el buen humor (A. Bryce Echenique, Peru)	I had understood how all that never had anything to do with humour or good temper
¿Qué hay de aquello/eso de los billetes falsos?	What's happening about that business of the forged notes?
¿Cómo podía yo pensar que aquello que parecía tan mentira era verdadero? (J. Cortázar, Argentina, dialogue)	How could I think that that thing which seemed such a lie was true?

Notes

(i) *Aquello de (que)* or *eso de (que)* often correspond to 'the saying that': *Spengler dijo aquello de que "la civilización en última instancia siempre es salvada por un puñado de soldados"* (*Cambio 16*, Spain) 'Spengler made that remark that "in the final instance civilization is always saved by a handful of soldiers"', *pensé que lo más parecido que existe a eso de ir por lana y volver trasquilado era . . .* (A. Bryce Echenique, Peru) 'I thought that the nearest thing to that saying "to go for wool and come back fleeced" was . . .' (the proverb describes an unexpected outcome).

(ii) The choice between a neuter or non-neuter demonstrative may cause problems: compare **esto** *es un soneto* 'this is a sonnet' and **éste/este**[3] *es un soneto – los demás sólo/solo tienen trece versos* 'this (*poema*) is a sonnet – the rest have only thirteen lines'. If the speaker has in mind a specific noun, the masculine or feminine pronoun must be used as appropriate unless the speaker is referring to a type of thing. For example, pointing to a coat in a shop window one could say **eso** *es lo que quiero* 'that's the (type of) thing I want' or **ése/ese** *es el que quiero* 'that's the **one** I want'. Sometimes it appears that the neuter and gendered forms are interchangeable. Examples: *ésa/esa es la verdad/eso es (la) verdad* 'that's the truth', *no tengo ni talento, ni fuerza. . . . Ésa/Esa es la verdad* (E. Sábato, Argentina, dialogue; *eso* also possible because it refers to the whole of the statement) 'I have neither talent nor strength. That's the truth', *esto es una operación militar* (G. García Márquez, Colombia, dialogue; *ésta/esta es . . .* also possible) 'this is a military operation', *ésa/esa es otra de las invenciones de ustedes* (M. Vargas Llosa, Peru, dialogue) 'that's another of your inventions', *¿qué es esto?* 'what's this?', *¿quién es éste/este?* 'who's this (man or boy)?', *éste/este es el problema* 'this is **the** problem', *esto es un problema* 'this is **a** problem'.

When the subject of the verb is a noun, the pronoun agrees with it: *la verdad es ésta/esta* 'the truth is this', *los problemas son éstos/estos* 'the problems are these.'

---

[3] For the use of the accent here and in the following examples – preferred by most writers and editors but optional according to the Academy – see 6.3.

8

Possessive adjectives and pronouns

8.1 General

Spanish possessives have two forms. The short forms, *mi, tu, su*, etc., are the normal, unstressed possessive adjectives and appear in front of a noun or noun phrase. These correspond to the English 'my', 'your', 'his', 'her': *mi libro* 'my book', *su casa* 'her/his/your house', *nuestra opinión*, etc. The full forms, *mío, tuyo, suyo*, etc., roughly correspond to the English 'mine', 'yours', 'hers', etc., and can only follow a noun or stand alone: *un amigo mío* 'a friend of mine', *de los dos prefiero el tuyo* 'of the two I prefer yours', etc.

Number and gender agreement is determined by the number and gender of the noun possessed, not of the possessor. All forms agree in number, but only those whose masculine singular ends in *-o* agree in gender. Points to watch are:

(a) Replacement of the possessive adjectives by the definite article when the identity of the possessor is obvious: *me he roto el brazo* 'I've broken my arm', *dame la mano* 'give me your hand' (see 8.3.4). This occurs much more frequently than in French and is sometimes confusing for English-speaking students;
(b) the difference between *es mío* and *es el mío* (see 8.4.2);
(c) the fact that *su/sus* can have six different English translations (see 8.5a).

8.2 Forms of the possessives

8.2.1 Short forms of possessives

Personal pronoun		Singular	Plural	
yo		*mi*	*mis*	my
tú (and Argentine *vos*)		*tu*	*tus*	your (familiar)
él/ella		*su*	*sus*	his/her
usted		*su*	*sus*	your (polite)
ellos/ellas		*su*	*sus*	their
ustedes		*su*	*sus*	your (polite)
Only *nuestro* and *vuestro* are marked for gender:				
nosotros/nosotras	**masc.**	*nuestro*	*nuestros*	our
	fem.	*nuestra*	*nuestras*	
vosotros/vosotras and	**masc.**	*vuestro*	*vuestros*	your (familiar)
archaic *vos*	**fem.**	*vuestra*	*vuestras*	

Vuestro is not used in Latin America and is replaced by *su/sus*. See 8.6 for discussion.

8.2.2 Long forms of possessives

All are marked for number and gender (*suyo/suyos/suya/suyas* replaces *vuestro* in Lat. Am.):

Personal pronoun	Masculine singular/ plural	Feminine singular/ plural	
yo	mío/míos	mía/mías	mine
tú/vos	tuyo/tuyos	tuya/tuyas	yours
él/ella	suyo/suyos	suya/suyas	his/hers
usted	suyo/suyos	suya/suyas	yours
nosotros / nosotras	nuestro/nuestros	nuestra/nuestras	ours
vosotros / vosotras	vuestro/vuestros	vuestra/vuestras	yours
ellos/ellas	suyo/suyos	suya/suyas	theirs
ustedes	suyo/suyos	suya/suyas	yours

8.3 Use of the short form of possessives

8.3.1 Basic uses

Possessive agrees in number with the possession; *nuestro* and *vuestro* agree in gender as well:

mi padre/mis padres	my father/my parents
mi madre/mis flores	my mother/my flowers
¿Dónde está tu coche?	Where's your car?
¿Dónde están tus zapatos?	Where are your shoes?
Me fío de su amigo	I trust his/her/your friend
Me fío de sus amigos	I trust his/her/your friends
nuestro dinero/nuestra dignidad	our money/our dignity
vuestra casa/vuestras casas	your house/your houses
Si ustedes quieren dejar sus cosas aquí . . .	If you want to leave your/his/her/ their things here . . .
Si ellos no quieren dejarnos su cortacésped . . .	If *they* don't want to lend us their lawnmower . . .

For ways of removing the ambiguities of *su/sus* see 8.5a.

8.3.2 Possessives with more than one noun

If a possessive refers to more than one noun, Spanish differs from English in deleting possessives only if the following nouns refer to the same or aspects of the same thing. One says *mi padre y mi madre* 'my father and mother' (different people) but *mi amigo y colega* 'my friend and colleague' (same person), *su paciencia y valor* 'his patience and courage' (aspects of a single virtue), *nuestros cuentos y (nuestras) novelas* 'our short stories and novels' (aspects of a single *oeuvre*), but *mi chaqueta y mi corbata* 'my jacket and tie'.

8.3.3 Possessive in military usage

In military circles, possessives are used to address officers: *sí, mi general* 'yes, General', *no, mi coronel* 'no, Colonel'.

8.3.4 Definite article instead of possessives[1]

Spanish uses possessive adjectives much more sparingly than English and French and very frequently replaces them with the definite article. A sentence like *sacó su pañuelo de su bolsillo* '(s)he took his handkerchief out of his/her pocket', although grammatically correct, sounds unnatural: *sacó el pañuelo del bolsillo* (if the pocket is someone else's) or *se sacó el pañuelo del bolsillo* (from his/her own pocket) are much more idiomatic. The Academy's *Esbozo* . . . , 3.10.9a, remarks that sentences like *pase sus vacaciones en la playa de X*, 'spend your holidays/vacation on the beach at X' for *pase las vacaciones* . . . have a foreign ring to them. Possessive adjectives are replaced by the definite article:

(a) If context makes it clear that the thing possessed belongs to the speaker or to the person who is the focus of the sentence, use of the definite article being normal with parts of the body, clothing and other intimate possessions, especially articles of which one normally has only one, e.g. wristwatch, purse, wallet/notebook, pen, pencil, glasses, etc. This feature of Spanish may confuse English speakers. 'Have you got the passport?' normally implies that we do not know to whom the passport belongs, otherwise we say 'his', 'her', 'your' as appropriate. *¿Tienes el pasaporte?* is taken to mean 'have you got **your** passport?' unless context shows that some other passport is involved. Spanish thus often relies on context to make possession clear. In the following sentence only the fact that women usually carry purses indicates that we should translate *el monedero* as 'my purse' (the speaker is a woman): *metí en una bolsa de playa el bronceador, las toallas, la radio portátil, el libro que estoy leyendo, dos camisetas, **el** monedero* . . . (Carmen Rico-Godoy, Spain) 'I put the suntan lotion, the towels, the portable radio, the book I'm reading, two T-shirts, **my** purse . . . in a beach-bag.' Further examples:

Cierre la boca	Shut your mouth
Llegó con los zapatos cubiertos de lodo	He arrived with his shoes covered in mud
Tengo los ojos azules	My eyes are blue/I've got blue eyes
Llegaba a pensar que Alicia había perdido la razón (S. Puértolas, Spain)	I was coming to think that Alicia had lost her reason
Junté las manos y bajé la cabeza (C. Fuentes, Mexico, dialogue)	I joined my hands and lowered my head
Introduje la mano izquierda en el bolsillo derecho del pantalón (A. Bryce Echenique, Peru)	I inserted my left hand in the right pocket of my trousers (*sic!*)

(b) When the thing possessed belongs to the person indicated by an indirect object pronoun. Compare *he corregido tu redacción* 'I've marked/graded your essay/paper' and *te he corregido la redacción*, same meaning, or also 'I've marked/graded your essay/paper for you'.

Ricardo se aflojó la corbata	Richard loosened his (own) tie
Bébete el café	Drink your coffee
Me quité los calcetines (*las medias = los calcetines* in some parts of Latin America)	I took off my socks
Arréglate el pelo	Tidy your hair

---

[1] Some of the examples and arguments in this section are inspired by S. Repiso Repiso (1989), 37–44.

María se muerde las uñas	Maria bites her nails
Le quiero ver los anteojos nuevos (M. Puig, Argentina, dialogue. Spain *las gafas* for *los anteojos*)	I want to see her new glasses
Se sacó de la manga una camándula de oro (G. García Márquez, Colombia. In Spain *camándula = rosario*)	She took a gold rosary from her sleeve

However, when the thing possessed is emphasized or particularized by context, by an adjective or by other words, or whenever ambiguity must be avoided, the possessive adjective usually reappears:

*Usted póngase **su** camisa, no **la mía***	You put on your shirt, not mine
*Vi **sus** ojos grandes, fatigados, sonrientes y como lacrimosos* (F. Umbral, Spain)	I saw her eyes, big, tired, smiling and seemingly tearful
Seguía con su saco y su corbatita de lazo (M. Vargas Llosa, Peru; Spain *saco = chaqueta* and *pajarita* = 'bow tie')	He was still wearing his jacket and his bow tie
*Acerqué **mi** cabeza a la suya* (C. Fuentes, Mexico, dialogue; contrast)	I moved my head close to his
*X deja **sus** manos suaves y perfumadas* (or *le deja las manos . . .*)	X leaves your hands soft and perfumed
*Toco **tus** labios . . .* (popular song)	I touch your lips . . .

Notes

(i) Use of the definite article downplays the thing possessed. *Te toco los labios* can sound accidental or matter-of-fact. A mother says *dame la mano, que vamos a cruzar la calle* 'hold my hand, we're going to cross the road', but an old-fashioned lover might say *dame tu mano y te haré feliz* 'give me your hand (i.e. 'in marriage') and I will make you happy'.

For this reason, one does not, in polite speech, use the definite article when the thing possessed is a human being: *¡cuánto echo de menos a **mis** hijas!* 'I miss my daughters so much!', *siempre voy de vacaciones con **mi** mujer/mi novia* (?*con la mujer/la novia* is either humorous or popular, cf. popular British English 'with the wife') 'I always go on holiday/vacation with my wife/girlfriend', *ha despedido a **su** secretaria* 'he's fired his secretary'.

(ii) As was mentioned above, the possessive adjective must be used when the object possessed is the subject of a verb, unless an indirect object pronoun identifies the possessor: *su cabeza se destacaba contra el cielo* 'his head stood out against the sky', ***sus** ojos parecían cansados* 'her eyes seemed tired', but *se le cae **el** pelo* 'his hair's falling out', *le dolían **las** piernas* 'her legs hurt'.

(iii) In spoken Latin-American Spanish possessive adjectives are often used in combination with indirect object pronouns even when it is obvious who is the possessor: *les pintamos su casa* (street sign, Oaxaca, Mexico) 'we'll paint your house for you', *me duele mi cabeza* (popular colloquial Mexican) 'my head aches', standard Spanish *me duele la cabeza*.

8.4 Long or pronominal forms of the possessives

8.4.1 Use of the long or pronominal forms of the possessive

(a) To translate English '. . . of mine/yours/his/ours', etc.:

un amigo mío	a friend of mine
un conocido tuyo	an acquaintance of yours
un pariente vuestro	a relation of yours(s)
un poema muy malo mío (interview in *Granma*, Cuba; Spain *un poema mío muy malo*)	a very bad poem of mine
Antonio ha vuelto a hacer una de las suyas	Antonio's up to his usual tricks again (lit. 'a trick of his')

una actitud muy suya	a very typical attitude of his/hers/yours/ theirs
algo mío/nada nuestro	something of mine/nothing of ours

(b) As a literary, rather stilted variation on the usual possessive:

en mi novela/en la novela mía	in my novel/in this novel of mine
nuestro pan/el pan nuestro de cada día	our daily bread

(c) In Spain, in formulas of address:

Bueno, hijo mío/hija mía, me voy   Well, dear, I'm off
(lit. 'my son'/'my daughter', a term of endearment used between friends, especially by women)
Te aconsejo que no, amigo mío   I advise you not to, my friend

Lat.-Am. Spanish characteristically says *mi hijo, mi hija, mi amigo,* etc.:

No, mi amiga. Me quedaré en casa. Iré otro día (A. Arrafut, Cuba, dialogue)	No my friend. I'll stay at home. I'll go another day

This gives rise to terms of endearment like *mijita* (= *mi hijita*), *mi amor,* etc. Several expressions of endearment in Spain optionally use the normal order, e.g. *mi vida/vida mía, mi cielo/cielo mío, mi cielín,* etc., 'darling'/(US 'honey'), etc.

(d) To translate the pronouns 'mine', 'yours' (see the following section for the use of the definite article in this construction):

—¿De quién es este bloc?—Mío—	'Whose notepad is this?' 'Mine'
Este garabato es tuyo	This scrawl is yours
Éste/Este es el vuestro, ¿verdad?	This one is yours, isn't it?

Note

The long forms are used in a number of set phrases: *de nuestra parte/de parte nuestra* 'for our part', *a pesar mío/suyo* 'despite me/despite him/her/you', *a costa mía* 'at my cost', *en torno suyo* 'around him/her/them/you', *a propuesta suya* 'at his suggestion', *muy señor mío* (Southern Cone *de mi con-sideración*) 'Dear Sir' (in letters).

8.4.2 Definite article with the long forms

The definite article is obligatory in the following cases:

(a) After prepositions. Compare —*¿De quién es el coche?* —*Mío* 'Whose car is it?' 'Mine' and —*¿En qué coche vamos?* —*En el mío* 'Which car are we going in?' 'In mine.' Further examples:

No hablo del tuyo sino del nuestro	I'm not talking about yours but ours
A tu primo sí lo/le conozco, pero no al suyo	I know your cousin, but not his/hers

(b) When the pronoun is the subject or object of a verb (even though the verb may be deleted):

Toma el mío	Take mine
Tu padre te deja salir, el mío no	Your father lets you go out, mine doesn't
Qué vida tan triste la suya	What a sad life his/hers/yours/theirs is
Los dos vídeos son buenos, pero el nuestro es mejor	The two videos are good but ours is better

(c) After *ser* 'to be', omission of the article stresses actual possession. Thus one would say *esta casa es mía* 'this house is mine' (it is my property or I live in it), but in an office where there are several telephones one would say *ese teléfono que* *suena es **el** tuyo* 'that phone that's ringing is yours' (i.e. the one you use, not your property). Compare:

Este libro es mío	This book belongs to me
la casa de Jeremiah Saint-Amour, que desde ahora era suya (G. García Márquez, Colombia)	Jeremiah Saint-Amour's house, which from now on was hers
Pero estas cualidades eran mucho más suyas que mías (A. Bryce Echenique, Peru)	But these qualities were much more hers than mine

and

*¿Ves estas tres camas? . . . Ésta/Esta es **la** mía, ésa/esa es la tuya y aquélla/aquella es la de Rafael* (implies use, not possession)	Do you see these three beds? This is mine, that's yours and that one's Rafael's

8.4.3 The neuter article with *lo mío, lo suyo*, etc.

The neuter form of the possessive has various meanings (discussed in detail at 7.2.1):

Mi marido sabe lo nuestro	My husband knows about us
Ahora estás en lo tuyo	Now you're in your element
Lo vuestro es alucinante	What happened to you is mind-boggling

8.5 Replacement of possessive by *de* + pronoun

In some cases a possessive can optionally be replaced by *de* + a pronoun. This happens:

(a) When it is necessary to clarify the meaning of *su/suyo*, which can have six translations: 'his', 'her', 'its', 'your' (*usted*), 'their', 'your' (*ustedes*). Context nearly always makes the meaning clear, but ownership can be stressed or ambiguities removed by using *de él/ella, de usted, de ellos/ellas, de ustedes*: *los paraguas de ustedes* 'your (plural) umbrellas', *la camisa de él* 'his shirt'.

In Spain, *su* is assumed out of context to be third-person, so that *de usted/ustedes* may be needed to show that the meaning is 'your'. (For Latin-American usage, see 8.6.) The possibility of ambiguity is illustrated by the question 'is this handkerchief yours or hers?', which one would probably say *¿este pañuelo es de usted o de ella?* whereas *¿este pañuelo es suyo?* 'is this handkerchief yours?' is clear if no one else is present. Examples:

Conozco a la madre de él	I know **his** mother
¿Este sombrero es de usted?	Is this hat yours?

(b) When *de* means 'from' and not 'of', as in

Hace tiempo que no tengo noticias vuestras/de vosotros	It's been some time since I've had news of you

8.6 Possessives: Latin-American usage

Latin-American usage differs from European in a number of ways:

(a) Possessives in areas of *voseo*:

Tu/tuyo are the forms corresponding to *vos* in *voseo* areas of Latin America: cf. *vos tenés tu birome* (Argentina, *la birome* is feminine) 'you've got your ballpoint pen' Spain *tú tienes tu bolígrafo*.[2]

(b) Possessives corresponding to *usted/ustedes* and to third-person pronouns: *vosotros* is not used in everyday Latin-American Spanish, except in liturgical and ceremonial language, and occasionally in business letters (see 11.3.3): it is everywhere replaced by *ustedes*. *Su/sus* is therefore the only second-person plural possessive form in all styles.

(c) In Latin America *su/suyo* is assumed, out of context, to mean *de usted/de ustedes* 'of you'. Third-person possession may be represented in everyday speech by *de él* his/its (masc.), *de ella* her/its (fem.), *de ellos* their (masc.), *de ellas* their (fem.). Examples:

¿Quieres que vayamos al cuarto de él a ver si está? (Costa Rican dialogue, quoted Kany, 69; Spain *a su cuarto*)	Do you want to go to his room to see if he's there?
En la oficina de ella no hay la mitad de trabajo que en la mía (M. Puig, Argentina, dialogue. Spain *en su oficina*)	There isn't half the work in her office that there is in mine

(d) *De nosotros* for *nuestro* is also common in Latin-American speech: *la casa de nosotros está en la esquina* (Colombian informant, standard Spanish *nuestra casa*) 'our house is on the corner', *—¿A quién se lo entregó? —Al jefe de nosotros* (*Vindicación de Cuba*, Cuba, dialogue) '"Whom did you hand it over to?" "To our boss"', standard Spanish *a nuestro jefe*.

8.7 Possessives after prepositions and adverbs

A common construction in colloquial Latin-American Spanish, also found in popular speech in Spain, is the use of possessive pronoun forms after prepositions followed by *de*, and after some adverbs: *?detrás mío* = *detrás de mí* 'behind me', and even, in substandard speech, *?entró antes mío* (from Carnicer 1969) 'he went in before me', for *entró antes que yo*. This usage is so deep-rooted in Argentina that it is found in the best writers, but it is considered colloquial in other Latin-American countries and incorrect in Spain and Mexico:

Adentro mío yo soy igual que todos los reaccionarios (M. Puig, Argentina, dialogue; Spain *dentro de mí* or *por dentro*)	Inside (me) I'm the same as all the reactionaries
Quiero estar cerca tuyo (ibid., Spain *cerca de ti*)	I want to be near you
No lo consiguió por lo intimidado que estaba en mi delante (M. Vargas Llosa, Peru, dialogue; Spain *delante de mí*)	He was so intimidated in my presence that he didn't manage it
La oficina de Atesa está detrás nuestro (reply at the information desk, Barcelona airport = *detrás de nosotros*)	The Atesa (car-hire) office is behind us

---

[2] 'Ballpoint pen' has numerous possible translations elsewhere in Latin America: *el lápiz (de pasta)* (Chile), *el lápiz* (Cuba), *el esfero(gráfico)* (Colombia), *la pluma (atómica)* (Mexico).

Pero un segundo autobús que iba por		But a second bus travelling behind
detrás suyo lo embistió con gran violencia		collided violently with it
(*El País*, Spain: it should be *detrás de él*)		

and also (the bracketed forms are used in standard Spanish):

?*alrededor mío*	(*a mi alrededor*/*alrededor de mí*)	around me
?*encima mía*	(*encima de mí*)	above/over me
?*enfrente suyo*	(*enfrente de él/ella/usted/ustedes/ellos/ ellas*)	opposite him/her/you/them
?*aparte suyo*	(*aparte de él/ella*, etc.)	apart from him/her, etc.
?*fuera suyo*	(*fuera de él/ella*, etc.)	apart from him/her, etc.

Foreign students should avoid this construction. However, *en torno nuestro* (literary) 'around us' is considered correct.

Note

Both *contra mí/ti* and *en contra mía/tuya*, 'against me/you', etc., are correct, but there is a tendency to make the possessive precede in Latin America, and this seems to be spreading to Spain: *está en mi contra* (Peanuts, Argentina) '(s)he/it is against me', *el hecho de que el teléfono se hubiera puesto en mi contra* . . . (S. Puértolas, Spain) 'the fact that the phone had turned against me . . .'.

9

Miscellaneous words

Many of the words discussed in this chapter are of problematic classification and have multiple uses as adjectives, pronouns or adverbs. For easy reference they are, where possible, discussed under a single heading.

9.1 *Ajeno*: adjective, marked for number and gender

A rather literary word meaning 'someone else's': *el dolor ajeno* (*el dolor de otros*) 'other people's sorrow', *en casa ajena* (*en casa de otro*) 'in another person's house':

> *Se preocupa demasiado por lo ajeno*   (S)he concerns her(him)self too much with other people's business

It is not used in this meaning after *ser: esta agenda es de otro* 'this is someone else's diary'.

Note

Ajeno often translates 'a stranger to', 'remote from': *éstos/estos son problemas ajenos a mi responsabilidad* 'these are problems outside my responsibility', ... *una mujer adulta pero atractiva que tomaba el sol tumbada y ajena, aparentemente, a todo* (C. Rico-Godoy, Spain) '. . . an adult but attractive woman who was lying there sunbathing and apparently oblivious to everything'.

9.2 *Algo*: invariable pronoun/adverb

The usual equivalent of 'something' or, in questions or after *poco* and a few other words discussed at 23.4, 'anything' (French *quelque chose*):

> *Aquí hay algo que no me suena*   There's something here that doesn't sound right to me
>
> *Detrás se veía algo grande, negro*   Behind one could see something big, black
> *¿Ves algo?*   Can you see anything?
> *Serán pocos los que hayan traído algo*   There probably won't be many who have brought anything
>
> *Aquella frase era el preámbulo de algo muy grave* (G. García Márquez, Colombia)   That phrase was the prelude to something very serious

Adverbially it means 'rather', 'somewhat', though *un poco, un tanto* or *más bien* are equally common in speech:

> *Estamos algo inquietos*   We're rather worried
> *. . . achinada y de hermosas piernas, aunque algo cargada de caderas* (L. Otero, Cuba)   (she had an) oriental face and lovely legs, although she was rather heavy in the hips

Notes

(i) *Algo así, algo así como* are translations of 'something like . . .': *pesa algo así como siete kilos* 'it weighs around 7 kilos', *se llama Nicanora, o algo así* 'she's called Nicanora, or something like that'.
(ii) In negative sentences *nada* translates 'anything': *no sabe nada* 'he doesn't know anything', *yo no sé dónde está nada en esta casa* 'I don't know where anything is in this house'.
(iii) The English sentence-opener 'do you know something . . .?' is *¿sabes una cosa? ¿Sabes algo?* means 'do you know anything?'

9.3 *Alguien*: invariable pronoun

'Someone'/'somebody'. It also translates 'anyone'/'anybody' in questions and certain other types of sentence. It is not marked for gender:

¿Conoces a alguien que pueda darme un presupuesto para reparar el coche?	Do you know anyone who could give me an estimate for mending my car?
Le pidió a Andrés que se quedara en casa por si alguien llamara (G. García Márquez, Colombia)	He asked Andrés to stay at home in case someone phoned

Notes

(i) **Alguien de los estudiantes, *alguien de ellos* is rejected by grammarians: *alguno de los estudiantes, alguno de (entre) ellos* are preferred, although *alguien de entre ustedes* is accepted by some authorities: *si alguien de entre ustedes/alguno de ustedes lo sabe, que lo diga* 'if someone among you/any of you knows, say so'. Occasionally *alguien de* is necessary since, unlike *alguno*, it does not indicate gender: *yo creo que alude a alguien de esta casa* 'I think he's alluding to someone in this house'.
(ii) María Moliner notes that *?darle una cosa a alguien que él no desea* offends the ear since *alguien* is too vague for a specifically masculine pronoun: *darle una cosa a alguien que no lo desea* 'to give something to someone who doesn't want it'.
(iii) 'Give it to someone else' is *dáselo a algún otro/alguna otra/alguna otra persona*. **Alguien otro* is not Spanish.
(iv) *Uno* is sometimes colloquially used for 'someone' when gender is an important part of the message (for other uses of *uno* as a pronoun see 28.7.1): *se ha peleado con uno en la calle* 'he's had a fight with some man in the street', *se casó con una de Valencia* 'he married some girl from Valencia'.

9.4 *Algún, alguno, algunos; alguna, algunas*: adjective/pronoun marked for number and gender

9.4.1 General uses of *alguno*

The appropriate form of *alguno* may be used either as an adjective or (except for the short form *algún*) as a pronoun.

(a) As an adjective:
The usual translation is 'some', French *quelque(s)*. It is shortened to *algún* before a singular masculine noun or noun phrase: *algún día* 'some day', *algún remoto rincón de Extremadura* 'some remote corner of Extremadura', but *alguna región* 'some region'.

Alguna is pronounced 'algún' immediately before feminine nouns beginning with a stressed *a-* or *ha-*, i.e. *algún alma perdida* 'some lost soul', *algún arma defensiva* 'some defensive weapon'; but Seco (1998), 36, says that this is usually avoided in careful language and *alguna* should be used in writing. When it is followed by *que* and a masculine noun phrase, either the short or long form may be used, i.e. *algún que otro libro* or *alguno que otro libro* 'some book or other', the short form being commoner (Seco, ibid.). Only *alguna que otra* is allowed with feminine nouns.

In the singular, *alguno* and *uno* are often interchangeable (provided *uno* is not being used as a number), but *alguno* often means 'one or maybe more' and is roughly equivalent to 'one or another', 'some or other'. (For the difference between *unos* and *algunos*, see 9.4.2):

En algún momento de la historia de nuestra lengua . . .	At one time or another in the history of our language . . .
Alguna vez la echaba de menos (S. Puértolas, Spain; *algunas veces* is more common in everyday speech)	At times he used to miss her
Deben cuidar bien esos platos. Alguna vez, en el futuro, podrían donarlos a un museo (L. Otero, Cuba, dialogue)	You should look after those plates well. One day (lit. 'some time') in the future you could donate them to a museum
—¿Tiene usted algún manual de programación?—Sí, alguno hay	'Do you have any programming manuals?' 'Yes, there may be one or two'

Note

In formal style *alguno* may follow a noun, in which case it is an emphatic equivalent of *ninguno*, 'none', 'no . . . at all': *no cultivaba forma alguna de contacto con el pueblo* (J. Marsé, Spain) 'he cultivated absolutely no kind of contact with the common people', *sin duda alguna ésa tenía alguna falla* (A. Bryce Echenique, Peru; or *esa*) 'there was absolutely no doubt that that one (a ballpoint refill, *la recarga de un bolígrafo*) had some defect', . . . *o mejor una lista de palabras que no tuviera orden alguno* (G. Cabrera Infante, Cuba, dialogue) '. . . or better a list of words with no order at all'.

(b) *Alguno* as a pronoun:

Se había puesto de acuerdo con alguno de sus compañeros	(S)he'd made an agreement with one or other of his/her workmates
Se lo habrá llevado alguna de las dependientas (Lat. Am. *vendedoras*)	One of the salesgirls must have taken it away
—¿Has recibido cartas de tu familia? *—Bueno, alguna, sí*	'Have you had any letters from your family?' 'Well, one or two, yes'

In the plural 'some' or 'a few' are the usual translations:

Con algunos de tercero vas a tener que hacer ejercicios de verbos irregulares	You're going to have to do irregular verb exercises with some of the third year
Algunos ya están deseando marcharse	Some already want to go

Notes

(i) When the singular of *alguno* is combined with a second-person pronoun, the verb agrees optionally with the pronoun or with the third person, although the latter is more usual: *si alguno de vosotros lo sabéis/lo sabe* 'if any of you know(s) it'. In the plural, agreement is always with the pronoun: *algunas de vosotras lo sabéis* 'some of you women know'. This is also true of the first-person plural: *algunas de nosotras generalmente caminamos despacito* (*La Jornada*, Mexico) 'some of us women generally walk slowly'.

(ii) 'Some' (and 'any') has no visible equivalent in Spanish when it precedes a partitive noun, i.e. a noun that denotes only part of what it refers to, as in 'give me some water' *dame agua*, 'you haven't bought any pins' *no has comprado alfileres*.

In some cases *un poco* or *ninguno* may be appropriate translations of 'some'. 'Any' in the sense of 'it doesn't matter which' is *cualquiera* (see 9.8): *¿tiene usted pan integral?* 'have you got any wholemeal bread?', *yo también quiero un poco*, 'I want some (a little) too', *¿chuletas de ternera? No tenemos* 'veal chops? We haven't got any', *no tenemos ninguno* 'we haven't got a single one' (masc.), *no queda apenas ninguna* 'there are hardly any (fem.) left', *comidas a cualquier hora* 'meals at any time'.

(iii) When *alguno* is the object, direct or indirect, and is placed before the verb for purposes of focus, agreement is governed by the number of an accompanying noun or pronoun: *a alguno de vosotros* **os** *quisiera ver yo en un lío como éste/este* 'I'd like to see one of you in a mess like this', *a alguno de ellos* **les** *quiere dar el premio* 'it's one of them that he wants to give the prize to'.

9.4.2 *Unos* and *algunos* contrasted

English speakers often have difficulty in differentiating these two plural words. *Unos* has several other uses discussed at 3.4.

(a) *Algunos . . . otros* and *unos . . . otros*
The two words are interchangeable when accompanied by *otros/otras*:

Algunos/unos vinieron, otros no	Some came, others didn't
. . . las explicaciones teológicas que hacían plausible la venta de unos terrenos y la compra de otros (A. Mastretta, Mexico; or *algunos terrenos*)	. . . the theological explanations that made plausible/acceptable the sale of some plots of land and the purchase of others
Algunos/Unos días estoy de mal humor, otros no	Some days I'm in a bad mood, others I'm not

(b) Only *algunos* is possible in the phrase *algunos de*: *salí a cenar con algunos de los alumnos* 'I went out to dinner with some of the students'. *Algunos* is also used when no identification of individuals is intended or possible: *algunos mexicanos hablan tres idiomas* 'some Mexicans speak three languages'.

(c) *Unos* 'some' and *unos cuantos* 'a few' can both be used when no specific reference to quantity is intended: *tráeme unas (cuantas) patatas* (Lat. Am. and Canary Islands *papas*) 'bring me a few/some/a couple of potatoes', *esta tarde vinieron unos (cuantos) amigos* 'some/a few friends came this afternoon', *he traído unas (cuantas) cerezas* 'I've brought some/a few cherries'. However, sentences like *salí anoche con unos amigos de Barcelona* 'I went out last night with some friends from Barcelona' and *. . . con unos cuantos amigos de Barcelona* '. . . with *a few* friends from Barcelona' may mean slightly different things, as they do in English.

(d) *Algunos/unos cuantos* are interchangeable in the meaning of 'a few': *—¿Tienes monedas de cinco pesetas? —Algunas/Unas cuantas* 'Have you got any 5-peseta coins?' 'A few', *. . . o cuando arriesgábamos algunos dólares en el casino* (A. Bryce Echenique, Peru; or *unos cuantos*) '. . . or when we gambled a few dollars in the casino'.

9.5 *Ambos*: adjective marked for number and gender

'Both', though it is rather literary and *los/las dos* usually replaces it in speech:

en ambos/los dos casos	in both cases
La idea de una pelea de novios le pareció tan ridícula a la edad y en la situación de ambos (G. García Márquez, Colombia)	The idea of a lovers' quarrel seemed so ridiculous to her given the age and situation of both of them
—¿Cuál de los dos es correcto? *—Ambos/Los dos*	'Which of the two is correct?' 'Both'

9.6 *Cada*: invariable

'Each', 'every'. *Cada* always precedes the noun:

Cada loco con su tema	'Each to his own' (lit. 'every madman with his obsession')
un libro por cada tres alumnos	one book for every three students
Me llama a cada momento	He's constantly on the phone to me
cada vez que te miro . . .	every time I look at you . . .
Cada día me preocupa más esto de la taquicardia (A. Bryce Echenique, Peru)	Every day I'm more worried by this tachycardia business (increased heart-rate)

Notes

(i) *Cada vez más/menos* usually translate 'more and more' and 'less and less': *es cada vez más complicado* 'it gets more and more complicated', *era cada vez menos generosa* 'she was less and less generous'.
(ii) In colloquial speech in Spain and Lat. Am. *cada* means 'all sorts of . . .': *dice cada tontería* 'the nonsense he talks . . .', *hay cada ladrón por ahí* 'there are all sorts of thieves there . . .', *¡me hace usted cada pregunta!* (S. Pitol, Mexico, dialogue), 'the things you ask me!'
(iii) 'Each one', 'each person': *que cada uno* (or *cada cual/cada quien*) *haga la lectura que le parezca conveniente* 'let each person read it as it suits him/her'.
(iv) ?*Me baño cada día* or ?*voy cada mañana* for . . . *todos los días*, . . . *todas las mañanas* are spreading, but are rejected by careful speakers. They are, however, correct when followed by a number: *cada tres días*. See 9.17 note (i).

9.7 *Cierto*: adjective, marked for number and gender

'Certain' i.e. 'specific'. Used thus it precedes the noun:

en ciertos casos	in certain cases
cierto alemán	a certain German
en cierta novela suya	in a certain novel of his/hers/yours/theirs
Y esto, claro, flotaba de cierta manera en el ambiente (A. Bryce Echenique, Peru)	And this, of course, was to some extent floating in the atmosphere

Determinado is a more formal synonym: *en determinados trenes existe un servicio de camareros* 'on certain trains waiter service is provided'.

Notes

(i) *Un cierto/una cierta* for 'a certain' are sometimes condemned as Gallicisms or Anglicisms, but are very common in all styles. *Un cierto* is found before partitive nouns – *yo era consciente de (una) cierta tendencia suya a exagerar* 'I was aware of a certain tendency of his to exaggerate' – and as a colloquial alternative to *un tal*: *se casó con un cierto Dionisio de México* 'she married a certain Dionisio from Mexico'.
(ii) Placed after a noun or verb *cierto* means 'fixed', 'accurate', 'true': *hemos tenido noticias ciertas de otro enfrentamiento en la frontera* 'we have received accurate reports of another frontier clash', *¿Está enfermo? ¿Es cierto o no?* (M. Puig, Argentina, dialogue) 'Is he ill/sick? Is it true or not?'

9.8 *Cualquier, cualquiera, cualesquiera*: adjective/pronoun, marked for number

As an adjective 'any'; as a pronoun 'anybody'/'any one' (Fr. *n'importe quel*).

(a) As an adjective:
Before any noun or noun phrase, the *a* of *cualquiera* (but not, usually, of *cualesquiera*) is dropped: *en cualquier momento* 'at any moment', *cualquier mujer* 'any

woman', *yo puedo andar con cualquier complejo* (L. Otero, Cuba, dialogue. *Andar* can mean 'to work properly' in Lat. Am. In Spain the verb is *funcionar*) 'I can function with any complex' (i.e. whatever complexes I may have), *inventan cualquier motivo para justificarse* 'they invent any motive to justify themselves', *en cualesquiera circunstancias* 'in any circumstances'.

However, the plural adjective *cualesquiera* is nowadays normally expressed by the singular since the meaning is almost the same: *cualquier mujer que no simpatice con el feminismo* ... 'any woman who doesn't/any women who don't sympathize with feminism ...'.

Cualquier(a) normally precedes the noun: *duerme a cualquier hora del día* '(s)he sleeps at any hour of the day', *se puede pagar con cualquier moneda* 'one can pay in any currency'. The idea of random choice is strengthened if it follows the noun, cf. English 'any at all'. When used thus of people the effect is often pejorative, as is the English 'any old':

Tráeme un libro cualquiera	Bring me any (old) book
... *no una muerte cualquiera, sino la muerte propia* (M. Benedetti, Uruguay)	... not any old death, but one's own death
Un martes cualquiera ... *él dijo de un modo que apareciera casual* (G. García Márquez, Colombia)	One Thursday (stresses 'no particular Thursday', 'one Thursday out of the blue') he said, in a way designed to seem casual ...
Vamos a pasear por una calle cualquiera	Let's just walk down any street
Su esposa no es una mujer cualquiera	His wife isn't just any woman (i.e. she is something special)

Notes

(i) *Cualquiera* before a feminine noun is an occasional and doubtful colloquial variant, cf. ?*de cualquiera manera* (dialogue in C. Fuentes, Mexico), ?*y más malvados que cualquiera otra tribu* (M. Vargas Llosa, Peru, dialogue) 'and more wicked than any other tribe'. It is, however, attested in Ortega y Gasset, Valera and a few other pre-mid-twentieth-century stylists.

(ii) For the use of *cualquiera* where *cualesquiera* is required see the note to (b).

(iii) *Una cualquiera* is heard colloquially with the meaning 'trollop', 'slut'.

(b) As a pronoun (the final -*a* is always retained).

cualquiera de estos tres modelos	any one of these three models
Cualquiera que sea el resultado	Whatever the result is
Cualquiera diría que eres un millonario	Anybody would think you're a millionaire
... *la necesidad en que se ven* ... *de desahogarse con cualquiera* (A. Bryce Echenique, Peru)	... the need they find themselves in to let off steam in front of anybody
No cualquiera tiene un auto como el de nosotros (S. Vodanovic, Chile, dialogue; Spain *el nuestro*)	Not everyone (lit. 'not anyone') has a car like ours
Cualesquiera que sean los desafíos en el camino de la construcción del comunismo ... *este pueblo y este partido los sabrán vencer* (Fidel Castro, speech)	Whatever the challenges along the path to the building of Communism ... this people and this Party will know how to overcome them

Note

There is a tendency in spontaneous speech and even in informal written styles to use the singular where the plural is required; this applies to both the pronoun and the adjective. Careful speakers usually reject this: *se les garantiza plaza escolar a sus hijos cualquiera que sean sus estudios* (*El País*, Spain; better *cualesquiera*) 'their children are guaranteed school places, whatever their studies' (i.e. whatever they have studied).

9.9 *Demasiado*: adjective marked for number and gender, or invariable adverb

As an adjective 'too many'/'too much'; as an adverb 'too'/'too well'.

(a) Used as an adjective, it must agree in number and gender:

Has comido demasiadas uvas	You've eaten too many grapes
No (le) conviene al trigo que caiga demasiada lluvia	It isn't good for the wheat for too much rain to fall
Llévate un poco de carne – has traído demasiada	Take away a bit of meat – you've brought too much
... pero el calor era demasiado hasta para una danza tan calma (M. Puig, Argentina, dialogue)	... but the heat was too much even for such a placid dance
Has traído demasiados pocos tornillos (*demasiado* is treated as an adjective before *poco*)	You've brought too few screws

Nowadays *demasiado* is always placed before the noun.

(b) As an adverb (invariable in form)

Tú hablas demasiado	You talk too much
A ése/ese me lo conozco demasiado	I know him only too well
No cuentes demasiado conmigo	Don't count on me too much

9.10 *Medio*

In standard Peninsular usage this word functions as an adverb (invariable in form) or as an adjective (inflected for number and gender), both meaning 'half':

Están medio borrachos	They're half drunk
La recogieron medio muerta	They picked her up half dead
media pinta/media luna	half a pint/half-moon
media hora	half an hour

It is also often used colloquially to mean 'rather', 'pretty' as in *es medio guapa/* (Lat. Am. *linda*) 'she's pretty good-looking', *son medio tontos* 'they're pretty stupid', *yo también estoy medio enredado estos días* (L. Otero, Cuba dialogue) 'I'm pretty tied up too these days'.

In Galicia and throughout Latin America there is a widespread colloquial tendency in spontaneous speech to make the adverb agree in gender: *ella es media loca* 'she's half crazy', for *medio loca*; *es media chiquita la casa* (Spain *es bastante pequeña*) 'the house is pretty small', *llegó media desilusionada* (popular Mexican, quoted Kany 55) 'she arrived pretty disillusioned, *la tenía media atragantada* (M. Puig, Argentina, popular dialogue) '... she had it half stuck down her throat'.

9.11 *Mismo* (and Latin-American variants): adjective, marked for gender and number

(a) 'The same':

When it means 'the same', which is its most common meaning on both continents, it is always placed before any noun or noun phrase that it qualifies:

Lleváis la misma blusa	You're wearing the same blouse
... con los mismos mozos pero un día griegos, otro andaluces, otro franceses, aunque vinieran de donde vinieran (A. Bryce Echenique, Peru. In Spain *mozos = camareros*)	... with the same waiters, but (dressed as) Greeks one day, Andalusians another, French on yet another, regardless of where they came from
Estos dos casos son el mismo	These two cases are the same (i.e. identical)
Estos dos son los mismos	These two are the same (i.e. as before)
—¿Es usted don Francisco? —El mismo	'Are you Don Francisco?' 'I am indeed' (lit. 'the same')

Notes

(i) *Lo mismo* may mean *la misma cosa*, or it may be adverbial. *Lo mismo* is also heard in familiar European Spanish with the meaning 'perhaps': *como me vuelvan a decir lo mismo/la misma cosa ...* 'if they say the same thing to me again ...', *lo mismo hace imitaciones de políticos que juegos de manos* '(s)he just as easily does imitations of politicians as conjuring tricks', *no nos divertimos lo mismo que si hubieras estado tú* 'we didn't have such a good time as we would have if you'd been there', *lo mismo te da una propina* (Spain only; familiar) 'maybe he'll give you a tip'. **Lo mismo como* is substandard for *lo mismo que* 'the same as'.

(ii) The following should be noted: *esa casa es lo mismo que (igual que) aquélla/aquella* 'that house is the same as that other one' (i.e. the same thing is true of it, not that they are the same house), *esa casa es la misma que compró Agustín* 'that house is the same one that Agustín bought'.

(b) Placed either before or after a noun, but always after a pronoun, *mismo* means 'selfsame'/'very'/'right':

Vivo en Madrid mismo/en el mismo Madrid	I live in Madrid itself
Aparca el helicóptero en su mismo jardín/su jardín mismo	He parks the helicopter right in his garden

If there is danger of ambiguity, *mismo* must be placed after the noun if it means 'very', 'selfsame': *el mismo Papa* 'the Pope himself' or 'the same Pope', *el Papa mismo* = only 'the Pope himself'. *Propio* (see 9.14b), placed before the noun, means the same as *mismo* in this sense, but it is not used with pronouns.

(c) Placed after a pronoun it emphasizes the pronoun e.g. *yo mismo* 'I myself', *ella misma* 'she herself':

—¿Quién construyó el chalet?[1]—Yo mismo/misma	'Who built the house?' 'I did myself'
Parece que convencí a Graciela, pero yo mismo ¿estoy convencido? (M. Benedetti, Uruguay)	It seems I convinced Graciela, but am I convinced myself?

(d) Placed after an adverb or adverbial phrase, *mismo* is itself an adverb and is therefore invariable:

---

[1] *El chalet* (Spain) 'detached house'.

por eso mismo	for that very reason
ahora mismo/ya mismo	right now/right away
aquí mismo	right here
Mañana mismo empiezo a escribir (A. Bryce Echenique, Peru, *Mañana*, when it means 'tomorrow', is an adverb)	I'll start writing *tomorrow* (the emphasis given here by *mismo* is not easily translated)

But if the adverbial phrase contains a noun not accompanied by the definite article, *mismo* may or may not agree with it (Seco (1998), 298, recommends agreement):

esta noche mismo/misma	this very night
Vino esta mañana mismo/misma	It came this very morning
En España mismo/misma no se pudo evitar la llegada del bikini	In Spain itself it was impossible to prevent the arrival of the bikini

When the definite article is present, *mismo* is an adjective and must agree in number and gender: *lo descubrieron en la chimenea misma* 'they found it in the chimney itself'.

Notes

(i) *Mismísimo* is a colloquial emphatic form of *mismo* in sense **(b)**: *el mismísimo presidente le/lo felicitó* 'the President himself congratulated him'.

(ii) Mexican and Central-American spontaneous speech often uses *mero* in contexts under **(b)**: *en la mera (misma) esquina* 'right on the corner', *lo hizo él mero (él mismo)* 'he did it himself', *ya mero (ahora mismo)* 'right now'. In various parts of Latin America, from Chile to Mexico, *puro* may be used in the same way: *en la pura cabeza (en la misma cabeza)* 'right on the head', etc. (from Kany, 57ff), *a puro Villa* (said by a bus-driver in Tabasco, Mexico) '(I'm going) only to Villahermosa', Spain *sólo/solo a . . .* ; *había puras mujeres* (colloquial Chilean, informant) 'there were only women there' (Spain *no había más que mujeres*).

(iii) *Mismamente* (= *igual*) is rustic or jocular.

(iv) *Mismito* can also be used in familiar speech to emphasize a pronoun or an adverb: *yo mismito me encargo de ello* 'I'll do it myself', *ahora mismito* 'right now', *aquí mismito* 'just here'.

9.12 *Mucho* and *poco*: adjectives, marked for number and gender, or invariable adverbs

'Much', 'little'. Used as adjectives they agree in number and gender. Used as adverbs they are invariable.

(a) Adjectival uses:

Mis hijos no me hacen mucho caso	My children don't pay much attention to me
En el patio hay muchos limoneros	There are a lot of lemon trees in the patio
Pon poca pimienta	Don't put much pepper on/in it
Somos muchos/pocos	There are a lot/not many of us
su poca paciencia	her scant patience
—¿Cuánta harina has comprado? —*Poca*	'How much flour have you bought?' 'Not much'
Lo poco gusta, lo mucho cansa	Brevity is the soul of wit (lit. 'little pleases, much tires')
Muchas se quejan de las nuevas horas de apertura	Many women are complaining about the new opening hours

Notes

(i) In the following sentences *mucho* and *poco* do not agree with the preceding noun, but refer to the general idea underlying the sentence: *¿trescientos mil dólares? Es mucho* '300,000 dollars? It's a lot', *¿tres cajas de ciruelas? es poco* 'three boxes of plums? that's not much'. Compare *mil cajas para cien días son pocas* '1000 boxes for 100 days isn't/aren't a lot', *setenta libros por estante son muchos* 'seventy books to a shelf is/are a lot', *y será mucha la cerveza que consumirán, para provecho del dueño* (M. Puig, Argentina, dialogue) 'and great will be the quantities of beer that they'll consume, to the owner's benefit'.

(ii) When the noun is preceded by an article *mucho* follows the article: *el mucho comer no es bueno* 'it isn't good to eat a lot.'

(b) Adverbial uses:

Estoy añorando mucho a mi patria	I'm missing my home country a lot
Poco antes de las siete llegó su hijo Andrés (G. García Márquez, Colombia)	Shortly before seven his son Andrés arrived
Sale poco últimamente	(S)he hasn't been out much lately
Por mucho que te quejes . . .	However much you complain . . .
Por poco que lo quieras . . .	However little you want it . . .
No sabes lo poco que me gusta ese hombre	You don't know how little I like that man

Notes

(i) Before *más, menos, mayor* and *menor*, when these are followed by a noun (present or implied), *mucho* or *poco* agree in number and gender – a fact that English-speakers are prone to forget: *tienen much**os** más hijos que tú/tienen much**os** más que tú* 'they have many more children than you'/'they have many more than you', *no en balde han transcurrido 27 años, hay much**a** más experiencia, much**a** más madurez* (Fidel Castro, Cuba) 'twenty-seven years have not passed in vain, there is much more experience, much more maturity'. This construction is not obligatory in Latin America: *cuando me jubile, me pasarán sin duda much**o** menos cosas* (M. Benedetti, Uruguay; Spain *much**as** menos cosas*) 'when I retire, no doubt a lot less things will happen to me'. Informants from Peru and Mexico found this acceptable, but it is rejected by Spaniards.

Before adjectives and adverbs, *mucho* and *poco* are adverbs and invariable in form: *los problemas eran mucho mayores* 'the problems were much greater'. See 5.10.

(ii) *Muy* 'very' can be thought of as a shortened form of *mucho*, used before adjectives and adverbs. The full form therefore reappears when it is used alone: *—¿Es laborioso? —Mucho.* 'Is he hard-working?' 'Very.'

(iii) *Poco* (but not *un poco*) negates a following adverb: *poco frecuente* = 'not frequent'. See 4.13.

(iv) 'Very much' = *muchísimo. Muy mucho* is archaic or jocular.

(v) *Un poco de* is invariable, but phrases like *?una poca de sal* 'a bit of salt' are heard in very popular or jocular speech.

9.13 *Otro*: adjective/pronoun, marked for number and gender

Adjectivally 'other'/'another'; pronominally 'another one'/'others':

Otra persona no te creería	Another person wouldn't believe you
Ponle otro sello (Lat. Am. *estampilla*)	Put another stamp on it
en circunstancias otras que aquellas en que . . .	in circumstances other than those in which . . .
El que lo hizo fue otro	The one who did it was someone else
Hay quienes ven la vida lógica y ordenada, otros la sabemos absurda y confusa (G. Cabrera Infante, Cuba, dialogue)	There are some who see life as logical and ordered, others of us know it's absurd and confused
Se lanzaban la pelota unos a otros	They were throwing the ball to one another

Notes

(i) **Un otro* 'another' (Fr. *un autre*, Catalan *un altre*) is not Spanish: *dame otro* 'give me another'. *El otro/la otra*, etc., means 'the other one'.

(ii) The possessives *mi, tu, su, nuestro, vuestro* precede *otro*, but other adjectives follow it, although *mucho* may appear in either position: *tu otro pantalón* 'your other trousers', *sé que estoy manipulada como otra mucha gente* (interview in *Cambio 16*, also *mucha otra ...*) 'I know I'm being manipulated like a lot of other people', ... *cosa que sólo celebraron Carmen Serdán y otras cuatro maestras* (A. Mastretta, Mexico, dialogue) '... something that only Carmen Serdán and four other women teachers greeted enthusiastically', *en otros pocos casos* (cf. *en pocos otros casos* 'in not many other cases') 'in a few other cases', *pero agravó la condición de otros varios millones de campesinos* (M. Vargas Llosa, Peru) 'but it worsened the condition of several million other peasants'.

(iii) *Los/las demás* may be a synonym of *los otros/las otras* if the latter means 'the rest'/'the remaining': *todos los demás países europeos* 'all the other European countries', *si de mí dependiera ya le habría regalado todos los demás muebles* (A. Bryce Echenique, Peru, dialogue) 'if it had depended on me, I'd have made you a present of all the other furniture'.

(iv) The phrase *alguno ... que otro* is noteworthy: *... y todo porque un día les habrá colocado alguna amonestación que otra* (M. Puig, Argentina, dialogue) '... and all because one day he gave them some sort of dressing down'. For the choice between *algún que otro* and *alguno que otro* before masculine nouns, see 9.4.1(a).

9.14 *Propio*: adjective, marked for number and gender

(a) Usually it means 'own', as in:

mi propio taxi/tus propias convicciones	my own taxi/your own convictions
Tiene chófer propio	He has his own driver
Intentar comprender su realidad es comprender mejor la tuya propia (Queen Sofía of Spain, quoted in *El País*)	Trying to understand their [i.e. artists'] reality is to understand your own better

(b) Placed before a noun, 'selfsame', 'very', etc. (same as *mismo* at 9.11b):

Las tachaduras son del propio autor	The crossing out is by the author himself
Nos dio audiencia el propio obispo	The Bishop himself granted us an audience

(c) 'Appropriate', 'right', 'peculiar', 'characteristic':

Ese olor es propio del butano	That smell is characteristic of butane
Ese lenguaje no es propio de un diplomático	That language is not suitable for a diplomat
Es propio de ella llegar tres horas tarde	It's like her/typical of her to arrive three hours late

9.15 *Solo*: adjective, marked for number and gender; *sólo* or *solo*: invariable adverb

The adjective means 'alone'; the adverb means 'only' (i.e. *solamente*). The adverb was always distinguished by the written accent, but the Academy's *Nuevas normas* of 1959 decree that an accent is necessary only to avoid ambiguity, so one may now write *solo tres* or *sólo tres* for 'only three'; this view is endorsed by Seco (1998), 417. However, forty years later most editors and publishers still follow the old rule. Ambiguity is only possible with the masculine singular adjective, e.g.

un hombre solo/un hombre sólo	a man alone/only one man
solo en casa/sólo en casa	alone in the house/only at home

(a) Adjectival uses:

Yo me quedé solo	I was left alone
Octavia me dijo que tenía que regresar sola (A. Bryce Echenique, Peru)	Octavia told me she had to go back alone
Por el solo tono de la voz comprendió que era una llamada alarmante (G. García Márquez, Colombia)	By the tone of the voice alone he understood that it was an alarming phone-call
dos cafés solos	two black coffees
(cf. *dos cafés sólo/solo*	only two coffees)

(b) Adverbial examples:

Sólo/Solo así se solucionarán estos problemas	Only in this way will these problems be solved
Millones de personas disfrutan de la luz eléctrica con sólo/solo accionar un simple conmutador	Millions of people enjoy electric light merely at the press of a switch
Tan sólo se me ocurrió en ese instante lo que podría haber pedido Graciela (M. Puig, Argentina, dialogue)	It only occurred to me at that moment what Graciela might have asked for

Notes

(i) A negative + *más . . . que* is a common way of translating 'only' (cf. French *ne . . . que . . .*): *no hizo más que reírse* 'all he did was laugh', *no piensa más que en sí misma* 'she only thinks of herself'. *Más que* must not be confused with *más de*. The latter is used with numerical values and means 'more than'. See 5.5 for discussion.

(ii) *A solas* strictly means 'alone' (i.e. unaccompanied), and is occasionally required for the sake of clarity, e.g. in: *lo solucionó a solas* 'he solved it alone (no one else present)', *lo solucionó solo* 'he solved it alone' (without help), *pero nunca había fumado a solas* (G. García Márquez, Colombia) 'but she had never smoked on her own'.

A *solas* cannot be used of inanimate things. In sentences like *estuvo a solas con sus pensamientos* 'he was alone with his thoughts' it is an elegant, rather poetic alternative to *solo*.

(iii) 'Not only . . . but also' is translated by *no sólo/solo . . . sino que*. See 33.1.

(iv) Translating 'the only . . .', 'the only one . . .', 'his only', etc. *Único* is required if no noun follows: *él es el único que sabe conducir* 'he's the only one who can drive', *es lo único concreto que tenemos* (L. Otero, Cuba) 'it's the only real thing we have', *lo único es que no sé nadar* 'the only thing is I can't swim', *es hijo único* 'he's an only child'. Compare *el único/solo ser por quien deseo vivir* 'the only person I want to live for', *son el único/solo sustento del gobierno* 'they're the government's only support'.

(v) In some Latin-American countries, e.g. Cuba, *único* may be used as an adverb meaning 'only', where other regions use *únicamente*, e.g. *?único* (for *únicamente/solamente/sólo*) *en esta región* 'only in this region.'

9.16 *Tanto*: adjective, marked for number and gender; or invariable adverb

For the use of *tanto* and *tan* in comparisons see 5.15.1.

This word basically means 'so much', 'so many' (French *tant de*):

(a) As an adjective it must agree in number and gender:

tanta nieve/tantas hormigas/tantos problemas	so much snow/so many ants/so many problems
. . . uno de tantos consuelos del pobre (M. Puig, Argentina, dialogue)	. . . one of so many consolations that the poor have

It can also function as a noun or pronoun (invariable form *tanto*):

No creí que se atreviera/atreviese a tanto	I didn't think (s)he/you would be that daring
Es un tanto místico	He's a bit of a mystic (or 'he lives in the clouds')
Cobran un tanto por ciento de comisión	They take a certain percentage as commission

(b) As an adverb it is invariable in form:

—Hay más de tres kilos. —¡No tanto!	'There are more than three kilos.' 'Not that much!'
Corrió tanto que no podía hablar	He ran so much that he couldn't speak
tanto era así que . . . (see note (ii) for *?tan era así . . .*).	so much was it so that . . .
tanto mejor/tanto peor para ellos	all the better/so much the worse for them
—Es nada menos que de cincuenta pesos. —¡Tanto mejor! (J. J. Arreola, Mexico, dialogue)	'It's all of fifty pesos.' 'So much the better!'
Es tanto un problema para la oposición como para el Gobierno	It's as much a problem for the opposition as for the government

Notes

(i) Before adjectives or adverbs, *tan* is required: *usted ha sido tan acogedor* 'you've been so welcoming', *se levanta tan de mañana que nadie le ve salir* 'he gets up so early in the morning that no one sees him leave', *tan a propósito* 'so much on purpose'/'so relevantly', *te lo enviaré tan pronto como pueda* 'I'll send it to you as soon as I can'.

Mejor, peor, mayor and *menor* are exceptions: *tanto mejor/peor para usted* 'so much the better/worse for you', *el peligro era tanto mayor debido a la radiactividad* 'the danger was so much greater due to radioactivity'.

(ii) *?Tan es así* for *tanto es así* 'it was so true' is considered substandard in Spain but is found in Latin-American speech and writing.

(iii) *Tanto* plus a singular noun is a colloquial expression for 'lots of', 'so many': *hay tanto ricacho por aquí* 'there are loads of stinking rich people round here'.

(iv) *Tanto . . . que* for 'as much as' is not Spanish: *no viaja tanto como tú* 'he doesn't travel as much as you'. *Tanto . . . que* can only mean 'so much . . . that'. For details see 5.15.1.

9.17 *Todo*: adjective/pronoun, marked for number and gender

'All', 'every', 'the whole of', 'any'.

(a) When not followed by a definite or indefinite article it usually means 'every' or 'any':

todo producto alimenticio que contenga colorantes artificiales . . .	any food product containing artificial colouring . . .
todo español sabe que . . .	every Spaniard knows that . . .
en todo caso	in any case

In all these cases *cualquier* could replace *todo*.

(b) With the definite article, possessives or demonstratives, or before proper names, its usual translation is 'the whole of'/'all':

toda la noche	all night
todos los cinco	all five of them

Varadero. Es una playa increíble. Todos los extranjeros nos envidian (L. Otero, Cuba, dialogue)	Varadero. It's an incredible beach. All the foreigners envy us.
Incluso Ricardo, con toda su paciencia, se salió del seminario	Even Ricardo, with all his patience, walked out of the seminar
Todo Barcelona habla de ello (see 1.4.7, note, for the gender of *todo* in this example)	All Barcelona's talking about it

(c) With the definite article and periods of time it means 'every':

El fontanero (Lat. Am. *plomero*) *viene todos los meses*	The plumber comes every/once a month
todos los viernes/años	every Friday/year

Notes

(i) *Cada* must be used if the actions are new ones rather than repetitions, or when the period of time is preceded by a number: *cada día sale con una chica nueva* 'every day he goes out with a new girl', *cada diez minutos sale con alguna nueva burrada* 'every ten minutes he comes out with some new nonsense', *tres gotas cada cuatro horas* 'three drops every four hours'.

(ii) Moliner, II, 1330, notes that *al . . .* is more elegant than *todos los . . .* when describing rate or quantity per period of time: *se fuma cuatro paquetes al día* 'he smokes four packs/(Brit. packets) a day', *lee un par de novelas a la semana* 'he reads a couple of novels a week', etc.

(iii) *Cuanto* may be used to translate 'absolutely every': *no es cosa de obligar a leer cuanto libro se ha escrito* (E. Sábato, Argentina, interview) 'it's not a question of obliging people to read every book that was ever written'. *Cuanto* is not used thus in phrases like *todos los días* 'every day'.

Cuanto or *todo cuanto* may also translate 'absolutely everything': *heredó de él una tremenda bronca a (todo) cuanto sonara a autoridad* (L. Sepúlveda, Chile; in Spain *bronca* means 'row'/'argument'. *Rabia* would be used here) 'he inherited from him a tremendous rage against everything that sounded like authority.'

(d) Pronominally, the singular means 'everything', the plural 'everyone'/'everybody'/'all of them': *se enfada por todo* 'he gets cross about everything', *es todo propaganda* 'it's all propaganda':

—¿Dónde están las fresas? —Me las he comido todas	'Where are the strawberries?' 'I've eaten them all'
Pago por todos	I'm paying for everyone

Note

After a neuter *todo* – as after all singular nouns and pronouns – Spanish usually makes the verb *ser* (and one or two others) agree with a following plural noun: *con nuestro nuevo plan de ahorros, todo **son** ventajas* 'with our new savings plan it's all advantages'. See 2.3.3 for further discussion.

(e) Agreement of *todo* should be noted in the following examples:

Su cara era toda pecas	Her face was all freckles
El cielo era todo nubes	The sky was all clouds
Esa niña es toda ojos (from Moliner, II, 1930)	That girl's all eyes

But the adverbial *todo* is found in some constructions, sometimes arbitrarily. *Soy toda oídos* 'I'm all ears' is normal for a female speaker, but one hears both *es toda sonrisas/todo sonrisas esta mañana* 'she's all smiles this morning'. The invariable *todo* makes the expression unambiguous with plural nouns: *esos hombres son todo músculo* means 'those men are all muscle', whereas . . . *todos músculos* sounds like '. . . all belong to the Muscle family/tribe'. Therefore *estas chuletas son todo hueso* is most likely for 'these chops are all bone'.

(f) Relative clauses involving *todo*:

The following sentences illustrate some translation problems:

todos los que dicen eso	all who say that
todo el que diga eso/todo aquel que diga eso (the latter is literary)	anyone who says that
Todo lo que escribe es bueno	Everything he writes is good
Cuanto/Todo cuanto escribe es bueno (literary)	Everything he writes is good
este poeta, cuyas palabras todas quedarán grabadas en nuestro corazón	this poet, whose every word will remain engraved on our hearts
el césped, por toda cuya superficie crecían malas hierbas	the lawn, over all of whose surface weeds were growing
esta ciudad, de la que conozco todas las iglesias	this city, all of whose churches I know
estas novelas, todas las cuales he leído	these novels, all of which I have read
estos niños, los padres de todos los cuales yo conozco	these children, all of whose parents I know
Estas páginas, escritas todas ellas en japonés	These pages, all of which are written in Japanese
el palacio, del que no hay habitación que yo no haya visitado	the palace, all of whose rooms I have visited

Notes

(i) *Todo* occasionally follows the noun in flowery styles: *el cielo todo estaba sembrado de estrellas* 'the whole sky was strewn with stars', *el mundo todo le parecía un jardín encantado* 'the whole world seemed to him an enchanted garden'.

(ii) *Todo el mundo* (singular agreement) is a set phrase meaning 'everybody'.

(iii) *Todo* followed by the indefinite article usually translates 'a whole . . .': *se comió toda una tarta de melocotones* 'he ate a whole peach tart', *hubo toda una serie de malentendidos* 'there was a whole series of misunderstandings'.

9.18 *Varios*: adjective, marked for number and gender

(a) 'Several', in which case it normally – but not invariably – precedes the noun: *en varias partes del país* 'in several parts of the country', *mis motivos son varios* 'my motives are several', *los aspectos varios de la cuestión* (literary: from Moliner, II, 1442) 'the several aspects of the question'.

(b) 'Various', 'varied', in which it can also follow or precede the noun. When used with *hay* or *ser* it precedes the noun:

flores de varios colores/de colores varios (the second option is more literary)	flowers of various colo(u)rs
La fauna de esta zona es muy varia/variada	The fauna of this zone is very varied

Note

Translating 'various': *en **diversas** ocasiones* 'on various occasions', *en **diferentes** puntos de los Andes* 'in various places in the Andes.'

10
Numerals

Spanish numerals are neither complex nor plagued with exceptions, although this makes the three unexpected forms *quinientos* 500 (**not** **cinco cientos*), *setecientos* 700 (**not** **sietecientos*) and *novecientos* 900 (**not** **nuevecientos*) easier to forget. It is also easy to forget that 16–19 and 21–29 are written as one word, whereas the other numbers are joined by *y*.

Spanish cardinal numerals (i.e. the numbers used for counting) are invariable in form, with the exception of *uno* 'one' and *cientos* 'hundreds', which agree in gender with the noun counted.

The ordinal numbers above *décimo* 'tenth' are usually avoided in informal language and are replaced by the corresponding cardinal numbers; see 10.12.2.

10.1 Cardinal numbers

0 *cero*	11 *once*	22 *veintidós*	40 *cuarenta*
1 *uno/una*	12 *doce*	23 *veintitrés*	41 *cuarenta y uno/una*
2 *dos*	13 *trece*	24 *veinticuatro*	50 *cincuenta*
3 *tres*	14 *catorce*	25 *veinticinco*	60 *sesenta*
4 *cuatro*	15 *quince*	26 *veintiséis*	70 *setenta*
5 *cinco*	16 *dieciséis*	27 *veintisiete*	80 *ochenta*
6 *seis*	17 *diecisiete*	28 *veintiocho*	90 *noventa*
7 *siete*	18 *dieciocho*	29 *veintinueve*	100 *cien/ciento*
8 *ocho*	19 *diecinueve*	30 *treinta*	101 *ciento uno/una*
9 *nueve*	20 *veinte*	31 *treinta y uno/una*	102 *ciento dos*
10 *diez*	21 *veintiuno/a*	32 *treinta y dos*	

185 *ciento ochenta y cinco*	400 *cuatrocientos/ cuatrocientas*	1001 see note (iv)
200 *doscientos/ doscientas*	500 **quinientos/quinientas**	1006 *mil seis*
205 *doscientos cinco/ doscientas cinco*	600 *seiscientos/seiscientas*	1107 *mil ciento siete*
300 *trescientos/trescientas*	700 **setecientos/setecientas**	1998 *mil novecientos/as noventa y ocho*
357 *trescientos((/as) cincuenta y siete*	800 *ochocientos/ ochocientas*	2022 *dos mil veintidós*
	900 **novecientos/ novecientas**	5000 *cinco mil*
	1000 *mil*	10.000 *diez mil*

500.014 *quinientos/as mil catorce*   936.257 *novecientos/as treinta y seis mil doscientos/as cincuenta y siete*

1.000.000 *un millón*   100.000.000 *cien millones*
$1.000.000 *un millón de dólares* (for the use of *de* see 10.4)

7.678.456 *pesetas: siete millones seiscientas setenta y ocho mil cuatrocientas cincuenta y seis pesetas*

    1.000.000.000 *mil millones*   1.000.000.000.000 *un billón*[1]

Notes

(i) 16–19 and 21–29 are arbitrarily written as one word, as are 200, 300, 400, 500, 600, 700, 800, 900. Forms like *diez y seis* for *dieciséis* are old-fashioned.

(ii) *Uno* is not used before *ciento* and *mil* except in rare cases of ambiguity: *una pareja de ratas es capaz de procrear más de ciento veinte crias por año* 'a pair of rats is capable of producing more than 120 offspring per year', *más de mil colegios equipados con televisores en color* 'more than one thousand schools equipped with colo(u)r television', but compare *trescientos/as un mil ochenta y cuatro* 301.084 and *trescientos/as mil ochenta y cuatro* 300.084.

(iii) A point (period) is used to separate thousands: *19.000 dólares* = $19,000. Years are sometimes written with a point, especially by typists, e.g. 1.998, but all the best authorities condemn this. A comma is used to separate decimals: *3,45* (pronounced *tres coma cuarenta y cinco*, not **tres coma cuatro cinco*) = British/American 3.45. However, Mexico, Puerto Rico and Central America use the system of the English-speaking world, i.e. 20,550 = *veinte mil quinientos cincuenta* and 1.25, pronounced *uno punto veinticinco*.

(iv) 1001 is theoretically *mil uno*. Seco (1998), 446, notes that *mil y uno* comes from the famous book *Las mil y una noches* 'One Thousand and One Nights' and is correct only in the vague sense of 'a lot': *tengo mil y una cosas que hacer* 'I've got a thousand and one things to do', *es sólo un ejemplo de los **mil y un** casos de todos los días* (*El País*, quoted Gerboin and Leroy, 91) 'it's only one example among the thousand and one of every day'. However, the form ... *y uno* is commonly used in speech after thousands: *mil y una pesetas* '1001 pesetas', *tres mil y un dólares* '3001 dollars'. Forms like *mil una pesetas* are confined to formal writing and are uncommon even there.

(v) Certain forms ending in *-ón* are used pejoratively to refer to people of a specific age: *un cuarentón* 'a forty-year-old man', *un cincuentón* 'a fifty-year-old', *una sesentona* 'a sixty-year-old woman'. Forms ending in *-añero* are merely descriptive, e.g. *un quinceañero* 'a fifteen-year-old', *una veinteañera* (C. Martín Gaite, Spain) 'a twenty-year-old woman'.

According to *El País's Libro de estilo* (1998), 368–9, the word *el/la joven* signifies a person aged between 13 and 18, and is therefore nearly equivalent to our 'teenager'.

10.2 Gender of numbers

Numbers, unlike letters of the alphabet, are masculine:

Yo puse un siete, no un nueve	I put a 7, not a 9
Los dos ochos del anuncio giraban velozmente en sentido contrario (C. Martín Gaite, Spain)	The two 8s on the advertisement were rotating rapidly in opposite directions
un cinco de bastos	a five of clubs
Tú eres el cinco	You're number five

This is also true of *cientos* and *miles* when they are used as nouns (i.e. when they are followed by *de*):

los miles de víctimas de los tifones	the thousands of victims of the typhoons
los escasos cientos de personas que asistían a la manifestación	the few hundred persons present at the demonstration

---

[1] Hispanic usage reflects the ruling of the International Conference on Weights and Measures of 1948 that a billion is a million million in all countries except the USA. Usage in Britain and many countries has fallen into line with the USA, so our billion is *mil millones* in Spanish. However, North-American influence on Latin America, and careless translating from English, means that *un billón* may sometimes stand for a thousand million.

Note

In informal styles *miles de* is quite often made feminine before a feminine noun: *la acumulación de los plaguicidas es un continuo peligro de envenenamiento para **las** miles de aves* (*La Vanguardia*, Spain) 'the accumulation of pesticides represents (lit. 'is') a continual threat of poisoning for the thousands of birds'. ***Los** miles de aves* is recommended: Seco (1998), 297, condemns *las miles* as 'abnormal'.

10.3 Agreement of *uno* and the hundreds

Uno and *cientos* (but not *ciento*/*cien*) must agree in gender with the noun counted – a rule constantly overlooked by foreign students:

un peso/*una peseta*	one peso/one peseta
veintiuna pesetas	twenty-one pesetas
quinientos dólares	five hundred dollars
setecientas libras	seven hundred pounds
en la página quinientas catorce	on page 514
Yo duermo en la cuatrocientas (*habitación* omitted)	I'm sleeping in (room) 400

Note

Combinations of tens plus one and thousands (21,000, 31,000, 41,000, etc.) are problematic. Logically one should say *veintiuna mil pesetas/mujeres* '21,000 pesetas/women' since the nouns are feminine and *mil* is in this case an adjective, not a masculine noun: cf. *se han visto afectadas treinta y **una** mil personas* 'thirty-one thousand people have been affected' (TVE broadcast). However, forms like *veintiún mil pesetas*, *treinta y un mil mujeres* '31,000 women', etc., are in fact in general use and most speakers will not accept *veintiuna/treinta y una mil*. Seco, in his latest edition (1998), 445, points out that the masculine is in fact the traditional form.

When thousands are multiplied by hundreds the expected gender agreement must be used: *doscien**tas** mil pesetas* '200,000 pesetas', never **doscientos mil pesetas*.

10.4 Millions

Millón is a masculine noun and is connected by *de* to the following noun or noun phrase:

*Este plan prevé una inversión global de más de 6.000 millones **de** pesetas, de **los** que mil millones se invertirán el próximo año* (*El País*, Spain)	This plan provides for an overall investment of more than 6,000 million pesetas, of which 1,000 million will be invested next year

Un millón is a singular noun and a following verb or noun must agree accordingly: *el millón y medio restante **fue** invertido. . .* 'the remaining million and a half were/was invested . . . '

10.5 *Un* or *uno*?

Uno loses its final vowel before a masculine noun or noun phrase, as does *una* before nouns beginning with stressed *a-* or *ha-*. *Veintiuno* is shortened to *veintiún* in the same contexts:

un tigre, dos tigres, tres tigres	one tiger, two tigers, three tigers (a tongue-twister)
veintiún mil hombres	21,000 men
veintiún mil mujeres (see note to 10.3)	21,000 women
un águila, veintiún armas, treinta y un hachas	one eagle, 21 weapons, 31 axes

In the following examples the final vowel is retained since the numeral does not precede a noun:

No hay más que veintiuno	There are only twenty-one
párrafo ciento uno	paragraph 101
Inglaterra, país tradicional de los fantasmas,	England, the traditional land of
ve uno nuevo por sus calles	ghosts, is witnessing a new one
(*Cambio16*, Spain)	in its streets

10.6 *Cien* or *ciento*?

Ciento is shortened to *cien* before another numeral which it multiplies, or before a noun or noun phrase:

cien mil bolívares	100,000 bolivares
cien millones	100 million
cien buenas razones	100 good reasons

but

ciento once	one hundred and eleven
en la página ciento dieciocho	on page one hundred and eighteen

The old rule (still respected by some purists and by some older speakers in Spain) was that *ciento* should be used when the number stands alone: —*¿Cuántos son?* —*¿Ciento* 'How many are there?' 'A hundred.' But this rule is completely obsolete in Latin America and virtually extinct in Spain:

Yo vivo en el cien	I live in number 100
Pues faltan cien o sobran cincuenta	Well, there are either a hundred
(A. Mastretta, Mexico, dialogue)	missing or fifty too many

However, *ciento* is used in percentages: see next section.

10.7 Expression of percentages

Ciento is used with all numbers, although the phrase *cien por cien* 'one hundred per cent' is also found for *ciento por ciento*. Forms like *cincuenta por cien*, *diez por cien* are heard colloquially in Latin America (and occasionally in Spain), but ... *por ciento* is used in writing on both continents:

el cuarenta y tres por ciento	forty-three per cent
tanto por ciento	so much per cent
El PCE sólo obtuvo el 8 y pico por ciento	The Spanish Communist Party only
de los votos (*El País*, Spain)	obtained slightly more than 8 per cent
	of the votes
el costo de la construcción creció el	building costs rose 0.7 per cent
0,7 por ciento (*La Nación*, Argentina)	
la seguridad, cien por cien, de que los	a hundred-per-cent guarantee that the
vertidos son inocuos (*El País*, Spain)	material to be dumped is harmless

10.8 Collective numerals

There is a series of collective numerals, cf. our 'score', sometimes used to express approximate quantities:

un par de veces a couple of times	*la cuarentena* about forty/quarantine
una decena ten	*una cincuentena* about fifty
una docena a dozen (often approximate, used less than in English)	*un centenar* about a hundred
una veintena a score/about twenty	*un millar* about a thousand

Notes

(i) *Cuatro* is used colloquially in Spain, Mexico and no doubt elsewhere to mean 'a couple'/'a handful': *no hay más que cuatro gatos* 'there's not a soul about' (lit.'only four cats about'), *no son más que cuatro desgraciados los que ponen las pegatinas fascistas* 'it's only a handful of wretches who put up fascist stickers'.

(ii) *Centenar* and *millar* are used for expressing rate: *mil dólares el centenar/millar* '1,000 dollars the hundred/the thousand' (or, more colloquially, *cada cien/por cada cien, cada mil*).

(iii) Like all collective nouns, collective numerals are often treated as singular: *una veintena de casas se ordenaba formando una calle frente al río* (L. Sepúlveda, Chile) 'a score of houses were laid out to form a street in front of the river'. See 2.3.1 for further remarks on agreement with collective nouns.

(iv) Another, more colloquial way of expressing approximations is by using *y pico*, as in *el piso veintipico* (M. Vázquez Montalbán, Spain) 'flat twenty-something', *treinta y pico* 'thirty and a bit'.

10.9 Mathematical expressions

Dos y tres son cinco	Two plus three equals five
Dos por tres son seis	Two times three equals six
Ocho dividido por dos son cuatro (or *ocho entre dos* . . .)	Eight divided by two is four
Once menos nueve son dos	Eleven minus nine equals two
Tres es la raíz cuadrada de nueve	Three is the square root of nine
Nueve es el cuadrado de tres	Nine is three squared
Forma un cuadrado de diez metros	It's ten metres square
dos metros cuadrados	Two square metres
menos veinte	minus twenty

The division sign is a colon, e.g. *3: 6 = 0,5 (tres dividido por seis son cero coma cinco)* '3 ÷ 6 = 0.5'.

10.10 Fractions

In both languages the more complex fractions like 'four twenty-sevenths' are usually nowadays expressed as percentages or decimals. Mathematical language uses forms that are uncommon in everyday speech. There are nouns to express some lower fractions, e.g. *la/una mitad* 'the/a half' , *el/un tercio* 'the/a third', *dos tercios* 'two-thirds', *el/un cuarto* 'the/a quarter'. From 'fifth' to 'tenth' the masculine ordinal numeral can be used: *un quinto/sexto/séptimo/octavo/noveno/décimo* 'a fifth/sixth/seventh/eighth/ninth/tenth', but this is more typical of mathematical, technical or sporting language (although not unknown in educated speech): *ganó por tres quintos de segundo* '(s)he won by three-fifths of a second'.

Everyday language uses the forms *quinta parte, sexta parte, séptima parte*, etc., although usage is fickle in a few cases and the *parte* may be dropped: one always says *tengo unas décimas de fiebre* 'I've got a couple of tenths of a degree of fever', but *un décimo* is the name given to a tenth share in a national lottery number. *La tercera parte* is also usual in non-mathematical speech for *el tercio*. Examples:

La mitad se salvó	Half were saved
un cuarto (de) kilo	a quarter (of a) kilo
Un tercio/La tercera parte de los españoles	A third of Spaniards think that . . .
piensa(n) que . . .	
Alaska y Venezuela sólo nos aseguran las dos	Alaska and Venezuela only guarantee
terceras partes de ese suministro	us two-thirds of that supply
(C. Fuentes, Mexico, dialogue)	

For twentieths to ninetieths (but not for the intermediate values like twenty-sixths, eighty-seconds, etc.) the ordinal forms (see 10.12) followed by *parte* are supposed to be used: *la vigésima parte* '1/20th', *tres trigésimas partes* '3/30ths', *la quincuagésima parte* '1/50th', etc. But the ordinal numbers between eleventh and ninety-ninth are considered pedantic, the more so the higher one goes, so the tendency (especially in Spain) is to use cardinal numbers: *la cuarenta parte* '1/40th', *la ochenta parte* '1/80th', and also for intermediate values: *la cincuenta y tres parte* '1/53rd'.

Ordinal forms with *parte* are used in everyday language for hundredths, thousandths, millionths and billionths: *la centésima/milésima/millonésima parte, tres doscentésimas* '3/200ths'. However, the word *parte* is often dropped:

A partir de la primera cienmilésima de	After the first one-hundred-thousandth
segundo, el Universo empieza a cobrar un	of a second the Universe
aspecto conocido (*Abc*, Spain)	begins to take on a familiar appearance
Greene corrió el fin de semana pasado en	Greene clocked (lit 'ran') 6.4 seconds
Atlanta en 6,40, una centésima de segundo	last weekend in Atlanta, a
menos que . . . (*Abc*, Spain)	hundredth of a second less than . . .

All the smaller fractions can alternatively be expressed, and generally are in mathematical language, by adding the suffix *-avo* to the ordinal number: *la veinticincava parte* '1/25th', *tres ochenta y seisavas partes* '3/86ths'. Mathematical language may alternatively use the masculine form, e.g. *tres ochenta y seisavos*. If two *a*s come together after *-avo* is added, one may optionally be dropped and usually is in non-mathematical discourse: *treinta(a)vo* '30th'.

Note

Medio/a/os/as is the adjectival form for 'half': *una media docena/pinta* 'a half-dozen/half-pint'; *la mitad* is the noun 'the half'. *Cuarto* may function as an adjective or noun: *un cuarto kilo* or *un cuarto de kilo* '1/4 kilo', but always *un cuarto de hora* '1/4 hour'.

10.11 Articles with numbers

Certain common numerical expressions, especially percentages, usually appear with the article. This is particularly true when the numerical value is preceded by a preposition and after *cumplir, al llegar a . . .* meaning 'to reach the age of':

Vivo en el cinco	I live in number 5
La inflación ha subido en un tres por ciento	Inflation has risen by 3 per cent
El 20 por ciento de los mexicanos	20 per cent of Mexicans say that . . .
dice(n) que. . .	
Cuando George Burns cumplió los	When George Burns reached the age of
noventa años . . . (*La Jornada*, Mexico)	ninety . . .
Lo dijo al llegar a los ochenta años	He said it when he reached eighty

But:

Ha costado entre tres mil y cinco mil pesetas	It cost between 3,000 and 5,000 pesetas
Tengo cuarenta y tres años (años can be omitted in approximations: *tiene cuarenta y pico* '(s)he's forty and a bit')	I'm forty-three

Use of the article with percentages is, however, subject to regional fluctuations: cf. *el año pasado el gasto programable representó 18.2 por ciento del PIB; para este año la cifra alcanzará 18.3 por ciento* (*La Jornada*, Mexico): (Mexico uses points and commas as in English) 'last year the predicted cost represented 18.2% of GDP; for this year the figure will reach 18.3%'.

10.12 Ordinal numbers

10.12.1 Ordinals first to tenth

These must agree in number and gender: *el quinto libro/la quinta casa* 'the fifth book'/'the fifth house'. Ordinals 1st–10th are in everyday use, but the cardinals encroach even on them in phrases like *el siglo nueve/noveno* 'the ninth century', *Alfonso diez/décimo* 'Alfonso the tenth', the ordinal being considered more correct:

primer(o) first	*quinto* fifth	*octavo* eighth
segundo second	*sexto* sixth	*noveno* ninth
tercer(o) third	*séptimo/sétimo* seventh	*décimo* tenth
cuarto fourth		

Examples:

el tercer hombre the third man	*la tercera vez* the third time
Carlos III (tercero) Charles III	*el siglo décimo/diez* the tenth century
Fernando VII (séptimo) Ferdinand VII	

Notes

(i) *Primero* and *tercero* lose their final vowel before a masculine singular noun or noun phrase: *el primer récord mundial* 'the first world record', *el tercer gran éxito* 'the third great success'.
(ii) *Séptimo* is often pronounced *sétimo* and the Academy approves of this as an alternative spelling. Many Spanish-speakers do not.
(iii) *Nono* is used for *noveno* when referring to popes: *Pío nono* 'Pope Pius IX'.
(iv) See 32.9.1 for how to say and write dates.
(v) In the titles of royalty and popes, the usual rule is that the ordinal number is used below eleven, the cardinal for numbers above ten: *Enrique V* (*Enrique quinto*) 'Henry the Fifth', but *Juan XXIII* (*Juan veintitrés*) 'John 23rd'.

10.12.2 Ordinal numbers above tenth

The use of special ordinal forms for these numbers is declining, and they are now mainly used only in official or formal language. Forms in bold type are used for fractions in technical language: *tres doceavos* 'three-twelfths'. They are used as ordinals in Lat. Am.: *la doceava parte de un sexenio* (Carlos Fuentes, Mexico, dialogue) 'one-twelfth of six years', and occasionally in Spain, but this is condemned by Manuel Seco (1998, 70) and by the *Libro de estilo* of *El País*.

undécimo eleventh **onceavo**	*quincuagésimo* fiftieth **cincuenta(a)vo**
duodécimo twelfth **doceavo**	*sexagésimo* sixtieth **sesenta(a)vo**
decimotercero thirteenth **treceavo**	*septuagésimo* seventieth **setenta(a)vo**
decimocuarto fourteenth **catorceavo**	*octogésimo* eightieth **ochenta(a)vo**
decimoquinto fifteenth **quinceavo**	*nonagésimo* ninetieth **noventa(a)vo**

decimosexto sixteenth ***dieciseisavo***
decimoséptimo seventeenth ***diecisieteavo***
decimoctavo eighteenth ***dieciochavo***
decimonoveno/decimonono nineteenth
 diecinueveavo
vigésimo twentieth ***veinteavo***
vigésimo/a primero/a twenty-first
vigésimo/a quinto/a etc. twenty-fifth
 veinticincavo
trigésimo thirtieth ***treinta(a)vo***
trigésimo/a sexto/a thirty-sixth
 treintiseisavo
cuadragésimo fortieth ***cuarenta(a)vo***

centésimo (in common use) hundredth
centavo
ducentésimo two-hundredth
tricentésimo three-hundredth
cuadringentésimo four-hundredth
quingentésimo five-hundredth
sexcentésimo six-hundredth
septingentésimo seven-hundredth
octingentésimo eight-hundredth
noningentésimo nine-hundredth
milésimo (in common use) thousandth
dosmilésimo two-thousandth
cuatrocientosmilésimo four-hundred
 thousandth
millonésimo millionth

Notes

(i) In informal styles, written and spoken, ordinal forms over tenth are either avoided, e.g. *mañana cumple treinta años* 'tomorrow's his thirtieth birthday', *—¿En qué capítulo viene? —En el trece* '"What chapter's it in"?' '"Thirteen"'; or the ordinary cardinal number is used, e.g. *el veinticinco aniversario* 'the twenty-fifth anniversary', *la trescientas cincuenta reunión del comité* 'the 350th meeting of the committee', *faltaban quince días para mi cincuenta cumpleaños* (C. Martín Gaite, Spain, dialogue) 'there were fifteen days to go to my fiftieth birthday', *el tren de alta velocidad español está a punto de contabilizar su pasajero medio millón* (El País) 'the Spanish High Speed Train is about to get (lit. 'to enter into its accounts') its 500,000th passenger'.

(ii) **Decimoprimero*, **decimosegundo*, for *undécimo*, *duodécimo*, are common mistakes in spoken Spanish.

(iii) Forms like *décimo tercero*, *décimo cuarto*, in which both words agree in number and gender, are nowadays old-fashioned. Forms like *vigesimoquinto/a*, *vigesimoséptimo/a*, etc. are also increasingly common for 21st–29th.

(iv) When addition of the suffix *-avo* creates a double *a*, as in *treinta(a)vo*, the *as* may be written single or double, the latter being usual among mathematicians, the former among non-specialists.

10.12.3 Position of ordinals

They usually precede, but used contrastively, or with titles, they may follow the noun, sometimes with a change of meaning:

en el tercer capítulo/en el capítulo tercero
 (latter order unusual)
 in the third chapter

los tres párrafos primeros
 the first three paragraphs (i.e. paras 1,2 and 3)

los tres primeros párrafos
 the three first paragraphs (i.e. paragraph 1 of three different chapters)

Isabel segunda (Isabel II)
 Elizabeth the second

por la enésima vez
 for the umpteenth time

10.13 Distribution

cada cinco meses
 every five months
Cada uno paga lo suyo
 Each will pay his share
Di cien mil pesos a cada uno
 I gave 100,000 pesos to each of them
Traían sendos ramilletes de flores
 Each bore a bouquet of flowers/Each one
 (literary style, informally *cada uno traía*
 was carrying a bouquet
 un ramillete)

Note

The use of *sendos* to mean 'several' (i.e. *varios*) is a common mistake on both continents.

10.14 Single, twofold, double, treble, etc.

un billete de ida	a single ticket
una habitación individual	a single room
todos y cada uno de los problemas	every single problem
con una sola excepción/con una excepción única	with a single exception
ni uno solo	not a single one
Mi sueldo es el doble del suyo	My salary is double his
el doble acristalamiento	double glazing
una cama de matrimonio	double bed
Duplicaron la suma	They doubled the sum
Esta cantidad es el triple de ésa/esa	This quantity is triple that

10.15 Dimensions and other numerical expressions

Este cuarto mide 2,5 (dos coma cinco) por 3,75 (tres coma setenta y cinco)	This room measures 2.5 by 3.75
El área es de tres metros cuadrados	The area is 3 square metres
Forma un cuadrado de dos metros	It's two metres square
mil centímetros cúbicos	1,000 cubic centimeters (cc)
El cable tiene cien metros de largo/de longitud	The cable's 100 meters long
Tiene cinco metros de hondo/ancho	It's five metres/(US 'meters') deep/wide
un motor de ocho caballos	an 8-horsepower engine
un motor de dos tiempos	a two-stroke engine
un ángulo de treinta grados	a 30-degree angle
Forma un ángulo recto	It makes a right angle
Debe de haber cinco bajo cero	It must be five degrees below zero
números pares/impares/ primos	even/odd/prime numbers
dos nueveavos dividido por tres sieteavos (see 10.12.2 for discussion of *-avo*)	two-ninths divided by three-sevenths
diez elevado al cubo/sexto/noveno	ten to the third/sixth/ninth

10.16 Numerals: rules for writing

There is no universal agreement about the rules for writing numbers. The following recommendations reflect Martínez de Sousa (1974), 294–5, checked against the *Libro de estilo* of *El País*. Figures are used:

(a) for all numbers over nine;

(b) for all numbers, when some of them are over nine: *3 ministros, 45 senadores y 100 diputados* 'three ministers, 45 senators and 100 members of Congress' (example from *Libro de estilo de El País*). Approximate numbers are, however, spelt out. See **(b)** below;

(c) in timetables: *salida a las 20.30* 'departure at 2030', *llegada a las 09.15* 'arrival at 0915';

(d) for dates: *el 23 de marzo de 1995* (occasionally seen written 1.995, although use of the point is censured by all the authorities). See 32.9 for discussion of the format of dates. Numbers are used for years (*1998, 2005*) but not for decades: *los años noventa* 'the nineties'.

(e) For exact figures, including addresses: *2,38 kilómetros* '2.38 km', *58 por ciento* '58 per cent', *419 páginas* '419 pages', *63 grados bajo cero* '63 degrees below zero',

223 habitantes '223 inhabitants', *Avenida de la Libertad 7, 2° izquierdo* '7 Liberty Avenue, left-hand flat/apartment on second floor'.

Words are used:

(a) for time elapsed: *veinticinco años* 'twenty-five years', *han pasado quince segundos* 'fifteen seconds have gone by';
(b) for approximate figures: *hubo más de quinientos heridos* 'there were more than five hundred injured';
(c) for numbers that are quoted as spoken by someone: *me dijo que quería comprar quince* 'he told me wanted to buy fifteen';
(d) for telling the time (in literary works): *llegó a las diez y media/a las cuatro cuarenta y cinco* 'he arrived a 10.30'/'at 4.45'.

Note

It is considered bad written style to begin a sentence with a number except in headlines and abbreviated messages. *El País* expressly forbids its journalists to open with *Diez personas resultaron heridas* . . . 'Ten persons were injured . . .': this should be recast as *Un total de diez personas resultaron heridas* (*Libro de estilo*, 10.10).

10.17 Telephone numbers

The *Libro de estilo* of *El País* recommends that phone numbers should be expressed by pairs: 54-06-72, spoken as *cincuenta y cuatro-cero seis-setenta y dos*, and this is indeed the usual way that phone numbers are said in Spanish. If the number of figures is uneven, the first group may be said as a combination of hundreds: *542-67-22*, spoken as *quinientos-cuarenta y dos-sesenta y siete-veintidós*. *Cinco-cuarenta y dos-sesenta y siete-veintidós* is also common in speech. Codes and extensions are sometimes written in brackets: (033) 527-76-89 (19) = 033-527 7689 (ext. 19). As the examples show, phone numbers are optionally written with hyphens separating the figures that are spoken as single numbers.

11

Personal pronouns

Index to chapter

The use of the third-person object pronouns *le* and *lo* is discussed separately in Chapter 12. For possessive adjectives and pronouns, see Chapter 8. For the pronoun *se* and pronominal (i.e. 'reflexive') verbs in general, see Chapters 26 and 28.

11.1 Classification and forms

'Subject' pronouns are used to emphasize the subject of a verb: *yo hablo*, 'I am talking', *él duerme* '*he* is sleeping'. See 11.2.1 for details of their use.

'Object' pronouns (other than third-person) are used either for both direct objects and indirect objects: *te quiero* 'I love you', *te hablo* 'I'm talking **to** you', *nos vio* 'he saw us', *nos dio* 'he gave **(to)** us'. This dual function means that there is usually no need to distinguish between 'direct' and 'indirect' object pronouns in Spanish except in the case of the third person, where the difference between the 'direct' object forms (*lo/la/los/las*) and the 'indirect' forms (*le/les*) only partly coincides with the traditional distinction between direct and indirect objects. This latter problem is discussed separately in Chapter 12.

Spanish has an incomplete set of prepositional personal pronouns (*mí*, *ti*, *sí*) which must be used after prepositions. The ordinary subject pronouns are used in the other persons. See 11.5.

Se is traditionally called a 'reflexive' third-person object pronoun, but it is usually not reflexive and it sometimes apparently functions as a subject. It is discussed at length in Chapters 26 and 28.

This table contains all the personal pronoun forms currently in use:

Person	Emphatic subject	Object	Prepositional	
		Singular		
1st	*yo*	*me*	*mí*	I
2nd	*tú*	*te*	*ti*	you (familiar)
	vos	*te*	*vos*	you (familiar)[1]
	usted	*lo/la/le*	*usted*	you (polite)
3rd	*él*	*lo/le*	*él*	he, it
	ella	*la/le*	*ella*	she, it
	ello[2]	*lo/le*	*ello*	it (neuter)
		se[3]	*sí*	'reflexive'
		Plural		
1st	*nosotros*	*nos*	*nosotros*	we (masculine)
	nosotras	*nos*	*nosotras*	we (feminine)
2nd	*vosotros*	*os*	*vosotros*	you (familiar masculine, Spain)
	vosotras	*os*	*vosotras*	you (familiar feminine, Spain)
	ustedes	*los/las/les*	*ustedes*	you (polite, also familiar in Latin America)
3rd	*ellos*	*los/les*	*ellos*	they (masculine)
	ellas	*las/les*	*ellas*	they (feminine)
		se[3]	*sí*	'reflexive'

11.2 Use of subject pronouns

11.2.1 Emphasis

The ordinary subject pronoun is expressed by the verb ending: *hablo* 'I speak', *habló* 'he/she/you/it spoke', *vendimos* 'we sold', *salieron* 'they/you went out', etc. The forms *yo/tú/él/ella/ustedes/ellos/ellas* are therefore usually only required for emphasis or contrast:

Estuve enfermo	I was ill/sick
Yo estuve enfermo	*I* was ill/sick
Hablas mucho	You talk a lot
Tú hablas mucho	*You* talk a lot
Es contable	(S)he is/You (*usted*) are an accountant

It is a bad error, common among English speakers, to use Spanish subject pronouns unnecessarily. To do so draws confusing attention to the subject of the verb, as in an English sentence pronounced with unnecessary stress on the pronoun, e.g. '*I* got up at eight, *I* showered, *I* had coffee, *I* went to work ... '. Spanish subject pronouns are used only:

---

[1] In parts of Latin America only: acceptability dependent on country and style: see 11.3.1.
[2] Discussed at 7.3.
[3] Discussed in Chapters 26 and 28.

(a) when the pronoun stands alone:

—*¿Quién ha venido?* —**Ellos**	'Who's come?' 'They have'
—*¿Quién lo ha hecho?* —**Nosotros**	'Who did it?' 'We did'
—*¿Quién es?* —**Yo**	'Who is it?' 'Me'

(b) When there is a change of subject (not necessarily within the same sentence) and the subjects are contrasted with one another:

Tú *eres listo, pero* **ella** *es genial*	You're clever, but she's a genius
Mi mujer trabaja y **yo** *me quedo en casa con los niños*	My wife works and I stay at home with the children
¿Mami le cuenta a Dios que Mita no va a misa y que **yo** *me porto mal?* (M. Puig, Argentina, dialogue)	Does Mummy tell God that Mita doesn't go to Mass and that I'm naughty?
——*A París no llegamos nunca —le dio la razón Tita. —Perfecto —celebré* **yo** (A. Bryce Echenique, Peru, dialogue)	'We'll never get to Paris,' Tita agreed. 'Great,' I said enthusiastically.

(c) To stress the subject pronoun (this is really only an instance of **b** in which the other subject has been omitted):

Pues **yo** *no quiero salir*	Well **I** don't want to go out (even if you do)
Tú *haz lo que te dé la gana*	**You** do whatever you like (implies 'what do I care?')

(d) *Usted/ustedes* / 'you' are used more frequently, either to avoid ambiguity or to stress the polite tone of an utterance:

¿Adónde van ustedes?	Where are you going?
Si (usted) quiere, iré con usted	If you like, I'll go with you

(e) Subject pronouns may occasionally be used to clarify ambiguous verb endings: *yo tenía/él tenía* 'I had' / 'he had', *que yo fuese/que él fuese* 'that I should go/be' / 'that he should go/be'. However, in both cases context usually makes the meaning clear.

Note

English can focus or emphasize almost any word simply by pronouncing it louder, e.g. 'you want to talk to **her** not to her brother' (first 'her' loud). Spanish uses other devices, e.g. cleft sentences (*es con ella con la que deberías hablar, no con su hermano*) or word order: *con ella deberías hablar, no con su hermano*. The English system of stress and intonation usually produces an unfortunate effect when carried over into Spanish. Further examples (bold type in English shows stress and loudness): 'where are **you** going?'*¿tú adónde vas?/¿adónde vas tú?*, 'I'm talking to **you**' *contigo es con quien estoy hablando*, 'what's **he** doing?'*¿y él qué está haciendo?/¿qué está haciendo él?*, '**you're** not coming with **us**' *con nosotros no vienes tú/tú con nosotros no vienes*'. See 11.15 and 37.5 for more remarks on this subject.

11.2.2 Subject pronouns for inanimate nouns

Él/ella/ellos/ellas may translate 'it' or 'them' when applied to inanimate things, but they are usually taken to stand for human beings when they are used as the subject of a verb. One does not therefore pronominalize *el viento sopla* 'the wind's blowing' as **él sopla*, which is understood as '(s)he's blowing'; *sopla* = 'it's blowing'. But subject pronouns are sometimes used in Latin America for an inanimate subject where Peninsular speakers would use either no pronoun at all or an appropriate form of *éste* 'this' / 'the latter':

*La "oposición" ha desaparecido de la radio, de la televisión y de la prensa diaria en el Perú. **Ella** subsiste, mínima, hostigada, desde las columnas de todos los periódicos* (M. Vargas Llosa, Peru)	The 'opposition' has vanished from radio, television and daily press in Peru. It continues to operate, minimal, harassed, from the opinion columns of all the newspapers

11.3 Formal and informal modes of address

11.3.1 *Voseo*

In Spain, *vos* occurs only in archaic styles. But *vos* is still used instead of *tú* in many parts of Latin America, although it may be too intimate for casual use by foreigners. It is everywhere stylistically informal, and is replaced by *tú* in prayers and other solemn language: God, Jesus and the Virgin are usually addressed as *tú*, not as *vos*. It is used in the spoken language of all social circles in Argentina, and in most social circles in Uruguay, Paraguay and most of Central America. It is also used in the extreme south of Mexico. In Colombia, Chile, Ecuador and Venezuela it is often heard, is possibly spreading, but may be considered 'lower-class' or provincial, although usage and attitudes vary locally: in Chile, for example, it is shunned by middle and upper-class persons. It is not usual in Bolivia, Peru, Panama, Cuba, Mexico and Puerto Rico, but there are local pockets of *voseo* in some of these countries. Even where *voseo* is current in speech, *tú* is often written, even in intimate letters.

The possessive adjective for *vos* is *tu/tus*, the object pronoun is *te*, and the prepositional form is *vos*: *¿**te** das cuenta de que estoy hablando de **vos** y de **tu** amiga?* 'do you realize I'm talking about you and your friend?' The verb forms used with *vos* fluctuate according to region and are best learnt locally. For details on the verb forms used with Argentine *voseo* see 13.1. and 16.2.8.

Note

Voseo descends from the Golden-Age use of *vos* as a polite second-person singular pronoun. *Vos* was still heard in early nineteenth-century Spain, to judge from Larra's *Artículos de costumbres* of the 1830s, and it survives in Spain in ritual language in official documents, in some prayers, when addressing the king on very formal occasions, and in pseudo-archaic style, e.g. in Buero Vallejo's play *Las meninas* (in this case it is comparable to the use of 'thou' in modern English). In Spain this archaic singular pronoun *vos* takes the normal verb endings for *vosotros*, and the possessive adjective/pronoun is *vuestro/a/os/as*.

11.3.2 *Tú* (*vos*) or *usted*?

The basic rule as far as Spain is concerned is that *tú* is used for anyone with whom one is on first-name terms.[4] *Tú* is therefore required between friends, family members, when speaking to children or to animals, generally between strangers under the age of about thirty, and in some prayers.[5]

---

[4] An exception would be an employer talking to an employee of long standing, when both first name and *usted* might be appropriate, as in this remark by a woman to her maid: —*Bueno, Pura, pues hasta mañana. Y cierre al salir.* (C. Martín Gaite, Spain, dialogue) 'Right, Pura, well, see you tomorrow. And shut the door on the way out.'

[5] The archaic *vos* is sometimes found in traditional prayers, e.g. *a mí me pesa, pésame Señor de haber**os** ofendido . . . por ser **vos** quien sois, bondad infinita, y porque **os** amo sobre todas las cosas* 'I am sorry, I am sorry, oh Lord, infinite goodness, for offending Thee, for I love Thee above all things', etc.

It therefore follows that, in Spain, *tú* is used much more readily than the French *tu* or German *Du*. It is much more widespread than fifty years ago, and it is sometimes considered the mark of a democratic outlook. However, *tú/vos* should not be said to persons in authority or to older strangers or elderly persons unless they invite its use. Use of *tú* where *usted* is expected may express contempt or threat: criminals call their victims *tú*, not *usted*.

Note

Generalization about the use of *tú* and *usted* is hazardous. In most of Latin America *tú/vos* is not used so readily as in Spain, and one also finds varieties (e.g. Antioquía, Colombia) where all three pronouns, *usted*, *tú* and *vos*, may be found addressed to the same person, depending on the degree of intimacy reached at any moment. Chilean Spanish is unusual in that *usted* can also be used for familiar address, which produces curious mixtures of pronouns in a single utterance. In the following extract from a Chilean play an upper-class mother sitting on the beach calls to her little son: *Alvarito, **métase** un poco al agua. **Mójese** las patitas siquiera* ... *¿**Ves** que es rica el agüita?* (S. Vodanovic) 'Alvarito, go into the water a bit. At least get your feet wet ... Do you see how lovely the water is?'

11.3.3 *Vosotros/as* or *ustedes*?

Vosotros (*vosotras* to two or more females) is the plural of *tú* and is used in Spain for two or more persons with whom the speaker is on first-name terms. It is used in all styles in standard European Spanish, but in Latin America it is replaced by *ustedes* in all but archaic styles, a phenomenon also found in the Canary Islands and locally in popular speech in southern Spain. A mother in Latin America addresses her child as *tú* or, in some places, as *vos*, and her children as *ustedes*. Even animals are called *ustedes* in Latin America.

Note

Vosotros and its possessive *vuestro* is found in business correspondence, flowery speeches and similar solemn or formal texts in Latin America, cf ... *dada la recomposición de relaciones entre la Argentina y vuestro país* ' ... given the re-establishment of relations between Argentina and your country' (from a business letter sent to England). The reasoning behind this is, apparently, that since *vosotros* is archaic in Latin America, it must therefore be suitable for very formal or elevated styles. But in Spain it is, in fact, familiar in tone.

11.3.4 Use of *usted, ustedes*

These are polite forms roughly equivalent to French *vous*, German *Sie* – but French and German usage is a poor guide, so see 11.3.2 and 11.3.3 for details of the relationship between *tú/vos* and *usted/ustedes*. Since they descend from the archaic formula *Vuestra Merced* 'Your Grace', these pronouns require third-person verb forms: *usted habla* 'you speak', *ustedes hablan* 'you (plural) speak'. In writing, *usted/ustedes* may optionally be abbreviated to *V./Vs., Vd./Vds.,* or, most usually in the twentieth century, *Ud./Uds.* Object forms of *usted/ustedes* are discussed under third-person pronouns (11.7.3).

Notes

(i) As subject pronouns *usted/ustedes* need only appear once at the beginning of a text or utterance and then occasionally thereafter to recall the politeness of tone. Whereas total omission of *usted/ustedes* may sound too informal, constant repetition may sound obsequious.

(ii) Agreement when one subject is *tú* and the other *usted* or *ustedes*, or one *vosotros* and the other *usted/ustedes*, is as for *ustedes*: *tú y usted, quédense aquí* 'you and you stay here'.

11.4 *Nosotros/as, nos*

Females referring to themselves and to other females should use *nosotras*.

The first-person plural is constantly used in books and articles when the author is modestly referring to her/himself. It is less pompous than the English 'royal we': *en este trabajo* **hemos** *procurado enfocar el problema de la inflación desde . . .* 'in this work I ('we') have tried to approach the problem of inflation from . . . '.

Nos for *nosotros* is obsolete, but is used by popes, bishops and monarchs in official documents or ritual utterances.

Note

The following construction is peculiar to Latin America, especially Argentina and other southern countries: **fuimos con** *mi hermano* (Spain *fui con mi hermano/mi hermano y yo fuimos*) 'I went with my brother' (lit. 'we went with my brother'), *y así nos fuimos a la Patagonia, con Matilde* (E. Sábato, Argentina, interview; Spain *fui con Matilde/Matilde y yo fuimos*) 'so Matilde and I went to Patagonia'.

11.5 Forms of pronouns after prepositions

11.5.1 Use after prepositions

Only *yo, tú* and *se* have separate prepositional forms: *mí, ti* and *sí* (the latter is discussed at 11.5.3). In the other cases the normal subject forms, *él, ella, ello, nosotros, vosotros, usted/ustedes, ellos/ellas*, are used after prepositions. *Mí* and *sí* are written with an accent to distinguish them from *mi* 'my' and *si* 'if'. *Ti* is not written with an accent, a fact constantly forgotten by foreigners and natives alike.

No sabe nada de mí	He knows nothing about me
No tengo nada contra ti	I've nothing against you
Creo en vos (Argentina, etc.)	I believe in you
no delante de usted	not in front of you
Me refiero a él/ella	I'm referring to him/her
Confiamos en ustedes/vosotros/vosotras	We trust in you
Corrió tras ellos	He ran after them
aparte de ellas	except for them (fem.)

However, seven prepositions or preposition-like words require the ordinary form of all the subject pronouns (but the pronoun *se* obeys slightly different rules – see 11.5.3 note i). These are: *entre* 'between'/'among' but see note (iii); *excepto* 'except', *hasta* when it means 'even' rather than 'as far as', *incluso* 'including'/'even', *menos* 'except' *salvo* 'except'/'save', *según* 'according to':

Todos lo hicieron menos/excepto/salvo tú	They all did it except/save you
Que se quede entre tú y yo	Let's keep it between you and me
Hasta tú puedes hacer eso . . .	Even you can do that . . .
según tú y él	according to you and him

Notes

(i) Note also the set phrases *de* **tú** *a* **tú** 'on equal terms', *hablar de* **tú** (i.e. *tutear*) 'to address someone as *tú*'.

(ii) For constructions like *?detrás tuyo* for *detrás de ti* 'behind you', or *?delante mío* for *delante de mí* 'in front of me' (frequent in colloquial Latin-American Spanish, substandard or popular in Spain), see 8.7.

(iii) *Mí* is used after *entre* in the set phrase *entre mí* as in *esto va a acabar mal, decía entre mí* 'this is going to end badly, I said to myself'.

There is a popular tendency in some regions to use the prepositional forms with *entre* when this refers to actual spatial location: *esta noche a la Inés la voy a poner a dormir en mi cama, entre mí y la Pelusa* (M. Puig, Argentina, dialogue) 'tonight I'm going to put Inés to sleep in my bed between me and Pelusa' (*la Inés* for *Inés* is popular style; see 3.2.21).

11.5.2 *Conmigo, contigo*

These special forms are used instead of *con + yo, con + tú*: *¿vienes conmigo?* 'are you coming with me?', *no quiero discutir contigo* 'I don't want to argue with you'. In areas of *voseo*, *contigo* is rarely heard: *no quiero discutir con vos* 'I don't want to argue with you'.

11.5.3 *Sí, consigo*

These are special prepositional forms of the pronoun *se*. *Sí* is used after prepositions other than *con*. The accent distinguishes it from *si* meaning 'if'. *Consigo* is used for *con + se* and means 'with himself/herself'. *Sí* is often combined with *mismo* when it is used reflexively:

No se refiere a sí misma	She's not referring to herself
Este fenómeno ya es muy interesante de por sí	This phenomenon is in itself very interesting
Un brillante que para sí lo quisieran muchos (advertisement)	a diamond many would like for themselves
Volvió en sí	(S)he came round (regained consciousness)
Colocó el vaso junto a sí (L. Otero, Cuba)	He put the glass next to himself
. . . tan perezosa que difícilmente era capaz de leer por sí sola	. . . so lazy that she was hardly able to read by herself
No puede dar más de sí	(S)he's doing the best (s)he can
Está disgustada consigo misma	She's cross with herself

Notes

(i) *Se* is unique in being the only pronoun requiring a prepositional form after *entre*: *entre* **tú** y **yo** 'between you and me', but *entre* **sí** 'among themselves': *hablan castellano entre sí* (or *entre ellos*) 'they speak Spanish among themselves'. *Entre sí* may also mean 'to himself': *dijo entre sí* 'he said to himself'/'he murmured under his breath'.

(ii) *Sí* is not always really 'reflexive' as the following example shows: *el acento sirve para que se distingan los ingleses entre sí* 'accent enables Englishmen to distinguish themselves from one another'.

(iii) There is a curious colloquial tendency to reject other persons of *volver en sí* 'to regain consciousness' and *dar de sí* 'to give of oneself'. One hears *recobré el conocimiento* (correct) or even *?volví en sí*, but the expected *volví en mí* is often avoided, even by educated speakers (although it is heard, especially when the pronoun is first-person: the last of the following examples reflects the hesitation of some speakers): *volví en sí ya estando en la clínica* (interview, *El Nacional*, Mexico) 'I came round when I was (lit. 'already being') in the clinic', —*Perdona, ¿no te importa ponerte de pie para que te veamos?* —*Estoy de pie, es que no doy más de sí* (E. Arenas, dialogue, Spain) 'Excuse me, would you mind standing up so we can see you?' 'I *am* standing up. This is all there is of me', *cuando volví en sí, o en mí, escuché un rumor* (S. Puértolas, dialogue, Spain) 'when I came round I heard a noise'.

(iv) There is a good deal of disagreement about *sí* in the modern language. *Sí* is required when it does not refer to identified persons: *hay muchos que hablan mucho de sí (mismos)* 'there are a lot of people who talk about themselves a lot', but when *sí* refers to a specific person, the modern tendency is to prefer a non-reflexive prepositional pronoun. In answer to a questionnaire, the great majority of informants (professional people and students, Spanish) rejected *sí* in the following sentences:[6] *hablan francés entre* **ellos** (*?entre sí*) 'they speak French among themselves', *lo mantuvo contra* **ella** *con uno de sus brazos* (E. Sábato, Argentina) 'she held him against herself with one arm', *tenía las manos apoyadas en la barra, delante de* **él** (*ante sí*) 'his hands were resting on the bar, in front of him(self)'. In the previous example, *ante sí* is tolerable, since *ante* is itself literary. But *delante de él* is normal in speech, although some speakers respect the difference between 'in front of him(self)' and 'in front of him' (someone else).

(v) *Sí* seems to be avoided with *usted*, probably because the latter is unconsciously felt to be second-person and the former third-person: *usted tiene ante* **usted** *a un hombre que . . .* (interview, *El Nacional*, Mexico) 'you have before you a man who . . .', *guárdeselo para* **usted** 'keep it for yourself', *yo sé que usted toca para* **usted** *misma* (J. Cortázar, Argentina, dialogue; *?para sí misma*) 'I know you play (music) for yourself'.

(vi) The French pronoun *soi* has suffered a similar erosion over the years, and has been replaced in many contexts by *lui-même, elle-même* (*él mismo, ella misma*).

11.6 Pronoun agreement in English and Spanish

Verbs sometimes agree with personal pronouns in ways unfamiliar to English speakers:

Soy yo/Somos nosotros/Fuisteis vosotros/Fueron ellos	It's me/It's us/It was you/It was them (lit. 'I am me', 'we are we', 'you were you', 'they were they')
El feo de la foto **eres** *tú*	The ugly one in the photo is you
Debería volver a escribir, pero no tiene estímulos ya. Y luego que tampoco la **ayudamos** **nadie** (C. Martín Gaite, Spain, dialogue)	She ought to start writing again, but there's nothing to stimulate her any more. And after all, none of us help her either
—*¿Quién ha dicho eso?*—**He** *sido yo* (Lat. Am. *¿Quién dijo eso? Fui yo*)	'Who said that?' 'It was me'

When answering the phone one says *soy Ana* 'it's Ana (here)' (lit. 'I'm Ana'), *soy Antonio* 'it's Antonio speaking'. *Es Ana* 'it's Ana' is only possible when said by someone else about her.

11.7 Object pronouns

The term 'object pronouns' is used in this book to refer to the forms *me, te, lo, la, le, nos, os, los, las, les* and *se* – although the latter apparently sometimes functions as a grammatical subject, as in *se vive* 'one lives', *se está mejor aquí* 'one's better off here'. See 28.6 for further discussion of this construction. Traditional grammars often divide these pronouns into two lists, 'accusative' or 'direct object' pronouns and 'dative' or 'indirect object' pronouns; but only the third-person set has two forms (*le/les* as opposed to *lo/la/los/las*), and the difference between them only partly coincides with the traditional distinction between 'indirect' and 'direct' objects. This difference is discussed separately in Chapter 12. For 'pronominal' verbs (sometimes inaccurately called 'reflexive' verbs), see Chapter 26.

---

[6] G. DeMello's (1996) survey of spoken Spanish in twelve capitals shows that use of *sí* is more common than generally supposed, especially in phrases like *de por sí* 'in itself', *por sí, en sí (mismo)* 'in itself'.

11.7.1 Forms of first- and second-person object pronouns

	Singular	Plural
First person	*me*	*nos*
Second person	*te*	*os* (see note iii)

Notes

(i) *Usted/Ustedes* take third-person object pronouns: *los vi a ustedes ayer* 'I saw you (plural) yes-terday'. See 11.7.3.

(ii) *Te* is the object form of *tú* and of *vos* (where *vos* is used): *vos sabés que te vi ayer* (Argentina) 'you know I saw you yesterday', *vos te arrepentirás* (Argentina) 'you'll be sorry'.

(iii) *Os* corresponds to *vosotros* and is therefore not heard in Latin America, where *ustedes* is used for both polite and familiar address; see 11.3.3 for discussion.

11.7.2 Use of first- and second-person object pronouns

The main problem raised for the English-speaking learner by these (and by the third-person) object pronouns is the variety of translations possible for each form. Spanish object pronouns merely indicate the person 'affected' by a verb phrase: they do not clearly indicate *how* the object is affected – this must be worked out from the meaning of the verb, from context or by common sense. English makes the meaning much more explicit, as can be seen from the following thirteen different translations of *me*:

Me han visto	They've seen **me**
Me dejó una finca	He left an estate **to me**
Me ha aparcado el coche	She's parked the car **for me**
Me compró una agenda	He bought a diary **off/from me**
Me sacaron tres balas	They took three bullets **out of me**
Me han quitado a mis hijos	They've taken my children **from me** (note translation)
Me tiene envidia	She's envious **of me**
Me tiró una bola de nieve	He threw a snowball **at me**
Me encontraron mil pesetas	They found 1,000 pesetas **on me**
Me echaron una manta	They threw a blanket **over me**
Voy a comprarme un helado	I'm going to buy **myself** an ice cream
Siempre me pone pegas	She always finds fault **with me**
Me rompió el brazo	He broke **my** arm

Lists A and B (at 12.3 and 12.4) show numerous further examples of sentences in which *me/te/os/nos* could be substituted for *le/les* or *lo/la/los* where the meaning is appropriate. A special case arises when the object pronoun and the subject pronoun (usually indicated by the verb ending) refer to the same person or thing, e.g. *me lavo* 'I'm washing (myself)', *te equivocaste* 'you were mistaken', *Miguel se va* 'Miguel's leaving', *nos caímos* 'we fell over'. We call such verbs 'pronominal verbs' and discuss them in Chapter 26.

11.7.3 Use of third-person object pronouns

The distinction between *le/les* and *lo/la/los/las* is discussed in Chapter 12. These overworked pronouns also have a second-person meaning since they are used for *usted/ustedes* 'you':

Doctora Smith, le aseguro que la llamé ayer	Dr Smith (fem.), I assure you I rang you/her yesterday
Le vi ayer (Spain only; see 12.5.1 and 12.5.2)	I saw you/him yesterday
Lo vi ayer (Latin America and, optionally, Spain too)	I saw it/him/you yesterday
Los vi ayer	I saw you/them yesterday

11.7.4 Constraints on the number of object pronouns

As far as the meaning of object pronouns is concerned, Spanish allows the following combinations of personal object pronouns before a verb:

(a) One direct object pronoun: *la vi* 'I saw her/it'.
(b) One indirect object pronoun *me dijiste* 'you said to me'.
(c) An indirect object pronoun followed by a direct object pronoun *me lo diste* 'you gave it to me', *se lo dieron* 'they gave it to him/her/you/them'.
(d) Occasionally, two indirect object pronouns: *me le has estropeado la camisa* 'you've spoilt his shirt for me!' This is not very common: see 11.11 and 11.12 for a discussion.
(e) Infrequently, a direct object followed by an indirect object, as in *¡qué guapa te me has puesto!* 'how attractive you have made yourself for me!': see 11.12 note (iii).

The combination of two **direct** object pronouns is not possible in Spanish and very peculiar in English, cf. ?'he was declared president, and after they declared **him it**, he went on to . . . ', which would have to be recast in Spanish: *después de que le/lo nombraran presidente, pasó a . . .* This constraint on the use of direct object pronouns in Spanish clarifies the difference between passive and impersonal *se*. See 28.4.1.

11.8 Pronouns with verbs of motion

Object pronouns cannot replace the preposition *a* plus a noun if mere physical arrival or approach is involved: *voy a la reunión – voy allí* (not **le voy*) 'I'm going to the meeting' – 'I'm going to it'; *acude a ella* 'he goes to her', not **le acude*:

Cuando tiene problemas siempre va a ella	When he has problems he always goes to her
Me dirijo a ustedes	I'm turning to you/addressing you/writing to you
todo el occidente que vino a nosotros . . . (M. Vargas Llosa, Peru)	the whole of the West (i.e. western world) which came to us . . .
Suele recurrir a él cuando no le queda más remedio	(S)he usually turns to him when (s)he has no alternative

However, object pronouns are often used colloquially with the following verbs, particularly if the verb is third-person:

Él se le acercó por la espalda (J. Marsé, Spain)	He approached her from behind
Ella se le reunió al doblar la esquina (L. Goytisolo, Spain)	She caught up with him as she turned the corner
Hoy, el que se te acerca es a menudo un drogadicto (A. Bryce Echenique, dialogue, Peru)	Nowadays, the person coming up to you is often a drug-addict
No sólo los sollozos de los niños se alzaron entonces, sino que se les unieron los de los sirvientes (José Donoso, Chile)	Not only did sobbing from the children break out then, but the servants' (sobs) were added to it

Notes

(i) This construction is rare in the first and second persons: *se le opuso* 'he opposed him', but *te opusiste a él* 'you opposed him' rather than *?te le opusiste*. Forms with first and second-person subjects occur in Latin America, especially in Mexico (J. Lope Blanch 1991, 20), and sentences like *me le acerqué* (i.e. *me acerqué a él*) 'I approached him', *te ruego que te nos incorpores* (for . . . *que te incorpores a nosotros*) 'I'm asking you to join us' are common, cf. *me le acerqué y le dije* . . . (J. L. Borges, Argentina) 'I went up to him and said to him . . .'.

(ii) *Se le puso delante, se me puso delante* '(s)he stood in front of him', '(s)he/you stood in front of me' occur colloquially for *se puso delante de él/se puso delante de mí*, and are more emotional in tone.

(iii) The example from José Donoso is an exception to the rule that object pronouns are not used with such verbs when the sentence refers to a non-human entity: the normal construction would be *se acercó al puente* 'he approached the bridge' > *se acercó a él* 'he approached it', not **se le acercó*.

(iv) Object pronouns are used to denote a person affected by *llegar* and *venirse* (if their subject is inanimate), and by *venir con*: *siempre me viene con pejigueras* 'he's always coming to me with irritating details', *cuando me llegó la noticia de su triunfo* . . . 'when news of his triumph reached me . . .', *el armario se le vino encima* 'the cupboard/(US 'closet') collapsed on him/her/you', *a mí no me venga usted con cuentos porque yo todo lo sé* (A. Bryce Echenique, dialogue, Peru) 'don't come to me with stories because I know all about it'.

(v) In *le viene a decir que* . . . 'he's coming to tell him that . . .' the *le* belongs to the *decir*: *viene a decirle que* . . . . In *le viene bien* 'it suits him' and *¿qué tal te va?* 'how are things going'/'how're you doing?', advantage, not motion, is involved.

11.9 Pronouns with *ser* and *resultar*

(a) With adjectives:

The choice is between *me es necesario* and *es necesario para mí* 'it's necessary for me'. The former is possible with *ser* only if the adjective expresses a meaning included in List A, 12.3. *Resultar* allows the construction with a wider range of adjectives, and may be thought of as the 'involving' counterpart of *ser*:

Les es/resulta necesario	It's necessary for them
Me es/resulta importante	It's important to me
Nos era imprescindible contactar a sus padres	It was absolutely necessary for us to contact her parents
Le era más fácil soportar los dolores ajenos que los propios (G. García Márquez, Colombia)	It was easier for him to put up with other people's suffering rather than his own
Voy a serle muy franca (A. Bryce Echenique, dialogue, Peru)	I'm going to be very frank with you

but

 La casa era demasiado blanca para mí/me The house was too white for me
  resultaba demasiado blanca (not *me era
  demasiado blanca)
 Era muy feo para ella **It** was very ugly for her
 Le resultaba muy feo **He** seemed very ugly to her

The following list will give an idea of the kind of adjective that can take object pronouns with *ser*:

agradable/desagradable agreeable/
 disagreeable
conocido/desconocido known/unknown
conveniente/inconveniente suitable/
 unsuitable
fácil/difícil easy/difficult
grato/ingrato pleasing/displeasing
indiferente indifferent
leal loyal

molesto bothersome
necesario/innecesario necessary/unnecessary
permitido/prohibido allowed/prohibited
posible/imposible possible/impossible
simpático/antipático nice/nasty (persons)
sincero, franco sincere, frank
suficiente/insuficiente sufficient/insufficient
urgente urgent
útil/inútil useful/useless

Notes

(i) Many of these adjectives could also be constructed with *para* or *con*: *es conveniente para ellos/les es conveniente* 'it's suitable for/to them', *voy a ser franco con usted/le voy a ser franco* 'I'll be frank with you'. The object pronouns convey a higher level of personal involvement.
(ii) *Grande, pequeño* take *le/les* if they mean 'too big', 'too small': *ese puesto le está grande* 'that job's too big for him'. Otherwise *resultar* or *ser para* must be used: *es grande para él* 'it's big to/for him', etc.
(iii) The nuance conveyed by *resultar* is often virtually untranslatable. Compare *es feo* = 'it/he's ugly' and *resulta feo* 'the effect is ugly'/'he/it is ugly as a result'.

(b) *Ser* plus personal pronouns with nouns:

This occurs only with a few nouns, most derived from or close in meaning to the adjectives listed above:

 Si le es molestia, dígamelo If it's a nuisance for you, tell me
 Nos es de interés . . . It's of interest to us . . .
 Me/Le era un gran placer/Era un gran placer It was a great pleasure for/to
  para mí/él me/him, etc.

Notes

(i) Spanish does not allow a pronominal construction in translations of sentences like 'I was always a good mother **to him**': *siempre fui una buena madre para él* (not **siempre le fui . . .*).
(ii) *Resultar* has limited use with nouns: *pues atrévase a contarla . . . Resultaría una gran novela* (C. Martín Gaite, dialogue, Spain) 'well, have the courage to tell it [*la historia*]. It would make a great novel', *mi temporada aquí me está resultando un verdadero viaje de estudios* (J. L. Borges, Argentina, letter style) 'my stay here is turning out to be a real study trip for me', *la señorita María ha resultado una excelente secretaria* (J. J. Arreola, Mexico) 'Señorita María has turned out to be an excellent secretary', *si le resulta un problema . . .* 'if it turns out to be a problem to you . . .'.

11.10 'Resumptive' *lo* with *ser, estar, parecer* and *hay*

The predicate of *ser, estar* and *parecer* is 'echoed' or resumed by *lo*: —*Parece buena la tierra desde aquí.* —*Lo es.* '"The land looks good from here." "It is."' This construction is discussed at 7.4, note (i). For *lo hay, los hay/las hay*, etc., see 30.2.2.

11.11 Object pronouns used to denote personal involvement

Object pronouns may simply show that a person is intensely affected, as in the indignant Frenchman's *regardez-moi* ça! 'just look at that for me!', 'just look at that, will you!' Usually the effect is untranslatable in standard English, but popular English sometimes uses 'on me', 'on you', etc., in order to include the person affected: *se me han ido de casa* 'they've left home "on me"', *se le ha averiado el coche* 'his car's broken down "on him"'. In Spanish this device is most common when there is a strong emotional involvement on the speaker's part, e.g. when parents are speaking about their child:

Me le has estropeado tres camisas	You've spoilt three of his shirts for me
—*Pues, yo eché a una porque me fumaba y ahora tengo otra que, además de fumar, me bebe* (E. Arenas, Spain, dialogue, very colloquial)	Well, I fired one [maid] because she smoked ('on me') and now I've got another who not only smokes but drinks ('on me')
Los alumnos se me habían largado a una manifestación (A. Bryce Echenique, dialogue, Peru)	The students (better 'my students') had gone off to a demonstration
No estará pensando embalsamarnos al Presidente . . . (I. Allende, Chile, dialogue)	You aren't thinking of having the President embalmed for us?
Mi suegra compró un reloj y al mes no le caminaba (A. Arrafut, dialogue, Cuba; Spain *no le funcionaba*)	My mother-in-law bought a watch and a month later it didn't work ('on her')
Sírvamele un café a la señorita (Argentina, quoted García (1975); possible, but rare in Spain)	Serve a coffee to the young lady for me
Cuídamele (or *cuídamelo*) *bien*	Look after him well for me
Péiname al niño	Do the child's hair for me

This device of including an interested party is used more in parts of Latin America than in Spain. *Me le pintaste la mesa* 'you painted the table for him for me' is apparently acceptable for some Latin American speakers. Peninsular Spanish tends to avoid clusters of two object pronouns when neither is a direct object, as is explained in note (i) of the next section.

11.12 Order of object pronouns

The invariable order of object pronouns when two or more appear together is:

1	2	3	4
se	*te/os*	*me/nos*	*le/lo/la/les/los/las*

i.e. *se*, if it occurs, comes first, second person precedes first person, and third-person pronouns come last:

María te lo dijo	Maria told it to you
Me lo habré dejado en casa	I must have left it at home
No querían comunicárnoslo	They didn't want to tell it to us
¿Por qué no se lo prueba?	Why don't you try it on?
Se te ha caído la tinta	You've dropped the ink
Nos los vamos a comprar	We're going to buy them for ourselves
Se nos ha vuelto listísimo	He's turned into a genius 'on us'

> *Yo me le fui encima, pero ella chilló*   I lunged at her, but she screamed
> (J. Cortázar, Argentina; Spain *yo me*
> *le eché encima*)

Notes

(i) As was mentioned at 11.7.4, the combinations of two indirect object pronouns occurs, albeit sporadically, in colloquial Peninsular Spanish, e.g. **te le** *dieron una paliza terrible* 'they gave him a terrific blow "on you"/"for you"', *écha****me****le un vistazo a esta carta* 'have a look at this letter for me'. But in practice it is usually avoided when the first pronoun is not *me*. Thus the following are not found: **te le dieron malas notas* 'they gave him bad grades "on you"', **nos te dieron una multa* 'they gave you a fine "on us"'.

In Spain *le* is constantly used as a direct object pronoun referring to a human male, so sentences like the following are possible: *al abuelo **nos le** llevamos de vacaciones todos los años* 'we take grandfather with us on holiday every year'. However, even in Spain this combination is usually avoided by replacing the *le* by *lo*: *al abuelo nos lo llevamos . . . .*

(ii) Reversal of the correct order with *se*, e.g. *?me se ha caído* for *se me ha caído* 'I've dropped it' (lit. 'it's fallen down "on me"'), *?¿me se oye?* for *¿se me oye?* 'can anyone hear me?'/'is anyone listening?', is a classic mistake of uneducated speech.

(iii) In the examples shown so far, the pronouns are all in the order indirect object–direct object (*te lo doy* 'I give it to you', etc.). As was mentioned at 11.7.4, the reverse order is occasionally seen, as in **te me** *han elogiado/alabado/encomiado mucho* 'they've praised/recommended you highly to me', *¡qué guapa* **te me** *has puesto!* 'how lovely you have become for/to me!' But generally the combination is avoided: one says *te han denunciado a ellos* 'they've reported you to them' not **te les han denunciado*, *nos mandaron a ellos* 'they sent us to them' not **nos les mandamos*.

11.13 Replacement of *le* by *se*

11.13.1 Se for *le* when the latter is followed by a pronoun beginning with *l*

If *le* or *les* are immediately followed by an object pronoun beginning with *l*, i.e. by *lo*, *la*, *los* or *las*, the *le* or *les* must be replaced by *se*: *le doy* 'I give to him/her/you' + *lo* 'it' > *se lo doy* 'I give **it** to him/her/you' – **never** **le lo doy*:

Quiero dárselo	I want to give it to him/her/you/them
Se lo dije a ella	I told her
Se lo dije a ellos	I told them (masc.)
*¿Quiere usted que **se** lo envuelva?*	Do you want me to wrap it for you?
*El guiso está a punto, pero no **se** lo voy a servir todavía*	The stew's ready but I'm not going to serve it to you (*usted* or *ustedes*) yet

Note

This phenomenon, which has no counterpart in French, Italian or Portuguese, is traditionally explained by the alleged ugliness of too many *l*s. This explanation is implausible, but it helps to remember that in Spanish two object pronouns beginning with *l* can never stand side by side. This is a strong rule: combinations of pronouns like **lelo*, **lela*, **lelos*, **leslo*, **leslos* are not heard anywhere in the Spanish-speaking world.

11.13.2 Latin American *se los* for *se lo*

The combination *se lo* is very ambiguous. For example, *se lo dije* may mean 'I told it to him, her, you (*usted*)', 'them' (*ellos* or *ellas*) or 'you' (*ustedes*)'. *A él/ella/usted/ ellos/ellas/ ustedes* may be added if context does not make the issue clear: *se lo dije a ustedes* 'I told **you**', etc.

There is a universal but grammatically illogical tendency in spontaneous Latin-American speech to show that *se* stands for *les* by pluralizing the direct object pronoun, i.e. ?*se los dije*, for *se lo dije* 'I told it to them':

*A un policía le había gustado más bien poco la gracia y se **los** había dicho* (J.Cortázar, Argentina, dialogue, for *se lo había dicho*)	One policeman didn't really like the joke and told them so
—Se los dije, hijos, ganó "Tierra y Libertad" (A. Mastretta, Mexico, dialogue; Spain *se lo dije* or, in this case, *os lo dije*)	I told you all/(US) 'I told you guys, "Land and Liberty" won'

This construction is very deep-rooted in Latin-American speech but it is vehemently rejected by Spaniards.[7] It is not accepted in formal written styles in Latin America.

11.14 Position of object pronouns

The position of object pronouns in relation to a verb depends on the form of the verb.

11.14.1 Pronouns with verbs in finite verbs

Pronouns come immediately before finite verb forms (i.e. all forms save the infinitive, gerund, participle and imperative) in the order given at 11.12. In compound tenses the pronouns are placed before the auxiliary verb:

Se los entregamos	We gave them (masc.) to him/her/it/them/you
Te los enviaré luego	I'll send you them (masc.) later
Os las guardaré (Spain)	I'll keep them (fem.) for you
La he visto	I've seen her/it/you
Se me ha roto el cinturón	My belt's broken

Notes

(i) No word may come between the object pronouns and a verb. In pronunciation these pronouns are unstressed: *te lo dijo* 'he said it to you' is pronounced *telodijo*, *os lo daré* 'I'll give it to you' is pronounced *oslodaré*, etc.

(ii) In pre-twentieth-century literary style, object pronouns were often joined to verbs in finite tenses: *contestóles así* 'he answered them thus' = *les contestó así*, *encontrábase exiliado* 'he found himself exiled' = *se encontraba exiliado*, *ocurriósele* 'it occurred to him/her' = *se le ocurrió*. Rules for this construction are omitted here since it is now extinct for practical purposes except in a few set phrases, e.g. *habráse visto* ... 'well, did you ever ...', *diríase* (literary) 'one might say', *dícese* (literary) 'it is said' (the latter survives in various forms in spoken Latin-American Spanish, e.g. *dizque*. See 28.4, etc. The construction is still occasionally found in burlesque or very flowery styles, and also in headlines in some Latin-American countries: *entrevístanse Gorbachov y Fidel en Moscú* (*Granma*, Cuba) 'Gorbachev and Fidel hold talks in Moscow'.

---

[7] DeMello (1992, 1) reports that in Mexico City the phenomenon is about equally frequent in educated and uneducated speech. His survey suggests that it is on the way to tacit acceptance throughout Latin America, although it is less common in Lima, La Paz and a few other places.

11.14.2 Position with imperatives: see 17.4.

11.14.3 Position with infinitives

(a) If the infinitive is used as a noun or follows an adjective or a participle plus a preposition, pronouns are suffixed to it in the usual order:

*Sería una locura decír***selo**	It would be madness to tell it to him
*Mejor enviár***selo** *ahora*	Best send it to him/her/them now
*Rechazaron el proyecto por considerar***lo** *demasiado caro*	They rejected the project on the grounds it was too expensive
*Estamos hartos de oír***telo**	We're fed up with hearing it from you
*Usted no puede quitár***mela**. *Eso sí sería de mal agüero* (G. García Márquez, Colombia, dialogue)	You can't take it (a gold chain) off me. That *would* be a bad omen

As the examples show, when more than one pronoun is attached to the infinitive a written accent is needed to show that the position of the stress has not changed.

(b) If the infinitive depends on a previous verb, there are two possibilities:

(1) Join the pronouns to the infinitive as in the previous examples:

*Quiero hacer***lo**	I want to do it
*Pudieron salvar***la**	They managed to save her
*Intentaron robár***noslo**	They tried to steal it from us
*Propusieron alquilár***noslos**	They suggested renting them to us
*Acabo de dár***telo**	I've just given it to you

This is the safest, and in the view of some excessively strict purists the only correct construction (Marsá 1986, 6.1.2). But Cervantes's *Don Quijote*, the purists' Bible, contains many instances of shifted pronouns.

(2) Place the pronouns before the finite verb: *lo quiero hacer*, etc. See the following section for discussion.

11.14.4 *Quiero verlo or lo quiero ver?*

Suffixed object pronouns are very often shifted leftwards when the infinitive depends on a preceding verb: *quiero verlo* > *lo quiero ver* 'I want to see it', etc. This construction, which has a long history, is possible with a large number of common verbs, but it is subject to controversy and apparently arbitrary constraints. When shifting is possible, both the suffixed and the shifted forms are equally acceptable in spoken Spanish. In Spain the two constructions seem to occur with about equal frequency in ordinary speech, but to judge by the dialogue of modern novels, Latin-American speech strongly prefers the shifted forms. The suffixed forms are everywhere considered rather more literary and are preferred in formal written styles. The following are everyday examples current on both continents:

querer

Te la quiero enviar/Quiero enviártela	I want to send it (fem.) to you
Por mucho que yo os lo quiera dar/quiera dároslo, no puedo	However much I want to give it (masc.) to you, I can't

poder

No puedo atenderle/No le puedo atender en este momento	I can't attend to you/her/him at this moment

Usted no me la puede quitar (compare the example from García Márquez in the previous section)	You can't take it off me

deber

Deberías explicárnoslo/Nos lo deberías explicar	You ought to explain it to us

tener que/haber que

Tiene que devolvértelo/Te lo tiene que devolver	He has to give it back to you
Hay que hacerlo/Lo hay que hacer	You have to do it

acabar de

¡Pero acabo de verlo/lo acabo de ver!	But I've just seen him!

llegar a

Incluso llegué a caerme/me llegué a caer por unas escaleras	I even managed to fall down a flight of stairs

haber de

He de consultarlo/Lo he de consultar con la almohada	I'd better sleep on it (lit. 'consult my pillow')

dejar de

No dejes de llamarla/No la dejes de llamar	Don't forget to phone her

ir a

Me temía que Roberto fuera a contárselo/se lo fuera a contar a mamá	I was worried that Roberto would go and tell it to mother

volver a

Como vuelvas a decírmelo/Como me lo vuelvas a decir, me voy	If you say it to me again, I'm going

hacer

Me hizo abrirlo/Me lo hizo abrir	He made me open it

The list at 18.2.3 indicates those common verbs which allow this shifting of suffixed pronouns, although some verbs, e.g. *fingir*, are controversial.

Notes

(i) Pronouns cannot be shifted if the verb on which the infinitive depends is a 'pronominal' verb (see Chapter 26 for a discussion of pronominal verbs). *Volverse* 'to turn round' is a pronominal verb (it has other meanings, discussed at 26.6.13 and 27.3.2), so one says *se volvió a mirarla* 'he turned to look at her' but not *se la volvió a mirar*. The latter is only possible if *volver* is not a pronominal verb, in which case we would take the *se* to stand for *le*, as in *el médico volvió a mirarle la lengua* 'the doctor looked at his/her tongue again' > *se la volvió a mirar* 'he looked at it again'. Compare the following examples in which *ver* and *dejar* are not pronominal verbs and therefore allow pronoun shifting: *nos ha visto hacerlo/nos lo ha visto hacer* 'he saw us do it', *os dejaron llamarla/os la dejaron llamar* 'they let you call her'.

Other common pronominal verbs that appear with an infinitive are: *ponerse a* 'to begin', *echarse a* 'to begin' (the non-pronominal verb of the same meaning, *echar a*, also does not allow pronoun shifting), *meterse a* 'to begin', *atreverse a* 'to dare'. The asterisked forms in the following examples are not correct Spanish: *se puso a hacerlo* (not **se lo puso a hacer*) 'he started to do it', *(se) lo echó a perder* (not **(se) echó a perderlo*) (roughly) 'he lost it'/'off he goes and loses it', *se metió a venderlos* (not **se los metió a vender*) 'he started to sell them', *se atrevió a hacerlo* (not **se lo atrevió a hacer*) 'he tried to do it'.

(ii) Pronouns cannot be shifted if any other word intervenes between the verb phrase and the following infinitive: *quisiera no hacerlo* 'I'd prefer not to do it' but not **lo quisiera no hacer; deseo* *mucho verla*, not **la deseo mucho ver* 'I really want to see her', etc. An exception is made of a few common verb phrases that include a preposition, usually *a* or *de*, or the conjunction *que: lo trató* **de** *hacer/trató de hacerlo* 'he tried to do it', *le tengo* **que** *hablar/tengo que hablarle* 'I've got to talk to her', *lo empezó* **a** *hacer/empezó a hacerlo* 'he began to do it'. The rule is also often broken in familiar speech, cf. *no le tengo* **nada** *que envidiar*, familiar for *no tengo nada que envidiarle* 'I've got nothing to envy him/her/you for', *el que no se tiene que andar metiendo eres tú* (A. Mastretta, Mexico, dialogue) 'the one who shouldn't go round getting involved is you'.

(iii) Pronouns are not shifted if the main verb is a positive imperative: *procura hacerlo* 'try to do it', *venga a verla* 'come and see her'. But in a negative imperative shifting may occur in familiar speech: *no intentes hacerlo/no lo intentes hacer* 'don't try to do it', *cuidado no lo vayas a manchar/no vayas a mancharlo* 'be careful not to make it dirty', *no te empieces a incluir tú en las culpas* (C. Martín Gaite, Spain, dialogue) 'don't start including yourself among the guilty ones'/'don't start blaming yourself as well', for *no empieces a incluirte tú en las culpas*.

(iv) In *voy a verla* 'I'm going to see her' either motion or futurity is meant. Usually *la voy a ver* can only be interpreted as a future form of the verb: 'I'll see her'/'I intend to see her', although familiar speech may allow shifting with both meanings: *ellos me fueron a comprar el billete* (Interview in *Triunfo*, Spain) 'they went and bought my ticket for me'.

(v) If more than one infinitive is involved in a construction that allows pronoun shifting, several solutions are possible, the first being safest for foreigners: *no quiero volver a decírtelo/no quiero volvértelo a decir/no te lo quiero volver a decir* 'I don't want to tell you it again', *puedes empezar a hacerlo/puedes empezarlo a hacer/lo puedes empezar a hacer* 'you can start to do it', *debes tratar de hacerlo/debes tratarlo de hacer/lo debes tratar de hacer* 'you must try to do it'.

However, if two pronouns are joined as suffixes they must stay together if they are shifted. In other words, starting from *tendrás que encargárselo a Enrique*, the only permitted shift is *se lo tendrás que encargar a Enrique* 'you'll have to ask Enrique to do it' **never** **le tendrás que encargarlo a Enrique*. Further examples: *¿quieres bebértelo ahora/te lo quieres beber ahora?* 'do you want to drink it now?', *¿vas a entregárselo ahora/se lo vas a entregar ahora?* 'are you going to hand it over to him/her now?', *¿vino a decírtelo ayer/te lo vino a decir ayer?* 'did (s)he come and tell it to you yesterday?'

(vi) It is difficult to explain why some verbal phrases allow pronoun shifting whereas others do not. The difference between a phrase like *tratar de* 'to try', which allows pronoun shifting, and *tardar en* 'to be late in'/'to take time over . . .', which does not, is presumably that the preposition *de* has become so intimately fused to *tratar* that the two words are processed by the speaker as a single word. A list of verbs that allow shifting appears at 18.2.3.

11.14.5 Position of pronouns with the gerund

(a) In combination with *estar* (continuous verb forms) and a few other auxiliary verbs like *andar, ir, venir*, the pronouns may be either attached or shifted:

Te lo estoy contando/Estoy contándotelo	I'm telling you it
Nos estuvieron esperando/Estuvieron esperándonos	They waited for us
Os lo estoy diciendo/Estoy diciéndooslo (note the double *o*)	I'm saying it to you (*vosotros*)
Se lo va contando a todos/ Va contándoselo a todos	He goes around telling it to everyone
Se me quedó mirando/Se quedó mirándome (the *se* belongs to *quedarse*)	He remained gazing at me

The second construction is slightly more formal and is probably safer for foreign students.

(b) In other cases the pronouns are always attached to the gerund: *disfruta mirándolo* 'he enjoys himself looking at it', *se divierte quemándolos* 'he amuses himself by burning them', *contesta insultándolos* 'he replies by insulting them', *llevo horas esperándote* 'I've been waiting for you for hours', etc.

Notes

(i) *Seguir* allows both constructions, but some native speakers did not accept pronoun shifting with *continuar: se seguían viendo/seguían viéndose* 'they went on seeing one another', *me sigue dando la lata/sigue dándome la lata* 'he's still pestering me', but *continuaban viéndose, continúa dándome la lata*. Compare *ella lo siguió encontrando todo muy natural* (A. Bryce Echenique, Peru) 'she continued to find it all very natural'.

(ii) In case **(a)**, if the auxiliary verb is an infinitive preceded by one of the verbs that allow pronoun shifting (see 11.14.4), several solutions are possible: *debe estar recordándolo/debe estarlo recordando/lo debe estar recordando* 'he must be remembering it/him', *tenía que quedarse mirándola/tenía que quedársela mirando/se la tenía que quedar mirando* 'he had to remain looking at her'.

11.14.6 Position with past participles

Pronouns come before the auxiliary verb:

Se ha equivocado	She's made a mistake
Se lo ha traído de (la) China	He's brought it from China
Te lo hemos mandado ya	We've already sent it to you

Notes

(i) In phrases in which pronoun shifting is possible (discussed at 11.14.4), there are two options: *se lo hemos tenido que vender/hemos tenido que vendérselo* 'we had to sell it to him', *la he vuelto a ver/he vuelto a verla* 'I've seen her again', *no he podido abrirlo/no lo he podido abrir* 'I couldn't open it', *ha debido hablarle/le ha debido hablar* '(s)he must have spoken to him/her'.

(ii) Literary language used to join personal pronouns to past participles, especially when the auxiliary verb was deleted, but this construction is obsolete except, occasionally, in flowery styles in some Latin-American republics.[8] The example given in Ramsey and Spaulding (1958), 4.15, *era un propietario rico de Cáceres, donde había nacido y* **criádose** 'he was a rich landowner from Cáceres, where he had been born and brought up' would nowadays be recast as . . . *donde había nacido y se había criado*.

11.15 Emphasis of object pronouns

(a) Object pronouns may be emphasized by adding *a* and the prepositional form of the pronoun:

*La vi **a ella**, pero no **a él***	I saw **her** but not **him**
*Te lo darán **a ti**, pero no **a él***	They'll give it **to you**, but not **to him**
*¡**A mí** me lo dices!*	You're telling **me**!?
*Si me retirara, pues, tampoco lo vería **a usted***	If I retired, well, I wouldn't see **you**
(S. Galindo, dialogue, Mexico)	either

(b) Reflexive phrases may be emphasized by the appropriate number and gender of *mismo* added to a prepositional pronoun. Reciprocal sentences can be emphasized by the appropriate form of *el uno* and *el otro*:

Se lavaron	They washed (themselves)/They were washed
*Se lavaron **a sí mismos***	They washed **themselves**
Es difícil vivir con quien no se estima a sí mismo (Abc, Spain)	It is difficult to live with someone who does not value himself/herself

---

[8] Kany (1970), 156, cites *un accidente ocurrídole en el corral de yeguas* 'an accident that happened to him in the yard where the mares are kept' from Uruguay. Seco (1998), 334, considers the construction 'inelegant'.

Se quieren el uno al otro	They love one another
Se quieren la una a la otra (two females)	They love one another
Se envidian los unos a los otros	They envy one another (more than two people involved)

Note

If both males and females are involved in a reciprocal sentence the logical form might be thought to be *el uno a la otra*, but both pronouns are left in the masculine in order to preserve the idea of reciprocity: *Antonio y María se quieren **el uno al otro*** 'Antonio and Maria love one another' (?*el uno a la otra* might imply that he loved her but not she him).

11.16 Redundant object pronouns

Spanish makes constant use of object pronouns even when the thing they refer to is already named by a noun. Some of these redundant pronouns are virtually obligatory, others are more typical of informal styles.

11.16.1 Redundancy when object precedes verb

If, for purposes of emphasis or focus, the direct or indirect object of a verb precedes the verb, a redundant pronoun is usually obligatory. Compare *compré esta casa hace cinco años* and *esta casa **la** compré hace cinco años* 'I bought this house five years ago'. Examples:

*Eso no me **lo** negarás*	You won't deny me that
*Aviones **los** tenemos a patadas* (quantity stated: see note (iii))	We've got tons/heaps of aircraft
*A alguno de vosotros **os** quisiera ver yo en un buen fregado* (D. Sueiro, familiar Spanish dialogue)	I'd like to see one of you in a real mess
*Al profesor Berlin no **le** parece tan importante que Maquiavelo propusiera esa disyuntiva* (M. Vargas Llosa, Peru)	It does not seem so important to Professor Berlin that Machiavelli suggested this dilemma

Notes

(i) The pronoun is omitted after *eso* in such phrases as *eso creo yo* 'that's what I think', *eso digo yo* 'that's what I think' (but compare *eso lo digo yo* 'that's what I **say**').
(ii) For a discussion of the effect of putting the object before the verb see 28.2.3c.
(iii) The redundant pronoun is not used when the object noun is indefinite, i.e. it refers to an unspecified or unidentified quantity or number, as in: *mucha prisa ha debido tener* 'he *must* have been in a hurry', *muchas cosas quiero contarte* 'I want to tell you a lot of things', *aviones tenemos aquí que han costado más de cincuenta millones* 'we've got (some) planes here that cost more than 50 million', *¡cuántas tonterías dices!* 'what a lot of nonsense you talk!'

11.16.2 Redundant pronouns and indirect objects

A redundant pronoun is very frequently inserted to show that a noun is 'involved', by the verb in one of the ways listed in List A at 12.3 (i.e. 'receiving', 'losing', 'advantage', 'involvement', etc.). In other words, an indirect object is often reinforced by a redundant indirect object pronoun:

*Lo que a usted **le** conviene . . .*	What would suit you . . .
*Bueno, si no **le** dicen a uno cómo hay que hacerlo . . .*	Well, if they don't tell one how to do it . . .
*Esta solución **le** pareció a doña Matilde la más acertada* (J. M. Guelbenzu, Spain)	This solution seemed to be the best one to Doña Matilde

*Se **le** notan cada vez más los años*	You can tell Martínez's age more
a Martínez	and more
***Les** tenía mucho miedo a los truenos*	He was very frightened of thunder
*A vos **te** la tienen jurada* (M. Puig, Argentina,	They've got it in for you
dialogue; Spain, *a ti* . . .)	
Le puso un nuevo conmutador a la radio	(S)he put a new knob on the radio
Tráigale un jugo[9] de naranja a la niña	Bring the girl an orange juice
(A. Mastretta, Mexico, dialogue)	

Note

Omission of the redundant pronoun depersonalizes the indirect object and would be appropriate in formal writing, official documents or business letters when a distant tone is required: *escriba una carta al Ministerio de Hacienda* 'write a letter to the Ministry of Finance', *comunique los detalles al señor Presidente* 'inform the President of the details', *esto no corresponde a Odradek* (J. L. Borges: Odradek is a non-human creature) 'this is not a trait of Odradek's', *es necesario dar cera a este tipo de suelo todas las semanas* (instruction leaflet, Spain) 'this type of floor must be waxed every week'.

In most other cases the redundant pronoun is used, more so than fifty years ago and always with proper names: *dáselo a Mario* 'Give it to Mario', *se lo robaron a Mariluz* 'they stole it from Mariluz' (*robar a* . . . 'to steal from . . .'). However, the redundant pronoun is sometimes omitted with other nouns, cf. *una forma estudiada de acentuar la ironía que gusta a todas las mujeres* (J. Marías, Spain) 'a studied way of emphasizing irony that all women like', where *les gusta a las mujeres* is less literary; or *todo lo que sobra de esta mañana lo podés dar a las gallinas* (M. Puig, Argentina, dialogue; or *se lo podés dar a las gallinas*; Spain *puedes* for the *vos* form *podés*) 'you can give the chickens everything left over from this morning'.

11.16.3 *Le* for redundant *les*

There is a strong tendency in spontaneous language everywhere to use the singular *le* in this construction for the plural *les*, especially (but not exclusively) when the pronoun refers to something inanimate:[10]

*Cualquiera **le** da vuelta a las razones por las*	Anyone might ponder on the reasons
que te viniste conmigo (J. M.	why you came to me
Guelbenzu, Spain, dialogue)	
*no dar**le** importancia a los detalles*	not to ascribe importance to details
*¿Quieres devolver**le** la isla de Manhattan a*	Do you want to give Manhattan Island
los Algonquins? (C. Fuentes, Mexico,	back to the Algonquins?
dialogue)	
Y ese pequeño elemento ya justificaría que	And that little detail would be enough
*yo **le** pusiera la firma a sus papeles* (M.	to justify my signing your papers
Puig, Argentina, dialogue)	
*?**Le** viene natural a los niños* (educated	It comes naturally to children
Spaniard, overheard; not universally	
accepted in Spain)	
*Bayardo San Román **le** puso término a*	Bayardo San Román put an end to so
tantas conjeturas con un recurso simple	much conjecture by a simple
(G. García Márquez, Colombia)	stratagem

---

[9] In Spain *el zumo* is used for the juice of fruits and vegetables, *el jugo* for meat juices.

[10] DeMello (1992, 2) reports that in Latin America it is equally common with animate and inanimate pronouns, but Peninsular informants generally reported it as less acceptable with animate pronouns. DeMello's study reveals the use of *le* for *les* to be very widespread even in quite formal speech.

This tendency is so deep-rooted, even in educated speech, that sentences like *él les* (for *le*) *da mucha importancia a las apariencias* 'he ascribes a lot of importance to appearances' sound frankly odd to many speakers. But use of the singular *le* for *les* is technically 'wrong', and should be avoided in formal writing – e.g. in this case by omitting the redundant pronoun altogether.

11.16.4 Redundant direct object pronouns

As was said at 11.16.1, a redundant pronoun is usually obligatory when an object precedes the verb, as in *las flores **las** compré ayer* 'I bought the flowers yesterday'. When the direct object *follows* the verb, use of a redundant object pronoun is common with *todo*: *ahora me **lo** tienes que contar todo* 'now you have to tell me everything'. It is also required when it is necessary to reinforce an object pronoun, e.g. *la vi a ella pero no a él* 'I saw *her* but not *him*' (not **vi a ella*). In other cases use of a redundant pronoun with direct objects is generally avoided in Spain. But it is very common in Latin America in spontaneous speech and in Argentina it appears even in literary styles, especially with proper names:

Le quiere mucho a ese hijo (Spain, familiar)	She loves that son a lot
*Morgan . . . también **lo** mandó llamar a Abdulmalik* (J. L. Borges, Argentina) dialogue; Spain . . . *mandó llamar a Abdulmalik*	Morgan also had Abdulmalik sent for
*No **lo** conocen a Perón en Córdoba, lo confunden con un cantante de tangos* (J. Asís, dialogue, Argentina; Spain *no conocen . . .*)	They've never heard of Perón in Córdoba. They think he's a tango singer
*Convénze**lo** a su amigo de que acepte la beca* (M. Vargas Llosa, Peru, dialogue; Spain *convenza a su amigo . . .*)	Persuade your friend to accept the grant

11.16.5 Redundant pronouns in relative clauses

Redundant pronouns occur in spoken Spanish in relative clauses to 'resume' or echo a direct or indirect object relative pronoun, especially in non-restrictive clauses, and may appear in writing, particularly if several words separate the *que* and the verb that depends on it:

*Los gramáticos aconsejan muchas cosas que nadie **las** dice* (Spain, informant)	Grammarians recommend lots of things that no one says
*Te voy a hacer una confesión que nunca me animé a hacer**la** a nadie* (Lat. Am., from Kany, 1970, 150)	I'm going to make you a confession I never had the courage to make to anybody
*Sólo por ti dejaría a don Memo a quien tanto **le** debo* (C. Fuentes, Mexico, dialogue)	Only for you would I leave Don Memo, whom I owe so much

This construction may sound uneducated, especially in restrictive clauses (the first two examples), and is best left to native speakers.[11]

---

[11] The survey by DeMello (1992, 4) of the educated spoken Spanish in eleven cities in Spain and Latin America shows that the construction is in fact very widespread, even in quite formal speech.

12

Le/les *and* lo/la/los/las

This chapter is devoted to the problem of the relationship between the third-person object pronouns *le/les* and *lo/la/los/las*. For first and second-person pronouns (including *usted* and *ustedes*) and for third-person subject pronouns (*él, ella, ellos, ellos*), see Chapter 11.

12.1 The *le/lo* controversy: summary of the arguments contained in this chapter

The rules governing the correct choice of third-person object pronouns are complex and vary a great deal throughout the Spanish-speaking world. The situation may be summarized thus: the personal pronoun used for third-person **direct** objects, human and non-human, in more than 90 per cent of the Spanish-speaking world is *lo/la* for the singular and *los/las* for the plural. *Le* and *les* are used for indirect objects as defined at 11.7.2 and 12.3. This scheme is recommended for beginners pending deeper knowledge of the language. However, *le* and *les* are also used for direct objects in the following cases:

(a) In the standard language of Spain when the direct object is singular, human and male: *yo le vi* 'I saw him' instead of *yo lo vi*. See 12.5.1.
(b) Sometimes as the object pronoun for *ustedes* in order to denote respect. See 12.6.1.
(c) Frequently when the subject of the verb is inanimate and the direct object is human, when the human object is reacting to the action described. See 12.6.2.
(d) Frequently, when the subject is impersonal *se* and the direct object is human. See 12.6.3.
(e) In all countries, *le/les* is used with certain verbs, listed at 12.6.4.

12.2 Third-person object pronouns: basic rules

Beginners can apply the following scheme, which is based on the Academy's current preferences and is valid for all of Latin America and acceptable to most Spaniards. These rules will produce correct sentences in over 90 per cent of cases:

Preferred third-person object pronouns (from the Academy's *Esbozo de una nueva gramática de la lengua española*, 3.10.5c)

	Direct object	Indirect object
Singular		
masculine	*lo*	*le*
feminine	*la*	*le*
Plural		
masculine	*los*	*les*
feminine	*las*	*les*

Examples:

Ángela vio a Antonio Angela saw Antonio
Antonio vio a Ángela Antonio saw Angela
Vio el libro (S)he saw the book
Vio la casa (S)he saw the house
María dijo hola a Juan Maria said hello to Juan
Juan dijo hola a María Juan said hello to Maria
Vio a los hombres (S)he saw the men
Vio a las mujeres (S)he saw the women
Vio los libros (S)he saw the books
Vio las casas (S)he saw the houses
Dijo hola a María y a José (S)he said hello to Maria and José
Dijo hola a María y a Ángela (S)he said hello to Maria and Angela

Lo vio She saw him
La vio He saw her
Lo vio (S)he saw it
La vio (S)he saw it
Le dijo hola She said hello to him

Le dijo hola He said hello to her

Los vio (S)he saw them
Las vio (S)he saw them
Los vio (S)he saw them
Las vio (S)he saw them
Les dijo hola (S)he said hello to them

Les dijo hola (S)he said hello to them

Notes

(i) Standard European Spanish prefers the form *le* for a **human** male direct object – *le vi* 'I saw him' – although *lo vi* is now considered by the Academy to be the preferable form and is much more common in Spain than in the past; see 12.5.1 for details. In the plural *los* is more common than *les* for male human direct objects and is generally preferred; see 12.5.2 for details.

(ii) *Usted/ustedes* 'you' (polite) takes third-person object pronouns: *lo vi ayer* 'I saw him/it/you yesterday', *le vi ayer* (Spain only) 'I saw you (masc.)/him yesterday', *los vi ayer* 'I saw them/you, yesterday', *las vi ayer* 'I saw them/you (fem.) yesterday'. This possibility that a third-person object pronoun may also indicate *ustede(es)* is not systematically shown in the translations of examples in this book.

12.3 Use of *le/les* as 'indirect object' pronouns: detailed rules

(*Le/les* are sometimes also used as direct object pronouns: see 12.5–12.6.)

Le/les are often described as third-person 'indirect object' pronouns (*pronombres de complemento indirecto*). However, 'indirect object' is a term that covers many different meanings and the more general principle underlying the use of *le/les* seems to be the following: *le/les* **replace any person or thing gaining from**

or losing by the action described in the verb phrase.[1] The nature of these gains or losses must be inferred from the meaning of the verb phrase or from clues provided by context. Whatever departures from these examples they may hear, foreign students are advised to use *le/les* in the following contexts:

List A Typical uses of *le/les*

Le can be translated 'him', 'her', 'it', 'you'; *les* as 'you' or 'them'. The choice in the following translations may be dictated by context, but in some cases it is arbitrary.

(a) Receiving or acquiring any thing, impression or sensation:

Le di la carta	I gave her/him/you the letter
Voy a darle una mano de pintura	I'll give it a coat of paint
No le dije la verdad	I didn't tell you/him/her the truth
Les suministramos acero y petróleo	We supply them steel and crude oil
Ángel le alcanzó un cuchillo	Angel handed him a knife
Le tirábamos bolas de nieve	We were throwing snowballs at her
Le dio una vuelta[2]	She turned it (lit. 'gave it a turn')
Les llegaba un olor de madreselva	A smell of honeysuckle reached them
Le pusieron una inyección	They gave you an injection
Le echaron una sábana	They threw a sheet over him
Se le agrega queso rallado	Grated cheese is added to it
Se le pegó una brizna de hierba	A blade of grass stuck to her
Le valió una sonrisa	It earned him a smile
Su padre le contagió sus locuras	His father infected him with his mad ways
Les enseñé el camino	I showed them the way
Le tocó el premio gordo	She got first prize
Les corresponde la mitad	They're/You're entitled to half
Les interesa callarlo	It's in their/your interest to keep it quiet
Le convenía que fuera así	It suited him that way
No les es ventajoso	It's not advantageous to them
Esa chaqueta no le va	That jacket doesn't suit him/her
Las cosas le iban mal	Things were going badly for her
Le hemos lavado tres camisas	We've washed three shirts for him
Enciéndele un cigarrillo	Light a cigarette for her
Le prometió que haría un esfuerzo	He promised her he'd make an effort
No le pasó nada	Nothing happened to him
Le sobrevino una tremenda tragedia	A great tragedy happened to him
Cuando se le sube el whisky	When the whisky goes to her head
Se le ocurrió llamar a la policía	He had the idea of phoning the police
No le parece mucho	It doesn't seem much to him
Le constaba que . . .	It was a fact to him that . . .
Le suena mal	It sounds wrong to her
Le da igual	It's all the same to him
La secretaria le cayó bien	He took a liking to the secretary
Le gusta la miel	(S)he/It likes honey
Le agradó la respuesta	The reply pleased her
Les dolía que sus padres no contestasen/contestaran	It pained them that their parents didn't reply
Cuánto les pesaba haber hablado	How sorry they were for having talked

---

[1] In contrast, an indirect object in English can only *receive*: we cannot say * 'they stole him 50 dollars'.

[2] In the Southern Cone *dar vuelta* is treated as a transitive verb: *dio vuelta la tortilla* '(s)he turned the pancake over', *la dio vuelta* '(s)he turned it over'; Spain *dio vuelta **a** la tortilla*.

(b) Loss or removal from:

Les han robado un millón de pesos	They've stolen a million pesos from them/you
Esto le ha quitado un peso de encima	This has taken a weight off her mind
Mario le ha quitado a Ana	Mario's taken Ana away from him (note the personal *a*)
Le he comprado un cuadro	I've bought a picture from him
Le están sacando una muela	They're taking one of her teeth out
Le costó un dineral	It cost her a fortune
Se le cae el pelo	His hair's falling out
Se le ha muerto un hijo	A son of his has died
Se le pasa pronto	She gets over it quickly
Le arrancaron la pistola	They seized the pistol off him

(c) Sufficiency, insufficiency, lack, excess:

Les basta decir que sí	All they have to do is say 'yes'
Le faltan mil pesos	She's 1,000 pesos short
Le faltaba un dedo meñique	One of his little fingers was missing
Mil pesetas al día le alcanzaban para vivir	She could manage on 1,000 pesetas a day
Le sobraba (la) razón	He was only too right
El traje le está grande	Her suit is too big for her

(d) Requesting, requiring, ordering:

Le hicieron varias preguntas	They asked her several questions
Le pidieron sus señas	They asked him his name and address
Les rogaron que se sentasen/sentaran	They requested them to sit down
Les ordenaron rendirse	They ordered them to surrender
Les exigía un esfuerzo continuo	It required continuous effort from them
Les llamó la atención	He/It attracted their attention (or 'he told them off')

Note

Compare *le mandó que comprara/comprase pan* '(s)he ordered her/him to buy bread' and *la mandó a comprar pan* '(s)he sent her to buy bread'.

(e) Numerous phrases involving *tener* plus an emotion (although the equivalent verbs *respetar*, *temer*, etc., may take *lo/la/las/los*):

Le tiene miedo	He fears him/her/you
Su madre le tenía poco cariño	His mother felt little fondness for him
Le tiene ojeriza	She has it in for him
Le tenías una envidia tremenda	You were enormously envious of her/him

(f) Numerous set phrases consisting of *hacer* plus a noun:

El frío les hacía mucho daño	The cold did them a lot of harm
El chico le hizo una mueca	The boy pulled a face at him
Mi nieto nunca les hacía caso	My grandson never heeded them
Tienes que hacerle frente a la realidad	You have to face up to reality
Le hacía falta reflexionar	(S)he needed to reflect

(g) To indicate persons or things affected by something done to a part of their body or to some intimate possession (for further details about this construction and for the omission of the possessive adjective with parts of the body and intimate possessions, see 8.3.4):

¡Le estás pisando los pies!	You're treading on his feet!
Los fríos le hielan los dedos	The cold weather freezes her fingers
A esa edad se les ablanda el cerebro	Their brains go soft at that age
Don Juan le acariciaba las mejillas	Don Juan was stroking her cheeks
Los nervios le jugaban malas partidas	His nerves were playing tricks on him
Se le ha hundido la moral	Her morale has collapsed
No le veo la gracia	I don't see what's funny in it
Los labriegos se amotinaron porque	The peasants revolted because they
les volvieron a gravar el aceite	taxed their olive oil again
Le he roto la camisa	I've torn his shirt
Le dejaron las gafas hechas añicos	They shattered her glasses
(las gafas = Lat. Am. *los anteojos* or *los lentes)*	

(h) In a number of less easily classified cases which may all be perceived to convey ideas of 'giving', 'removing', 'benefiting', 'involving', 'affecting intimately':

¿Qué le vamos a hacer?	What can be done about it?
No le hace (Southern Cone; Spain *no tiene que ver*)	That's irrelevant
¡Dale!	Hit him!/Go on!/Get moving!
Le agradezco	I thank you
El cura les (also *los*) *aconsejaba que no lo hicieran/hiciesen*	The priest advised them not to do it
Le encontraron mil pesos	They found 1,000 pesos on her
La respuesta de su hija le afectó mucho (*lo* or *le* possible in Latin America)	His daughter's reply affected him a lot

Note

This multiplicity of meanings can give rise to ambiguities: *le compré un vestido* 'I bought a dress off her/for her', *cómprame algo* 'buy something for/off me', *Ángel me robó una manzana* 'Ángel stole an apple from me/for me/on my behalf.' Context nearly always makes the sense plain, or the sentence can be recast: *compró una calculadora para mí* 'he/she bought a calculator for me', etc.

12.4 Uses of *lo/la/los/las*

Lo/la/los/las are the third-person 'direct object' pronouns, 'direct' object understood here as the person or thing directly affected by a verb phrase but not 'losing' or 'gaining' in the ways described in List A above. In the following list of examples it will be seen that even when dramatically affected by the verb phrase (as in 'they killed her') the person or thing denoted by the pronoun is not actively involved as a participant in the action or as an interested party. In fact the condition of the pronoun is very often literally that of an object which merely has the action of the verb done to it.

List B: Contexts normally requiring *lo/la/los/las* (direct object)

The use of *lo* for human males in this list reflects standard Latin American usage and the Academy's current recommendation. The second of the alternative forms reflects widespread, preferred, but not obligatory usage in Spain. See 12.2 and 12.5.1 for discussion.

(a) Direct physical actions (although there are exceptions, like *le pega* '(s)he beats him/her'; see 12.6.4):

Lo/Le interrogaron	They interrogated him
La operaron	They operated on her/you (*usted*)
Coge estos papeles y quémalos	Take these papers and burn them
A usted lo durmieron con algún mejunje en la sidra (J. L. Borges, Argentina, dialogue; Spain *le*)	They put you to sleep with some potion in the cider
Saca el carburador y límpialo	Take out the carburettor and clean it
—¿Y tu cámara?—La he perdido	'What about your camera?' 'I've lost it'

(b) Verbs of perception, e.g. 'seeing', 'hearing', 'knowing', etc.:

Al director no lo/le conozco	I don't know the director
La vi ayer en el mercado	I saw her/you yesterday in the market
Sabía que el ladrón estaba en la habitación porque lo/le oí	I knew the thief was in the room because I heard him
El agente lo/le miraba	The policeman was looking at him
El padre lo miraba con orgullo (J. Aldecoa, Spain; or *le*)	His father gazed at him with pride
A uno de ellos lo identifiqué enseguida (J. Marías, Spain; or *le*)	One of them I identified immediately

(c) Praise, blame, admiration, love, hatred and other actions denoting attitudes towards a person or thing:

Sus profesores lo/le alaban	His teachers praise him/you
A las monjas las envidio mucho	I envy nuns a lot
Lo/Le admiro profundamente	I admire him deeply
Su marido la adora	Her/Your husband adores her
La considero una amiga	I consider her/you a friend
Yo la quiero mucho	I love her a lot

(d) 'Naming', 'nominating', 'describing' (but see 12.6.4 for the verb *llamar*):

Los denominaron 'los decadentes'	They named them 'the decadents'
Lo/Le nombraron alcalde	They nominated him mayor
Las describió en términos despectivos	He described them (fem.) in pejorative terms
Lo calificó de tragedia	He described it as a tragedy

(e) Many other actions done to things or persons but not 'involving' them in the ways described in List A above:

La crisis energética no la podrá solucionar ningún gobierno elegido	The energy crisis can't be solved by any elected government
El Canciller los recibirá a las siete y cuarto	The Chancellor will receive you/them at 7.15
Este país no hay quien sepa gobernarlo	There's no one who knows how to govern this country
Habrá que defenderlos	We'll have to defend them
No pude convencerla	I couldn't convince her
Yo intentaba evitarlos	I was trying to avoid them

Notes

(i) *Lo/la/los/las* agree in gender with the noun they replace. If they do not replace a specific noun, *lo* is used: *dijo que llegaría a las siete, pero no* **lo** *creo* 'he said he'd arrive at seven, but I don't believe it', *esto no* **lo** *aguanta nadie* 'no one can stand this'. This neuter use of *lo* is discussed at 7.4.

(ii) The first and second-person pronouns *me/te/nos/os* could be used in any of the above sentences in place of the third-person pronoun, provided the result makes sense.

12.5 The *le/lo* controversy: general remarks

Interminable controversy surrounds the use of *le/les* as a **direct object** pronoun. Beginners may follow the scheme given in 12.2, but they will soon come across at least some of the variants described hereafter. Some of these are local or dialectal and not to be imitated by foreigners. But some of them are basic features of Spanish and fluent foreigners will need to use them. Section 12.5 describes regional variations. Section 12.6 describes certain subtleties in the use of *le* and *lo* found in the best written and spoken styles throughout the Spanish-speaking world.

12.5.1 Le for lo in Spain (leísmo): further details

The standard language of Spain, i.e. the variety used in the media and by most educated speakers in Madrid and central regions of Spain, favours *le vi* for *lo vi* when the sentence means 'I saw **him**' as opposed to 'I saw it':

—¿Has visto a Miguel?—No, no **le** he visto   'Have you seen Miguel?' 'No, I haven't seen him'

—¿Has visto mi boli?—No, no **lo** he visto   'Have you seen my ballpoint pen?' 'No, I haven't seen it'

There is much disagreement about this phenomenon, and the Academy has itself changed its mind on the subject several times in the last 150 years and now advocates the Latin-American preference for *lo* for both human males and masculine non-human direct objects. But in the face of massive resistance in Spain the Academy officially 'tolerates' forms like *le vi* for 'I saw **him**'.[3] Feminists will note that in the *leísta* system only males are differentiated from inanimate objects: *la vi* means both 'I saw her' and 'I saw it'.

Leísmo is very deeply entrenched in central Spain and students may still encounter a certain amount of anti-*loísta* prejudice in those regions: some Spaniards still claim that *lo vi* applied to a male human being sounds vaguely substandard or regional. However, students will also note much inconsistency in the use of *le* or *lo* with reference to human males in Spain, *lo* being more frequent in the South and increasingly common, it seems, in all circles, cf. *lo tiene por vecino de calle y desde la ventana lo ve pasar todos los días* (Carlos Casares, *El País*, Spain) 'he assumes that he's a neighbour from the same street and from the window he sees him go by every day'. Advanced students of Latin-American Spanish will also notice from section 12.6 that, although rare, the use of *le* in Latin America for human direct objects, male and female, is in fact more common in certain countries and circumstances than is usually claimed.

The Academy's current dislike of *le* as a 'direct object' pronoun, based on an inaccurate definition of 'direct' and 'indirect' objects, does not in fact do justice to the complexities of Spanish on either continent. The following pages attempt to provide a succinct account of the problem. For a full discussion see García (1975).

---

[3] The Academy now prefers *lo* on historical grounds. The argument in the *Esbozo* . . . is that since *lo* comes from the Classical Latin accusative *illum* and *le* from the dative *illi*, 'I saw him' should be *lo vi* in Modern Spanish and 'I said **to** him' *le dije*.

12.5.2 *Les* for *los* in Spain

Use of *les* for *los*, e.g. *les vi* 'I saw them' (masc.) is also frequently heard in colloquial language in Spain, especially in Castile, when the pronoun refers to human males, but this construction is less common than *los vi* and is in fact not 'tolerated' by the Academy or favoured in writing. Seco (1998), 180, says of *no les he visto* applied to human males that 'literary language does not generally admit it, although examples are not infrequent in good writers', as the following examples attest:

Les *llevaron a una casa donde estuvieron mucho rato esperando* (Juan Benet, Spain, for *los llevaron . . .*)	They took them to a house where they waited for a long time
La colonización **les** *explotó* (P. Laín Entralgo, Spain)	Colonization exploited them

12.5.3 *Le* for *la* in Spain: regional usage

Speakers from north-western Spain, especially Navarre and the Basque provinces, often use *le* for female human direct objects as well as for males: *le vi* = both 'I saw him' and 'I saw her', *lo vi* (masc.) and *la vi* (fem.) 'I saw it'. This usage sometimes appears in literature and is generally accepted as a regional variant. The same phenomenon is sporadically heard elsewhere, e.g. in Valencia and in Paraguay.

12.5.4 *La* for *le* (*a ella*) in Spain (*laísmo*)

Older speakers in Madrid and speakers in the countryside of central Spain often use *la* for the **indirect** object pronoun to refer to a female or feminine noun:

?*Yo* **la** *dije la verdad* (for *yo le dije la verdad*)	I told her the truth
?*Yo* **la** *alabo el gusto* (M. Delibes, Spain, dialogue; for *yo le alabo el gusto*	I praise her taste
¿Desde entonces yo **la** *he escrito varias veces* (A. Martín, Spain, dialogue, for *le he escrito*)	Since then I've written to her several times
?*A una de estas bujías se* **la** *exige un rendimiento cinco veces superior* (Cambio16, Spain, for *se le exige . . .*)	These spark plugs are expected to yield a five times greater output

Schoolteachers have waged a long war against this type of *laísmo* and it is now apparently disappearing in the speech of Madrid. It is common in pre-twentieth-century literature. Foreign students should avoid it.

12.5.5 *Lo* for *le* in Latin America

Extreme *loísmo*, i.e. use of *lo* for the indirect object, is reported in popular speech in many parts of Latin America: Kany (1970), 137, cites from Guatemala *ya no tarda en llegar. ¿Quiere hablarlo?* 'he won't be long now. Do you want to speak to him?' (for *hablarle*). The same phenomenon is occasionally heard in dialects in Spain. It should not be imitated.

12.5.6 *Le* for *lo/la* applied to inanimate objects in Spain

In familiar speech in Madrid and in pre-twentieth-century texts, one finds *le* used as the direct object pronoun even for inanimate nouns: ?*no* **le** *he leído todavía*

'I haven't read it [*el libro*] yet', ?*unos niegan el hecho, otros le afirman* 'some deny the fact, others assert it' (B. Feijoo, mid-eighteenth century). This extreme *leísmo*, endorsed by the Academy until the 1850s, is nowadays considered substandard or dialect unless it is a rare instance of genuine personification. However, it occasionally appears in written language, e.g.:

En esta historia mal concertada hacen que San Prudencio y otros obispos maldigan al pueblo y le destruyan (J. Caro Baroja, Spain)	In this disjointed story they make St Prudentius and other bishops curse the village and destroy it

12.6 Le used for human direct objects throughout the Spanish-speaking world

Even when all the regional and dialectal factors are excluded, *le* is still found as a direct object pronoun in the best styles in Spain where *la/las* would be expected, and in Latin America where *lo/los* or *la/las* would be predicted. This problem arises because a simple distinction between 'direct' and 'indirect' objects is not made in Spanish, as is clear from translation of the following sentences, in both of which 'her' is the direct object of 'flattered':

(a) he flattered her
(b) the joke flattered her

We expect the Spanish translation to be **(a)** *él la halagó*, **(b)** *la broma la halagó*, and this indeed is what many native speakers accept. However, many speakers, Spanish and Latin-American, translate **(b)** as *la broma le halagó*, this being the more common form in educated speech.[4] As a result, although the rules for the use of *le/les* already given at 12.3 and the rules for *lo/la/los/las* given at 12.4 will enable foreign learners to form sentences that are acceptable to the majority of native speakers, they do not always explain the actual use of these pronouns.

12.6.1 Le to denote respect

In certain areas some speakers use *le* for human direct objects as a mark of respect. Spaniards who say *lo vi* for 'I saw him' may prefer *le vi* for the polite *usted* form: *le vi* 'I saw you'. Argentine informants were convinced that they would say *no quería molestarle* 'I didn't mean to bother you' when speaking to their boss, but *molestarlo* when speaking about him. Colombian informants said *molestarlo* in both cases. Examples of *le* used with *usted*:

¡Buenas tardes, hijitos! Les encuentro muy alegres (A. Buero Vallejo, Spain, dialogue)	Good afternoon, my dears! I find you very cheerful

---

[4] In an attempt to replicate García's (1975) experiments on natives of Buenos Aires, we issued a questionnaire to twenty-eight educated speakers (mostly university students or professionals, 80% from Madrid) asking them to insert *la* or *le* in the following sentences: (i) *A María todo el mundo . . . halaga* 'everyone flatters Maria', (ii) *María comprendió que fue una broma, pero . . . halagó que esa broma fuera posible* 'Maria understood it was a joke, but it flattered her that the joke was possible.' In (i) 87% put *la*, in (ii) 90% put *le*. When the sample was increased by adding twenty Latin Americans from five different countries the picture did not change.

Si le molesta el humo, señora, lo apago	If the smoke troubles you, Señora, I'll put it out

but

Lo apagué porque la molestaba el humo	I put it out because the smoke was bothering her

It is possible that, for some speakers of European Spanish, use of *lo* can, on the other hand, express the idea that the male person referred to is helpless or held in low esteem, although this distinction is not made in central Spain, where there is no detectable difference of meaning between *lo* and *le* when they are used as direct object pronouns for males. The following examples may show *lo* used with the nuance described, but the choice seems arbitrary and *le* is clearly preferred in the singular for human males:

***Lo** agarramos por los sobacos y por las piernas y **lo** subimos . . . dejándole tendido en la puerta de aquel pisito* (J. Marsé, Spain, dialogue about a drunkard; inconsistent use of *le/lo*)	We grabbed hold of him under the arms and by the legs, and carried him up and left him lying in the doorway to that little flat/apartment
*Después **lo** hemos traído aquí* (A. Buero Vallejo: refers to the dead Ignacio in *En la ardiente oscuridad*)	Then we brought him here

In some parts of Latin America the nuance operates more clearly. García (1975) reports that some speakers in Buenos Aires detect a difference between *le llevaron al hospital* and *lo llevaron al hospital*, 'they took him to the hospital', the former implying that the patient was walking or co-operative, the latter that he was carried; and it seems that some Spaniards also accept the distinction. For Colombian informants only *lo llevaron* was possible.

12.6.2 *Le/les* preferred when subject is inanimate

Le/le are often the preferred direct object pronouns when they denote a human being and the subject of the verb is inanimate; this statement applies both to Spain and to Latin America.[5] Compare the following sentences: *la espera su marido* 'her husband's waiting for her' and *le espera una catástrofe* 'a catastrophe awaits her/him'. *Le* is used when the human direct object is *reacting* emotionally, as in sentences like 'it surprised him', 'it shocked her', 'he doesn't know what's awaiting him'. The phenomenon is vividly illustrated in this Peruvian sentence where *le* reflects an inanimate subject (a tooth) and a human direct object, but the *lo* reflects both a human subject (the dentist who is speaking) and a human direct object: *si [la muela] le molesta mucho, lo puedo atender hoy mismo* (Peruvian dentist to male patient, from *Variedades*, 238) 'if it [the tooth] is troubling you a lot, I can attend to you today'. Further examples (all Latin American except the first):

---

[5] García notes of Buenos Aires speakers that whereas only 14% of a sample would translate 'he convinced him' as *él le convenció* (the rest say *él lo convenció*), 54% say *este color no le convence* 'this colo(u)r doesn't convince him/her'. We found that of twenty-three educated Spaniards, mostly from Madrid, only 20% used *le* in *yo la convencí* 'I convinced her', but 70% preferred *le* in *si a tu suegra este color no le convence, que elija otro* 'if this colour doesn't convince your mother-in-law, let her choose another'.

Le amargaba la idea de haber estrangulado las palabras que estaba a punto de dirigirle (C. Martín Gaite, Spain)	She was embittered by the idea of having choked back (lit. 'strangled') the words she was about to say to him
Él se miraba la sangre que le había salpicado (M. Vargas Llosa, Peru)	He looked at the blood that had spattered him
Sin embargo, le molestaba encararse con Parodi (J. L. Borges, Argentina)	Yet it troubled him to come face to face with Parodi
Durante mucho tiempo le angustió esa novedad (E. Sábato, Argentina)	For a long while that new turn of events (lit. 'novelty') filled him with anguish
. . . lo que más le preocupaba de la muerte al doctor Urbino . . . (G. García Márquez, Colombia)	. . . what worried Dr Urbino most about the death . . .

The following are some verbs that take *le/les* when their subject is inanimate:

Le acometió una duda	A doubt assailed him/her
La angustia le acompañaba siempre	Anguish went with her always
Yo la acompañaba siempre	I always went with her
A Consuelo le admiró que no contestase	It surprised Consuelo that he did not reply
A Consuelo la admiro mucho	I admire Consuelo a great deal
El dolor que le afligía . . .	The pain that afflicted him/her . . .
No sabe la suerte que le aguarda	(S)he doesn't know the fate that's waiting for him/her
Yo la aguardé (likewise *esperar*)	I awaited her
No le alcanzan mil pesetas para vivir	1,000 pesetas aren't enough for him/her to live on
No pude alcanzarla	I couldn't catch up with her
El gas les hace reír	The gas makes them laugh
Yo los haré reír	I'll make them laugh

And similarly such verbs as the following: *asustar* 'to frighten', *ayudar* 'to help', *calmar* 'to calm', *coger* 'to catch', *complacer* 'to please', *convencer* 'to convince', *distraer* 'to amuse'/'distract', *encantar* 'to enchant'/'charm', *estorbar* 'to impede'/ 'get in the way of', *exasperar* 'to exasperate', *fascinar* 'to fascinate', *fatigar* 'to fatigue', *indignar* 'to outrage', *inquietar* 'to worry', *molestar* 'to trouble', *preocupar* 'to worry', *seducir* 'to charm', *tranquilizar* 'to calm', etc.

Note

The rules given in this section reflect what seems to be the best usage in Spain, the Southern Cone and Mexico, but it must be remembered that many native speakers do not exploit all the potential of these subtleties so they will often disagree about the correct pronoun to use. Moreover, strongly *loísta* speakers, e.g. Colombians, may use *lo/la* where others prefer *le*.

12.6.3 Preference for *le/les* after impersonal or reflexive *se*

If impersonal (or, occasionally, reflexive *se*) precedes a third-person pronoun there is a widespread tendency to prefer *le/les* as the direct object pronouns when the object is human.[6]

---

[6] The verb *llevarse* seems always to prefer *lo* for a direct object pronoun, human or not. In the following sentences distributed to fifty-five Spaniards from Madrid, Segovia and Valladolid, the immense majority preferred *lo* to *le*, despite the fact that the area is heavily *leísta*: *se rompió una pierna y se . . . llevaron al hospital en ambulancia* 'he broke a leg and they took him to hospital in an ambulance' (*lo* 75%, *le* 25%); *a mi padre me . . . voy a llevar a pasar las vacaciones con nosotros* 'I'm going to take my father on holiday with us' (*lo* 62%, *le* 38%).

Se le notaba tímida y cortada (L. Goytisolo, Spain)	One could see she was timid and embarrassed
Se le notaba alegre (M. Vargas Llosa, Peru, *lo* expected)	One could see he was cheerful
Entonces se le leerá como se le debió leer siempre . . . (M. Vargas Llosa, Peru, essay on Camus; *lo* expected)	Then he will be read as he always should have been read . . .
Hola doctor, ¡qué bien se le ve! (Peruvian speaker, *Variedades* 238, *lo* expected)	Hello doctor, you're looking well!
Licha se le prendió de la solapa (C. Fuentes, Mexico)	Licha pulled him to her by his lapels
Licha se le volvió a abrazar (ibid.)	Licha put her arms round him again/Licha drew him to herself again

Notes

(i) Use of *le/les* for the direct object is here a device for removing some of the ambiguities that arise in Spanish from the scarcity of object pronoun forms. Use of *lo/la* after *se* invites the interpretation of *se* as a substitute for *le* by the rule that two object pronouns beginning with *l* cannot occur side by side (see 11.13.1). Thus *le cortó la cabeza* '(s)he cut his/her head off' is pronominalized *se la cortó* '(s)he cut it off (him/her)' (for the expected **se la cortó*). For this reason *se la notaba pálida* may suggest 'he noticed that his/her/their hand, face, head, cheek, chin (or some other grammatically feminine noun) was pale'; *se le notaba . . .* shows that the object is the whole person. Compare the following examples in which *se* replaces *le* and the object is not human: *se lo cobró* 'he took **it** (money) off him/her/you', *se la vendió a ella* 'he sold **it** (fem.) to her', *se lo leyó a su padre* '(s)he read **it** to his/her father'.

(ii) In Spain *le* is occasionally seen even for non-human direct objects after impersonal *se*, although in this example *los* would be more usual: *a los esperpentos de Valle-Inclán siempre se les ha considerado ejemplos de expresionismo español* (A. Buero Vallejo, Spain) 'Valle-Inclán's esperpentos have always been considered examples of Spanish expressionism.'

(iii) Use of *la* after impersonal *se* to refer to a female and of *lo* to refer to a male is not, however, impossible, as in *la luz se apagó y apenas se lo veía* (M. Vargas Llosa, Peru) 'the light went out and one could scarcely see him', *se lo veía pálido en las fotos* (J. Marías, Spain) 'he looked pale in the photographs', *al término de la temporada* **se le** *dio de baja,* **se lo** *traspasó al fútbol francés* (J. Marías, Spain) 'at the end of the season he was released and transferred to French soccer', *—No se le acusa de ningún hecho.—Y entonces ¿de qué se lo acusa?* (interview *La Nación*, Argentina) '"He's not being accused of any action." "What is he being accused of, then?"'

12.6.4 *Le/les* preferred with certain verbs

The following verbs take *le* for their object pronoun, even though in most cases it would seem to English-speaking students that the pronoun is a direct object:[7]

Creer 'to believe', when its object is human: *yo no le creo, señora,* 'Señora, I don't believe you', but *sí que lo creo* 'I do believe it'.

Discutir 'argue'/'discuss' when it means 'to answer back': *¿desde cuándo le discutía?* 'since when had she been answering him back?' (M. Vargas Llosa, Peruvian dialogue).

Enseñar when its object is human: *les enseñaba* 'he taught/showed them' but *lo enseñaba* 'he showed it'.

This is presumably a peculiarity of the verb *llevar*: *le* is reserved for the meaning 'carry *to* him/her', and *lo* for the meaning 'to take' or 'to wear'.

[7] Most native speakers of Spanish would, on formal grounds, analyse the *le* in *le gusta* as an 'indirect object', whereas English speakers usually perceive the 'him' of 'it pleases him' as a 'direct object' exactly as in 'it frightened him', and they would find it quite strange to think of the *le* of *su marido le pega* as an 'indirect object'.

Entender 'understand' when its object is human: *no le entiendo* 'I don't understand him/her/you' but *lo entiendo* 'I understand it'.

Gustar/agradar/complacer/placer 'to please', and all verbs of similar or opposite meaning: *le gusta la miel* 'he/she/it likes honey/you like honey', *le disgustaba encontrarse sola* 'she disliked finding herself alone'.

Importar 'to matter'/'concern', *concernir* 'to concern' and verbs of similar meaning: *no les importa que no tengan dinero* 'they don't care that they have no money'; *eso no le concierne a usted* 'that doesn't concern you'.

Interesar: reiteró que sólo/solo un hombre le interesaba en el mundo 'she repeated that only one man in the world interested her'.

Llamar: Many speakers prefer *le/les* when the verb means 'to give a name': *todo el mundo le llama 'Chelo'*, 'everybody calls her "Chelo"', *se nos informó en un 'briefing', que le llaman* (Cuban TV interview) 'we were told in a "briefing", as they call it'; but this usage is not universal: *al más alegre lo llamaban el Trompo* (G. García Márquez, Colombia) 'they called the most cheerful one "Spinning Top". (For christening, educated usage says *le pusieron María de nombre* 'they called her "Maria"'). *La/lo/(le)/los/las* are the usual object pronouns used when the verb means 'phone' or 'call to': *yo la llamaré apenas haya alguna novedad* 'I'll call you/her as soon as there's news'.

Obedecer 'obey': *¿le han obedecido a Mademoiselle Durand?* 'did you obey Mlle Durand?' (E. Poniatowska, Mexico, dialogue), although the verb is also found with *la/lo*.

Pegar 'to beat': *[Lalita] te contó que le pegué* (dialogue in M. Vargas Llosa, Peru) 'Lalita told you I hit her', *dicen que le pega mucho* 'they say he hits him/her/you a lot'. *Pegarlo/pegarla*, etc., is assumed to mean 'to stick (i.e. glue) it'. *La pegaba* for '(s)he beat her is, however, heard in familiar language, cf. *luego él cambió y le daba achares y la pegaba* (Rosa Montero, Spain) 'then he changed and made her jealous and hit her', *la insultaba y la pegaba* (S. Puértolas, Spain) 'he insulted her and hit her'. Foreigners should probably stick to *le/les*.

Preocupar, inquietar 'to worry': *le preocupa* 'it worries him/her/you'.

Recordar when it means 'to remind': *la recuerdo* 'I remember her', but *recuérdale que viene esta noche* 'remind her/him that (s)he's coming tonight'.

Tirar, when it means 'to pull' rather than to 'throw' or 'throw away': *la amiga le tiraba de la mano* (Javier Marías, Spain) 'her friend was pulling her by the hand'. Compare *lo/la tiró* '(s)he threw it/(s)he threw it away'.

Tocar, when it means 'to be the turn of' rather than 'to touch': compare *le toca a usted, señora* 'it's your turn, Señora' and *la tocó a usted, señora* 'he touched you, Señora'.

12.6.5 *Le/les* in double accusative constructions

In *Juan la oyó* 'John heard her' *la* is normal since 'she' is not 'actively participant' in any of the ways described at 12.3 List A. In 'John heard her sing an aria' there are two objects, one, 'aria', less active than the other, 'her'. Spanish speakers normally use *le* to denote the more active object: *Juan le oyó cantar un aria* (*la* occurs, particularly in Spain, but may be rejected by educated speakers). Questionnaires, based on examples from García (1975), elicited the following replies from twenty educated *madrileños*, which confirmed García's finding with Latin-American speakers: *María no quería venir, pero ... obligamos a venir* (*la* 70%, *le* 30%) 'Maria didn't want to come, but we obliged her to come' (single accusative); *pobre María, su padre siempre . . . obliga a decir la verdad* (*la* 35%, *le* 65%) 'poor Maria, her father always obliges her to tell the truth' (two objects, 'her' and *a decir la verdad*).

Notes

(i) *Ver* normally takes *lo* (in Spain *le*)/*la/los/las*: *yo me quedé con ella porque quería ver**la** firmar el contrato* 'I stayed with her because I wanted to see her sign the contract'.

(ii) *Dejar* 'to let' may take *la* (and in Latin America *lo*): ***la** dejaron hacerlo* 'they let her do it'. *Permitir* takes *le*: ***le** permitieron hacerlo*.

12.7 Pronouns with verbs of motion

For *acude a ella* 'he goes to her', *se les acercó* '(s)he approached them', see 11.8.

12.8 'Resumptive' or 'echoing' *lo* with *ser, estar* and *haber*

The predicate of *ser, estar, parecer* and *haber* is resumed or 'echoed' by *lo*: *parecía alemana y **lo** era* 'she looked German and she was', *pensé que había un error pero no **lo** había* 'I thought there was a mistake, but there wasn't'. See 7.4.1 note (i) and 30.2.2 for details.

12.9 *Se* for *le/les* when they are followed by *lo/la/los/las*

For the obligatory replacement of *le* by *se* when it precedes *lo/la/los/las*, as in *se lo di* 'I gave it to him' (**never** **le lo di*), see 11.13.1.

12.10 Latin America *se los* for *se lo*

For the colloquial Latin American form *?se los dije* 'I told them/you (plural)' for the standard *se lo dije a ellos/ellas/ustedes*, see 11.13.2.

12.11 *Le* for *les*

For the universal colloquial tendency to use *le* for *les* when the latter is a 'redundant' pronoun, as in *siempre **le** digo la verdad a mis padres* 'I always tell my parents the truth', for *les digo la verdad*, see 11.16.3.

13

Forms of verbs

The conjugation of regular verbs is shown at 13.5.2. Regular spelling changes are shown at 13.5.3. Compound tenses are shown at 13.5.4. Irregular verbs are listed at 13.4.

Argentine *vos* forms are mentioned in this chapter since they are used in educated speech in that country. *Voseo* is discussed in more detail at 11.3.1.

13.1 General remarks about the Spanish verb system

13.1.1 The three conjugations

All Spanish verbs belong to one of three conjugations distinguished by the vowel of the infinitive: (1) *-ar* (2) *-er* (3) *-ir*, or *-ír* in the case of the half-dozen verbs listed at 13.1.4f.

The endings of verbs of the *-ir* conjugation are the same as those of the *-er* conjugations except for: **(a)** *vosotros* forms of the imperative: *comed* 'eat' but *vivid* 'live'; **(b)** *nosotros* forms of the present indicative: *comemos* 'we eat' but *vivimos* 'we live'; **(c)** *vosotros* form of the present indicative: *coméis* 'you eat' but *vivís* 'you live'; **(d)** *vos* forms of the present indicative in those countries, e.g. Argentina and most of Central America, where this pronoun is used instead of *tú*: *vos comés* 'you eat' (= *tú comes*), but *vos vivís* 'you live' (= *tú vives*); **(e)** forms based on the infinitive, i.e. the future and the conditional: *comerá* 'he'll eat', *vivirá* 'he'll live', *comería* 'he'd eat' but *viviría* 'he'd live'.

The full conjugation of three typical regular verbs in *-ar*, *-er* and *-ir* is shown at 13.5.2.

13.1.2 Regular spelling changes

There are predictable spelling changes that affect all verbs. They are discussed at 13.5.3.

13.1.3 Irregular verbs : general remarks

Only about two dozen Spanish verbs (not counting compound verbs formed from them) are traditionally defined as truly 'irregular'. These are:

andar to walk 13.3.5	*estar* to be 13.3.21	*poder* to be able 13.3.34
asir to seize (rarely used) 13.3.6	*haber* auxiliary verb or	*poner* to put (and several
caber to fit into 13.3.8	'there is/are' 13.3.22	compounds) 13.3.35
caer to fall (and some	*hacer* 'to do'/'to make'	*producir* to produce (and
compounds) 13.3.9	13.3.23	all verbs ending in
dar to give 13.3.15	*ir* to go 13.3.24	*-ducir*) 13.3.37
decir to say 13.3.16	*oír* to hear 13.3.29	*querer* to want 13.3.38

saber to know 13.3.42
salir to go out 13.3.43
ser to be 13.3.45
tener to have (and several
  compounds) 13.3.46

traer to bring (and a few
  compounds) 13.3.47
valer to be worth (and
  compounds) 13.3.48

venir to come (and
  compounds) 13.3.49
ver to see 13.3.50

13.1.4 Radical changing verbs

'Radical changing' verbs are numerous: several hundred are in everyday use, although many of them are derived from more familiar verbs, e.g. *descontar* 'to discount', conjugated like *contar* 'to count'/'to tell a story'. Radical changing verbs have regular endings, but a vowel in the stem is modified in some forms, cf. *contar* 'to tell a story' > *cuenta* 'he tells', *perder* 'to lose' > *pierdo* 'I lose', *sentir* 'to feel' > *siente* 'he feels' > *sintió* 'he felt', etc.

Grammarians have traditionally been reluctant to call these verbs 'irregular', but their forms cannot be predicted since their infinitive is no guide to whether they are radical changing or not. Compare *renovar* 'to renovate', which is a radical changing verb, and *innovar* 'to innovate' which is not.

A few verbs are uncertain or have become regular. These include: *cimentar* 'to cement' like *cerrar* or, more usually, regular; *derrocar* 'to overthrow', nowadays regular; *mentar* 'to mention', though educated usage still prefers to conjugate it like *cerrar*; *derrengarse* 'to be exhausted', nowadays regular; *plegar* 'to fold' like *cerrar* or optionally regular. Note also the following:

When conjugated regularly	When conjugated like
apostar = to post a sentry	*contar* = to bet
aterrar = to terrorize	*cerrar* = to level/raze to the ground
asolar = to parch	*contar* = to level/raze to ground[1]

The following list shows the common types of radical changing verbs and a selection of verbs that occur constantly and should be learnt first.

(a) Conjugated like *contar* 'tell'/'count', 13.3.14:
acordarse de 'to remember', *acostarse* 'to go to bed', *apostar* 'to bet', *aprobar* 'to approve'/'to pass an exam', *avergonzarse* 'to be ashamed', *colarse* 'to slip through'/'gatecrash', *colgar* 'to hang', *comprobar* 'to check', *consolar* 'to console', *costar* 'to cost', *demostrar* 'to demonstrate' (a fact or technique), *desaprobar* 'to disapprove', *encontrar* 'to find'/'to meet', *esforzarse* 'to make an effort', *mostrar* 'to show', *probar* 'to prove'/'to try' (i.e. 'to sample', 'to test'), *recordar* 'to remember'/'to remind', *renovar* 'to renew', *rodar* 'to roll', *soltar* 'to release'/'let out', *sonar* 'to sound', *soñar* 'to dream', *tronar* 'to thunder', *volar* 'to fly'.
(b) Conjugated like *cerrar* 'to close', 13.3.11:
acertar 'to get right'/'to hit the mark', *apretar* 'to squeeze/tighten', *atravesar* 'to cross', *calentar* 'to heat', *comenzar* 'to begin', *confesar* 'to confess', *despertar(se)* 'to wake up', *empezar* 'to begin', *encerrar* 'to lock/shut in', *enterrar* 'to bury', *gobernar* 'to govern', *helar* 'to freeze' (liquids), *manifestarse* 'to demonstrate' (i.e. protest), *negar* 'to deny', *nevar* 'to snow', *pensar* 'to think', *recomendar* 'to recommend', *sentarse* 'to sit down', *temblar* 'to tremble', *tropezar* 'to stumble'.

---

[1] The regular form is becoming standardized for both meanings.

(c) Conjugated like *mover* 'to move', 13.3.28:
desenvolverse 'to develop', *devolver* 'to give back', *disolver* 'to dissolve', *doler* 'to hurt', *envolver* 'to wrap up', *llover* 'to rain', *morder* 'to bite', *oler* 'to smell' (see 13.3.30), *remover* 'to stir up' (Lat. Am. 'to remove'), *resolver* 'to resolve', *soler* 'to be accustomed to' (+ infinitive), *volver(se)* 'to return'/'to become', etc.

(d) Conjugated like *perder* 'to lose', 13.3.32:
atender 'to attend' (i.e. pay attention), *defender* 'to defend', *encender* 'to light/set fire to', *entender* 'to understand', *extenderse* 'to extend/stretch' (over a distance), *tender a* 'to tend to'.

(e) Conjugated like *pedir* 'to ask for' (13.3.31):
competir 'to compete', *concebir* 'to conceive', *conseguir* 'to achieve'/'to manage', *corregir* 'to correct', *derretirse* 'to melt', *despedir* 'to fire' (i.e. dismiss from job), *despedirse* 'to say goodbye', *elegir* 'to elect'/'to choose', *gemir* 'to groan', *impedir* 'to hinder'/'to impede', *medir* 'to measure', *perseguir* 'to persecute'/'to chase', *proseguir* 'to pursue' (a course of action), *rendirse* 'to surrender', *repetir* 'to repeat', *reñir* 'to scold' (see 13.3.40), *seguir* 'to follow', *servir* 'to serve'/'to be useful', *vestir(se)* 'to wear'/'to dress'.

(f) Conjugated like *reír* 'to laugh', 13.3.39:
desleír(se) 'to dissolve/melt', *engreírse* 'to grow conceited', *(re)freír* 'to fry', *sonreír* 'to smile'.

(g) Conjugated like *sentir* 'to feel', 13.3.44:
advertir 'to warn', *arrepentirse* 'to repent', *consentir* 'to consent', *convertir* 'to convert'; *convertirse en* 'to turn into', *desmentir* 'to deny', *disentir* 'to dissent', *divertir(se)* 'to amuse oneself', *herir* 'to wound', *interferir* 'to interfere', *invertir* 'to invest', *mentir* 'to tell lies', *preferir* 'to prefer', *referirse a* 'to refer to', *sugerir* 'to suggest'.

(h) *dormir* 'to sleep' and *morir* 'to die', 13.3.18.

(i) *jugar* 'to play', 13.3.25.

(j) *adquirir* 'to acquire', 13.3.3.

(k) Conjugated like *discernir* 'to discern', 13.3.17: *cernirse* 'to hover'/'to loom', *concernir* 'to concern' (third-person only).

13.1.5 Forms of the present indicative

The endings of the present indicative of regular verbs and of all but a few irregular verbs are shown at 13.5.2. However, there are numerous verbs in the *-er* and *-ir* conjugations in which the first-person singular ending is attached to an irregular stem, e.g. *producir* 'to produce' > *produzco* 'I produce', *poner* 'to put' > *pongo* 'I put', etc. These must be learnt separately.

Four irregular verbs have a first-person singular ending in *-y*: *dar* > *doy*, *estar* > *estoy*, *ir* > *voy*, *ser* > *soy*.

Argentine *vos* forms of the present tense can be found by dropping any unstressed *i* from the ending of the European Spanish *vosotros* form: *vosotros habláis* > *vos hablás* 'you speak', *vosotros teméis* > *vos temés* 'you fear', *vosotros sois* > *vos sos* 'you are'; but *vosotros vivís* > *vos vivís* 'you live', *vosotros decís* > *vos decís* 'you say'.

13.1.6 Forms of the imperfect indicative

The endings of the imperfect indicative are shown at 13.5.2. The Argentine *vos* endings are the same as the standard *tú* endings. The endings are added to the stem left after removing the infinitive ending. There are only three exceptions:

ser to be	*era, eras, era, éramos, erais, eran*
ir to go	*iba, ibas, iba, íbamos, ibais, iban*
ver to see	*veía, veías, veía, veíamos, veíais, veían*
(instead of the expected* *vía, *vías*, etc.)	

13.1.7 Forms of the preterite[2]

The endings of the preterite are shown at 13.5.2: Argentine *vos* forms are the same as for *tú* in standard Spanish. The third-person plural ending is -*eron* in the case of the preterite of:

conducir 'to drive', and all verbs whose infinitive ends in -*ducir*	*condujeron*
decir to say	*dijeron*
ser and *ir* 'to be' and 'to go'	*fueron*
traer to bring	*trajeron*

Verbs whose infinitive ends in -*ñer*, -*ñir* or -*llir* also lose the *i* in the third-person singular and third-person plural endings. See 13.5.3(6).

Most of the irregular verbs listed at 13.1.3 have an irregular preterite stem, and many of them have unexpected first-person and third-person singular endings with an unstressed final vowel. *Hacer* 'to do' and *caber* 'to fit into' are typical:

hacer: *hice, hiciste, hizo, hicimos, hicisteis, hicieron*
caber: *cupe, cupiste, cupo, cupimos, cupisteis, cupieron*

Verbs conjugated like *sentir* 'to feel', *pedir* 'to ask', and *dormir* 'to sleep' have irregularities in the third person of the preterite:

sintió > sintieron	*pidió > pidieron*	*durmió > durmieron*

13.1.8 The future and the conditional

The endings of the future and conditional tenses are identical for all verbs, regular and irregular and are shown at 13.5.2 (Argentine *vos* forms are the same as for *tú*). These endings are always added to the infinitive except in the cases of the following twelve verbs:

caber to fit in: ***cabr–***	*poder* to be able: ***podr–***	*salir* to go out: ***saldr–***
decir to say: ***dir–***	*poner* to put: ***pondr–***	*tener* to have: ***tendr–***
haber (aux. verb): ***habr–***	*querer* to want: ***querr–***	*valer* to be worth: ***valdr–***
hacer to do/make: ***har–***	*saber* to know: ***sabr–***	*venir* to come: ***vendr–***

13.1.9 Forms of the present subjunctive

The endings of the present subjunctive are easily memorized: -***ar*** verbs take the endings of the present indicative of regular -*er* verbs except that the first-person -*o* is replaced by -*e*; -***er*** and -***ir*** verbs take the endings of the present indicative of regular -*ar* verbs, except that first-person -*o* is replaced by -*a*. See 13.5.2 for examples.

---

[2] The British spelling of the US 'preterit' is used throughout this book.

As far as regular verbs and most irregular verbs are concerned, these endings are added to the stem left after removing the *-o* of the first-person present indicative: e.g. *vengo* 'I come' > *venga*, *conduzco* 'I drive' > *conduzca*, *quepo* 'there's room for me' > *quepa* (from *caber*, 13.3.8), etc. The six exceptions among the irregular verbs are:

dar to give	*dé, des, dé*, etc.[3]
estar to be	*esté, estés, esté, estemos, estéis, estén*
haber	*haya, hayas, haya, hayamos, hayáis, hayan*
ir to go	*vaya, vayas, vaya, vayamos, vayáis, vayan*
saber to know	*sepa, sepas, sepa, sepamos, sepáis, sepan*
ser to be	*sea, seas, sea, seamos, seáis, sean*

In the case of radical changing verbs, the usual vowel changes occur, e.g. *cuente, cuentes, cuente, contemos, contéis, cuenten* (from *contar*, see 13.3.14). Verbs like *sentir* 'to feel' have another irregularity in the present subjunctive: *sienta, sientas, sienta, sintamos, sintáis, sientan*.

Morir 'to die' and *dormir* 'to sleep' also show have extra irregularities in the present subjunctive. See 13.3.18 for details.

In Argentina the *vos* forms of the present subjunctive used by careful speakers are the same as the standard *tú* forms. See 16.2.8 for further comments on this topic.

13.1.10 Forms of the past (imperfect) and future subjunctives

There are two sets of imperfect subjunctive endings: these are the imperfect subjunctive in *-ra* and the imperfect subjunctive in *-se*. They are shown at 13.5.2 (Argentine *vos* forms are the same as the standard *tú* forms). When used as subjunctive forms, these two sets of forms are interchangeable. For the slight differences between their uses see 16.2.3.

The endings of the future subjunctive (virtually obsolete, so foreign learners will not need to use it: its limited uses in modern Spanish are discussed at 16.17) are identical to those of the *-ra* past subjunctive, except that the last *a* is replaced by *e*: *-ar* verbs: *-are, -ares, -are, -áremos, -areis, -aren*; *-er* and *-ir* verbs: *-iere, -ieres, -iere, -iéremos, -iereis, -ieren*.

The past (imperfect) and future subjunctive endings are added to the stem of the third-person singular of the preterite indicative. In the case of regular verbs this stem is found by removing the infinitive ending, e.g. *habl(ar)* > *habl-*: *yo hablara/hablase, tú hablaras/hablases, él hablara/hablase*, etc. But in the case of irregular verbs the preterite stem is often irregular, e.g.

Infinitive	**Third-person preterite stem**	**Past and future subjunctives**
sentir 'to feel' and verbs like it	*sint(ió)*	*sintiera/sintiese/sintiere,*
pedir 'to request' and verbs like it	*pid(ió)*	*pidiera/pidiese/pidiere*, etc.
ser 'to be'	*fu(e)*	*fuera/fuese/fuere*, etc.

---

[3] The accent merely distinguishes the forms from the preposition *de*.

producir 'to produce', and all verbs ending in *-ducir*	*produj(o)*	*produjera/produjese/produjere*, etc.
tener 'to have'	*tuv(o)*	*tuviera/tuviese/tuviere*, etc.

Morir and *dormir* have the third-person preterite stems *mur(ió)* and *durm(ió)*, so the past subjunctives are *muriera/muriese*, *durmiera/durmiese*, etc.

The forms *-ese*, *-era*, *-ere*, etc, (i.e. not *-iese*, *-iera*, *-iere*) are used with the following verbs:

decir to say	*dijera/dijese/dijere*, etc.
ir 'to go' and *ser* 'to be'	*fuera/fuese/fuere*, etc.
traer to bring	*trajera/trajese/trajere*, etc.
all verbs whose infinitive ends in *-ducir*	*condujera, produjese*, etc.
all verbs whose infinitive ends in *-ñer, -ñir* or *-llir*	*bullera, tañese*, etc.

13.1.11 The imperative: see Chapter 17

13.1.12 Forms of the past participle: see 19.2.1

13.1.13 The compound tenses

The compound tenses, e.g. *he hablado* 'I have spoken', *has visto* 'you've seen', *habían tenido* 'they'd had', *habrán hecho* 'they'll have made', etc., are always predictable if one can conjugate *haber* (see 13.3.22) and knows the past participle of the verb. For this reason individual compound tenses are not listed, but the full compound tense forms of *ver* 'to see' is shown in 13.5.4. The use of the compound tenses is discussed at 14.8.–14.10.

13.1.14 Forms of the gerund: see 20.2

13.1.15 Forms of the adjectival participle

This refers to forms like *preocupante* 'worrying', *convincente* 'convincing', discussed at 19.4.

13.1.16 Continuous forms of verbs

Spanish has a full range of continuous forms, e.g. *estoy hablando* 'I'm talking', *estuve esperando* 'I was waiting'/'I waited for a time', etc. They are all formed from the appropriate tense of *estar* (see 13.3.21) and the invariable gerund. Their use is discussed in Chapter 15.

13.1.17 Forms of the passive: see 13.5.1

13.2 Variants and spelling rules

13.2.1 Colloquial variants

The Spanish verb system is remarkably stable throughout the Spanish-speaking world, despite the large number of forms and exceptions. Popular regularizations of irregular forms, e.g. **cabo* for *quepo* (from *caber* 'to fit into'), **produció* for *produjo* (from *producir* 'to produce'), **andé* for *anduve* (from *andar* 'to walk') are stigmatized.

Three other popular spoken forms are very common, although all but **(a)** are stigmatized as uneducated and should be avoided by foreigners:

(a) use of the infinitive for the *vosotros* form of the imperative: *dar* for *dad* 'give', *callaros* for *callaos* 'shut up!'/'be quiet', *iros* for *idos* 'go away', etc. This is widespread in Spain (*vosotros* forms are not used in Latin America). For discussion see 17.2.4;

(b) addition of *-s* to the second-person preterite singular, e.g. ?*distes* for *diste* 'you gave', ?*hablastes* for *hablaste* 'you spoke'. This is common on both continents, but it is stigmatized and is not seen in printed texts;

(c) pluralization of forms *haber* (other than *hay*) when it means 'there is'/'there are', e.g. ?*habían muchos* for *había muchos* 'there were many'. This is very common in Catalonia and Latin America but it is stigmatized in Castilian-speaking Spain. See 30.2.1 note (i).

There is also a tendency in some Latin-American dialects to regularize radical changing verbs, e.g. **cuentamos* for *contamos* 'we tell', **detiénete* for *detente* 'stop'. Such forms sometimes appear in printed dialogue, but foreigners should avoid them.

13.2.2 General spelling rules

Certain spelling changes are applied systematically throughout the verb system, e.g. *pago > pagué, saco > saqué, rezo > recé*. The most common are shown at 13.5.3.

13.2.3 Spelling and pronunciation of *aislar, reunir, prohibir* and similar verbs whose stem contains a diphthong

When the last syllable but one of an infinitive contains a falling diphthong (one whose second letter is *i* or *u*), this diphthong may or may not be broken into two syllables when it is stressed, e.g.

prohibir to prohibit	[proɣβír] (two syllables)
prohíbe (s)he prohibits	[proíβe] (three syllables)
reunir to join together	[rrewnír] (two syllables)
reúnen they join	[rreúnen] (three syllables)

Compare the following verb in which the diphthong is not broken:

causar to cause	[kawsár] (two syllables)
causa it causes	[káwsas] (two syllables)

Since 1959 the stressed vowel in such broken diphthongs has been written with an accent. In the Academy's view the fact that *-h-* appears between the two vowels makes no difference. This ruling affects the following forms of the verb (bracketed forms are unaffected):

tú imperative:	*aísla*	*reúne*	*prohíbe*
usted(es) imperative:	*aísle/aíslen*	*reúna/reúnan*	*prohíba/prohíban*

Present indicative
aislar 'to isolate': *aíslo, aíslas, aísla, (aislamos), (aisláis), aíslan*
reunir 'to bring together':[4] *reúne, reúnes, reúne, (reunimos), (reunís), reúnen*
prohibir 'to prohibit': *prohíbe, prohíbes, prohíbe, (prohibimos), (prohibís), prohíben*

---

[4] *Reunirse* 'to hold a meeting'.

Present subjunctive
aislar: aísle, aísles, aísle, (aislemos), (aisléis), aíslen
reunir: reúna, reúnas, reúna, (reunamos), (reunáis), reúnan
prohibir: prohíba, prohíbas, prohíba,(prohibamos), (prohibáis), prohíban

The following verbs are similarly affected, but bracketed verbs are now archaic or rare:

ahijar to adopt (child)	*(airar* to anger)	*(desahitarse* to digest[5])	*maullar* to meow
(ahilar to line up)	*amohinar* to vex	*enraizar* to take root	*prohijar* to adopt
(ahincar to urge)	*arcaizar* to archaize	*europeizar* to	*rehilar* to quiver
(ahitar to cloy)	*aullar* to howl	Europeanize	*rehusar* to refuse
ahumar to smoke (food)	*aunar* to unite	*hebraizar* to hebraicize	*sahumar* to incense
	aupar to help up	*judaizar* to judaize	*sobrehilar* to over-
	cohibir to restrain		cast (in sewing)

The new spelling is in general use in printed texts in Spain, but most people still omit the accent in handwriting and many Latin-American publishers use the old, unaccented forms.

In other verbs the diphthong is not broken: when the diphthong is stressed the accent falls on its first vowel and no written accent appears, e.g. *arraigarse* 'to take root' > *arraigo*, *encausar* 'to sue' > *encausa*, etc. Similar are *amainar* 'to shorten'/'to calm', *causar* 'to cause', *desahuciar* 'to evict'/'to give up hope for' (variable, usually the diphthong is retained), *desenvainar* 'to unsheathe', *embaucar* 'to swindle', *embaular* 'to pack' (a trunk/suitcase: variable – the verb is hardly ever used), *envainar* 'to sheathe', *peinar* 'to comb'/'to do someone's hair', *reinar* to reign', etc.

13.2.4 Verbs whose infinitive ends in *-iar*

These are of two types. The majority conjugate like *cambiar* 'to change': the *-ia* survives as a diphthong throughout and is always pronounced [ya], so the verb is conjugated as a regular *-ar* throughout and no accent appears on the *i*.

But about fifty verbs conjugate like *liar* 'to tie in a bundle'. These verbs are conjugated like *cambiar* (i.e. regularly) except that the *i* of the diphthong is stressed in the following cases (bracketed forms are regular):

Imperative: (*tú*) *lía*, (*usted*) *líe*, (*ustedes*) *líen*
Present indicative: *lío, lías, lía, (liamos), (liáis), lían*
Present subjunctive: *líe, líes, líe, (liemos), (liéis), líen*

The following list shows common verbs which conjugate like *liar* 'tie up'/ 'wrap up':

agriar to sour (usu. like *cambiar*)	*descarriar* to misdirect	*inventariar* to inventory
aliar to ally	*desliar* to untie	*litografiar* to lithograph
amnistiar to grant an amnesty to	*desvariar* to rave	*malcriar* to pamper
	desviar to divert	*mecanografiar* to type
ampliar to expand/enlarge	*enfriar* to chill	*paliar* to palliate (usually like *cambiar*)
ansiar to yearn for	*enviar* to send	
arriar to flood/to haul down	*escalofriar* to feel shivery	*piar* to cheep
	espiar to spy	*porfiar* to argue stubbornly

---

[5] More accurately, 'to get rid of a sensation of excessive fullness'. The verb is rarely used.

ataviar to array (with clothes)
autografiar to autograph
auxiliar to aid (disputed, usually like *cambiar*)
averiar to damage
aviar to fit out
biografiar to write the biography of
conciliar to reconcile (usually like *cambiar*)
contrariar to counter
criar to breed/raise
desafiar to challenge

expatriarse to emigrate (also like *cambiar*)
expiar to expiate
extasiar to make ecstatic (usually like *liar*)
extraviar to mislead
fiar to confide
fotografiar to photograph
gloriar(se) to glory
guiar to guide
hastiar to weary
historiar to chronicle (usually like *cambiar*)

radiografiar to x-ray
resfriarse to catch a cold
rociar to sprinkle
telegrafiar to telegraph
vaciar to empty
vanagloriarse to be boastful (almost always like *cambiar*)
variar to vary
vidriar to glaze (also like *cambiar*)

13.2.5 Verbs whose infinitive ends in *-uar*

Nearly all conjugate like *actuar* 'to act', i.e. the *u* may be stressed. The only forms affected are (bracketed forms are as a regular *-ar* verb, as are all the unlisted forms):

Imperative: (*tú*) *actúa*, (*usted*) *actúe*, (*ustedes*) *actúen*
Present indicative: *actúo, actúas, actúa, (actuamos) (actuáis) actúan*
Present subjunctive: *actúe, actúes, actúe, (actuemos), (actuéis), actúen*

Verbs that conjugate like *actuar*:

acentuar to emphasize
atenuar to attenuate
conceptuar to deem
continuar to continue
desvirtuar to spoil
efectuar to carry out
evaluar to assess
exceptuar to except

extenuar to emaciate
fluctuar to fluctuate
graduar to grade
habituar to habituate
individuar to individualize
infatuar to infatuate
insinuar to hint

preceptuar to establish as a norm/precept
puntuar to punctuate/ to assess
redituar yield (profit, etc.)
situar to situate
valuar to value

Averiguar ('to find out') is conjugated as a regular *-ar* verb and the *u* is never stressed, i.e. it is always pronounced [w]. A dieresis is written over the *u* before a following *e* in order to preserve the pronunciation [gw]. The only forms with a dieresis are (bracketed forms are unaffected):

Imperative: (*usted*) *averigüe* (*ustedes*) *averigüen*
Preterite: *averigüé, (averiguaste), (averiguó), (averiguamos), (averiguasteis), (averiguaron)*
Present subjunctive: *averigüe, averigües, averigüe, averigüemos, averigüéis, averigüen*

Notes

(i) Verbs ending in *-cuar, evacuar* being the most common, should officially be conjugated like *averiguar* (without the dieresis), but conjugation like *actuar* is common in Spain and accepted in some Latin-American countries.
(ii) Like *averiguar* is *aguar* 'to spoil' (a party, fun, etc.).

13.2.6 Verbs ending in -*ear*

All regular: the penultimate *e* is never written with an accent, cf. *pasear* 'to go for a walk':

Present indicative: *paseo, paseas, pasea, paseamos, paseáis, pasean*
Present subjunctive: *pasee, pasees, pasee, paseemos, paseéis, paseen*

13.2.7 Verbs ending in -*cer*

If the infinitive ends in -*cer* the spelling changes shown at 13.5.3 are applied in the case of a few verbs (*c* > *z* before *a, o*). However, the only verbs ending in -*cer* that are conjugated in this way are:

(a) those in which the *c/z* occurs after a consonant:

coercer to coerce	*ejercer* to practise/(US 'to	*(re)torcer* to twist (radical
convencer to convince	practice')	changing; see 13.3.12)
destorcer to untwist		*vencer* to defeat

(b) the following exceptional verbs:

(re)cocer to boil (food) (radical changing; see 13.3.12)
escocerse to sting/smart (conj. like *cocer; picar* 'to sting' is more usual)
mecer to rock/swing; *mecerse* to sway

The rest are like *parecer*, i.e. -*zc*- replaces -*c*- before -*o* or -*a*. See 13.3.10.

13.2.8 Verbs ending in -*eer*: see 13.3.36

13.2.9 Verbs ending in -*cir*

The spelling change shown at 13.5.3 must be applied if the infinitive ends in -*cir*: *c* > *z* before *a, o*. But the only totally regular verbs ending in -*cir* are *esparcir* 'to scatter/strew', *fruncir* 'to pucker/wrinkle' (the eyebrows), *resarcir* 'to repay (effort)', *uncir* 'to yoke' and *zurcir* 'to darn'/'to sew together'. Any others, e.g. *producir*, should be viewed with suspicion and checked in the list at 13.4.

13.2.10 Verbs whose infinitive ends in -*uir*: see *construir* 'to build', 13.3.13

13.3 Irregular verbs

13.3.1 General

Irregular verbs and model radical changing verbs are listed in alphabetical order. The list omits oddities like the archaic *abarse*, found only in the form *ábate* 'get thee hence!', or *usucapir* 'to acquire property rights through customary use', used in legal jargon and only in the infinitive. In general, only the irregular forms are shown, except in the cases of some very common verbs.

13.3.2 *Abolir* 'to abolish'

Defective verb. Only those forms are used in which the verb ending begins with -*i*.
Infinitive *abolir*: Gerund *aboliendo*   **Past participle** *abolido*
Imperative *abolid*. (*abole is not used)
Present indicative: only *abolimos*, and *abolís* are used.

Present subjunctive: not used

All other tenses are regular. Unused forms are replaced, e.g. **sin que se abola* by *sin que sea abolido*. A few other verbs are defective, but only *abolir* and *agredir* are common nowadays:

aguerrir 'to inure'/'to harden' (only past participle in current use)
agredir see 13.3.4
arrecirse (Lat. Am.) 'to be frozen stiff'
aterirse 'to be numb with cold' (only infinitive and participle in current use)
blandir 'to brandish'

despavorir 'to be terrified' (only past participle in current use)
empedernir 'to harden'/'to petrify' (only participle in current use)
garantir 'to guarantee' (replaced in Spain by *garantizar* but still used in Peru and the Southern Cone, where it is often conjugated regularly)

13.3.3 *Adquirir* 'to acquire' (also *inquirir* 'to enquire', US 'inquire')

The infinitive was once *adquerir*, hence *-ie-* when the stem vowel is stressed. Bracketed forms are regular, as are all forms not shown, e.g. *adquirí*, *adquiría*, *adquiriré*, *adquiriera*, etc.

Imperative: (*tú*) *adquiere*, (*usted*) *adquiera*, (*ustedes*) *adquieran*
Present indicative: *adquiero*, *adquieres*, *adquiere*, (*adquirimos*), (*adquirís*), *adquieren*
Present subjunctive: *adquiera*, *adquiera*s *adquiera*, (*adquiramos*), (*adquiráis*), *adquieran*

13.3.4 *Agredir* 'to assault'/'to attack'

Classified by some as defective (like *abolir* 13.3.2), by others as a regular *-ir* verb, the former usage being the more conservative.

13.3.5 *Andar* 'to walk'/'to go about'

A regular *-ar* verb except for the preterite and the past subjunctive:

Preterite: *anduve*, *anduviste*, *anduvo*, *anduvimos*, *anduvisteis*, *anduvieron*
Imperfect subjunctive (-ra): *anduviera*, *anduvieras*, *anduviera*, *anduviéramos*, *anduvierais*, *anduvieran*
Imperfect subjunctive (-se): *anduviese*, *anduvieses*, *anduviese*, *anduviésemos*, *anduvieseis*, *anduviesen*

Preterite forms like **andé*, **andaste* are sometimes heard, but are strongly stigmatized.

13.3.6 *Asir* 'to grasp'/'to seize'

Usually nowadays replaced by *agarrarse*. Forms that contain a *g* are avoided, but other forms are occasionally heard, e.g. *me así a una rama para no caerme* 'I clutched hold of a branch so as not to fall'. It is conjugated like a regular *-ir* verb except for (bracketed forms are regular):

Imperative: (*usted*) *asga*, (*ustedes*) *asgan*
Present indicative: *asgo*, (*ases*, *ase*, *asimos*, *asís*, *asen*)
Present subjunctive: *asga*, *asgas*, *asga*, *asgamos*, *asgáis*, *asgan*

13.3.7 *Balbucir* 'to stammer'

Nowadays found only in those forms whose ending begins with *i*, e.g. *balbucía*, *balbució*. Other forms are replaced by the regular *balbucear*, which has replaced it in everyday speech.

13.3.8 *Caber* 'to fit in'

Numerous irregularities.

Gerund *cabiendo*   **Past participle** *cabido*
Imperative: (*tú*) *cabe*, (*vosotros*) *cabed*, (*usted*) *quepa*, (*ustedes*) *quepan*
Present indicative: *quepo, cabes, cabe, cabemos, cabéis, caben*
Imperfect (regular): *cabía, cabías, cabía, cabíamos, cabíais, cabían*
Preterite: *cupe, cupiste, cupo, cupimos, cupisteis, cupieron*
Future: *cabré, cabrás, cabrá, cabremos, cabréis, cabrán*   **Conditional:** *cabría*, etc.
Present subjunctive: *quepa, quepas, quepas, quepamos, quepáis, quepan*
Imperfect subjunctive (-ra): *cupiera, cupieras, cupiera, cupiéramos, cupierais, cupieran*
Imperfect subjunctive (-se): *cupiese, cupieses, cupiese, cupiésemos, cupieseis, cupiesen*

   Usage: *¿quepo yo?* 'is there room for me?', *no cabe* 'it won't fit', *no cabíamos* 'there wasn't room for us'.

13.3.9 *Caer* 'to fall'

Gerund *cayendo*   **Past participle** *caído*
Imperative: (*tú*) *cae*, (*vosotros*) *caed*, (*usted*) *caiga*, (*ustedes*) *caigan*
Present indicative: *caigo, caes, cae, caímos, caéis, caen*
Imperfect (regular): *caía, caías, caía, caíamos, caíais, caían*
Preterite: *caí, caíste, cayó, caímos, caísteis, cayeron*
Future (regular): *caeré*, etc.   **Conditional (regular):** *caería*, etc.
Present subjunctive: *caiga, caigas, caiga, caigamos, caigáis, caigan*
Imperfect subjunctive (-ra): *cayera, cayeras, cayera, cayéramos, cayerais, cayeran*
Imperfect subjunctive (-se): *cayese, cayeses, cayese, cayésemos, cayeseis, cayesen*

13.3.10 Verbs ending in *-cer*

All verbs ending in *-cer* conjugate like *nacer*, shown below, except the regular verbs *coercer, ejercer, (con)vencer* and *mecer*, for which see 13.5.3 item (1), and the radical-changing verbs *escocer, (re)cocer* and *(re)torcer*, for which see 13.3.12 and 13.2.7a. In all other verbs ending in *-cer c > zc* before *a* or *o*. All forms are as for a regular *-er* verb except for the following (bracketed forms are regular):

Imperative: (*usted*) *nazca*, (*ustedes*) *nazcan*
Present indicative: *nazco*, (*naces, nace, nacemos, nacéis, nacen*)
Present subjunctive: *nazca, nazcas, nazca, nazcamos, nazcáis, nazcan*

13.3.11 *Cerrar* 'to shut'/'to close'

A common type of radical changing verb. The endings are those of regular *-ar* verbs, but the *e* of the stem changes to *ie* when stressed. All forms are as for a regular *-ar* verb, save (bracketed forms are regular):

Imperative: (*tú*) *cierra*, (*usted*) *cierre*, (*ustedes*) *cierren*
Present indicative: *cierro, cierras, cierra, (cerramos), (cerráis), cierran*
Present subjunctive: *cierre, cierres, cierre, (cerremos), (cerréis), cierren*

13.3.12 *Cocer* 'to boil' (food)

This, and three verbs like it, *torcer* 'to twist', *destorcer*, 'to untwist' and *retorcer* 'to wring'/'to twist', conjugate exactly like *mover* save for the predictable spelling change *c* > *z* before *a*, *o* (bracketed forms are regular):

Imperative: (*tú*) *cuece*, (*usted*) *cueza*, (*ustedes*) *cuezan*
Present indicative: *cuezo, cueces, cuece, (cocemos), (cocéis), cuecen*
Present subjunctive: *cueza, cuezas, cueza, (cozamos), (cozáis), cuezan*

13.3.13 *Construir* 'to build'

Verbs ending in *-uir* are quite common. An unstressed *i* between vowels is spelt *y*, e.g. *construyó* for the expected **construió*, and an unexpected *y* is inserted in a number of forms, e.g. *construyes* for the predicted **construes*.

Gerund: *construyendo*   **Past participle:** *construido* (no accent! See 39.2.3b note (i) for explanation)

Imperative: (*tú*) *construye*, (*vosotros*) *construid*, (*usted*) *construya*, (*ustedes*) *construyan*

Present indicative: *construyo, construyes, construye, construimos* (no accent!), *construís, construyen*

Imperfect (regular): *construía, construías, construía, construíamos, construíais, construían*

Preterite: *construí, construiste, construyó, construimos, construisteis, construyeron*
Future (regular): *construiré*, etc.   **Conditional (regular):** *construiría*, etc.

Present subjunctive: *construya, construyas, construya, construyamos, construyáis, construyan*

Imperfect subjunctive (-ra): *construyera, construyeras, construyera, construyéramos, construyerais, construyeran*

Imperfect subjunctive (-se): *construyese, construyeses, construyese, construyésemos, construyeseis, construyesen*

Argüir 'to argue (a point)' is spelt with a dieresis whenever the *u* is followed by *i*. This preserves the pronunciation [gw]: *arguyo, argüimos, argüí, arguya*, etc.

13.3.14 *Contar* 'to count'/'to tell a story'

A common type of radical changing verb: the *o* of the stem changes to *ue* when it is stressed. All forms are as for a regular *-ar* verb except (bracketed forms are regular):

Imperative: (*tú*) *cuenta*, (*usted*) *cuente*, (*ustedes*) *cuenten*
Present indicative: *cuento, cuentas, cuenta, (contamos), (contáis), cuentan*
Present subjunctive: *cuente, cuentes, cuente, (contemos), (contéis), cuenten*

13.3.15 *Dar* 'to give'

Gerund: *dando*   **Past participle:** *dado*
Imperative: (*tú*) *da*, (*vosotros*) *dad*, (*usted*) *dé*, (*ustedes*) *den*

Present indicative: *doy, das, da, damos, dais, dan*
Imperfect (regular): *daba, dabas, daba, dábamos, dabais, daban*
Preterite: *di, diste, dio* (no accent!), *dimos, disteis, dieron*
Future (regular): *daré*, etc. **Conditional (regular):** *daría*, etc.
Present subjunctive: *dé, des, dé, demos, deis, den*
Imperfect subjunctive (-ra): *diera, dieras, diera, diéramos, dierais, dieran*
Imperfect subjunctive (-se): *diese, dieses, diese, diésemos, dieseis, diesen*

The accent on the present subjunctive forms distinguishes them from the preposition *de* 'of'. This accent becomes unnecessary when a pronoun is suffixed: *dele, deles.*

13.3.16 *Decir* 'to say'

Gerund *diciendo* **Past participle** *dicho*
Imperative: (*tú*) *di*, (*vosotros*) *decid*, (*usted*) *diga*, (*ustedes*) *digan*
Present indicative: *digo, dices, dice, decimos, decís, dicen*
Imperfect (regular): *decía, decías, decía, decíamos, decíais, decían*
Preterite: *dije, dijiste, dijo, dijimos, dijisteis, dijeron*
Future: *diré, dirás, dirá, diremos, diréis, dirán* **Conditional:** *diría*, etc.
Present subjunctive: *diga, digas, diga, digamos, digáis, digan*
Imperfect subjunctive (-ra): *dijera, dijeras, dijera, dijéramos, dijerais, dijeran*
Imperfect subjunctive (-se): *dijese, dijeses, dijese, dijésemos, dijeseis, dijesen*

13.3.17 *Discernir*, 'to discern'

This shows the common radical changing modification *e > ie*, but verbs like *discernir* are very unusual in the *-ir* conjugation: only *cernir* 'to hover'/'to loom', *concernir* (third person only) 'to concern' and *hendir* (in Spain also *hender*, like *entender*) 'to cleave' conjugate like it (bracketed forms are regular):

Imperative: (*tú*) *discierne*, (*usted*) *discierna*, (*ustedes*) *disciernan*
Present indicative: *discierno, disciernes, discierne*, (*discernimos*), (*discernís*), *disciernen*
Preterite (regular): *discerní, discerniste, discernió*, discernimos, discernisteis, discernieron**
Present subjunctive: *discierna, disciernas, discierna*, (*discernamos*), (*discernáis*) *disciernan*
Imperfect subjunctive (-ra) (regular): *discerniera*, etc.
Imperfect subjunctive (-se) (regular): *discerniese*, etc.

*Not the expected **discirnió, *discirnieron.*

All other forms are as for a regular *-ir* verb.

13.3.18 *Dormir* 'to sleep', *morir* 'to die'

Dormir and *morir* are the only verbs of this kind. Apart from the common change *o>ue*, the third-person preterite stem vowel is *u*. The *u* also appears in the first and second plural of the present subjunctive and in the gerund. Forms in brackets are regular:

Gerund *durmiendo* **Past participle** *dormido* (reg.), but *muerto* is the p.p. of *morir*

Imperative (*tú*) *duerme,* (*vosotros*) *dormid,* (*usted*) *duerma,* (*ustedes*) *duerman*
Present indicative: *duermo, duermes, duerme,* (*dormimos*), (*dormís*), *duermen*
Imperfect (regular): *dormía, dormías, dormía, dormíamos, dormíais, dormían*
Preterite: (*dormí*), (*dormiste*), *durmió,* (*dormimos*), (*dormisteis*), *durmieron*
Future (regular): *dormiré,* etc.　　　　　**Conditional (regular):** *dormiría,* etc.
Present subjunctive: *duerma, duermas, duerma, durmamos, durmáis, duerman*
Imperfect subjunctive (-ra): *durmiera, durmieras, durmiera, durmiéramos, durmierais, durmieran*
Imperfect subjunctive (-se): *durmiese, durmieses, durmiese, durmiésemos, durmieseis, durmiesen*

13.3.19 *Erguir(se)* 'to rear up'/'to sit up straight'

This verb has alternative forms in some of its tenses, the forms with *y-* being more common.

Gerund *irguiendo*　　　　　　　　　　**Past participle** *erguido*
Imperative (*tú*) *yergue* / *irgue,* (*vosotros*) *erguid,* (*usted*) *yerga*/*irga,* (*ustedes*) *yergan*/*irgan*
Present indicative: *yergo*/*irgo, yergues*/*irgues, yergue*/*irgue,* (*erguimos*), (*erguís*), *yerguen*/*irguen*
Preterite: *erguí, erguiste, irguió, erguimos, erguisteis, irguieron*
Present subjunctive: *yerga*/*irga, yergas*/*irgas, yerga*/*irga, yergamos*/*irgamos, yergáis*/*irgáis, yergan*/*irgan*
Imperfect subjunctive (-ra): *irguiera, irguieras, irguiera, irguiéramos, irguierais, irguieran*
Imperfect subjunctive (-se): *irguiese, irguieses, irguiese, irguiésemos, irguieseis, irguiesen*

All other forms are regular. Usage: *no te agaches – ponte erguido* 'stop slouching – sit up straight', *se irguió como una serpiente* 'it rose up like a snake', *el perro irguió las orejas* 'the dog pricked up its ears', etc.

13.3.20 *Errar* 'to wander'/'to err'

This verb conjugates like *cerrar*, i.e. *e > ie* when stressed, but the *ie* is written *ye*. In the Southern Cone and Colombia, and in some other parts of Latin America, it is regular, i.e. *erro, erras, erra,* etc. Conjugated like a regular -*ar* verb except for (bracketed forms are regular):

Imperative: (*tú*) *yerra,* (*usted*) *yerre,* (*ustedes*) *yerren*
Present Indicative: *yerro, yerras, yerra,* (*erramos*), (*erráis*), *yerran*
Present Subjunctive: *yerre, yerres, yerre,* (*erremos*), (*erréis*), *yerren*

13.3.21 *Estar* 'to be'

This constantly occurring irregular verb is conjugated like a regular -*ar* verb except for the final stressed vowel in several forms of the present indicative and subjunctive, and except also for the preterite, which is unexpected. The difference between *estar* and *ser* is discussed in Chapter 29.

Gerund (regular): *estando*　　　　　　　**Past participle (regular):** *estado*
Imperative: (*tú*) *está,* (*vosotros estad,* regular), (*usted*) *esté,* (*ustedes*) *estén*

Present indicative: *estoy, estás, está, estamos, estáis, están*
Imperfect (regular): *estaba, estabas, estaba, estábamos, estabais, estaban*
Preterite: *estuve, estuviste, estuvo, estuvimos, estuvisteis, estuvieron*
Future (regular): *estaré,* etc.   **Conditional (regular):** *estaría,* etc.
Present subjunctive: *esté, estés, esté, estemos, estéis, estén*
Imperfect subjunctive (-ra): *estuviera, estuvieras, estuviera, estuviéramos, estuvie-rais, estuvieran*
Imperfect subjunctive (-se): *estuviese, estuvieses, estuviese, estuviésemos, estuvie-seis, estuviesen*

Notes

(i) The imperative is often formed from the pronominal ('reflexive') form, i.e. *estate, estaos, estese, estense*. These should not be (but frequently are) spelt with an accent, e.g. *estáte*, better *estate*.
(ii) *Estar* is never used in the continuous form: **está estando* is not Spanish.

13.3.22 *Haber* auxiliary verb, and also 'there is', 'there are', 'there were', etc.

This common verb is used to form the compound tenses of all regular and irregular verbs (for discussion of compound tenses see 14.8). It is also used in the third person only as the main 'existential' verb, cf. *había muchos* 'there were a lot', *habrá menos de cinco* 'there will be less than five'. When used thus its present indicative form is *hay*: see Chapter 30 for discussion.

Gerund (regular): *habiendo*   **Past participle:** *habido*
Imperative: (not used)
Present indicative: *he, has, ha (hay), hemos, habéis, han*
Imperfect (regular): *había, habías, había, habíamos, habíais, habían*
Preterite: *hube, hubiste, hubo, hubimos, hubisteis, hubieron*
Future: *habré, habrás, habrá, habremos, habréis, habrán*
Conditional: *habría, habrías, habría, habríamos, habríais, habrían*
Present subjunctive: *haya, hayas, haya, hayamos, hayáis, hayan*
Imperfect subjunctive (-ra): *hubiera, hubieras, hubiera, hubiéramos, hubierais, hubieran*
Imperfect subjunctive (-se): *hubiese, hubieses, hubiese, hubiésemos, hubieseis, hubiesen*

Notes

(i) The *-ra* subjunctive form is also commonly used to form the conditional perfect, i.e. *te hubiera llamado* for *te habría llamado* 'I would have phoned you'. See 14.7.5 for discussion
(ii) When it means 'there is/was/will be', etc., this verb is always singular: *había cinco* 'there were five'. Forms like *?habían cinco* are unacceptable in Castilian-speaking Spain and in careful writing everywhere, but are usual in spoken Spanish in Catalonia and Latin America.
(iii) *Habemos* is used in the phrase *nos las habemos* 'we're dealing with', e.g. *en don Luis nos las habemos nuevamente con el Hombre y la Mujer* ('in Don Luis we are dealing once again with Man and Woman' J. Montesinos, quoted by Seco (1998), 237).
(iv) The form *?haiga* is sometimes heard for the subjunctive *haya* but it is stigmatized as rustic or illiterate.

13.3.23 *Hacer* 'to do'/'to make'

There are several compounds, e.g. *deshacer* 'to undo', *contrahacer* 'to counterfeit':

Gerund: *haciendo*   **Past participle:** *hecho*
Imperative: *(tú) haz, (vosotros) haced, (usted) haga, (ustedes) hagan*
Present indicative: *hago, haces, hace, hacemos, hacéis, hacen*
Imperfect (regular): *hacía, hacías, hacía, hacíamos, hacíais, hacían*
Preterite: *hice, hiciste, hizo, hicimos, hicisteis, hicieron*
Future: *haré, harás, hará, haremos, haréis, harán*   **Conditional:** *haría*, etc.
Present subjunctive: *haga, hagas, haga, hagamos, hagáis, hagan*
Imperfect subjunctive (-ra): *hiciera, hicieras, hiciera, hiciéramos, hicierais, hicieran*
Imperfect subjunctive (-se): *hiciese, hicieses, hiciese, hiciésemos, hicieseis, hiciesen*

13.3.24 *Ir* 'to go'

Gerund: *yendo*   **Past participle:** *ido*
Imperative: *(tú) ve, (vosotros) id* (see note)*, (usted) vaya, (ustedes) vayan*
Present indicative: *voy, vas, va, vamos, vais, van*
Imperfect: *iba, ibas, iba, íbamos, ibais, iban*
Preterite: *fui* (no accent!)*, fuiste,* **fue** (no accent!)*, fuimos, fuisteis,* **fueron**
Future (regular): *iré, irás, irá, iremos, iréis, irán*   **Conditional (regular):** *iría*, etc.
Present subjunctive: *vaya, vayas, vaya, vayamos, vayáis, vayan*
Imperfect subjunctive (-ra): *fuera, fueras, fuera, fuéramos, fuerais, fueran*
Imperfect subjunctive (-se): *fuese, fueses, fuese, fuésemos, fueseis, fuesen*

Note

The *vosotros* imperative of *irse* is irregularly *idos* (for the predicted **íos*). See 17.2.4 for further discussion of this form.

13.3.25 *Jugar* 'to play'[6]

This verb is unique in that *u > ue* when stressed. Note also *g > gu* before *e*. All forms are as for a regular *-ar* verb except (bracketed forms are regular):

Imperative: *(tú) juega, (usted) juegue, (ustedes) jueguen*
Present indicative: *juego, juegas, juega, (jugamos), (jugáis), juegan*
Preterite (regular): *jugué, jugaste, jugó, jugamos, jugasteis, jugaron*
Present subjunctive: *juegue, juegues, juegue, (juguemos), (juguéis), jueguen*

13.3.26 *Lucir* 'to show off' (transitive)

C > zc before *a* or *o*. All other forms are as for a regular *-ir* verb (bracketed forms are also regular):
Imperative: *(usted) luzca, (ustedes) luzcan*
Present indicative: *luzco, (luces, luce, lucimos, lucís, lucen)*
Present subjunctive: *luzca, luzcas, luzca, luzcamos, luzcáis, luzcan*

---

[6] i.e. 'play a game'. *Tocar* = 'to play an instrument'.

Note

Verbs ending in *-ducir* are conjugated like *producir* shown at 13.3.37.

13.3.27 *Maldecir* 'to curse', *bendecir* 'to bless'

Conjugated like *decir* in some tenses, and regularly in others. Forms that differ from *decir* are shown in bold type:

Gerund: *maldiciendo*   Past Participle: *maldecido*
Imperative: *(tú)* **maldice**, *(vosotros)* maldecid, *(usted)* maldiga, *(ustedes)* maldigan
Present indicative: *maldigo, maldices, maldice, maldecimos, maldecís, maldicen*
Imperfect (regular): *maldecía,* etc.
Preterite: *maldije, maldijiste, maldijo, maldijimos, maldijisteis, maldijeron*
Future (regular): **maldeciré, maldecirás, maldecirá, maldeciremos, maldeciréis, maldecirán**
Conditional (regular): **maldeciría, maldecirías, maldeciría, maldeciríamos, maldeciríais, maldecirían**
Present subjunctive: *maldiga, maldigas, maldiga, maldigamos, maldigáis, maldigan*
Imperfect subjunctive (*-ra*): *maldijera, maldijeras, maldijera, maldijéramos, maldijerais, maldijeran*
Imperfect subjunctive (*-se*): *maldijese, maldijeses, maldijese, maldijésemos, maldijeseis, maldijesen*

13.3.28 *Mover* 'to move'

A common type of radical changing verb. The *o* of the stem changes to *ue* when stressed. All other forms (including bracketed ones) as for regular *-er* verbs:

Imperative: *(tú)* mueve, *(usted)* mueva, *(ustedes)* muevan
Present indicative: *muevo, mueves, mueve, (movemos), (movéis), mueven*
Present subjunctive: *mueva, muevas, mueva, (movamos), (mováis), muevan*

13.3.29 *Oír* 'to hear' (also *desoír* 'to disregard', 'to turn a deaf ear to')

Gerund: *oyendo*   Past participle: *oído*
Imperative: *(tú)* oye, *(vosotros)* oíd, *(usted)* oiga, *(ustedes)* oigan
Present indicative: *oigo, oyes, oye, oímos, oís, oyen*
Imperfect (regular): *oía, oías, oía, oíamos, oíais, oían*
Preterite: *oí, oíste, oyó, oímos, oísteis, oyeron*
Future (regular): *oiré,* etc.   Conditional (regular): *oiría,* etc.
Present subjunctive: *oiga, oigas, oiga, oigamos, oigáis, oigan*
Imperfect subjunctive (*-ra*): *oyera, oyeras, oyera, oyéramos, oyerais, oyeran*
Imperfect subjunctive (*-se*): *oyese, oyeses, oyese, oyésemos, oyeseis, oyesen*

13.3.30 *Oler* 'to smell'

Oler is conjugated like *mover* but shows the predictable spelling *hue* for *ue* when this diphthong is at the beginning of a word. All forms, including bracketed ones, as for a regular *-er* verb except:

Imperative: *(tú)* huele, *(usted)* huela, *(ustedes)* huelan
Present indicative: *huelo, hueles, huele, (olemos), (oléis), huelen*
Present subjunctive: *huela, huelas, huela, (olamos), (oláis), huelan*

13.3.31 *Pedir* 'to ask for'

The endings are regular, but the *e* of the stem changes to *i* when stressed, and also in the gerund, third-person preterite and imperfect subjunctive:

Gerund: *pidiendo* **Past participle:** *pedido*
Imperative: *(tú) pide, (vosotros) pedid, (usted) pida, (ustedes) pidan*
Present indicative: *pido, pides, pide, pedimos, pedís, piden*
Imperfect (regular): *pedía, pedías, pedía, pedíamos, pedíais, pedían*
Preterite: *pedí, pediste, pidió, pedimos, pedisteis, pidieron*
Future (regular): *pediré*, etc. **Conditional (regular):** *pediría*, etc.
Present subjunctive: *pida, pidas, pida, pidamos, pidáis, pidan*
Imperfect subjunctive (-ra): *pidiera, pidieras, pidiera, pidiéramos, pidierais, pidieran*
Imperfect subjunctive: (-se): *pidiese, pidieses, pidiese, pidiésemos, pidieseis, pidiesen*

13.3.32 *Perder* 'to lose'

A common type of radical changing verb. The endings are regular, but the *e* of the stem changes to *ie* when stressed. All forms, including bracketed ones, are as for a regular *-er* verb except:

Imperative: *(tú) pierde, (usted) pierda, (ustedes) pierdan*
Present indicative: *pierdo, pierdes, pierde, (perdemos), (perdéis), pierden*
Present subjunctive: *pierda, pierdas, pierda, (perdamos), (perdáis), pierdan*

13.3.33 *Placer* 'to please'

Found only in the third person and nowadays very rare: *gustar* (regular) is the usual word for 'to please'. It is conjugated like *nacer* (see 13.3.10) except that irregular alternatives (none nowadays used) exist for the following third-person forms:

Preterite	**Present subjunctive**	**Imperfect subjunctive**
sing. *plugo*, plural *pluguieron*	*plega*	*pluguiera/pluguiese*

13.3.34 *Poder* 'to be able'

Gerund: *pudiendo* **Past Participle:** *podido*
Imperative: not used
Present indicative: *puedo, puedes, puede, podemos, podéis, pueden*
Imperfect (regular): *podía, podías, podía, podíamos, podíais, podían*
Preterite: *pude, pudiste, pudo, pudimos, pudisteis, pudieron*
Future: *podré, podrás, podrá, podremos, podréis, podrán* **Conditional:** *podría*, etc.
Present subjunctive: *pueda, puedas, pueda, podamos, podáis, puedan*
Imperfect subjunctive (-ra): *pudiera, pudieras, pudiera, pudiéramos, pudierais, pudieran*
Imperfect subjunctive (-se): *pudiese, pudieses, pudiese, pudiésemos, pudieseis, pudiesen*

13.3.35 *Poner* 'to put'

Gerund: *poniendo*   **Past participle:** *puesto*
Imperative: (*tú*) *pon*, (*vosotros*) *poned*, (*usted*) *ponga*, (*ustedes*) *pongan*
Present indicative: *pongo, pones, pone, ponemos, ponéis, ponen*
Imperfect (regular): *ponía, ponías, ponía, poníamos, poníais, ponían*
Preterite: *puse, pusiste, puso, pusimos, pusisteis, pusieron*
Future: *pondré, pondrás, pondrá, pondremos, pondréis, pondrán*
Conditional: *pondría*, etc.
Present subjunctive: *ponga, pongas, ponga, pongamos, pongáis, pongan*
Imperfect subjunctive (-*ra*): *pusiera, pusieras, pusiera, pusiéramos, pusierais, pusieran*
Imperfect subjunctive (-*se*): *pusiese, pusieses, pusiese, pusiésemos, pusieseis, pusiesen*

Also compounds like *componer* 'to compose', *imponer* 'to impose', *proponer* 'to propose', *descomponer* 'to split something up', *suponer* 'to suppose', etc. An accent is written on the *tú* imperative of these compounds, e.g. *componer* 'to compose' > *compón*, *posponer* 'to postpone' > *pospón*.

13.3.36 *Poseer* 'to possess'

This verb and others like it, e.g. *leer* 'to read', *creer* 'to believe', requires that a *y* sound between vowels should be written *y* and not *i*. This is a spelling rule, not an irregularity:

Gerund: *poseyendo*   **Past participle:** *poseído*
Imperative: (*tú*) *posee*, (*vosotros*) *poseed*, (*usted*) *posea*, (*ustedes*) *posean*
Present indicative: *poseo, posees, posee, poseemos, poseéis, poseen*
Imperfect (regular): *poseía, poseías, poseía, poseíamos, poseíais, poseían*
Preterite: *poseí, poseíste, poseyó, poseímos, poseísteis, poseyeron*
Future (regular): *poseeré*, etc.   **Conditional (regular):** *poseería*, etc.
Present subjunctive: *posea, poseas, posea, poseamos, poseáis, posean*
Imperfect subjunctive (-*ra*): *poseyera, poseyeras, poseyera, poseyéramos, poseyerais, poseyeran*
Imperfect subjunctive (-*se*): *poseyese, poseyeses, poseyese, poseyésemos, poseyeseis, poseyesen*

13.3.37 *Producir* 'to produce'

Conjugated like *lucir* except for the preterite and for forms (imperfect and future subjunctive) based on the preterite stem. The preterite endings, and therefore the past and future subjunctive endings, are -*eron*, -*era*, -*ese*, etc., not -*ieron*, -*iera*, -*iese*:

Imperative: (*tú*) *produce*, (*vosotros*) *producid*, (*usted*) *produzca*, (*ustedes*) *produzcan*
Present indicative: *produzco, produces, produce, producimos, producís, producen*
Imperfect (regular): *producía*, etc.
Preterite: *produje, produjiste, produjo, produjimos, produjisteis, produjeron*
Future (regular): *produciré*, etc.   **Conditional (regular):** *produciría*, etc.
Present subjunctive: *produzca, produzcas, produzca, produzcamos, produzcáis, produzcan*

Imperfect subjunctive (-ra): *produjera, produjeras, produjera, produjéramos, produjerais, produjeran*

Imperfect subjunctive (-se): *produjese, produjeses, produjese, produjésemos, produjeseis, produjesen*

Preterite forms like **produció, *conducí* are common mistakes, but they are stigmatized.

13.3.38 *Querer* 'to want'/'to love'

Gerund: *queriendo*   **Past participle:** *querido*
Imperative (little-used): *(tú) quiere, (vosotros) quered, (usted) quiera, (ustedes) quieran*
Present indicative: *quiero, quieres, quiere, queremos, queréis, quieren*
Imperfect (regular): *quería, querías, quería, queríamos, queríais, querían*
Preterite: *quise, quisiste, quiso, quisimos, quisisteis, quisieron*
Future: *querré, querrás, querrá, querremos, querréis, querrán* **Conditional:** *querría,* etc.
Present subjunctive: *quiera, quieras, quiera, queramos, queráis, quieran*
Imperfect subjunctive (-ra): *quisiera, quisieras, quisiera, quisiéramos, quisierais, quisieran*
Imperfect subjunctive (-se): *quisiese, quisieses, quisiese, quisiésemos, quisieseis, quisiesen*

13.3.39 *Reír* 'to laugh'

This verb is in fact conjugated in almost the same way as *pedir*, although the absence of a consonant between the vowels obscures the similarity:

Gerund: *riendo*   **Past participle:** *reído*
Imperative: *(tú) ríe, (vosotros) reíd, (usted) ría, (ustedes) rían*
Present indicative: *río, ríes, ríe, reímos, reís, ríen*
Imperfect (regular): *reía, reías, reía, reíamos, reíais, reían*
Preterite: *reí, reíste, rió,* reímos, reísteis, rieron*
Future (regular): *reiré, reirás, reirá, reiremos, reiréis, reirán*
Conditional (regular): *reiría,* etc.
Present subjunctive: *ría, rías, ría, riamos, riáis, rían*
Imperfect subjunctive (-ra): *riera, rieras, riera, riéramos, rierais, rieran*
Imperfect subjunctive (-se): *riese, rieses, riese, riésemos, rieseis, riesen*

*Note the written accent. The only third-person singular preterites ending in *-io* that have no written accent are *dio* (from *dar*) and *vio* (from *ver*); see 39.2.3 note (i) for further remarks.

13.3.40 *Reñir* 'to scold'

This and other verbs in *-eñir* are conjugated like *pedir*, except that, as usual, *ie>e* and *ió>ó* after *ñ*; see 13.5.3. Only the forms that differ from *pedir* are shown, and bracketed forms are also regular:

Gerund: *riñendo*
Preterite: *(reñí), (reñiste), riñó, (reñimos), (reñisteis), riñeron*
Imperfect subjunctive (-ra): *riñera, riñeras, riñera, riñéramos, riñerais, riñeran*
Imperfect subjunctive (-se): *riñese, riñeses, riñese, riñésemos, riñeseis, riñesen*

13.3.41 *Roer* 'to gnaw'

The bracketed forms are little-used alternatives. In practice the first-person singular indicative is avoided and may be expressed by *estoy royendo* 'I'm gnawing'.

Gerund: *royendo*   **Past participle:** *roído*
Imperative: *(tú) roe, (vosotros) roed, (usted) roa(roiga/roya), (ustedes) roan(roigan/royan)*
Present indicative: *roo (roigo/royo), roes, roe, roemos, roéis, roen*
Imperfect (regular): *roía, roías, roía, roíamos, roíais, roían*
Preterite: *roí, roíste, royó, roímos, roísteis, royeron*
Future (regular): *roeré,* etc.   **Conditional (regular):** *roería,* etc.
Present subjunctive: *roa (roiga/roya), roas (roigas/royas), roa (roiga/roya), roamos
  (roigamos/royamos), roáis (roigáis/royáis), roan (roigan/royan)*
Imperfect subjunctive (-ra): *royera, royeras, royera, royéramos, royerais, royeran*
Imperfect subjunctive (-se): *royese, royeses, royese, royésemos, royeseis, royesen*

13.3.42 *Saber* 'to know'

Gerund: *sabiendo*   **Past participle:** *sabido*
Imperative (rarely used): *(tú) sabe, (vosotros) sabed, (usted) sepa, (ustedes) sepan*
Present indicative: *sé, sabes, sabe, sabemos, sabéis, saben*
Imperfect (regular): *sabía, sabías, sabía, sabíamos, sabíais, sabían*
Preterite: *supe, supiste, supo, supimos, supisteis, supieron*
Future: *sabré, sabrás, sabrá, sabremos, sabréis, sabrán*   **Conditional:** *sabría,* etc.
Present subjunctive: *sepa, sepas, sepa, sepamos, sepáis, sepan*
Imperfect subjunctive (-ra): *supiera, supieras, supiera, supiéramos, supierais,
  supieran*
Imperfect subjunctive (-se): *supiese, supieses, supiese, supiésemos, supieseis,
  supiesen*

13.3.43 *Salir* 'to go out'/'to leave'

Gerund: *saliendo*   **Past participle:** *salido*
Imperative: *(tú) sal, (vosotros) salid, (usted) salga, (ustedes) salgan*
Present indicative: *salgo, sales, sale, salimos, salís, salen*
Imperfect and preterite: regular
Future: *saldré, saldrás, saldrá, saldremos, saldréis, saldrán* **Conditional:** *saldría,* etc.
Present subjunctive: *salga, salgas, salga, salgamos, salgáis, salgan*
Imperfect subjunctive (-ra): *saliera,* etc.
Imperfect subjunctive (-se): *saliese,* etc.

13.3.44 *Sentir* 'to feel'

A common type of *-ir* verb. The endings are regular, but the stem vowel changes to *ie* or to *i* in certain forms. All forms as for a regular *-ir* verb (including bracketed ones), except:

Gerund: *sintiendo*
Imperative: *(tú) siente, (usted) sienta, (ustedes) sientan*
Present indicative: *siento, sientes, siente, (sentimos), (sentís), sienten*
Preterite: *(sentí), (sentiste), sintió, (sentimos), (sentisteis), sintieron*
Present subjunctive: *sienta, sientas, sienta, sintamos, sintáis, sientan*

Imperfect subjunctive (-ra): *sintiera, sintieras, sintiera, sintiéramos, sintierais, sintieran*

Imperfect subjunctive (-se): *sintiese, sintieses, sintiese, sintiésemos, sintieseis, sintiesen*

13.3.45 *Ser* 'to be'

A very common verb. For its relationship with the verb *estar* see Chapter 29:

Gerund: *siendo*   **Past participle:** *sido*
Imperative: *(tú) sé* (see note), *(vosotros) sed, (usted) sea, (ustedes) sean*
Present indicative: *soy, eres, es, somos, sois, son*
Imperfect: *era, eras, era, éramos, erais, eran*
Preterite: *fui* (no accent!), *fuiste, fue* (no accent!), *fuimos, fuisteis, fueron*
Future (regular): *seré, serás, será, seremos, seréis, serán*
Conditional (regular): *sería,* etc.
Present subjunctive: *sea, seas, sea, seamos, seáis, sean*
Imperfect subjunctive (-ra): *fuera, fueras, fuera, fuéramos, fuerais, fueran*
Imperfect subjunctive (-se): *fuese, fueses, fuese, fuésemos, fueseis, fuesen*

Note

The accent distinguishes this word from the pronoun *se*.

13.3.46 *Tener* 'to have'

Gerund: *teniendo*   **Past participle:** *tenido*
Imperative: *(tú) ten, (vosotros) tened, (usted) tenga, (ustedes) tengan*
Present Indicative: *tengo, tienes, tiene, tenemos, tenéis, tienen*
Imperfect (regular): *tenía, tenías, tenía, teníamos, teníais, tenían*
Preterite: *tuve, tuviste, tuvo, tuvimos, tuvisteis, tuvieron*
Future: *tendré, tendrás, tendrá, tendremos, tendréis, tendrán*
Conditional: *tendría,* etc.
Present subjunctive: *tenga, tengas, tenga, tengamos, tengáis, tengan*
Imperfect subjunctive (-ra): *tuviera, tuvieras, tuviera, tuviéramos, tuvierais, tuvieran*
Imperfect subjunctive (-se): *tuviese, tuvieses, tuviese, tuviésemos, tuvieseis, tuviesen*

13.3.47 *Traer* 'to bring'

Gerund: *trayendo*   **Past participle:** *traído*
Imperative: *(tú) trae, (vosotros) traed, (usted) traiga, (ustedes) traigan*
Present indicative: *traigo, traes, trae, traemos, traéis, traen*
Imperfect (regular): *traía, traías, traía, traíamos, traíais, traían*
Preterite: *traje, trajiste, trajo, trajimos, trajisteis, trajeron* (**not** **trajieron*)
Future (regular): *traeré,* etc.   **Conditional (regular):** *traería,* etc.
Present subjunctive: *traiga, traigas, traiga, traigamos, traigáis, traigan*
Imperfect subjunctive (-ra): *trajera, trajeras, trajera, trajéramos, trajerais, trajeran*
Imperfect subjunctive (-se): *trajese, trajeses, trajese, trajésemos, trajeseis, trajesen*

The preterite *truje, trujiste,* etc. is found in Golden-Age texts and occasionally in dialects.

13.3.48 *Valer* 'to be worth'

Gerund: *valiendo*   **Past participle:** *valido*
Imperative: (*tú*) *vale*, (*vosotros*) *valed*, (*usted*) *valga*, (*ustedes*) *valgan*
Present indicative: *valgo, vales, vale, valemos, valéis, valen*
Imperfect (regular): *valía, valías, valía, valíamos, valíais, valían*
Preterite (regular): *valí, valiste, valió, valimos, valisteis, valieron*
Future: *valdré, valdrás, valdrá, valdremos, valdréis, valdrán*
Conditional: *valdría*, etc.
Present subjunctive: *valga, valgas, valga, valgamos, valgáis, valgan*
Imperfect subjunctive (-ra): *valiera, valieras, valiera, valiéramos, valierais, valieran*
Imperfect subjunctive (-se): *valiese, valieses, valiese, valiésemos, valieseis, valiesen*

13.3.49 *Venir* 'to come'

Gerund: *viniendo*   **Past participle:** *venido*
Imperative: (*tú*) *ven*, (*vosotros*) *venid*, (*usted*) *venga*, (*ustedes*) *vengan*
Present indicative: *vengo, vienes, viene, venimos, venís, vienen*
Imperfect (regular): *venía, venías, venía, veníamos, veníais, venían*
Preterite: *vine, viniste, vino, vinimos, vinisteis, vinieron*
Future: *vendré, vendrás, vendrá, vendremos, vendréis, vendrán*
Conditional: *vendría*, etc.
Present subjunctive: *venga, vengas, venga, vengamos, vengáis, vengan*
Imperfect subjunctive (-ra): *viniera, vinieras, viniera, viniéramos, vinierais, vinieran*
Imperfect subjunctive (-se): *viniese, vinieses, viniese, viniésemos, vinieseis, viniesen*

13.3.50 *Ver* 'to see'

Gerund: *viendo*   **Past participle:** *visto*
Imperative: (*tú*) *ve*, (*vosotros*) *ved*, (*usted*) *vea*, (*ustedes*) *vean*
Present indicative: *veo, ves, ve, vemos, veis, ven*
Imperfect: *veía, veías, veía, veíamos, veíais, veían*
Preterite: *vi* (no accent!), *viste, vio* (no accent!), *vimos, visteis, vieron*
Future (regular): *veré*, etc.   **Conditional (regular):** *vería*, etc.
Present subjunctive: *vea, veas, veas, veamos, veáis, vean*
Imperfect subjunctive (-ra): *viera, vieras, viera, viéramos, vierais, vieran*
Imperfect subjunctive (-se): *viese, vieses, viese, viésemos, vieseis, viesen*

The root verb is stressed in compound form in the first-person and third-person singular of the preterite and the third-person singular present indicative, e.g. *entreví* 'I glimpsed', *entrevió* '(s)he glimpsed', *prevé* '(s)he foresees'.

13.3.51 *Yacer* 'to lie' (as in 'he lay there') (US 'to lay')

Almost never used nowadays: *estar tumbado, estar acostado* are the usual translations. It is conjugated like *nacer*, except for the alternative forms shown in brackets:

Imperative: (*usted*) *yazca* (*yaga/yazga*), (*ustedes*) *yazcan* (*yagan/yazgan*)
Present indicative: *yazco* (*yago, yazgo*), other persons regular
Present subjunctive: *yazca* (*yaga/ yazga*), etc.

13.4 List of irregular verbs

A number of very rare verbs have been omitted, but this is no guarantee that all of the verbs listed are in common use today. Bracketed forms indicate verbs which are found in the infinitive or past participle forms, which are often the only surviving remains of the verbs that are otherwise obsolete (cf. *aterirse*). For verbs beginning with the prefix in *re-* that are not listed here see the root verb.

abastecer: -cer 13.3.10
abolir: see 13.3.2
aborrecer: -cer 13.3.10
abrir: past participle
  abierto
absolver: mover 13.3.28
  past participle *absuelto*
abstenerse: tener 13.3.46
abstraer: traer 13.3.47
acaecer: -cer 13.3.10
acertar: cerrar 13.3.11
acontecer: -cer 13.3.10
acordar: contar 13.3.14
acostar(se): contar 13.3.14
acrecentar: cerrar 13.3.11
adherir: sentir 13.3.44
adolecer: -cer 13.3.10
adormecer: -cer 13.3.10
adquirir: see 13.3.3
aducir: producir 13.3.37
advertir: sentir 13.3.44
aferrar(se): cerrar 13.3.11
  but usually regular
agradecer: -cer 13.3.10
agredir: see 13.3.4
(aguerrir: abolir 13.3.2)
alentar: cerrar 13.3.11
almorzar: contar 13.3.14
  z>c before *e*
amanecer: -cer 13.3.10
andar: see 13.3.5
anochecer: -cer 13.3.10
anteponer: poner 13.3.35
apacentar: cerrar 13.3.11
aparecer: -cer 13.3.10
apetecer: -cer 13.3.10
apostar: contar 13.3.14
  reg. in meaning 'to
  station'
apretar: cerrar 13.3.11
aprobar: contar 13.3.14
argüir: construir 13.3.13
arrecirse: abolir 13.3.2
arrendar: cerrar 13.3.11
arrepentirse: sentir
  13.3.44

ascender: perder 13.3.32
asentar: cerrar 13.3.11
asentir: sentir 13.3.44
asir: see 13.3.6
asolar: contar 13.3.14 if it
  means 'to parch', but
  usually reg. nowadays
atañer: see 13.5.3, item 6
  third-person sing. only
atender: perder 13.3.32
atenerse: tener 13.3.46
(aterirse: abolir 13.3.2)
atraer: traer 13.3.47
atravesar: cerrar 13.3.11
atribuir: construir
  13.3.13
avenir: venir 13.3.49
aventar: cerrar 13.3.11
avergonzar: contar 13.3.14
  z>c before *e*.
  Diphthong spelt *üe*,
  e.g. subjunctive
  avergüence, etc.
balbucir: see 13.3.7
bendecir: maldecir 13.3.27
blandir: abolir 13.3.2
bruñir: gruñir see 13.5.3,
  item 6
bullir: zambullir see
  13.5.3, item 6
caber: see 13.3.8
caer: see 13.3.9
calentar: cerrar 13.3.11
carecer: -cer 13.3.10
cegar: cerrar 13.3.11 *g>gu*
  before *e*
ceñir: reñir 13.3.40
cerner: perder 13.3.32
cernir: discernir 13.3.17
cerrar: see 13.3.11
circunscribir: irreg. past
  participle *circunscrito*
cocer: see 13.3.12
colar: contar 13.3.14
colegir: pedir 13.3.31 *-g>j*
  before *a, o*

colgar: contar 13.3.14
  g>gu before *e*
comenzar: cerrar 13.3.11
  z>c before *e*
compadecer: -cer 13.3.10
comparecer: -cer 13.3.10
competir: pedir 13.3.31
complacer: -cer 13.3.10
componer: poner 13.3.35
comprobar: contar
  13.3.14
concebir: pedir 13.3.31
concernir: discernir
  13.3.17
concertar: cerrar 13.3.11
concluir: construir 13.3.13
concordar: contar 13.3.14
condescender: perder
  13.3.32
condolerse: mover 13.3.28
conducir: producir 13.3.37
conferir: sentir 13.3.44
confesar: cerrar 13.3.11
confluir: construir 13.3.13
conmover: mover 13.3.28
conocer: -cer 13.3.10
conseguir: pedir 13.3.31
  gu>g before *a, o*
consentir: sentir 13.3.44
consolar: contar 13.3.14
consonar: contar 13.3.14
constituir: construir
  13.3.13
constreñir: reñir 13.3.40
construir: see 13.3.13
contar: see 13.3.14
contender: perder 13.3.32
contener: tener 13.3.46
contradecir: decir 13.3.16
contraer: traer 13.3.47
contrahacer: hacer 13.3.23
contraponer: poner
  13.3.35
contravenir: venir 13.3.49
contribuir: construir
  13.3.13

controvertir: sentir
13.3.44
convalecer: -cer 13.3.10
convenir: venir 13.3.49
convertir: sentir 13.3.44
corregir: pedir 13.3.31 *g>j*
before *a, o*
costar: contar 13.3.14
crecer: -cer 13.3.10
creer: poseer 13.3.36
cubrir: irreg. past
participle *cubierto*
dar: see 13.3.15
decaer: caer 13.3.9
decir: see 13.3.16
decrecer: -cer 13.3.10
deducir: producir 13.3.37
defender: perder 13.3.32
deferir: sentir 13.3.44
degollar: contar 13.3.14,
diphthong spelt *üe*
demoler: mover 13.3.28
demostrar: contar 13.3.14
denegar: cerrar 13.3.11
g>gu before *e*
denostar: contar 13.3.14
dentar: cerrar 13.3.11
often *dientar* (reg.)
nowadays
deponer: poner 13.3.35
derrengar: cerrar 13.3.11
often regular
nowadays; *g>gu*
before *e*
derretir: pedir 13.3.31
derrocar: nowadays
regular; *c>qu* before *e*
desacertar: cerrar 13.3.11
desacordar: contar
13.3.14
desagradecer: -cer 13.3.10
desalentar: cerrar 13.3.11
desandar: andar 13.3.5
desaparecer: -cer 13.3.10
desapretar: cerrar 13.3.11
desaprobar: contar 13.3.14
desasosegar: cerrar 13.3.11
g>gu before *e*
desatender: perder 13.3.32
desavenir: venir 13.3.49
descender: perder 13.3.32
desceñir: reñir 13.3.40
descolgar: contar 13.3.14
g>gu before *e*
descollar: contar 13.3.14
descomedirse: pedir
13.3.31

descomponer: poner
13.3.35
desconcertar: cerrar
13.3.11
desconocer: -cer 13.3.10
desconsolar: contar
13.3.14
descontar: contar 13.3.14
desconvenir: venir 13.3.49
describir: past participle
descrito
descubrir: past participle
descubierto
desdecir: decir 13.3.16
desempedrar: cerrar
13.3.11
desengrosar: contar
13.3.14
desentenderse: perder
13.3.32
desenterrar: cerrar 13.3.11
desenvolver: mover
13.3.28, past participle
desenvuelto
desfallecer: -cer 13.3.10
desgobernar: cerrar
13.3.11
deshacer: hacer 13.3.23
deshelar: cerrar 13.3.11
desherrar: cerrar 13.3.11
desleír: reír 13.3.39
deslucir: lucir 13.3.26
desmembrar: cerrar
13.3.11
desmentir: sentir 13.3.44
desmerecer: -cer 13.3.10
desobedecer: -cer 13.3.10
desoír: oír 13.3.29
desollar: contar 13.3.14
despedir: pedir 13.3.31
despedrar: cerrar 13.3.11
despertar: cerrar 13.3.11
despezar: cerrar 13.3.11
usually *despiezar*,
regular; *z>c* before *e*
desplacer: -cer 13.3.10
desplegar: cerrar 13.3.11
g>gu before *e*; now
often regular
despoblar: contar 13.3.14
desproveer: poseer 13.3.36,
past participle
desprovisto/desproveído
desteñir: reñir 13.3.40
desterrar: cerrar 13.3.11
destituir: construir
13.3.13

destruir: construir 13.3.13
desvanecer: -cer 13.3.10
desvergonzarse: contar
13.3.14; *z>c* before *e*;
diphthong spelt *üe*
detener: tener 13.3.46
detraer: traer 13.3.47
devolver: mover 13.3.28,
past participle *devuelto*
diferir: sentir 13.3.44
digerir: sentir 13.3.44
diluir: construir 13.3.13
discernir: see 13.3.17
disentir: sentir 13.3.44
disminuir: construir
13.3.13
disolver: mover 13.3.28 ,
past participle *disuelto*
disponer: poner 13.3.35
distender: perder 13.3.32
distraer: traer 13.3.47
distribuir: construir
13.3.13
divertir: sentir 13.3.44
doler: mover 13.3.28
dormir: see 13.3.18
elegir: pedir 13.3.31 *g>j*
before *a, o*
embebecer: -cer 13.3.10
embellecer: -cer 13.3.10
embestir: pedir 13.3.31
embravecer: -cer 13.3.10
embrutecer: -cer 13.3.10
empedrar: cerrar 13.3.11
empequeñecer: -cer
13.3.10
empezar: cerrar 13.3.11
z>c before *e*
empobrecer: -cer 13.3.10
enaltecer: -cer 13.3.10
enardecer: -cer 13.3.10
encanecer: -cer 13.3.10
encarecer: -cer 13.3.10
encender: perder 13.3.32
encerrar: cerrar 13.3.11
encomendar: cerrar
13.3.11
encontrar: contar 13.3.14
encubrir: past participle
encubierto
endurecer: -cer 13.3.10
enflaquecer: -cer 13.3.10
enfurecer: -cer 13.3.10
engrandecer: -cer 13.3.10
engreírse: reír 13.3.39
engrosar: contar 13.3.14
now usually regular

engullir: *zambullir* see
13.5.3, item 6
enloquecer: *-cer* 13.3.10
enmendar: *cerrar* 13.3.11
enmohecer: *-cer* 13.3.10
enmudecer: *-cer* 13.3.10
ennegrecer: *-cer* 13.3.10
ennoblecer: *-cer* 13.3.10
enorgullecer: *-cer* 13.3.10
enriquecer: *-cer* 13.3.10
enronquecer: *-cer* 13.3.10
ensangrentar: *cerrar*
13.3.11
ensoberbecer(se)-cer
13.3.10
ensordecer: *-cer* 13.3.10
entender: *perder* 13.3.32
enternecer: *-cer* 13.3.10
enterrar: *cerrar* 13.3.11
entreabrir: past participle
entreabierto
entredecir: *decir* 13.3.16
entreoír: *oír* 13.3.29
entretener: *tener* 13.3.46
entrever: *ver* 13.3.50
third-person present
singular *entrevé*
entristecer: *-cer* 13.3.10
entumecer(se)-cer 13.3.10
envanecer: *-cer* 13.3.10
envejecer: *-cer* 13.3.10
envilecer: *-cer* 13.3.10
envolver: *mover* 13.3.28
past participle *envuelto*
equivaler: *valer* 13.3.48
erguir: see 13.3.19
errar: see 13.3.20
escabullirse: *zambullir* see
13.5.3, item 6
escarmentar: *cerrar*
13.3.11
escarnecer: *-cer* 13.3.10
escocer: *cocer* 13.3.12
escribir: past. participle
escrito
esforzar: *contar* 13.3.14
z>c before *e*
establecer: *-cer* 13.3.10
estar: 13.3.21
estremecer: *-cer* 13.3.10
estreñir: *reñir* 13.3.40
excluir: *construir* 13.3.13
expedir: *pedir* 13.3.31
exponer: *poner* 13.3.35
extender: *perder* 13.3.32

extraer: *traer* 13.3.47
fallecer: *-cer* 13.3.10
favorecer: *-cer* 13.3.10
florecer: *-cer* 13.3.10
fluir: *construir* 13.3.13
fortalecer: *-cer* 13.3.10
forzar: *contar* 13.3.14 *z>c*
before *e*
fregar: *cerrar* 13.3.11
g>gu before *e*
freír: *reír* 13.3.39 past
participle *frito*
gemir: *pedir* 13.3.31
gobernar: *cerrar* 13.3.11
gruñir: see 13.5.3, item 6
guarecer: *-cer* 13.3.10
guarnecer: *-cer* 13.3.10
haber: 13.3.22
hacer: see 13.3.23
heder: *perder* 13.3.32
helar: *cerrar* 13.3.11
henchir: *pedir* 13.3.31
hender: *perder* 13.3.32
hendir: *discernir* 13.3.17
herir: *sentir* 13.3.44
herrar: *cerrar* 13.3.11
hervir: *sentir* 13.3.44
holgar: *contar* 13.3.14
g>gu before *e*
hollar: *contar* 13.3.14
huir: *construir* 13.3.13
humedecer: *-cer* 13.3.10
impedir: *pedir* 13.3.31
imponer: *poner* 13.3.35
imperative singular
impón
incensar: *cerrar* 13.3.11
incluir: *construir* 13.3.13
indisponer: *poner* 13.3.35
inducir: *producir* 13.3.37
inferir: *sentir* 13.3.44
influir: *construir* 13.3.13
ingerir: *sentir* 13.3.44
injerir: *sentir* 13.3.44
inquirir: *adquirir* 13.3.3
instituir: *construir*
13.3.13
instruir: *construir*
13.3.13
interferir: *sentir* 13.3.44
interponer: *poner* 13.3.35
intervenir: *venir* 13.3.49
introducir: *producir*
13.3.37
intuir: *construir* 13.3.13

invernar: *cerrar* 13.3.11
now usually regular
invertir: *sentir* 13.3.44
investir: *pedir* 13.3.31
ir: see 13.3.24
jugar: see 13.3.25
languidecer: *-cer* 13.3.10
leer: *poseer* 13.3.36
llover: *mover* 13.3.28
lucir: see 13.3.26
maldecir: see 13.3.27
manifestar: *cerrar* 13.3.11
mantener: *tener* 13.3.46
medir: *pedir* 13.3.31
mentar: *cerrar* 13.3.11
mentir: *sentir* 13.3.44
merecer: *-cer* 13.3.10
merendar: *cerrar* 13.3.11
moler: *mover* 13.3.28
morder: *mover* 13.3.28
morir: see 13.3.18
mostrar: *contar* 13.3.14
mover: see 13.3.28
mullir: *zambullir* see
13.5.3, item 6
nacer: *-cer* 13.3.10
negar: *cerrar* 13.3.11 *g>gu*
before *e*
nevar: *cerrar* 13.3.11
obedecer: *-cer* 13.3.10
obstruir: *construir* 13.3.13
obtener: *tener* 13.3.46
ofrecer: *-cer* 13.3.10
oír: see 13.3.29
oler: see 13.3.30
oponer: *poner* 13.3.35
oscurecer: *-cer* 13.3.10[7]
pacer: *-cer* 13.3.10
padecer: *-cer* 13.3.10
palidecer: *-cer* 13.3.10
parecer: *-cer* 13.3.10
pedir: see 13.3.31
pensar: *cerrar* 13.3.11
perecer: *-cer* 13.3.10
permanecer: *-cer* 13.3.10
perseguir: *pedir* 13.3.31
gu>g before *a, o*
pertenecer: *-cer* 13.3.10
pervertir: *sentir* 13.3.44
placer: see 13.3.33
plegar: *cerrar* 13.3.11
g>gu before *e*
poblar: *contar* 13.3.14
poder: see 13.3.34
podrir: variant of *pudrir*,

---

[7] *Obscurecer, obscuro* are older spellings.

common in Lat. Am.,
rare in Spain: *-u-*
used for all other
forms save past part.
podrido
poner: see 13.3.35
poseer: see 13.3.36
posponer: *poner* 13.3.35
  tú imperative *pospón*
predecir: *decir* 13.3.16
predisponer: *poner* 13.3.35
preferir: *sentir* 13.3.44
prescribir: past participle
  prescrito
presuponer: *poner* 13.3.35
prevalecer: *-cer* 13.3.10
prevaler: *valer* 13.3.48
prevenir: *venir* 13.3.49
prever: *ver* 13.3.50 third-
  pers. present *prevé*,
  prevén
probar: *contar* 13.3.14
producir: see 13.3.37
proferir: *sentir* 13.3.44
promover: *mover* 13.3.28
proponer: *poner* 13.3.35
proseguir: *pedir* 13.3.31
  gu>g before *a*
prostituir: *construir*
  13.3.13
proveer: *poseer* 13.3.36
  past participle
  provisto/proveído
provenir: *venir* 13.3.49
pudrir: regular; see also
  podrir
quebrar: *cerrar* 13.3.11
querer: see 13.3.38
raer: *caer* 13.3.9 *rayo* is
  an alternative to *raigo*
reaparecer: *-cer* 13.3.10
reblandecer: *-cer* 13.3.10
recaer: *caer* 13.3.9
recluir: *construir* 13.3.13
recocer: *cocer* 13.3.12
recomendar: *cerrar* 13.3.11
reconocer: *-cer* 13.3.10
reconvenir: *venir* 13.3.49
recordar: *contar* 13.3.14
recostar(se): *contar*
  13.3.14
reducir: *producir* 13.3.37
reelegir: *pedir* 13.3.31 *g>j*
  before *a, o*
referir: *sentir* 13.3.44
reforzar: *contar* 13.3.14
  z>c before *e*

refregar: *cerrar* 13.3.11
regar: *cerrar* 13.3.11 *g>gu*
  before *e*
regir: *pedir* 13.3.31 *g>j*
  before *a, o*
rehacer: *hacer* 13.3.23
reír: see 13.3.39
rejuvenecer: *-cer* 13.3.10
remendar: *cerrar* 13.3.11
remorder: *mover* 13.3.28
remover: *mover* 13.3.28
rendir: *pedir* 13.3.31
renegar: *cerrar* 13.3.11
  g>gu before *e*
renovar: *contar* 13.3.14
reñir: see 13.3.40
repetir: *pedir* 13.3.31
replegar: *cerrar* 13.3.11
  g>gu before *e*
repoblar: *contar* 13.3.14
reponer: *poner* 13.3.35
reprobar: *contar* 13.3.14
reproducir: *producir*
  13.3.37
requebrar: *cerrar* 13.3.11
requerir: *sentir* 13.3.44
resentirse: *sentir* 13.3.44
resollar: *contar* 13.3.14
resolver: *mover* 13.3.28,
  past participle *resuelto*
resonar: *contar* 13.3.14
resplandecer: *-cer* 13.3.10
restablecer: *-cer* 13.3.10
restituir: *construir* 13.3.13
restregar: *cerrar* 13.3.11
  g>gu before *e*
retemblar: *cerrar* 13.3.11
retener: *tener* 13.3.46
reteñir: *reñir* 13.3.40
retorcer: *cocer* 13.3.12 *c>z*
  before *a, o*
retraer: *traer* 13.3.47
retribuir: *construir*
  13.3.13
retrotraer: *traer* 13.3.47
reventar: *cerrar* 13.3.11
reverdecer: *-cer* 13.3.10
reverter: *perder* 13.3.32
revestir: *pedir* 13.3.31
revolar: *contar* 13.3.14
revolcar(se): *contar*
  13.3.14 *c>qu* before *e*
revolver: *mover* 13.3.28
  past participle *revuelto*
robustecer: *-cer* 13.3.10
rodar: *contar* 13.3.14
roer: see 13.3.41

rogar: *contar* 13.3.14
  g>gu before *e*
romper: past participle
  roto
saber: see 13.3.42
salir: see 13.3.43
satisfacer: *hacer* 13.3.23
seducir: *producir* 13.3.37
segar: *cerrar* 13.3.11 *g>gu*
  before *e*
seguir: *pedir* 13.3.31 *gu>g*
  before *a* or *o*
sembrar: *cerrar* 13.3.11
sentar: *cerrar* 13.3.11
sentir: see 13.3.44
ser: see 13.3.45
serrar: *cerrar* 13.3.11
servir: *pedir* 13.3.31
sobre(e)ntender: *perder*
  13.3.32
sobreponer: *poner* 13.3.35
sobresalir: *salir* 13.3.43
sobrevenir: *venir* 13.3.49
sofreír: *reír* 13.3.39, past
  participle *sofrito*
soldar: *contar* 13.3.14
soler: *mover* 13.3.28
  future, conditional
  and past and future
  subjunctives not
  used
soltar: *contar* 13.3.14
sonar: *contar* 13.3.14
sonreír: *reír* 13.3.39
soñar: *contar* 13.3.14
sosegar: *cerrar* 13.3.11
  g>gu before *e*
sostener: *tener* 13.3.46
soterrar: *cerrar* 13.3.11
subarrendar: *cerrar*
  13.3.11
subscribir: see *suscribir*
subvenir: *venir* 13.3.49
subvertir: *sentir* 13.3.44
sugerir: *sentir* 13.3.44
suponer: *poner* 13.3.35
suscribir: past participle
  suscrito
sustituir: *construir*
  13.3.13
sustraer: *traer* 13.3.47
tañer: see 13.5.3, item 6
temblar: *cerrar* 13.3.11
tender: *perder* 13.3.32
tener: see 13.3.46
tentar: *cerrar* 13.3.11
teñir: *reñir* 13.3.40

torcer: cocer 13.3.12 *c>z*
  before *a, o*
tostar: contar 13.3.14
traducir: producir
  13.3.37
traer: see 13.3.47
transcribir: past
  participle *transcrito*
transferir: sentir 13.3.44
transgredir: abolir
  13.3.2 sometimes
  regular
transponer: poner 13.3.35
trascender: perder 13.3.32

trasegar: cerrar 13.3.11
  g>gu before *e*
traslucir: lucir 13.3.26
trasponer: poner 13.3.35
trastrocar: contar 13.3.14
  c>qu before *e*
trocar: contar 13.3.14
  c>qu before *e*
tronar: contar 13.3.14
tropezar: cerrar 13.3.11
  z>c before *e*
tullir: zambullir see
  13.5.3, item 6
valer: see 13.3.48

venir: see 13.3.49
ver: see 13.3.50
verter: perder 13.3.32
vestir: pedir 13.3.31
volar: contar 13.3.14
volcar: contar 13.3.14
  c>qu before *e*
volver: mover 13.3.28
  past participle *vuelto*
yacer: see 13.3.51
zaherir: sentir 13.3.44
zambullir: see 13.5.3,
  item 6

13.5 Regular verb forms

The following remarks apply throughout these verb tables:

(i)   *Vosotros* forms are replaced by *ustedes* forms throughout Latin America.
(ii) The imperfect subjunctive *-ra* form of *haber* (*hubiera*, etc.) is an optional
      alternative for the conditional *habría* in the conditional tenses of the perfect.
(iii) The future subjunctive is almost obsolete. See 16.17.
(iv) All compound tenses are formed with the auxiliary *haber* (see 13.3.22) and
      the past participle, which is invariable in form in these tenses.

13.5.1 Overview of the Spanish verb

Spanish verbs may appear in the following forms:

Infinitive   *hablar* discussed in Chapter 18
Gerund   *hablando* discussed in Chapter 20
Past participle *hablado* discussed in Chapter 19
Imperative   *habla* (*tú*), *hablad* (*vosotros/vosotras*) discussed in
                     Chapter 17
                     hable (*usted*), *hablen* (*ustedes*)

ACTIVE VOICE

Indicative mood

The uses of the indicative tense forms are discussed in Chapter 14.

Present   *yo hablo*, etc. I speak
Imperfect   *yo hablaba*, etc. I was speaking
Preterite   *yo hablé*, etc. I spoke
Future   *yo hablaré*, etc. I shall/will speak
Conditional *yo hablaría*, etc. I would speak

Perfect	*yo he hablado*, etc. I have spoken
Pluperfect	*yo había hablado*, etc. I had spoken
Future perfect	*yo habré hablado*, etc. I will have spoken
Conditional perfect	*yo habría hablado*, etc. or *yo hubiera hablado* I would have spoken
Pretérito anterior	*yo hube hablado* I had spoken, etc. (see 14.10.4)

CONTINUOUS (DISCUSSED IN CHAPTER 15)

Present	*yo estoy hablando*, etc. I am speaking
Imperfect	*yo estaba hablando*, etc. I was speaking
Preterite	*yo estuve hablando*, etc. I spoke/had a talk
Future	*yo estaré hablando*, etc. I will be speaking
Conditional	*yo estaría hablando*, etc. I would be speaking
Perfect	*yo he estado hablando*, etc. I have been speaking
Pluperfect	*yo había estado hablando*, etc. I had been speaking
Future perfect	*yo habré estado hablando*, etc. I shall/will have been speaking
Conditional perfect	*yo habría estado hablando*, etc. I would have been speaking

Subjunctive mood (no English translation)

Present	*(que) yo hable*, etc.
Imperfect	*(que) yo hablara/(que) yo hablase*, etc.
Future	*(que) yo hablare*, etc. (obsolete, except in third person in very formal styles)
Perfect	*(que) yo haya hablado*, etc.
Pluperfect	*(que) yo hubiera/hubiese hablado*, etc.
Future perfect	*(que) yo hubiere hablado*, etc. (obsolete)

CONTINUOUS

Present	*(que) yo esté hablando*, etc.
Imperfect	*(que) yo estuviera/estuviese hablando*, etc.
Future	*(que) yo estuviere hablando*, etc.
Perfect	*(que) yo haya estado hablando*, etc.
Pluperfect	*(que) yo hubiera/hubiese estado hablando*, etc.
Future perfect	*(que) yo hubiere estado hablando* (obsolete)

PASSIVE VOICE

There are a number of ways of translating the English passive, the most common being the passive with *ser*, e.g. *esta novela fue publicada en México*, or (in the case of the third person) passive *se*, e.g. *esta novela se publicó en México*. These forms, not always interchangeable, are discussed in Chapter 28, but a selection of the chief tenses are shown here by way of illustration. The participle in the *ser* form must agree in number and gender with the subject of *ser*:

Indicative (third person only shown)

Present	*es publicado/se publica* it is published
Imperfect	*era publicado/se publicaba* it used to be published
Preterite	*fue publicado/se publicó* it was published
Future	*será publicado/se publicará* it will be published
Conditional	*sería publicado/se publicaría* it would be published
Perfect	*ha sido publicado/se ha publicado* it has been published
Pluperfect	*había sido publicado/se había publicado* it had been published
Future perfect	*habrá sido publicado/se habrá publicado* it will have been published
Conditional perfect	*habría sido publicado/se habría publicado* it would have been published

CONTINUOUS

The passive continuous with *ser* is not very common. It is discussed at 15.4.

Present	*está siendo publicado/está publicándose*[8] it is being published
Imperfect	*estaba siendo publicado/estaba publicándose* it was being published
Future	*estará siendo publicado/estará publicándose* it will be being published
Conditional	*estaría siendo publicado/estaría publicándose* it would be being published
Perfect	*ha estado siendo publicado/ha estado publicándose*
Pluperfect	*había estado siendo publicado/había estado publicándose*
Future perfect	*habrá estado siendo publicado/habrá estado publicándose*
Conditional Perfect	*habría estado siendo publicado/habría estado publicándose*

Subjunctive

Present	*(que) sea publicado/(que) se publique*
Imperfect	*(que) fuera publicado/(que) se publicara/(que) fuese publicado/(que) se publicase*
Future	*(que) fuere publicado/(que) se publicare* (almost obsolete)
Perfect	*(que) haya sido publicado/que se haya publicado*
Pluperfect	*(que) hubiese/hubiera sido publicado/que se hubiera/hubiese publicado*

CONTINUOUS

The subjunctive continuous passive is also rare in practice.

Present	*(que) esté siendo publicado/(que) se esté publicando*

---

[8] The pronoun may optionally be shifted in all these continuous forms, i.e. *se está publicando*, etc.

Imperfect	(que) estuviera/estuviese siendo publicado/(que) se estuviera/estuviese publicando
Perfect	(que) haya estado siendo publicado/que haya estado publicándose
Pluperfect	(que) hubiera/hubiese estado siendo publicado/que hubiera/hubiese estado publicándose

13.5.2 Conjugation of regular verbs

The three verbs *hablar* 'to speak', *comer* 'to eat' and *vivir* 'to live' conjugate regularly throughout and are unaffected by spelling changes.

(Stem	*habl-*	*com-*	*viv-*)
Infinitive	hablar	comer	vivir
Gerund	hablando	comiendo	viviendo
Past participle	hablado	comido	vivido
Imperative			
(*tú*)	habla	come	vive
(*vosotros/as*)	hablad	comed	vivid
(*usted*)	hable	coma	viva
(*ustedes*)	hablen	coman	vivan

Indicative

Present

hablo	hablamos	como	comemos	vivo	vivimos
hablas	habláis	comes	coméis	vives	vivís
habla	hablan	come	comen	vive	viven

Perfect

he hablado, etc.   he comido, etc.   he vivido, etc.

Imperfect

hablaba	hablábamos	comía	comíamos	vivía	vivíamos
hablabas	hablabais	comías	comíais	vivías	vivíais
hablaba	hablaban	comía	comían	vivía	vivían

Preterite

hablé	hablamos	comí	comimos	viví	vivimos
hablaste	hablasteis	comiste	comisteis	viviste	vivisteis
habló	hablaron	comió	comieron	vivió	vivieron

Pluperfect   *Pretérito anterior*

había hablado, etc.	hube hablado, etc.
había comido, etc.	hube comido, etc.
había vivido, etc.	hube vivido, etc.

Future

hablaré	hablaremos	comeré	comeremos	viviré	viviremos
hablarás	hablaréis	comerás	comeréis	vivirás	viviréis
hablará	hablarán	comerá	comerán	vivirá	vivirán

Future perfect
habré hablado, etc.   *habré comido*, etc.   *habré vivido*, etc.

Conditional
hablaría hablaríamos	*comería comeríamos*	*viviría viviríamos*
hablarías hablaríais	*comerías comeríais*	*vivirías viviríais*
hablaría hablarían	*comería comerían*	*viviría vivirían*

Perfect conditional
habría hablado, etc. *habría comido*, etc. *habría vivido*, etc., or
hubiera hablado, etc. *hubiera comido*, etc. *hubiera vivido*, etc.

Subjunctive

Present
hable *hablemos*	*coma* *comamos*	*viva* *vivamos*
hables *habléis*	*comas* *comáis*	*vivas* *viváis*
hable *hablen*	*coma* *coman*	*viva* *vivan*

Perfect
haya hablado, etc.   *haya comido*, etc.   *haya vivido*, etc.

Imperfect
(a) *-ra* form
hablara habláramos	*comiera comiéramos*	*viviera viviéramos*
hablaras hablarais	*comieras comierais*	*vivieras vivierais*
hablara hablaran	*comiera comieran*	*viviera vivieran*

(b) *-se* form
hablase hablásemos	*comiese comiésemos*	*viviese viviésemos*
hablases hablaseis	*comieses comieseis*	*vivieses vivieseis*
hablase hablasen	*comiese comiesen*	*viviese viviesen*

Pluperfect
hubiera hablado, etc.   *hubiera comido*, etc.   *hubiera vivido*, etc.
hubiese hablado, etc.   *hubiese comido*, etc.   *hubiese vivido*, etc.

Future
hablare habláremos	*comiere comiéremos*	*viviere viviéremos*
hablares hablareis	*comieres comiereis*	*vivieres viviereis*
hablare hablaren	*comiere comieren*	*viviere vivieren*

13.5.3 Spelling changes in the verb system

The following spelling rules apply to all Spanish verbs, regular and irregular:

(1) Infinitives ending in *-zar*, *-cer* and *-cir*:

> *z* is spelt *c* before *i* or *e*.
> *c* is spelt *z* before *a* or *o* (although in the majority of verbs ending in *-cer*, *c* becomes *zc* before *a*, and *o*)

	rezar 'to pray'	*vencer* 'to defeat'	*esparcir* 'to scatter'
Gerund	*rezando*	*venciendo*	*esparciendo*

Past participle	*rezado*		*vencido*		*esparcido*	
Present indicative						
	rezo	*rezamos*	*venzo*	*vencemos*	*esparzo*	*esparcimos*
	rezas	*rezáis*	*vences*	*vencéis*	*esparces*	*esparcís*
	reza	*rezan*	*vence*	*vencen*	*esparce*	*esparcen*
Preterite						
	recé	*rezamos*	*vencí*	*vencimos*	*esparcí*	*esparcimos*
	rezaste	*rezasteis*	*venciste*	*vencisteis*	*esparciste*	*esparcisteis*
	rezó	*rezaron*	*venció*	*vencieron*	*esparció*	*esparcieron*
Present subjunctive						
	rece	*recemos*	*venza*	*venzamos*	*esparza*	*esparzamos*
	reces	*recéis*	*venzas*	*venzáis*	*esparzas*	*esparzáis*
	rece	*recen*	*venza*	*venzan*	*esparza*	*esparzan*

No other forms affected.

Verbs ending in *-cer* or *-cir* are usually irregular and should be checked against the list at 13.4.

(2) Infinitives ending in *-car, -quir:*

> *c* is spelt *qu* before *e* or *u*.
> *qu* is spelt *c* before *a* or *o*.

	sacar 'to take out'		*delinquir* 'to commit a crime'	
Present indicative				
	saco	*sacamos*	*delinco*	*delinquimos*
	sacas	*sacáis*	*delinques*	*delinquís*
	saca	*sacan*	*delinque*	*delinquen*
Preterite				
	saqué	*sacamos*	*delinquí*	*delinquimos*
	sacaste	*sacasteis*	*delinquiste*	*delinquisteis*
	sacó	*sacaron*	*delinquió*	*delinquieron*
Present subjunctive				
	saque	*saquemos*	*delinca*	*delincamos*
	saques	*saquéis*	*delincas*	*delincáis*
	saque	*saquen*	*delinca*	*delincan*

No other forms affected.

Delinquir seems to be the only living example of a verb ending in *-quir* and it is very rarely used.

(3) Infinitives ending in *-gar, -guir:*

> *g* is spelt *gu* before *i* or *e*.
> *gu* is spelt *g* before *a* or *o*.

	llegar 'to arrive'	*seguir* 'to follow' (radical changing, like *pedir* 13.3.34)
Past participle	*llegado*	*seguido*

Present indicative

llego	llegamos	s**i**go	seguimos
llegas	llegáis	sigues	seguís
llega	llegan	sigue	siguen

Preterite

lle**gué**	llegamos	seguí	seguimos
llegaste	llegasteis	seguiste	seguisteis
llegó	llegaron	siguió	siguieron

Present subjunctive

lle**gue**	lle**gue**mos	si**g**a	si**g**amos
lle**gue**s	lle**gu**éis	si**g**as	si**g**áis
lle**gue**	lle**gu**en	si**g**a	si**g**an

No other forms affected.

(4) Infinitives ending in -*guar*:
  The *u* is written *ü* before *e*. See 13.2.5 for examples.

(5) Infinitives ending in -*ger*, -*gir:*
  g is spelt *j* before *a* or *o*.

Present indicative

proteger 'to protect'		*fingir* 'to pretend'	
prote**j**o	protegemos	fin**j**o	fingimos
proteges	protegéis	finges	fingís
protege	protegen	finge	fingen

Present subjunctive

prote**j**a	prote**j**amos	fin**j**a	fin**j**amos
prote**j**as	prote**j**áis	fin**j**as	fin**j**áis
prote**j**a	prote**j**an	fin**j**a	fin**j**an

No other forms affected.
Verbs ending in -*jar*, e.g. *amortajar*, and -*jer*, e.g. *tejer*, retain the *j* throughout.

(6) Infinitive in -*ñer*, *ñir*, -*llir*.

  ie is spelt *e*.
  ió is spelt *ó*.

	tañer 'to chime'	*gruñir* 'to grunt'	*zambullir* 'to dive'
Gerund	tañendo	gruñendo	zambullendo
Preterite			

tañí tañimos	gruñí gruñimos	zambullí zambullimos
tañiste tañisteis	gruñiste gruñisteis	zambulliste zambullisteis
tañó tañeron	gruñó gruñeron	zambulló zambulleron

Imperfect subjunctive

tañera tañéramos	gruñera gruñéramos	zambullera zambulléramos
tañeras tañerais	gruñeras gruñerais	zambulleras zambullerais
tañera tañeran	gruñera gruñeran	zambullera zambulleran

tañese tañésemos gruñese gruñésemos zambullese zambullésemos
tañeses tañeseis gruñeses gruñeseis zambullese zambulleseis
tañese tañesen gruñese gruñesen zambullese zambullesen

Future subjunctive (almost obsolete)
tañere, etc., *gruñere*, etc., *zambullere*, etc.

(7) Verbs in *-eer*: all conjugate like *poseer* at 13.3.36.
(8) Verbs in *-uir*: all conjugate like *construir* at 13.3.13.

13.5.4 Full conjugation of the compound tenses of *ver*

The forms of the compound tenses are completely predictable provided one knows the full conjugation of *haber* (13.3.22) and the past participle of the verb.

The conjugation of the compound tenses of *ver* 'to see' is shown here as an example. Note the irregular past participle, *visto*.

Indicative

Perfect 'I have seen', etc.
he visto *hemos visto*
has visto *habéis visto*
ha visto *han visto*

Pluperfect 'I had seen', etc.
había visto *habíamos visto*
habías visto *habíais visto*
había visto *habían visto*

Future perfect 'I shall have seen' etc.
habré visto *habremos visto*
habrás visto *habréis visto*
habrá visto *habrán visto*

Conditional 'I would have seen', etc.
habría visto *habríamos visto*
habrías visto *habríais visto*
habría visto *habrían visto*

Pretérito anterior 'I had seen' etc.
hube visto *hubimos visto*
hubiste visto *hubisteis visto*
hubo visto *hubieron visto*

Subjunctive

Perfect
haya visto *hayamos visto*
hayas visto *hayáis visto*
haya visto *hayan visto*

Imperfect
hubiera visto *hubiéramos visto* or
hubieras visto *hubierais visto*
hubiera visto *hubieran visto*

hubiese visto *hubiésemos visto*
hubieses visto *hubieseis visto*
hubiese visto *hubiesen visto*

14

Use of indicative (non-continuous) verb forms

Continuous forms (*estoy hablando, estamos trabajando*, etc.) are discussed in Chapter 15; the subjunctive is discussed in Chapter 16. The possible forms of a typical regular verb are shown at 13.5.1.

14.1 Names of the tenses

There is little consensus among grammarians of Spanish about the names of the tenses, and another source of difficulty is the fact that in Spanish *pretérito* simply means 'past' (one can talk of *las glorias pretéritas* 'former glories'/'bygone glories'), whereas 'preterite' (US 'preterit') refers only to one Spanish past tense.

The following names are used by various grammarians: **Imperfect indicative** (B&B, R&S, H&N,[1] i.e. *hablaba, decía*): *pretérito imperfecto* (Academia, Seco), *copretérito* (Bello). **Preterite** (B&B, R&S, i.e. *hablé, dije*): *pretérito perfecto simple* (Academia), *pretérito indefinido* (Seco), *pretérito perfecto absoluto* (Gili Gaya), *pretérito* (Bello), past definite (H&N). **Perfect** (B&B, R&S, H&N, i.e. *he hablado*, also sometimes called in English 'present perfect' to distinguish it from the future perfect, pluperfect and conditional perfect): *pretérito perfecto compuesto* (Academia), *pretérito perfecto* (Seco), *pretérito perfecto actual* (Gili Gaya), *ante-presente* (Bello). **Pluperfect** (B&B, R&S, H&N, i.e. *había hablado, había dicho*): *pretérito pluscuamperfecto* (Academia, Seco), *antecopretérito* (Bello). *Pretérito anterior* (B&B, Academia, Seco, i.e. *hube hablado, hube dicho*): preterite perfect (R&S), *antepretérito* (Gili Gaya, Bello), past anterior (H&N). **Conditional** (i.e. *hablaría, diría*): normally called the 'conditional' in English and *el condicional* by most Hispanic writers and by the Academy, but *el potencial* by Manuel Seco and a few other authorities, *pospretérito* by Bello and *futuro hipotético* by Gili Gaya. **Future (indicative)** (i.e. *hablaré, diré*): called the 'future' or 'future indicative' in English and *futuro* in most Spanish texts, but *futuro imperfecto* by Seco to distinguish it from the future perfect/*futuro perfecto* (*habré hablado, habrán dicho*).

14.2 Tense in Spanish: general remarks

Any attempt at a brief overview of the role of the various tenses in the Spanish verb system would be confusing, but the following points deserve emphasis:

---

[1] B&B: Butt and Benjamin; R&S: Ramsey and Spaulding (1958); H&N: Harmer and Norton (1957).

(a) There is no 'present' tense in Spanish, if by present tense is meant a tense form whose exclusive function is to express present time. The uses of the simple 'present' tense, *hablo, fumas, van*, etc., are several and varied. See 14.3 for further discussion.

(b) There is no 'future tense' in Spanish, in the sense that there is no verb form whose exclusive function is to indicate future time. The following sentences are all 'future' and all mean 'I'll call you tonight', but they express different nuances: *te llamo esta noche, te llamaré esta noche, te voy a llamar esta noche.* See 14.6 for further discussion.

(c) The difference between the imperfect and the preterite tenses, e.g. between *hablaba* and *hablé*, often involves a distinction between past events viewed as incomplete at the time (imperfect tense) and past events viewed as complete at the time (preterite tense). English does not systematically make this distinction, so without further information one cannot tell whether to translate a form like 'I went' as *fui* (viewed as a completed action) or *iba* (viewed as an incomplete or as a habitual action). This difference in Spanish is especially subtle for English speakers when the verb *ser* 'to be' is involved. See 14.4 for discussion.[2]

(d) Unlike French and German, Spanish has a full range of continuous forms which resemble English progressive forms: *está lloviendo* 'it's raining', *estabas pensando* 'you were thinking', *he estado comiendo* 'I've been eating'. The resemblance to the English progressive forms is misleading: see 15.2.1 for details.

(e) The difference between the preterite *hablé* 'I spoke' and the perfect *he hablado* 'I've spoken' is maintained in spoken and written Spanish whereas it is blurred in French, Italian and German. However, the difference in Spanish only partly coincides with the distinction between 'I spoke' and 'I've spoken'; see particularly 14.9. Use of the perfect tense is also governed by different rules in most of Latin America. See 14.9.8 for more details.

14.3 Uses of the present tense

For the use of the present in conditional sentences, e.g. *si sales, compra pan* 'if you go out, buy some bread', see 25.2. For the use of the present as a future tense see 14.6.3.

14.3.1 Present tense to indicate timeless or habitual events that still occur

The simple present tense is used to express eternal or timeless truths or habitual events. This is probably the commonest use of this verb form:

---

[2] Earlier editions of this grammar described the difference between the preterite and imperfect as a difference between 'perfective aspect' and 'imperfective aspect' or 'completed' events and 'incomplete' events. This was misleading since it suggested that the preterite always indicates that a past event was always really completed rather than merely *viewed* as complete. *Trabajé con ella el año pasado* 'I worked with her last year' is possible even if you are still working with her. A pro-Franco poster from the Spanish Civil War reads *España fue, es y será inmortal* 'Spain was, is and will be immortal', and there is obviously no implication that her past immortality ended: the idea is that the country was uninterruptedly immortal *throughout* the past and still is in the present. Viewing an action as completed reflects the point of view of the speaker; it does not always mean that the action literally ended.

Llueve mucho en Irlanda	It rains a lot in Ireland
Fumo más de sesenta al día	I smoke more than sixty a day
María es venezolana	Maria's Venezuelan
Los sonetos tienen catorce versos	Sonnets have 14 lines
No tengo tarjeta de crédito	I don't have a credit card
Me deprime comer sola	Eating on my own depresses me
(C. Martín Gaite, Spain)	
Los que son creyentes tienen ese consuelo	Those who are believers have that
(M. Puig, Argentina)	consolation

As in English, use of the present continuous for what seems to be a habitual event makes the event in some ways unusual or temporary: *últimamente estoy fumando más de sesenta al día* 'lately I'm smoking more than sixty a day'.

14.3.2 The present tense for events occurring in the present

The simple present in Spanish can simply indicate that an action is happening in the present: *fuma* can mean 'she is smoking' as well as 'she smokes'. The chief problem here is how to distinguish between this use of the present tense and the present continuous, *está fumando*. In English there is little overlap between the simple present and the progressive: 'he comes' for 'he is coming' is nowadays very archaic. But the difference between the Spanish simple present and the present continuous is not so clear-cut. The following remarks should therefore be read together with the discussion of the continuous form in Chapter 15.

(a) With some verbs and in some contexts there is often only a slight difference between the simple present and the continuous:

Escribe una novela/ Está escribiendo una novela	He's writing a novel
¿Qué haces?/¿Qué estás haciendo?	What are you doing?
(they mean the same when they express surprise)	
¡Mira cómo llueve!/¡Mira cómo está lloviendo!	Look at the way it's raining!

(b) The simple present, and not the continuous, is used with verbs that denote states rather than actions, e.g. *parece cansada* 'she seems tired', *brilla la luna* 'the moon is shining', *hoy lleva traje de chaqueta* 'she's wearing a suit today'. See 15.3b for discussion.

Occasionally the continuous may be optionally used to emphasize an unusual or surprising state, as in *está haciendo mucho calor* 'it's very hot (lately)'. See 15.2.2 for explanation.

(c) The simple present is much used for events that happen in the present but are not necessarily actually in progress **now**. In other words, it is used for events that are just about to happen or have just happened or which are really states or habitual actions rather than events that are actually in progress:

Acusamos recibo de su carta del 3 de enero	We acknowledge receipt of your letter of 3 January
A mí me suena poco natural	It sounds unnatural to me
La oposición considera una maniobra el aperturismo anunciado por el régimen	The opposition considers the liberalization policy announced by the regime to be a manoeuvre
¿Por qué te metes en ese asunto?	Why are you getting involved in that business?

¿Qué dices? (= *¿qué estás diciendo?* when indignation or surprise are intended)	What did you say (just then)?' or 'What do you say?' or 'What are you saying?'
¿No oyes los perros?	Can't you hear the dogs?
¡Que me ahogo!	I'm drowning!
¡Ya voy!/Disiento	I'm coming!/I disagree
Merino pasa la pelota a Andreas	Merino passes the ball to Andreas
¿Vienes?/¿Interrumpo?	Are you coming?/Am I interrupting?

None of the sentences under **(c)** refers to an event which is strictly speaking in progress now, but to events that have either just happened or are just about to happen (*¿qué dices?*, *pasa la pelota*, *¿interrumpo?*, *¡que me ahogo!*), or which are present but not necessarily happening at this moment, e.g. *la oposición considera . . .* , *¿por qué te metes? . . . , yo disiento*. Failure to observe the rule that the present continuous can only be used for events that are actually in progress is a common mistake among English-speakers. See 15.1.2–3 for further discussion.

14.3.3 The *presente histórico* or historic present

Use of the present tense to refer to the past is much more favoured than in English as a way of dramatizing descriptive narrative in literature, but it also constantly occurs in colloquial Spanish, more commonly than the equivalent in popular English (e.g. 'Mrs Brown comes up to me and says . . . ').

Frena a la mula y sus ojos claros, ávidos, buscan en una y otra dirección. Por fin, distingue a unos pasos, acuclillado, a un hombre con sandalias y sombrero de cuero (M. Vargas Llosa, Peru)	He stopped (stops) his mule and his bright, eager eyes sought (seek) in both directions. Eventually he spotted (spots), a few paces away, a man in leather sandals and hat, crouching
—Bueno, pues me llama —decía, riéndose, y me dice que por qué no nos vemos. ¿Vernos? ¿Dónde?, le digo yo. En cualquier sitio. Podemos ir al teatro, al cine, a bailar, dice. Pero, ¿qué es lo que les pasa a tus amiguitas?, le digo. Es que no son tan guapas como tú, me dice. —Se reía—. A buenas horas lo has descubierto, le digo, yo ya no tengo nada que ver contigo. ¡Pero si estamos casados!, me dice él (S. Puértolas, Spain, dialogue; very colloquial)	'Anyway, he rings me,' she said, laughing, 'and he asks me why don't we meet. Meet one another? Where?, I say to him. "Anywhere. We can go to the theatre, to the movies, dancing," he says. But what's happened to your lady friends? I say to him. "Actually they're not as attractive as you," he says to me.' She was laughing. 'A fine time to discover that, I say to him, I don't have anything to do with you any more. "But we're married!" he says to me.'

Note

The historic present is almost always used in everyday speech after *por poco* 'all but' and often after *casi* 'nearly': *me caí por unas escaleras y por poco/casi me **rompo/me rompí** el tobillo* 'I fell down a flight of stairs and nearly broke my ankle', *casi me **mata**, lo cual no era nada difícil por aquel entonces* (A. Bryce Echenique, Peru) 'she nearly killed me, which wasn't at all difficult at that time', *casi **enloquezco** al abrir el telegrama* (ibid.) 'I nearly went crazy on opening the telegram'. Occasional exceptions can be found on both continents: *por poco me **hizo** llorar de lo cariñosa que es* (M. Vargas Llosa, Peru, dialogue) 'she's so affectionate she nearly made me cry'.

14.3.4 Present tense used as an imperative

This is frequent in everyday speech to produce a rather abrupt imperative: *tú te callas* 'you just keep quiet'. All matters connected with the imperative are discussed in Chapter 17.

14.3.5 Use of the present to ask permission

The present is much used when asking for someone's consent:

¿Te lo traigo yo?	Shall I bring it for you?
¿Escribo a los abuelos para decírselo?	Shall I write to our grandparents to tell them?
¿Llamo para ver si ha venido?	Shall I ring to see whether (s)he's come?
¿Vamos al cine esta noche?	Do you want to go to the cinema (US 'movies') tonight?

14.3.6 Use of the present as a future tense

Spanish makes constant use of the simple present to refer to the future: *mañana vamos a California* 'we're going to California tomorrow', *te veo luego* 'I'll see you later'. See 14.6.3 for discussion.

14.3.7 Present in sentences like 'it's the first time I've seen you' and in other expressions of time

English-speaking learners should note the use of the present tense where our language uses the perfect in sentences of the type 'this is the first time that . . . ' and 'I've been . . . for *n* days/weeks', etc.:

*Es la primera vez que la **veo***	It's the first time I **have seen** her
*No es la primera vez que los noruegos **entran** en Nueva York* (J. L. Borges, Argentina)	It isn't the first time that the Norwegians **have entered** New York
*Hace tres años que no **vengo***	I haven't been here for three years
Desde hace dos días estoy tratando de comunicarme con el señor Morales (*Prensalibre*, Guatemala, dialogue)	I've been trying to contact Mr Morales for two days

The past tense used in such constructions is the imperfect. See 14.5.3.

14.4 The preterite: general

The Spanish preterite refers to actions that were completed in the past or are *viewed* as completed in the past (the reason for this distinction is clarified at 14.4.1). Occasionally it refers to events as beginning in the past (see 14.4.8). The difference in meaning between the preterite and the imperfect tense is sometimes difficult for English speakers. It is easy to explain that the preterite is used to describe completed 'one-off' past events like *aquel día **se rompió** una pierna* 'that day (s)he broke a leg'. ?*Aquel día se rompía una pierna* 'that day (s)he was breaking a leg' is hardly likely (but see 14.5.8 for a rare exception). It is also possible to say confidently that the preterite is used for events that continue for the whole of a specified period or for the whole of a number of specified periods in the past: *fue rey durante ocho años* 'he was king for eight years', *habló tres veces durante cuatro horas* 'he spoke three times for four hours (each time)'. But a difficulty arises when the past event is habitual or prolonged, since one can often optionally describe such events with the imperfect or with the preterite, as in *mi padre fumó mucho cuando era joven* or *fumaba mucho cuando era joven* 'my father smoked a lot when he was young' or *la Guerra Civil era un desastre/la Guerra Civil fue un desastre* 'the Civil War was a disaster'; see 14.4.3 and 14.4.4 for a discussion.

The preterite is very often used in Latin-American Spanish where the perfect tense is used in Spain. See 14.9.8 for discussion.

14.4.1 Preterite for events occurring throughout a finite period

The preterite tense must be used for an event that continued throughout the whole of a finite period of time, regardless of whether the action then ended or not.[3] By 'finite' is meant a period of time of a specific length, i.e. whose beginning and end are stated or implied:

Estuve destinado en Bilbao dos años	I was stationed in Bilbao for two years
Te olvidas del tiempo que estuviste casado	You forget the time you were married
Por un instante pensé que me caía	For a moment I thought that I was falling
Los dinosaurios reinaron sobre la tierra durante millones de años	The dinosaurs reigned on Earth for millions of years
La ETA tuvo menos actividad durante el régimen de Franco que al instalarse la democracia (M. Vargas Llosa, Peru)	ETA (Basque terrorists) was less active during the Franco regime than when democracy was introduced
Durante años no pudimos hablar de otra cosa (G. García Márquez, Colombia)	For years we could talk of nothing else
En toda mi vida supe de dos casos (D. Navarro Gómez, Spain)	In all my life I've known of two cases
La fiesta fue un éxito	The party was a success (from start to finish)
Fue un día magnífico	It was a magnificent day (from start to finish)

Notes

(i) Compare *cuando llegué vi que la fiesta era/estaba siendo un éxito* 'when I arrived I saw that the party was a success' (but it wasn't over yet) and *como era un día magnífico, fuimos al zoo* 'as it was a magnificent day, we went to the zoo' (but it may have rained later).

(ii) Words like *siempre* and *nunca* often indicate actions continuing throughout the whole of a period of time: *siempre procuré pasarlo bien* 'I always tried to have a good time', *nunca me hizo gracia ese hombre* 'I never really liked that man', *nunca Fermín Eguren me pudo ver* (J. L. Borges, Argentina) 'Fermín Eguren never was able to stand me' (i.e. throughout the time I'm referring to). But words like *siempre* or *nunca* may refer to habitual actions that occur over no specified period and therefore require an imperfect verb, as in *antes siempre iba a misa* 'I/(s)he/you always used to go to Mass', *nunca hacía tanto calor como ahora* 'it never used to be as hot as now'.

(iii) In sentences involving phrases like *todos los días*, *todos los años* either tense may be possible, depending on whether we look at the action as complete or as going on at the time: *todos los veranos veraneaban en San Sebastián/veranearon en San Sebastián* 'every summer they spent their holidays/vacation in San Sebastian', *aquella semana regaba/regó el jardín todas las mañanas* 'that week he watered the garden every morning', but *cuando yo era pequeño yo lo/le veía pasar casi todos los días* (not *lo/le vi* since the period is too vague) 'when I was little I saw him pass nearly every day'.

(iv) Actions performed throughout a period of time can, of course, be performed habitually, in which case the imperfect is used, as in *hablaba durante tres horas* (or *solía hablar*

---

[3] The issue is whether the period ended, not the action: *habló durante dos horas, y luego continuó hablando durante tres horas más* 'he talked for two hours and then went on talking for three more hours' is correct. For the possible alternative *estuvo hablando durante dos horas* see 15.2.3.

durante tres horas) 'he used to speak for three hours' (on an unspecified number of different occasions).

14.4.2 Preterite used to indicate single events or sets of events completed in the past

A single completed past event, or a single set of completed past events, is expressed by the preterite:

La Segunda Guerra Mundial empezó en 1939	World War Two began in 1939
Hubo una explosión	There was an explosion (i.e. at that moment)
Momentos después Pepe tosió	A few moments later Pepe coughed
Lo primero que escribí fue un cuento (A. Grandes, Spain)	The first thing I wrote was a short story
... el día que el muchacho cumplió veinte años (I. Allende, Chile)	... the day the boy reached the age of twenty
Martín la abrazó cuatro veces	Martín embraced her four times
Lo escribió ochenta veces	(S)he wrote it eighty times

Notes

(i) The preterite is used to describe a series of completed events that occurred separately (in whichever order), whereas the imperfect suggests events that occurred simultaneously or habitually. Compare: *lloró, gritó, se rió* 'she wept, shouted, laughed' (separate actions), and *lloraba, gritaba, se reía ...* '(s)he was weeping, shouting, laughing' (simultaneously) or 'she used to weep', etc.
(ii) The imperfect is, nevertheless, occasionally also used in literary styles for a single completed event. See 14.5.8.

14.4.3 Preterite used to distinguish narrative from description

It follows from the preceding section that the preterite is sometimes used to show that an event is part of the narrative whereas the imperfect shows that it is descriptive background. In other words, the preterite suggests an 'event'. This difference is clearest for English speakers in a sentence like *tuvieron tres niños* 'they had (i.e. 'produced') three children', which is (usually) three events, and *tenían tres niños*, which is merely a state of affairs. Less obvious is the difference between *querían hacerlo* 'they wanted to do it', which indicates merely a state of mind, and *quisieron hacerlo*, which points to an event or outcome, i.e. it means that that they wanted to do it *and tried to*, whether successfully or not (in fact it usually implies failure).

English speakers find this distinction most confusing with the verb *ser*. María Luz Gutiérrez Araus (1995), 32, quotes an interesting example from García Márquez: *un perro ... irrumpió en los vericuetos del mercado ... y mordió a cuatro personas que se le atravesaron en el camino. Tres **eran** esclavos negros. La otra **fue** Sierva María de todos los Ángeles* 'a dog rushed into the narrow alleyways of the market and bit four people who got in its way. Three were black slaves. The other was Sierva María de todos los Ángeles.' Luz Gutiérrez explains the difference between *era* and *fue* in this example as a difference between the 'nonactive', i.e. 'descriptive', imperfect and the 'active' (i.e. 'narrative') preterite. The preterite brings Sierva María into the foreground – she is a major character in the novel. The imperfect pushes the other three characters into the descriptive background. But such examples are rare and literary: ordinary language would say *era*.

In the following example, the preterite presents the publication of the statistics as events while the imperfect paints the background:

*En noviembre se registraron 851.320 contratos, de los cuales 83.419 **fueron** indefinidos. Es decir, las colocaciones han caído significativamente respecto a la cifra récord del pasado octubre, que **fue** de más de un millón. El paro ha caído en 157.444 personas desde noviembre de 1996, cuando la tasa de paro **era** del 14,04% (El País, Spain)*

851,320 labour contracts were registered in November, of which 83,419 were long-term. In other words, the number of persons hired has fallen significantly compared with last October's record figure, which was more than half a million. Unemployment has fallen by 157,444 persons since November 1996, when the unemployment rate was 14.04%.

14.4.4 Use of the preterite to denote habitual events

Habitual events in the past are usually expressed by the imperfect, as explained at 14.5.2. But the preterite can describe habitual or prolonged events in the past: the preterite views the event as having gone on uninterruptedly during a finite period whereas the imperfect merely describes it as going on at the time or as part of the background against which events are being narrated. In the sentence *mi padre **fumaba**/**fumó** mucho cuando era joven* 'my father smoked a lot when he was young', either tense is possible, whether or not he carried on smoking afterwards and whether or not he is still alive.[4] The imperfect tense views the habit as in progress at the time; the preterite looks back on it as an event viewed as a whole, i.e. as something that continued throughout whichever period of time the speaker has in mind (his youth, those years, that period I'm talking about, etc.).

The upshot of all this is that, since the speaker or writer is free to adopt differing points of view about the narrative or descriptive status of an event, and since we cannot always know what is in the speaker's or writer's mind, it often happens that either the preterite or the imperfect can be used in Spanish with a difference of nuance that is virtually untranslatable in English:

*Mi niñez **fue**/**era** feliz*
My childhood was happy

*Recuerdo que **llovió**/**llovía** mucho cuando vivíamos en Irlanda*
I remember it rained a lot when we lived in Ireland

*Alonso se **levantó**/se **levantaba** todos los días a las ocho para ir al trabajo*
Alonso got up every day at eight to go to work

*Cuando vivíamos juntos no **tuvimos**/**teníamos** problemas*
When we lived together we had no problems

*Siempre dormía como **durmió** su padre, con el arma escondida dentro de la funda de la almohada (G. García Márquez, Colombia; siempre **durmió** como **dormía** su padre would have meant almost the same thing)*
He always used to sleep as his father (had) slept, with his gun hidden in his pillowcase.

Intrinsic characteristics are likely to be expressed by the imperfect since they tend to be part of a general background. Thus *la casa era muy grande* 'the house was very big', *mi padre era gallego/blanco* 'my father was Galician/white'; use of

---

[4] It is this possibility that makes the terms 'perfective aspect' and 'imperfective aspect' unhelpful for learners, even though they may be correct technical descriptions.

fue in these cases is very unlikely since such descriptions are obviously not 'events'. Verbs expressing location, position or state of mind are also descriptions and therefore expressed by the imperfect: *estaba de rodillas/cansado/saltando de alegría* '(s)he was kneeling, tired, jumping for joy', etc. Non-intrinsic characteristics can take either tense, but are more likely to appear with the imperfect if they refer to some more or less permanent attribute. However, choice of tense depends whether we consider an event viewed as a whole (preterite) or whether we are focusing on what was true at the time (imperfect), as in *yo, de pequeño, fui tímido* or *era tímido* 'as a child I was/used to be timid'. Students are advised to use the imperfect in such cases, since use of the preterite for a more or less inherent characteristic can sound strange or very literary, as in *Sir Thomas Browne (1605–82) supo el griego, el latín, el francés, el italiano y el español, y fue uno de los primeros hombres de letras que estudiaron anglosajón* (J. L. Borges, Argentina, more usually *sabía griego*) 'Sir Thomas Browne (1605–82) knew Greek, Latin, French, Italian and Spanish, and was one of the first men of letters to study Anglo-Saxon.'

14.4.5 Use of the preterite to denote an event that has reached completion

The preterite may indicate that a process has finally reached completion, as in

*Una vez el dinero **estuvo** en mis manos, compré la casa*	As soon as the money came into my hands, I bought the house
Estuvo lista a las once (G. García Márquez, Colombia)	She was ready by eleven
*Cuando el café **estuvo** listo le alcanzó una tacita* (E. Sábato, Argentina)	When the coffee was ready she handed him a small cup
*La conversación se **fue** espaciando* (*ir* + gerund suggests a longish process, *fue* shows the process is complete)	The conversation gradually petered out

14.4.6 Use of the preterite to indicate an event that actually happened

Sometimes the preterite clearly indicates that the event referred to happened, while the imperfect does not give us this information. Compare: *tuvimos que atravesar dos desiertos para llegar al oasis* 'we had to cross two deserts to get to the oasis' (and we did), and *teníamos que atravesar dos desiertos para llegar al oasis* 'we had (still) to cross two deserts to get to the oasis'. The first looks back on the crossing as an action that took place, the second envisages the crossing as still to be made and does not tell us whether it took place or not. Further examples:

***Fue** un error decírselo*	It was a mistake to tell him (we committed it)
***Era** un error decírselo*	It was a mistake to tell him (we may or may not have committed it)
***Costó** trabajo conseguirlo*	It was hard work getting it (but we did)
***Costaba** trabajo conseguirlo*	It was hard work to get it (we may or may not have done)

It is therefore not possible to say **fue un error devolverle el dinero, por eso no lo hice* which has the absurd meaning ***'I committed the mistake of giving him back the money, so I didn't'; *era un error . . .* must be used.

14.4.7 Preterite to denote a rapid or short-lived event

The preterite can sometimes show that an event lasted only a moment. The imperfect would, in these cases, indicate an event that had not yet ended at the time referred to:

Hubo una nota de alarma en su voz	There was a (brief) note of alarm in his/her voice
Cuando abrí el horno, se sintió calor	When I opened the oven it felt hot (i.e. there was a gust of heat)
Creí que hablabas en serio	I thought (for a second) that you were talking seriously
Estuvo a punto de pensar que esas manos no eran suyas (C. Fuentes, Mexico, dialogue)	(For a second) he was on the verge of thinking that those hands weren't his own

14.4.8 Preterite used to indicate the beginning of a state or action

The preterite may occasionally be inchoative or inceptive in meaning, i.e. it may indicate the beginning of an action. Compare *mi hija habló a los once meses* (i.e. *empezó a hablar*) 'my daughter started talking at eleven months', and *mi hija hablaba a los once meses* 'my daughter was talking **by** eleven months'. Also:

Me cayó bien (cf. *me caía bien* 'I was getting on well with him/her')	I took a liking to her/him
Ana me gustó desde el primer momento	I liked ('took a liking to') Ana right from the start
De repente Marta sintió/sentía ganas de cantar	Marta suddenly felt an urge to sing

14.4.9 Preterite used to indicate certainties in the future

The preterite is occasionally used to indicate an absolute certainty in the future:

Cuando llegue, llegó	She'll be here when she's here (and that's that!)
Cuando se acabe, se acabó	When it's finished, it's finished/It'll be finished when it's finished

This construction is more common in Latin America than in Spain. The following three examples are not heard in Spain:

Para las dos ya lo acabé (Mexican example from J. M. Lope Blanch, 1991; Spain *ya lo tengo/tendré acabado*)	I'll have it finished by two o'clock
Mañana ya llegó el día (L. Rafael Sánchez, Puerto Rico, dialogue; Spain *mañana es el día*)	Tomorrow's the day!
Nos fuimos (colloquial Latin American; Spain *nos vamos*)	We're going/We're leaving right now (lit. 'we left')

14.4.10 Special meanings of the preterite of some verbs

Some verbs require special translations when they appear in the preterite. This is especially true of the modal verbs *deber, poder, querer, saber*, which are discussed in Chapter 21. Two other verbs affected are:

Tener: the preterite may mean 'to receive'/'to get', the imperfect means 'had' in the sense of 'was in my possession':

tuve la impresión de que . . .	I got the impression that . . .
tenía la impresión de que . . .	I had the impression that . . .
Tuve una carta	I got/received a letter
Tenía una carta	I had a letter
Cuando tuvo ocasión de estudiar consiguió con la universidad a distancia el título de ingeniero (Cambio16, Spain)	When he got the chance to study, he graduated as an engineer from the Open University[5]

This does not override the rule given at 14.4.1 that the preterite must be used for actions continuing throughout a specified period: *tuvo fiebre durante tres días* '(s)he had a fever for three days'.

Conocer: the preterite means 'meet for the first time', the imperfect means 'to be acquainted with':

Conocí a Antonia	I met Antonia (for the first time)
Conocía a Antonia	I knew Antonia

14.5 The imperfect: general

The Spanish imperfect form expresses past time and it indicates an event viewed as not yet complete at the time referred to. The imperfect is therefore much used as a background tense to describe something that was in progress when another event occurred, as in *yo **dormía** cuando empezó la tormenta* 'I **was sleeping** when the storm started'. It is also much used to describe habitual events in the past, but the preterite can also sometimes describe habitual events, as explained at 14.4.4.

In colloquial language the Spanish imperfect may be a substitute for the conditional. See 14.5.4 and 25.5 for discussion.

14.5.1 Imperfect tense to denote past events in progress when something else happened

The imperfect is much used to indicate any state or event that was already in progress when something else happened. It is thus the correct tense for background descriptions, the preterite being used for events that happened against the background:

*Yo **volvía** del cine cuando vi a Niso*	I was coming back from the cinema when I saw Niso
*Miró por encima del hombro para estar segura de que nadie la **acechaba** (G. García Márquez, Colombia)*	She looked over her shoulder to be sure that no one was lying in wait for her
*Cuando entré en el cuarto noté que **olía** a quemado*	When I entered the room I noticed there was a smell of burning
*Los monumentos y estatuas que **adornaban** los paseos y las plazas fueron triturados (E. Mendoza, Spain)*	The monuments and statues that adorned the avenues and squares were pulverized
*Volví a la sala, pero él ya no **estaba** (A. Mastretta, Mexico, dialogue: i.e. his absence was still continuing when I arrived)*	I went back to the living room, but he was no longer there

---

[5] The public university whose courses are transmitted on radio and TV.

Me marchaba ya cuando has llamado I was just leaving when you rang
   (Latin America *llamaste*)[6]

For the possible use of the continuous imperfect, e.g. *estaba acechando*, instead of the simple imperfect see 14.5.5.

14.5.2 Imperfect used to denote events that continued in the past for an unspecified period

The imperfect can indicate that an event continued in the past for an unspecified period (and may or may not have continued). It is thus much used for characteristics, situations, habitual actions and other events that have no clear beginning and end:

*Las catapultas romanas **lanzaban** piedras*	Roman catapults threw stones
*Me enfadé porque Pepe me había dicho que yo **era** tonto*	I got angry because Pepe had told me that I was stupid
*Cada vez que os **veíais** lo **decía*** (J. Aldecoa, Spain, dialogue)	He used to say it every time you met
*Le **exasperaban** estas comidas mexicanas de cuatro o cinco horas de duración* (C. Fuentes, Mexico)	These four- or five-hour Mexican meals exasperated him
*A veces le **dolían** el aire y la tierra que **pisaba**, el sol del amanecer, las cuencas de los ojos* (A. Mastretta, Mexico)	Sometimes the air and the ground she trod on hurt her; and the rising sun, her eye-sockets

The preterite must be used if a period of time is specified, as in 'he was president **for eight years**', see 14.4.1.

14.5.3 Imperfect in phrases of time of the kind 'I hadn't seen her for years', 'it was the first time that . . . '

English speakers should note the use of the imperfect in the following type of sentence where English uses the pluperfect tense (for the use of the present tense in sentences of this type see note to 14.3.7):

*Hacía años que no la **veía***	I **hadn't** seen her for years
*Era la primera vez que la **veía***	It was the first time I **had seen** her

14.5.4 Imperfect for the conditional

The imperfect is often used in familiar speech instead of the conditional. This most commonly occurs in four cases:

(a) When the conditional would refer to an immediate future. In this case Spanish resembles English: one can say 'he said he would come' or 'he said he was coming':

*Prometió que **venía/vendría***	He promised he was coming/would come
*Juró que lo **hacía/haría***	He swore he'd do it
*Pensé que ya no **venías/vendrías***	I thought you weren't coming/wouldn't come any more

---

[6] In Spain *llamaste* would mean that the phone conversation is no longer in progress.

Me encontraba menos nervioso porque sabía que los refuerzos llegaban/llegarían de un momento para otro	I felt less nervous because I knew the reinforcements were arriving/ would arrive at any moment

But this is not possible with *ser* or if the future is not immediate:

Creía que sería/iba a ser posible	I/(s)he thought it would be possible
Juró que me amaría siempre (not *amaba . . .*[7])	(S)he swore (s)he would love me always

(b) With *deber* and *poder*, in which case the imperfect is slightly more colloquial:

Podía ser una solución, mira . . . (C. Martín Gaite, Spain, dialogue)	It could be a solution, you know . . .
Debías/deberías hacerlo ahora	You should do it now

This usage is especially frequent with *poder* and *deber* to show that someone should or could have acted differently in the past, e.g. *podías/podrías haberlo hecho, ¿no?* 'you could have done it, couldn't you?'; see 21.2.3d and 21.3.3 for details.

(c) In 'remote' and 'unfulfilled' conditions in familiar Spanish (see 25.5 for more details):

Aunque no me gustara, me casaba/casaría con ella	I'd marry her even if I didn't like her
No tenía más que decírmelo y le cambiaba el vaso (very colloquial for *le habría cambiado*)	He only had to tell me and I'd have changed his glass
Un paso más y te rompías el pescuezo (colloquial for *te habrías roto/te hubieras roto*)	One more step and you'd have broken your neck

Note

The imperfect cannot replace the conditional when the later indicates a guess or estimate (as explained at 14.7.2).

(d) In familiar Spanish, to express a wish:

Ya le decía yo cuatro verdades!	I wouldn't mind giving him/her a piece of my mind! (lit. 'telling him/her four truths')
Tenían que hacer un monumento al tío que inventó el café (M. Delibes, Spain, dialogue)	They ought to build a monument for the guy who invented coffee
Yo ahora me tomaba un helado y me quedaba tan bien	I'd (like to have) have an ice-cream now and I'd feel great

14.5.5 *Hablaba* or *estaba hablando*?

If the action is not habitual and is truly past (e.g. 'I was leaving the next day' is in fact a future in the past), the difference between the continuous and non-continuous imperfect is often neutralized, although modern Spanish prefers the continuous form in this case if the verb is one of those which allow the continuous form (see Chapter 15): *yo hablaba/estaba hablando con los vecinos cuando llegaron los bomberos* (*estaba hablando* is preferred) 'I was talking to the neighbo(u)rs when the firemen arrived'.

---

[7] *Querer* means to love a person in all senses, as a friend, relative or lover. *Amar* is used between people who are passionately in love and also for religious love: *amar a Dios* 'to love God', *ama al pecador* 'love the sinner'.

14.5.6 Imperfect in children's language

An interesting use of the imperfect is found in children's language (called the *imperfecto lúdico* or 'imperfect of play'): *vamos a jugar a que yo era un vaquero y tú eras un indio* 'let's pretend I'm a cowboy and you're an Indian'.

14.5.7 Imperfect to make courteous requests

The imperfect can be used to show courtesy in requests and enquiries:

¿Qué deseaba?	What would you like?
Perdone, quería hablar con el director	Excuse me, I'd like a word with the manager

14.5.8 Imperfect used for preterite in literary styles

In literary styles, especially sensational journalism, the imperfect is sometimes used as an alternative to the preterite for dramatic effect. Normally the sentence includes an adverb of time that shows that the action is a single completed event:

*la historia de cómo un hombre de cincuenta años **mataba** en la noche vieja a su amante, una niña de 14 años . . .* (*Cambio16*, Spain; or *mató*)	The story of how, on New Year's Eve, a man of fifty killed his lover, a girl of 14 . . .
*Un cuarto de hora después dos grapos **asesinaban** a un policía armado* (or *asesinaron*)	A quarter of an hour later two members of GRAPO[8] murdered an armed policeman
*Un día antes, en Santiago de Cuba, **era** asesinado Frank País* (*Granma*, Cuba)	The day before, in Santiago de Cuba, Frank País was murdered

This construction is not particularly common in Spanish, but it is frequent in literary French (the *imparfait dramatique*) and is therefore often found in Frenchified Spanish, e.g. in the works of the *modernistas* of the early twentieth century.

14.5.9 Imperfect used in reported speech and in 'stream of consciousness' (*monólogo interior*)

In reported speech the present tense becomes an imperfect and the perfect tense becomes a pluperfect. The following is an extract in direct speech from a letter in a novel written by J. Aldecoa, Spain. Annick writes to David: *Lo que ocurre es que tu carta me ha dejado inquieta. No hablo de tus planteamientos generales; sabes que los comparto. Pero estoy libre de emociones viscerales . . . . Y me preocupo por ti. No se trata de tu seguridad sino de tu pérdida de rumbo. Temo que estás buscándote salidas nobles pero falsas, porque tú, no te engañes, eres un diletante, un señorito que juega a derribar tiranías.* 'The thing is that your letter has left me worried. I'm not referring to your views in general; you know I share them. But I'm not prone to gut reactions . . . And I worry about you. Not about your safety but about your loss of direction. I'm afraid you're looking for a noble but false way out, because, don't fool yourself, you're a dilettante, an upper-class boy playing at overthrowing tyrants.'

In reported speech, this would read: *Annick le decía en su carta que lo que **ocurría era** que su carta la **había dejado** inquieta. **No hablaba** de sus planteamientos*

---

[8] A terrorist group active in Spain in the 1980s.

generales; ya **sabía** *él que ella los* **compartía**. *Pero ella* **estaba** *libre de emociones viscerales . . . Y se* **preocupaba** *por él.* **No se trataba** *de su seguridad, sino de su pérdida de rumbo.* **Temía** *que* **se estaba buscando** *salidas nobles pero falsas porque, no se* **debía** *engañar, él* **era** *un diletante, un señorito que* **jugaba** *a derribar tiranías.*

The following paragraph is an example of 'stream of consciousness' (*monólogo interior*): *sola en la tienda, Felicitas se quedó reflexionando. Vaya, al chico le* **parecía** *mejor que esperase la visita del director (. . . .) Ella* **quería** *trabajar en el hotel y el director* **decía** *que* **quería** *una chica como ella (. . .) Ya no* **parecía** *fácil el acceso a la recepción del hotel, que* **hacía** *unos días se* **había** *abierto ante sus ojos como una visión prometedora, pero* **debía** *trazarse un plan de acción* (S. Puértolas, Spain) 'alone in the shop Felicitas was thinking. So the boy thought it was better for her to wait for the manager to come and see her. She wanted to work in the hotel and the manager said he wanted a girl like her. It didn't seem easy any more to get a job in the hotel reception, which a few days ago had seemed to her a promising possibility, but a plan of action had to be drawn up.'

14.6 Future tense: general

Spanish has several ways of expressing the future, and the so-called 'future tense' (*hablaré, vendrás*) is not the most common in everyday speech (from which it is said to be disappearing except in its 'suppositional' role described at 14.6.5):

(a) *Esta noche vamos al cine*	Tonight we're going to the cinema
(b) *Esta noche vamos a ir al cine*	Tonight we're going to go to the cinema
(c) *Esta noche iremos al cine*	Tonight we'll go to the cinema
(d) *Esta noche hemos de ir al cine*	Tonight we're to go/we have to go to the cinema

(a) describes an event which is pre-arranged or a fixture due to happen in the immediate future; **(b)** is a foreseen or 'intentional' future and it is also often an informal substitute for the future tense proper *iremos, seré*, etc.; **(c)** is less common in colloquial language and very often excludes the idea of pre-arrangement. Consequently it may sound rather uncertain or, depending on tone and context, may sound like an order or promise; **(d)** is discussed at 21.4.1. It is sometimes heard in Latin America with a future meaning, but in Castilian-speaking areas of Spain it usually implies obligation and is now old-fashioned, rather like the English 'tonight we **are to go** to the cinema'; but it has other, still current, uses, discussed at 21.4.1. It is very common in Mexico as an alternative to *deber de*; the latter is discussed at 21.3.2, the Mexican construction at 21.4.1b).

As was mentioned earlier, the future tense is disappearing from spoken (but not written) Spanish, this process being more advanced in Latin America than in Spain and more deep-rooted in familiar or popular styles. It is usually replaced by the simple present – *te llamo mañana* 'I'll call you tomorrow' (see 14.6.3) – or by *ir a* + infinitive: *la voy a ver mañana* 'I'm going to see her tomorrow' (see 14.6.4).

14.6.1 Uses of the future tense form to denote future time

Often, particularly in informal speech, the present and future forms are interchangeable. However, the future is used:

(a) For provisional or less certain statements about the future, e.g. for predictions, or for statements about the future when no other word makes it clear that the future is meant:

Si llueve se aplazará el partido	If it rains the match will be postponed
En el remoto futuro el sol se apagará	In the remote future the sun will go out
Para entonces todos estaremos calvos	We'll all be bald by then (said of something that will take a long time)
Me ha dado diez mil pesetas. Con esto tiraré hasta la semana próxima, y luego veremos (*luego vemos* is impossible here)	He gave me 10,000 pesetas. I'll manage with that until next week, and then we'll see
En cuanto pasemos el túnel ya verás cómo cambia el tiempo. Hará más frío (I. Aldecoa, Spain, dialogue)	When we get through the tunnel you'll see how the weather changes. It'll be colder
Por la noche nos iremos al cine Juan y yo (A. Buero Vallejo, Spain, dialogue, *nos vamos* possible; *nos iremos is* more tentative)	This evening Juan and I will go/are going to the cinema
Nos veremos mañana en Palacio para el premio al profesor Bernstein, ¿no es cierto? (C. Fuentes, Mexico, dialogue. *Nos vemos* . . . implies more certainty)	We'll see one another tomorrow at the Palace for the prize-giving to Professor Bernstein, won't we?

Notes

(i) Nevertheless, the difference between sentences like *te veo mañana* and *te veré mañana* 'I'll see you tomorrow' is slight. The former is informal and indicates something so firmly prearranged as to be felt to be a present reality. The latter is slightly less certain. Thus *esta noche vamos al teatro* 'tonight we're going to the theatre' is usual, but if uttered in the morning, with the prospect of many other chores intervening, one might say *esta noche, cuando lo tengamos todo hecho, iremos al teatro* 'tonight, when we've got everything done, we'll go to the theatre'.

(ii) *acaso, tal vez, quizá(s)*, which means 'perhaps', *posiblemente* 'possibly' and *probablemente* 'probably' may, when they refer to some future event, appear either with the future tense or conditional, but more usually with the present subjunctive: *quizá/tal vez venga/vendrá mañana* 'perhaps (s)he'll come tomorrow'. See 16.3.2 for details. **Tal vez/quizá/acaso* **viene** *mañana* is not correct.

(b) The future is much used for promises, especially long-term ones, since these by nature are not prearrangements:

Ten confianza en mí. No te decepcionaré	Have confidence in me. I won't disappoint you
¡No pasarán!	They shall not pass!
Hoy eres la Cenicienta, pero mañana serás una princesa	Today you're Cinderella, but tomorrow you'll be a princess
Pero cuídalo como si fuera ya mío, porque en ese caso algún día será de mis hijas (A. Bryce Echenique, Peru, dialogue)	But look after it as though it already belonged to me, because in that case one day it will belong to my daughters
Una verdadera revolución no admitirá jamás la impunidad (*Vindicación de Cuba*, Cuba)	A true revolution will never allow crimes to go unpunished

However, the present can be used colloquially (but not with *ser* 'to be') for short-term promises presented as prearrangements, e.g. *no te preocupes, te lo devuelvo mañana* 'don't worry, I'll give it back to you tomorrow'.

14.6.2 Future tense used for stern commands

The future is occasionally used for very solemn or stern commands, as in English:

No matarás	Thou shalt not kill
No saldrás de esta casa hasta que yo no te lo permita	You will not leave this house until I allow you to

14.6.3 Present tense with future meaning

The present is much used in informal language to refer to the immediate future. If the subject is human this conveys an idea of prearrangement and is therefore especially used for fixtures or appointments, cf. English 'I'm going to Spain next year', 'we attack tomorrow'. If the subject is inanimate, the action is foreseen as a certainty or a fixture, e.g. *el tren sale mañana a las 7* 'the train's leaving tomorrow at 7' (scheduled departure). Compare *el tren* **saldrá** *mañana a las siete* 'the train **will leave** tomorrow at seven', which implies an unscheduled departure in both languages.

The fact that the verb refers to the future is normally shown by some time phrase like *mañana, esta noche, el año que viene*:

Vamos a España el año que viene	We're going to Spain next year
Te llamo esta noche	I'll ring you tonight
Nos vemos	Goodbye/See you again
Si viene por aquí, ¿qué digo?	If he comes round here, what shall I say?
Esta noche hay tormenta, verás	Tonight there'll be a storm, you'll see
Espera, lo hago en un momento	Wait, I'll do it in a moment
El día menos pensado le tiran a tu madre la casa (C. Martín Gaite, Spain, dialogue; expresses certainty)	One fine day (lit. 'the day least expected') they're going to knock your mother's house down
¡Repite eso y te mato! (A. Bryce Echenique, Peru, dialogue)	Say that again and I'll kill you!

Notes

(i) This use of the present tense is particularly common with verbs of motion (*ir, venir, salir, llegar*).

(ii) Events predicted in an unspecified future are by nature less certain, so the present tense should not be used: *si las cosas continúan así, ya no* **habrá** *árboles* 'if things go on like this there will be no more trees left'.

(iii) If there is nothing in the sentence or context that clearly shows that the statement refers to the future, the present tense is assumed to be a true present and the future must be shown by some unambiguous form, e.g. *ir a* + infinitive or the future tense proper. Compare *me parece que no hay sitio* 'I think there's no room' and *me parece que no habrá/va a haber sitio* 'I think there won't be room'.

(iv) The present tense of *ser* is usually used for the future only for calendar statements: *mañana es jueves* 'tomorrow is Thursday', but *mañana el discurso* **será** *pronunciado por el presidente* 'tomorrow the speech will be delivered by the president'.

14.6.4 *Ir a . . .* + infinitive

The future is very often expressed by *ir a* + the infinitive. This form may express intention or it may simply be a colloquial substitute for the future tense (but not for the suppositional future mentioned at 14.6.5). In this second use it is so frequent that it virtually replaces the ordinary future tense form in the speech of many people. Kany (1970), 192, gives several Latin-American examples like *ya va usted a querer pelear con nosotros por semejante porquería* (Peru, popular; Spain *se va usted a pelear con nosotros por . . .*) 'sure, you'll want to fight us over a bit of rubbish like this', *¿cuánto va a querer, señor?* (Mexico, popular; Spain *¿cuánto va a ser?/¿cuánto quiere?*) 'how much will you want, Sir?' But the future tense is by no means extinct in spoken Spanish in Spain or in Latin America, as can be seen in this passage of colloquial Cuban:

—*¿Y qué harás entre estas cuatro paredes? —Limpiaré el cuarto, me lavaré la cabeza, plancharé una blusita para ir al trabajo el lunes, me sentaré en la butaca, sacaré un crucigrama, me asomaré al balcón, cocinaré, me comeré las uñas. ¡No tengo ni un solo minuto libre!* (A. Arrufat, Cuba, dialogue; Spain *haré un crucigrama*)	'And what'll you do (shut up) between these four walls?' 'I'll clean my room, wash my hair, iron a blouse for work on Monday, sit in the armchair, do a crossword, look out of the window, cook, bite my nails . . . I don't have a single minute free!'

Note

The imperfect *iba a*, etc., may also be used as a future in the past. See 14.7.3.

14.6.5 Suppositional future

An important function of the future tense in ordinary Spanish, especially in Europe, is to express suppositions or approximations. Use of the future in approximations often produces much more idiomatic Spanish than clumsy sentences involving *aproximadamente* or *alrededor de*. In questions, the future expresses wonder, incredulity or conjecture:

Serán las nueve y media, por ahí (C. Martín Gaite, Spain, dialogue)	It must be around 9.30
Albert Hoffman descubrió el LSD hará 50 años (*El País*, Spain)	Albert Hoffman discovered LSD about 50 years ago
Un par de años hará . . . Gannon me escribió de Gualeguaychu (J. L. Borges, Argentina)	It must be a couple of years ago that Gannon wrote to me from Gualeguaychu
Pase usted, por favor. Siéntese. Estará cansado (J. de Jesús Martínez, Panama, dialogue)	Please come in. Sit down. You must be tired
—*¿Dónde está tu monedero? —Me lo habré dejado en casa*	'Where's your purse?' 'I must have left it at home'
¡Habráse visto semejante tontería!	Did anyone ever see such nonsense!
¿Qué será esto?	I wonder what this is
¿Qué hora será? (Lat. Am.*¿Qué horas serán?*)	I wonder what the time is
¿Qué estará tramando ella?	I wonder what she's up to . . .
. . . eh, no querrás que mi jefe vea eso (J. Marías, Spain)	. . . hey, you won't want my boss to see that, do you?

Notes

(i) Kany (1970), 190, notes that this use of the future is more common in Spain than in Latin America, where *deber (de)* . . . often replaces it: *deben (de) ser las cinco = serán las cinco*. See 21.3.2 for *deber de*, which is also used in Spain.

(ii) In Mexico *haber de* is commonly used for *deber de* in this construction. See 21.4.1.

(iii) For additional remarks on the use of the future perfect tense for conjectures, see 14.11.

14.7 The conditional: general

(For the forms of the conditional see 13.1.8.) The name 'conditional' is apt insofar as it often shows that an event is conditional on some other factor, as in *podríamos ir mañana* 'we could go tomorrow' (if the weather's nice, if we're free, etc.). But it has other functions that have nothing to do with the idea of conditionality, especially the expression of suppositions or approximations in the past (14.7.2) and the expression of the future in the past (14.7.3).

For the purpose of agreement, the conditional counts as a past tense, so the subjunctive in a subordinate clause governed by the conditional must also be in the past. Compare *es absurdo que vengas mañana* 'it's absurd for you to come tomorrow' and *sería absurdo que **vinieras/vinieses** mañana* 'it would be absurd for you to come tomorrow' (see 16.16 for detailed discussion).

Colloquial language may, in some contexts, replace the conditional by the imperfect, especially in conditional sentences (see 14.5.4 and 25.5 for discussion). Replacement of the imperfect subjunctive by the conditional, e.g. *?si yo tendría dinero* for *si yo tuviera dinero* 'if I had some money' is very common in popular speech in Navarre and neighbouring regions, in Argentina and perhaps locally elsewhere, but foreigners should avoid it.

14.7.1 Uses of the conditional to express conditions

(For the conditional in conditional sentences, see Chapter 25.) The conditional is also used for implied conditions, i.e. conditional statements in which the if-clause has been deleted:

Sería una locura ponerlo en marcha sin aceite	It would be crazy to start it up with no oil
¿Quieres ir a la manifestación? Sería interesante	Do you want to go to the demonstration? It would be interesting
De nada serviría un nuevo golpe porque sólo perjudicaría al país (Headline, Bolivian press)	Another coup d'état would be pointless because it would only damage the country

14.7.2 Conditional for suppositions about the past

The conditional is used for suppositions and approximations about the past in the same way as the future is for the present (see 14.6.5 and 14.11):

Aquel día andaríamos más de cincuenta kilómetros	That day we must have walked more than 50 km
Tendría (or *tenía/debía de tener*) *unos treinta años*	He must have been about thirty
Los guardé algún tiempo . . . ; luego supongo que los quemaría (C. Martín Gaite, Spain, dialogue)	I kept them (*los diarios* – 'the diaries') for a while. Then I guess I must have burnt them
Llevaba un saco sport que en algún tiempo habría sido azul marino (E. Sábato, Argentina. *Saco = americana* or *chaqueta* in Spain)	He was wearing a sports jacket which must once have been navy blue

In some styles, especially journalism and more so in Latin America, the conditional is used for rumours, inferences or unsubstantiated reports. This construction is condemned by grammarians, and by the editors of *El País*, as a Gallicism:

*Nos han informado que el ministro Brunner **habría dicho** que **seríamos** un pequeño*	We've been told that minister Brunner is reported to have said that we are

grupo de personas que estamos obstaculizando la llegada del gas natural hacia Santiago (*La Época*, Chile)	allegedly a small group of people who are holding up the arrival of natural gas in Santiago
Gregorius habría nacido en Glasgow . . . (J. Cortázar, Argentina)	Gregorius was reportedly born in Glasgow . . .
La desaparición de los etarras estaría motivada por cuestiones de seguridad (*Abc*, Spain)	Security reasons are said to be the motive for the disappearance of the ETA members (ETA is a Basque separatist movement)

Notes

(i) For more details about this construction and *deber de* + infinitive, see note to 21.3.2.

(ii) In questions, the conditional perfect may express amazement or anxiety. See 14.11.

14.7.3 Conditional for the future in the past

The conditional is used to express the future in the past (i.e. as a close equivalent of *iba a . . .* + infinitive).

Yo sabía que papá bajaría/bajaba/iba a bajar a las once	I knew father would come down at 11 o'clock
Cerró la puerta con cuidado; su mujer dormía profundamente. Dormiría hasta que el sol hiciera su primera presencia en la ventana (I. Aldecoa, Spain)	He shut the door carefully; his wife was fast asleep. She would sleep until the sun first showed at the window
Entonces tuvo una aventura que se desarrollaría en tres etapas diferentes	He then had an adventure that was to develop in three different stages
En un rato todo el mundo se iría a dormir la siesta (A. Mastretta, Mexico, dialogue. Spain *dentro de un rato*)	Soon everyone would go and take a siesta

14.7.4 Conditional in rhetorical questions

As in English, the conditional is much used for questions to which the speaker already knows the answer:

¿Alguien se atrevería a decir que la 'socialización' ha hecho más libres a los diarios? (M. Vargas Llosa, Peru)	Would anyone dare to say that 'socialization' has made newspapers more free?

14.7.5 Replacement of the conditional by the *-ra* form of the subjunctive

The *-ra* subjunctive form is a stylistic variant for the conditional when this is used as a true conditional (and not, for example, as a suppositional tense or future in the past). This is normal with the auxiliary *haber*: *habría sido mejor/hubiera sido mejor* 'it would have been better'. Use of the *-ra* form instead of the conditional is slightly more formal in tone:

Hubiera podido ser una buena novela de misterio . . . (C. Martín Gaite, Spain dialogue)	It could have been a good mystery novel . . .
El mal lo mismo se hubiera colado por alguna grieta de las piedras del castillo (M. Puig, Argentina, dialogue)	The disease would have crept in just the same through some crack in the walls of the castle

A lo mejor me hubiera hecho mucho bien seguir con la terapia (A. Mastretta, Mexico, interview)	Perhaps it would have done me a lot of good to continue with therapy

It is also common with *querer* and *deber*, although it is more formal than the plain conditional: *yo querría/quisiera hacerlo* 'I'd like to do it'; *deberías/debieras haberlo hecho* 'you should have done it'. With *poder* it is literary: *podría haber sido/pudiera haber sido* 'it could have been'. See Chapter 21 for discussion of these modal verbs. With other verbs it is nowadays uncommon and archaic:

Abril, sin tu asistencia clara, **fuera** *invierno de caídos esplendores . . .* (Juan Ramón Jiménez, poetry; i.e. *sería . . .*)	'April, without thy bright presence, would be a winter of fallen splendours . . .'
Un libro **fuera** *poco . . . para dar cauce a un país como La Mancha* (C. J. Cela, Spain)	A book would be little (lit. 'were little . . .') . . . to do justice to (lit. 'to give channel to') a land like La Mancha

It is commonly used in the Latin-American literary formula *pareciera que . . .* (for *parecería que . . .*) 'it would seem that . . . ', cf. *pareciera que al señor Doens se le detuvo la historia nacional en 1992* (interview in *La Prensa*, Panama) 'it would seem that for Mr Doens the country's history stopped in 1992'.

Notes

(i) Use of the *-se* subjunctive in place of the *-ra* form for the conditional is not favoured by the grammarians: it is explicitly banned by the *Libro de estilo* of *El País*. But it is commonly heard in spontaneous speech: **y hubiese** (for *hubiera/habría*) *sido muy sospechoso que yo me negase* (M. Puig, Argentina dialogue) 'and it would have been very suspicious if I'd refused'.

(ii) In pre-eighteenth century Spanish the use of the *-ra* form for the conditional with all verbs was very common: *y si estas calamidades no me acontecieran, no me* **tuviera** *yo por caballero andante* (Cervantes, *Don Quijote*) 'and had these calamities not befallen me, I would not consider myself a knight errant'. This is analogous to the archaic English pluperfect construction ' . . . I had not considered myself a knight errant'.

14.8 Compound tenses: general remarks

The compound tenses are as follows:

Perfect (14.9)	*he hablado*, etc.	I have spoken
Pluperfect (14.10)	*había hablado*, etc.	I had spoken
Pretérito anterior (14.10.4)	*hube hablado*, etc.	I had spoken
Future perfect (14.11)	*habré hablado*, etc.	I will have spoken
Conditional perfect (14.11)	*habría hablado*, etc.	I would have spoken
Perfect subjunctive (14.9.9)	*haya hablado*, etc.	(no exact translation)
Pluperfect subjunctive (14.10.5)	*hubiera* or *hubiese hablado*, etc.	(no exact translation)

Most of these can also appear in the continuous form (see Chapter 15):

Perfect	*he estado hablando*, etc.	I've been speaking
Pluperfect	*había estado hablando*, etc.	I had been speaking
Future perfect	*habré estado hablando*, etc.	I will have been speaking
Conditional perfect	*habría estado hablando*, etc.	I would have been speaking
Perfect subjunctive	*haya estado hablando*, etc.	(no exact translation)
Pluperfect subjunctive	*hubiera* or *hubiese estado hablando*, etc.	(no exact translation)

The compound tenses all use the auxiliary *haber* or, much less commonly and the *pretérito anterior* excepted, *tener* (see 14.8.3). No Spanish verbs form the perfect with *ser* 'to be' as an auxiliary (*llegar, ir, venir* are very rare archaic or journalistic exceptions, cf. *el verano es ido* 'summer is gone', *Cambio16*, Spain).

Unlike French and Italian, the past participle is invariable and does not agree in number and gender with the object of the verb (unless *tener* is used instead of *haber*: see 14.8.3). For an example of a verb conjugated in the compound tenses, see 13.5.4.

14.8.1 Compound tenses: word order

Learners should respect the rule that no words may come between the auxiliary and the participle: French *j'ai toujours dit* = *siempre he dicho*. *Yo he siempre dicho* is not heard in normal Spanish. However this rule is occasionally broken in literary style with such words as *ni siquiera, incluso, todavía, aún, ya, nunca, jamás, más que, quizá(s), tal vez*:

Se habrá tal vez olvidado	You may have forgotten
Se ha más que duplicado la cifra	The figure has more than doubled
(From *Hoja del lunes*, Spain)	
... en buena parte por no habérselo	... to a great extent because he had
aún propuesto con entera seriedad	not yet suggested it to him in all
(S. Pitol, Mexico)	seriousness

Note

When *haber* is in the infinitive or the gerund form, the pronouns are always attached to it: *... habérselo propuesto* '... to have suggested it to him/her/you', *habiéndolo recibido* 'having received it'.

14.8.2 Suppression of *haber* and of the past participle in compound tenses

The auxiliary verb *haber* may optionally be suppressed to avoid repetition:

Yo también he pasado por baches y conocido	I've been through rough patches as well
la duda (L. Goytisolo, Spain, dialogue)	and known doubt
No sólo había tocado la mano y mirado los	Not only had he touched the hand and
ojos de la mujer que más le gustaba tocar	looked at the eyes of the woman he
y mirar del mundo ... (C. Fuentes,	most liked to touch and look at in the
Mexico)	world ...

Note

The past participle may be deleted in English, but not in Spanish: '"Have you tried the sausages?" "Yes, I have."' —*¿Has probado las salchichas? —Sí* or —*Sí, las he **probado***. However, deletion occasionally occurs with the pluperfect tense, to judge by *¿Se había reído? Sí, se había. Pero esta vez sin sarcasmo* (M. Vargas Llosa, Peru, dialogue) 'Had he laughed? Yes, he had. But without sarcasm this time.' Spanish informants thought that this might be more typical of Latin-American Spanish.

14.8.3 *Tengo hecho, tengo comprado*, etc.

Tener is occasionally used as an auxiliary, like the English 'to have **got**', to denote the successful acquisition of some object or the fulfilment of some task. Compare 'I've painted the windows' and 'I've got all the windows painted' or 'I've done my homework' and 'I've got all my homework done.' The participle must agree in number and gender with the object of the verb. The verb must be transitive and it must have a direct object (**tengo sido*, cf. Portuguese *tenho sido* 'I have been', is not Spanish):

Ya tengo compradas las entradas	I've already bought the tickets
Para el viernes tendré hechos todos mis deberes	By Friday I'll have all my homework done
Yo tenía concertada hora con el jefe	I had arranged an appointment with the boss
Que persigan a los pillos que tienen tomadas las calles (*El Tiempo*, Colombia)	Let them chase after the hoodlums that have taken over the streets
Tenía pensado cruzar a la orilla derecha y beber vino en el cafecito de la rue des Lombards (J. Cortázar, Argentina, dialogue)	I had planned to cross to the right bank and drink wine in the little café in the Rue des Lombards

Note

Llevar is also occasionally used in the same way for accumulative actions: *llevo tomadas tres aspirinas, pero todavía me duele la cabeza* 'I've taken three aspirins, but my head still aches', *y le llevan encontradas ya creo que hasta tres calaveras en la catedral de Lima* (A. Bryce Echenique, Peru, dialogue; Spain *y llevan encontradas* ...) 'I think they've already found three of his skulls in Lima Cathedral'(refers to a famous saint), *yo llevo vendidos cuatrocientos* (Mexico City, overheard) 'I've sold four hundred'.

14.9 The perfect tense

European Spanish and literary Latin-American Spanish differs sharply from French, German and Italian, and broadly resembles English in that the difference between the preterite, *hablé* 'I spoke', and the perfect, *he hablado* 'I've spoken', is respected both in written and spoken language. Students of languages in which the difference is blurred or lost in the spoken language must avoid translating sentences like *je l'ai vu hier, ich habe ihn gestern gesehen, l'ho visto ieri* 'I saw him yesterday' as **lo/le he visto ayer* (correctly *lo/le vi ayer*). Such misuse of the perfect is sometimes heard in popular Madrid speech.

European Spanish usually uses the perfect wherever English does, but the converse is not true: the European Spanish perfect often requires translation by the English simple past. Moreover, in most of the Spanish-speaking world (Galicia, Asturias and most of Latin America) the preterite is in fact more common than the perfect, cf. *no vino todavía* (Latin America) 'he didn't come yet' (US English[9]: Britain 'he hasn't come yet') and *no ha venido todavía* (Spain), 'he hasn't come yet'. See 14.9.8 for further remarks on the perfect tense in Latin America.

14.9.1 Perfect to denote events occurring in time that includes the present

The perfect is used for events that have happened in a period of time that includes the present, e.g. today, this afternoon, this week, this month, this year, this century, always, already, never, still, yet. In this respect, English – especially British English – and European Spanish coincide:

---

[9] Some varieties of North-American English resemble Latin-American Spanish in using the simple past in preference to the compound perfect.

No he visto a tu madre esta semana	I haven't seen your mother this week
Hemos ido dos veces este mes	We've been twice this month
En sólo dos generaciones se ha desertizado un 43% de la superficie terrestre (advertisement in *Abc*)	In only two generations 43% of the earth's surface has been reduced to desert
Ya han llegado	They've already arrived
Siempre he pensado que . . .	I have always thought that . . .
Aún/Todavía no han llegado	They haven't arrived yet

Notes

(i) The preterite may be used with the effect of severing the link between the event and the present moment. Compare *vi a tu suegra esta mañana* and *he visto a tu suegra esta mañana* 'I saw/have seen your mother-in-law this morning'. Use of the preterite suggests either that the statement was made after mid-day (the most likely explanation), or that the speaker feels that the event is by now further in the past.

(ii) Words like *siempre, nunca* may or may not include the present: compare *yo siempre he sido un problema para mis padres* 'I've always been a problem for my parents' (and still am) and *yo siempre fui un problema para mis padres* 'I always was a problem for my parents' (e.g. when I was young). But some speakers do not systematically respect the difference of meaning in either language.

(iii) For the Latin-American (and Canary Islands) use of the preterite in the above contexts see 14.9.8.

14.9.2 Perfect for events whose effects are still relevant in the present

The perfect is used for recent past events that are relevant to or explain the present:

Alguien ha fumado un cigarrillo aquí. Huelo el humo	Someone has smoked a cigarette here. I can smell the smoke
¿Quién ha roto esta ventana?	Who's broken this window?
Todo el mundo habla de Fulano porque ha publicado otra novela	Everyone's talking about so-and-so because he's published a new novel
Es evidente que Simone de Beauvoir ha leído con detenimiento a estos autores y aprovechado sus técnicas . . . (M. Vargas Llosa, Peru)	It is obvious that Simone de Beauvoir has read these authors closely and (has) taken advantage of their techniques . . .

Notes

(i) This use of the perfect is also common in literary Latin-American styles, but everyday Latin-American speech in many regions favours the preterite for any completed event. See 14.9.8.

(ii) One finds the perfect used in European Spanish in conjunction with some word or phrase that refers to a past not continuing into the present, e.g. 'yesterday', 'two months ago'. This may express the idea that an event is relevant to or explains something in the present, as in *está en muy mala edad para cambiar. Ha cumplido cincuenta años en junio* (C. Martín Gaite, Spain, dialogue) 'he's really not the best age for changing. He was fifty last June', *mi padre ha muerto hace un par de meses* 'my father died a couple of months ago' (which explains why I'm still sad). Seco (1998, 357) comments that use of the perfect as opposed to the preterite in such cases shows that the action took place in what for the speaker is the 'psychological present'. But many Spaniards from the north and most Latin Americans insist on the preterite in such cases and in sentences like the following:[10] *ayer, a la caída de la tarde, cuando el gran acantilado es de cinabrio, he vuelto a la isla* (I. Aldecoa, Spain) 'yesterday, at nightfall, when the big cliff is the colour of cinnabar, I returned to the island', *se trata de un ejercicio que ha perdido la iniciativa hace meses* (*Cambio 16*, Spain) 'it involves an exercise which lost its initiative months ago', *a mí todo lo que me ha sucedido me ha sucedido*

---

[10] DeMello (1994, 1) reports that the corpus of spoken educated Spanish records this use of the perfect in the speech of Madrid, Seville and also in Latin America in Lima and La Paz, but there are virtually no examples from other Latin-American capitals.

ayer, anoche a más tardar (J. Cortázar, Argentina, dialogue) 'everything that has happened to me happened yesterday, last night at the latest', *hace pocos días, un pacifista danés ha sido acusado de espionaje a favor de Moscú* (*La Vanguardia*, Spain) 'a few days ago a Danish pacifist was accused of spying for Moscow'.

The following sentence was judged by informants from north-west Spain to be incorrect, but it is acceptable to many speakers from the centre, south and east: *bueno, **he ido** a hacerme el análisis hace quince días y mañana o pasado me dan los resultados* (interview in *Cambio 16*, Spain: *madrileña* speaker) 'anyway, I went and got a test done two weeks ago and tomorrow or the day after they'll give me the results'.

14.9.3 Perfect of recency

In Spain, but less so in Latin America, the perfect may optionally be used for any very recent event, in practice any event that has happened since midnight. Very recent events (e.g. seconds ago) are almost always expressed by the perfect tenses in Peninsular Spanish:

Esta mañana me he levantado/me levanté a las seis	I got up at six this morning
¿Has oído la explosión?	Did you hear the explosion?
—¿Quién ha dicho eso? —No he sido yo. Ha sido él	'Who said that (just now)?' 'It wasn't me. It was him'
La he visto hace un momento	I saw her a moment ago
No he podido hacerlo	I couldn't do it
Perdone, no he entendido bien lo que ha dicho (C. Martín Gaite, Spain, dialogue)	Sorry, I didn't fully understand what you said (just now)
—Te he hecho daño porque no has entendido nada (A. Bryce Echenique, Peru, dialogue; the perfect is rather more alive in Peru than further south)	I hurt you because you didn't understand a thing
Ha muerto Franco (Headline)	Franco is dead
¿Qué has dicho?	What did you say?

Notes

(i) The perfect of recency is more typical of European Spanish, although Kany (1970), 200, reports its colloquial use in Bolivia and Peru. Other Latin-American regions favour the preterite in these examples, but for many speakers of European Spanish *?la vi hace un momento* sounds wrong because the event is very recent. In north-western Spain the preterite is more common, and natives of that region sometimes comment on the frequency with which *madrileños* use the perfect of recency.[11] Many persons from the north-west insist on the preterite in examples like *me he levantado a las ocho* or *la he visto hace un momento* on the grounds that the perfect cannot be used when the time of the event is specified.

(ii) The above examples are chosen to show how European Spanish freely uses the perfect of recency with verbs like *querer, ser*, where English allows only the simple past: *no he querido hacerlo* 'I didn't want to do it', *¿quién ha sido el gracioso que se ha llevado las llaves?* 'who's the clown who took the keys away with him (just now)?'

(iii) European Spanish thus differs from English in that the perfect is used of any very recent event, completed or not. English allows 'have you heard the news?' since the news can still be heard, but not **'have you heard that explosion?'* cf. *¿habéis visto el relámpago?* 'did you see the flash?'

(iv) In view of the frequent occurrence of the perfect of recency in Spain, it is not easy to explain the use of the preterite by Peninsular radio announcers who end programmes with remarks like **oyeron** *la novena sinfonía de Beethoven* 'you have been listening to Beethoven's Ninth Symphony' (more usually *acaban de oír . . .*).

---

[11] A. Moreira Rodríguez, private communication, recalls a friend's eight-year-old daughter, a native of Galicia, rebuking her little cousin from Madrid: *¡Siempre estás con 'he corrido', 'he visto', 'he ido'. Hablas mal. Hay que decir 'corrí', 'vi', 'fui'!*

14.9.4 Perfect in time phrases

The perfect is often used, especially in Spain, in negative time phrases of the sort *hace años que no te he visto* (or *no te veo*; Latin Americans and Spaniards from the northwest may not accept the perfect) 'I haven't seen you for years'. Positive sentences of this type usually require the present tense: *hace años que lo/le veo todos los días* 'I've been seeing him every day for years'. See Chapter 32 (Expressions of Time).

14.9.5 Use of the perfect for quotations

The perfect is sometimes used for famous quotations, e.g. *Aristóteles ha dicho que . . .* 'Aristotle said . . .', though Carnicer (1972), 176, censures this usage. The present, preterite or imperfect is safer.

14.9.6 Perfect used for future certainties

The perfect is occasionally used in familiar European Spanish, at least in central Spain, for future actions that are described as certainties. Formal usage would require the future perfect: *cuando vuelvas ya he acabado/ya lo habré acabado* (Lat. Am. *ya acabé*) 'I'll have finished by the time you come back.' See 14.4.9 for the Latin-American tendency to use the preterite in similar sentences.

14.9.7 Perfect with future reference in conditional sentences

As in English, the perfect may refer to the future in the if-clause of a conditional sentence: *si la situación no ha cambiado para el viernes, avísame* 'if the situation hasn't changed by Friday, let me know'.

14.9.8 The perfect tense in Latin America

In Latin America all completed actions tend to be expressed by the preterite tense, more so in some regions than others. This solution is so favoured in informal styles in some regions that the perfect tense is rarely heard:

*¿Todavía no **llegó** tu padre?*	Hasn't your father come yet?
Aún no salieron del cine	They haven't come out of the cinema yet
¿Qué hubo? (Colombia, Venezuela, etc.; Spain *¿Qué hay?*)	How're things?
Ya nos llegó la moderna solución (advertisement in *El Tiempo*, Colombia)	Now we've got the modern answer!
En el curso de los últimos años se lograron (Spain *se han logrado . . .*) *notables progresos en el conocimiento de la función de los riñones* (Chilean press, quoted in *Variedades*, 220)	In recent years notable progress has been made in (our) knowledge of the function of the kidneys
—¿Ya organizaste? —le pregunté. —Sí, ya organicé (A. Mastretta, Mexico, dialogue; Spain *has organizado, he organizado*)	'Have you organized it?', I asked him. 'Yes, I've organized it'
¿Nunca te fijaste en eso? (ibid., Spain *nunca te has fijado*)	Haven't you ever noticed/Didn't you ever notice that?

This use of the preterite is especially typical of spoken language in the Southern Cone: the perfect tense is a rarity in everyday speech in Buenos Aires city and is said to sound bookish. However, colloquial usage varies from one region to another. In the spoken language of Bolivia and Peru the perfect is more frequent and its use seems to correspond quite closely to standard European usage. Kany

(1970), 201, notes that in popular Bolivian and Peruvian speech one even hears constructions like *?he tenido un mal sueño anoche* 'I had a bad dream last night', where all other regions, including Spain, require the preterite.[12]

Lope Blanch describes the situation in spoken Mexican Spanish as follows:[13] the preterite is used (as in many places in Latin America) for all completed actions, however recent: *estudié mucho este mes* 'I've done a lot of studying this month' (and now I've stopped), *¿ya viste la película? Sí, la vi* 'have you seen the film? Yes, I have', *la vi dos veces esta semana* 'I've seen her twice this week', *nos podemos ir. El maestro no vino* 'we can go. The teacher hasn't come' (and he won't be coming now).

The perfect is used for actions that are still continuing or being repeated in the present and for events that may still occur – in this respect Mexican and European Spanish broadly coincide: *he estudiado mucho este mes* 'I've been doing a lot of studying this month (and I still am)', *siempre he usado anteojos* (Spain *anteojos* = *las gafas*) 'I've always used glasses (and still do)', *el maestro no ha venido* 'the teacher hasn't come yet' (but he may still come), *aún no ha llamado* 'he hasn't phoned yet' (but may still phone).

Mexican Spanish therefore differs from European in that the perfect is not used to indicate a past action that is still relevant to the present, and would use the preterite in the European sentence *alguien ha fumado un cigarrillo aquí* 'someone's smoked a cigarette here' (I can still smell it). The Mexican perfect indicates an action that is *continuing* in the present or the future: Mexican *he fumado mucho* = 'I have been smoking a lot and still am smoking'.

Lope Blanch further notes that the perfect may occasionally replace the preterite in exclamations. In this case it has a strong emotional emphasis: compare *esta mañana llovió mucho* 'it rained a lot this morning' and *¡esta mañana ha llovido mucho!* 'did it rain a lot this morning!'

The tendency, mentioned earlier, to use the perfect with a present meaning is taken to extremes further south in Latin America. Kany (1970), 205ff, notes that in colloquial Ecuadorian and southern Colombian Spanish the perfect is used, even in educated speech, as an equivalent to the present tense: *?ya ha sido tarde* = *ya es tarde* 'it's late', *?piernas gordas ha tenido la Laura* (i.e. *tiene*) 'Laura's got fat legs'. Occasionally it may even be used as a future: *??el año que viene ha sido* (i.e. *será*) *bisiesto* 'next year will be a leap year'. Kany further notes that, south from Ecuador, and especially in Argentina, even the pluperfect of *ser* is locally heard in popular speech with a present meaning: *??había sido tarde* = *es tarde*. However, these forms, which are very aberrant with respect to normal usage elsewhere, tend to have the special function of expressing surprise.

14.9.9 The perfect subjunctive

In general, the perfect subjunctive, *haya dicho, hayamos contestado*, etc., is used when the rules of Spanish grammar require that a perfect indicative verb must be put in the subjunctive mood, and the imperfect subjunctive is used when the original sentence would have had the preterite or imperfect indicative. Compare

---

[12] But note European *anoche* **dormí** *mal* 'I slept badly last night' and *esta noche* **he dormido** *mal*, same meaning.

[13] 'Sobre el uso del pretérito en el español de México' in Lope Blanch (1991), 131–43.

creo que lo ha hecho 'I think he did it' and *no creo que lo **haya** hecho* 'I don't think that he did it', but *creo que lo hizo/lo hacía* 'I think he did it/used to do it' and *no creo que lo hiciera* 'I don't think (s)he did it'. But it often seems that the perfect and imperfect subjunctives can be used interchangeably:

Es imposible que lo haya hecho/que lo hiciera/hiciese	It's impossible that (s)he did it
Niega que su mujer le abriera/abriese/le haya abierto la puerta	He denies that his wife opened the door for him/her
Algunos no aceptan que Colón descubriera/ descubriese/haya descubierto América	Some people don't accept that Columbus discovered America

14.10 The pluperfect: general

The pluperfect is formed with the imperfect of *haber* plus a past participle: *habías comido* 'you had eaten', *habían llegado* 'they/you had arrived'. The *-ra* form of the verb can also sometimes have an indicative pluperfect meaning in literary Spanish. See 14.10.2.

14.10.1 Uses of the pluperfect

The use of the Spanish pluperfect corresponds quite closely to the English pluperfect. It is used for events or states that preceded some past event and are felt to be relevant to it:

Ya se habían dado cuenta de que no estabas	They had already realized you weren't there
Sabíamos que ya había vendido el coche	We knew that he had already sold the car
Yo me había levantado, duchado y desayunado, y estaba esperando a Octavia en la ventana, cuando sonó el teléfono (A. Bryce Echenique, Peru)	I had got up, showered and breakfasted and was awaiting Octavia at the window when the phone rang

Notes

(i) Colloquially the pluperfect may be avoided, especially in Latin-American Spanish, where it is commonly replaced by the preterite or, when it refers to habitual actions, by the imperfect: *lo encontré donde lo dejé* (for ... *donde lo había dejado*) (from Lope Blanch (Mexico), 1991, 152) 'I found it where I'd left it/where I left it', *cuando terminábamos* (for *habíamos terminado*) *volvíamos a casa* (habitual) 'when we had finished, we used to return home', *le faltaban dos dientes y nunca se puso* (Spain *se había puesto/se ponía*) *a dieta ni fue* (Spain *había ido/iba*) *al gimnasio* (A. Mastretta, Mexico, dialogue) 'he had two teeth missing and he had never been on a diet or gone to the gym'.
(ii) In some cases the English pluperfect will require translation by the preterite. Occasionally, English uses a simple past where a Spanish pluperfect is required: 'I didn't imagine ahead to parties ... or nights alone in the double bed after a divorce which left me stranded' (Mary Ingram, *Now we are Thirty*) *no podía imaginarme el futuro, fiestas ... noches sola en la cama matrimonial después de un divorcio que me **había dejado** abandonada sin saber qué hacer.*

14.10.2 Pluperfect in *-ra*

The *-ra* form of Spanish verbs descends from the Latin indicative pluperfect: Latin *fueram* 'I had been' > Spanish *fuera*. The Spanish form gradually acquired a subjunctive meaning and for most purposes it is now identical in use to the *-se* imperfect subjunctive (see 16.2.3 for further details). But the old indicative pluperfect use of the *-ra* forms survives in literature and journalism as a supposedly elegant alternative for the ordinary pluperfect with *había*. This is very common in Latin America, but it is also found in Spain among those who think of themselves as stylists. Lorenzo (1980), 135, echoes a typical European attitude to this construction: *evidentemente, la sentimos como afectada, pero hay muchas gentes que lo son . . . .*

When used thus, the *-ra* form has no subjunctive meaning at all. However, this construction seems to have been contaminated by a feature of the subjunctive: it only occurs in subordinate, chiefly relative clauses: *el libro que había leído* 'the book he had read' can be re-cast in supposedly 'elegant' style as *el libro que leyera*, but the sentence *había leído el libro* 'he had read the book' cannot be rewritten **leyera el libro*. Examples:

*Fue el único rastro que dejó en el que **fuera** su hogar de casada por cinco horas* (G. García Márquez, Colombia; for *había sido*)	It was the only trace she left in what had been her marital home for five hours
*Parece ser además que en el solar donde se **construyera** el hotel se alzaba antes el palacio* (A. Grosso, Spain; he is addicted to the construction)	It seems, moreover, that the palace once stood on the land where the hotel had been built

Notes

(i) One even finds examples of the imperfect subjunctive in *-se* used as an indicative pluperfect in the same contexts as the *-ra* form described above: *así había dado con el hombre capaz, muy versado en asuntos económicos, que conociese en la Logia* (A. Carpentier, Cuba; for *había conocido* or *conociera*) 'he had thus come across the able man, well versed in economic matters, whom he had met in the (Masonic) Lodge'. But this is very rare on both continents and rather forced.

(ii) Use of the *-ra* pluperfect in spoken Spanish is typical of Galicians since the *-ra* form still has an indicative pluperfect meaning in Gallego (and in Portuguese).

14.10.3 *-ra* and *-se* verb forms after *después de que, desde que, luego (de) que*, etc.

The rule for the choice of verb form after *después (de) que* and *luego de que* 'after', and *a los pocos días de que* 'a few days after' is subjunctive for as yet unfulfilled events, *comeremos después de que lleguen los demás* 'we'll eat after the rest arrive', and indicative for fulfilled events: *comimos después de que **llegaron** los demás* 'we ate after the rest arrived'. If the subject of both verbs is the same *después (de) que* is replaced by *después de* + infinitive: *nos fuimos después de haber hecho todo* 'we left after we had done everything'. Further examples:

. . . después de que las hijas mayores la ayudaron a poner un poco de orden en los estragos de la boda (G. García Márquez, Colombia)	. . . after the elder daughters (had) helped her to put a bit of order in the devastation left by the wedding
. . . después de que Victoriano Huerta mató a Madero (A. Mastretta, Mexico, dialogue)	. . . after Victoriano Huerta killed Madero
*Desde que se **casó**, Octavia nunca volvió a besarme* (A. Bryce Echenique, Peru; *desde que* can only refer to fulfilled events)	From the moment she got married, Octavia never kissed me again
Él le entregó . . . los planos, las copias. Luego que ella los hubo recogido de sus manos . . . dijo . . . (J. Aldecoa, Spain: *pretérito anterior*, discussed at 14.10.4)	He gave her . . . the maps, the copies. After she had taken them from his hands . . . he said . . .

However, the media everywhere frequently use the *-ra* or *-se* verb forms even for fulfilled events in the past and even with subordinators like *desde que* 'from the moment that . . . ', which obviously introduces fulfilled events:

. . . *después de que Nigeria* **hiciese** *pública su decisión de firmar el acta* (*El País*, Spain)	. . . after Nigeria made public its decision to sign the communiqué/ minutes
Vargas Llosa, que conserva muchos amigos en Barcelona desde que **residiera** *en España* (*Abc*, Spain)	Vargas Llosa, who has kept many friends in Barcelona from when he lived in Spain
El asalto se produjo veinte minutos después de que **salieran** *con el dinero del Banco de la Nación* (*La República*, Peru)	The attack took place twenty minutes after they (had) left the National Bank with the money
. . . *luego de que por problemas de tipo legal les* **fuera** *impedido el paso ayer en la mañana* (*La Época*, Chile)	. . . after their entry had been prevented for legal reasons yesterday morning

14.10.4 *Pretérito anterior:* **hube hablado, hube acabado,** etc.

This tense, formed with the preterite of *haber* plus the past participle, is used to indicate an event completed just before a following past event. It is normally confined to literature and it is now extremely rare in speech:

Cuando hubieron terminado de reírse, examinaron mi situación personal (A. Cancela, quoted *Esbozo*, 3.14.7)	When they had finished laughing they examined my personal situation
Le escribió el mismo día, no bien se hubo marchado (L. Goytisolo, Spain)	He wrote to her the same day, when she had only just left
Así que después de que se hubo marchado la enfermera hizo un par de llamadas telefónicas (E. Lynch, Argentina)	So once the nurse had left he made a couple of telephone calls
. . . *así que, una vez que me hube quitado la blusa* . . . (E. Sábato, Argentina, dialogue)	. . . so as soon as I had taken my blouse off . . .
. . . *porque no bien hube entrado a Octavia Carrión* (A. Bryce Echenique, Peru)	. . . because I'd scarcely carried Octavia Carrión in . . .

Notes

(i) This tense is only used after *después (de) que* 'after', *luego que, así que, no bien, enseguida que, en cuanto, tan pronto como* and *apenas*, all translatable as 'as soon as', and after *cuando* and other phrases of similar meaning, to emphasize that the event was completed just before the main event in the sentence. In ordinary language it is replaced by the preterite: *tan pronto como llegamos, pasamos al comedor* 'as soon as we (had) arrived, we went through to the dining room', *pero apenas entró cambió de opinión* (J. Ibargüengoitia, Mexico, dialogue) 'but he'd hardly entered when he changed his mind', *apenas terminamos el almuerzo llegó Casals* (M. Puig, Argentina, dialogue) 'we'd scarcely finished lunch when Casals arrived'; or, less commonly, by the pluperfect:[14] *apenas* **había ordenado** *el señor juez el levantamiento del cadáver para llevarlo al depósito judicial, rompieron el silencio unos gritos de mujer* (F. García Pavón, Spain) 'the judge had scarcely ordered the removal of the body to the official morgue when the silence was broken by women shouting'.

(ii) The *pretérito anterior* refers to a single completed event. After the same time phrases, repeated or habitual events are expressed by the ordinary pluperfect – *en cuanto habíamos terminado el trabajo, volvíamos a casa* 'as soon as we had finished work, we used to return home' – or, colloquially, by the imperfect: *en cuanto terminábamos el trabajo, volvíamos a casa.*

(iii) The French equivalent of *hube terminado* is *j'eus fini*, or in popular French *j'ai eu fini*. Whereas this tense survives in French, the *pretérito anterior* is moribund in Spanish.

14.10.5 The pluperfect subjunctive

Normally this form, *hubiera hablado, hubiese hablado*, is used when the rules of Spanish grammar require that a pluperfect indicative form must be rewritten in

---

[14] Replacement by the pluperfect is uncommon. Busquets and Bonzi (1983), 69, 267, give numerous examples as alternatives to the preterite.

the subjunctive. Compare *yo estaba convencido de que Manuel lo **había hecho** 'I was convinced Manuel had done it' and *yo no estaba convencido de que Manuel **lo hubiera/hubiese hecho** 'I wasn't convinced that Manuel had done it'. These rules are explained in Chapter 16.

Students must beware of confusing the pluperfect subjunctive with the conditional perfect. The latter may be formed either with the conditional or the *-ra* form of *haber*: *habría sido mejor* and *hubiera sido mejor* both mean 'it would have been better'. The pluperfect subjunctive can only be formed with the *-ra* or *-se* forms.

14.11 The future perfect and conditional perfect

The future perfect, *habré hecho* 'I will have done' and the conditional perfect *habría hecho* or *hubiera hecho* 'I would have done' are used in more or less the same ways as their English equivalents. But the following points are worthy of note:

(a) The future perfect is much used to express conjecture or, in questions, mystification or perplexity: *se lo habrá dicho Miguel* 'Miguel must have told him/her/you', *¿dónde lo habrá puesto?* 'where *can* (s)he have put it?' The negative expresses a conjecture or may make a statement rhetorical, i.e. it expects or hopes for the answer 'of course not': *no lo habrán hecho* 'I guess they haven't done it' or 'they *can't* have done it'. In questions, the negative may make a tentative suggestion: *¿no se lo habrán llevado a casa?* 'do you think that possibly they've taken it home'/'could it possibly be that they've taken it home?', *¿no será que ya han tomado la decisión?* 'couldn't it be that they've already taken the decision?' It may also make a question rhetorical (i.e. it expects or hopes for the answer 'no'): *¿no la habrás vuelto a llamar?* 'you haven't called her again, have you?!'
(b) The conditional perfect frequently occurs in conditional sentences of the type 'if I had had enough money **I would have bought** it' *si hubiera tenido suficiente dinero, lo **habría/hubiera comprado***. Use of the *-ra* form of *haber* in this tense is a common alternative, as explained at 1 4.7.5.

It may also express a conjecture or supposition about the past: *se lo habría dicho Miguel* 'Miguel must have told him/her'. In questions it adds a note of conjecture or perplexity: *¿no se lo habría dicho Miguel?* 'it couldn't be that Miguel told her, could it?' Further examples:

¿La habría oído? (C. Martín Gaite, Spain, dialogue)	Could he possibly have heard her?
¿Cómo era posible que Papá se hubiera enterado? ¿Se lo habría contado mi hermana?	How was it possible that Father had found out? Could my sister have told him?

14.12 Tense agreement

Tense agreement with the subjunctive is discussed in full at 16.16.

As far as the indicative tenses are concerned, Spanish is stricter than English about the agreement of past with past. In sentences like 'John said he is/was coming' English seems optionally to use either tense in the subordinate clause. Spanish requires *Juan dijo que venía*. Sentences like ?*Juan dijo que viene* usually sound careless or substandard. The present is, however, possible with the perfect tense when John's arrival is still awaited: *Juan ha dicho que viene*.

15

Continuous forms of the verb

15.1 General

15.1.1 Forms and equivalents of the continuous

Spanish has a full range of continuous verb forms based on the appropriate tense of *estar* 'to be' and the gerund: *estoy hablando* 'I'm talking', *estuve cenando* 'I was having dinner/supper', *estaremos escribiendo* 'we'll be writing', etc. The formation of the gerund is discussed at 20.2. French has a close equivalent of the Spanish continuous: *je suis en train de parler* 'I'm (in the process of) speaking' stresses an ongoing action in much the same way as *estoy hablando*, but the Spanish continuous is used much more frequently. Students of Spanish who know French well should recall that if *en train de* . . . is impossible in French, the continuous will usually be impossible in Spanish. *Je pars demain* = *salgo mañana*. **Je suis en train de partir demain*/**Estoy saliendo mañana* are both impossible for 'I'm leaving tomorrow' (the latter, at least, in most countries; but see 15.5b).

The Italian continuous, *sto lavorando* (= *estoy trabajando* 'I'm working'), is more restricted in use than its Spanish counterpart. The Spanish continuous can appear in any tense except the *pretérito anterior*, whereas in the past only the imperfect continuous *stavo lavorando* is used in Italian.

The Spanish continuous form is apparently more common than fifty years ago and some of its current uses seem to reflect the influence of English. The Academy's *Esbozo* . . . , 3.12.5, complains bitterly about the abuse of the continuous. English-speaking learners constantly over-use the continuous and produce sentences like *en este capítulo el autor **está diciendo** que* . . . 'in this chapter the author is saying that . . .' instead of the correct ***dice** que* . . . These errors usually arise from a failure to apply the rule that the continuous usually refers only to actions that are really in progress. In this case the author is obviously not actually saying the words *now*.

15.1.2 The Spanish continuous and the English progressive compared

Spanish continuous forms, e.g. *estoy leyendo, estaban hablando*, etc., misleadingly resemble the much-used English progressive verb form, e.g. 'I'm reading', 'they were talking'. The Spanish continuous differs from its English counterpart in several important respects:

(a) The present and imperfect tenses of the Spanish continuous can only refer to actions that are or were actually in progress or are or were in the process of being repeated, whereas the English progressive doubles as a future tense and also, sometimes, as a habitual form:

Estoy comiendo	I'm (actually) eating
Estabas hablando	You were (in the process of) talking

But

Llegamos mañana	**We're arriving** tomorrow (future)
Si te pones así, me voy	If you get like that, **I'm going** (future)
Mi hijo va a un colegio mixto	My son **is going** to a mixed (i.e. co-educational) school (habitual)
Te envío ésta para decirte que . . .	**I'm sending** you this to tell you that . . . (really means 'I shall send': you haven't sent it yet)
Solicito un puesto en la Administración (*estoy solicitando* suggests you are actually filling out the form)	**I'm applying** for a job in the Civil Service (really means 'I've applied for' or 'I'm going to apply')
Se casan (*se están casando* suggests they are in mid-ceremony)	**They're getting** married (i.e. they are going to get married)
Yo salía a la mañana siguiente para París	**I was leaving** the following morning for Paris (future in the past)
Hoy el Barça juega en casa	Today Barcelona **is/are playing** at home (*está jugando* possible only if the game is in progress)

See 15.5b for exceptions to this rule in the Spanish of some Latin-American regions.

(b) The Spanish continuous is very rarely used with the common verbs of motion *ir*, *venir*, *volver* (but see 15.5a for exceptions in parts of Latin America):

¿Adónde vas?	Where **are you going**?
Ya voy	I'm **coming**[1]
Viene la policía	The police **are coming**
Yo volvía cuando te vi	I **was coming back** when I saw you

(c) The Spanish continuous adds a nuance to, but does not substantially alter the meaning of the non-continuous verb form, so that the two forms are sometimes virtually interchangeable. This should be clear in the following examples:

¿No hueles que se queman/se están quemando las salchichas?	Can't you smell that the sausages **are burning**?
Yo hablaba con Mario	I **was talking** to Mario/I used to talk to Mario
Yo estaba hablando con Mario	I **was talking** to Mario
Ana lee/está leyendo un libro	Ana **is reading** a book
—¿Qué haces?—Leo esta revista (S. Vodanovic, Chile, dialogue; could equally well have been expressed *¿Qué estás haciendo?—(Estoy) leyendo esta revista*. Some Peninsular informants preferred the continuous)	'What **are you doing**?' '(I'm) **reading** this magazine'
No te conocía, ¿qué te pasa? Hablas raro (C. Martín Gaite, Spain, dialogue)	I didn't recognize you. What's the matter with you. **You're talking** strangely

---

[1] In Spanish 'to go' must be used when referring to the departure point and 'to come' when referring to the arrival point; English is vague in this respect. Thus *no voy a tu fiesta esta noche* = 'I'm not **coming/going** to your party tonight', but not **no vengo a tu fiesta . . .*'. *—¿Vienes conmigo? —No, no voy contigo* 'Are you coming with me?' 'No, I'm not coming/going with you.'

Dígame en qué piensa, por favor (ibid.)	Tell me what **you're thinking** about?
¿Qué es la libertad? El otro hombre está	What is freedom? The other man is thinking
pensando en ello. Está sentado en un	about it. He is sitting in an armchair. **He**
sillón. Fuma (*El País*, Spain)	**is smoking**

(d) A number of common Spanish verbs do not appear in the continuous form, whereas their English counterparts do. See 15.3 for discussion.

15.1.3 Further remarks on the relationship between the simple present tense and the present continuous

The difference between the simple present and the continuous present is particularly subtle for English speakers. The Spanish continuous form is normally possible only when the action is clearly happening *now* or is being repeated now. The Spanish present tense, *escribo*, *hago*, etc., is imprecise: it may indicate present, future, habitual events, eternal truths or even past events (see 14.3 and 14.6.3). Continuous forms are much more specifically present: compare *fuma* 'he smokes' or 'he's smoking' and *está fumando* 'he's (actually) smoking'.

An action must be perceived to be actually in progress for the continuous to be possible. Peninsular informants[2] said *está lloviendo* on seeing rain through a window, and thought that *llueve*, in this case, sounded vaguely poetic or archaic. But most avoided the continuous in the sentences *asómate a ver si **llueve*** 'look out and see if it's raining' and *¿**llueve** o no llueve?* 'is it raining or not?', the reason being that someone who asks whether it is raining has obviously not actually seen or heard rain falling. Similarly, when someone up a tree shouts 'I'm falling!', (s)he literally means 'I'm going to fall!', not 'I'm already in mid-air!': a Spanish speaker shouts *¡que me caigo!*, not *¡que me estoy cayendo!*, which has the figurative meaning 'I'm ready to drop', i.e. 'I'm exhausted'.

With some verbs that refer to actions that are self-evidently more or less prolonged events, e.g. *leer* 'to read', *charlar* 'to chat', or where the duration of an action is emphasized, the continuous is more appropriate than the simple form. The answer *está leyendo* 'he's reading' is better than *lee* in reply to the question *¿qué hace Miguel?* 'what's Miguel doing?'

When an action is by nature more or less instantaneous, i.e. it cannot be extended, as is the case with verbs like *toser* 'to cough', *romper* 'to break', *firmar* 'to sign', etc., the continuous indicates a series of repeated actions, as in English: *estaba tosiendo* '(s)he was coughing'.

15.2 Uses of the continuous forms

15.2.1 Continuous used to emphasize events in progress

The continuous forms of the present and imperfect tenses are often used to show that an event is or was actually in progress at the time. In cases in which the action is emphatically in progress at the time, the continuous is obligatory:

Ahora no se puede poner – está haciendo	He can't come to the phone now – he's
sus cuentas (not . . . *hace sus cuentas*)	doing his accounts

---

[2] In this and several other cases, Latin-American informants tended to use the continuous more readily than Peninsular informants.

No quería molestarla, porque estaba trabajando/trabajaba	I didn't want to bother her/you because she was/you were working
Arriba golpearon dos veces, sin mucha fuerza.—Está matando las cucarachas— propuso Gregorius (J. Cortázar, Argentina, dialogue)	There were two knocks from upstairs, not very loud. 'He's killing the cockroaches,' Gregorius suggested
Octavia estaba abriendo la puerta cuando regresé (A. Bryce Echenique, Peru)	Octavia was (just) opening the door when I returned
Pero ¡si te estoy escuchando!/¡si te escucho!	But I *am* listening to you!

Notes

(i) In the case of the imperfect tense, the continuous and non-continuous are sometimes more or less interchangeable if they really refer to the past and the action is not habitual; i.e. *pensaba* and *estaba pensando* both mean 'I/(s)he was thinking'/'you were thinking'. See 14.5.5 for discussion.

(ii) As far as the present and imperfect are concerned, English speakers will often find that if the phrase 'in the middle of' makes at least possible sense in the translation, the Spanish continuous is possible. 'Octavia was in the middle of opening the door' makes sense, so *estaba abriendo* is correct. But ?? 'I think that the President is in the middle of defending stricter laws' sounds peculiar, so *defiende*, not *está defendiendo* is called for.

(iii) The preterite, perfect and pluperfect continuous, e.g. *estuve hablando, he estado hablando*, differ in meaning from the non-continuous equivalents of these tenses. See 15.2.3.

15.2.2 Continuous used to denote temporary or surprising events

The continuous may optionally be used to show that an action is temporary or in some way unusual or surprising:

Vive en París, pero últimamente está viviendo/vive en Madrid	He lives in Paris, but at the moment he's living in Madrid
Me estoy sintiendo mal/Me siento mal	I'm (suddenly) feeling ill
¡Qué sueño me está entrando! (C. Martín Gaite, Spain, dialogue)	I suddenly feel so sleepy!
Pero ¿qué estás haciendo?/¿Qué haces?	But what *are* you doing?
¿Qué me estás contando?/¿Qué me cuentas?	What *are* you telling me!?
—¿En qué estábamos pensando tú y yo cuando engendramos a estos seres, me quieres explicar?—le pregunta la madre al padre (Carmen Rico-Godoy, Spain, dialogue; or . . . *en qué pensábamos*)	'Do you mind explaining to me what you and I were thinking of when we conceived these creatures?', the mother asks the father

15.2.3 Preterite, perfect, pluperfect and periphrastic future continuous used to denote prolonged events

The preterite, perfect, pluperfect and the periphrastic future (*ir a* + infinitive) continuous show that an action is, was or will be prolonged over a period of time:

Estuve hablando dos horas con tu hermano	I was talking with your brother for two hours
Pero, ¿vas a estar esperándola todo el día?	But are you going to keep on waiting for her all day?
Estuve andando hasta el amanecer (S. Puértolas, Spain)	I was walking/walked until dawn
Acuérdense, el señor ese con el que estuvimos tomando nieves en el zócalo de Atlixco . . . (A. Mastretta, Mexico, dialogue; *nieves* = *helados* in Spain)	Remember, that gentleman we had an ice cream with in the main square in Atlixco . . .

He estado pensando que tú no siempre dices la verdad	I've been thinking that you don't always tell the truth
El rostro de María sonreía. Es decir, ya no sonreía, pero había estado sonriendo un décimo de segundo antes (E. Sábato, Argentina)	Maria's face was smiling. I mean, it wasn't smiling now, but it had been smiling a tenth of a second before

Note

The preterite continuous, *estuve hablando/comiendo* 'I was speaking/eating for a time' indicates an action that was prolonged in the past but is viewed as finished,[3] unlike the imperfect forms *hablaba/estaba hablando*, which merely indicate that an action was going on at the time. It has no clear counterpart in English or French: *ahí está el libro que me hizo perder pie ... lo estuve buscando antes no sé cuánto rato* (C. Martín Gaite, Spain, dialogue) 'there's the book I tripped over ... I don't know how long I spent looking for it earlier', *abandonó la sala y corrió en busca del teléfono ... . Estuvo hablando horas* (A. Bryce Echenique, Peru) 'she left the room and ran in search of the phone. ... She spent hours talking/She talked for hours'.

This use of the continuous is really only possible with verbs that refer to drawn-out actions, e.g. 'think', 'talk', 'read', 'wait', 'eat', etc. Verbs that refer to instantaneous actions cannot be extended: **estuvo rompiendo una ventana* 'he was breaking a window (for a certain time)' is not possible, and *estaba rompiendo una ventana* is only possible with the unlikely meaning 'he was (in the middle of) breaking a window'. Instantaneous actions can, however, be repeated over a period of time: *estuvo disparando al aire durante tres minutos* 'he spent three minutes firing into the air'.

15.2.4 Continuous to express repeated events:

The continuous may express the idea that an event is or has been constantly recurring:

Está yendo mucho al cine estos días	He's going to the cinema a lot these days
La estás viendo demasiado, hijo	You're seeing too much of her, son
Lleva años que se está yendo pero nunca acaba de irse	He's been leaving for years but never gets round to going
Está haciendo frío	It's been cold lately/The weather's cold at the moment
Estamos cansados de que los nicaragüenses se estén metiendo en aguas hondureñas para capturar pescadores (interview in *La Prensa*, Honduras)	We're tired of the Nicaraguans (constantly) entering Honduran waters to capture fishermen
Pero está usted tomando muy seguido esas hierbas y seguido hacen daño (A. Mastretta, Mexico, dialogue)	But you're taking those herbs over long periods, and they cause harm when taken over long periods

Venir and *ir* may appear in the continuous form in this sense, but not usually, at least in standard varieties of the language, in other contexts.

15.2.5 Future and conditional continuous

The future continuous is used either **(a)** to describe events which will be in progress at a certain time, or **(b)** to conjecture about what may actually be happening now:

Mañana a estas horas estaremos volando sobre el Pacífico	Tomorrow at this time we'll be flying over the Pacific

---

[3] Or that the period during which the event took place came to an end, regardless of whether the action itself terminated: *estuve leyendo durante tres horas, y continué leyendo hasta el amanecer* 'I read for three hours then went on reading until morning' is possible.

¿Qué sabes tú lo que es vivir para ponerle las zapatillas a un hombre? Pruébalo dos meses y al tercero ya estarás maldiciendo tu destino (T. Moix, Spain, dialogue)	What do you know about living in order to put a man's slippers on? Try it for two months and by the third you'll be cursing your fate!
Estarán comiendo a estas horas	They'll probably be eating at this time of day
¿Me estarán viendo/Me ven desde esa ventana?	I wonder if they can see me from that window

The future perfect continuous can also be used to express conjectures: *no me habrás estado esperando, ya te dije que no te preocuparas* (C. Martín Gaite, Spain, dialogue) 'I hope you haven't been waiting for me, I told you not to worry'.

The conditional continuous is used like its English counterpart 'would be . . . -ing': *yo sabía que a esa hora estarían comiendo* 'I knew that at that time they would be eating'. It can also express conjectures or suppositions about events that may have been going on: *—¿Por qué no contestaba al teléfono?—Estaría durmiendo* ' "Why wasn't she answering the phone?" "She must have been sleeping." '

15.3 Restrictions on the use of the continuous

(a) Continuous forms are not normally used with certain verbs that refer to inner mental activities, e.g. *aborrecer* 'to loathe', *amar* 'to love', *odiar* 'to hate', *saber* 'to know', e.g. *odio tener que quedarme en casa* 'I hate having to stay at home'. In this respect Spanish and English coincide, but some verbs which denote inner states or 'invisible' actions may appear in the continuous in Spanish but not in English, e.g.:

Me estoy creyendo todo lo que dices	?I'm believing everything you say
Estoy viendo que vamos a acabar mal	I can see we're going to end badly
Te estás mereciendo una bofetada	You deserve (i.e. 'are asking for') a slap
Estoy temiendo que va a llegar tarde	I'm afraid he's going to arrive late

Note

Doler 'to hurt' may appear in either form, much as in English: *me duele/me está doliendo la barriga* 'my stomach aches/is aching'.[4]

(b) The continuous is not used to describe states rather than actions (English often allows the progressive form for states):

Normalmente lleva corbata azul, pero hoy lleva una corbata roja	Normally he wears a blue tie, but today he's wearing a red tie
Tres arañas de luces colgaban del techo	Three chandeliers were hanging from the roof
Lo que falta es . . .	What's lacking is . . .
La luna brillaba sobre las olas	The moon was shining on the waves
Parece cansada	She's looking tired
¡Qué bien huele la madreselva hoy!	Isn't the honeysuckle smelling good today!

(c) The continuous is not used with *estar* (**estar estando* is not Spanish), *poder, haber* or, usually (at least in European and standard literary Spanish), with *ir, venir, regresar, volver, andar*, except in the frequentative sense discussed at (15.2.4):

¿Adónde vas?	Where are you going?

---

[4] More accurately, 'my belly aches'. Spanish-speakers are often confused by English-speakers who fastidiously call their intestines their 'stomach' (*estómago*). *Los intestinos, las tripas* or *la barriga* are not considered indelicate words.

Viene ahora	He's coming now
Cuando volvíamos del cine (me) subí un momento a ver a la abuela	When we were coming back from the cinema I went up to see grandmother for a moment
Estás estúpido hoy	You're being stupid today

(d) Finite forms of verbs that describe physical posture or position can refer only to an action, not to a state. English speakers are often misled by forms like 'he was sitting down' which almost always means *estaba sentado* 'he was seated'. *Estaba sentándose* = 'he was in the process of sitting down', and *se sentaba* means 'he used to sit down'. Further examples:

Estaban tumbados	They were lying down
Estaba agachada	She was crouching down
(compare *estaba agachándose*	(S)he was in the process of bending down)

Notes

(i) *Tener* 'to have' is not used in the continuous, except in the frequentative sense described earlier: *me dijo que estaba teniendo problemas con su vecino* 'he told me he was having problems with his neighbour'.

(ii) *Llevar* is used in the continuous only with the sense of 'to take from one place to another': *lleva camisa* 'he's wearing a shirt', *llevabas una maleta en la mano*' 'you were carrying (= 'holding') a suitcase in your hand', but *está llevando/lleva una camisa a su madre* 'he's taking a shirt to his mother'.

(iii) *Parecer* 'to seem' occasionally appears in the continuous: *la situación me está pareciendo/me parece cada vez más fea* 'the situation's looking uglier and uglier to me'.

(iv) The continuous of *ir*, *venir* and, regionally, of some other of these verbs of motion is found in colloquial speech in parts of Latin America. See 15.5 for Latin-American usage.

15.4 Continuous forms of *ser*

Some grammarians frown on continuous forms of *ser* like *está siendo* on the grounds that they are borrowed from English, but they are not uncommon, especially in Latin America, and they occur in speech as well as in writing to judge by the dialogue of some novels. It seems unreasonable to deny to the language the nuance provided by a continuous form of *ser*, e.g.:

Por un instante pensó que de algún modo él, Martín, estaba de verdad siendo necesario a aquel ser atormentado (E. Sábato, Argentina)	For an instant he thought that he, Martin, was really being necessary to that tormented creature
La convocatoria a las distintas manifestaciones está siendo variada (La Vanguardia, Spain)	The people attending the demonstrations come from various sources (lit. 'the calling to the various demonstrations is varied')
Yo no estoy siendo juzgado (C. Fuentes, Mexico, dialogue)	I'm not being judged
Estás siendo muy bueno hoy	You're being very good today

But unless the passive with *ser* must be used, it seems wise to observe Carnicer's rejection (1972), 43ff, of sentences like *la fachada está siendo reparada* 'the front of the building is being repaired' in favour of *se está reparando la fachada* or *están reparando la fachada*.

15.5 Latin-American uses of the continuous

Written – or at least printed – Latin-American Spanish seems to obey the same rules as European Spanish as far as the use of the continuous is concerned. However, there are numerous regional variants in colloquial usage and it seems, in general, that the continuous is used more extensively in Latin-American speech than in Spain.

(a) In many places the continuous of *ir*, *venir* and other verbs of motion is regularly heard:

—*Estamos yendo a Pato Huachana* —*dijo Lalita* (M. Vargas Llosa, Peru, dialogue)	'We're going to Pato Huachana,' Lalita said
Estaba yendo a tomar un café con leche en Brosa (M. Vargas Llosa, Peru, dialogue)	I was on my way to Brosa to have a white coffee
¿Cómo le va yendo? (Chile, quoted in Kany, 1970, 282; Spain *¿Cómo le va?*)	How are things with you?

(b) In colloquial Peruvian, Bolivian and Chilean Spanish, and perhaps locally elsewhere in Latin America, the present continuous is used, as in English, to express a pre-scheduled future where standard language uses the non-continuous present: *mañana estoy yendo a París* 'tomorrow I'm going to Paris' (= *mañana voy a París*). This is not possible in European Spanish.

(c) Kany (1970), 282ff, reports that in the Andean region, including Chile, verbs like *poder*, *tener*, *haber* also appear in the continuous form, especially in popular styles: *estás pudiendo* = *puedes* 'you can', *¿está habiendo?* 'is there any?' (Spain *¿hay?*). This usage is not heard in standard Spanish. The Peninsular colloquial form *irse yendo* is worth noting: *me voy a ir yendo ¿sabes?* (C. Martín Gaite, Spain, dialogue), 'I'm on my way/I'm off'/(US 'I'm out of here').

(d) In colloquial, but not written Mexican, *andar* is much used instead of *estar* to form the continuous: *ando trabajando* 'I'm working', *¿qué andas haciendo?* 'what are you doing?' Similar forms with *andar* are sometimes heard in popular speech in Spain, e.g. *¿qué andas haciendo?* for *¿qué estás haciendo?*, but *andar* + gerund normally means 'to go around doing something'; see 20.8.1 for discussion and examples.

16

The subjunctive

Index to chapter

16.1 Summary of the main uses of the subjunctive

The following chart indexes the main uses of the Spanish subjunctive after phrases and clauses + *que*, e.g. *quiero que . . ., es necesario que, la idea de que . . .* (the charts do not include every point raised in the chapter).

Meaning or type of phrase or clause	Subjunctive?		Meaning or type of phrase or clause	Subjunctive?	
any negative verb	usually	16.2.9	doubt	usually	16.8
possibility, probability	always	16.3	fear	usually	16.9
depending on	always	16.4	'the fact that . . .'	usually	16.10
wanting	always	16.5	other nouns + *de que*	variable	16.10
needing	always	16.5	believing and suspecting	only if negated	16.11.1, 16.7
ordering	variable	16.5	stating, declaring	only if negated	16.7
requesting, allowing, forbidding, avoiding	always (if *que* is used)	16.5	knowing	only if negated	16.7
emotional reactions	usually	16.6	understanding	variable	16.11.2
value judg(e)ments	usually	16.6	hoping	usual	16.11.3
denial	usually	16.7			

The following chart summarizes the main uses of the Spanish subjunctive after subordinators (e.g. *cuando, para que, con tal de que*, etc.):

Meaning	Subjunctive?		Meaning	Subjunctive?	
perhaps	variable	16.3	after	variable	16.12.7
in order to	always	16.12.3	while/as (time)	variable	16.12.7
in order that not .../ lest	always	16.12.3	since (time)	variable	16.12.7
because	variable	16.12.4	as soon as	variable	16.12.7
so that (manner)	variable	16.12.5a	until	variable	16.12.7
como (= 'as')	variable	16.12.5b	provided/ on condition	always	16.12.8a
without	always	16.12.5c	except	variable	16.12.8b
in case	variable	16.12.6	unless	variable	16.12.8b
before	always	16.12.7	although	variable	16.12.9
when	variable	16.12.7	in spite of	variable	16.12.9

Other uses of the subjunctive:

to translate 'whoever', 'whatever', 'whenever', 'however', 'wherever', 'the more . . . the more'.	depends on meaning	16.13
in relative clauses	depends on meaning	16.14
after *donde* and *cuanto* introducing clauses	depends on meaning	16.14.4
after superlatives	depends on style	16.14.5
for affirmative imperatives	with *usted*	16.15.1
to make negative imperatives	always	16.15.1
after words expressing wishes (e.g. *ojalá*)	always	16.15.2
in conditional sentences	variable	Ch. 25
in a few set phrases	always	16.15.3

16.2 General remarks on the subjunctive

16.2.1 The importance of the Spanish subjunctive

The subjunctive is a very important feature of Spanish and there is no conclusive evidence that it is dying out, although it is true that spontaneous speech, especially Latin-American, occasionally uses the indicative where formal styles require the subjunctive. The subjunctive allows Spanish to express shades of meaning that English ignores – see 16.14.1 for a vivid example. Students will also often note that the subjunctive often removes ambiguities that affect English – especially the British variety – now that it has more or less lost the subjunctive. Compare the tendency of British speakers to say 'we insist that the children are looked after properly' both to state a fact (indicative) and to express a wish, i.e. '. . . *be* looked after properly'.

16.2.2 Forms of the subjunctive

There are three simple (i.e. non-compound) tenses of the Spanish subjunctive: present, imperfect and future. Only two are in common use: the present, formed as explained at 13.1.9, and the imperfect, of which there are two forms, one in -*ra* and one in -*se*. These forms are explained at 13.1.10 and all the forms are shown at 13.5.2. The relationship between the two forms is discussed in the next section. The future subjunctive, discussed at 16.17, is virtually obsolete and has been replaced by the present or the imperfect subjunctive.

Compound tenses of the subjunctive, e.g. *haya hablado, hubiera/hubiese hablado* (also mentioned at 14.9.9 and 14.10.5), and continuous forms of the subjunctive, e.g. *esté hablando, estuviera/estuviese hablando*, are also common.

16.2.3 The *-ra* and *-se* forms compared

When the *-ra* and *-se* forms are used as subjunctives they seem to be completely interchangeable and the two forms are shown side by side in the following examples.[1] The *-ra* form is more frequent everywhere, and in some parts of Latin America has all but replaced the *-se* form, but not in Argentina, to judge by the popular dialogue in Manuel Puig's novels. The *-ra* form also has a few uses as an indicative form which it does not share with the *-se* form, at least in normal styles:

(a) It may be a supposedly elegant literary variant for the indicative pluperfect, especially in Latin-American texts: *el hombre que ella conociera años antes* 'the man she had met years ago', for *que había conocido . . . .* See 14.10.2 for discussion.

(b) It can replace the conditional of *haber – habría sido mejor/**hubiera** sido mejor* 'it would have been better' – and less commonly of a few other verbs. See 14.7.5 for discussion.

(c) It is used in a few set phrases: e.g. *acabáramos* 'now I see what you're getting at . . .', *otro gallo nos cantara* 'that would be another story . . .'.

16.2.4 Tense agreement and the subjunctive

This is discussed in detail at 16.16. The idea that there is a 'Rule of Agreement' that dictates which tense of the subjunctive must be used in Spanish is one of the myths of traditional grammar, but in the vast majority of cases the following scheme applies:

Tense of verb in main clause	Tense of subjunctive verb
Present, perfect, future, imperative	Present
Conditional, imperfect, preterite, pluperfect	Imperfect

Examples: *le digo/he dicho/diré que se **vaya*** 'I tell/have told/will tell him to go away'; *le diría/decía/dije/había dicho que se **fuera/fuese*** 'I would tell/was telling/told/had told him to go away'.

16.2.5 When the subjunctive is not used in clauses introduced by *que*

It is much easier to state categorically when the subjunctive is **not** used in clauses introduced by *que* than to list all the cases in which it is used. The subjunctive is **not** used:

(a) After affirmative statements that simply declare that an event happened, is happening or will happen: *es cierto que **hubo** una conspiración* 'it's true that there was a conspiracy', *era obvio que lo **había** hecho* 'it was obvious that he'd done it', *se prevé que **habrá** déficit* 'a deficit is forecasted', *se queja de que está cansada* (*quejarse de* is treated as a verb of statement) 'she complains she's tired'.

---

[1] The view, argued by Bolinger (1991), 274–82, that they mean slightly different things is not generally accepted.

(b) After affirmative statements that declare the subject's belief or opinion:[2] *creo/me parece que **habla** inglés* 'I think she speaks English', *yo pensaba que él **era** más honrado* 'I thought he was more honest', *dice que **viene*** 'she says she's coming', *parece que su mujer **está** enferma* 'it seems that his wife is ill/sick'. There are occasional exceptions to **(b)** discussed at 16.11.1.

However, negative verbs + *que* usually require the subjunctive, e.g. *no creo/no me parece que **hable** inglés* 'I don't think she speaks English'. See 16.2.9.

(c) After subordinators (words like *cuando, después de que, mientras que,* etc.), when the verb refers to an action that either habitually happens or had already happened at the time of the main verb. Compare *le pagaré cuando **llegue*** 'I'll pay him when he arrives' and *le pago cuando **llega**/le pagué cuando **llegó*** 'I pay him when he arrives' (habitual)/'I paid him when he arrived' (past). See 16.12.1 for further discussion.

(d) When the subject of the main verb and the subordinate verb are the same, in which case the infinitive is often used. See next section.

16.2.6 Subjunctive or infinitive?

In many cases a subjunctive can – or must be – avoided by using an infinitive. As far as phrases and clauses + *que* are concerned, a subjunctive subordinate verb is usually only required when the subject of the verb in the main clause and the subject of the subordinate verb are different. When they are the same the infinitive is used. Thus *yo quiero* 'I want' + *yo voy* 'I go' must be expressed as *yo quiero **ir*** 'I want to go' (same subject), but *yo quiero* + *él va* 'he goes' = *yo quiero que él **vaya,*** 'I want him to go' (different subjects, subjunctive obligatory). However, verbs of prohibiting, permitting, requesting, suggesting and advising – i.e. most verbs that can be constructed with an indirect object pronoun – may allow either construction (see 16.5.2).

The infinitive may also be used after certain subordinators when the subjects are identical, e.g. *la llamé después de llegar a casa* 'I rang her after I got home'. See 16.12.2.

16.2.7 The subjunctive does not always indicate doubt or uncertainty

One common misconception about the Spanish subjunctive is that it expresses doubt or uncertainty. This is sometimes true, but the subjunctive is not in fact always obligatory after some common words that express uncertainty (e.g. 'perhaps', 'probably' – see 16.3.2 – and 'to doubt', see 16.8), and the sentence *me acostaré cuando se **ponga** el sol* 'I'll go to bed when the sun sets' does not doubt that the sun will set: the subjunctive is required after *cuando* simply because the sunset is still in the future.

In this respect students of French or Italian must remember that Spanish uses the present subjunctive to indicate the future in subordinate clauses after words like 'when', 'after', 'as soon as', etc., where the other two languages often use the future indicative. Compare *on y ira quand il **fera** beau temps* and *ci andremo quando*

---

[2] In this respect Spanish differs from Italian and resembles French. Compare *creo que **es** verdad/je crois que c'est vrai* (both subordinate verbs indicative) and Italian *credo che **sia** certo* (second verb subjunctive).

farà bel tempo (both verbs future indicative) with *iremos allí cuando* **haga** *buen tiempo* (second verb present subjunctive). Portuguese differs from all three in using a future subjunctive in this context: *iremos lá quando* **fizer** *bom tempo*.

The subjunctive also expresses certainties in other types of sentence. In *el hecho de que España no* **tenga** *petróleo explica en parte las dificultades económicas del país* 'the fact that Spain has no oil explains in part the country's economic difficulties' there is no doubt about Spain's having no oil. It is simply a rule of Spanish grammar that phrases meaning 'the fact that' usually require the subjunctive, possibly because an idea of cause is involved. See 16.10.1 for further discussion.

16.2.8 Regional variations in the use of the subjunctive

There is very little variation in the use of the subjunctive in educated speech throughout the Spanish-speaking world. In some regions, especially Navarre, the Basque Provinces and Argentina, there is a strong tendency in familiar speech to replace the imperfect subjunctive by the conditional, e.g. *?si tendría dinero, lo compraría* for *si tuviera/tuviese dinero lo compraría* 'If I had some money, I'd buy it'. This should not be imitated by foreign learners, although it is acknowledged (at least in Spain and not in writing) as a well-known regionalism.

Also to be avoided is the tendency, heard in popular speech in parts of Latin America, to replace the subjunctive by the indicative after subordinators of time that point to the future, e.g. *?se lo diré cuando viene* for *se lo diré cuando venga* 'I'll tell him when he comes'. The future indicative is quite often heard in Latin-American speech after phrases like *es posible que* 'it is possible that'; see 16.3.

In Argentina, where *voseo* is normal and accepted in conversation among all social groups, careful speakers may nevertheless use standard Spanish subjunctive forms with *vos*. The expected *vos* forms with a stressed final vowel are considered a shade too popular for many tastes. In the following examples the speakers address one another as *vos*: *tengo miedo que no vengas . . . que aflojes* (J. Asís, Argentina; Spain . . . *miedo* **de** *que*) 'I'm scared you won't come . . . that you'll go off the idea', *no digas nada pero papá fue a matar un pollo . . .* (M. Puig, Argentina, dialogue) 'don't say anything, but father went to kill a chicken . . . '. Compare this example of very familiar language: *yo no tengo inconveniente en hablar de perros todo lo que* **querás** (Mafalda cartoon, Joaquín Salvador Lavado (Quino) Argentina; 'correct' style *todo lo que* **quieras**) 'I don't mind talking about dogs as much as you like'. See 11.3.1 for more remarks about Argentine *voseo*.

16.2.9 Subjunctive required after negative statements + *que*

As a general rule, sentences of the type Negative Statement + *que* are followed by the subjunctive. Compare the following pairs:

Es cierto que su mujer está enferma	It's true that his wife is ill
No es cierto que su mujer **esté** *enferma*	It isn't true that his wife is ill
Parece que es verdad	It seems that it's true
No parece que **sea** *verdad*	It doesn't seem that it's true
Es que quiero verla	It's that/The fact is that I want to see her/it
No es que **quiera** *verla*	It isn't that I want to see her/it
Significa que forma parte del movimiento	It means that (s)he is part of the movement
No significa que **forme** *parte del movimiento*	It doesn't mean that (s)he is part of the movement

. . . porque habla ruso	. . . because he speaks Russian
*. . . no porque **hable** ruso*	. . . not because he speaks Russian

Exceptions to this rule occur, especially after *no saber que* 'not to know that', *no decir que* 'not to say (i.e. 'state') that' and *no ser que* 'not to be that'. See section 16.7.1.

16.3 Subjunctive after statements of possibility and probability (including words meaning 'perhaps')

16.3.1 *Es posible/probable que* . . . and similar statements

In sentences of the pattern Statement of Possibility/Probability/Plausibility + *que* + subordinate verb, the latter is in the subjunctive. 'Possibility' also includes meanings like 'the risk that . . .', 'the danger that. . .', 'it is inevitable that . . .', etc.

*Es posible que **haya** tormenta*	There may be a storm
*Era probable que **sucediera**/**sucediese** así*	It was probable that it would happen that way
*Es previsible que para el año 2500 **tengamos** ordenadores* (Lat. Am. *computadoras*) *que les darán ciento y raya a sus inventores humanos*	It's foreseeable that by the year 2500 we will have super-intelligent computers that leave their human inventors standing
*Puede ser que este auge se **prolongue** y **enriquezca** con escritores más originales y propios* (M. Vargas Llosa, Peru)	This boom may last and be enriched by more original and more native authors
*La sola posibilidad de que aquella muchacha no lo **viese** más lo desesperaba* (E. Sábato, Argentina)	The mere possibility that that girl wouldn't see him again filled him with despair
*Corrías el riesgo de que te **vieran**/**viesen***	You were running the risk of them seeing you
*Es inevitable que los autores . . . **entren** en decadencia y **pierdan** su capacidad creadora* (J. Marías, Spain)	It is inevitable that authors . . . will go into decline and lose their creative ability
*También puede ocurrir que Santiago **prefiera** tener a Graciela en una relación deteriorada . . .* (M. Benedetti, Uruguay, dialogue)	It may also be the case that Santiago prefers being with (lit. 'having') Graciela in a shaky relationship . . .

Notes

(i) *Pueda que* is a common Latin-American alternative for *puede que/puede ser que* 'maybe'/ 'it may be that': *pueda que algo te den y te mejores* (M. Puig, Argentina, dialogue) 'maybe they'll give you something and you'll get better'.

(ii) The future indicative, or, when the verb in the main clause is in the past, the conditional, are quite often found in informal Latin-American Spanish after such statements, e.g. *. . . la posibilidad de que no **podrán** (Spain *puedan*) moler fábricas que no cuenten con caña suficiente* (*Granma Internacional*, Cuba) '. . . the possibility that mills that do not have enough sugar-cane will not be able to do any crushing'.

(iii) Use of *capaz que*, usually, but apparently not always, with the subjunctive, is typical of familiar Latin-American speech: *capaz que a la semana siguiente se lo **ofrecen** [sic] a Jane Fonda y para que acepte **convierten** el personaje en mujer* (*La Jornada*, Mexico) 'it's possible that the following week they'll offer it (the part) to Jane Fonda and make the character a woman so that she'll accept'. This construction is banned from formal styles and unheard in the standard language of Spain, although it is found in regional dialects.

16.3.2 Subjunctive after words meaning 'perhaps', 'possibly', 'probably'

There are several commonly used words meaning 'perhaps': *acaso, tal vez, quizá(s),*[3] *a lo mejor, igual, lo mismo, posiblemente.*These adverbs may appear in main or subordinate clauses, but they are discussed here in order to group them with statements of possibility.

(a) *Tal vez* (written *talvez* in Latin America), *quizá(s)* and *acaso* all mean 'perhaps'. *Acaso* is rather literary in this meaning, but it has another common use described at 16.3.3. With all these words, when the event referred to is happening in the present or happened in the past, use of the subjunctive is optional.[4] The subjunctive makes the possibility rather weaker:

*Tal vez **fuese** una discusión auténtica. Tal vez **representaban** una comedia en mi honor* (interview, Madrid press; both moods used)	Maybe it was a real argument. Maybe they were putting on an act for my benefit
*Tal vez **debió** irse* (*El País*, Spain)	Perhaps he should have gone (i.e. 'resigned')
*Tal vez **tengamos** algo de culpa nosotros mismos* (S. Vodanovic, dialogue, Chile)	Perhaps we're partly to blame ourselves
*Quizá ni siquiera **entabláramos** conversación* (J. Marías, Spain; *entablamos* possible)	Perhaps we didn't even start up a conversation
*Quizá por eso **hayan dejado** de ser ya escritores* (R. Arenas, Cuba)	Perhaps that's the reason they are no longer writers
*Quizá **era** pena lo que se traslucía en la sonrisa de . . . mi padre* (idem, *fuera/fuese* possible)	Perhaps it was sorrow that came through in my father's smile

If the event is still in the future, the present subjunctive or, much less commonly, the future indicative, is used, but not the present indicative:

*Quizá/tal vez **venga/vendrá** mañana* (not* *viene mañana*)	Perhaps she'll come tomorrow
*Quizá éste **sea** el destino auténtico de la humanidad* (E. Mendoza, Spain)	Perhaps this is humanity's true fate
*Tal vez me **toque** mi turno para ir a la libertad* (C. Solórzano, Mexico, dialogue)	Perhaps it's my turn to go to 'freedom'
*Quizá España **podrá** desempeñar un papel particularmente activo en el restablecimiento de la paz en Europa Central* (*El País*, Spain; *pueda* is possible, but expresses more uncertainty)	Perhaps Spain will be able to play a particularly active part in re-establishing peace in Central Europe

But the conditional of *haber* and *poder* is common after these words to make the statement more tentative: *quizá **habría** que revisar asimismo estos conceptos* (A. Gala, Spain) 'it may also possibly be necessary to modify these ideas'.

If the event *was* still in the future, only the imperfect subjunctive or the conditional can be used: *quizá/tal vez **vinieran/viniesen/vendrían** al día siguiente* (not *venían*) 'perhaps they would come the following day', . . . *una generación que acaso no **volviera** a ser feliz fuera de sus retratos* (G. García Márquez, Colombia) '. . . a generation that would perhaps never again be happy outside its portraits'.

---

[3] *Quizá* is more frequent than *quizás* and is preferred in written Spanish in memory of the original spoken Latin form *quis sapit*, which did not end in an *s*.
[4] Use of the indicative is increasingly usual, but it may still sound incorrect to some older speakers.

The subjunctive can only be used if *quizá(s)* or *tal vez* precede the verb they modify: one can only say *era, tal vez, un efecto de esta política* . . . 'it was, perhaps, an effect of this policy . . .'.

(b) *A lo mejor* also means 'perhaps', but it does not take the subjunctive.[5] It is heard everywhere on both continents, but it is confined to spoken language or informal writing:

A lo mejor se ha quedado en casa	Perhaps/Maybe (s)he's stayed at home
Ni siquiera la nombró. A lo mejor se ha olvidado de ella (M. Vargas Llosa, Peru, dialogue)	He didn't even mention her. Maybe he's forgotten her

(c) In Spain *igual* and *lo mismo* are also used in familiar speech in the meaning 'perhaps': *si te viera todos los días, igual acabaría despreciándote* (J. A. Zunzunegui, Spain, dialogue, quoted Steel, 1976, 134) 'if I saw you every day maybe I'd end up despising you', *llama a la puerta. Lo mismo te da una propina* 'Knock on the door. Maybe he'll give you a tip.' These two constructions are considered substandard by some speakers and they are not heard in Latin America. See 5.15.3 for a Latin-American use of *igual*.

(d) In many parts of Latin America *de repente* is used colloquially to mean 'perhaps'; the word means 'suddenly' in Spain and in standard language. It does not take the subjunctive: *de repente viene mañana* = *a lo mejor viene mañana* 'perhaps she's coming tomorrow'.

(e) *Posiblemente* 'possibly' and *probablemente* 'probably' obey the same rules as *tal vez* and *quizá(s)*: they can be followed by a subjunctive or by an indicative form when they refer to events in the present or past, but if they refer to the future or to the future in the past they can be followed by the subjunctive or by a future or conditional tense, but not by any other indicative tense:

Posiblemente **quedara** *algo de alcohol etílico en nuestras venas humorísticas* (G. García Márquez, Colombia; *quedaba* or *quedase* possible)	Perhaps there was still some ethyl alcohol left in the veins of our humo(u)r
Posiblemente lo más criollo de nuestra cocina **radica** *en las sopas y los guisos* (*Cuba Internacional*, Cuba; *radique* possible; Spain *consiste en*; *guiso* more or less interchangeable with *guisado* in Spain)	Possibly the most authentic (lit. 'creole') aspect of our cuisine lies in the soups and stews
Posiblemente lleguen/llegarán mañana (not *llegan*)	Possibly they'll arrive tomorrow
. . . alguna oscura sensación de incertidumbre, que probablemente **será** *tan incierta como el resto* (J. Cortázar, Argentina)	. . . some obscure sensation of uncertainty, which will probably be as uncertain as the rest
Probablemente en ningún momento te **fuiste** *del cuarto* (ibid.)	Probably you never left the room at any time
Probablemente el mérito **sea** *de Ada* (C. Rico-Godoy, Spain, dialogue)	You can probably thank Ada for that

As a direct verbal modifier *posiblemente* is not particularly colloquial: *ser posible que* . . . (always followed by subjunctive), *quizá* or *tal vez* are more common.

---

[5] Navas Ruiz (1986), 36, says that the subjunctive is 'infrequent' with *a lo mejor*, but he gives no examples. We have seen it with the subjunctive in the Colombian press but we doubt whether this is accepted usage.

16.3.3 Further remarks on *acaso*

Acaso is frequently followed by the indicative mood in all styles as a way of adding a sarcastic note to questions or to make a rhetorical question. It then loses the element of doubt associated with the meaning 'perhaps' and suggests that the answer to the question is obvious:

¿Acaso has visto alguna vez que no llueva en verano? (implying 'of course you haven't . . .')	Have you ever known it not to rain in summer? (lit. 'have you ever seen that it didn't rain in summer?')
¿Acaso todos los paganos no odian a los huambisas? (M. Vargas Llosa, Peru, dialogue)	Don't all the Indians (lit. 'pagans') hate the Huambisa tribe?

16.4 'Depending'

Statements + *que* that mean 'to depend on . . .' require the subjunctive:

*Yo dependo de que me **devuelvan** el dinero a tiempo*	I'm depending on them giving me the money back in time
*De las mujeres depende que se **coma** en el mundo* (A. Mastretta, Mexico, dialogue)	It's women who ensure that people eat in this world (lit. 'that one eats in this world depends on women')
*Miguel contaba con que lo/le **llamaran**/ **llamasen** aquella noche*	Miguel was counting on them ringing him that night

16.5 Statements of 'influence' + *que*

16.5.1 General

By 'influence' is meant any attempt to influence the outcome of the action in the subordinate clause by such actions as wanting, ordering, needing, causing, allowing, prohibiting, advising, persuading, encouraging it to happen, or avoiding or excluding it.

When the subject of the main verb is not the same as the subject of the subordinate verb, the subjunctive must be used for the latter: *yo quiero que Mario lo* ***haga*** 'I want Mario to do it'. When the subjects are the same, the infinitive is used: *yo quiero **hacerlo*** 'I want to do it'; see 16.5.2a. However, some verbs of 'influence', especially verbs of permitting and prohibiting and other verbs that can take an indirect object, can also optionally be used with an infinitive even when the subjects are different. This possibility is discussed in 16.5.2c.

The following verbs always require the subjunctive when the subject of the subordinate verb is different from the subject of the main verb (although asterisked forms can be used impersonally with the infinitive. See 16.5.2b):

causar que to cause . . .	*necesitar que* to need to . . .
conseguir/lograr que to succeed in . . .	*oponerse a que* to be against . . .
contribuir a que to contribute to . . .	*pedir que* (but see 16.5.3) to ask/request
cuidar de que to take care that . . .	that . .
decir que§ to tell someone to . . .	*preferir que* to prefer that . . .
dificultar que to hinder . . .	*pretender que* . . . to aim for/to aspire to
esforzarse porque to make an effort	*querer/desear que* to want . . .
to . . .	*salvar de que* to rescue/save from . . .
evitar*/impedir que to avoid . . .	*ser necesario que* to be necessary that . . .
exigir* que to require that . . .	*suplicar que* to implore to . . .
hacer falta* que to be necessary that . . .	*vigilar que/asegurarse de que* to make sure
insistir/empeñarse en que to insist on . . .	that . . .

§ Not *decir de*, which is not Spanish: cf. French *dire à quelqu'un de faire quelque chose* = *decirle a alguien que **haga** algo* 'to tell someone to do something'. However *decir de* occurs in popular speech in the Southern Cone.

But there are many alternative ways of expressing the ideas associated with these verbs, e.g. by using adjectives, as in *es necesario/deseable que . . .* 'it's necessary/desirable that . . .', or nouns, as in *la petición/obligación de que . . .* 'the request/obligation that . . .', and these also require the subjunctive when they are followed by *que*, e.g. *su insistencia en que contestaran/contestasen en seguida* 'his insistence on their replying immediately'. Examples:

Quiero que estudies más	I want you to study more
Se esforzaba porque los demás vivieran/viviesen en mejores condiciones (*esforzarse por* 'to make an effort to . . .')	He strove to ensure that the others lived in better conditions
Organicé que todas nos vistiéramos como ellas (A. Mastretta, Mexico, dialogue)	I arranged it so that all of us women should dress like them
Soy partidario de que lo publiquen	I support their publishing it
Esto dio como resultado que no le hicieran/hiciesen caso	The upshot of this was that they ignored him/her
Me salvé de puro milagro de que los ladrones me mataran/matasen	By a sheer miracle I avoided being killed by the thieves
Cierta impaciencia generosa no ha consentido que yo aprendiera a leer (J. L. Borges, Argentina)	A certain generous impatience did not allow me to learn to read
No puedes pretender que cambien las cosas (J. Aldecoa, Spain, dialogue)	You can't try to change things
El primer paso, le dijo, era lograr que ella se diera cuenta de su interés (G. García Márquez, Colombia)	The first thing to do, she said to him, was to get her to notice his interest
Nadie impidió que Hemingway escribiera y publicase sus libros (G. Cabrera Infante, Cuba)	Nobody prevented Hemingway from writing and publishing his books
Hay que evitar que ellos se enteren	We have to avoid them finding out
Es necesario/imprescindible que lo reciban para mañana	It is necessary/essential that they receive it by tomorrow

Notes

(i) As was mentioned earlier, a noun phrase like *la decisión de que* 'the decision that', *la orden de que* 'the order that', *el deseo de que* 'the wish that', etc., can replace the main verb: *la orden de que se apagaran/apagasen las luces* 'the order for the lights to be turned off', *el anhelo de que Dios exista* 'the longing for God to exist', *la idea era que las chicas ayudasen/ayudaran a los chicos* 'the idea was that the girls should help the boys', *la petición de que se la indultara/indultase no llegó a tiempo* 'the petition for her reprieve didn't arrive in time'. When such a noun phrase immediately precedes *que*, *de* is inserted: *la necesidad **de** que nos mantengan informados* 'the need for them to keep us informed'. See 33.4.2 for details and exceptions.

(ii) Some verbs may or may not imply 'influence', according to their meaning. They take the subjunctive only when an order or wish is implied: *decidió que lo **firmaran/firmasen*** 'he decided that they should sign it', *decidió que lo **habían firmado*** 'he decided (i.e. 'came to the conclusion') that they had signed it', *dijo que se **terminara/terminase*** 'he said (ordered) that it should be finished', *dijo que se **había terminado*** 'he said (i.e. 'announced') that it was finished'; and likewise *establecer que* 'to stipulate that' (subjunctive)/'to establish the truth that' (indicative), *pretender que* 'to try to'/'to aim at'/'wish that' (subjunctive)/'to claim that' (indicative), *escribir* 'to write that' (indicative) 'to write instructing that' (subjunctive).

(iii) Statements of 'hope' are discussed at 16.11.3.

16.5.2 Use of the infinitive with verbs of 'influence'

Some of the verbs listed under 16.5.1, and certain other verbs of influence not mentioned so far, may appear with an infinitive construction in the following circumstances (for *pedir* and similar verbs of requesting, see 16.5.3):

(a) if the subject of the main clause and the subject of the subordinate clause are co-referential, i.e. they refer to the same person or thing (see also 18.3 for more remarks on this use of the infinitive):

Quiero hacerlo but *Quiero que **tú** lo hagas*	I want to do it/I want you to do it
No se deja pensar en ella	He doesn't let himself think of her
No pude evitar caerme (but) *No pude evitar que se cayera/cayese*	I couldn't help falling (but) I couldn't stop him/her falling
Ya has logrado enfadarme/Ya has logrado que me enfade	Now you've managed to make me angry
Pidió ir/Pidió que fueran/fuesen (but see 16.5.3)	He asked to go/He asked them to go

(b) In impersonal constructions (i.e. when there is no identifiable subject):

Hacía falta conseguir más gasolina	It was necessary to get more petrol/US 'gas'
Se evitaba hablar de ellos	People avoided talking about them
Se exigía presentar los documentos	The documents were required to be presented/Presentation of the documents was required
Esto obliga a pensar que . . .	This obliges one to think that . . .

(c) With certain verbs, even when they are not impersonal and have different subjects. These are verbs that can be constructed with an indirect object, as in *te ayudaré a **conseguir**/a que **consigas** lo que quieres* 'I'll help you to get what you want'.

Many of these are always followed by the preposition *a*, and the infinitive is almost always then used in preference to the subjunctive. The most common of these verbs are:

acostumbrar a to get used to	*enseñar a* to teach to	*mandar a* to send
ayudar a to help to	*forzar a* to force to	someone to do
autorizar a to authorize to	*impulsar a* to impel to	something
animar a to encourage to	*incitar a* to encourage to	*obligar a* to oblige to
condenar a to condemn to	*inducir a* to persuade to	*persuadir a* to persuade to
contribuir a to contribute to	*instar a* to urge to	*retar a* to challenge to
convidar a to invite to	*invitar a* to invite to	*tentar a* to tempt to
desafiar a to challenge to		

Thus we can say:

Le acostumbré/animé/autoricé/ayudé a hacerlo/a que lo hiciera/hiciese	I accustomed/encouraged/allowed/helped him/her to do it
Le condené/desafié/enseñé/forcé/impulsé/incité a hacerlo/a que lo hiciese/hiciera	I condemned/challenged/taught/forced/impelled/incited him to do it
Le induje/invité/mandé/obligué/persuadí/reté/tenté a hacerlo/a que lo hiciera/hiciese	I induced/invited/sent/obliged/persuaded/challenged/tempted her to do it

Verbs followed directly by *que* (i.e. that are not followed by *a*) can be divided into two categories. The following are usually followed by the infinitive, although the subjunctive is also found:

consentir to allow   *impedir* to prevent   *permitir* to allow/
dejar to let   *mandar* to order   to permit
hacer to make (i.e. cause to)   *ordenar* to order   *prohibir* to forbid

Examples:

Le dejó/hizo hacerlo/que lo hiciera/hiciese	She let/made him do it
Le impidió hacerlo/que lo hiciese/hiciera	She prevented him/her from doing it
Le mandó/permitió/prohibió hacerlo/que lo hiciera/hiciese	He ordered/allowed/prohibited her from doing it
Déjanos a los hombres conversar en paz (M. Vargas Llosa, Peru, dialogue)	Leave us men to talk in peace
La dosis de vanidad que todos tenemos dentro hizo que me sintiera el hombre más orgulloso de la Tierra (Che Guevara, quoted in *Granma*, Cuba)	The dose of vanity that we all have within us made me feel the proudest man on Earth
Los gritos y las piedras no me amedrentarán, puesto que estos actos sólo hacen perder la confianza en la democracia (President Eduardo Frei in *La Época*, Chile)	Shouts and stones will not make me afraid, since these actions only make one lose confidence in democracy
Irala me convidó a acompañarla (J. L. Borges, Argentina, dialogue; *a que la acompañara* also possible)	Irala invited me to accompany her
Había ordenado retirarse a todas sus sirvientas (A. Gala, Spain; or . . . *a todas sus sirvientas que se retirasen/retiraran*)	She had ordered all her ladies-in-waiting to withdraw

Finally, there is a series of verbs that are in a transitional state. The conservative construction is with the subjunctive and this is safer for foreigners, but the infinitive construction is frequently heard colloquially and is creeping into newspapers. Such verbs are:

aconsejar to advise   *pedir* to ask (but see 16.5.3)   *recomendar* to recommend
obstaculizar to hinder   *proponer* to propose   *sugerir* to suggest

*Te propuse **hacerlo**/que lo hiciéramos/hiciésemos*	I suggested to you that we should do it
*Te confieso que te propuse **fugarnos*** (A. Bryce Echenique, Peru, dialogue)	I admit that I suggested to you that we should elope
*Además, aprende de Octavia, a quien una vez **le sugerí pasar** a la otra parte* (ibid.)	Moreover, learn from Octavia, to whom I once suggested that she should go over to the other side
*Incluso las radioemisoras aconsejaron con insistencia a los capitalinos **abstenerse** de salir* (*La Jornada*, Mexico)	Even the radio stations strongly advised residents of the capital to avoid going out

Notes

(i) Some of these verbs can appear without an object in their main clause where English requires a 'dummy' object like 'one' or 'people': *un delgado vestido que impedía **llevar** nada bajo él/ . . . que se **llevara/llevase** nada debajo de él* 'a thin dress that prevented **one** from wearing anything underneath it', *que hagan respetar los derechos humanos* (*El Tiempo*, Colombia) 'let them get **people** to respect human rights', *esto permite pensar que . . .* 'this allows one to think that . . .'.

(ii) When the object is inanimate and the subject is human the subjunctive should be used. One can say *la hiciste llorar* 'you made **her** cry', but not **se puede hacer un texto significar cualquier cosa* for . . . *hacer que un texto signifique cualquier cosa* 'one can make a text mean anything' (impersonal *se* counts as a human subject); *el experto técnico puede hacer que el acompañamiento se oiga menos* 'the technical expert can make the accompaniment sound less loud' but not * . . . *puede hacer al acompañamiento oírse menos*.

When both subject and object are inanimate it seems that either construction is possible, although the safe option is the subjunctive: *el embalse permite que las aguas del río alcancen unos niveles adecuados* (possibly *permite a las aguas alcanzar . . .*) 'the dam allows the water of the river to reach suitable levels', . . . *vientos flojos que harán bajar las temperaturas* (Radio Nacional de España, 20-3-97) '. . . light winds that will cause temperatures to fall.'

16.5.3 Use of the infinitive with *pedir* and verbs of similar meaning

Pedir and other verbs of similar meaning, e.g. *rogar* 'to request', seem to be in a complex transitional state with respect to the use of the infinitive. They may appear in certain requests with the infinitive when the subjects are identical – *pidió* **hablar** *con el director* 'he asked to speak to the director', *pidió* **verme** *a las seis* 'he asked to see me at six o'clock' – but these are best thought of as set phrases. They normally require the subjunctive when the subjects are different, as do other verbs of requesting: *pidió/suplicó/rogó que* **contestaran/contestasen** *cuanto antes* '(s)he asked/ implored/requested them to answer as soon as possible'. Nevertheless, when the subject of the main verb is impersonal *se*, the infinitive is found in public notices of the type *se ruega a los residentes no llevar las toallas a la piscina* 'residents are asked not to take towels to the swimming-pool'.

In other cases, use of the infinitive when the subjects differ is not normally accepted as correct in standard language, but it is heard in familiar Latin-American speech and sometimes appears in Latin-American writing: *piden restituir a empleados de Correos que fueron despedidos* (*La Prensa*, Panama) '(unions) ask for reinstatement of dismissed Post Office workers', normally . . . *piden que se restituya a los empleados . . .* ; *le pidió dejarlo solo con los varones* (G. García Márquez, Colombia) 'he asked her to leave him alone with the men', normally *le pidió que lo dejara/dejase solo*; *te pido exigir que te den lo que nos ofrecieron* (ibid., dialogue) 'I ask you to insist on them giving us what they offered us', usually *te pido que exijas que . . .* ; *hoy nos hemos reunido por lo del wáter y les ruego permanecer sentados hasta que se solucione el problema* (A. Bryce Echenique, Peru, dialogue) 'we've met today over the question of the lavatory and I ask you to remain seated until the problem is solved', usually . . . *que permanezcan sentados*.

This infinitive construction is rejected in Spain, but it is increasingly common in journalistic styles, especially headlines, e.g. ?*Amnistía Internacional pide al gobierno español presionar* (better *que presione*) *a Chile* (*El País*, Spain) 'Amnesty International asks Spanish Government to pressure Chile'. Moreover, sentences like ?*me pidió salir con él* 'he asked me to go out with him' are common in the informal speech of young Spaniards. This seems to be limited to this constantly occurring third-person singular dating formula: informants who thought that these forms were natural would not accept **nos pidieron ir con ellos al cine* for *nos pidieron que fuéramos/fuésemos con ellos*, or **les pedimos salir con nosotros* for *les pedimos que salieran/saliesen con nosotros*.

16.6 Emotional reactions and value judg(e)ments

16.6.1 Emotional reaction or value judg(e)ment + *que* + subjunctive

See also 26.4.2 for further remarks on the use and non-use of *de que* with such expressions.

In standard Spanish, the subjunctive is used in sentences of the pattern Emotional Reaction + *que* + Subordinate Verb. 'Emotional reaction' covers a vast range of possibilities including regret, pleasure, blame, displeasure, surprise, understanding, toleration, excusing, rejection, statements of sufficiency and insufficiency, importance, etc. It also includes value judg(e)ments like 'it's logical that . . .', 'it's natural that . . .', 'it's enough that . . .'. Examples:

*Es natural / comprensible que **esté** alterada*	It's natural/understandable for her to be upset
Que estuviera todo tal cual, era hasta cierto punto lógico (E. Lynch, Argentina; subordinate clause precedes main clause)	It was logical to some extent that everything was as it was
*Sería mejor que lo **hiciera**/**hiciese** de otra manera*	It would be better if he did it some other way
*No aguanto/**perdono** que me **hablen** de esa manera*	I can't stand them/anyone talking to me like that
Está mal que bromees con eso (M. Puig, Argentina, dialogue)	It's wrong to make fun of that
No podemos aceptar que unos pocos impongan a la gran mayoría sus intereses individuales (E. Frei in *La Época*, Chile)	We cannot accept that a few persons should impose their individual interests on the great majority
Es curioso que todos los asamblearios se fíen más de lo que escuchan por los auriculares (J. Marías, Spain)	It's curious that all conference members have more confidence in what they hear over their headphones
Basta que les des la mitad ahora	It's enough for you to give them half now
¡Qué rabia que no nos suban el sueldo!	It's so infuriating that we aren't getting a salary rise!
Estoy hasta el moño de que tengamos que ser siempre nosotras las que debamos recoger la mesa (C. Rico-Godoy, Spain)	I'm sick to death of the fact that it's always us women who have to clear the table
Andrés era el culpable de que me pasaran todas esas cosas (A. Mastretta, Mexico, dialogue)	It was Andrés's fault that all these things were happening to me

It is important in Spanish to differentiate between emotional reactions and value judg(e)ments on the one hand, and statements of fact like *es verdad que* 'it's true that', *es obvio/evidente que* 'it's obvious that', *es indiscutible que* 'it is beyond dispute that', *afirma/pretende que . . .* '(s)he claims that . . .'. The latter require the indicative, even though the distinction may sometimes appear arbitrary to English-speakers, particularly when they notice that *ser natural que* 'to be natural that' takes the subjunctive whereas *quejarse de que* 'to complain that' takes the indicative, despite seeming to be an emotional reaction; see note to 16.6.2. For statements like 'it is **not** true that', see 16.7.1.

Notes

(i) *Menos mal que* 'thank heavens that' takes the indicative: *menos mal que no se **ha** roto* 'thank heavens it's not broken'.

(ii) The form *mejor . . .* 'it would be best that . . .' is also followed by the indicative. This abbreviation of *sería mejor que* is very common in Latin America, but it is also heard in colloquial language in Spain: *mejor lo dejamos para más tarde* 'we'd better leave it for later'. Compare *sería mejor que lo **dejáramos/dejásemos** para más tarde* 'it would be better if we left it until later'.

(iii) In spontaneous language in Latin America (and to a lesser extent in some parts of Spain) an emotional reaction to a past, present or habitual event may be expressed by the indicative. This construction is sometimes seen in writing in Latin America, especially in Argentina:[6] *el innegable genio de Joyce era puramente verbal; lástima que lo* **gastó** *en la novela* (J. L. Borges, Argentina). 'Joyce's undeniable genius was purely verbal; a pity that he wasted it on the novel', *es curioso que uno no* **puede** *estar sin encariñarse con algo* (M. Puig, Argentina, dialogue) 'it's strange that one can't manage (lit. 'can't be') without getting fond of something', *me da lástima que* **terminó** (ibid., dialogue) 'I'm sorry it's ended', *me parece raro que este hombre* **baja** *y dice "Mire . . ."* (Venezuelan spontaneous speech, quoted DeMello, 1996, 367) 'it seems strange to me that this man should get out and say "Look . . ."', *se asombra de que todo el mundo* **tiene** *un ticket* (ibid.; Madrid speech) '(s)he's surprised everyone's got a ticket'.

This tendency is rather stronger with verbs followed by *de que*: see 16.6.2. Use of the indicative after emotional reactions and value judg(e)ments seems to be spreading in familiar speech in Spain, but it is not accepted in careful styles. It is, however, sometimes found in medieval and Golden Age texts.

(iv) English speakers should beware of over-using *si* 'if' in sentences involving a value judg(e)ment: *sería maravilloso* **que**/*si no hubiera/hubiese hambre en el mundo* 'It would be wonderful **if** there were no hunger in the world'.

(v) The subjunctive is still required when the main clause is deleted: *. . . pero que él diga eso . . .* (some phrase like *es increíble que . . .* having been deleted from the sentence) ' . . . that he should say that . . .'/' . . . that he should have the nerve to say that . . .'.

16.6.2 Further remarks on emotional reactions followed by *de que*

For further remarks on the use or non-use of *de que* after such expressions, see 26.4.2.

It was stated in 16.6.1 that the subjunctive is used with expressions of emotion and foreigners should respect this rule. But when the verb is followed by *de que* the indicative mood is sometimes heard in relaxed speech when the verb is in the present or past. This tendency should not be imitated by foreign students:

Me alegré de que (pensaban)/pensaran/ pensasen hacerlo	I was glad that they intended to do it
Se indignaba de que sus suegros (creían)/ creyeran/creyesen en la pena de muerte	(S)he was outraged that his/her in-laws believed in the death penalty

Note

Quejarse de que . . . 'to complain that . . .' seems to foreign learners to be an emotional reaction, but it is followed by the indicative: *se queja de que Berta la* **hace** *quedarse a dormir la siesta* (M. Puig, Argentina, dialogue) 'she complains about Berta making her stay in to sleep in the afternoon'. *Lamentar que* 'to regret the fact that' takes the subjunctive. *Lamentarse de que* 'to lament the fact that . . .' takes the subjunctive when it expresses an emotional reaction and the indicative when it merely makes a statement. *Protestar de que* 'to protest that' takes the indicative: *protestaba de que/se lamentaba de que el gobierno* **había** *subido los impuestos* 'he was protesting at/lamenting the fact that the government had raised taxes', *lamento que ustedes no me* **hayan** *comprendido* 'I regret that you did not understand me'.

16.6.3 *Lo* + emotional reactions

If a value judg(e)ment is expressed by a phrase involving the 'neuter article' *lo*, the rules for the use of the subjunctive are as follows:

---

[6] The phenomenon is reviewed in DeMello (1996, 2). Recordings of educated speech from eleven Hispanic cities suggest that colloquial language differentiates between value judg(e)ments accompanied by emotional reaction (subjunctive) and value judg(e)ments that merely inform the speaker of a fact (s)he didn't know (indicative). But he notes that the indicative is found in 57% of Latin-American sentences involving value judg(e)ments and only 36% in Spain. Literary language strongly prefers the subjunctive.

(a) *Lo lógico es que . . . / lo normal es que . . . / lo habitual / corriente es que . . .* are followed by a subjunctive:

Lo lógico / lo normal / lo habitual es que no venga	The logical thing / the normal thing / the usual thing is that he doesn't come
*En nuestro país, lo habitual es que en todo asunto en que una persona pobre reclama de algún abuso . . . **termine** con problemas mayores que aquellos por los cuales reclama,* (*La Época*, Chile);	In our country, the usual thing is that, in any matter over which a poor person complains about some abuse, (s)he ends up having worse problems than the ones (s)he is complaining about

(b) *Lo peor es que / lo mejor es que . . . / lo malo es que . . . / lo terrible es que . . . / lo molesto es que . . .*, etc., are followed by a subjunctive when the verb in the main clause points to an event still in the future:

*Lo peor será que no **venga** nadie*	The worst thing will be if no one comes
*Lo malo sería que no **terminaran / terminasen** el trabajo a tiempo*	The problem would be if they didn't finish the work on time
*Lo más provocante de la ley es que **provoque** una reacción violenta del gobierno cubano* (*La Jornada*, Mexico)	The most provocative thing about the law is that it may produce a violent reaction from the Cuban government

But if the main verb is timeless, habitual or in the past, the verb is usually in the indicative, although the subjunctive is also possible:

Lo malo fue que no terminaron el trabajo a tiempo	The bad thing was that they didn't finish the work on time
*Lo peor fue que no **vino** nadie*	The worst thing was that no one came
*Lo que me indigna es que la sociedad todavía **condena** los amores o amoríos entre una señora madura y un jovencito ,* (C. Rico-Godoy Spain)	What makes me mad is that society still condemns romances or love affairs between a mature woman and a young man
*Lo malo es que **soñé** nuevamente con Emilio* (M. Benedetti, Uruguay, dialogue)	The worst is that I dreamt of Emilio again
*Lo que más me sorprendió . . . fue que . . . se **habían** detenido y vuelto* (J. Marías, Spain)	What surprised me most . . . was that . . . they had stopped and turned round

Note

In some cases use of the subjunctive depends on the meaning: *lo increíble era que Pedro no lo **sabía*** or ***supiera/supiese*** 'the incredible thing was that Pedro didn't know about it'. Here there is a slight difference of meaning between moods: the indicative assumes that Pedro did not know, whereas the subjunctive leaves open the question whether he knew or not. The choice depends on whether the action denoted by the subordinate verb is a reality to the speaker. Compare: *lo peor es que mi padre nunca **dice** nada* 'the worst thing is that my father never says anything', and a possible reply to this: *sí, lo peor es que no **diga** nada* 'yes, the worst thing is that he doesn't say anything' (i.e. *if* that is the case). In the second example the speaker does not claim knowledge of the facts described by the first speaker. This subtle distinction will be found to operate in many examples of subjunctive use.

16.7 Subjunctive after denials

16.7.1 Subjunctive after denials

In sentences of the pattern Denial + *que* + Subordinate Clause, the subordinate verb is usually in the subjunctive:

Mayta negó que hubiera intervenido en el rapto (M. Vargas Llosa, Peru, dialogue; or *hubiese*)	Mayta denied he was involved in the kidnapping
Yo no he dicho que seas una histérica (C. Rico-Godoy, Spain, dialogue)	I never said you were a hysteric
Esto no significa que haya que esperar un cambio radical de actitud (J. Cortázar, Argentina)	This doesn't mean that one must expect a radical change of attitude
Fue tan sólo un segundo pero no creo que se le haya borrado a ninguno de los espectadores (J. Marías, Spain)	It was only for a second but I don't think any of the spectators has ever forgotten it
No ocurre/sucede que haya eclipse todos los días	It doesn't happen that there's an eclipse every day
No se trata de que tengas que quedarte todos los días hasta las nueve de la noche	It's not a question of your having to stay until 9 p.m. every day
*Pero nunca creí que Marta se **acostumbrara** a vivir en un pueblo* (M. Puig, Argentina, dialogue)	But I never thought Marta would get used to living in a small town
*Nunca pensé que **fueras** así* (A. Arrafut, Cuba, dialogue)	I never imagined you were like that

However, the subjunctive is sometimes optional after verbs of knowing or believing, depending on the degree of uncertainty involved. Choice of the subjunctive in such cases depends on the speaker's background knowledge. If one knows for a fact that X is a thief, one says *no confesaba que **había** robado el dinero* '(s)he didn't confess to stealing the money'. If X may be innocent one says *no confesaba que **hubiese/hubiera** robado el dinero*. For this reason, statements of ascertainable fact, e.g. *yo no sabía que la puerta **estaba** abierta* 'I didn't know the door was open' (it was) are more likely to take the indicative, and matters of opinion, e.g. *no creo que sea muy útil* 'I don't think it's very useful', are almost certain to take the subjunctive:

*Yo sabía que él estaba ahí/Yo no sabía que él **estaba** ahí* (concedes that (s)he was there)	I knew (s)he was there/I didn't know (s)he was there
*Yo no sabía que él **estuviera/estuviese** ahí* (suggests that the speaker is still not convinced (s)he was there)	I didn't know (s)he was there
*No es seguro que el gobierno **reduzca/reducirá** los impuestos fiscales*	It's not certain that the Government will lower income taxes
*Yo no creía/pensaba que **vendría***	I didn't think (s)he'd come

Notes

(i) The indicative is occasionally found after *negar que* and verbs of similar meaning, although this construction is unusual, especially in Spain: *niego que hubo bronca* (*Proceso*, Mexico; usually *hubiera*, *hubiese* or *haya habido bronca*) 'I deny there was a row', *¿también va Vd. a negar que los ingleses se lavan?* (J. Camba, Spain; the indicative is appropriate here because a denial would be unreasonable) 'are you also going to deny that the English wash?', *pero negaban tozudamente que transportaban marihuana en esta ocasión* (*Granma*, Cuba) 'but they stubbornly denied that they were carrying marihuana on this occasion', *rechaza que Dios existe*[7] (usually *exista*) '(s)he denies that God exists'.
(ii) Negative questions and negative orders take the indicative. See note (v).
(iii) *No ser que* and *no que . . .* are denials and are normally followed by the subjunctive, except that *no ser que* takes the indicative in questions: *no es que yo **diga** que es mentira* 'it's not that I'm saying that it's a lie', *no es que se dijeran grandes cosas* (J. Marías, Spain) 'it isn't that important (lit. 'great')

---

[7] Example from Navas Ruiz (1986), 69.

things were said', *no era que no hubiese pobres por toda la ciudad* (A. Mastretta, Mexico) 'it wasn't that there were no poor people all over the city', *no que yo sea más inteligente que ustedes* 'not that I'm more intelligent than you'. But *¿no será que no quiere hacerlo?* 'isn't it the case that he doesn't want to do it?', *¿no sería que no quedaban más?* 'wouldn't it be the case that there were none left?'

Exceptionally, *no ser que* is followed by the indicative, in which case the denial is more confident and assertive: *no era que tomaba posesión del mundo* (M. de Unamuno, Spain) 'it wasn't that he was taking possession of the world'.

The special formula *no sea que* 'lest'/'so that not . . .' takes the subjunctive: *págalo, oye, no sea que nos **denuncie** a la policía* 'listen, pay it, in case he reports (i.e. so he doesn't report) us to the police'.

(iv) Compare the different translations of *decir* in the following examples: *ha dicho que **venía*** '(s)he said (s)he was coming', *no he dicho que **venía*** 'I didn't say I was coming', *no he dicho que **viniera/viniese*** 'I didn't tell him/her to come'.

(v) Negative questions and negative orders do not amount to denials, so the indicative is used: *¿no es verdad que **ha** dicho eso?* 'isn't it true that he said that?', *¿no sientes que el corazón se te **ensancha** al ver esto?* (J. Ibargüengoitia, Mexico, dialogue) 'don't you feel your heart getting bigger when you see this?', *no digas que es verdad* 'don't say it's true', *no creas que esto **es** lo único que hacemos* (A. Mastretta, Mexico, dialogue) 'don't think that this is the only thing we do', *pero no crean ustedes que me vio* (C. Rico-Godoy, Spain, dialogue) 'but don't get the idea that he saw me'.

16.8 Statements of doubt

Dudar que takes the subjunctive, but used in the negative it is followed by an indicative when it really means 'to be sure that':

*Dudo que **sea** verdad*	I doubt whether it's true
*No dudo que **sea** verdad lo que dices*	I don't doubt whether what you say is true (tentative remark)

But

*No dudo que **es** verdad lo que dices*	I don't doubt (i.e. 'I'm convinced') that what you say is true
*No dudo que **vendrá/venga***	I don't doubt he'll come
*Dudo que yo **pueda** venir mañana/Dudo poder venir mañana* (infinitive possible since the verbs are in the same person)	I doubt I can come tomorrow
*No hay duda que ella **puede** ser discutida* (M. Vargas Llosa, Peru; Spain *no hay duda de que . . .*)	There is no doubt that it can be debated

16.9 Statements of fear

Temer/tener miedo de que 'to fear' and other statements of similar meaning usually take the subjunctive or a future indicative tense (including future time expressed by *ir a* 'to be going to . . .') or, if they refer to the past, a past subjunctive or an indicative future in the past. For *temerse que* see note (ii):

*Temo que le **moleste**/Temo que le va a molestar/**molestará**/le **vaya** a molestar*	I'm afraid it may upset him/her
*Temíamos que le **molestara/molestase/molestaría**/Temíamos que le **iba/fuera** a molestar*	We were afraid it would upset him/her
*Yo tenía miedo de que te **hubieras** ido* (G. Cabrera Infante, Cuba, dialogue)	I was scared that you'd gone
*. . . para no ver el mar por la escotilla porque nos da miedo de que **entre*** (E. Poniatowska, Mexico)	. . . so as not to see the sea through the hatchway, because we're afraid it'll come in

The subjunctive is always used if the main verb is negated: *no temía que me fuera/fuese a atacar* 'I wasn't afraid he/she/it was going to attack me'.

Notes

(i) Use of redundant *no* (see 23.2.4) instead of *que* after *temer(se)* changes the meaning: the subjunctive is then obligatory. Compare *temo que no te **va** a gustar* 'I'm afraid you're not going to like it' and redundant *no* in *temo no te **vaya** a gustar demasiado* 'I'm afraid in case/lest you're going to like it too much', *temo no te **vayas** a enfadar* 'I'm afraid in case/lest you get cross'.

(ii) *Temerse que* usually means little more than 'I'm sorry to say that . . .' and it therefore takes the indicative: *me temo que no **he** sido muy delicado* 'I fear I haven't been very discreet', *de eso me temo que no **puedo** hablarte* (L. Sepúlveda, Chile, dialogue) 'I'm afraid I can't talk to you about that.'

(iii) *Temer que* may also be found with the indicative when it refers to timeless or habitual actions: *temo que la verdadera frontera la **trae** cada uno dentro* (C. Fuentes, Mexico, dialogue) 'I fear that each one of us carries the real frontier inside ourselves', *empezaba a temer que las imágenes de los dos mundos . . . **pertenecían** a dos caras de la misma moneda* (J. Aldecoa, Spain) 'I was beginning to believe that the images of the two worlds . . . belonged to two sides of the same coin'.

16.10 Subjunctive after 'the fact that . . .' and after other noun phrases

16.10.1 'The fact that . . .'

There are three common ways of translating 'the fact that': *el hecho de que, el que,* and *que*; the latter two items have various other meanings, for which see the Index.

(a) With all of these the subjunctive is used whenever any kind of value judg(e)ment or emotional reaction is involved, or whenever any idea of cause or influence is involved:

*(El) que no **diga** nada no debería afectar tu decisión*	The fact that he says nothing shouldn't affect your decision
*No hay duda de que el hecho de que me **hayan** dado el Nobel va a dar mayor resonancia a todo lo que diga y haga* (G. García Márquez, Colombia)	There is no doubt that the fact that they've given me the Nobel Prize will give more weight to everything I say and do
*Lo que me hace insoportable tu vanidad es el hecho de que **hiera** la mía* (cartoon by J. Ballesta in *Cambio16*, Spain)	What makes your vanity unbearable is the fact that it wounds mine
*El que yo **escriba** un diario se debe también a Virginia* (J. J. Arreola, Mexico, dialogue; in Spain *diario* = *la agenda*)	The fact that I keep a diary is also due to Virginia
*Que tres aviones se **destrocen**, se **desplome** un tren, . . . **arda** una discoteca, y todo en menos de un mes quizá sea simplemente casualidad* (*Cambio16*, Spain)	The fact that three aeroplanes/(US 'airplanes') are destroyed, a train plunges into a ravine . . . a discotheque catches fire, and all in less than a month, is perhaps pure chance

(b) The indicative is required when the main verb is a verb of knowing or perceiving (e.g. *enterarse de* 'to find out', *darse cuenta de* 'to realize'). When *el hecho de que* is preceded by a preposition it also almost always takes the indicative:

*Se ha dado cuenta del hecho de que **tiene** que trabajar para vivir*	(S)he has realized (s)he has to work in order to live

*Le disgustaría que usted no viniera sólo/solo por el hecho de que **viene** él*	(S)he would be upset if you didn't come only because he was coming
*Que el poder **tiende** al abuso . . . no debe escandalizar a nadie (El País)*	That power tends to abuse is a . . . fact that should scandalize no one
*Quizá tenga ello también algo que ver con el hecho de que la actividad artística misma **está** moviéndose ahora hacia la recuperación de esa funcionalidad (Cambio16, Spain)*	Perhaps it may also have something to do with the fact that artistic activity itself is moving now towards recovering that function

(c) In some cases the subjunctive and indicative appear to be interchangeable. We can detect no difference of meaning between the following alternatives, but foreigners will not go wrong if they apply the rules set out in (**a**) and (**b**):

*Le molesta el hecho de que no **venga/viene** a verlo/le*	The fact that she doesn't come to see him annoys him
*No le daba importancia al hecho de que él no le **hacía/hiciera/hiciese** caso*	(S)he didn't mind the fact that he paid her/him no attention
*No quiero que el hecho de que te **conozco/ conozca** sea un obstáculo*	I don't want the fact that I know you to be an obstacle
*El hecho de que no me **veía/viera/viese** me hacía sentirme seguro*	The fact that she couldn't see me made me feel safe

Note

El que 'the fact that' must be differentiated from *el que* 'the person that'. Sometimes only context makes the sense clear: *el que haya dicho eso no sabe lo que dice* 'the person who/whoever said that doesn't know what (s)he's talking about', *el que haya dicho eso no tiene importancia* '**the fact** that (s)he said that has no importance'.

16.10.2 Subjunctive after other noun phrases used as subordinators

When a noun phrase replaces a verb phrase it is normally connected to a following subordinate clause by *de que*: compare *esperamos **que** llueva* 'we hope it will rain' and *la esperanza **de que** llueva* 'the hope that it will rain': see 33.4.2 for more detailed discussion of the use of *de que* after nouns.

In general the mood of the subordinate verb after such noun phrases is governed by the rules that would affect verb phrases of the same meaning, i.e. *la posibilidad de que . . .* 'the possibility that . . . ' requires the subjunctive because *es posible que . . .* 'it's possible that . . . ' does. However, there is a series of miscellaneous noun phrases after which choice between the subjunctive and indicative is determined by meaning. Two factors may combine or operate independently to invoke the subjunctive: (**a**) the type of verb in the main clause, (**b**) the reality or non-reality of the event expressed by the subordinate clause.

(a) In the following examples the verb in the main clause is of a type (emotional reaction, possibility, etc.) which would itself require the subjunctive:

*Le contrarió la casualidad de que **encontrase/ encontrara** ahí a su primo*	(S)he was annoyed by happening to find his/her cousin there
*No podía soportar la idea de que no le **dieran/ diesen** el puesto*	He couldn't stand the idea of not getting the job

(b) In the following sentences the indicative is used because the subordinate verb indicates an established fact or reality, even though in some cases the person affected may not yet know the truth of the situation:

*Siempre daba la casualidad de que no **llegaban** a tiempo*	It always happened that they never arrived on time (habitual fact)
*Se tenían que enfrentar con el problema de que no **tenían** dinero*	They had to face up to the problem of not having any money (fact)
*Consiguió que aceptara la idea de que no le **darían** el puesto*	(S)he managed to get him to accept the idea that they wouldn't give him/her the job (i.e. accepting a fact)
*Tengo la convicción de que no **hace** nada*	I'm convinced (s)he doesn't do anything (knowledge)
*Se encontró con la sorpresa de que **estaba** de mal humor*	(S)he was surprised to find that (s)he was in a bad mood (factual)
*Le atormentaba la obsesión de que su mujer le **engañaba***	He was tormented by the obsession that his wife was being unfaithful to him (factual, as far as he knows)

(c) There remains a small number of cases in which the choice between subjunctive and indicative is either more or less optional or is dictated by some principle so obscure that we cannot explain it. The following examples must speak for themselves:

*Tuve la suerte de que no me **viera**/**vio***	I was lucky in that he didn't see me (on that occasion; factual, but subjunctive more usual)

But

*Tenía la suerte de que no me **veía***	I was lucky in that he didn't see me (on one or several occasions; indicative only)
*Tenía siempre la preocupación de que le **iba**/**fuera** a pasar algo*	She always worried that something might happen to her
*Vivía con la pesadilla de que **perdería** su dinero*	He lived with the nightmare of losing his money (indicative only)
*Le animaba la ilusión de que lo **conseguiría***	She was encouraged by the dream of getting it (same subject for both verbs)
*Le animaba la ilusión de que ella lo **conseguiría**/**consiguiera**/**consiguiese***	(S)he was encouraged by the dream that (s)he would get it (different subjects)

16.11 Subjunctive after special verbs

16.11.1 Subjunctive after *creer, parecer, suponer* and *sospechar*

We said at 16.2.5b and 16.7.1 that expressions of belief + *que* take the indicative – *creo que Dios existe* 'I believe that God exists' – unless they are negated: *no creo que Dios exista* 'I don't believe God exists'. However, the subjunctive occasionally appears after these verbs even when they are affirmative. The meaning is then more hypothetical or hesitant, but the difference can barely be translated into English:

*Sospecho que **es**/**sea** mentira*	I suspect it's a lie
*Como si la Historia fuera una especie de saltamontes; y parece que lo **sea** pero en otro sentido* (A. Sastre, Spain, dialogue)	As if History were a sort of grasshopper; and it seems that it is, but in a different sense
*¿Por qué estás así? Parece que te **estuvieras** ahogando* (E. Bryce Echenique, Peru, dialogue)	Why are you like that? It looks as though you were drowning

Use of the subjunctive to make a question ironic (i.e. it expects the answer 'no') seems to be confined to Latin-American Spanish:

*¿Usted cree que esto **ayude**?* (Manuel Puig,   Do you really think that this helps?
Argentina, dialogue; incredulous tone)
*¿Usted cree que yo **quiera** lastimar a esta niña*   Do you really think I want to hurt
preciosa? (A. Mastretta, Mexico, dialogue)   this lovely girl?

In Spain the indicative (*ayuda, quiero*) would have been used.

16.11.2 Subjunctive after *comprender/entender que, explicar que*

All of these verbs take the subjunctive when they are negated, e.g. *no entiendo que ahora me **pregunten** sobre la ponencia* (interview in *El País*, Spain) 'I don't understand why people are asking me now about the written statement/paper'.

Comprender takes the subjunctive when it means 'to sympathize with':

*Yo comprendo que los concejales **defendieran***   I understand the councillors (US
sus posiciones dentro del partido (Santiago   'councilors') defending their
Carrillo in *Cambio16*, Spain; or *defendiesen*)   positions inside the party

Explicar usually takes the indicative when it really means 'to state' or 'to say': *Manuel explicó que **había** estado enfermo* 'Manuel explained that he had been ill.' But the subjunctive is used when the verb means 'gives the reason why': *esto explica que las mutaciones de la literatura **estén** estrechamente ligadas a las innovaciones técnicas* 'this explains how changes in literature are intimately linked to technical innovations'.

16.11.3 Subjunctive after *esperar que*

Esperar 'to hope' may be followed by the subjunctive, by the future indicative, by the indicative of *ir a*, or by the conditional. The subjunctive is by far the commoner form when the verb means 'to hope'. Use of the indicative of these tenses suggests the meaning 'to expect':

*Espero que le **convenzas**/**convencerás***   I hope/expect you'll convince him
*. . . con la esperanza de que ella **haría** lo*   . . . in the hope that she'd do the same
mismo (C. Fuentes, Mexico)
Por un momento la invadió la esperanza de que   For a moment she was overcome by
*su marido no **habitara** ya el reino de los vivos*   (lit. 'invaded by') the hope that her
(S. Pitol, Mexico; or *habitase*)   husband no longer dwelt in the
    realm of the living
*Espero que me **vas** a pagar*   I hope you're going to pay me

Notes

(i) *Esperar **a** que* and *aguardar **a** que* 'to wait for . . .' take the subjunctive: *yo estaba esperando/aguardando a que **fuera**/**fuese** otro el que lo **hiciera**/**hiciese*** 'I was waiting for someone else to do it.'
(ii) *No esperar que* always takes the subjunctive: *yo no esperaba que me **fuera** a escribir* 'I didn't expect (s)he was going to write to me.'

16.12 The subjunctive after subordinators

16.12.1 Introductory

Subordinators are such words as 'before', 'after', 'provided that', 'because', 'when', 'unless', which introduce subordinate clauses. The general rule governing the mood of the verb after subordinators is: if the event referred to has or had occurred, the verb is in the indicative; if the event has or had not yet occurred, the verb is in the subjunctive.[8] Example:

*Se lo di cuando **llegó***	I gave it to him when he arrived
*Se lo daré cuando **llegue***	I'll give it to him when he arrives
*Yo iba a dárselo cuando **llegara/llegase***	I was going to give it to him when he arrived

It follows from this that a few subordinators, e.g. *antes de que* 'before', *para que/a que* 'in order that', always take the subjunctive because they always refer to something that has or had not yet happened. In some cases, e.g. *puesto que* 'since' (i.e. 'because'), *debido a que* 'due to the fact that', the event referred to has obviously already taken place and the indicative is obligatory (these subordinators are also discussed in Chapter 33). But in most cases the mood depends on the rule given above.

As in English, the subordinate clause may precede or follow the main clause: *después de que llegaron, empezamos a hablar/empezamos a hablar después de que llegaron* 'after they arrived we started talking'/'we started talking after they arrived'.

16.12.2 Replacement of the subjunctive by the infinitive after subordinators (see also 18.3)

The infinitive is used after certain subordinators when both verbs have the same subject. Compare *entré sin verla* 'I came in without seeing her' (same subject 'I') and *entré sin que ella me **viera/viese*** 'I came in without **her** seeing me' (different subjects). This is possible with the following subordinators:

(a) All those that include the word *de*,[9] e.g. *con tal de que* 'provided that', *antes de que*, 'before', *después de que* 'after', *bajo la condición de que'* 'on condition that', *con el objeto de que/a fin de que* 'with the intention of', *a cambio de que* 'in return for', *a pesar de que* 'despite', *en caso de que* 'in the event of', *el hecho de que* 'the fact that', etc. The *que* is dropped before the infinitive:

Lo haré antes de salir	I'll do it before I go out
Lo escribió con el objeto de criticar a sus colegas	(S)he wrote it with the intention of criticizing his/her colleagues
El hecho de saber cuatro lenguas me ayuda	The fact of knowing four languages helps me

---

[8] This does not refer to interrogative forms like *cuándo, dónde, cómo*, which are not subordinating conjunctions and are best thought of as different words. These words are followed by the indicative: *¿sabes cuándo **llega**?* 'do you know when (s)he's coming?', *¿te acordarás de dónde lo **has/habrás dejado**?* 'will you remember where you've left it?', *dudo que sepa cómo se **dice*** 'I doubt (s)he knows how one says it'. Note that *depender* and *según* are followed by non-interrogative forms: *depende de cuando **lleguen*** 'it depends when they arrive', *según quien **sea*** 'according to who it is'.

[9] Except *en vista de que* 'in view of the fact that', which is always followed by an indicative finite verb.

(b) *Sin que* 'without', *para que/porque/a que* 'in order to', *nada más* 'as soon as', *hasta que* 'until'. The *que* is dropped before an infinitive: compare: *entré sin hacer ruido* 'I came in without making any noise', *entré sin que me viera/viese* 'I came in without him/her seeing me'; *fue al dentista a que le sacara/sacase una muela* 'she went to the dentist for him to take one of her teeth out' and *fui al supermercado a comprar pan* 'I went to the supermarket to buy bread'. Compare also *cerré los ojos por no llorar* 'I shut my eyes so as not to cry', *estábamos cruzando la plaza de San Martín para tomar el colectivo* (M. Vargas Llosa, Peru, dialogue) 'we were crossing San Martín square in order to get the bus'.

In the case of the other subordinators, e.g. *cuando, mientras que* 'while', *en cuanto* 'as soon as', a subordinate finite verb cannot be replaced by an infinitive: *te lo diré cuando te vea* 'I'll tell you when I see you', never **te lo diré cuando verte*, which is not Spanish.

The subordinators that allow the infinitive construction are found with an infinitive in very informal speech even when the subjects are not the same, as in *?cómprame unas postales para mandarlas yo a mi madre* for *cómprame unas postales para que yo se las mande a mi madre* 'buy me some postcards for me to send to my mother'; but this is barred from careful language and should be avoided by foreigners.

16.12.3 Subjunctive with subordinators of purpose

(a) Phrases meaning 'in order to' such as *a fin de que, para que/porque, con el objeto de que, con el propósito de que, con la intención de que* and *a que* (which also has other meanings, e.g. *a que sí* 'I bet it's true'), are always followed by a subjunctive because they obviously point to an event that has or had not yet happened. (When the subjects of the verbs are identical the infinitive is used, e.g. *lo hice para fastidiarte* 'I did it to annoy you'; see 16.12.2b):

*Afuera, para que la solidaridad se **sienta**, hay que reunir un millar de personas* (M. Benedetti, Uruguay, dialogue)	Outside, so that people should sense the (level of) solidarity, one ought to assemble about a thousand people
*Me callé porque/para que no me **acusaran/acusasen** de metomentodo*	I kept silent so that they wouldn't accuse me of interfering
*He escrito una circular a fin de que se **enteren** todos*	I've written a circular so that everybody knows about it

Note

For the difference between *por* and *para* when both mean 'in order to', see 34.14.7.

(b) A number of phrases express negative intention or avoidance, i.e. 'so that not', and always take the subjunctive. They are awkward to translate now that the word 'lest' has fallen into disuse. These phrases do not allow replacement of the subjunctive by an infinitive:

*Trabaja más, no sea que te **despidan***	Work harder so that they don't (lit. 'lest they') fire you
Me subí al coche en tres minutos no se me fuera a arrepentir de la invitación (A. Mastretta, Mexico, dialogue)	I got into the car within three minutes lest he regretted/so that he wouldn't regret the invitation
No corras tanto, no vaya a darte un infarto	Don't hurry (lit. 'run') so much – you don't want to give yourself a heart attack

Devuélvele el dinero, no ocurra que nos **demande**	Give her back the money. We don't want her to sue us

16.12.4 Subjunctive with subordinators of cause and consequence

(a) The following are always followed by the indicative and do not allow replacement of the finite verb by an infinitive:

pues because (see 33.5.3) *ya que* since/seeing that *debido a que* due to the fact that
puesto que since *en vista de que* seeing that

Como, when it means 'since'/'because', is also usually followed by the indicative. It is discussed in detail at 33.5.2. When followed by the subjunctive *como* means 'if' and is discussed at 25.8.2. For the use of *como* use in sentences like *hazlo como quieras* 'do it as/how you like', see 16.12.5b. *Cómo* means 'how' in direct and indirect questions, and is best thought of as a different word: see 24.7.

Invítame ya que/puesto que **tienes** *tanto dinero/***Como** *tienes tanto dinero me puedes invitar* (in this meaning *como* must appear at the head of the clause; see 33.5.2 for further discussion)	Since you have so much money you can pay for me

(b) *Porque* is usually followed by an indicative but requires the subjunctive when it means 'just because'/'only because' or 'not because' and the main verb is negated. Sometimes it can be preceded by *sólo/solo*:

No lo hago porque tú lo **digas**	I'm not doing it just because *you* say so
Que nadie venga a nosotros porque **piense** *que va a obtener enchufes*[10] (*Cambio16*, Spain)	Let no one come to us (just) because they think that they'll get special favo(u)rs
Me perdí y llegué tarde. No porque yo me oriente mal, sino porque iba un poco sonada (C. Martín Gaite, Spain)	I lost my way and was late. Not because I have no sense of direction but because I was a bit high

But:

No lo hago porque tú lo **dices**	I won't do it **because** you say so/said I should
No lo hago sólo/solo porque tú lo **dices**	I'm doing it, but not simply because you're telling me to
No salgo contigo sólo/solo porque **tienes** *un Ferrari*	The fact that you have a Ferrari isn't the only reason I go out with you

Compare also: *sólo/solo porque* **tengas** *un Ferrari no voy a salir contigo* 'the fact that you have a Ferrari isn't a good enough reason for me to go out with you'.

The subjunctive is used after *bien porque . . . o/ya porque . . . o, fuera porque . . . fuera porque* meaning 'whether . . . or':

Bien/Ya porque **tuviera** *algo que hacer o porque* **estuviera** *cansado, el caso es que no estuvo muy amable con nosotros*	Whether he had something to do or whether he was tired, the fact is that he wasn't very kind to us

---

[10] *El enchufe*, literally 'plug', is also used in Spain to mean 'connections': *está muy enchufado* 'he's well connected', *el enchufismo* 'the old boy network', 'the inside favo(u)rs system', also *el amiguismo*.

. . . *ya fuese para apuntalar al Gobierno, ya para atacarlo (ABC Color*, Paraguay)	. . . whether in order to support the government, or to attack it
Fuera porque no sea costumbre de los arrabales estadounidenses, fuera porque a nadie le interesara demasiado su vida . . . (S. Puértolas, Spain; *bien porque . . . o porque* could have been used)	Whether because it wasn't usual in the suburbs of the USA, or because her life didn't interest people too much . . .

Note

If *porque* means *para que* (as it does after verbs like *esforzarse porque* 'to make an effort in order to . . .'), the verb is always subjunctive: *nos esforzamos porque/para que todos* **tengan** *agua limpia* 'we're making an effort to ensure that everyone has clean water', *estoy un tanto apurado y como impaciente porque* **pase** *el trago* 'I'm a bit worried and rather impatient for this unpleasantness to pass'.

(c) *De ahí que* 'hence the fact that' is almost always followed by a subjunctive:

De ahí que el Papa haya incluso presionado al nuevo Gobierno (El País, Spain)	This is why the Pope has even put pressure on the new Government
De ahí que visitar nuestra casa se convirtiese de vez en cuando en motivo de excursión (L. Goytisolo, Spain)	This is why visiting our house occasionally became the pretext for an excursion

(d) *Dado que* takes the indicative if it means 'given that', the subjunctive if it means 'if it is the case that':

dado que él **quiera** *hacerlo*	if it's the case that he wants to do it . . .
dado que es así . . .	given that this is the case . . .

16.12.5 Subjunctive with subordinators of result, aim and manner

The basic rule is that these take the indicative when they imply result and the subjunctive when they refer to an aim or intention. They do not allow replacement of the finite verb by an infinitive.

(a) When they indicate the result of an action the following take the indicative:

así que so (= 'as a result')
conque so (esp. in questions, e.g.
    ¿conque lo has hecho tú? 'so it was
    you that did it?')
de modo que in such a way that/so

de manera que in such a way that/so
de suerte que in such a way that/so
de forma que in such a way that/so

Tú tienes la culpa, de modo que/así que/ conque no te **puedes** *quejar*	You're to blame so you can't complain
Se han dispuesto helicópteros que sobrevuelen la zona, de manera que **podría** *ser factible hacerlo por esa vía (La Época*, Chile)	Helicopters have been ordered to over-fly the area, so it could be feasible to do it (i.e. 'enter the area') using that route

De modo que/de manera que/de forma que may also indicate aim or purpose, in which case they take the subjunctive. Unfortunately some varieties of English, especially British, no longer systematically clarify the difference between result and aim in this kind of sentence, so *lo hizo de modo que nadie se* **enteró** and *lo hizo de modo que nadie se* **enterase/enterara** may both be translated 'he did it so no one realized', despite the fact that they mean entirely different things in Spanish (the indicative implies that no one realized, the subjunctive that he *hoped* that no one would).

It seems that North Americans usually differentiate 'he did it so no one realized' (indicative) and 'he did it so no one **would** realize' (subjunctive), but translating from British English often poses the dilemma that there is no way of knowing whether the original implies result or aim. Examples:

*Compórtate de modo/manera que no **sospeche***	Behave so as to avoid him/her suspecting
*Entró silenciosamente de modo/manera que yo no la **oyera/oyese***	She came in quietly so that I wouldn't hear her
*Entró silenciosamente de modo/manera que no la **oí***	(S)he came in quietly so (i.e. 'and') I didn't hear her
*Alguien debería . . . modificar el sistema de enseñanza, de forma que el colegio de los niños **empezara** en junio* (C. Rico-Godoy, Spain)	Someone ought . . . to modify the educational system so that the children's school starts in June
*—Está sobreactuando —me dijo a mí en el pasillo, de forma que nuestra madre no le **pudiera** oír* (S. Puértolas, Spain)	'She's over-acting,' he said to me in the corridor so that our mother wouldn't hear her

(b) *Como* requires the subjunctive when it refers to an action which is or was still in the future:[11]

*Hazlo como **quieras***	Do it however you like
*Lo hizo como **quiso***	(S)he did it the way (s)he wanted
*Te dije que podías venir como **quisieras/ quisieses***	I told you could come any way you liked

For *como* + subjunctive meaning 'if' see 25.8.2; for *como* meaning 'as' (i.e. 'seeing that') see 33.5.2.

(c) *Como si* 'as if', *cual si* (literary) 'as if', and *sin que* 'without' always take the subjunctive (but for *como si* = 'just as if'/'it's just the same as when', see note ii):

*Me miró como si no me **viera/viese***	(S)he looked at me as if (s)he couldn't see me
*Las trató con gran familiaridad, como si las **viera** todos los días* (C. Fuentes, Mexico)	He treated them very familiarly, just as if he saw them every day
Uno . . . espera ese vistazo cual si fuera una maravilla (M. Benedetti, Uruguay)	One . . . awaits that vision as though it were a miracle
*Debes hacerlo sin que yo **tenga** que decírtelo*	You must do it without my having to tell you

Notes

(i) *Comme si* takes the indicative in French: *comme si elle avait quinze ans* = *como si **tuviera** quince años* 'as if she was fifteen years old'.

(ii) *Hacer como si* 'to act as if' and *ser como si* 'to be as if . . .' take the indicative when *como si* means the same as *como cuando . . .'. . .* the same as when . . .': *hicieron como si no se enteraban* (S. Puértolas, Spain) 'they acted as if they didn't understand', *es como si/cuando no **puedes** respirar y te asustas* 'it's the same as when you can't breathe and you get scared', *el niño pasa de todo, como si le llevo a una manifestación en favor del divorcio . . . o contra los bocadillos de calamares* (M. Vázquez

---

[11] In literary styles, *como* is occasionally found with the *-se* or *-ra* forms when it refers to a past action: *como se diese/diera cuenta de que . . .* 'as/when he realized that . . .'.

Montalbán, Spain, dialogue) 'my little boy doesn't worry about anything: it's the same whether I take him on a march in support of divorce or against squid sandwiches'.

Como si ... is also found colloquially in Spain with the indicative to mean 'even if': —*No iré hasta las ocho.* —*Como si no* **vienes**, *a mí me da igual* (Spain, colloquial) '"I won't come until eight o'clock." "Even if you don't come it's the same to me."'

(iii) *Tan* ... *como que* ... 'such ... as that ...' takes the subjunctive: *dos héroes como nosotros no pueden retroceder por cosas tan sin importancia como que le* **coma** *a uno un gigante* (children's story book, Spain) 'two heroes like us can't turn back because of such unimportant things as being eaten by a giant' (lit. 'as that a giant eats one').

(iv) *Como que*, which can also mean 'as if', takes the indicative: *últimamente lo he venido notando preocupado, como que desea comunicarme algo* (J. J. Arreola, Mexico, dialogue) 'lately I've been noticing that he's preoccupied, as if he wanted to tell me something'.

16.12.6 Subjunctive with subordinators of possibility (words meaning 'perhaps' are discussed at 16.3.2)

En caso de que and *en el caso de que* call for the subjunctive:

En caso de que no **esté**, *llámame*	If she's not in call me
Esperaremos dos minutos para darle tiempo de ponerse cómodo, en el caso de que se **esté** *usted duchando* (A. Bryce Echenique, Peru)	We'll wait two minutes for you to make yourself comfortable if it should happen that you're having a shower
Las puse en la maleta en caso de que las **necesitaras/necesitases**	I put them in the suitcase in case you you needed them

But *por si* usually (but not invariably) takes the indicative, although *por si* **acaso** may take either mood:

Llévate el paraguas por si (acaso) **llueve/** **lloviera/lloviese**	Take the umbrella in case it rains
Está apuntando hacia la otra acera, por si **hay** *un ataque por retaguardia* (J. Ibargüengoitia, Mexico, dialogue)	He's aiming at the other pavement/(US 'sidewalk') in case there's an attack from the rear
Por si fuera poco ... (set phrase)	As if this wasn't enough ...
Conviene que vayas enterado por si alguien te **pidiera** *una aclaración* (E. Mendoza, Spain, or *pidiese*)	It would be best if you were informed (lit. 'went informed') in case anyone asks you for an explanation

Note

Suponiendo que 'supposing that' requires the subjunctive: *suponiendo que* **venga**, *¿le vas a dejar entrar?* 'supposing he comes, are you going to let him in?'

16.12.7 Subjunctive with subordinators of time

a medida que/ *según/conforme*	as	*en cuanto/nada más/* *apenas/tan pronto como/*	as soon as
antes (de) que	before	*nomás que* (Lat. Am.)	
cuando	when	*hasta que*	until
desde que	since	*mientras que*	as long as
después (de) que	after	*siempre que*	every time

These include such words and phrases as the following:

After subordinators of time the subordinate verb is in the subjunctive when its action is or was still in the future. Students of French and Italian must resist the temptation to use the future tense after these subordinators. Compare *je lui donnerai son livre quand il* **arrivera**, *gli darò il suo libro quando* **arriverà** and *le daré su libro cuando* **llegue** 'I'll give him his book when he arrives':

*Llegamos antes de que **empezara**/**empezase*** *a nevar* (for *antes de que* see note i)	We arrived before it started snowing
*No sea muy dura con su empleada, después que se **haya** tranquilizado* (S. Vodanovic, Chile, dialogue; Spain *después de que* . . .)	Don't be very hard on your maid after she's calmed down (or possibly, 'after you've calmed down')
*Me saludará cuando **llegue***	She'll greet me when I arrive/she arrives
*Me saluda cuando **llega***	She greets me when she arrives (habitual)
*Tú conoces a mi prima. Cuando **venga** le diré que te lo cuente* (A. Arrafut, Cuba, dialogue)	You know my cousin. When she comes I'll tell her to tell you about it
*Iban a cenar cuando **llegaran**/**llegasen** los demás*	They were going to have supper when the rest arrived (i.e. they had not yet arrived)
*Las ideas se irán haciendo más y más claras en la medida en que nos **aventuremos** más y más por la senda que iremos construyendo* (C. Almeyda in *El País*)	The ideas will get increasingly clear as we venture further along the path we will be building
*Me doy cuenta, a medida que Rosita **pasa** mis notas a máquina, de que he reunido cerca de doscientas páginas* (C. Fuentes, Mexico)	I realize, as Rosita types out my notes, that I've assembled more than 200 sheets of paper
*tan pronto como **acabe** la huelga . . .*	as soon as the strike is over . . .
*tan pronto como **acabó** la huelga . . .*	as soon as the strike was over . . .
*En cuanto **pueda** me compraré un reloj* (M. Benedetti, Uruguay, dialogue)	As soon as I can, I'll buy a watch
*Nomás que **oscurezca** te vas por la carretera* (J. Ibargüengoitia, Mexico, dialogue; Spain *en cuanto oscurezca* . . .; for the Latin-American word *nomás* see 23.2.5)	As soon as it gets dark you go down the road . . .
*Apenas **pueda**, te llamo* (J. Asís, Argentina; *apenas* is discussed more fully at 23.5.7; see also note i)	As soon as I can, I'll ring you
*Hasta que no **llegue** a ser ministro no se quedará contento*	He won't be satisfied until he becomes a minister
*Hasta que no **llegó** a ser ministro no se quedó contento*	He wasn't satisfied until he became a minister
*Siempre que la **vea** se lo diré*	I'll tell her every time I see her

Notes

(i) Of these subordinators of time, only *antes de, después de, hasta* and *nada más* (and in Latin America *nomás*) can take an infinitive construction when the subjects of both verbs are identical. In the case of *nada más*, the subjects do not need to be identical: *me fui después de comer* 'I went after I had eaten', *hazlo antes de acostarte* 'do it before you go to bed', *trabajó hasta no poder más* 'he worked until he could work no longer', *la llamaré nada más llegar a casa* 'I'll call her as soon as I get home', *salí nada más entrar ella* 'I left as soon as she came in'. *Apenas* is heard with the infinitive in very informal speech when the subjects are identical, although this is stigmatized: *?lo hice apenas llegar a casa* (good Spanish *lo hice apenas llegué a casa*) 'I did it as soon as I got home'. The rest allow only a finite verb, indicative or subjunctive according to the rule given.

(ii) *Antes de que* is always followed by the subjunctive because it must refer to a subsequent and therefore future event. Both *antes de que* and *antes que* are correct, the former being more common in Spain. *Antes que* also means 'rather than' and must not be confused with *antes (de) que* 'before': *cualquier cosa antes que casarse* 'anything rather than get married'.

(iii) *Después (de) que* 'after' and similar phrases, e.g. *a los pocos días de que*, 'a few days after', *desde que* 'since', *luego de que* 'after', always take the subjunctive when they refer to an action still in the future. If they refer to a past action they should logically take the indicative, but in written Spanish the *-ra* and *-se* forms are quite common. (For a more detailed discussion see 14.10.3.)

(iv) *Mientras* 'as long as'/'while' is variable with respect to the subjunctive. When it means 'on condition that'/'provided that', the subjunctive is obligatory: *no irá a la cárcel mientras no robe* 'he won't go to prison provided/as long as he doesn't steal anything'. When it refers to simultaneous events in the past or the present, or to habitual events, the indicative is used: *ayer me arreglé el abrigo mientras oía la radio* 'yesterday I mended my coat while I listened to the radio', *siempre pongo la televisión mientras como* 'I always switch the television on while I eat'. When it refers to simultaneous actions in the future the subjunctive or indicative can be used: *mañana puedes hacer la comida mientras yo arreglo/arregle la casa* 'tomorrow you can do the cooking while I tidy the house'.

In all the above contexts *mientras que* may be heard instead of *mientras*, but students are advised to use *mientras* alone (see Seco, 1998, 296). However, when contrast is implied (i.e. when it means 'on the other hand'), the *que* is usual: *él es inaguantable mientras que ella es muy simpática* 'he's unbearable, while she's very nice'.

(v) *Nada más* is followed by an indicative when it means *sólo*: *sólo/nada más voy un momento a comprar el periódico* 'I'm just going out for a moment to buy a newspaper'.

16.12.8 Subjunctive with subordinators of condition and exception

They all call for the subjunctive. (For *si* 'if' and *como* when it means 'if' see 25.8.1 and 25.8.2). Those that include the word *de*, e.g. *con tal de . . .* , are used with infinitive when the subject of both verbs is identical, as explained at 16.12.2, e.g. *me lo llevaré a condición de no tener que leerlo* 'I'll take it on condition that I don't hFave to read it'.

(a) Condition. All the following mean 'provided that', 'on condition that':

con tal (de) que	*a condición de que*	*a cambio de que* (also 'in
siempre que (also 'whenever')	*con la condición de que*	return for')
siempre y cuando (emphatic)	*bajo (la) condición de que*	

*El Gobierno está dispuesto a negociar siempre que/siempre y cuando/con tal (de) que/a condición de que **sean** razonables*	The government is ready to negotiate provided they are reasonable
*. . . sin la condición previa de que se **anule** el contrato . . .* (*El País*, Spain)	. . . without the precondition that the contract should be cancelled . . .
*. . . siempre que no **haya** daño o riesgo para otros . . .*	. . . provided there is no danger or risk to others . . .
*Añadió cincuenta mil pesetas a la minuta a cambio de que yo **hiciera** esta llamada telefónica* (M. Vázquez Montalbán, Spain)	He added fifty thousand pesetas to my professional fees in return for my making this telephone call

(b) Exception (occasionally followed by indicative in cases discussed in note i). The infinitive cannot be used with these subordinators:

a no ser que unless	*a menos que* unless	*como no (sea que)* unless
salvo que unless/save that	*fuera de que* (less common)	(in suggestions)
excepto que unless/except that	unless	*como no fuera que* unless

*Me casaré contigo a no ser que/salvo que/como no sea que/a menos que **hayas** cambiado de idea*	I'll marry you unless you've changed your mind
*Íbamos de vacaciones en agosto salvo/a no ser que/como no fuera que yo **estuviera/estuviese** muy ocupado*	We took our holidays (US 'vacation') in August unless I was very busy

No sé qué sugerir. Como no (sea que) vayamos al teatro . . .	I don't know what to suggest unless we go to the theatre . . .

Note

Excepto/salvo que and *con la salvedad de que* are followed by the indicative when they mean 'except for **the fact that**': *ella hablaba mejor, excepto que/salvo que/con la salvedad de que* **pronunciaba** *mal las eñes* 'she spoke better/best, except (for the fact) that she pronounced the eñes badly'.

16.12.9 Subjunctive with subordinators of concession

There are several ways of saying 'although', of which *aunque* is the most common:

aunque	*siquiera*	*si bien*	*así*	*aun cuando*	*y eso que*

Words meaning 'despite the fact that' have a similar meaning:

a pesar de que	*pese a que* (literary)	*a despecho de que* (literary)

With the exception of *si bien que* and *y eso que*, which are always used with the indicative (see 33.6), these require the subjunctive if they point to an event which is or was still in the future. *Así* always requires the subjunctive when it means 'although'. Those that contain the word *de* may be constructed with an infinitive in the circumstances described at 16.12.2:

Es un valiente, no lo confesará así/ aunque le **maten**	He's a brave man: he won't admit it even if they kill him
No lo confesó aunque le **ofrecieron** *dinero*	He didn't confess although they offered him money
No lo confesaría aunque le **mataran/matasen**	He wouldn't confess it even if they killed him
A estas alturas de la campaña nadie aguanta un rollo de estos así le **den** *veinte duros* (M. Delibes, Spain, dialogue)	At this stage in the [election] campaign no one's going to put up with a lot of old nonsense like that even if they give them a hundred pesetas
. . . tienen que cumplir, así **caminen** *bajo la lluvia* (La Jornada, Mexico)	. . . they have to fulfil/(US 'fulfill') their mission, even if they walk in the rain
Vendieron la finca, a pesar de que el abuelo se **oponía**	They sold the estate, despite the fact that grandfather opposed it
Venderán la finca, a pesar de que el abuelo se **oponga**	They'll sell the estate, despite the fact that grandfather will/may oppose it
Dijeron que venderían la finca, a pesar de que el abuelo se **opusiera/opusiese**	They said they would sell the estate despite the fact that grandfather would/might oppose it
. . . pese a que muchos de quienes iniciaron la tarea ya no están ahora (ABC Color, Paraguay)	. . . despite the fact that many who began the task are no longer here now

Notes

(i) The subjunctive may be used with *aunque* to refer to past or habitual events. In this case it strengthens the concession, making it an equivalent to a strong 'even though': *jamás culparé a Octavia, aunque lo haya intentado alguna vez* (A. Bryce Echenique, Peru, dialogue) 'I'll never blame Octavia, even though I may have tried to sometimes', *aunque no te* **gusten** *las películas ésta/esta te va a gustar* 'even though you don't like films you'll like this one', *aunque* **sea** *español no me gustan los toros* 'even though I'm Spanish I don't like bullfights'.

(ii) When *siquiera* is used to mean 'although' (literary style) it requires the subjunctive: . . . *dos fuentes independientes . . . a las que se aludirá, siquiera* **sea** *vagamente* (*Libro de estilo de El País*, Spain) ' . . . two independent sources . . . which will be mentioned, even if in vague terms'.

16.13 Translating 'whether . . . or', 'however', 'whatever', 'whoever', 'whichever' and 'the more . . . the more . . . '

The phrases discussed in this section are often translated by the *forma reduplicativa*, i.e. constructions in which the subjunctive verb is repeated, as in ***digan*** lo que ***digan*** 'whatever they say', ***pase*** lo que ***pase*** 'whatever happens', *no hay salida para ti,* ***hagas*** *lo que* ***hagas***, *vayas a donde* ***vayas*** (C. Fuentes, Mexico, dialogue) 'there's no way out for you, whatever you do, wherever you go'. After a negative the second verb is sometimes omitted: *quieras o no (quieras)* 'whether you want to or not'.

16.13.1 'Whether . . . or'

The *forma reduplicativa* is used:

Lo único que tengo que hacer es informar sobre unos hechos escuetos, que son los que son, guste o disguste a unos u otros (*El Mundo*, Spain)	The only thing I have to do is to inform about certain simple facts, which are what they are whether certain people like it or not
Escuchaba las conversaciones con sus amigas, repararan o no repararan en mí (S. Puértolas, Spain)	I listened to her (lit. 'the') conversations with her women friends, whether they noticed me or not

The second verb is sometimes replaced by *hacer* or, in negative phrases, omitted altogether:

trabaje en una red, o lo ***haga*** *desde un PC en casa* . . . (Spanish computer manual)	whether you work on a network, or from a PC at home . . .
Estuviese o no enfermo, lo cierto es que no vino al trabajo	Whether he was ill/(US) 'sick' or not, the fact is he didn't come to work
Estaré de tu parte, tengas razón o no (la tengas)	I'll be on your side, whether you're right or wrong

16.13.2 'However'

Por mucho que/por más que + verb, *por mucho* + noun + verb, *por (muy)* + adjective + verb. Use of the subjunctive follows the usual rule: if the event referred to is or was a reality, the indicative is used: *por mucho que/más que se lo dijo, no lo hizo* '(s)he didn't do it however much she asked him/her', but *por mucho que se lo digas, no lo hará* 'he won't do it however much you ask him'. Further examples:

Por mucho calor que haga, no abrirá la ventana	However hot it gets she won't open the window
Por más que las esperanzas de Eulalia y su padre crecían, no lograban contagiar a Andrés (A. Mastretta, Mexico, dialogue; real event)	However much Eulalia's and her father's hopes grew, they didn't manage to inspire (lit. 'infect') Andrés
Por más que llueva no se le van a resucitar los novillos muertos (M. Puig, Argentina)	However much it rains, his dead steers won't come back to life
Por buena vista que uno tenga no alcanza a ver más que piedras (J. Ibargüengoitia, Mexico, dialogue)	However good one's eyesight is/may be, one can see nothing but stones

Notes

(i) The subjunctive may appear even though the action is a reality; the force of the concession is then stronger: *por mucho que/más que se lo dijera, no lo hacía* 'however often she told him, he didn't do it', *en Mendoza a esa hora cae el frío, por más sol que haya habido durante el día* (M. Puig, Argentina, dialogue; subjunctive, because it happens whether there was sun or not) 'the cold sets in at that time in Mendoza, however sunny it may have been during the day'.

(ii) To translate 'however it is', 'however it was', etc., either the *forma reduplicativa* is used or *como quiera que* + subjunctive, e.g. *. . . pero como quiera que sea, yo he comprado . . . una media docena por lo menos* (J. J. Arreola, Mexico) '. . . but however it is/but all the same, I've bought . . . at least a half a dozen', or *. . . sea como sea . . .*

16.13.3 'The more . . . the more'

Cuanto/a/os/as más . . . más is the standard formula. The general rule is applied: if the event is a reality the indicative is used:

Cuanto más coma más querrá	The more he **eats** the more he'll **want**
Cuanto más comía, más quería	The more he **ate** the more he **wanted**
Cuanta más leche eches, más espesará	The more milk you add, the thicker it'll get
Yo sabía que cuanto más bebiera/bebiese más me emborracharía	I knew that the more I drank, the drunker I would get

For the use of *mientras* in this construction, and, in parts of Latin America (e.g. Mexico), of *entre* instead of *cuanto*, see 5.11.

16.13.4 'Whatever'

The *forma reduplicativa* is normally used to translate 'whatever':

diga lo que diga	whatever he says
haga lo que haga	whatever she does
Den lo que den, siempre vamos al Metropolitan (E. Poniatowska, Mexico, dialogue)	Whatever's on (lit. 'whatever they give'), we always go to the Metropolitan cinema
Cómpralo sea como sea	'Buy it whatever it looks like' or 'buy it whatever the cost'
Dijo que lo compraría fuera como fuera/fuese como fuese	He said he'd buy it, whatever it was like

Comoquiera que sea and *comoquiera que fuera* could be used in the last two examples, but they are less usual. *Como quiera* is a less frequently seen alternative spelling.

Lo que + the subjunctive may also be used in some contexts:

Aquella novela o lo que quiera que fuese era muy difícilmente publicable (J. Marías, Spain)	That novel, or whatever it was, was very unlikely to be publishable
. . . por temor, por pereza o por lo que sea . . . (S. Puértolas, Spain)	. . . because of fear, laziness, or whatever . . .

Note

The English 'whatever' may mean 'whichever', in which case it is best translated by an appropriate tense form of *sea cual sea . . . .* This construction is preferred in written and spoken language to the rather stilted *cualquiera que* and *comoquiera que* (for a general discussion of *cualquiera* see 9.8): *las camelias, cualquiera que/sea cual sea su color, son bonitas* 'camellias are pretty whatever their colo(u)r'.

When 'whatever' means 'everything' it will usually be translated by *todo lo que* or *cuanto*: *trae todo lo que puedas* 'bring whatever/everything you can', *aprenderé todo lo que/cuanto pueda* 'I'll learn whatever/everything I can'.

16.13.5 'Whichever'

When this word means 'which', 'whichever one' or 'the one that' it is usually translated by *que* or *el que* + subjunctive (for more details on the subjunctive in relative clauses, see 16.14):

Escoge la maceta que más te guste	Choose whichever flowerpot you like most
—¿Cuál me llevo?— El que usted quiera	'Which should I take?' 'Whichever you like'

16.13.6 'Whenever'

Cuando with the subjunctive when the event referred to is or was still in the future, and the indicative in all other cases:

Vienen cuando quieren	They come whenever they like
Vendrán cuando quieran	They'll come whenever they like

Cuando quiera que is old-fashioned for *cuando*, but it is used as an occasional literary alternative for *siempre que*: . . . *cuando quiera que en la vida española se ponen tensos los ánimos* . . . (R. Pérez de Ayala, Spain, quoted by Seco, 1998, 139) 'whenever passions are stirred in Spanish life'.

16.13.7 'Anyone who . . .', 'whoever . . .'

Cualquiera que 'anyone who . . . ' cannot be replaced by the *forma reduplicativa*:

Cualquiera que te vea pensará que vas a una fiesta	Anyone who sees you will think you're going to a party

If 'anyone who . . . ' means 'those who . . . ', 'people who . . . ', a nominalizer plus the subjunctive is used, i.e. *quien* or *el que*:

El que/quien se crea eso está loco	Anyone who believes that is mad

Quienquiera . . . is also found. Seco (1998), 378, says it is, in Spain, exclusively literary, but the following example suggests that it survives colloquially elsewhere:

Quienquiera se crea eso está loco (G. Cabrera Infante, Cuba, dialogue; Spain *el que crea* . . . or *quien crea* . . .)	Anyone who thinks that is mad

But *quienquiera que sea* 'whoever it is' seems to be in free variation with the *forma reduplicativa*:

No abras la puerta, sea quien sea/quienquiera que sea	Don't open the door, whoever it is
. . . *íntimo amigo del Jefe del Gobierno, fuera el que fuese* (M. Vázquez Montalbán, Spain; or *quienquiera que fuera/fuese*)	. . . a close friend of the Prime Minister, whoever he happened to be

16.13.8 'Wherever'

Dondequiera or *forma reduplicativa*:

Dondequiera que voy/Vaya donde vaya me lo/le encuentro	Wherever I go I meet him

Dondequiera que vaya/Vaya donde vaya *me lo/le encontraré*	Wherever I go I'll meet him
Dondequiera que fuese/Fuese donde fuese, *me lo/le encontraba* (or *fuera* . . .)	Wherever I went I met him

Notes

(i) The *que* is sometimes omitted, e.g. *dondequiera se encuentren* 'wherever they're found', but this is censured by Seco (1998), 170.

(ii) *Adondequiera* should be used with verbs of motion when it means 'wherever . . . to': *adondequiera que vayan* 'wherever they go' or *vayan a donde vayan*.

16.14 Subjunctive in relative clauses

In this section nominalizers such as *el que* 'the one that', *quien* 'the one who', *aquellos que* 'those who', etc., are treated as relative pronouns. They are also discussed under Nominalizers at 36.1. See 16.13. for *cualquiera que, quienquiera que, cuandoquiera que, dondequiera*.

16.14.1 Subjunctive in relative clauses when the antecedent is not yet identified

Spanish uses the subjunctive in such cases to express a nuance that English usually ignores. Compare *los que **digan** eso* 'those who say that' (if anyone does) and *los que **dicen** eso* 'those who say that' (some do). The difference in Spanish is striking. Contrast *prefiero un coche que **tenga** cuatro puertas* 'I prefer a car with four doors' (i.e. any car), *prefiero ese coche que **tiene** cuatro puertas* 'I prefer that car with four doors'; *busco un médico que **sepa** acupuntura* (note: no personal *a*) 'I'm looking for a doctor (i.e. 'any doctor') who knows acupuncture', *conozco a un médico que **sabe** acupuntura* 'I know a doctor who knows acupuncture'. Further examples:

Me voy a casar con el primero que me lo
  pida
	I'm going to marry the first man who
	  asks me

*Haz lo que **quieras***	Do whatever you like

*. . . cualquier reacción que uno **pueda** tener*
  suena a sobreactuado (C. Rico-Godoy,
  Spain)
	. . . any reaction one might have sounds
	  like over-acting/sounds overdone

Me pregunto si hay alguien en el mundo a
  *quien no le **haya** ocurrido lo mismo*
  (J. Marías, Spain)
	I wonder if there is anyone in the world
	  to whom the same thing hasn't occurred
	  (i.e. 'hasn't had the same thought')

*¿Sabes de alguien que **tenga** apellido en este*
  país? (E. Sábato, Argentina, dialogue)
	Do you know anyone in this country
	  who has a surname (i.e. an illustrious
	  name)?

¿Habrá en la tierra algo sagrado y algo que
  *no lo **sea**?* (J. L. Borges, Argentina)
	Is there anything sacred on earth, and
	  anything that isn't?

*Dígame qué tienen que **esté** muy sabroso*
  (J. Ibargü engoitia, Mexico, dialogue)
	Tell me what you've got that tastes
	  really good

Mi trabajo consistía en buscar los libros que
  *las personas **solicitasen*** (R. Arenas,
  Cuba, dialogue)
	My work consisted in searching for
	  whatever books people asked for

Note

In literary styles, the subjunctive is common in relative clauses when the main clause is introduced by como 'like' or como si fuera/fuese 'as if it were . . .' . . . *como un ángel que **perdiera/perdiese** las alas* ' . . . like an angel that had lost its wings', *el sol se pone súbitamente – como si **fuera** un interruptor* *que lo apagara* (J. Marías, Spain; or *fuese*) 'the sun sets suddenly – as if it were a switch that had turned it off'.

16.14.2 Subjunctive in relative clauses when the existence of the antecedent is denied

If the antecedent does not exist the verb in the relative clause is in the subjunctive:

*No hay nadie que **sepa** tocar más de un violín a la vez*	There is no one who can play more than one violin at the same time
*No había mendigo a quien él no **diera**/ **diese** limosna*	There was no beggar to whom he wouldn't give alms
*No hay quien le **entienda***	There's no one who can understand him
*En realidad no existen culturas 'dependientes' y emancipadas ni nada que se les **parezca*** (M. Vargas Llosa, Peru)	In reality there are no 'dependent' and emancipated cultures or anything like them
*¿A quiénes conoces que se **vean** feas esperando un hijo?* (A. Mastretta, Mexico, dialogue; *se vean* = *estén* in Spain)	What women do you know who look ugly when they're expecting a baby?

16.14.3 Subjunctive in relative clauses when the main verb is in the future tense

The subjunctive is also normal when the verb in the main clause refers to the future:

*Seré yo el que **tenga** que solucionar mis propios problemas* (cf. *soy yo el que **tengo**/**tiene** que solucionar . . .*)	I'll be the one who has to solve my own problems
*No será hasta el primer Consejo de Ministros que se celebre tras las vacaciones estivales, cuando el Gobierno **apruebe** el proyecto de ley* (*La Vanguardia*, Spain; for the obligatory use of *cuando* here see 36.2.3)	It won't be until the first Cabinet Meeting to be held after the summer vacation that the government will approve the draft law

Compare French *j'apprendrai ce que je pourrai* (future indicative) and Spanish *aprenderé lo que **pueda*** 'I'll learn what I can'.

16.14.4 Subjunctive after the relatives *donde* and *cuanto* (for *dondequiera que* see 16.13.8).

The subjunctive is used if the reference is to a yet unknown or to a non-existent entity:

*Comeré en el pueblo donde me **pare***	I'll eat in **whichever** village I stop in
*Comí en el pueblo donde me **paré***	I ate in the village where I stopped
*Buscó una zona donde el mar **llegara** debilitado* (M. Vázquez Montalbán, Spain)	He looked for an area where the sea was coming in with less force
*Te daré cuanto/todo lo que me **pidas***	I'll give you anything you ask
*Le di (todo) cuanto/todo lo que me **pidió***	I gave her everything she asked

16.14.5 Subjunctive in relative clauses after superlative expressions

The subjunctive may appear in literary styles in relative clauses following superlative statements, but it is unusual in everyday written or spoken language:

*El mayor incendio que jamás se **ha**/**haya** visto*	The greatest fire ever seen
La mayor transacción con divisas fuertes que se	The largest hard-currency transaction

> *haya hecho en el Río de la Plata* (E. Sábato, Argentina)
>
> ... *y el aburrimiento general más importante que haya presenciado en mi vida* (A. Bryce Echenique, Peru)

> ever made in the River Plate region
>
> ... and the greatest general boredom I've ever witnessed in my life

Compare these less literary examples:

> *Eres la chica más simpática que he conocido*
>
> *Yo debía ser el extranjero más inteligente que madame Forestier había visto en su vida* (A. Bryce Echenique, Peru)
>
> *Dijo que era la mayor barbaridad que a nadie se le había ocurrido*

> You're the most likeable girl I've ever met
>
> I must have been the most intelligent foreigner Madame Forestier had seen in her life
>
> He said it was the greatest stupidity anybody had ever thought of

16.15 Subjunctive in main clauses

The subjunctive is primarily a feature of subordinate clauses, but it may appear in a main clause in certain circumstances.

16.15.1 Subjunctive with the imperative

(a) The subjunctive is used to form all negative imperatives: *no me hables* 'don't talk to me', *no se vayan ustedes* 'don't go away'.

(b) The subjunctive is used for affirmative (i.e. not negative) imperatives with the pronouns *usted* and *ustedes*: *guarden silencio* 'keep quiet', *váyase* 'go away'.

(c) The subjunctive is used to form first- and third-person imperatives, e.g. *sentémonos* 'let's sit down', *que entre* 'let him/her come in'.

The imperative is discussed in detail in Chapter 17.

16.15.2 Subjunctive to express wishes

The verb is usually preceded by *ojalá*, by *quién* or simply by *que* – the latter is omitted in some set phrases. *Así*, used jokingly, parodies a typical gypsy curse and is frequently heard in colloquial language (at least in Spain):

> *¡Ojalá nos toquen las quinielas!*
>
> *Ojalá se le queme el arroz* (A. Arrafut, Cuba, dialogue)
>
> *¡Quién fuera millonario!*
>
> ... *y pensé quién fuera escritor* ... (A. Bryce Echenique, Peru)

> Let's hope we win the pools!
>
> I hope your/his/her rice burns
>
> If only I were a millionaire!
>
> ... and I thought if only one were a writer ...

(*Quién* in this construction should not be confused with the word meaning 'who'.)

> *¡Que no se vaya!* —*pensaba* —*¡que no eche a volar!* (A. Mastretta, Mexico, dialogue)
>
> *Bendita seas, cuñada* ... (A. Mastretta, Mexico, dialogue)
>
> *¡Dios se lo pague!*
>
> *¡Así se te pegue mi catarro!*

> 'Please don't let him leave!' I thought, 'don't let him fly away!'
>
> God bless you, sister-in-law ...
>
> May God repay you!
>
> I hope you get my cold!

There is also a less common expression with the same meaning as *ojalá*: ***fueran*** (or *así/ya fueran*) *como tú todas las mujeres*... 'if only all women were like you ...'.

16.15.3 Subjunctive in some common set phrases

(a) *O sea que* 'in other words':

Ha dicho que tiene que trabajar, o sea que no quiere venir	He said he had to work, in other words he doesn't want to come

(b) In the phrases *que . . . sepa / que . . . recuerde*:

Que yo recuerde es la primera vez que le/lo veo	As far as I remember it's the first time I've seen him
Nada que yo sepa (J. Madrid, Spain)	Nothing as far as I know
Que se sepa nadie lo ha hecho antes	As far as anybody knows, it hasn't been done before

(c) In a few other set phrases:

¡Acabáramos!	Now I see what you're getting at!
Otro gallo nos cantara si le hubiéramos / hubiésemos hecho caso	It would have been another story if we had listened to him
¡Cómo tiras el dinero! Ni que fueras millonario . . .	The way you throw money about any-one would think you're a millionaire
¡Vaya tontería!	What nonsense!

16.16 Tense agreement: subjunctive

Despite the claims of many traditional grammars, there are no rigidly fixed rules of tense agreement between main and subordinate clauses, but the following are by far the most usual combinations:

(a) Main clause in present indicative
(1) Present subjunctive:

*Me **gusta** que **hable***	I like her to talk
***Quiero** que **dejes** de fumar*	I want you to stop smoking

(2) Perfect subjunctive:

*Me **encanta** que **hayas** venido*	I'm delighted you've come

(3) Imperfect subjunctive (see note i):

*Es imposible que lo **dijera/dijese***	It's impossible that he said it

(b) Main clause in future: present subjunctive:

*Nos **contentaremos** con que **terminen** para finales del mes*	We'll be content with them finishing by the end of the month
*¡Jamás soportaré que mi sobrina **se case** con un tipo que va por el mundo vestido de profesor en vacaciones!* (A. Bryce Echenique, Peru, dialogue)	I'll never tolerate my niece marrying a guy who goes around dressed like a teacher on holiday (US 'vacation')!

(c) Main clause in conditional or conditional perfect: imperfect subjunctive:

*Nos **contentaríamos** con que **terminaran/ terminasen** para finales del mes*	We'd be content with them finishing by the end of the month
*Yo habría preferido que se **pintara/pintase** de negro*	I'd have preferred it to be painted black

(d) Main clause in perfect (see note (ii)): present, perfect or imperfect subjunctive:

> *Le **he dicho** que se **siente*** (A. Gala, Spain, dialogue; perfect of recency)
> I told you to sit down
>
> *Ha **sido** un milagro que no te **hayan** reconocido/reconocieran/reconociesen*
> It was a miracle that they didn't recognize you

(e) Main clause in imperfect, preterite or pluperfect (see notes iii and iv)
(1) Imperfect subjunctive:

> *La idea **era** que **cobrarais/cobraseis** los viernes*
> The idea was that you'd get paid on Fridays
>
> *Me **sorprendió** que **fuera/fuese** tan alto*
> It surprised me that he was so tall
>
> *Yo te **había pedido** que me **prestaras/ prestases** cien dólares*
> I'd asked you to lend me 100 dollars

(2) Pluperfect subjunctive:

> *Me **sorprendía** que **hubiera/hubiese** protestado*
> I was surprised that he had protested

(f) Main clause in imperative: present subjunctive

> *Díganles que se **den** prisa*
> Tell them to hurry

Notes

(i) The combination present + imperfect or perfect subjunctive occurs when a comment is being made about a past event. There seems to be little difference between the perfect and imperfect subjunctive in this case, and occasionally the present subjunctive can also be used: *algunos **niegan** que Cristóbal Colón **fuera/fuese/haya sido/sea** el primer descubridor de América* 'some deny that Christopher Columbus was the first discoverer of America'.

(ii) The perfect (*ha dicho, ha ordenado*, etc.) is strictly speaking classified as a present tense for the purposes of agreement, but the imperfect subjunctive is occasionally used with it when the event in the subordinate clause is also in the past. Compare *ha **dado** órdenes de que nos **rindamos*** 'he's given orders for us to surrender' and *el clima que se está creando **ha llevado** a que se **hablara** de intervención del Ejército* (*Cambio16*, Spain; also *hable*) 'the climate that is being created has led to talk of Army intervention'.

(iii) The combination past indicative + present subjunctive is optionally possible when the subordinate clause refers to a timeless or perpetual event: *Dios **decretó** que las serpientes no **tengan/tuvieran/tuviesen patas**[12]* 'God decreed that snakes should have no legs'.

(iv) When the subordinate event is in the future and the time of the main verb is the recent past, the present subjunctive is sometimes found in the subordinate clause: *el Gobierno vasco **reclamó** ayer que se le **transfiera** el mando efectivo de las fuerzas de seguridad del Estado en el País Vasco* (*El País*) 'the Basque Government demanded yesterday that effective control over the State security forces in the Basque Country should be transferred to itself'.

Use of the present when both verbs refer to the past is common in popular Latin-American speech but is unacceptable to Peninsular speakers, although examples are increasingly frequent in the media and not unknown in spontaneous speech – a tendency that suggests that the Spanish imperfect subjunctive may one day become obsolescent, like its French counterpart. Examples: *el inspector aduanero le **pidió** a la muchacha que le **muestre** su casaca* (*La Prensa*, Peru; Spain *mostrara/mostrase*. In Spain *la casaca* = 'frock-coat') 'the customs inspector asked the girl to show him her coat', *Eva abogó por Perón, pidió, clamó, imploró, para que **entiendan** lo que quería decirles* (A. Posse, Argentina; normally *entendieran* or *entendiesen*) 'Eva pleaded for Perón, asked, clamo(u)red, implored them [i.e. the Communists] to understand what he was trying to say to them', *logró impedir que frases como ésta **destruyan** mi vida* (A. Bryce Echenique, Peru; for *destruyeran/destruyesen*) 'she managed to prevent phrases like this from destroying my life'.

(v) After *como si* 'as if', *igual que si/lo mismo que si* 'the same as if', the verb is always in the imperfect subjunctive: *le hablaré **como si** yo no **supiese/supiera** hablar bien el castellano* 'I'll talk to him as if I didn't know how to speak Spanish well.' See also 16.12.5c for *como si*.

---

[12] *Las piernas* is used only of human legs

16.17 The future subjunctive

The forms of the future subjunctive are discussed at 13.1.10.

The future subjunctive is nowadays obsolete in standard Spanish except in a few literary variants of set phrases such as *sea lo que fuere* (more usually *sea lo que sea*) 'whatever it may be', *venga lo que viniere* (usually *venga lo que venga*) 'come what may'. It is still much used in legal documents, printed regulations, charters and similar official documents after formulas of the kind 'a person who . . . ':

> *APUESTA: Contrato bilateral en el que se acuerda que el que **acertare** un pronóstico o **tuviere** razón en una disputa recibirá del perdedor lo pactado* (from a Spanish legal dictionary)

> BET: A bilateral contract whereby it is agreed that a person who makes an accurate forecast or wins an argument shall receive the amount agreed from the loser

It occasionally appears in flowery language to indicate a very remote possibility:

> *. . . lo cual ofrece amplísimas ventajas en la extracción del motor o en reparaciones, caso de que las **hubiere*** (advertisement, Spain; *hubiera/hubiese* more normal)

> . . . which offers very extensive advantages when removing the engine or in repair work – if such a thing should ever arise

It is quite common in Latin-American newspaper style in some regions: Kany (1970), 225, notes examples in written usage from nine American republics:

> *. . . sólo la aplicación de un plan de estrictas medidas, aun cuando éstas **resultaren** antipopulares, permitirá salir de la actual situación* (*La Nación*, Buenos Aires)

> . . . only the application of a plan of strict measures, even if these were unpopular, would allow us to get out of the present situation

17

The imperative

17.1 General remarks

The imperative is used to give orders or to make requests. There are various ways of making an imperative sound less abrupt: in this respect intonation and attitude are as important in Spanish as in any language, and a friendly manner counts for much more than the constant use of *por favor* or *haga el favor* 'please', which, like *gracias*, English speakers constantly use unnecessarily. In Spain, *por favor* is strictly speaking required only when one is asking a favo(u)r, and since barmen, waiters or salespersons are not doing favo(u)rs simply by serving customers, *por favor* is not really necessary. However, the formula *por favor* seems nowadays to be heard much more often than before.[1] Other points to watch are: **(a)** all negative imperatives (e.g. 'don't do', 'don't say') are formed with the subjunctive: *vete* 'go away', *no te **vayas*** 'don't go away; **(b)** for Latin Americans there is no *vosotros* imperative: *ustedes* is used for both strangers and friends, and even for little children and animals.

17.2 Affirmative forms of the imperative

17.2.1 General

(For negative imperatives 'don't do', 'don't say', etc. see 17.3.) Addition of a subject pronoun to an imperative can make an order emphatic and brusque:

¡*Tú* bájate de ahí!/*Usted* bájese	You! Get down from there!
¡*Vosotros* callaos! (colloquially *callaros*)	You shut up!

17.2.2 The tú imperative

The familiar singular imperative (*tú* form) is, with eight exceptions, formed by removing the -s of the second-person singular of the present indicative: *llamas*>*llama*, *lees*>*lee*. The exceptions are:

decir to say: ***di***	*poner* to put: ***pon***	*venir* to come: ***ven***
hacer to do/make: ***haz***	*salir* to leave/go out: ***sal***	*tener* to have: ***ten***
ir to go: ***ve*** (*vete* = 'go away')	*ser* to be: ***sé***	

Examples:

Anda, sé bueno y márchate (J. Madrid, Spain)	Come on, be good and go away

---

[1] Mexican speech, characteristically very attentive to politeness, uses *por favor* constantly.

Ven a tomar el café cuando quieras   Come and have coffee whenever you want
   (I. Grasa, Spain)

Notes

(i) *Tú* imperatives are nowadays constantly seen in advertisements on both continents. This usage is presumably designed to make the reader feel young, cf. *si el precio de tu seguro es un obstáculo, no le des más vueltas* (*El País*, Spain) 'if the cost of your insurance is getting in your way, stop worrying about it'.

(ii) Note idiomatic uses of *tener*: *ténmelo preparado* 'have it ready for me', *tenme al corriente* 'keep me informed', etc.

(iii) The *tú* imperative of *haber* is theoretically *he*, but it is never used. As Seco (1998), 243, points out, the nowadays rather stilted literary expression *he aquí*, 'here is . . .'/'what follows is . . . ' (French *voici* . . .) is not the imperative of *haber*: *he aquí una imagen de* . . . 'this is an image of . . .', *he aquí un resultado cuidadosamente escondido* (*El País*, Uruguay) 'this is a carefully concealed result.'

17.2.3 The *vos* imperative

The imperative form corresponding to *vos* (Southern Cone, especially Argentina, and Central America) can usually be found by removing the *-d* from the European *vosotros* form; the final vowel is therefore usually stressed: *tened>tené, contad>contá, decid>decí*. Pronominal verbs take the pronoun *te*, so the imperative of *lavarse* is *lavate* (stressed on the second *a*; the standard form is *lávate*). Further examples (all from Argentina; the *tú* form is included for comparison. Stressed vowels are shown in bold):

*Deci**l**e que pase* (*di**l**e que pase*)	Tell him to come in
*Ven**í** cuando puedas* (*ven cuando puedas*;	Come when you can
see 16.2.8 for *ven**í** cuando pod**á**s*)	
*Levant**a**te* (*lev**á**ntate*)	Get up
*O**í**me, Pozzi* (M. Puig, Argentina; *ó**y**eme*)	Listen, Pozzi
*Esch**á** esto* (ibid.; *escucha*)	Listen, to this

17.2.4 The *vosotros* imperative

The familiar European Spanish plural (*vosotros*/*vosotras*) imperative is formed by replacing the *-r* of the infinitive by *-d*:

ser to be: ***sed***	*tener* to have: ***tened***	*cantar* to sing: ***cantad***
ir to go: ***id***	*venir* to come: ***venid***	

The *-d* is dropped in the pronominal form: *dad* + *os* = *daos* as in *daos la mano* 'shake hands', *lavad* + *os* = *lavaos*: *lavaos el pelo* 'wash your hair'. There is one exception: *id* + *os* = *idos* 'go away!' from *irse*, although in everyday speech *iros* is nowadays much more usual.

This form is replaced by the *ustedes* form of the imperative in Latin America except in very formal styles (e.g. liturgical language), but it is in everyday use in Spain.

Note

In informal spoken language in Spain this imperative is often replaced by the infinitive: *venid* = *venir*, *id* = *ir*, *daos* = *daros*, *veníos* = *veniros*, *lavaos las manos* 'wash your hands' = *lavaros las manos*, etc. Although it apparently has a long history, this construction is still considered slovenly by some speakers, but it is very widespread. Example: *a mí no me gusta criticar, pero tener* (for *tened*) *cuidado con Socorro que ya se ha cargado tres matrimonios y yo creo que va a conseguir el cuarto* (E. Arenas, Spain, popular dialogue) 'I don't like to criticize, but watch out for Socorro – she's already messed up three marriages and I reckon she's going to make it four'.

Formal and written styles require the forms in *-d*. For further remarks on the use of the infinitive as an imperative, see 17.9.

17.2.5 The *usted/ustedes* imperative

The pronouns *usted* and *ustedes* have no independent imperative forms: they use the third-person singular or plural present subjunctive endings respectively: *dígame* 'tell me', *tenga* 'take'/'have', *díganme (ustedes)*, 'tell (plural) me', *avancen* 'move on'/'go on', etc. The plural forms are used for both polite and informal address in Latin America: a Latin-American mother addresses her children as *ustedes*, which sounds strange to Spaniards. *Vosotros* forms of the verb are unfamiliar to most Latin Americans:

Vaya a descansar. Preséntese aquí a las 11 (M. Vázquez Montalbán, Spain)	Go and have a rest. Be here at 11 o'clock
¡Ayúdeme, doctora! (M. Vargas Llosa, Peru)	Help me, doctor!
Perdone si parezco impertinente (L. Ortiz, Spain)	Excuse me if I seem impertinent

Notes

(i) For the position of the pronouns and the Latin-American form *?siéntensen*, see 17.4.

(ii) Spoken Mexican usage regularly adds *le* to certain common imperatives, e.g. *aváncenle* 'move on', *pásenle* 'come in', *ándale* 'wow!'

17.2.6 The imperative of *estar*

For the affirmative imperative of *estar* 'to be' the pronominal form is frequently (but not exclusively) used: *estate quieto* 'be still'/'stop fidgeting', *estense listas para las ocho* 'be ready by eight'. With *usted* the non-pronominal form is more common, but not exclusively used:

No esté tan segura de que era un miedo distinto (C. Martín Gaite, Spain, dialogue)	Don't be so sure that it was a different fear
—*Esté tranquila* —*le dijo . . . si se mueve le va mal, así que estese tranquila* (G. García Márquez, Colombia, dialogue)	'Keep calm', he told her . . . 'If you move it'll go badly for you, so keep calm'

This is most common in the *tú* imperative because the non-pronominal form is easily confused with the third-person present singular, *está*. But the pronominal construction is not universal: the following example would have been expressed *estate lista* in Spain:—*Paso a cambiarme como a las ocho. Por favor, está lista* (C. Fuentes, Mexico, dialogue) 'I'll be home around eight to get changed. Please be ready.'

Note

Much uncertainty surrounds the question whether one should write *estate* or *estáte*, *estese/estense* or *estése/esténse*; the Academy does not seem to have pronounced unambiguously on the matter. We use the unaccented forms on the grounds that the accent is unnecessary. One does not write **deténlo* for *detenlo* 'arrest him', even though the imperative form is *detén*.

17.3 Negative forms of the imperative

To express a negative imperative, the present subjunctive must be used:

Affirmative imperative		Negative imperative	
canta	sing	*no cantes*	don't sing
vete	go away	*no te vayas*	don't go away
(usted) levántese	stand up	*no se levante*	don't stand up
(vosotros) sentaos	sit down	*no os sentéis*	don't sit down
(ustedes) dénselo	give it to him/her/them	*no se lo den*	don't give it to him/her/them

No vuelvas antes de las 9 (I. Grasa, Spain)	Don't come back before 9

Oye, no lo tomes a mal, sobrino
  (M. Vargas Llosa, Peru, dialogue)
	Listen, nephew, don't get me
	  wrong

Notes

(i) The Argentinian *vos* forms obey the same rules and foreign students should use the standard subjunctive forms with them for the reasons explained at 16.2.8: *levantate* > *no te levantes* (*no te levantés* is a shade too 'popular' for some Argentinians).

(ii) Affirmative forms of the imperative are occasionally used in the negative in popular Spanish speech, e.g. *?no rechistad* 'don't answer back!' for *no rechistéis*. This should not be imitated.

17.4 Position of object pronouns with the imperative

When an imperative form is used with an object pronoun, the following rules apply:

(a) If the imperative is affirmative, the pronouns are attached to the verb in the normal order (shown at 11.12):

(Tú) dame la mano	Hold my hand
(Tú) ponte la chaqueta (Argentina, *[vos]* *ponete el saco*)	Put your jacket on
(Usted) démelo	Give it to me
(Vosotros/as) dádmelo	Give it to me
(Vosotros) despertaos (colloquial *despertaros*; see 17.2.4)	Wake up
(Ustedes) dénnoslo	Give it to us
Dime lo que sea, venga (C. Martín Gaite, Spain, dialogue)	Tell me, whatever it is. Come on
Léelo con toda tranquilidad (S. Puértolas, Spain, dialogue)	Read it in your own time
Déjamelo ver, déjamelo ver (A. Mastretta, Mexico, dialogue)	Let me see it, let me see it

(b) If the imperative is **negative**, the pronouns precede it in the normal way (shown at 11.12):

No me des la lata	Stop pestering me
No te pongas la chaqueta	Don't put your jacket on
No me lo dé (Usted)	Don't give it to me
No os quejéis (vosotros)	Don't complain
No se lo enseñen (Ustedes)	Don't show it to him/her/them

Es una chica que trabaja conmigo no te
  vayas a creer (C. Martín Gaite,
  Spain, dialogue)
	She's a girl who works with me, don't
	  imagine anything else

Notes

(i) When a pronoun ending in a vowel is attached to an affirmative *ustedes* imperative there is a widespread tendency in popular Latin-American speech either to repeat the plural *-n* at the end of the word or to shift it to the end of the word: *?levántensen* or *?levántesen* (for *levántense*) 'get up', *?díganselon* or *?dígaselon* (for *díganselo*) 'tell it to him'. Kany, 143ff, gives examples from seventeen Latin-American republics, and in some places these forms are heard even in spontaneous educated speech. This construction is unknown in standard European Spanish and is banned from Latin-American written styles.

(ii) In some northern regions of Spain, popular language puts the pronouns before an affirmative imperative verb and uses a redundant pronoun even for a direct object (this construction should not be confused with imperatives preceded by *que*, discussed at 17.6) : *?¡le dé el juguete al niño!* (for *dele el juguete al niño!*) 'give the toy to the child', *?las riegue las plantas* (for *riegue las plantas*) 'water the plants'. This construction is usually stigmatized as uneducated and should not be imitated.

(iii) There is some uncertainty about the correct spelling of the imperative of *dar* (*dé*) when a single pronoun is attached: *dele* or *déle* for 'give him'? Since the accent is used only to distinguish *dé* 'give' from *de* 'of', it is not really required on an unambiguous form like *dele, denos*.

17.5 First-person plural imperatives

The present subjunctive can be used to make a first-person plural imperative, e.g. 'let's go!', 'let's begin'. If the verb is pronominal, the final *-s* is dropped before adding *-nos*:

Empecemos	Let's get started
Asegurémonos primero de la verdad de los hechos	Let us first assure ourselves of the truth of the facts
No nos enfademos (Lat. Am. *no nos enojemos*)	Let's not get angry/Don't let us get angry

Notes

(i) *Ir* forms its first-person plural imperative irregularly: *vamos, vámonos* 'let's go'. The expected form *vayámonos* is nowadays virtually extinct and *vayamos* is used as an imperative only in set phrases, e.g. *vayamos al grano* 'let's get to the point'.

(ii) With the exception of *vámonos* 'let's go', informal spoken language tends to avoid this construction. This is usually done by using *ir a* or sometimes simply *a* and an infinitive, e.g. *vamos a sentarnos* 'let's sit down', *bueno, a levantarse* 'OK, let's get up' (note third-person pronoun), *vamos a verlo/a ver* 'let's have a look'/'let's see'. Thus *no nos enfademos* 'let's not get angry' may be expressed by *no vale la pena enfadarse, no nos vamos a enfadar, no vamos a enfadarnos*. However, *no nos enfademos* is perfectly acceptable in spoken language.

(iii) Double *s* is not found in Spanish, so one *s* is dropped in cases like the following: *digámoselo* 'let's tell it to him/her/them' (not **digámosselo*), *démoselos* 'let's give them to him/her/them' – although such forms have fallen into disuse for the reason given in note (i).

17.6 Third-person imperatives

Third-person imperative forms consisting of *que* + a subjunctive are common. They are usually translatable by some formula like 'let him/her/them . . . ', 'tell him/her/them to . . . ':

—*Que llaman preguntando por su marido.* —*Pues que le/lo llamen a la oficina*	'There's a phone call for your husband.' 'Then tell them to call him at his office'

Que nos cuente qué política económica querría que hiciéramos (Felipe González in *El País*, Spain)	Let him tell us what economic policy he'd like us to follow (lit 'make')
Que ella los bañara, los vistiera, oyera sus preguntas, los enseñara a rezar y a creer en algo (A. Mastretta, Mexico, dialogue)	[As far as I was concerned] let her bathe them, clothe them, listen to their questions, teach them to pray and believe in something

Note

Third-person imperatives without *que* are found in set phrases: *¡Dios nos coja confesados!* (archaic or humorous) 'Good God!'/ 'Heavens above!' (lit.'may God take us after we've confessed!'), *¡sálvese quien pueda!* 'every man for himself!' (or woman: the Spanish phrase is not sexist).

17.7 Second-person imperatives preceded by *que*

An imperative can be formed from a second-person subjunctive preceded by *que*. This makes the order more emphatic or presents it as a reminder:

¡Que tengas un buen fin de semana!	Have a good weekend!
¡Que no perdáis el dinero!	Don't lose the money!
¡Que se diviertan!	Have a good time! (*ustedes*)

17.8 Impersonal imperatives (passive *se* imperatives)

It is possible to form an imperative with passive *se*, the resulting construction having no exact equivalent in English. It is much used in formal written Spanish to give instructions without directly addressing the reader:

Rellénese en mayúsculas	Fill out in capital letters (lit. 'let it be filled out . . . ')
Véase el capítulo siguiente	See following chapter
Tradúzcanse al castellano las siguientes frases	Translate the following phrases into Spanish
Cuézanse las patatas durante 15 minutos, córtense en rodajitas, déjense enfriar y cúbranse con mayonesa	Boil the potatoes for 15 minutes, cut into slices, leave to cool and cover with mayonnaise

As the last two examples show, the verb agrees in number with the logical object of the verb (in these cases with *frases* and *patatas*).

Note

There is a modern tendency, not universally approved, to replace this impersonal imperative by the infinitive. See the next section.

17.9 The infinitive used as an imperative

The infinitive can sometimes be used as an imperative:

(a) In spoken European Spanish as a familiar replacement for the standard affirmative *vosotros* imperative ending in *-d*: *decirme la verdad* = *decidme la verdad* 'tell me the truth'. This is discussed in the note to 17.2.4.

(b) Everywhere, as a brief, impersonal alternative to the *usted/ustedes* imperative, useful for public notices or instructions, e.g. in technical manuals or cookery books. Its growing popularity seems to be due to a perception that the impersonal imperative described at 17.8 is formal or slightly old-fashioned.

This use of the infinitive is controversial. Some grammarians reject the use of the infinitive for affirmative commands and admit only negative forms like *no fumar* 'no smoking', *no tocar* 'don't touch', *no fijar carteles* 'no bill-sticking', *no asomarse a la ventanilla* 'do not lean out of the window'. Such negative forms are nowadays seen everywhere in Spain and Mexico (and no doubt elsewhere), although they seem to be a recent development; one used to say **prohibido** *fumar*, etc. As far as affirmative forms are concerned, María Moliner says that an imperative like *callarse todos* for *cállense todos* 'everybody be quiet'/'be quiet all of you' is not acceptable in careful language. Nevertheless, the form is increasingly frequent in informal writing:

Empujar (notice on doors; better *empujen?*)	Push
No aparcar delante de las puertas (*no aparquen . . .*)	No parking in front of doors
Para servir, poner los medallones en un plato, salsearlos, y acompañarlos con las bolitas de papa, zanahorias y un ramito de brócoli (La Reforma, Mexico; *papas = patatas* in Spain; *salsear = sazonar*; *brócoli = brécol* in Spain)	To serve, put the medallions [of beef] on a plate, season them and serve them with the potato balls, carrots and a sprig of broccoli
Descolgar y esperar. Percibirá una señal acústica continua y uniforme. No demorar el marcar (instructions in Spanish phone book)	Lift receiver and wait. You will hear a continuous even tone. Do not delay dialling/(US 'dialing')
Le gustaba su marido. Adivinar la razón, porque él era espantoso (A. Mastretta, Mexico, dialogue)	She was fond of her (own) husband, God knows why (lit. 'guess why'), because he was ghastly

Note

Haber plus the past participle is often used to make a sarcastic imperative when a solution is no longer possible: —*Me arrepiento de haberla llamado.*—*Bueno, no haberlo hecho* '"I regret ringing her." "Well, we shouldn't have done it, should we?"', —*Me he pegado una mojadura.* —*Haber traído el paraguas* '"I've got soaked." "You should have brought your umbrella."'

(c) With the preposition *a*, the infinitive may be used to give orders in informal styles:

—*Lo he hecho mal.* —*Bueno, a hacerlo bien la segunda vez* (tends to look uneducated without the *a*)	'I've done it wrong'. 'Well do it right the second time'
—*¡No tengo novio todavía!* —*Las ganas no te faltan. ¡A buscarlo!* (A. Arrufat, Cuba, dialogue)	'I haven't got a boyfriend yet!' 'You're keen enough. So look for one!'
¡Todos a callar!	Be quiet everybody!
¡A dormir inmediatamente!	Go to sleep right now!

This type of imperative may sometimes include the speaker: *bueno, ahora a trabajar* 'OK, now let's get to work.'

Note

In Spain an infinitive is nowadays often used to introduce the last point in radio or TV news items. This is surely not an imperative but an abbreviation of some phrase like *sólo/solo nos queda . . .* or *sólo/solo falta* . . . 'all that remains is to . . .': *y finalmente,* **añadir** *que ésta no es la primera vez que el autor recibe un importante premio literario* 'and finally, we should add that this isn't the first time that the author has received an important literary prize'.

17.10 The present indicative used as an imperative

The present indicative is sometimes used as an imperative in speech, just as in English, e.g. 'you're getting up right now and going to school'. In both languages this tends to be a no-nonsense imperative and it can be brusque to the point of rudeness:

Si quieres, me **llamas** *mañana*	If you want to, call me tomorrow
Si tienes dinero, me lo **das**	If you've got money, give it to me
De acuerdo. No te guardo el sitio para mañana, pero pasado me **haces** *dos páginas* (C. Rico-Godoy, Spain, dialogue)	OK. I won't keep the space for you tomorrow, but the day after tomorrow you're doing two pages for me (editor to journalist)
Nomás que oscurezca te **vas** *por la carretera y* **tiras** *en una barranca el cuerpo de una muchacha que se murió* (J. Ibargüengoitia, Mexico, dialogue; *nomás que = en cuanto* or *nada más* . . . in Spain)	As soon as it gets dark, you go down the road and you throw the body of a girl who died into a ravine

17.11 Ways of mellowing the imperative

Imperative forms can sound more like an order than a polite request, especially if one gets the intonation wrong. There are numerous ways of making a request sound friendly, although in any language a politely worded request can still sound rude if the intonation is abrupt or irritable. Some ways of making a request sound more mellow are:

(a) Use the conditional or imperfect of *poder*:

*¿***Podrían***/***Podían** *hacer menos ruido (por favor)?*	Would you mind making less noise?/ Could you make less noise?
*¿***Podrías** *hacerme el favor de no fumar?*	Would you mind not smoking?

(b) Use *querer*. The conditional makes the imperative even milder:

*¿***Quieres** *decirme la verdad?*	Would you mind telling me the truth?
*¿***Querrías** *(hacerme el favor de) darle un recado a Pedro?*	Would you mind giving a message to Pedro?

The phrases *quieres/querrías/quiere usted hacerme el favor* are very common in everyday Spanish.

(c) Use the phrase *a ver* 'let's see . . .':

A ver si vienes a verme más a menudo	Try and come and see me more often
A ver si salimos un día	Let's go out one day/Why don't we go out one day?
A ver si me devuelves el dinero que te presté	Perhaps you could give me back the money I lent you

(d) Turn the request into a question:

¿Me pasas el agua (por favor)?	Pass the water, please
¿Me pone con el 261-84-50 (por favor)?[2]	Can you connect me to 261 8450 please?

(e) In Spain, use *tú* instead of *usted*:

Dame una cerveza	Give me a beer (friendly tone)

This is very widespread in Spain and appropriate between young people (say under forty) even when they are strangers, but it sounds over-familiar when said to older persons or to people in authority. In Latin America *tú* is used much less frequently between strangers.

(f) Add a diminutive suffix to the direct object noun:

This is a common way of making a request sound friendly. Compare *deme una barra de pan* 'give me a loaf of bread' and *deme una barrita de pan* 'I'll just take a loaf of bread, please', *tómate un cafelito* (J. Madrid, Spain, dialogue) 'have a coffee'. The diminutive does not necessarily imply smallness in this construction; it simply makes the tone warmer, as in *espere un momentito* 'just a second, please' (see 38.2.2).

(g) Add some tag like *¿eh?*, *¿puedes?* :

Vamos al cine, ¿quieres?/¿vale?[3]	Let's go the cinema, OK?
Abre la puerta, ¿puedes?	Open the door, would you?/(US) Do you want to open the door?
No chilles, ¿eh?	Stop screaming

17.12 Miscellaneous imperative constructions

Oye/Oiga (Usted) (por favor)	Excuse me!/Pardon me! (lit. 'hear!')
No lo vuelvas a hacer/No vuelvas a hacerlo	Don't do it again
Mira lo que he comprado	Look what I bought
Fíjate lo que me ha pasado	Look what happened to me
Imagínate qué disgusto	Imagine how upset I was (lit. 'imagine what displeasure')
Trae que te lleve la bolsa (colloquial, Spain only?)	Let me carry your bag
Trae aquí (colloquial, Spain only?)	Give it here/Let me take it
No se te ocurra hacer eso	Don't even think of doing that
No dejes de llamarme/No se te olvide llamarme	Don't forget to call me
Vete a saber	Goodness knows/Heaven knows why
No me digas (incredulous tone)	You don't say!

Note

English allows passive imperatives (normally only in the negative): 'don't be scared by him'. A different solution must be found in Spanish: *no te dejes engañar por lo que dice* 'don't be deceived by what he says', *no dejes que te hagan cantar a la fuerza* 'don't be bullied into singing', *no dejes que te mangoneen/no te dejes mangonear* 'don't let yourself be pushed around'.

---

[2] See 10.17 for how to say telephone numbers in Spanish.
[3] Constant use of *vale* 'fine'/'OK', is remarked on by Latin Americans as being typical of Peninsular Spanish.

18

The infinitive

18.1 Summary

Spanish infinitives end in *-ar*, *-er* or *-ir*. In the latter case a few infinitives, e.g. *freír*, *reír*, *sonreír*, have an accent on the *i*. These are listed at 13.1.4f.

The infinitive may act as a verb or noun. In the latter case it is masculine and usually singular: *fumar es malo para la salud* 'smoking is bad for the health'. This kind of English sentence must never be translated using the Spanish gerund: **fumando es malo para la salud* is emphatically not Spanish. When it acts as a verb, the Spanish infinitive cannot in itself express number, mood, time or person (this latter fact should be remembered by students of Portuguese). It is also sometimes ambiguous as to voice, i.e. it can sometimes be passive in meaning, as in *tres cartas sin terminar* 'three unfinished letters'.

Like the gerund, the infinitive often requires suffixed personal pronouns, e.g. *antes de hacerlo* 'before doing it', cf. French *avant de le faire*. When the infinitive is governed by a finite verb, position of the pronouns may in some cases be optional with variable stylistic effects, as in *quiero verlo* and *lo quiero ver* 'I want to see it': see 11.14.4 and below at 18.2.3. For the use of the infinitive as an imperative see 17.9. For *de* + infinitive to mean 'if . . . ', see 25.8.3.

18.2 Infinitive governed by a verb

This section refers to constructions like *sabe nadar* 'he can swim', *te desafío a hacerlo* 'I challenge you to do it', etc. These constructions have many parallels in English, although there are some surprises and Spanish is free of the complication raised by the unpredictable choice between the infinitive and the -ing form: compare 'he claimed **to have** done it' = *pretendía haberlo hecho* and 'he remembered **having** done it' = *se acordaba de haberlo hecho*.

18.2.1 Replacement of finite subordinate verbs by an infinitive

If the subject of the verb in a main clause and the verb in a subordinate clause are co-referential, i.e. they share the same subject, the verb in the subordinate clause is usually replaced by an infinitive. This is obligatory in most cases, as can be seen from the following pairs (the subjunctive construction is discussed at 16.5):

Él quiere que lo haga (different subjects)	He wants him/her (someone else) to do it
Él quiere hacerlo (same subjects)	He wants to do it
Prefiero que tú lo abras	I prefer you to open it
Prefiero abrirlo yo mismo	I prefer to open it myself

Some verbs always take an infinitive because they are always co-referential, i.e. one always says *se obstinaba en hacerlo* '(s)he insisted on doing it', *tienden a abstenerse* 'they tend to abstain': these are listed at 18.2.3. In the case of some other verbs, either construction (i.e. an infinitive or *que* + finite verb) is allowed when the subjects are the same, e.g. *Juan niega haberlo hecho* or *Juan niega que lo hiciera/hiciese/haya hecho* 'Juan denies having done it'/'Juan denies that he did it.' In such cases, use of the infinitive makes the sentence unambiguously co-referential in the third person, whereas *Juan niega que lo hiciera* could mean '. . . denies that (s)he (i.e. some other person) did it' or . . . 'you did it' as well as 'he (himself) did it': Compare these pairs:

Desmintieron que hubieran/hubiesen lanzado el misil	They denied that they'd launched the missile i.e. they themselves or someone else)
*Desmintieron **haber** lanzado el misil* (note use of *haber*)	They denied **launching** the missile
Reconozco que lo hice	I recognize I did it
Reconozco haberlo hecho	I recognize having done it
Afirmaba que era francés	He claimed he was French (himself or someone else)
Afirmaba ser francés	He claimed to be French
Recuerdo que lo compré	I remember I bought it
Recuerdo haberlo comprado	I remember having bought it

This construction is used with more verbs in Spanish than in English. See the next section.

18.2.2 Infinitive construction with certain verbs of saying, believing, affirming, etc.

Spanish allows an infinitive construction with a number of verbs of saying, believing, affirming, etc., a construction which may seem bizarre to English-speakers (one cannot say *'he says to be ill' for 'he says he's ill'). As was mentioned earlier, the infinitive construction has the advantage of eliminating the ambiguity of *dice que lo sabe* '(s)he says (s)he knows it', which may refer to a fourth person. Despite this advantage, the infinitive construction, *dice saberlo*, tends to be confined to formal styles and the ambiguous construction with *que* is much more usual in everyday language. Further examples:

Creo tener razón/Creo que tengo razón	I think I'm right
Dijo llamarse Simón . . . tener 42 años, ser casado, mexicano y estar radicado en el Salto de la Tuxpana (J. Ibargüengoitia, Mexico; the text imitates official language)	He said he was called Simón . . . was 42, married, Mexican and lived in Salto de la Tuxpana
Había creído volverse loco, pensado en matarse (M. Vargas Llosa, Peru)	He had imagined he was going mad, thought about killing himself
Los oceanógrafos estiman haber descubierto una variedad no registrada a la fecha (*El País*, Uruguay; Spain . . . *hasta la fecha*)	Oceanographers consider they have discovered a hitherto unrecorded variety
Dudo poder hacerlo/Dudo que pueda hacerlo[1]	I doubt I can do it
La información . . . revela ser falsa (C. Fuentes, Mexico, dialogue)	The information turns out to be false

Seat estudia reducir bruscamente sus   Seat is studying a sharp reduction in its
   modelos (Cambio16, Spain: ... *cómo*   (range of) models
   reducir/el modo de reducir is better)

Notes

(i) In written language an infinitive may appear in relative clauses when the subjects refer to different things and the clause includes a verb of saying or believing. This avoids the use of two *ques*: *las tres muchachas, que él creía **ser** hijas de don Mateo* (rather than *que él creía que eran ...*) 'the three girls, whom he believed to be the daughters of Don Mateo'.
(ii) The past equivalent of the infinitive is made with *haber* + past participle: *dice haberlo sabido desde hace tiempo* 'she says that she's known it for some time'.

18.2.3 Verbs followed by the infinitive

The following list shows some of the more common verbs that are followed by an infinitive. Common French equivalents are supplied as a reminder to students of that language to avoid all-too-frequent blunders like **se acercó de él* for *se acercó a él* (French *il s'est approché de lui*). Where no preposition is shown the verb is followed by an infinitive, as in *anhelaban hacerlo* 'they longed/yearned to do it'. Where 'see 16.5.2' appears, the verb may be used either with the infinitive or with a subjunctive, as explained in that section.

Verbs that are asterisked are followed by an infinitive even when the subject of this infinitive is different from the subject of the finite verb, as in *acusó a Miguel de haberlo hecho* 'he accused Miguel of having done it'. In other cases the infinitive construction requires that the subjects be identical, as in *me abstuve de hacer un comentario* 'I refrained from commenting'.

Verbs (plus prepositions) followed by infinitive
(Verbs marked § allow pronoun shifting. See note (i))

abstenerse de to refrain from
acabar de§: acabo de verla 'I've just seen her'
acabar por to end by
acercarse a to approach (Fr. *s'approcher de*)
aceptar to accept
acertar a§ to manage to/to succeed
aconsejar to advise (Fr. *conseiller de*) (see 16.5.2)
acordar§ to agree to
acordarse de to remember (cf. *recordar*, see note iv)
acostumbrar a§ to be accustomed to (or 'to make someone accustomed to ...'
acusar de* to accuse of
afanarse por to do one's best to
afirmar to claim/to state
alcanzar a§ to manage to: *es todo lo que alcancé a ver* 'it's all I managed to see'

amenazar (con) to threaten to (Fr. *menacer de*): *amenazó matarle* or *con matarle*
anhelar§ to long to
animar a to encourage to; see 16.5.2
ansiar§ to long to
aparentar§ to seem to
aprender a§ to learn to
apresurarse a to hasten to
arrepentirse de to regret/to repent
arriesgarse a to risk
asegurar§ to assure
atreverse a to dare to (cf. Fr. *oser faire*)
autorizar a to authorize to; see 16.5.2
avergonzarse de to be ashamed of
ayudar a§ to help to; see 16.5.2
bajar a to go down to
buscar to seek to (Fr. *chercher à*)
cansarse de to tire of
cesar de§ to cease from

---

[1] The infinitive is particularly common after *dudar* + *poder* 'to doubt one is able to ... ': *dudo poder hacerlo* 'I doubt I can do it'. However, it is not used to replace *dudar que* when the latter would require the subjunctive: *dudo que yo **sea** tan inteligente como ella dice* 'I doubt I'm as intelligent as she says', but not **dudo ser tan inteligente como ella dice*.

comenzar a§ to begin to
comenzar por to start by
comprometerse a to undertake to
conceder to concede to
condenar a to condemn to; see 16.5.2
conducir a to lead to; see 16.5.2
confesar to confess
conseguir§ to succeed in
consentir en to consent to (Fr. *consentir à*)
consistir en to consist of
contribuir a to contribute to
convenir en to agree to
convidar a to invite to; see 16.5.2
creer§ to believe
cuidar de to take care to
*culpar de** to blame someone for
deber must (see 21.3)
decidir§ to decide to (Fr. *décider de*)
decidirse a to make up one's mind to
decir tell (i.e. order; Fr. *dire de*); also
  'say'; see 16.5.2 and 18.2.2
declarar to declare
dejar§* to let/to allow: *le dejó hacerlo* or
  se lo dejó hacer 'he let her do it'; see 16.5.2
dejar de§ to leave off/to give up
demostrar§ to demonstrate (more
  usually with *que* + finite verb)
desafiar a to challenge to (Fr. *défier de*);
  see 16.5.2
desear§ to desire/to wish to
desesperar de to despair of
desvivirse por to do one's utmost to
dignarse to deign to
disponerse a to get ready to
*disuadir de** to dissuade from
divertirse en to amuse oneself by
  (usually with gerund; Fr. *s'amuser à*)
dudar en to hesitate over (Fr. *hésiter à*)
echar(se) a to begin to
elegir to choose to
empeñarse en to insist on
empecinarse en to insist on
empezar a§ to begin to
empezar por to start by
encargarse de to take charge of
enseñar a§ to show how to/teach; see
  16.5.2
enviar a to send to; see 16.5.2
escoger to choose
esforzarse por/en to strive to (Fr.
  s'efforcer de)
esperar§ to hope/to expect/to wait to
evitar§ to avoid (Fr. *éviter de*)
excitar a to excite to; see 16.5.2
figurarse to imagine
fingir to pretend to
forzar a§ to force to; see 16.5.2

guardarse de to take care not to
gustar de to like to (but usually *le gusta
  fumar*, etc.)
habituarse a to get used to
hacer§ to make (*la hizo callar*, etc.); see
  16.5.2
hartarse de to tire of/have enough of
imaginar to imagine
impedir§ to prevent from (Fr. *défendre
  de*); see 16.5.2
impulsar a to urge to see 16.5.2
incitar a to incite to; see 16.5.2
inclinar a to incline to; see 16.5.2
inducir a to induce/to persuade to; see
  16.5.2
insistir en to insist on (Fr. *insister pour*)
instar a to urge to; see 16.5.2
intentar§ to try to (Fr. *essayer de*)
interesarse en (or *por*) to interest in (Fr.
  s'intéresser à)
invitar a to invite to; see 16.5.2
ir a to go to (*esto va a hacerse pronto*
  'this is going to be done soon')
jactarse de to boast of
jurar§ to swear to
juzgar to judge (but usually with *que* . . .)
lamentar to regret to
limitarse a to limit oneself to
llegar a to become/to go so far as to . . .
llevar a to lead to; see 16.5.2
lograr to succeed in
luchar por struggle to
mandar§ to order to (Fr. *ordonner de*);
  see 16.5.2
mandar a to send to (do something);
  see 16.5.2
manifestar to state/to declare (usually
  with *que* . . .)
maravillarse de to marvel at (see also
  16.6)
merecer to deserve to (usually with *que*)
meterse a to start to
mover a to move to
necesitar§ to need to
negar to deny (*negarse a* refuse to); see
  18.2.2
obligar a§ to oblige to (Fr. *obliger de*);
  see 16.5.2
obstinarse en to insist obstinately on
  (Fr. *s'obstiner à*)
ofrecer to offer (usually with *que* . . .)
oír§ to hear (see 20.7)
olvidar, to forget; infinitive *olvidar,
  olvidarse de, olvidársele*; see 26.7.26
optar (usually *optar por*) to opt to/for
ordenar§ to order to (Fr. *ordonner de*);
  see 16.5.2.

parar de§ to stop
parecer§ to seem to; see 18.2.2
pasar a§ to go on to
pasar de to be uninterested in
pedir to ask to (Fr. *demander à, demander de*); see 16.5.2, note (v)
pensar§ *pienso hacerlo* 'I plan to do it'
pensar en to think of (Fr. *penser à*)
permitir§ to allow to (Fr. *permettre de*); see 16.5.2
persistir en to persist in (Fr. *persister à*)
persuadir a to persuade to (Fr. *persuader à quelqu'un de faire* . . .); see 16.5.2
poder§ to be able to
ponerse a to start to
precipitarse a to rush to
preferir§ to prefer to
prepararse a to get ready to
presumir de (approx.) to boast about
pretender§ to claim to/to try to
proceder a to proceed to
procurar§ to try hard to
prohibir§ to prohibit from (Fr. *défendre de*) 16.5.2
prometer§ to promise to (Fr. *promettre de*)
quedar en to agree to
querer§ to want to (see 21.5)
reconocer to acknowledge (more usually with *que*)
recordar§ to remember to (see note iv)

rehuir to shun/to avoid
rehusar§ to refuse to (Fr. *refuser de*)
renunciar a§ to renounce
resignarse a to resign oneself to
resistirse a to resist
resultar to turn out to be
resolver§ to resolve to (Fr. *résoudre de*)
saber§ to know how to (see 21.2)
sentir to regret/to be sorry for (see 16.6)
soler: solía hacerlo§ 'he habitually did it' (see 21.6)
solicitar§ to apply to; see 16.5.2
soñar con to dream of
tardar en to be late in/to be a long time in (Fr. *tarder à*)
temer§ to fear to
tender a§ to tend to
tener que to have to; see 21.3 (and also *hay que*)
tentar a to tempt to; see 16.5.2
terminar de§ to finish
tratar de§ try to
vacilar en to hesitate over
venir de to come from . . .
ver§ to see (see 20.7)
ver de to try to
volver a (hacer)§ to (do) again (see 32.6a)
votar por to vote for

Notes

(i) Verbs followed by § allow pronoun shifting, i.e. one can say *acabo de hacerlo* or *lo acabo de hacer, pienso mudarme mañana* 'I'm thinking of moving tomorrow' or *me pienso mudar mañana*. Doubtful verbs, e.g. *fingir, afirmar*, are not marked. Pronoun shifting is discussed in detail at 11.14.4.

(ii) Verbs of motion, e.g. *salir, bajar, ir, volver, entrar, acercar(se)*, always take *a* before an infinitive: *bajó a verla* 'he went down to see her', *entraron a saludar al profesor* 'they went in to say hello to the teacher', etc. When the subjects are not identical, *a que* + subjunctive is required: *bajó a que la viera/viese* 'she went down so he could see her'.

(iii) For the use of the infinitive as a noun, e.g. *es bueno jugar al tenis* 'it's good to play tennis'/'playing tennis is good', see 18.6.

(iv) The construction is *me acuerdo de haberla visto* or *recuerdo haberla visto* 'I remember seeing her'. *Recordarse* can only mean 'to remember oneself', as in *me recuerdo como un niño muy tímido* 'I remember myself as a very timid child'. However *recordarse* for 'to remember' is common in familiar Latin-American speech, although it is avoided in careful styles and is considered incorrect in Spain.

18.2.4 Verbs of permitting and forbidding, and other verbs constructed with an indirect object

Most (but not all) verbs that can be constructed with an indirect object, e.g. *prohibir a alguien que cante/prohibir a alguien cantar* 'to forbid someone to sing', allow either a subjunctive or an infinitive construction. They are discussed under the subjunctive at 16.5.2.

It is worth repeating here that when used with the infinitive, verbs of obliging, prohibiting and permitting can appear without an object in Spanish but not in

English: *esto prohíbe pensar que . . .* 'this prohibits **us/one** from thinking that . . . ' See 16.5.2, note (i).

18.2.5 Infinitive after verbs of perception

The infinitive is used after verbs like *ver*, *oír*, *sentir* to denote a completed action. An incomplete action is indicated by the gerund. English makes the same distinction: compare 'I saw him smoke a cigar' and 'I saw him smoking a cigar.' See 20.7 for more examples:

Te vi entrar	I saw you come in
Se lo oí decir	I heard her/him/you (*usted*) say it
Te lo vi firmar	I saw you sign it
Vimos llegar el avión (note word order)	We saw the plane arrive
No he oído nunca aullar a un lobo, pero sé que era un lobo (J. L. Borges, Argentina, dialogue)	I've never heard a wolf howl, but I know it was a wolf
Nunca te había visto antes mirarte las uñas (S. Vodanovic, Chile, dialogue)	I'd never seen you look at your fingernails before
Ya estoy harta de oírlo hablar como si en América latina todo fuera de extrema izquierda (A. Bryce Echenique, Peru, dialogue)	I'm fed up with hearing you talk as though everything in Latin America were extreme left-wing
Marés sentía desintegrarse día a día su personalidad (J. Marsé, Spain)	Marés felt his personality disintegrate day by day

Note

Since the Spanish infinitive is neutral as to voice (i.e. it can be either active or passive), a passive may be required in the English translation: *nunca la oí nombrar* 'I've never heard her mention**ed**', *vio matar a varios prisioneros* 'he saw several prisoners kill**ed**'. Given this ambiguity with respect to voice, a sentence like *vi matar a dos leones*, could, out of context, mean either 'I saw two lions killed' or 'I saw two lions kill'. The first meaning comes most readily to mind.

18.3 Infinitive after prepositions and subordinators

18.3.1 Infinitive after prepositions

The infinitive is used after prepositions and prepositional phrases: *fue la primera* **en** *enterarse* 'she was the first to find out', *estoy harto* **de** *decírtelo* 'I'm tired of telling you', *reprende a la banca* **por** *arriesgarse* (*El País*, Spain) 'he reproaches the banks for taking risks', *un líquido* **para** *quitar las manchas* 'a liquid to remove stains', *un abrigo* **sin** *estrenar* 'an unworn coat', etc. Prepositions are never used before a Spanish gerund: **estoy harto de diciéndolo* is emphatically not Spanish. For a solitary and archaic exception to this rule see 20.5.

Some prepositional phrases are subordinators and may require a finite verb preceded by *que*, e.g. *a cambio de que lo hagas tú* 'in return for you doing it', *para que él lo haga* 'in order for him to do it'. See the next section.

18.3.2 Choice between the infinitive and *que* + finite verb

An infinitive construction is possible after a number of subordinators, listed at 16.12.2, e.g. *hasta* 'until', *para* 'in order to', *sin* 'without', *nada más* 'as soon as' and those consisting of phrases that require the word *de que* before a finite verb, e.g. *antes de (que)* 'before', *después de (que)* 'after', *el hecho de (que)* 'the fact that', etc.

Foreign students should apply the rule of co-referentiality: the infinitive should be used with these subordinators only if the subject of the subordinate verb is the same as the main verbs, as in *lo hice antes de salir* 'I did it before I went out/before going out'.

If the subjects are different, the subjunctive or indicative must be used (although the rule is applied loosely with *antes de* and *después de*), the choice being determined by the rules laid out at 16.12.1. Compare *lo haré nada más acabar esto* 'I'll do it as soon as I've finished this' and *lo haré nada más que acabe esto* 'I'll do it as soon as this finishes'. The latter sentence could also, however, mean 'as soon as I finish this' or 'as soon as (s)he finishes/you finish . . . '. Further examples:

Lo haré después de comer/de que coma	I'll do it after I've had lunch
Lo haré después de que hayáis comido	I'll do it after you've had lunch
Entré sin verte	I entered without seeing you
Entré sin que tú me vieras/vieses	I entered without you seeing me
Se fue antes de contestar	He left before he answered
Se fue antes de que yo contestase/contestara	He left before I answered
Enfermó (Lat. Am. se enfermó) por no comer	He fell ill/(US 'sick') from not eating

Spontaneous language often uses an infinitive construction with these subordinators even when the subjects are not identical. Thus *lo terminé antes de que tú llegases/llegaras* 'I finished before you arrived' is correct, *lo terminé antes de llegar tú* is constantly heard in informal speech. This use of the infinitive when the subjects are different is best avoided by foreigners, but its use is spreading rapidly in colloquial language. Further examples:

?*Le miraba sin él darse cuenta* (J. Marsé, dialogue: *sin que él se diese/diera cuenta*)	He watched him without him realizing
?*¿Te voy a ver antes de irte?* (Spanish informant, i.e. . . . *antes de que te vayas*)	Am I going to see you before you go?
?*Llegamos antes de empezar la película* (*antes de que empezara/empezase . . .*)	We arrived before the film started
Es decir que había comprado marfil para usted vender (*Vindicación de Cuba*, Cuba, dialogue, for . . . *para que usted lo vendiera/vendiese*)	In other words he had bought ivory for you to sell
¿Me podés comprar postales para mandar yo? (Argentinian informant, i.e. *para que que yo las mande*; Spain *puedes* for *podés*)	Could you buy me some postcards for me to send?

18.3.3 *Al* + infinitive

In theory, *al* + infinitive ought probably to be confined to co-referential sentences, as in *me di cuenta al llegar* 'I realized on arriving/when I arrived'. But sentences like *me di cuenta al llegar Juan* literally ?'I realized on Juan's arriving' (not co-referential) are very common for *me di cuenta cuando llegó Juan* 'I realized when Juan arrived'. Further examples:

Se enfadó al enterarse	He got angry when he found out
Se hace camino al andar (Antonio Machado, Spain)	One makes one's path as one goes along

Al fumarlo los indios experimentaban una especie de éxtasis (*El País*, Spain)	When they smoked it the Indians experienced a sort of ecstasy
Al comprar uno de nuestros productos, te obsequiamos . . . (advertisement, Spain; not co-referential better *cuando compras . . .*)	When you buy one of our products we give you as a present . . .

18.4 Replacement of finite forms by the infinitive

(a) The infinitive may be used to give a brief answer a question:

—*¿Qué hacemos? —Esperar*	'What do we do?' 'Wait'
—*¿Qué me aconsejas? —No decir nada*	'What do you advise me?' 'Say nothing'
—*¿Pero se puede saber que está usted haciendo? —¡Sacar a mi mujer!* (E. Arenas, Spain, dialogue)	'But do you mind telling me what you're doing?' 'Getting my wife out!'
—*¿Y ahora qué vas a hacer, Martín? —Entrar por la puerta principal* (A. Bryce Echenique, Peru, dialogue)	'And what are you going to do now, Martín?' 'Go in through the front door'

(b) After *más que, menos, excepto*:

Yo siempre sospeché que había algo después de la muerte. Más que sospecharlo, lo sabía, casi con seguridad (J. de Jesús Martínez, Panama, dialogue)	I always suspected that there was something after death. More than suspect it, I knew, almost as a certainty
. . . ojos que más que mirar, retan (E. Arenas, Spain)	. . . eyes that rather than look, challenge
. . . todo, menos/excepto decirle la verdad	. . . anything, except tell him/her the truth

(c) For naming or listing actions, as in:

. . . y esto es lo que hacen los campesinos: arar, plantar, podar, regar	. . . and this is what peasants do: ploughing/(US 'plowing'), planting, pruning, watering
¿Sabéis lo que yo hago después de que vosotros os habéis ido a casa? Trabajar	Do you know what I do after you've gone home? Work

18.5 Infinitive: passive or active?

The Spanish infinitive may have a passive meaning, especially after *sin, por, a* and *para*:

Esto aún está por ver	This is still to be seen
una cerveza sin abrir	an unopened beer
casas a medio construir	half-built houses
Los republicanos llegan a la convención . . . con las tácticas electorales sin decidir (*El País*, Spain)	The Republicans are arriving at the Convention . . . with their electoral tactics undecided
Pasaba el tiempo sin sentir (C. Martín Gaite, Spain)	Time passed unnoticed
En su recámara había cuatro maletas a medio hacer (A. Mastretta, Mexico, dialogue; *recámara* = *dormitorio* in Spain)	In her bedroom there were four half-packed suitcases
Transcurrieron años sin tener noticias de lo ocurrido	Years passed without (lit. 'without having') news of what had happened being received

| *. . . trabajos para hacer por el estudiante* | *. . .* work to be done (lit. 'to do') by the student |

18.6 Infinitive as a noun

The infinitive may function as a noun, in which case it is sometimes translated by an English *-ing* form. Used as a noun, an infinitive is always masculine and usually singular:

Mañana me toca lavar el coche	It's my turn to wash the car tomorrow
Votar Comunista es votar contra el paro (election poster)	To vote Communist is to vote against unemployment
aquel fluir movedizo de los colores . . . (C. Martín Gaite, Spain)	that shifting flow of the colo(u)rs . . .
Mejor no hacerlo	Best not do it
Odio ordenar	I hate sorting/tidying
un atolondrado ir y venir	a mad coming and going
Contemplar en vídeo el sufrimiento auténtico de algún semejante es mucho peor que infligirlo uno mismo (E. Lynch, Argentina)	To watch the actual suffering of another human being on video is much worse than actually inflicting it on him

18.7 Definite articles before the infinitive

The definite article is used before the infinitive:

(a) In the common construction *al* + infinitive:

| *Al entrar, se dio cuenta de que no había nadie* | On entering, he realized no one was there |
| *Tómese una pastilla al acostarse* | Take a pill on going to bed |

(b) When the infinitive is qualified by an adjective or by a noun phrase joined to the infinitive, often by the preposition *de*:

Oyó el agitado girar de una cucharilla contra un vaso (L. Goytisolo, Spain)	He heard the agitated grating of a teaspoon against a glass
Cristina escuchó el percutir de las gotas de la ducha sobre los azulejos (L. Otero, Cuba)	Cristina heard the splatter of drops from the shower on the tiles
. . . el envejecer despacio entre laureles marchitos y ciénagas (G. García Márquez, Colombia)	. . . ageing slowly among withered laurels and swamps
con el andar de los años	as the years passed by

(c) The infinitive seems to be obligatory when it refers to some specific or personal action rather than to a general statement. Compare *vivir separados cuesta más* 'living apart costs more' (general statement) and *el vivir separados fue cosa de él* 'living apart was his idea' (specific, personal). Also:

| *Ayuda mucho dejar de fumar* | It helps to stop smoking |
| *Fue idea del médico **el** dejar de fumar* | Stopping smoking was the doctor's idea |

(d) In other cases when the infinitive is used as a noun, the definite article seems to be optional, although it is much less common in informal styles. The article is, however, quite often retained when the infinitive is the subject of a verb.

In all the following examples the definite article before the infinitive could have been omitted, although in the attributed examples it was in fact used. Omission would make the style slightly less literary:

Paula no pudo evitar (el) reírse (J. J. Plans, Spain)	Paula couldn't help laughing
¿Por qué no se lo deja permanentemente aquí y se evita así (el) estar trayéndolo y llevándolo? (J. de Jesús Martínez, Panama, dialogue)	Why don't you leave it here for him permanently? That way you'll avoid fetching it and taking it away (again)
En 1604 Jaime I de Inglaterra decía que (el) fumar era 'abominable para el ojo, odioso para la nariz, dañino para el cerebro y peligroso para los pulmones' (*Cambio16*, Spain)	In 1604 James I of England said that smoking was 'abominable to the eye, hateful to the nose, damaging to the brain and dangerous to the lungs'
(El) hacer esto le costó mucho trabajo	Doing this cost him a great deal of effort
Esto permite a los robots (el) ser reprogramados para . . .	This allows robots to be reprogrammed to . . .

(e) The article is required in some constructions involving *en*:

La moda en el vestir influye en la moda del maquillaje	Fashion in dressing influences fashion in make-up
Algunos españoles son un poco enfáticos en el hablar	Some Spaniards are rather ponderous in their manner of speaking
Le conocí en el andar	I recognized him from his way of walking

(f) After set verb phrases involving a preposition the article is omitted:

Hice mal en venir aquí	I did wrong in coming here
Tardaron horas en hacerlo	They took hours to do it
Acabaron por no hablarse con nadie	They ended up not talking to anyone
Tratábamos de contactarla	We were trying to contact her

(g) The indefinite article *un* is also found before a qualified infinitive:

en un abrir y cerrar de ojos	in the wink of an eye
Después de dos años de un agitado avanzar por el camino de la libertad . . .	after two years of agitated progress (lit. 'agitated progressing') along the road to liberty . . .

18.8 Infinitive as an imperative

The use of the infinitive as an imperative form is discussed at 17.9.

18.9 'Rhetorical' infinitive

The infinitive may be used in rhetorical questions or to express disbelief or indignation:

¡Pagar yo cien mil por eso!	What! Me pay 100,000 for that!
¡Enamorarme yo a mis años!	Me fall in love at my age!
Pero, ¿cómo abrirlo sin llave?	But how (on earth) does one open it without a key?

18.10 Adjective + de + infinitive

A sentence like *es difícil aprender español* 'it's difficult to learn Spanish' differs from *el español es difícil **de** aprender* 'Spanish is difficult to learn'. *De* is not used when the adjective modifies the infinitive itself:

No es fácil creerlo	It isn't easy to believe it
Es increíble pensar que el hombre ha pisado la luna	It's incredible to think that man has walked on the moon
Es imposible comprobar que . . .	It's difficult to prove that . . .

When the adjective does not modify the infinitive but some noun or pronoun (present or implied), *de* is used:

*(Eso) es difícil **de** averiguar (difícil modifies eso)*	That's difficult to check
*Creo que es cierto, pero es imposible **de** comprobar*	I think it's true, but it's impossible to prove
*Para este Día del Padre sorprenda a papá con un delicioso menú fácil y rápido **de** elaborar (La Reforma, Mexico)*	For today, Father's Day, surprise father with a delicious menu that's easy and quick to prepare

18.11 Infinitive preceded by *que*

The following construction must be noted, particularly by students of French: cf. *j'ai beaucoup **à** faire, je n'ai rien **à** faire*, etc.:

*Tengo mucho **que** hacer*	I've got a lot to do
*Voy a comprar algo **que/para** leer*	I'm going to buy something to read
*Dame algo **que/para** hacer*	Give me something to do
*Eso nos ha dado bastante **que** hacer*	This has given us enough to do
*Te queda mucho **que** sufrir en este mundo*	You've a lot left to suffer in this world

But this construction with *que* cannot be used with verbs of needing, requesting, searching:

*Necesito algo **para** comer*	I need something to eat
*Quiero algo **para** beber*	I want something to drink
*Pidió algo **para** calmar su dolor de muelas*	He asked for something to soothe his toothache
*Busco algo **para** . . .*	I'm looking for something to . . .

Note

The construction with *que* must be distinguished from the following similar construction with **qué** (stressed word) 'what'/'anything': *no tengo **qué** comer* 'I haven't got anything to eat', *no sabemos **qué** pensar* 'we don't know what to think'.

18.12 *El problema a resolver, un argumento a tomar en cuenta, etc.*

This combination of a noun + *a* + an infinitive is an increasingly fashionable alternative way of saying 'the problem to be solved', etc. Seco (1998), 5, says that it is a Gallicism reinforced by the influence of English – 'a problem to (be) solve(d)', *un problème à résoudre* – but he welcomes its brevity and points out that it is not strictly equivalent to *por* + infinitive: *cosas por hacer* = 'things still to be done', *cosas a hacer* = 'things to do'. The Academy's *Esbozo . . .*, 3.11.5, tolerates certain set expressions used in commerce and finance, e.g. *total a pagar* 'total payable', *cantidades a deducir* 'amounts deductible', *asuntos a tratar* 'business pending'/'agenda', but notes that the Academies of all Spanish-speaking countries condemn such sentences as *tengo terrenos a vender* 'I've got land to sell' (for *que*/*para vender*), *personas a convocar* 'people to call/summon' (for *que convocar*), etc.

This construction with *a* is more widely accepted in Latin America, cf. *los uniformados presentaron hace poco un nuevo texto a ser considerado* (*ABC Color*, Paraguay) 'the military recently presented a new text for consideration'. For more examples see 35.9.

19

Participles

This chapter discusses past participles, e.g. *hablado* 'spoken', *visto* 'seen', and adjectival or present participles ending in *-ante*, *-(i)ente*, e.g. *perteneciente* 'belonging', *inquietante* 'worrying'.

19.1 Past participle: general

The past participle has several functions:

(a) It is used with *haber* to form the compound tenses of verbs: *ha hablado* 'he has spoken', *yo la había visto* 'I had seen her'. See 14.8 for discussion.

(b) It is occasionally used with *tener* or *llevar* to emphasize the idea of acquisition or accumulation, as in *tengo compradas las entradas* 'I've bought the entrance tickets', *llevo tomados tres somníferos* 'I've taken three sleeping tablets'. See 14.8.3 for discussion.

(c) It is used to form the passive: *fue impreso* 'it was printed', *fueron observados/observadas* 'they were observed'. The passive is discussed in Chapter 28.

(d) It functions as an adjective, in which case it agrees in number and gender like any adjective: *una exagerada reacción* 'an exaggerated reaction', *un argumento improvisado* 'an improvised argument', *una desesperada tentativa* 'a desperate attempt', etc. These adjectival past participles can, like any adjective, be converted into nouns by the use of an article, demonstrative adjective, numeral or some other word that has the effect of turning adjectives into nouns: *un muerto* 'a dead person', *ese herido* 'that wounded person', *¿qué dirán por su parte los censurados?* 'what will those who have been censured have to say for themselves?', *varios condenados* 'several condemned persons'. Such forms can neatly replace an English relative clause: *nunca olvidaremos a los desaparecidos* 'we'll never forget those who disappeared', *¿dónde están los recién llegados?* 'where are the ones who've just arrived?'

Many words ending in *-ado*, *-ido* are used only as adjectives, e.g. *adecuado* 'appropriate'/'adequate', *desgraciado* 'unhappy', *desmesurado* 'disproportionate', *indiscriminado* 'indiscriminate', *descarado* 'shameless', etc. But the majority can function either as verbal participles (e.g. *había alarmado a los vecinos* 'he had alarmed the neighbours'/(US 'neighbors'), or as adjectives: *las caras alarmadas de los vecinos* 'the neighbo(u)rs' alarmed faces'. Further examples of the many participles that have this dual function are:

elevado elevated	*desconocido* unknown	*justificado* justified
debido due	*disecado* stuffed (animal)	*resignado* resigned
dedicado dedicated	*emocionado* excited	*supuesto* alleged/supposed

Most past participles that can function as adjectives can appear with *ser* without creating a passive sentence: *su reacción era exagerada* 'his reaction was exaggerated', *mi llanto era desesperado* 'my weeping was desperate', *su cara me era desconocida,* 'her/his face was unknown to me'. Verbal participles form passive sentences when used in the same way: *la ciudad fue destruida* 'the city was destroyed', *eran perseguidos* 'they were being persecuted/pursued'. In the latter case it may be possible to make the verbal participle adjectival by using *estar*, e.g. *la ciudad estaba destruida* 'the city was in a state of destruction'. See 28.2.5 for details.

19.2 Past participles: forms

19.2.1 Regular and irregular past participles

The past participle is formed in most cases by replacing the *-ar* of an infinitive by *-ado*, and *-er* and *-ir* by *-ido*: *hablar/hablado, tener/tenido, construir/construido* (no accent!), *ir/ido, ser/sido*, etc. There are a few common irregular past participles (shown in bold type):

absolver (and all verbs ending in *-solver*) **absuelto**	*imprimir* **impreso** (*imprimido* is also heard in compound tenses)
cubrir (and all verbs ending in *-cubrir*) **cubierto**	*morir* **muerto** (see note i)
decir (and all verbs ending in *-decir*§) **dicho**	*poner* (and all verbs ending in *-poner*) **puesto**
escribir (and all verbs ending in *-scribir*) **escrito**	*romper* **roto**
freír **frito**	*ver* (and compounds like *prever*) **visto**
hacer **hecho**	*volver* (and all verbs ending in *volver*) **vuelto**

(§See the next paragraph for *maldecir*.)

A few have separate adjectival and verbal participles; compare *está* **despierto** *porque lo/le he despertado* 'he's awake because I've woken him', *ahora que han* **soltado** *a los animales andan* **sueltos** 'now they've released the animals they're wandering free', *el agua que ha* **bendecido** *un cura se llama agua* **bendita** 'the water that a priest has blessed is called holy water'. In the following list the participles are in bold type, verbal participle first:

absorber **absorbido/absorto** absorbed	*maldecir* **maldecido/maldito** cursed
bendecir **bendecido/bendito** blessed	*prender* **prendido/preso** pinned on (see note iii)
confesar **confesado/confeso** confessed	
confundir **confundido/confuso** confused	*presumir* **presumido/presunto** presumed
despertar **despertado/despierto** woken up	*proveer* **proveído/provisto** equipped with
elegir **elegido/electo** elected	*soltar* **soltado/suelto** released
freír **(freído)/frito** fried (see note ii)	*suspender* **suspendido/suspenso** failed (e.g. exams)
imprimir **(imprimido)/impreso** printed	

Notes

(i) *Muerto* is also the passive past participle of *matar* 'to kill' when applied to human beings: *su padre fue* **muerto** *durante la guerra* 'his father was killed in the war' but *unos bandidos habían* **matado** *a su padre* 'some bandits had killed his father'; compare also *con el tiempo sería muerto por la Gestapo* (Ernesto Sábato, Argentina, interview) 'he was later to be killed by the Gestapo'.
(ii) *Frito* is nowadays used in all cases, and forms like *he freído* for *he frito* are considered archaic, although they are occasionally used by some speakers.
(iii) *Prender* has numerous meanings: *preso* often means an inmate (of a jail). In Latin America *prender* is often used for 'to switch on' lights, etc.; Spain *encender*.

19.2.2 Irregular past participles in Latin America

A number of irregular adjectival participle forms are more widely used in Latin America than in Spain, especially in Argentina. These are scholarly participles that are either obsolete in Spain or used only in set phrases, e.g. *el presidente electo* 'the president elect'. But they are regularly used in Latin America not only as adjectives but also in the formation of passives, e.g. *resultó electo candidato a la presidencia* (A. Mastretta, Mexico) 'he was elected as presidential candidate', Spain *salió elegido*. In the following list the standard form appears first:

convencer **convencido**/**convicto**
  convinced
corromper **corrompido**/**corrupto** corrupt
describir **descrito**/**descripto** described

dividir **dividido**/**diviso** divided
inscribir **inscrito**/**inscripto** entered (a
  written item)
prescribir **prescrito**/**prescripto** prescribed

Ocurre en las regiones antárticas descriptas con extraordinaria vividez . . . (J. L. Borges, Argentina, Spain *descritas*)

It happens in the Antarctic regions described with extraordinary vividness . . .

Incluye todos los shampoos prescriptos por médicos (*Gente*, Argentina; Spain *recetados*/*prescritos*)

It includes all the shampoos prescribed by doctors

. . . escritores que fueron conservadores convictos (M. Vargas Llosa, Peru; in Spain *convicto* = 'convicted')

. . . writers who were convinced conservatives

Latin Americans may reject the use of the regular participles in such sentences, but the irregular forms are not accepted by most Peninsular speakers, and certainly not in the formation of the passive.

Note

Both *una sociedad corrompida* and *una sociedad corrupta* 'a corrupt society' are said in Spain, the latter being now more usual. *Corrupto* is usual in Latin America, but compare . . . *los congresistas son corrompidos* (*El Tiempo*, Colombia) 'the Congressmen are corrupt'.

19.3 Participle clauses

Participle clauses are common in Spanish. These clauses often have exact English counterparts, but slight differences occur between the two languages (see also 31.3.4 for sentences like *aceptó irritada* 'she accepted irritably'):

Me fui, convencido de que él no sabía nada
José González, nacido el 23 de marzo
¿Dónde vas? preguntó alarmado
su padre, muerto en 1956 . . .

I left, convinced he knew nothing
José González, born on 23 March
Where are you going? he asked in alarm
his father, who died in 1956 . . .

> *. . . preguntado qué le había gustado de ella,*   . . . asked what he had liked about her,
> *contesta con un gruñido* (G. García   he replies with a grunt
> Márquez Colombia)

Absolute participle clauses (i.e. participles that do not depend on another verb in the sentence) are quite common, especially in literary styles. Some absolute participle constructions are stylistically normal, others are rather literary. They can rarely be translated word for word:

Llegados a Madrid, se alojaron en el mejor hotel (see note)	Having arrived in Madrid, they stayed at the best hotel
Concluidas las primeras investigaciones, la policía abandonó el lugar de autos	The initial investigations having been concluded, the police left the scene of the crime
. . . por fin, transcurridos siete años desde la publicación de su primera novela . . .	. . . at last, seven years having passed since the publication of his first novel . . .
Después de vendida la casa, nos arrepentimos (from Seco, 1998, 334)	Once the house was sold, we regretted it
Arrasado el jardín, profanados los cálices y las aras, entraron a caballo los hunos en la biblioteca monástica (J. L. Borges, Argentina; very literary)	Having demolished the garden and profaned chalices and altars, the Huns rode into the monastery library
Cortados el teléfono y el telégrafo e inutilizada la radio, la única manera es que alguien vaya a Huancayo a dar aviso (M. Vargas Llosa, Peru, dialogue; Latin American? Spain . . . *con el teléfono cortado*, etc.)	With the phone and telegraph cut and the radio out of action, the only way is for someone to go to Huancayo with a message

Note

Llegar seems to be the only verb of motion that allows this construction. One cannot say **entrada en el agua se puso a nadar* 'entering the water she began to swim': *cuando entró en el agua se puso a nadar*, or *bajados del tren for *cuando bajaron del tren* 'when they got out of the train'.

19.4 Participles in *-ante*, *-iente* or *-ente*

Adjectival present participles may be formed from many but by no means all verbs. Such participles function like the English adjectival forms in -ing: 'Sleeping Beauty' = *La Bella Durmiente*. New coinages are appearing constantly, many of them inspired by English adjectives ending in -ing.

Adjectival participles are formed thus:

-ar conjugation: replace the *-ar* of the infinitive by *-ante*: *alarmar>alarmante* 'alarming' *inquietar>inquietante* 'worrying';
-er conjugation: replace the *-er* of the infinitive by *-iente* or, in a few cases, by *-ente*
-ir conjugation: replace the *-iendo* of the gerund by *-iente* or *-ente*, the choice being unpredictable.

Examples from the *-er* and *-ir* conjugations:

crecer **creciendo>creciente** growing	*dormir* **durmiendo>durmiente** sleeping
proceder **procediendo>procedente** proceeding	*herir* **hiriendo>hiriente** wounding
sorprender **sorprendiendo>sorprendente** surprising	*producir* **produciendo>producente** producing (*contraproducente*, counter-productive)

*tender **tendiendo>tendente** tending (to)*
*concernir **concerniendo>concerniente***
concerning
*conducir **conduciendo>conducente***
leading (to)
*existir **existiendo>existente***
existing/extant

*sonreír **sonriendo>sonriente***
smiling
*reír **riendo>riente** laughing*
*salir **saliendo>saliente** outgoing, etc.*
*seguir **siguiendo>siguiente***
following

There are a few irregular forms (the gerund is shown in brackets):

convencer (convenciendo) convincente
convincing
convenir (conviniendo) conveniente suitable

fluir (fluyendo) fluente flowing/fluent
provenir (proviniendo) proveniente de
coming from

Forms in *-nte* cannot be made from all verbs and they should be learnt separately from the dictionary, especially in view of the remark in note (ii). They are often used in written, mainly journalistic style to replace relative clauses in the same way as English participles in *-ing*:

una situación cambiante/estresante	a changing/stressful situation
el ministro saliente/entrante	the outgoing/incoming minister
condiciones vinculantes (El País, Spain)	binding conditions
resultados sobresalientes	outstanding results
un éxito fulminante	a resounding success
el millón y medio restante	the remaining 1.5 million
157.000 personas, pertenecientes a diferentes clases sociales y procedentes de lugares muy distintos de nacimiento, votaron . . . (*El País*, Spain)	157,000 people, belonging to various social classes and originating from widely different places, voted . . .
. . . en fin, todo conducente a la violencia obtusa . . . (*Triunfo*, Spain)	. . . in short, anything leading to simple-minded violence . . .

Notes

(i) The gerund in *-ando* or *-iendo* could not be used instead of the *-nte* form in any of these examples. See 20.3 for discussion.

(ii) These participles are formed unpredictably. English speakers often invent non-existent words like **moviente* for 'moving': *piezas móviles* = 'moving parts', *espectáculo conmovedor* = 'moving spectacle'. Compare also *mesa plegable* 'folding table', *agua potable* 'drinking water', *confiado/crédulo* = 'confiding', *planta trepadora* = 'climbing plant', *resultados satisfactorios* 'satisfying results', *hechos reveladores* 'revealing facts', *un libro aburrido* 'a boring book', *es cansado* 'it's tiring', and many others.

(iii) Many forms in *-nte* are not strictly speaking participles but non-verbal adjectives, e.g. *brillante* 'shining', *corriente* 'current'/'ordinary', *aparente* 'apparent', *reciente* 'recent', etc.

(iv) With the exception of a few slang or popular words, e.g. *dominanta* 'bossy' (of a woman), *currante>curranta* (familiar Peninsular Spanish for 'hard-working'), *atorrante>atorranta* (Lat. Am.) 'slacker'/'layabout'/(US 'bum'), *golfante>golfanta* (popular Peninsular Spanish for 'rascal'/'no-good'), neither participles nor adjectives ending in *-nte* have a separate feminine form. However, a few nouns in *-nte* make their feminine with *-nta*. See 1.2.5.

20

The gerund

For the use of the gerund to form the continuous aspect of verbs, e.g. *estoy hablando* 'I'm talking', *estaba diciendo* 'he was saying', etc. see Chapter 15.

20.1 General

The gerund is invariable in form, but pronouns are sometimes attached to it. This may be obligatory, as in *contestó riéndose* 'she replied (by) laughing', or optional as in *estaba esperándolos* or *los estaba esperando* 'he was waiting for them'. See 11.14.5 for details.

The Spanish gerund is quite unlike the English -ing form, which serves as gerund, present participle, noun and adjective; and it is also unlike the French form ending in *-ant* which covers the functions of both the Spanish gerund and the adjectival form in *-ante, -(i)ente* (discussed at 19.4).

The Spanish gerund is theoretically a kind of adverb and can therefore properly only modify verbs, but not nouns. ?*Una caja conteniendo libros* 'a box containing books' is therefore bad Spanish since there is no verb: this mistake is very common among English-speakers and quite common among native speakers. See 20.3 for detailed discussion.

Except in one archaic construction described at 20.5, the Spanish gerund is never preceded by a preposition.

20.2 Forms of the gerund

(a) All verbs of the *-ar* conjugation, including radical changing verbs: replace the *-ar* of the infinitive by *-ando*: *hablar* 'to speak' > *hablando*, *dar* 'to give' > *dando*.
(b) Verbs of the *-er* and *-ir* conjugations: replace the infinitive ending with *-iendo*: *temer* 'to fear' > *temiendo*, *vivir* 'to live' > *viviendo*, *producir* 'to produce' > *produciendo*.

Irregular verbs form the gerund in the same way: *ser>siendo, tener>teniendo,* with the following exceptions:

decir and its compounds: *diciendo*	verbs ending in *-llir: bullendo*
dormir, morir: durmiendo, muriendo	verbs ending in *-ñir* or *-ñer: tañendo*
erguirse: irguiéndose	verbs like *construir: construyendo, huyendo*
ir: yendo (regular, despite appearances)	verbs like *pedir: pidiendo*
oír and its compounds: *oyendo*	verbs like *poseer: poseyendo, leyendo*
poder: pudiendo	verbs like *reír: riendo, sonriendo*
traer, caer and compounds:	verbs like *sentir: sintiendo, riñendo*
trayendo, cayendo	
venir and its compounds: *viniendo*	

20.3 'A box containing books' 'a girl speaking French', etc.

English and French regularly replace relative clauses by a participle construction using the -ing form or the -*ant* form of the verb:

We need a girl who speaks French
We need a girl speak**ing** French
He had a box that contained several books He had a box contain**ing** several books
C'est là une réponse qui équivaut à un refus/
C'est là une réponse équivalant à un refus
(That's a reply that amounts to a refusal)

Since the Spanish gerund can strictly speaking modify only verbs and not nouns, such sentences must usually be translated by a relative clause:

Necesitamos una chica que hable francés   We need a girl who speaks French
   (not **hablando francés*)
Tenía una caja que contenía varios libros   He had a box containing several books
   (not **conteniendo libros*)
Esa/Ésa es una respuesta que equivale a   That's a reply amounting to a refusal
   una negativa (not **equivaliendo a*)

The gerund is possible only when there is a verb in the main clause to which it can refer, e.g. *me escribió pidiéndome que fuera a verla* 'she wrote a letter asking me to go and see her'. *El cartero trajo una carta pidiendo dinero* 'the postman brought a letter asking for money' is therefore correct only if *pidiendo* refers to *trajo . . .* and not to *carta*, i.e. only if the postman himself is asking for money.
   However, this rule is broken:

(a) In captions to pictures

Dos 747 siendo preparados para el despegue   Two 747s being prepared for take-off
El Avante publicó mi foto quitándome los   *Avante* published a photo of me
   aretes (A. Mastretta, Mexico, dialogue)   taking off my earrings (lit. ear 'hoops')

(b) After verbs meaning 'hear', 'imagine', 'see', 'find', usually to show that the action is actually in progress. See 20.7 for more details.
(c) In the exceptional cases of the adjectives *ardiendo* 'burning' and *hirviendo* 'boiling'. See 4.4 for discussion.
(d) In official and administrative documents: *una ley decretando . . .* (= *una ley por la que se decreta* 'a law decreeing . . . '. This construction, sometimes called the *gerundio curialense* or 'lawyers' gerund', is deeply entrenched in certain documents, e.g. the *Boletín Oficial del Estado* (where Spanish laws are published), but Seco (1998), 228, condemns it, as does the Academy's *Esbozo . . .* , 3.16.8.
(e) Occasionally by writers whose style is presumably above reproach:

El propósito de Probo, el hombre solo   It was not possible to realize the goal
   afrontando a la multitud, no se pudo   of Probus, the man alone facing
   realizar (Seco, 1998, xvii)   the multitude

—despite his unequivocal condemnation of this very construction (Seco, 1998, 228).
(f) Constantly in spontaneous speech and informal writing:

. . . luego ya en mi habitación, recién limpia   then back in my room, (which was)
   y oliendo a ambientador de flores   recently cleaned and smelling of
   (C. Martín Gaite, Spain)   flower-scented air-freshener

Tenía mi edad y un hijo viviendo con su mamá (A. Mastretta, Mexico, dialogue)	She was my age and had a son living with her mother
el tenue ruido de un cuerpo moviéndose con sigilo (L. Sepúlveda, Chile)	the sound of a body moving stealthily
. . . con la luna ahí colgando para nosotros (A. Bryce Echenique, Peru)	. . . with the moon hanging there for us
Hombres trabajando a 400m (Mexican road sign)	Men working at 400 metres/ (US 'meters')

Foreign learners should probably avoid all these uses of the gerund except **(a)**, **(b)** and **(c)**. However, the grammarians' wholesale condemnation of **(d)** to **(f)** seems excessive, since in certain contexts these constructions are clearly acceptable to careful native speakers.

Notes

(i) The participle form ending in *-nte* may sometimes be used like the English *-ing* form: *. . . personas pertenecientes a diferentes clases sociales* ' . . . people belonging to different social classes'. This construction, possible only with a limited number of verbs and uncommon, is discussed at 19.4.

(ii) French also allows the *-ant* form to refer to a subject different from that of the main clause: *la pluie tombant à verse, le voyageur s'arrête sous un hangar*, **ya que** *llovía a cántaros, el viajero se detuvo bajo un granero*, '**since** it was pouring, the traveller (US 'traveler') stopped under a barn'.

20.4 Main uses of the gerund to modify the main verb in the sentence

20.4.1 Gerund used to indicate simultaneous actions

The gerund is used to indicate an action happening at the same time as the action of the main verb:

Se fue gritando	He went off shouting
Nos recibió bañándose	She received us while she was having a bath
Metió la carta en el sobre, cerrándolo a continuación	(S)he put the letter in the envelope, sealing it afterwards
Me bajé del caballo queriendo un zumo de naranja (A. Mastretta, Mexico)	I got down from my horse as I wanted (lit. 'wanting') an orange juice
. . . y en el séquito se habían metido Ariel y Remesa, **siendo** *el editor el que tenía que cambiar el paso constantemente* (M. Vázquez Montalbán, Spain)	. . . Ariel and Remesa had joined the gang/retinue, it being the publisher who had to make an effort to keep up

The action denoted by the gerund must be happening at the same time as, or almost simultaneously with, that of the main verb. Sentences like *?el ladrón huyó volviendo horas más tarde* 'the thief fled, returning hours later' should be expressed *el ladrón huyó y volvió horas más tarde*. *?Abriendo la puerta, entró en la casa* (better *abrió la puerta y entró en la casa*) is less acceptable in Spanish than 'opening the door, he entered the house'. Note also that the Spanish gerund should not be used to describe an action that is the result of a previous action: one says *el edificio se hundió y mató a varias personas* not *?se hundió matando a varias personas* 'the building collapsed **killing** several people' – although journalists and TV and radio announcers often break this rule in Spanish.

Note

With the verbs *ser* and *estar* the gerund can translate 'when' or 'while', a construction strange to English-speakers: *estando en París, me enteré de que su padre había muerto* 'while I was in Paris, I found out that his father had died', *le conocí siendo yo bombero* 'I met him while I was a fireman', *te lo diré, pero no estando aquí esta señora* 'I'll tell you, but not while this lady is here'.

20.4.2 Gerund used to indicate method

The gerund may indicate the method by which an action is performed. English usually requires the preposition 'by':

Hizo su fortuna comprando acciones a tiempo — He made his fortune (by) buying shares at the right time

Elijo libros a través de las sugerencias de los periódicos y yendo a numerosas conferencias (Queen Sofía, quoted in *El País*) — I choose books from suggestions in the newspapers and by going to numerous lectures

Hacéis divinamente no teniendo niños (Antonio Gala, Spain, dialogue) — You're doing just the right thing by not having children

Estás obligado a escribir otra novela. No publicando ésta/esta te he hecho un favor (M. Vázquez Montalbán, Spain, dialogue) — You're obliged to write another novel. I've done you a favo(u)r by not publishing this one

Conozco mucha gente que trabajando logró lo que quería (A. Arrafut, Cuba, dialogue) — I know a lot of people who got what they wanted by working

Note

This construction is often equivalent to a condition: *apretando/si lo aprietas de ese modo lo vas a romper* 'you'll break it if you squeeze it/by squeezing it like that', *poniéndose/si se pone así conmigo usted no conseguirá nada* 'you'll get nowhere if you get like that with me'.

20.4.3 Gerund used to express purpose (= *para* + infinitive)

This construction occurs with verbs of communication:

Me escribió diciéndome/para decirme que fuera/fuese a verle — He wrote telling me to come and see him

Nos llamó pidiendo/para pedir dinero — He rang us asking/to ask for money

Letonia y Estonia han aprobado leyes privando a la población rusa del derecho de ciudadanía (*El País*, Spain) — Latvia and Estonia have passed/ published laws depriving their Russian population of citizenship

20.4.4 Gerund used to indicate cause (= *ya que* ... , *puesto que* ... + finite verb)

Siendo estudiante, tendrá usted derecho a una beca — Since you're a student, you'll be entitled to a grant

Tratándose de usted, no faltaba más — Since it's you, there's no need to mention it

Confieso que, a mí, siendo editor, lo único que me preocupa es que no lean (*Cambio16*, Spain) — I admit that, being a publisher, the only thing that worries me is that they don't read

No queriendo molestar me fui — Not wanting to be a nuisance, I left

No sabiendo qué hacer se volvió a sentar cerca de la puerta — Not knowing what to do, he sat down again by the door

Un día, no teniendo nada que hacer, fue a verla — One day, not having anything to do, he went to see her

20.4.5 Gerund used to express concession (= *aunque* + finite verb)

The Spanish gerund occasionally signifies 'although', often in combination with *aun* 'even'.

Siendo inteligente como es, parece tonto	Although intelligent, he looks stupid
Aun estando enfermo nos resulta útil	He's useful to us, even though he's ill/(US 'sick')
Llegando tarde y todo, nos ayudó mucho	Although he arrived late, he helped us a lot
*Es probable que este servicio no se ofrezca en su provincia o que, **aun existiendo**, no se haya anunciado* (Spanish *Yellow Pages*)	It is probable that this service is not available in your province or, even if it exists (lit. 'even existing'), it has not been advertised
Usted, siendo católica, parece ignorar que los católicos peruanos también dependemos de Roma (A. Bryce Echenique, Peru, dialogue)	Even though you are a Catholic, you seem not to know that we Peruvian Catholics also depend on Rome

20.4.6 Gerund preceded by *como* to replace *como si*

Me miró como calculando mi edad (S. Puértolas, Spain; or *como si estuviera calculando . . .*)	She looked at me as if she were calculating my age
Julio se rascaba la cabeza, como diciendo . . . A. Bryce Echenique, Peru)	Julio scratched his head, as if saying . . .

20.5 *En* + gerund

In older language and in some dialects this is an equivalent of *al* + infinitive: *en llegando al bosque* = *al llegar al bosque* 'on arriving at the woods' (cf. French *en arrivant à*).

This construction seems to be virtually extinct in educated usage. Its modern equivalent, *al* + infinitive, is discussed at 18.3.3

20.6 Gerund used to qualify the object of a verb

Like the English -ing form, the Spanish gerund can also indicate an action performed by the direct object of certain kinds of verb:

(a) With verbs of 'perception' like 'see', 'hear', 'observe': see 20.7 for details.

(b) With verbs like *coger, pillar* ('to catch'), *arrestar* 'to arrest', *dejar* 'to leave', *encontrar* 'to find', *sorprender* 'to surprise':

La cogió/pilló robando	(S)he caught her stealing
La dejé llorando	I left her crying
Me sorprendí repitiendo entre dientes . . . (C. Martín Gaite, Spain)	I caught myself repeating between my teeth . . . (i.e. 'muttering')
Dejamos a Andrés durmiendo (A. Mastretta, Mexico, dialogue)	We left Andrés sleeping

(c) With verbs of representation like 'paint', 'draw', 'photograph', 'show', 'describe', 'imagine', 'represent', etc.:

La pintó tocando el clavicémbalo	He painted her playing the harpsichord
Esta fotografía muestra al rey bajando del avión	This photo shows the king getting out of the plane
Se la imaginó recogiendo sus enseres (C. Martín Gaite, Spain)	She imagined her gathering together her belongings
. . . y por eso los recuerdo siempre bebiendo (A. Bryce Echenique, Peru, dialogue)	. . . and that's why I remember them always drinking
Me los describió cazando leones	He described them to me hunting lions

Note

Captions under photos or other pictures fall into this category. In such captions the gerund very often appears with no accompanying finite verb. See 20.3a above.

20.7 Gerund after verbs of perception ('see', 'hear', etc.)

Commonly after the verb *ver* 'to see', and occasionally after *oír* 'to hear', *recordar* 'to remember', *olvidar* 'to forget' and *sentir* 'to feel'/'to hear', the gerund may be used to qualify the object of the main verb, as in *abrimos el periódico y vemos a niños muriéndose de hambre* (*El País*) 'we open newspapers and see children dying of hunger'. Usually the infinitive is also possible in this construction, the difference being one of aspect: the infinitive indicates an action that is completed and the gerund an action that is or was not yet complete. Compare *la vi fumando un cigarrillo* 'I saw her (while she was) smoking a cigarette' and *la vi fumar un cigarrillo* 'I saw her smoke a cigarette'. There is usually a colloquial alternative which uses a finite verb *la vi que fumaba un cigarrillo* 'I saw that she was smoking a cigarette'. Further examples:

No se me olvida mi hijo bailando con ella	I can't forget my son dancing with her
La recuerdo siempre cantando	I remember her always singing
. . . me gustaba salir sola a mojarme a las escaleras de atrás, sentir la lluvia azotando los avellanos de la huerta (C. Martín Gaite, Spain)	. . . I liked to go out to the back stairs alone to get wet and hear the rain lashing the hazelnut trees in the garden
Cuando Félix divisó al doctor leyendo una revista política . . . (C. Fuentes, Mexico)	When Felix caught sight of the doctor reading a political magazine . . .

With verbs of motion the gerund is not usually possible: 'I saw him coming towards me' is *lo/le vi venir hacia mí* or *lo/le vi que venía hacia mí* but not **lo/le vi viniendo hacia mí*.

Oír 'hear' may take a gerund, as in *desde allí oíamos al niño jugando en su cuarto* 'from there we could here the child playing in his/her room'. But it more often appears with either the infinitive or the construction with *que* and a finite verb. The infinitive is the safest option for foreign learners, since a gerund could sometimes be taken to refer to the subject of the main verb; e.g. *?la oí entrando* could mean 'I heard her while (I was) entering':

La oí toser/que tosía	I heard her coughing
Oí entrar a alguien/que alguien entraba	I heard someone come in
. . . oyendo a su padre hablar de que[1] Emiliano Zapata había tomado Chilpancingo (A. Mastretta, Mexico, dialogue)	. . . listening to her father talking about Emiliano Zapata having occupied Chipancingo

---

[1] *De que* is correct here. For misuse of *de que* after certain verbs, see 33.4.3.

But the gerund is possible if its subject is inanimate:

Cuando el sargento oye la corneta tocando la retirada (M. Vargas Llosa, Peru)
When the sergeant hears the trumpet sounding the retreat

Oí el ruido del yelo cayendo sobre un vaso (J. Marías, Spain; alternative and more usual spelling *hielo*)
I heard the noise of the ice falling on to a glass

20.8 Other uses of the gerund

20.8.1 Gerund with *andar*

This translates the English 'to go around doing something', with the same faintly pejorative implication of pointless activity. *Ir* can usually replace *andar* in this construction:

Siempre anda/va buscando camorra
He always goes round looking for trouble

Era profesor de geografía, y siempre anduvo solicitando traslados (C. Martín Gaite, Spain)
He was a geography teacher and was always applying for transfers (to other schools)

Anduve maldiciendo todo el jueves (A. Mastretta, Mexico, dialogue)
All that Thursday I went around swearing

Note

Spoken (not written) Mexican Spanish often uses *andar* for *estar* to form the continuous: *¿andas trabajando?* (for *¿estás trabajando?*) 'are you working?'; see 15.5.

20.8.2 Gerund with *ir*

(a) Expresses slow or gradual action:

Nos vamos haciendo viejos
We're (gradually) getting older

La conversación se fue espaciando
The conversation gradually became drawn-out

Ella se fue doblando hasta caer al suelo (*Cambio16*, Spain)
She gradually doubled up until she fell to the ground

Así ha ido perdiendo todos los clientes, por estar pensando en otra cosa (M. Puig, Argentina, dialogue)
That's how he's been losing all his customers, through thinking about other things

Poco a poco el consumidor ha ido descubriendo que las frutas de Cuba están a punto aunque sean de color amarillo verdoso (interview in *Granma*, Cuba)
Gradually the consumer has discovered that fruit from Cuba is ripe even if it is greenish yellow in colo(u)r

Note

Spoken Mexican Spanish also uses this construction to express an action that is just finishing (examples from Lope Blanch, 1991, 16): *espera un momento; voy acabando ya* (Spain *estoy acabando ya/estoy a punto de acabar*) 'wait a moment, I'm just finishing', *voy llegando ahorita* (Spain *acabo de llegar*) 'I've only just arrived'.

(b) By extension, to express careful, painstaking or laborious actions:

Ya puedes ir preparando todo para cuando lleguen
You can start getting things ready for when they arrive

Ve escribiendo todo lo que te dicte
Write down everything as I dictate it to you

Gano lo necesario para ir tirando
I earn enough to get by

20.8.3 Gerund with *llevar*

This provides a neat translation of 'for' in time expressions: *llevo dos meses pintando esta casa* 'I've been painting this house for six months'. This construction is discussed at 32.3.1.

20.8.4 Gerund with *quedarse*

This translates the idea of 'to continue to do something':

Me quedé ayudándolos un rato	I stayed on for a while to help them
Se quedó mirándome	She remained staring at me

20.8.5 Gerund with *salir*

Usually translates English phrases involving 'come out'/'go out':

Salió ganando	He came out the winner
Era lo único que quería: salir volando por la ventana (C. Martín Gaite, Spain, dialogue)	It was all I wanted to do – fly out of the window

20.8.6 Gerund with *seguir* and *continuar*

Seguir and *continuar* with the gerund translate 'to go on . . . -ing', 'to continue to . . . '. See 32.8 for discussion.

20.8.7 Gerund with *venir*

To express an action that accumulates or increases with time. It sometimes conveys mounting exasperation:

Hace años que viene diciendo lo mismo	He's been saying the same thing for years
Dice que hace mucho que la viene viendo	He says he's been seeing her for a long time
La sensación de aislamiento en la Moncloa viene siendo progresiva (*Cambio16*, Spain)	The sensation of isolation at the Moncloa (the Spanish Prime Minister's residence) is steadily growing
Los programas que se vienen ejecutando en el campo de la cardiología infantil (interview, *Granma*, Cuba)	the programmes (US 'programs') that have been carried out in the field of child cardiology

Note

The following construction is typically Mexican: *¿Qué, no lo viste? Ah, claro: tú vienes llegando apenas* (Spain *apenas acabas de llegar*) 'What? Didn't you see it? Oh, of course, you've only just arrived' (from Lope Blanch, 1991, 17).

20.8.8 Gerund with *acabar, terminar*

These verbs with the gerund mean 'end by':

Siempre acaba enfadándose	He always ends by getting mad
Acabarás haciendo lo que ella diga	You'll end by/up doing what she says
. . . porque con el tiempo terminaríamos no viéndonos nunca (A. Bryce Echenique, Peru)	. . . because with time we'd end by not seeing one another at all

Acabar por + infinitive is an equivalent and is the more common construction in negative statements: *acabarás por no salir nunca de casa* 'you'll end by/up never going out of the house.'

20.9 Translating the English -ing form

The following example consist mainly of cases where the English -ing form may not be translated by the Spanish gerund.

20.9.1 When the -ing form is the subject of a verb

This is normally translated by an infinitive or by a suitable noun:

Learning a language is fun	*Aprender un idioma es divertido*
Eating too much butter is bad for the heart	*Comer demasiada mantequilla es malo para el corazón*
No smoking	*Prohibido fumar*
Skiing is expensive	*Esquiar/El esquí cuesta mucho*
Salmon fishing is an art	*La pesca del salmón es un arte*

20.9.2 When the -ing form is the object of a verb

In this case there are two possibilities:

(a) When the same subject performs both actions, use an infinitive or a noun:

He dreads having to start	*Teme tener que empezar*
I like swimming	*Me gusta nadar/Me gusta la natación*
He gave up gambling	*Dejó de jugar/Dejó el juego*
Try ringing him	*Intenta llamarlo/le*
There's nothing I like better than working in the garden	*No hay nada que me guste más que trabajar en el jardín*

(b) When the actions are performed by different subjects, use a clause or noun. The subjunctive must be used where required by the rules laid out in Chapter 16:

I can't stand Pedro singing	*No puedo ver que Pedro cante*
I didn't mind him/his living here	*No me importaba que viviera/viviese aquí*
I recommended promoting her	*Recomendé su ascenso/que la ascendiesen/ ascendieran*
I approve of you(r) getting up early	*Me parece bien que te levantes temprano*

Note

Some verbs allow the gerund. See 20.7.

20.9.3 The -ing form used in a passive sense

Care is needed when the English -ing form replaces a passive infinitive, cf. 'your hair needs cutting' (= 'your hair needs to be cut'). In the Spanish translation an infinitive or a clause must be used:

Your hair needs cutting	*(Te) hace falta que te corten/te cortes el pelo*
This needs attending to	*Hace falta cuidarse de esto/Hay que atender a esto*
You're not worth listening to	*No vale la pena escucharte*
It wants/needs polishing	*Hace falta sacarle brillo*

20.9.4 The -ing form preceded by prepositions

Unless the preposition is 'by' (see 20.4.2) an infinitive or clause must be used:

I'm looking forward to seeing you	*Tengo ganas de verte*
I prefer swimming to running	*Prefiero nadar a correr*
He was punished for being late	*Lo/Le castigaron por llegar tarde*
This is a good opportunity for showing what you mean	*Ésta/Esta es una buena oportunidad para demostrar lo que quieres decir*
(S)he's thinking of starting a business	*Piensa empezar un negocio*
You get nothing in life without working	*No se consigue nada en esta vida sin trabajo/sin trabajar*
He was furious at being mistaken for his brother	*Le enfureció que le confundieran/ confundiesen con su hermano*

20.9.5 The -ing form before nouns

(a) If the -ing form is itself a noun, translation is usually by an infinitive or a noun:

driving licence	*el carnet/el permiso de conducir*
dancing shoes	*los zapatos de baile*
fishing rod	*la caña de pescar*

(b) If the -ing form is a participle (adjective) then a relative clause may be used, unless a participle in *-ante, -(i)ente* exists (see 19.4):

a walking doll	*un muñeco andante*
the chiming bells	*las campanas que tañen/tañían* (**tañente* does not exist)
a worrying problem	*un problema inquietante*
a convincing reply	*una respuesta convincente*

But often an idiomatic solution must be sought in either case:

flying planes	*aviones en vuelo*
turning point	*el punto decisivo/la vuelta de la marea*
steering wheel	*el volante*
dining-room	*el comedor*

Note

For the exceptional use of *hirviendo* 'boiling' and *ardiendo* 'burning' as adjectives, see 4.4.

21

Modal auxiliary verbs

21.1 General

This chapter discusses the following commonly occurring auxiliary verbs:

poder: to be able to, to be allowed to, can, could

soler: to be in the habit of

saber: to know how to

deber: must, ought to, should

querer: to want

haber (que, de): to have to

All, except *deber*, are conjugated irregularly. Their forms are shown at 13.3.

21.2 *Poder* and *saber* 'to be able to'/'to know how to'

21.2.1 *Poder* and *saber* contrasted

Both verbs are often equivalent to 'can' or 'could', but their meanings are slightly different: *saber*, as well as 'to know', means 'to know how to do something', and *poder* means 'to be able to do something'/'to be allowed to do something'. Sometimes the meanings overlap:

¿Sabes nadar?	Can you swim? (do you know how to?)
¿Puedes nadar hoy?	Can you swim today? (are you able to/are you allowed to?)
Nunca podía salir con sus amigas	She could never/was never allowed to go out with her girlfriends
Soy libre. Puedo hacer lo que quiero	I'm free. I can do whatever I want
Mi madre sabe guisar muy bien cuando quiere	My mother can cook very well when she wants to
Se sabe ganar/Sabe ganarse las simpatías de todo el mundo	She knows how to win people's affections
Nunca he sabido tocar el piano	I've never known how to play the piano

Notes

(i) Since 'can' and 'could' have no infinitives or participles in English, *poder* is translated by 'to be able to'/'to be allowed to' in compound and future tenses: *nunca había podido descifrarlo/nunca podrá descifrarlo* 'she had never been able to decipher it/she'll never be able to decipher it'.

(ii) *No poder (por) menos de* means the same as *no poder evitar* + infinitive: *no podré (por) menos de decírselo* 'I won't be able to stop myself from telling him/her'. The Latin-American equivalent is *no poder menos que*.

(iii) Idioms with *poder*: *no puedo más, estoy harta* 'I can't go on, I'm fed up', *al menos en ese terreno la vida no ha podido conmigo* (C. Martín Gaite, Spain) 'in this area at least, life hasn't got the better of me'.

21.2.2 Preterite and imperfect of *poder* and *saber*

The preterite refers to one occasion, the imperfect to a period of time usually made clear by the context. The positive preterite often means 'to manage to':

No pudo escaparse	He couldn't escape (he didn't manage to)
No podía escaparse	He couldn't escape (at that time; no information about whether he eventually did)
No me pudo ver porque estaba ocupada	She couldn't/didn't get to see me because she was busy
No podía verme porque estaba siempre ocupada	She couldn't see me because she was always busy

Notes

(i) Very often the preterite of *saber* 'to know' means 'found out'; the imperfect means 'knew': *cuando supe la verdad* 'when I found out/heard the truth', *sabía la verdad* 'I/(s)he knew the truth'.
(ii) Paradoxically, the positive preterite of *poder* can also mean the opposite, i.e. 'could have done but didn't'. See 21.2.3c.

21.2.3 *Poder* to express possibility and suggestions

Poder is usually translated by 'could' or 'may'. Except where indicated, either the imperfect or the conditional can be used.

(a) Possibility/suggestions:

Podía/Podría no haberla visto	He may not have seen her
Lo que podíamos/podríamos hacer es tirar este tabique	What we could do is to knock down this partition
Puedes/Podías/Podrías venir a comer mañana	You could come to lunch tomorrow
Puede/Podría/Podía haberle ocurrido algo	Something may/could have happened to him

Pudiera could be used also for *podría*, but it is less usual, at least in the spoken language.
(b) Polite requests:
The conditional is perhaps more usual than the imperfect in polite requests, but both are often heard:

¿Podría/Podía usted abrir la ventana?	Could you open the window?
¿Podrías/Podías decirle al jefe que estoy enfermo?	Could you tell the boss I'm ill?

(c) The positive preterite indicative may sometimes express something that could have happened but did not:

El día que pudo estallar la Tercera Guerra Mundial (Cambio16, Spain)	The day World War III could have broken out
. . . pensando en lo que pudo haber sido y no fue (J. Marsé, Spain)	. . . thinking of what might have been and wasn't
Pudo haberte demorado el amor, pero unos amigos te esperaban en el centro (P. Armando Fernández, Cuba)	Love could have delayed you, but some friends were waiting for you in the centre

The negative preterite means 'couldn't and didn't': *no pudo hacerlo* 'he didn't manage to do it'.

(d) The imperfect indicative (not the conditional) can also be used to reproach somebody for something done or left undone in the past:

Me lo podías haber dicho	You could have told me
Podías haber puesto algún adornito de Navidad (C. Rico-Godoy, Spain, dialogue)	You could have put up some Christmas decorations

Notes

(i) *Puede ser, podría/pudiera ser, podría/pudiera haber sido* are equivalent to 'it could be', 'it could have been'. *Pudiera* is less often used in the spoken language: *aun en el caso de que nuestro viejo profesor se hubiera muerto, que bien pudiera ser . . .* (C. Martín Gaite, Spain) 'even if our old teacher has died, which could well have happened.'

In answers, *puede ser* can be abbreviated to *puede: —¿Vas a pescar mañana? —Puede . . .* '"Are you going fishing tomorrow?" "Perhaps/Maybe . . ." '.

For the use of *puede ser que, pudiera ser que, podría ser que, podría/pudiera haber sido que* with the subjunctive, see 16.3.1.

21.2.4 *Poder* used in speculations

Ha llamado alguien. ¿Quién puede/podrá haber sido/ha podido ser?	Somebody rang. Who could it have been?
¿Dónde se puede haber ido/puede haberse ido?	Where can she have gone?
¿Crees que puede haber sido/ ha podido ser Juan?	Do you think it may have been John?

₂1.3 *Deber, deber de* and *tener que*

21.3.1 *Deber* to express obligation

Su hijo debe trabajar más si quiere aprobar el examen	Your son must work harder if he is to pass the examination
Debes decirme lo que sepas	You ought to/must tell me what you know
Hubo un verano en el que el marido debió ausentarse de más por razones profesionales (J. Marías, Spain)	There was a summer when her husband had to be away more often than usual for professional reasons

In the last three examples *tener que* could be used instead to strengthen the obligation:

Me dijo que tenía que hacerlo yo	She told me I had to do it
Tengo que pagar todos estos recibos	I have to pay all these bills
Como te levantas tarde, tienes que ir siempre corriendo a todas partes	Since you get up late you always have to be in a hurry

Notes

(i) The degree of obligation is reduced by using the conditional or, less often, the *-ra* form of *deber*. Since the imperfect may colloquially replace the conditional, *deberías hacerlo, debías hacerlo* and *debieras hacerlo* may therefore all mean 'you ought to do it', although *debiera* has a more literary flavour.

(ii) *No tener más remedio que* is a variation of *tener que* often used in everyday language to express strong obligation: *no tengo más remedio que despedirla* 'I've got no choice but to fire her'.

(iii) *Deber* **de** must not be used to express obligation. **Debes de hacerlo ahora* is bad Spanish for *debes hacerlo ahora* 'you've got to do it now'. This mistake is not uncommon in popular speech on both continents and even in writing, cf. **nos parece que debemos de hacer a un lado las argumentaciones electoreras* (Mexican politician quoted in *La Jornada*) 'it seems to us that we should put electioneering arguments to one side', for *debemos hacer a un lado*; also *si desea hacer alguna rectificación en la libreta electoral, debe de acreditarlo con documentación* (Peruvian official document) 'if you wish to make any change in the Electoral Register, you must provide documentary support'. See the next section for the correct use of *deber de*.

21.3.2 *Deber (de)* to express probability or supposition

Deber de can only express probability or supposition, although *deber* alone is nowadays also used with this meaning:

Debiste (de) llegar tarde	You must have arrived late
Debe (de) haber sido muy guapa	She must have been very beautiful
Deben (de) ser las cinco	It must be five o'clock
Mi madre debió de pensar que había que confiar en el destino (S. Puértolas, Spain)	My mother must have thought that she had better put her trust in fate
Y eso debe ser algo de lo que no se recupera uno nunca (J. Marías, Spain: or *debe de*)	And that must be something one never recovers from

The modern loss of the distinction between obligation (*deber*) and supposition (*deber de*) creates ambiguities. Use of *deber de* to translate 'must' would clarify the following examples:

Debió hacerlo Juan	John ought to have done it (on that occasion)/John must have done it
Debía hacerlo Juan	John used to have to do it/John ought to do it/John must have done it

Notes

(i) Mexican Spanish constantly uses *haber de* to express suppositions. See 21.4.1b
(ii) Like 'got to' in English, *tener que* can also indicate a strong supposition, as in *búscalo bien, tiene que estar ahí* 'check thoroughly, it's *got* to be there'.

21.3.3 Preterite, conditional and imperfect of *deber*

The preterite expresses something that should have been done; the negative something that should not have been done. The conditional and the imperfect express something that should be done:

Debió decírtelo antes	She ought to/should have told you before
Debía/debería decírtelo antes	She ought to/should tell you before
No debiste hacerlo	You shouldn't have done it
En ese momento debí desconfiarme, pero no lo hice (J. Ibargüengoitia, Mexico, dialogue)	At that moment I ought to/should have been suspicious, but I wasn't
Volvió al sitio del que nunca debió salir (E. Arenas, Spain, dialogue)	He went back to the place he ought never to have left/should never have left

However, when it is used to express suppositions, the preterite of *deber* may indicate an assumption or surmise so strong as to be a virtual certainty: *lo que ella le dijo debió convencerlo, ya que al día siguiente le dio cien mil dólares* 'what she told him must have convinced him since he gave her 100,000 dollars the following day'. The correct form to use here for a supposition is *debió **de** convencerlo*, as explained at 21.3.2, but there is an unfortunate universal tendency to omit the ***de***.

21.4 *Haber*

Haber is the modal auxiliary used for forming compound tenses, e.g. *he visto* 'I have seen', *habían vuelto* 'they had returned'. This use is discussed at 14.8. *Haber*, with the special present tense form *hay*, is used to translate 'there is', 'there are', 'there were', etc.: *hay cincuenta* 'there are fifty', *hubo una explosión* 'there was an explosion'. This is discussed in Chapter 30.

21.4.1 *Haber de*

Haber de has the following uses:

(a) It expresses mild obligation, or, sometimes, or future intention. This usage is nowadays literary and faintly archaic, at least outside Catalonia:

He de hacerlo cuanto antes	I have to do it as soon as possible
Si su compañía tiene bancos de datos que han de ser accesibles desde varias sedes, puede ahorrarse muchas complicaciones poniendo esos datos en Internet (Internet manual, Spain)	If your company has data banks that are to be accessed from several sites, you can save yourself many complications by putting this data on the Internet
Hubo de repetir el experimento (J. Marías, Spain)	(S)he had to repeat the experiment

Catalans often use this construction in Castilian to express obligation since their language uses *haver de* for obligation.

(b) It may express probability or suppositions:

Ha de haberle dicho todo	(S)he must have told her/him everything

This construction is also nowadays rare and literary except in Mexico, where it is very common, e.g. *para terminar, el capitán ha de haberse quejado de su soledad. Serafina ha de haberlo compadecido* (J. Ibargüengoitia, Mexico, dialogue) 'eventually the Captain must have complained about his solitude. Serafina must have taken pity on him', Spain *debió (de) haberse quejado, debió (de) haberlo/le compadecido*.

(c) In the conditional it translates an indignant or mystified 'should . . . '. This usage is normal, at least in Spain:

¿Por qué habría de ofenderse si yo no dije nada? (or, more colloquially, *iba a ofenderse*)	Why should she get offended if/when I didn't say anything?

21.4.2 *Haber que*

Haber que means 'to be necessary to . . .'. In this construction the verb is used only in the third-person singular. The present-tense form is *hay que*.

Hay que darles tiempo	One has to give them time/it's necessary to give them time
A los muertos hay que dejarlos irse (C. Martín Gaite, Spain)	The dead must be allowed to depart
No había que hacer autopsia (G. García Márquez, Colombia)	There was no need to do an autopsy
Hubo que llamar a los bomberos (with the implication 'and that's what we did')	It was necessary to call the firemen

21.5 *Querer* 'to want to'

This verb must not be confused with *querer* 'to love'. In the latter meaning it cannot precede an infinitive or a noun referring to something inanimate': ***me encanta*** *nadar* 'I love swimming', *me encanta/adoro el helado de vainilla* 'I love vanilla ice-cream'.

The imperfect of *querer* with an infinitive simply means 'wanted to' and does not tell us whether the wish was fulfilled or not:

Quería hablar con José	I wanted to talk to José (and may or may not have succeeded)

The preterite of *querer* plus an infinitive is peculiar in that out of context it is ambiguous. It may mean 'wanted to and failed':

Quise hablar con José	I wanted/tried to talk to José (but failed)

But in other contexts it may mean 'wanted to and did', especially when the speaker is being very assertive:

Lo hice porque quise	I did it because I wanted to

The negative preterite means 'to refuse to'. Compare *no quiso hacerlo* 'he didn't want to do it' (so he didn't) and *no quería hacerlo* 'he didn't want to do it' (no information about whether he did it or not).

The *-ra* imperfect subjunctive form can be used for the conditional: *no querría/quisiera volver a nacer* 'I wouldn't like to be born again'. The imperfect indicative can also be used instead of these two tenses in polite enquiries or requests: *querría/quisiera/quería hablar con el encargado* 'I would like to speak to the manager'.

21.6 *Soler*

Soler translates the idea of 'usually', 'to be used to'. It is not used in the future, conditional and preterite tenses:

No me suele doler la cabeza	I don't usually suffer from headaches
Los zapatos de tacón alto suelen ser incómodos	High-heeled shoes are usually uncomfortable
Solía hablar solo	He used to talk to himself
Ha solido portarse/acostumbrado a portarse bien conmigo	She's usually behaved well towards me

Notes

(i) *Acostumbrar a* 'to be in the habit of' may replace *soler* when conscious habits are involved (so not **acostumbraba a hablar solo*): *no acostumbro a/no suelo beber* 'I don't usually drink'. *Acostumbrar* (no *a*) was the classical construction in Spain and is common in Latin America; Seco (1998), 20, quotes the Argentinian A. di Benedetto: *un periodista que acostumbra contar cosas* 'a journalist who habitually tells things'.

(ii) In some spoken varieties of Latin-American Spanish, notably in the Southern Cone, *saber* is used for *soler*: *sabe levantarse a las ocho* for *suele levantarse a las ocho* 'he usually gets up at eight'. This usage is, however, popular or provincial.

21.7 *Deber, poder* and *tener que*: alternative construction with compound tenses

Deber and *poder* allow a variety of constructions in compound tenses, i.e. tenses based on *haber* and a participle. The option of pronoun shifting (discussed at 11.14.4) doubles the number of possibilities:

Debería haberlo hecho/Lo debería haber hecho   He ought to have done it
Habría debido hacerlo/Lo habría debido hacer
  (*debiera* can replace *debería* here)

Tener que may also appear in the same alternative constructions: *ha tenido que hacerlo/tiene que haberlo hecho/lo tiene que haber hecho* 'he had to do it'/'he must have done it', etc.

21.8 Translation of miscellaneous English modal verbs: 'would', 'shall', 'will' and 'need'

(a) 'Would'. This may form a conditional: 'it would be better' *sería mejor*. In English narrative it is often an equivalent of the imperfect meaning 'used to': 'every morning he would go out/he went out/he used to go out at seven' *todas las mañanas salía a las siete*.

(b) 'Should'. This may mean 'ought to', in which case the conditional of *deber* is the translation: 'this should work now' *debería funcionar ahora*. In older English it may be an equivalent of the conditional 'would': 'I should/would be very angry if you did it' *me enfadaría mucho si lo hicieras*.

(c) 'Ought to'. The conditional or imperfect of *deber* is the likely equivalent: 'you ought to eat less meat' *deberías/debieras/debías comer menos carne*. When it refers to the past, the preterite of *deber* is a common translation: *debiste hacerlo antes* 'you should have done it sooner'.

(d) 'Got to'. This may imply a strong obligation: 'you've got to work harder' *tienes que trabajar más*. In American English, and increasingly in British English, it expresses a supposition: 'it's got to/must be a lie' *debe (de) ser mentira/tiene que ser mentira*.

22

Personal a

22.1 Personal *a*: general

The use of the preposition *a* before certain kinds of direct object is so important in Spanish, and so unlike the use of the English preposition 'to', that it deserves a separate chapter. The basic rule is that identified or particularized human direct objects are marked by a preceding *a*: *vi a María* 'I saw Mary'. Compare *vi el coche* 'I saw the car' (non-human).[1] However, 'personal' *a* is a rather inaccurate label since the same *a* also sometimes appears with inanimate direct objects, particularly, but not only, whenever there might be doubt about which is the subject and which is the object, as sometimes happens in Spanish where word order is quite flexible.

22.2 Personal *a* before nouns denoting human beings or animals

Personal *a* is required before a direct object which denotes a known or identified human being, or a 'personified' animal, e.g. a pet or some other familiar animal.

Before a direct object which is a personal name or title – *Pedro, el jefe, mamá* – personal *a* is never omitted: *conozco a tu madre* 'I know your mother', *vi a Mario y a Elena* 'I saw Mario and Helen', *no aguantan al nuevo jefe* 'they can't stand the new boss'. With animals, use of personal *a* depends on the extent to which the creature is humanized. Pets virtually always take personal *a*, but in other cases use of *a* depends on factors of emotion or context: the more familiar the language, the more likely the use of *a*. At the zoo one is likely to say *vamos a ver a los monos* 'let's go and see the monkeys' but, probably, *vamos a ver los insectos* 'let's go and see the insects', monkeys being more lovable than cockroaches. Clinical or scientific language would naturally use personal *a* much more sparingly.

In the following examples personal *a* is obligatory:

No conozco a Feliciano	I don't know Feliciano
Acompañé a mi madre a la clínica	I accompanied my mother to the clinic
Llevó a las niñas al zoo	He took the girls to the zoo
¡Mira a los turistas!	Look at the (i.e. those) tourists!
La policía busca a un individuo con una	The police are seeking an individual

---

[1] The words 'identified' or 'particularized' are crucial here. Grammar books often imply that any human direct object requires personal *a*, but as the following section shows, this is not the case.

cicatriz en el labio inferior	with a scar on his lower lip
Admiran mucho al cámara (cf. *admiran la cámara* 'they admire the camera')	They admire the cameraman a great deal
¿Quieres pasear al perro?	Do you want to take the dog for a walk?
Dejad de atormentar al gato	Stop tormenting the cat

Compare the following sentences in which the object of the verb is not individually particularized:

Busco un marido que me ayude en la casa	I'm looking for a husband who will help me in the house
No conozco un solo farmacéutico en todo Bruselas (A. Bryce Echenique, Peru)	I don't know a single pharmacist in the whole of Brussels
Veía un chico que jugaba en silencio (E. Sábato, Argentina)	I saw a child playing in silence
Los universitarios eligieron una reina de belleza (I. Allende, Chile)	The university students elected a beauty queen
Amenazaron con no dejar un terrorista vivo en todo el país	They threatened not to leave a single terrorist alive in the whole country
Este DC-10 ha traído pasajeros desde Berlín	This DC-10 has brought passengers from Berlin
Mira los turistas, siempre gastando dinero	Look at tourists (for example), always spending money
Utilizaron un perro lobo para el experimento	They used an Alsatian dog for the experiment

Note

A proper name may occasionally denote an inanimate object, in which case personal *a* cannot be used: *dice conocer todo Shakespeare* 'he says he knows the whole of Shakespeare' (i.e. the works), *van a subastar un Turner* 'they're going to auction a Turner', *procura tomar la reina* 'try to take the queen' (in chess).

22.3 Personal *a* with nouns linked by *como*

A noun linked by *como* to a previous noun which itself has a personal *a*, or to a pronoun standing for such a noun, must also take personal *a* (although it may be omitted colloquially if there is no ambiguity):

Tuve que recoger a mi hermana como a un fardo	I had to pick my sister up as though she were a bundle
Su reacción fue de las primeras cosas que delató a Adriano Gómez como a un ser peligroso (J. Donoso, Chile)	His reaction was one of the first things to expose Adriano Gómez as a dangerous person
Me trataba como a una reina (A. Mastretta, Mexico, dialogue)	He treated me like a queen

?*Tuve que recoger a mi hermana como un fardo* sounds like ?'I had to pick up my sister as if I were a bundle.'

22.4 Personal a before pronouns

22.4.1 Before pronouns other than relative pronouns

When a pronoun stands for a person it takes personal *a*. These pronouns include *alguien, alguno, uno, ambos, cualquiera, nadie, otro, ninguno, este, ese, aquel, quien, todo, él, ella, usted* and other personal pronouns (excepting *me, te, se, nos, os, le, la, lo*). See next section for discussion of the use of personal *a* in relative clauses (pronouns like *alguien*, *nadie*, *cualquiera* are unusual in that they take personal *a* even though they do not refer to specific individuals):

He visto a alguien en el pasillo	I've seen someone in the corridor
Aunque yo no conozco a nadie de la gente	Although I don't know anyone among
que viene aquí . . . (C. Martín Gaite, Spain)	the people who come here . . .
Era capaz de insultar a cualquiera	He was capable of insulting anybody
¿A quién has visto?	Who(m) did you see?
La persona a quien yo más echaba de menos	The person I missed most
A ése/ese es al que quiere, no a ti	He's the one she loves, not you
Conoce a todo el mundo	He knows everyone

22.4.2 Personal *a* before relative pronouns

Personal *a* may appear before a direct object relative pronoun that refers to a human being, in which case the form of the relative pronoun will be *a quien*, *al que* or *al cual* (see 35.4.1 for discussion). If personal *a* is not used, *que* is the usual relative pronoun.

Personal *a* is not usual when the clause is clearly restrictive (as defined at 35.1.2). But if it is non-restrictive it must be used, though the difference is occasionally elusive. Peninsular informants generally insisted on *a* in the following examples:

*Tengo un profesor **al** que/**a** quien han*	I have a teacher whom they've appointed
nombrado miembro de la Academia	as a member of the Academy
Hace unos días, en el puerto, me dijiste que	A few days ago, at the harbour, you told
*yo era la primera persona **a** la que habías*	me I was the first person you had
querido (E. Sábato, Argentina, dialogue)	loved
*Plutón, esposo de Proserpina, **a** la que/*	Pluto, the husband of Proserpine, whom
***a** quien/**a** la cual robó*	he carried off

Notes

(i) The word *único* generates disagreement. One hears *tú eres el único que quiero* 'you're the only one I love'; some prefer . . . *al que quiero*, others accept both.

(ii) *El que* or *quien* are obligatory in all types of clause if *que* alone creates ambiguities, as it quite often does with human antecedents. Compare *ése/ese es el autor que siempre ataca* 'that's the author whom (s)he always attacks' or 'that's the author who always attacks'. *Al que* or *a quien* . . . show clearly that 'whom (s)he always attacks' is meant. Another example: *los militares que/a los que/a quienes han ascendido* 'the military men (whom) they have promoted', where use of personal *a* excludes the meaning 'who have ascended'.

(iii) Personal *a* is rare before relative pronouns referring to non-human objects, but it is found: *hemos encontrado enormes listas de coches a los que tenían controlados* (*Cambio16*, Spain) 'we have found enormous lists of cars that they had under surveillance'.

22.5 Personal *a* before personified nouns

A personified noun usually requires personal *a*. The decision as to whether a noun is personified or not is, however, dependent on complex factors of context:

*Tú temes **al** éxito tanto como al fracaso*	You fear success as much as failure
Se iba feliz a su casa para no seguir desafiando	He went off happily to his home
***al** azar* (G. García Márquez, Colombia)	so as not to go on tempting chance
Los cazas llevan bengalas de magnesio para	The fighters carry magnesium flares to

*confundir **a** un misil dirigido* (*Cambio16*, Spain)	confuse a guided missile

The last example shows how certain verbs, e.g. *confundir* 'confuse', *criticar* 'criticize', *temer* 'to fear', *satirizar* 'satirize', *insultar* 'insult', etc., tend, by their meaning, to personify their object because they suggest a human-like reaction on the part of the object. They therefore quite often appear with personal *a* even before inanimate nouns, which explains – but does not justify – the occurrence of sentences like ?*criticaba a las novelas de fulano* 'he criticized so-and-so's novels'.

22.6 Personal *a* after *tener, querer*

These verbs may acquire different meanings when used with personal *a*:

Tengo un hijo y una hija	I've got a son and a daughter
Tenemos una asistenta griega	We have a Greek maid

but:

*Así tiene **al** marido y **a** los hijos, a base de bocadillos, latas y congelados*	That's how she keeps her husband and children – on sandwiches, tins and frozen food
*Tengo **a** mi tío como fiador*	I've got my uncle to act as guarantor
*La humedad de la noche . . . tiene **a** las veredas resbaladizas y brillosas* (M. Vargas Llosa, Peru; *vereda* for Peninsular *acera* 'pavement'; *brillosas = brillantes*)	The dampness of the night . . . makes the pavements slippery and shiny
Quiere una secretaria	He wants a secretary
*Quiere **a** una secretaria*	He loves a secretary

22.7 Omission of personal *a* before numerals

Nouns preceded by a number tend to be unspecified or unidentified and personal *a* is often omitted before them:

Reclutaron (a) doscientos jóvenes	They recruited 200 young people
Bayardo San Román . . . vio las dos mujeres vestidas de negro (G. García Márquez, Colombia)	Bayardo San Román . . . saw the two women dressed in black
Sólo/Solo conozco un hombre capaz de componer esta emboscada maestra (. . . *a un hombre* also possible)	I only know one man capable of organizing this masterly ambush

Note

A clearly particularized or identified personal noun will, however, take personal *a*: *yo conocía personalmente **a** sus tres hijas* 'I knew his three daughters personally'.

22.8 Personal *a* combined with dative *a*

Ambiguity may arise when two *a*s occur in the same sentence, e.g. ?*presenté a mi marido a mi jefe* 'I introduced my husband to my boss' or 'I introduced my boss to my husband'? The common solution is to omit personal *a* and place the direct object after the verb and before the indirect object.

Presenté Miguel a Antonia	I introduced Miguel to Antonia
Denuncié el ladrón al guardia	I reported the thief to the policeman
Mande el paciente al especialista	Send the patient to the specialist
Yo prefiero Dickens a Balzac	I prefer Dickens to Balzac

22.9 Personal *a* before collective nouns

Personal *a* is normally used before collective nouns when these refer to human beings:

Sir Walter Raleigh enriqueció a la enclenque corte inglesa (*Cambio16*, Spain)	Sir Walter Raleigh enriched the feeble English court
*No conocía **al** resto del grupo*	I/(S)he didn't know the rest of the group
*. . . un paso que podría poner **a** Estados Unidos en una posición delicada* (*La Prensa*, Argentina)	. . . a step which could put the US in a delicate position

A is obligatory in all these examples. Compare the following sentences in which the nouns do not refer to inhabitants or members of a group, but to a place: *los turistas inundan México* 'tourists are inundating Mexico', *Hitler invadió la Unión Soviética* 'Hitler invaded the Soviet Union'.

Notes

(i) Before words like *país, nación, partido, movimiento*, when these words refer – or may refer – to people, *a* seems to be optional: *criticó duramente al/el movimiento anarquista* 'he criticized the anarchist movement severely', *será imposible gobernar a Euskadi* (*Cambio16*, Spain: omission possible) 'it will be impossible to govern the Basque country', *un potente terremoto sacudió el/al país* 'a powerful earthquake shook the country', *Luis García Meza, quien gobernó el país entre julio de 1980 y agosto de 1981* (*El País*, Spain; *al* possible) 'Luis García Meza, who governed the country between July 1980 and August 1981'.
(ii) Seeing, visiting, leaving, picturing or painting a place do not call for personal *a*:[2] *estamos deseando ver Lima* 'we're longing to see Lima', *se negó a visitar Rumania* 'he refused to visit Romania', *quería pintar Toledo* 'he wanted to paint Toledo', *abandonaron Madrid* 'they left Madrid'.

22.10 Personal *a* before inanimate direct objects

Personal *a* cannot appear before a noun denoting an inanimate direct object in straightforward sentences of the following kind:

He comprado un sacacorchos	I've bought a corkscrew
Escribe poesía	He writes poetry
Sus palabras delataban su derrotismo	His words betrayed his defeatism

But, despite its name, personal *a* is used before inanimate nouns:

(a) When there is likely to be ambiguity as to which is the subject and which is the direct object of a verb. Such ambiguity is very common in relative clauses, where the verb often precedes the subject:

*Este producto es el que mejor impermeabiliza **al** algodón*	This product is the one that best waterproofs cotton
*La trama conceptual que subyace **a** esta obra*	The network of concepts underlying this work
*Es difícil saber en qué medida afectó esto **a** la economía cubana* (M. Vargas Llosa, Peru)	It is difficult to know to what extent this affected the Cuban economy
*una organización que protege **a** su coche* (advertisement, *Cambio16*, Spain)	an organization which protects your car

---

[2] Although the Academy used to maintain that they did, and DeMello (1999, forthcoming) finds that it is still quite often used in spontaneous speech, although omission is the norm.

A tres Autos y un Comercio quemaron (Latin-American headline, strange to Peninsular speakers)	Three Cars and Store Burnt

A sentence like *es difícil saber en qué medida afectó esto la economía cubana* would be difficult to interpret: it could mean '. . . this affected the Cuban economy' or '. . . the Cuban economy affected this'. Personal *a* makes it clear which is the direct object.

(b) *A* also sometimes appears before inanimate direct objects when both subject and object are inanimate, even though there is apparently no danger of ambiguity.

It seems that this occurs only in those sentences in which the inanimate subject is also the true agent of the action. In a sentence like *la piedra rompió un cristal*, 'the stone broke a pane of glass' or *la novela causó una sensación* 'the novel caused a sensation' it can be argued that the agents of the action are the person who threw the stone or wrote the novel; *piedra* and *novela* are merely instruments. For this reason personal *a* is impossible. However, if the inanimate subject is the real agent of the action, personal *a* may **optionally** appear. It is as though the native speaker were not entirely confident that word order alone – loose in Spanish – sufficiently clarifies which is the subject and which the object. The issue is not in doubt if one of the nouns is a human being or is the instrument of a human being. But if both are of equal status, *a* identifies the object clearly:

*Ambos creían que los astros regían **a** las pasiones* (Octavio Paz, Mexico)	Both believed the stars ruled the passions
*Este morfema nominal concretiza **al** semantema* (F. Abad Nebot, Spain)	This nominal morpheme makes the semanteme concrete
*El suicidio de la muchacha . . . excitó **a** la opinión pública* (M. Vargas Llosa, Peru)	The girl's suicide . . . stirred public opinion
*. . . el artículo 516 del código penal, que considera **a** la homosexualidad como un delito* (La Hora, Ecuador)	. . . article 516 of the Penal code, which considers homosexuality as a crime

A could in fact be omitted in all these examples.

(c) *A* regularly appears after impersonal *se* so as to show that the *se* is indeed impersonal *se* and not any other kind of *se* such as reflexive *se* or passive *se*, etc.:

*. . . la plataforma, como se llama **a** los andenes en Inglaterra* (J. Marías, Spain)	. . . the 'platform', as they call the *andén* (of a railway station) in England
*En España se llamaba **a** la plata* (Sp. *dinero*) *de los cohechos y sobornos 'unto de México'* (O. Paz, Mexico; cf. *la plata se llamaba* 'money was called . . . ')	In Spain they used to call the money from bribery and graft 'Mexican grease'
*Demasiado a menudo se comparó **a** esos órganos con filtros* (Ercilla, Chile, in Variedades 220)	Too often these organs [the kidneys] were compared with filters
*La inversión es indispensable si se quiere convertir **al** sistema ferroviario en un sector atractivo para los inversionistas privados nacionales* (La Hora, Ecuador)	Investment is essential if one wishes to turn the railway (US 'railroad') system into an attractive sector for local (i.e. Ecuadorian) private investors

22.11 *A* obligatory or preferred with certain verbs

(a) Some verbs always take the preposition *a*, e.g. *agarrarse a* 'to hold on to', *asociarse a* 'to associate oneself with', *suceder a* 'to follow', *sustituir a* 'to substitute', *renunciar a* 'to renounce', *ayudar a*, *gustar/agradar* 'to please', etc. However, this *a* may not always be personal *a* but some other manifestation of the preposition *a*:

*Considera que la opción más sabia es renunciar gradualmente **a** la energía nuclear* (El País: not personal *a*)	He considers that the wisest option is gradually to give up nuclear energy
*Esto obedece **a** unas normas de comportamiento*	This obeys certain norms of behaviour
En cuanto a su marido, le gustaba todo lo que le gustara a su mujer, pero no que su mujer les gustara tanto a los hombres (M. Vázquez Montalbán, Spain)	As far as her husband was concerned, he liked everything his wife liked but he didn't like the fact that men liked his wife so much
*Este nuevo producto ayuda **al** cabello a recobrar su brillo natural* (*a* normal)	This new product helps the hair recover its natural shine
*Este nuevo tipo de transistor sustituye **a** los anteriores*	This new type of transistor replaces the former ones

It is worth recalling at this point that there is an important difference between personal *a* and the dative *a* meaning 'to' after verbs of giving, saying, pointing, etc. The latter *a* is usually reinforced by a redundant pronoun, whereas the former is not – at least in the Peninsula and in careful speech in much of Latin America. Thus one says *le dije a tu padre* 'I said to your father . . . ' (redundant *le*) but only *vi a tu padre* 'I saw your father' not *?le/lo vi a tu padre*. Reinforcement with a redundant pronoun is only required when the object precedes the verb: *a tu padre le/lo vi ayer . . .* 'I saw your father yesterday . . . '; this word order device is explained at 11.16.1 and 37.5.3. Sentences like *?lo vi a tu padre* are, however, accepted in the Southern Cone and are heard in familiar Latin American speech everywhere. See 11.16.4 for more details.

(b) *A* preferred after some verbs:

Some verbs often take *a* before an inanimate direct object. These include *afectar a* 'to affect', *reemplazar a* 'to replace', *superar a* 'to overcome/exceed', *acompañar a* 'accompany', *combatir a* 'to combat', *llamar a* 'to name/call', *seguir a* 'to follow', *sobrevivir a* 'to survive'. However, usage is uncertain with some of them and Spanish speakers sometimes disagree about the appropriateness of the use of *a* before an inanimate object:

Los historiadores británicos llaman "guerra peninsular" a lo que nosotros denominamos guerra de la independencia	British historians give the name 'Peninsular War' to what we call the War of Independence
Estas ventajas permiten al Volkswagen superar a sus rivales (*a* normal)	These advantages allow the Volkswagen to beat its rivals
El nuevo Ford ha reemplazado a la gama anterior	The new Ford has replaced the previous range
. . . y en las horas que siguieron a la muerte (I. Allende, Chile)	. . . and in the hours following the death
. . . y cuántas lágrimas de hiel tuvo que derramar encerrado en el retrete para sobrevivir a su desastre íntimo (G. García Márquez, Colombia)	. . . and how many bitter tears (lit 'tears of bile') he had to shed, while locked in the toilet, in order to survive his intimate personal disaster

23

Negation

23.1 General

Spanish negative words discussed in this chapter are:

no no/not
nunca/jamás never/ever
nada nothing
apenas hardly/scarcely
nadie nobody

en mi vida never in my
  life
ni nor/not
en absoluto absolutely not
ninguno none/no

tampoco not even/nor
nomás (Lat. Am.) just/
  only/scarcely

Matters requiring special attention are the stylistic consequences of use or non-use of the double negative, e.g. *no lo he visto nunca/nunca lo he visto* 'I've never seen it/him', the use of negative words in certain types of positive sentences, e.g. *¿quién ha dicho nunca eso?* 'who ever said that?', *más que nunca* 'more than ever'; and the use of redundant *no*, e.g. *¡cuántas veces no te habré dicho!* 'how many times must I have told you!'

23.2 *No*

23.2.1 Use and position

No usually precedes the word that it negates, but object pronouns are never separated from a verb: *no dije . . .* 'I didn't say', but *no se lo dije* 'I didn't say it to him/her/you/them':

Mario no estaba	Mario wasn't there
No perdamos tiempo	Let us not waste time
No todos son capaces de aprender idiomas	Not everyone is capable of learning languages
Arguyen – y no sin razón – que . . .	They argue – and not without reason – that . . .
No intentabas verla	You weren't trying to see her
Intentabas no verla	You were trying not to see her

If a verb has been deleted, *no* retains its position: *bebe cerveza pero no bebe vino* > *bebe cerveza, pero no vino* 'he drinks beer but not wine':

Viene mañana, pero no esta tarde	He's coming tomorrow, but not this afternoon/evening
—¿Sabéis nadar? —Yo sí, pero él no	'Can you swim?' 'I can, but he can't'

In very emphatic denials it may follow a noun or pronoun:

¡Bases nucleares no!	No nuclear bases!
ah no, eso no . . .	oh no, not that . . .
Aquí puede entrar todo el que quiera,	Anyone who wants to can come in here,
pero borrachos no (or *pero no borrachos*)	but not drunkards

Notes

(i) Compound tenses do not allow participle deletion in Spanish. In answer to *¿lo has visto?* 'have you seen him/it?' one says *sí* or *sí, lo he visto*, or *no* or *no, no lo he visto*, but not **no, no lo he . . .* (compare English 'no, I haven't . . . '). —*¿Has sido tú? —No, no he sido yo* '"Was it you?" "No, it wasn't"', —*¿Se lo has dado? —No, no se lo he dado* '"Did you give it to him/her/them?" "No, I didn't"'. This rule is occasionally broken in the pluperfect: see 14.8.2 for an example.

(ii) Deletion of a gerund or infinitive is, however, possible: —*¿Estabas comiendo* (Lat. Am. *almorzando*)? —*No, no estaba* '"Were you having lunch?" "No I wasn't"', —*¿Quieres venir? —No, no quiero* '"Do you want to come?" "No I don't".'

(iii) If it means 'non-' or 'un-', *no* precedes the noun or adjective: *yo estoy por la no violencia* 'I support non-violence', *la política de la no intervención* 'the non-intervention policy', *es la única imagen no real en todo el libro* (J. Marsé, Spain) 'it's the only non-real image in the whole book'.

23.2.2 'No' and *no* contrasted

The English word 'no' is versatile and may require translation in various ways:

Look, no hands!	*Mira, ¡sin manos!*
'What's the problem?' 'No money.'	—*¿Cuál es el problema? —No tengo/tiene/*
	tenemos/tienen (etc.) *dinero*
no petrol/(US 'no gas')	*No hay gasolina*
no smoking	*prohibido fumar/no fumar*
no way!	*¡ni hablar!*
no kidding?!	*¿en serio?*
There's no need for arguments	*No hay por qué discutir*

23.2.3 *No* as a question tag

¿No? at the end of a statement implies that the asker already knows the answer, cf. 'isn't it?', 'do you?':

Usted habla inglés, ¿no?	You speak English, don't you?
Mejor tarde que nunca, ¿no?	Better late than never, don't you think?

Note

A reply to a negative question is handled as in English: i.e. *no* confirms the negative. There is no Spanish equivalent of the contradicting 'yes' of French (*si!*) or German (*doch*): —*¿No vienes? —No* '"Aren't you coming?" "No (I'm not)"', —*¿No vas a enfadarte otra vez? —Sí* '"You aren't going to get cross again?" "Yes I am"', —*¿No cerraste con llave el armario? —Sí* '"Didn't you lock the cupboard?" "Yes. I did".'

23.2.4 'Redundant' *no*

An apparently superfluous *no* is inserted in certain types of sentence:

(a) Colloquially and optionally, to avoid two *ques* side by side:

*Más vale que vengas conmigo que (**no**)*	Better come with me than stay here alone
que te quedes solo aquí (or *. . . a que te*	
quedes solo . . .)	

(b) In informal language redundant *no* is often unnecessarily used in comparisons, especially before an infinitive:

*Mejor gastar cien mil ahora que (**no**) tener que comprar un coche nuevo para el verano*	Better spend one hundred thousand now than have to buy a new car by summer
*La obra de R. vale más para un conocimiento de la derecha que **no** para conocer la República* (M. Tuñón de Lara, Spain)	R.'s work is more useful for gaining knowledge of the Right than of the Republic
*. . . con los ojos más luminosos, más tristes y más agradecidos que ella **no** le vio nunca . . .* (G. García Márquez, Colombia)	. . . with the most luminous, saddest and most grateful eyes she had ever seen in him . . .

(c) Optionally in interjections involving *cuánto* or *qué de* 'how much', 'how many'. Use of *no* is rather literary nowadays:

*¡Cuántas veces **no** lo había soñado en los últimos tiempos!* (L. Goytisolo, Spain)	How often he had dreamt of it lately!
*¡Qué de angustias (**no**) habrán pasado!*	What anguish they must have suffered!
*¡Cuántas veces (**no**) te lo habré dicho!*	How many times must I have told you!

(d) Optionally after *hasta* and *a menos que* in negative sentences:

*Adolfito, hasta que **no** te tomes el bocadillo no te vas a jugar* (E. Arenas, Spain, dialogue)	Adolfo, you're not going out to play until you finish your sandwich
*No cobrarás hasta que (**no**) encuentre trabajo*	You won't get the money until she finds work
*No era noticia hasta que **no** la publicaba Abc* (*Cambio16*, Spain)	It wasn't news until *Abc* published it

But *no* is not used if the main clause is positive: *siguieron sin hacer nada hasta que llegó el capataz* 'they carried on doing nothing until the foreman arrived', *me quedaré aquí hasta que se ponga el sol* 'I'll stay here until the sun sets'.

(e) In literary usage, after expressions of fear. The *no* does not alter the sense. Note that *que* is used if the *no* is removed:

*Temo **no** le haya sucedido/Temo que le haya sucedido alguna desgracia*	I'm worried (s)he may have suffered some misfortune
*Tenía miedo **no** (or tenía miedo de que) lo/le vieran desde arriba*	He was afraid that they would see him from above

23.2.5 *Nomás* (occasionally written *no más*)

Throughout Latin America this phrase has a variety of meanings in colloquial language that it does not have in Spain. The form *nomás* is never used in Spain.

—¿Dónde está el hospital? —En la esquina nomás (Spain *justo en la esquina*)	'Where's the hospital?' 'Right on the corner'
La vi ayer nomás (Spain *la vi ayer mismo*)	I saw her only yesterday
Pase nomás (Spain *pase, pase*, etc.)	Do come in, please
nomás que venga . . . (en cuanto venga)	as soon as she/he arrives . . .
El gringo viejo se murió en México. Nomás porque cruzó la frontera (C. Fuentes, Mexico, dialogue)	The old gringo died in Mexico. Just because he crossed the frontier
Una invitación del señor Presidente nomás lo/no se rechaza (idem, dialogue)	You don't turn down an invitation from the President himself

Note

On both continents, *no . . . más que* means 'only' and must be distinguished from *no . . . más de* 'not more than'; see 5.5.

23.3 Double negative

One may say *nadie vino* or *no vino nadie* 'no one came'. As the second example shows, if a negative follows a verb, the verb must also be preceded by a negative: a negative sentence in Spanish requires that all the constituents of the sentence be negated if possible: *pero una **no** debe esperar **nunca nada** de un hombre sino malas noticias* (C. Rico-Godoy, Spain) 'but one (fem.) should never expect anything from a man except bad news', *nunca hay **nada nuevo** en **ninguna** parte* (C. Solórzano, Mexico, dialogue) 'there's never anything new anywhere'. Students of French should note that a verb preceded by a negative does not need negating again by another preceding negative. Compare *personne **ne** savait la vérité* and ***nadie** sabía la verdad* 'no one knew the truth' (never **nadie no sabía la verdad*), or *de ninguna manera pensaba hacerlo* 'in no way was she thinking of doing it' (never **de ninguna manera **no** pensaba . . .*):

No dice nada	He says nothing
Nadie dijo nada	No one said anything
Apenas come nada	She scarcely eats anything
Tampoco vino nadie	Nor did anyone come
Nunca trae ninguno	She never brings a single one
No sabe ni latín ni francés	He knows neither Latin nor French
No la he visto nunca con nadie	I've never seen her with anyone

Examples of single negatives:

Tampoco vino	He didn't come either
Apenas habla	(S)he scarcely talks
Nadie cree eso	No one believes that
Ninguna era más guapa que ella	No woman was more beautiful than her
Jamás/Nunca la volvería a ver	(S)he was never to see her again
Ni él ni ella podían decir si esa servidumbre recíproca se fundaba en el amor o la comodidad (G. García Márquez, Colombia)	Neither he nor she could have said whether this reciprocal servitude was based on love or convenience

The difference between a double and a single negative, e.g. between *nunca viene* and *no viene nunca*, is sometimes merely stylistic. References under the individual items give guidance on this subject.

Notes

(i) The double negative may occasionally be ambiguous, although intonation or context usually make the meaning clear: *lo que dice no es nada* 'what he says is nothing' (i.e. worthless) or 'what he says isn't nothing' (i.e. it isn't worthless); *no llora por nada* 'she doesn't cry over nothing'/'she doesn't cry over anything'; compare *llora por nada* 'she cries over nothing' (*no llora sin motivo* expresses the first idea unambiguously).

(ii) The double preceding negative *nunca nadie . . .* is found, as in *nunca nadie ha dicho eso* 'no one has ever said that' (or *nadie ha dicho eso nunca* or *nadie ha dicho nunca eso*); *nunca nadie supo decirle el porqué de esa Ynés con i griega* (J. Marsé, Spain) 'no one was ever able to tell him the reason for that "Ynés" with a "y"'. The same idea can be expressed by *nadie ha dicho eso nunca*, or *nunca ha dicho eso nadie*, or *no ha dicho eso nunca nadie*.

A compound preceding negative linked with *y* is also possible, at least in literary styles, as in *en ningún momento y en ninguna parte había visto que volara/volase un elefante* 'never and nowhere had he seen an elephant fly . . .' / 'he had never seen anywhere that an elephant could fly'.

23.4 *Nada, nadie, nunca, jamás, ninguno* in sentences that are affirmative in form or meaning

These words can have the meaning of 'anything', 'ever', 'anyone', 'anything' in the following contexts:

(a) After comparisons:

Más que nada, es taimado	More than anything, he's cunning
Salió más temprano que nunca (A. Mastretta, Mexico, dialogue; *jamás* not possible)	She went out earlier than ever before
En España son muchos los que se precian de asar el cordero mejor que nadie (*Cambio16*, Spain)	There are many in Spain who pride themselves on roasting lamb better than anyone else
... algo que les pareció más violento, más subversivo que nada que jamás oirían (José Donoso, Chile)	... something which seemed to them more violent, more subversive than anything they would ever hear
... y allí un capataz, el mejor que jamás hubiera (M. Puig, Argentina, dialogue)	... and a foreman there – the best that ever was
Este libro es más complicado que ninguno de los que yo he leído	This book is more complicated than any I've read
Es más inteligente que ninguna de las otras	She's more intelligent than any of the other girls/women

(b) In sentences which involve expressions of doubt, denial, abstention, impossibility, etc.:

Es dudoso que nadie pueda pasar por nativo en más de tres o cuatro idiomas	It's doubtful whether anyone can pass as a native in more than three or four languages
Durante todo aquel tiempo se abstuvo de todo contacto con nadie	During all that time he refrained from all contact with anyone
Se negó siquiera a hablar a nadie de la emisora (G. Cabrera Infante, Cuba)	He even refused to talk to anyone from the radio station
Es imposible ver nada de lo que está sucediendo	It's impossible to see anything of what's going on
Es horrible contar todo esto a nadie	It's horrible to tell all this to anyone
Es poco probable que ninguno haya sobrevivido	It's unlikely that any have survived
Yo no sé dónde está nada en esta maldita casa	I don't know where anything is in this damned house

(c) In questions or exclamations that expect a negative answer:

¿A usted cuándo le han preguntado nada?	When did anyone ask you anything?
¿Quién ha visto a nadie que trabaje más que él?	Who has ever seen anyone who works more than he does?
¿Para qué despedirme de nada ni de nadie? (A. Gala, Spain)	Why say goodbye to anyone or anything?
¿Quién puede pensar en nada cuando se está rodeado de idiotas? (C. Solórzano, Mexico, dialogue)	Who can think of anything when one's surrounded by idiots?
¿Quién hubiera pensado nunca/jamás que se casaría con Josefa?	Who would ever have thought he'd have married Josefa?

(d) After *antes de, antes que,* and *sin*:

He venido sin nada	I've come without anything
sin nadie que lo/le cuidara/cuidase	without anyone to look after him
Al otro día me levanté antes que nadie	The next day I got up before everyone
(J. Cortázar, Argentina, dialogue)	else (lit. 'before anyone')
Esto hay que hacerlo antes de empezar nada	This must be done before starting anything (else)

Notes

(i) Statements of emotion involve a subtlety: *me sorprendería que nadie me llamara/que no me llamara/nadie* 'I'd be surprised if nobody rang me', *me sorprendería que me llamara/llamase nadie* 'I'd be surprised if anyone rang me', *sentiría que nadie me viera así/que me viera/viese así nadie* 'I'd be sorry if anyone sees me (looking) like this'; *sentiría que nadie me viera/viese así/sentiría que no me viera/viese así nadie* 'I'd be sorry if no one sees me (looking) like this'.

(ii) In sentences in which English allows 'something' after 'without' Spanish allows *algo*: . . . *sin que nadie pudiera hacer algo para impedirlo* (L. Spota, Mexico; *hacer nada* also possible) '. . . without anyone being able to do anything/something to stop it', *no podía dormir sin que algo* (not *nada*) *la despertara/despertase* 'she couldn't sleep without something waking her up'.

23.5 Further remarks on individual negative words

23.5.1 *Nada, nadie*

(a) When *nada* or *nadie* are the direct object of a verb or its predicate, or follow a preposition, they usually appear in the double negative construction in ordinary language:

No sé nada	I know nothing/I don't know anything
No sé nada de nada	I don't know anything about anything
No conozco a nadie	I don't know anyone
No es nada/nadie	It's nothing/nobody
No hay nada/nadie	There's nothing/nobody
No lo haría por nada/nadie	I wouldn't do it for anything/anyone
Porque la palabra "felicidad" no era apropiada para nada que tuviera alguna vinculación con Alejandra (E. Sábato, Argentina)	Because the word 'happiness' was not appropriate for anything which had any link with Alejandra

But in literary or emotive styles they may precede the verb:

. . . *nada prometen que luego traicionen* (L. Cernuda, Spain, poetry)	. . . they [i.e. violets] promise nothing that they then betray
Dentro de la pensión reinaba el silencio, como si nadie la habitara (J. Marsé, Spain)	Inside the boarding-house silence reigned, as if no one were living in it
Nada en el mundo nos podrá separar (A. Arrafut, Cuba, dialogue)	Nothing in the world will be able to separate us
A nadie conozco más apto para esta labor literaria	I know no one more suited for this literary task
Por nada del mundo quisiera perderme eso (set phrase in everyday use)	I wouldn't miss that for anything in the world
. . . *como esos hombres silenciosos y solitarios que a nadie piden nada y con nadie hablan* (E. Sábato, Argentina)	. . . like those silent and solitary men who ask nothing from anyone and speak with no one

(b) When *nada, nadie* are the subject of a verb they usually precede it:

Nada parece cierto en todo esto	Nothing seems sure in all this
Nada en la pieza es histórico (M. Vargas Llosa, Peru)	Nothing in the play is historical

Nadie quiso creerle que era honrado . . . (M. Vargas Llosa, Peru, dialogue)	No one was willing to believe he was honest . . .
Nadie cree eso ya	No one believes that any more

But a double negative construction is used in questions:

¿No ha venido nadie?	Hasn't anyone come?
¿No ha llegado nada?	Hasn't anything arrived?

Note

With some verbs either construction may be used: *no me gusta nada/nada me gusta* (the second construction is more literary) 'I don't like anything', *nada de lo que tú hagas me molesta/no me molesta nada de lo que tú hagas* 'nothing you do bothers me'.

23.5.2 *Nada* as intensifier

Nada may be used adverbially with the meaning 'not at all':

Manuel no trabaja nada	Manuel does absolutely no work
No hemos dormido nada	We haven't slept a wink
La separación de su marido no había sido nada dramática (S. Puértolas, Spain)	The break with her husband had not been at all dramatic
No me gusta nada lo que acabas de decir (A. Bryce Echenique, Peru, dialogue)	I really don't like what you just said

23.5.3 Further remarks on *nadie*

Nadie takes personal *a* if it is the object of a verb:

Apenas conozco a nadie	I hardly know anybody
No se veía a nadie en la playa	There was no one to be seen on the beach

Note

Nadie de should not be followed by a plural noun or pronoun: *nadie de la clase* but **ninguno** *de los alumnos* 'none of the students', **ninguno** *de ellos* 'none of them', **ninguno** *de nosotros* 'none of us'.

23.5.4 *Ni*

'Nor', 'neither'. As with other negative words, if *ni* follows the verb to which it refers the verb must itself be negated. Compare *ni tú ni yo lo sabemos* 'neither you nor I know (it)' and *no lo sabemos ni tú ni yo*. Constructions like **ni tú ni yo no lo sabemos* are considered archaic or incorrect. Unlike 'nor', *ni* is usually repeated before each member of a list: *no han llegado (ni) Antonio, ni Pilar, ni Ana, ni Marta* 'neither Antonio, Pilar, Ana nor Marta has arrived' (the first *ni* is optional). Examples of the use of *ni*:

. . . ya que entonces no había en la tierra ni sólidos ni líquidos ni gases (J. L. Borges, Argentina)	. . . since at that time there were neither solids nor liquids nor gases on the earth
No tenemos ni coñac ni ron	We have neither cognac nor rum
Ni fumo ni bebo/No fumo ni bebo	I neither smoke nor drink
Ni era amable, ni se esforzaba en serlo (A. Gala, Spain)	She wasn't pleasant, nor did she make an effort to be
No hubo tiempo ni de llamar a una ambulancia (C. Martín Gaite, Spain)	There wasn't even time to call an ambulance
Ni con ella, ni con nadie, me puedo comunicar (M. Puig, Argentina, dialogue)	I can't communicate with her or with anybody
Ya no puede uno llorar ni en los entierros (A. Mastretta, Mexico)	One can't even cry at funerals any more

Notes

(i) *Ni* commonly translates 'not even'. It can be reinforced by *siquiera*: *ni (siquiera) en mis peo-res momentos soñé que esto pudiera/pudiese suceder* 'not even in my worst moments did I dream this could happen', *eres un inútil, no puedes ni (siquiera) freírte un huevo* 'you're useless, you can't even fry yourself an egg', ... *experiencia que no les sirvió ni para enfrentarse con un puñado de bandidos* (M. Vargas Llosa, Peru, dialogue) '... an experience that didn't even help you take on a handful of bandits' *¡ni se te ocurra (siquiera) venir a verme!* 'don't even get the idea of coming to see me!'

(ii) Before a noun it may be an emphatic denial: *—¿Sabes quién es? —Ni idea* '"Do you know who it is?" "No idea"', *—¿Cuánto ganabas? —Ni (siquiera) un céntimo* '"What were you earning?" "Not a cent"'.

(iii) *Ni* is required after *sin*: *vivía sin dinero ni ganas de tenerlo* 'she lived without money or the urge to have it', *sin mujer ni hijos* 'without wife or children', *el buque seguía aquellas vueltas y recodos sin vacilar ni equivocarse nunca* (from Ramsey and Spaulding, 11.45) 'the vessel followed those turns and bends without ever hesitating or making a mistake'.

(iv) The following Latin-American sentence, *si no te gusta lárgate, que ni haces falta* (A. Mastretta, Mexico, dialogue) 'if you don't like it go away, because you're not even wanted' would be expressed in Spain by ... *ni falta que haces*.

23.5.5 *Ninguno*

'No', 'none', 'nobody' (cf. French *aucun*, German *kein*). The double negative rule applies – if *ninguno* follows the verb, the verb must itself be negated: *ninguno de ellos lo sabe/no lo sabe ninguno de ellos* 'none of them knows it', *nunca compra ninguno* 'she never buys a single one'. In certain types of sentences, it may be an equivalent of 'any': see 23.4 for examples.

It may be either adjectival or pronominal. As an adjective it loses its final -*o* before a masculine noun or noun phrase: *en ningún momento pensé que* ... 'at no point did I think that ...', *en ningún miserable pueblo costero* ... 'in no wretched coastal village ...', *no aceptaremos ninguna solución parcial* 'we will accept no par-tial (or 'biased') solution'.

It is normally pronounced 'ningún' before feminine nouns beginning with stressed *a*- or *ha*-, and this is occasionally reflected in writing, e.g. *ningún arma nuclear* 'no nuclear weapon'. But the grammarians agree that the full form should be written before such nouns: *ninguna arma nuclear*.

The plural *ningunos/ningunas* is rare, presumably because there is little need to mention more than one of something that does not exist. But it does occur with nouns that are always plural: *ningunas vacaciones en Cataluña son completas sin una excursión al Pirineo* 'no holiday/vacation in Catalonia is complete without a trip to the Pyrenees', *total, tenía 18 años y ningunas ganas de volver al pueblo* (A. Mastretta, Mexico, dialogue) 'in short/in a word, he was eighteen and had no desire to go back to the village'. Further examples:

(a) Pronominal forms:

Ninguno de los que hablan un idioma está libre de dudas (M. Seco, Spain)	None of those who speak a language is free of doubts
O se lleva todos, o ninguno	Either you take/(s)he takes them all, or none
Si he sido insincero con ninguno/alguno de vosotros, decídmelo (*ninguno* is more literary)	If I have been insincere with any of you, tell me so

(b) Adjectival forms:

El ministro no hizo ningún comentario/no   The Minister made no comment
    hizo comentario ninguno/alguno
Tampoco recibimos ninguna contestación/   Neither did we receive any reply to
    recibimos contestación alguna a nuestra   our previous letter
    carta anterior
—Si es molestia, puedo esperar.   'If it's a nuisance I can wait.'
    —Molestia ninguna/Ninguna molestia   'No nuisance at all.'
Había llegado al climaterio con tres hijas y   She had reached the menopause with
    ningún varón (G. García Márquez,   three daughters and no male (offspring)
    Colombia)

Notes

(i) As the examples show, *alguno*, placed after the noun, may be used as an emphatic variant of *ninguno*: *en momento alguno* = *en ningún momento* 'at no moment at all'. See the note to 9.4.1a for details.

(ii) When *ninguno* is the subject of a verb, person and number agreement seems to be optional when the pronoun appears: *ninguna de nosotras **tiene/tenemos** marido* 'none of us women has/have a husband', *ninguno de vosotros **habéis/ha** traído el libro* 'none of you has/have brought the book'.

    If the pronoun is omitted, the verb ending must make the meaning clear: *ninguno **hemos** dicho eso* 'none of us said that', *¿no **salisteis** ninguna anoche?* 'didn't any of you girls/women go out last night?' (compare *¿no salió ninguna anoche?* 'didn't any of the girls/women go out last night?').

(iii) If *ninguno* is a direct or indirect object and is placed before the verb, the redundant pronoun agrees with the accompanying noun or pronoun: *a ninguno de ellos **los** conozco* 'I don't know any of them', *a ninguno de nosotros **nos** quiere dar el dinero* 'he doesn't want to give the money to any of us'.

23.5.6 *Nunca* and *jamás*

Both mean 'never' or, in certain sentences, 'ever'. *Jamás* is somewhat stronger and less common than *nunca*. It is usually, but not always, a synonym of *nunca*, but see note (i). The combination *nunca jamás* is strongly emphatic.

    Both require a double negative construction when they follow the verb phrase to which they refer: *nunca viene* = *no viene nunca* 'he never comes', *nadie viene jamás* 'no one ever comes'.

Nunca/Jamás conocí a nadie que hablase/   I've never met anyone who spoke
    hablara tan bien (el) español   Spanish so well
No sale nunca/jamás de casa   He never goes out of the house
¿Has oído nunca/jamás que un elefante   Have you ever heard of an elephant
    volase/volara? (see note ii)   flying?
Cabe dudar si nunca/jamás existió un   There is room to doubt whether there
    parentesco lingüístico entre el quechua y   ever existed a linguistic relationship
    el aymara   between Quechua and Aymara

Notes

(i) *Jamás* cannot appear after comparisons, i.e. after *más que* or *menos que*: *ahora más que nunca* 'now more than ever', *trabaja menos que nunca* 'he's working less than ever'.

(ii) In rhetorical questions inviting the answer 'no' *jamás/nunca* means 'ever': *¿se vio jamás/nunca tal cosa?* 'was such a thing ever seen?', *¿se ha oído jamás/nunca que un hombre mordiera a un perro?* 'who ever heard' (lit. 'was it ever heard') that a man bit a dog?' Compare non-rhetorical question: *¿has estado alguna vez en Madrid?* 'were you ever in Madrid?'

23.5.7 *Apenas* and other words meaning 'scarcely', 'hardly', 'as soon as'

The variant *apenas si* is much used for the meanings 'only' and 'scarcely': Seco (1998), 51, says it is especially common in literary styles. It is not used in time statements or when *apenas* follows the verb.

The subjunctive is required when the action is or was still in the future, as in *lo haré apenas lleguemos a casa* 'I'll do it as soon as we get home'. See 16.12.7. The *pretérito anterior* (*hubo llegado*, etc.) may be used to denote a completed past action in conjunction with words meaning 'scarcely', especially in literary styles, though it is very rare in speech. See 14.10.4 for discussion.

No te conozco apenas	I hardly know you
Apenas (si) te conozco	I hardly know you
En una semana apenas si cambió dos palabras con su tío (J. Marsé, Spain)	In the course of a week she barely exchanged two words with her uncle
Apenas llegamos/habíamos llegado hubimos llegado/cuando empezó a llover	We had scarcely arrived when it started raining
hace apenas seis años	barely six years ago
Apenas tengo lo suficiente para pagar la cena	I've barely got enough to pay for supper

Notes

(i) *No bien* (in Argentina and perhaps elsewhere *ni bien*) is an alternative: *no bien se hubo marchado/se marchó cuando . . .* '(s)he'd barely left when . . .', *no bien algo me produce una tristeza infinita, me convierto en un hombre de izquierda* (A. Bryce Echenique, Peru) 'as soon as something produces an infinite sadness in me, I turn into a man of the Left' (i.e. politically). *Nomás* (see 23.2.5) may also be used in Latin America to mean 'scarcely'.

(ii) *Nada más* is a colloquial alternative in time statements: *nada más llegar, pasé por su despacho* 'as soon as I arrived, I dropped in at his office', *lo haré nada más llegue* 'I'll do it as soon as I arrive' (or 'as soon as he/she/it arrives/you arrive').

23.5.8 *En mi vida, en toda la noche, en absoluto*

The phrases *en mi vida/en la vida*, 'in my life', *en toda la noche* 'in the whole night', *en absoluto* 'absolutely not' are occasionally used as negatives: *en mi vida lo/le he visto* (or *no lo/le he visto en mi vida*) 'I've never seen him in my life', *en toda la noche he podido dormir* 'I've not been able to sleep the whole night', *en mi vida he visto nada más francés ni más bonito que tú* (A. Bryce Echenique, Peru) 'I've never in my life seen anything more French or prettier than you', —*¿Te molesta?* —*En absoluto* "Does it bother you?" "Absolutely not/not at all".'

En toda la noche as a negative phrase is rather old-fashioned: *no he podido dormir en toda la noche* is more normal.

23.5.9 *Tampoco*

'Not . . . either', 'nor', 'neither' (cf. French *non plus*). It is the opposite of *también* 'also'. As with other negative particles, it requires a double negative construction if it follows a verb phrase: *tampoco creo en los ovnis* = *no creo en los ovnis tampoco* 'nor do I believe in UFOs'/'I don't believe in UFOs either':

—*¿Tienes la llave?* —*No.* —*Yo tampoco . . .*	'Do you have the key?' 'No.' 'Nor do I . . .'
Tampoco hay que olvidar que la inflación puede, en ciertas circunstancias, ser beneficiosa	Nor should one forget that inflation can, in certain circumstances, be beneficial

Tampoco dice nada a nadie	Nor does he say anything to anyone
Ellos tampoco hicieron ningún comentario	They didn't make any comment either

Ni or *y* can precede *tampoco*: *me dijo que no le gustaba el vino, y/ni tampoco la cerveza* 'he told me he didn't like wine or beer'. As this example shows, *ni* can only be combined with *tampoco* if a negative statement precedes.

24

Interrogation and exclamations

Frequent mistakes made by foreigners in interrogative or exclamatory sentences are: confusion between *qué* and *cuál*, failure to write accents on interrogative or exclamatory pronouns and adverbs, omission or wrong position of the upside-down question mark and exclamation mark, mistakes in the choice between *qué* and *lo que* in indirect questions.

24.1 Spelling

The interrogative pronouns and adverbs are:

¿cómo?	how? 24.7	*¿cuánto?*	how many/much? 24.6	*¿por qué?*	why? 24.10
¿cuál?	which?/what? 24.3	*¿dónde?*	where? 24.9	*¿qué?*	what? 24.4
¿cuándo?	when? 24.8	*¿para qué?*	what for? 24.10	*¿quién?*	who? 24.5

The accent, which appears in both direct and indirect questions, marks a real feature of pronunciation, i.e. that the interrogative and exclamatory forms are stressed words. Compare *yo sé que quiere comprar* and *yo sé **qué** quiere comprar* 'I know that he wants to buy', 'I know *what* he wants to buy'. Another example: *en Chiapas se creyó que lo peor había pasado. Ahora hay más muertos y ni siquiera hay acuerdo entorno a **cuántos** son y **cómo** murieron* (*La Reforma*, Mexico) 'it was thought that the worst was over in Chiapas. Now there are more dead and there isn't even any agreement about how many and how they died.'

24.2 Word order in interrogative sentences

When a sentence or clause begins with one of the above interrogative or exclamatory words, the order Verb–Subject is used:[1]

¿Qué hizo usted?	What did you do?
¿Cómo se llama tu hermana?	What's your sister called?
¿A qué viene la pregunta? (G. García Márquez, Colombia, dialogue)	What's the question for?
¡Qué tonterías dice Miguel!	What nonsense Miguel talks!

Word order in interrogative sentences is discussed more fully at 37.2.2.

---

[1] Although in Cuba and locally elsewhere in the Caribbean and in Central America, constructions like *¿qué usted hizo?* are commonly heard. See note to 37.2.2 note (ii).

24.3 *Cuál*

24.3.1 Basic uses of *cuál*

This word is a pronoun whose basic meaning is 'which one?' of a set:

¿Cuál prefieres?	Which one do you prefer?
¿A cuál prefieres?	Which of them (refers to persons) do you prefer?
¿A cuál de los tres se refiere usted?	To which of the three are you referring?

However, when persons are referred to, *quién* is preferred: *han venido algunos de tercero, pero no sé **quiénes*** (rather than *cuáles*) 'some of the third year have come, but I don't know which/who'.

24.3.2 Translating 'what is/are/were?', etc.

When translating sentences like 'what is the motive?', 'what's the difference?' one normally uses the phrase *¿cuál es/era el motivo/la diferencia?* (or *¿qué motivo/ diferencia* **hay/había**?). This is because such sentences basically mean '**which**, of the various possible motives, is the motive?', '**which** of the possible differences is the difference?' *¿Qué es?* literally means 'what thing?' or 'what kind of thing?', so it must be used when asking the definition of something's nature, as in 'what (kind of thing) is democracy?', 'what (kind of thing) is Vermouth?' Examples:

*¿**Cuál** es el problema?* (**¿Qué es el problema?* is not Spanish; *¿qué problema hay?* is possible)	What's the problem?
¿Cuál es su impresión de los acontecimientos?	What is your impression of the events?
Juan Pablo II . . . estaba impaciente por escuchar un resumen . . . de cuáles son las perspectivas actuales de la democracia en España (*Cambio16*, Spain)	John Paul II was impatient to hear a summary of what the present outlook is for democracy in Spain
Ya hay bastante desolación como para poder ver cuáles son los deberes del hombre (E. Sábato, Argentina)	There is already enough desolation for us to be able to see what man's duties are

Compare

¿Qué es la vida?	What is life?
¿Qué hora es?	What's the time?
¿Qué es su hermana?	What is his sister? (i.e. what does she do?)
¿Qué griterío es ése/ese?	What's that shouting?

Note

It is possible to say *ninguno de ellos sabe siquiera **cuál es** mi nombre* (L. Otero, Cuba, dialogue) 'none of them even knows what my name is', but far more usual is . . . *ninguno sabe cómo me llamo. ¿Cómo se llama?* means 'what's your/his/her/its name?', and one says *¿a qué fecha estamos?/¿a cuántos estamos?* for 'what's the date today?' or *¿qué fecha es hoy?* Compare *¿cuál es la fecha de la Batalla de Waterloo?* 'what's the date **of** the Battle of Waterloo?'

24.3.3 *Cuál*: dialect differences

In Spain and in some parts of Latin America, *cuál* is almost never used adjectivally (i.e. directly before a noun): one says *¿**qué** chicas vienen esta noche?* 'which girls are coming tonight?', not *¿cuáles chicas vienen esta noche?* However, sentences like the latter are common in many parts of Latin America:

No sé a cuáles asuntos se refiere (Chile, from Kany, 70; Spain *¿qué asuntos?*)	I don't know what matters he's referring to
¿Gatos? ¿Cuáles gatos? (C. Fuentes, Mexico, dialogue; Spain *¿qué gatos?*)	Cats? What cats?
¿Cuál vida me improviso para ustedes? (L. Rafael Sánchez, Puerto Rico, dialogue; Spain *¿qué vida?*)	What life should I take on (i.e. 'act out', 'invent') for you?

Sentences like *¿cuál sombrero prefieres?* may occasionally be heard in Spain, but learners of European Spanish should say *¿qué sombrero prefieres?* or *¿cuál de los sombreros prefieres?* or simply *¿cuál prefieres?*

24.4 Qué

For the conjunction *que* see 33.4. For the relative pronoun *que*, see Chapter 35.

24.4.1 Basic uses of qué

¿Qué? means 'what?', 'what sort of?', but not in sentences like *¿cuál es el problema?* 'what's the problem?', for which see 24.3.2. It is also used in exclamations like *¡qué inteligente es!* 'isn't (s)he intelligent!' See 24.4.4.

(a) *Qué* as a pronoun:

No sé qué decirte	I don't know what to say to you
De qué estás hablando?	What are you talking about?
Discutían sobre qué iban a decirle a Andrés	They were arguing about what they were going to say to Andrés
Por cierto, ¿qué fue de Antonio?	By the way, what became of Antonio?

(b) *Qué* as an adjective (see 24.3.3 for the Latin-American use of *cuál* in this context):

¿A qué párrafo te refieres?	Which paragraph are you referring to?
¿Qué animales prefiere fotografiar?	What animals do you prefer to photograph?
¿Con qué medios podemos contar?	What means can we count on?
Me pregunto en qué situación estará ahora	I wonder what situation he's in now

Notes

(i) *¿Qué?* is a familiar alternative for the more refined *¿cómo?/¿cómo dices?* when a repetition is requested:—*María es muy respondona.*—*¿Qué?* (polite *¿cómo?*, in Mexico *mande*) '"Maria answers back a lot." "What?"' (i.e. 'what did you say?').
(ii) *El qué* may occasionally be used as an interrogative, presumably to make clear that 'what?' is meant rather than 'I beg your pardon':—*Eso es extraño.*—*¿El qué?* '"That's odd." "What is?"', —*Se le olvidó traer el Malibu.*—*¿El qué?* '"(S)he forgot to bring the Malibu." "The what?"'
(iii) In the following sentence the word *que* is a conjunction and therefore does not take an accent: *¡que me llamen a las cinco!* 'let them call me at five o'clock!'/'tell them to call me at five'.

24.4.2 Qué and lo que in indirect questions

Either *qué* or *lo que* are possible in indirect questions except immediately before an infinitive, when *qué* is required and *lo que* may sound uneducated:

Sé de lo que te hablo (C. Fuentes, Mexico, dialogue; or *qué*)	I know what I'm talking to you about
Ni sé qué piensa y tampoco sé lo que pienso yo (E. Sábato, Argentina, dialogue)	I don't know what he thinks, and I don't know what I think either
No sé qué hacer (**not** **no sé lo que hacer*)	I don't know what to do

No sé lo que/qué voy a hacer	I don't know what I'm going to do
Pregúntale qué/lo que tiene	Ask him/her what (s)he's got

24.4.3 Qué: idiomatic uses

¿Qué tal?	How are you? How are things?
¿Qué tal estás?	How are you?
¿Qué te parece?	What do you think of it?
¿A santo de qué haces eso?	What on earth are you doing that for?
¿A mí qué?	What do I care?
¿y qué?	so what?
¿A qué viene esta compra? (J. Aldecoa, Spain, dialogue)	What's the point of this purchase?

24.4.4 Translating 'What a . . . !'

Qué is used without a following article to translate 'what a . . . !' in exclamations:

¡Qué vida ésta!	What a life!
¡Qué día más/tan hermoso!	What a lovely day!
¡Qué cara! (Spain, familiarly, *¡qué morro!*)	What a nerve/cheek!

A following adjective is preceded by *más* or *tan*:

¡Qué pareja más/tan moderna!	What a modern couple!
¡Qué libro más/tan aburrido!	What a boring book!
¡Qué nevera más/tan estúpida ésta/esta!	Isn't this a stupid refrigerator!

Notes

(i) Use of *cómo* before adjectives is an archaism that survives in Latin America: *¡cómo somos desgraciadas las mujeres!* (Spain *¡qué desgraciadas somos las mujeres!*) 'how unhappy we women are!', *¡cómo es difícil vivir!* (= *¡qué difícil es vivir!*) 'how difficult living is!'; (Argentinian and Uruguayan examples from Kany, 1970; 342–3). Lope Blanch (1991), 13, notes that this construction with *cómo* is used by all social classes in Mexico, but it is not used in Spain, cf. *cómo es díscola alguna gente* 'how unruly some people are' (A. Mastretta, Mexico, dialogue; Spain: *qué díscola es . . .*).

The colloquial *cómo . . . de* is common on both continents: *¡cómo estás de guapa!* 'aren't you attractive!', *pero ¡cómo está de gordo!* 'my, isn't he fat!'

(ii) *Qué de . . .* is a rather old-fashioned alternative for *cuánto* in exclamations: *¡qué de cosas/cuántas cosas tengo que contarte!* (familiarly *¡la de cosas que tengo que contarte!*) 'what a lot of things I've got to tell you!'

24.5 Quién

For *quien* as a relative pronoun see Chapter 35. For *quien* as a nominalizer (e.g. *quien dice eso . . .* 'people who say that . . .') see Chapter 36. *Quién/quiénes* translates 'who'/'whom' in direct and indirect questions:

¿Quién ha sido?	Who was it?
¿Quién iba a pensar que era médico?	Who would have thought he was a doctor?
¿Sabes en quién estoy pensando ahora?	Do you know who(m) I'm thinking of now?
¿Sabes quiénes van a estar?	Do you know who is going to be there?

Notes

(i) Historically *quien* had no plural (it descends from a Latin singular form *quem*), and popular speech still often uses the singular for the plural, e.g. *¿sabes quién* (instead of *quiénes*) *son?* 'do you know who they are?' This construction, frequent in older literature, should not be imitated.

(ii) *Quién* plus the imperfect subjunctive translates 'if only . . .'. See 16.15.2.

24.6 Cuánto

Cuánto may function as a pronoun/adjective or as an adverb. In the former case it agrees in number and gender with the noun; in the latter case it is invariable.

(a) 'How much', 'how many':

¿Cuánto es?	How much is it?
¿Cuánta mantequilla queda?	How much butter is left?
¿Cuántos vienen?	How many are coming?
No ha dicho cuánto pan quería	He didn't say how much bread he wanted
¿Cuánto han trabajado?	How much/long have they been working?

(b) In exclamations, 'how much!', 'what a lot!':

In exclamations *cuánto* is shortened to *cuán* before adverbs or adjectives other than *más, menos, mayor, menor, mejor, peor*. However, although it is not yet quite extinct in educated speech, *cuán* is nowadays usually found only in flowery styles, and *qué*, or *lo* + adjective or adverb (the latter discussed at 7.2.2) are more usual:

¡Cuántas veces (no) te lo habré dicho!	How many times have I told you!
¡Mira cuánta nieve!	Look at all that snow!
¡Cuánta falta le hace a este niño alguien que le enderece!	How much this child needs someone to keep him on the straight path!
¡Cuánto pesa esta mochila!	Isn't this rucksack heavy!
. . . ella misma se sorprendió de cuán lejos estaba de su vida (G. García Márquez, Colombia; or *. . . de lo lejos que estaba de su vida*)	. . . she herself was surprised at how distant he was from her life
Melania insistió, tosiendo un poquito para demostrar cuán mal estaba (J. Donoso, Chile, usually *. . . lo mal que estaba*)	Melania insisted, coughing slightly to demonstrate how ill she was
¡Cuánto más trágico!	How much more tragic!
¡Cuánto mejor estarías así!	How much better you'd be like that!

Notes

(i) In the comparative phrases *cuanto más/menos . . . más/menos* 'the more . . . the more' 'the less . . . the less', *cuanto* is not used exclamatorily and does not take an accent. See Chapter 5 for further discussion of this construction.

(ii) *Cuanto* may be used as a relative pronoun equivalent to *todo lo que: dime cuanto sabes* = *dime todo lo que sabes* 'tell me everything you know'.

24.7 Cómo

'How' in direct and indirect questions and in exclamations. Sometimes it means 'why?', and in this case it is more formal than the English 'how come?' (for *como* = 'as', 'since', see 33.5.2; for *como* + subjunctive = 'if' see 25.8.2):

¿Cómo te llamas?	What's your name?
¿Cómo quieres que me peine?	How do you want me to do my hair?
No sé cómo hacerlo	I don't know how to do it
¡Cómo está el mundo!	What a state the world is in!
¡Cómo llueve!	Look how it's raining!
¿Cómo/Por qué no me llamaste ayer?	Why didn't you ring me yesterday?
¿Cómo le dejas ir solo al cine a ese niño?	How can you let that child go to the cinema on his own?

> ... *su ignorancia sobre el cómo y el*
> *porqué* ... (J. Aldecoa, Spain)

> ... his ignorance about the how and
> why ...

Note

¿Cómo? Or *¿cómo dice (usted)?* (Mexico *mande*) are polite ways of requesting a repetition of something misheard or misunderstood.

24.8 *Cuándo* 'when'

Little need be said about this word in direct and indirect questions: *¿cuándo fue eso?* 'when was that?', *no sé cuándo llegarán* 'I don't know when they'll arrive'.[2]

When it is not a question word, *cuando* (no accent) may introduce relative clauses (see 35.12), or it may be a subordinator, often requiring the subjunctive (see 16.12.7). For 'whenever' see 16.13.6. For the use of *cuando* in cleft sentences, e.g. *fue entonces cuando* ... 'it was then that ... ' see 36.2. It may also occasionally function as a preposition meaning 'at the time of': *nos casamos cuando el terremoto* 'we got married at the time of the earthquake'.

24.9 *Dónde* 'where'

This word should be differentiated from *¿adónde?*, which means 'where to?' and is optionally used with verbs of motion: *¿adónde van ustedes?* or *¿dónde van ustedes?* Only *¿dónde?* can be used when no motion is involved: *¿dónde estamos?*, not *¿adónde estamos?*

When it is not a question word, *donde* (no accent) may introduce relative clauses (see 16.14.4 and 35.10), where the difference between *donde* and *a donde* is discussed. For 'wherever' see 16.13.8. For *donde* in cleft sentences, e.g. *fue allí donde* ... 'it was there that ... ' see 36.2.3. *Donde* may also mean 'at the house of' in some countries, especially Chile, Peru, Ecuador and Central America: *voy donde Miguel = voy a casa de Miguel*; this construction is also heard in regional popular speech in Spain. *Lo de* has the same meaning in Argentina: *voy a lo de Miguel*.

24.10 *Por qué, para qué*

Por qué 'why' (stressed *qué*) must be distinguished in spelling and pronunciation from *porque* 'because'. *¿Para qué?* 'what ... for?' must be distinguished from *para que* 'in order to'.

In questions *para qué* stresses intention, *por qué* stresses cause, and the difference is the same as between 'what for?' and 'why?': *¿para qué* (or *¿por qué) vamos a cambiarlo si todo está bien?* 'what are we changing it for if everything's OK?' Statistically *por qué* is much more frequent and can often be used instead of *para qué*, but not always, as the following example shows: *¿por qué se incendió la casa?* 'why did the house catch fire?' (not *para qué* or 'what for?').

---

[2] Foreign students sometimes wonder why the subjunctive is not used in such sentences, e.g. *no sé cuándo 'lleguen'*; but the subjunctive is not used after interrogative words (i.e. accented words like *cuándo, dónde*). See 16.12.1 for more details.

25

Conditional sentences

25.1 General

Conditional sentences have various structures, but the commonest patterns are:

(a) Open conditions:

Si viene me quedo/quedaré	If (s)he comes I'll stay
Si han llegado, me quedaré	If they have arrived, I'll stay

(b) Remote conditions:

Si viniera/viniese, me quedaría/quedaba	If he were to come, I'd stay

(c) Unfulfilled conditions:

Si hubiéramos/hubiésemos tenido más dinero, habríamos/hubiéramos comprado la casa	If we had had more money we'd have bought the house

(d) Fulfilled conditions:

Si no salía, era porque prefería quedarse en casa	If she didn't usually go out, it was because she preferred to stay at home
Si llegaba temprano comíamos a las doce	If he arrived early we had lunch at twelve

One point can hardly be over-emphasized: *si*, in the meaning of 'if', is never followed by the present subjunctive except in one rare construction. See 25.8.1 for details.

25.2 Open conditions

So called because fulfilment (US 'fulfillment') or non-fulfilment of the condition is equally possible. The subjunctive is not used in open conditions and the tense pattern is the same as in English:

(a) *Si* + present + present:

Si tenemos que pagar tanto no vale la pena	If we have to pay so much it's not worth it
Sólo concibo escribir algo si me divierto, y sólo puedo divertirme si me intereso (J. Marías, Spain)	I can only contemplate writing something if I enjoy it, and I can only enjoy it if I'm interested
Si (el elitismo) significa que selecciona sus miembros en razón de su aptitud, todas las	If elitism means that it selects its members according to their ability,

universidades del mundo son elitistas (M. Vargas Llosa, Peru)	every university in the world is elitist

(b) *Si* + present + future (or present with future meaning):

Si el contrato no está mañana en Londres, no hay trato	If the contract isn't in London by tomorrow, the deal's off
Si llueve me quedo/quedaré en casa	If it rains I'll stay at home
Si te oye tu papi se muere. (A. Mastretta, Mexico, dialogue)	If daddy hears you he'll die (figuratively or literally)

(c) *Si* + past tense + present or future, normally only possible when the subject of the verb in the main clause is not yet sure about the facts described in the if-clause:

Si han contestado ya, no les escribiré	If they've already answered, I won't write to them
Si terminaron la semana pasada nos queda poco por hacer	If they finished last week there isn't much left for us to do
Si llevaba minifalda su madre estará enfadadísima	If she was wearing a miniskirt her mother will be really cross

(d) *Si* + present + imperative

Si queréis ver el desfile salid al balcón	If you want to see the parade go out on to the balcony

(e) In reported speech referring to the past, the imperfect or pluperfect indicative appears in the if-clause, and the conditional (or colloquially the imperfect indicative) in the main clause: *me dijo que me pagaría si **había** terminado* 'he told me he'd pay me if I'd finished', *el médico dijo que la operarían si **tenía** algún hueso roto* 'the doctor said that they'd operate on her if she had any broken bones'. This construction is also very common in stream-of-consciousness style, i.e. when the text reports someone's unspoken thoughts: '(he knew that) if it rained everything would be spoilt' *(sabía que) si **llovía** se estropearía todo:*

*Si la policía la **detenía**, ya escarmentaría* (M. Vázquez Montalbán; Spain, unspoken thoughts)	If the police arrested her, that would teach her a lesson
*Si no **actuaba** pronto, Gianni terminaría por resquebrajarse, por acabar en una clínica psiquiátrica* (S. Pitol, Mexico)	If she didn't act promptly Gianni would break down, end up in a psychiatric clinic
*Me pareció que si me **mostraba** disponible te ibas a cansar* (M. Puig, Argentina, dialogue)	I thought that if I showed I was available you'd get tired of me

The frequent occurrence of this type of construction in passages of indirect speech sometimes encourages students to believe that the pattern *si* + imperfect indicative + conditional is also the usual way of forming remote conditions in Spanish, as in French and English, e.g. 'if I had money'/*si j'avais de l'argent . . .* , Spanish *si yo **tuviera**/**tuviese** dinero . . . .* The next section should correct any such misconception.

25.3 Remote conditions

In 'remote' conditions the verb in the if-clause is in the imperfect subjunctive (*-ra* or *-se* form); the verb in the other clause is normally in the conditional.

There are two types, which correspond to the English sentences 'if you paid now it would cost less' and 'if I were rich I'd buy you a house'. The first is fulfillable and is merely a slightly hypothetical variant of an equivalent open condition: there is little difference between *si pagaras ahora, costaría menos* 'if you **paid** now it would cost less' and *si pagas ahora, costará menos* 'if you **pay** now it will cost less'. In the second type the condition is contrary to fact and the subjunctive construction is the only possible one in Spanish: *si yo fuera/fuese rico, te compraría una casa,* 'if I were rich, I'd buy you a house' (but I'm not). As was mentioned at 25.2e, English and French-speaking students must avoid using the imperfect indicative in the if-clause (cf. *si j'étais riche . . .*):

Iría contigo si tuviera dinero	I'd go with you if I had any money
Si supieras hacer el nudo como todos los chicos	If you knew how to make a knot
de tu edad, no te tendrías que quejar	like all the boys of your age,
(I. Aldecoa, Spain, dialogue; *supieses* also possible)	you wouldn't have to complain
Si pagaran más las labores me convendría	If the needlework was better paid
tomar una sirvienta con cama (M. Puig,	it'd be worth my while getting
Argentina, dialogue)	a live-in maid
Si por lo menos se pudiera limitar el	If one could at least cut back
contrabando de cocaína, se ahorrarían muchas	cocaine smuggling, a lot of
muertes (M. Vargas Llosa, Peru,	deaths would be avoided
dialogue; or *pudiese*)	

Notes

(i) Use of the conditional in the if-clause is regional or substandard, but it is common in Navarre, the Basque Provinces and nearby parts of Spain, in popular Argentine speech and no doubt elsewhere, e.g. *?si no estaría preso, no lo habrían soltado* 'if he wasn't arrested they wouldn't have let him go' (M. Puig, Argentina, dialogue; for *estuviera/estuviese*). This should not be imitated.

(ii) For use of the *-ra* subjunctive form as an alternative for the conditional, see 25.6 and 14.7.5.

25.4 Unfulfilled conditions

These indicate a condition in the past that was not fulfilled. The verb in the if-clause is in the pluperfect subjunctive (*hubiera/hubiese hablado,* etc.) and the verb in the main clause is usually in the perfect conditional (*habría/hubiera hecho,* etc.):

Si él hubiera/hubiese tenido dinero, hubiera/habría	If he'd had money he'd have
saldado la cuenta	settled the bill
Si no hubiera sido por las contracciones del	If it hadn't been for the stomach
estómago, se habría sentido muy bien (J. Cortázar,	cramps, he'd have felt fine
Argentina, dialogue)	

Notes

(i) A number of simplifications of this type of conditional sentence are heard in spontaneous speech but are banned from writing or non-spontaneous language and are rather informal for foreign speakers: *si lo llego a saber, te habría llamado* 'If I'd found out, I'd have rung you', *si llegas a estar más rato, te juro que entro a cobrarles algo . . .* (C. Martín Gaite, Spain, dialogue) 'if you'd stayed there any longer, I swear I'd have gone in and charged them some money', *si sé que estás enfermo, no vengo* 'if I'd known you were ill, I wouldn't have come', *dio un tropezón y si se descuida, se cae* '(s)he slipped and (s)he'd have fallen down if (s)he hadn't taken care'.

(ii) *Si* + imperfect + imperfect is frequent in Argentine speech: *si me tocabas, te mataba con mi cuchillo* (E. Sábato, Argentina, dialogue) 'if you'd touched me, I'd have killed you with my knife'. Also *si* + imperfect + imperfect subjunctive: *si hace unos años yo veía* (for *hubiera visto*) *en la playa a alguien con esto, hubiera pensado: ese tipo es loco* (Mafalda cartoon, Joaquín Salvador Lavado (Quino)

Argentina; *está loco* in Spain) 'if I had seen someone a few years ago on the beach with that, I'd have thought: that guy's crazy'.

25.5 Imperfect indicative for conditional

The imperfect indicative frequently replaces the conditional tense in spontaneous speech on both sides of the Atlantic (the subject is further discussed at 14.5.4). This usage is perfectly acceptable in relaxed European Spanish but it is not allowed in formal styles and it may be less tolerated in some American republics than in others:

*Si tuviese/tuviera dinero, me **compraba** un coche* (for *compraría*)	If I had the money, I'd buy a car
Desde luego, si yo fuera hombre, no me casaba . . . (L. Goytisolo, Spain, dialogue)	Obviously, if I were a man I wouldn't get married . . .
Si de pronto tuviese/tuviera la certeza de que no voy a vivir más que dos días, de seguro me iba (for *iría*) *a confesar* (M. de Unamuno, Spain)	If I suddenly found out for certain that I'd only two days to live, I'd certainly go to confession
Si no fuera por vosotros iba yo a aguantar a vuestro padre . . . (set expression: *iría* not used)	If it weren't for you, would I put up with your father?

25.6 *-ra* forms instead of the conditional

Imperfect subjunctive in *-ra* (but not, at least in careful language, the *-se* form) is a very common alternative for the conditional of the auxiliary verb *haber* and also of some other verbs: *con él o sin él, hubiera/habría sido igual* 'with him or without him, it would have been the same'. See 14.7.5 for detailed discussion.

25.7 Fulfilled conditions

These are not really conditions at all but merely an elegant way of saying 'the reason why'/'just because'/'whenever'. The verb is never in the subjunctive:

Si me estaba contando todos aquellos proyectos era porque inexorablemente pensaba realizarlos (F. Umbral, Spain)	If he was telling me about all those plans it was because he was inevitably intending to carry them out
Si he tenido suerte, la culpa no es mía	It's not my fault if I've been lucky
Si teníamos dinero, íbamos al teatro	If (i.e. 'when') we had any money we used to go to the theatre
Si te traje a la playa es para que vigilaras a Alvarito y no para que te pusieras a leer (S. Vodanovic, Chile, dialogue)	If I brought you to the beach it's so you can keep an eye on little Álvaro, not so you could start reading

25.8 *Si* 'if'

25.8.1 *Si*: general

Si is never followed by the present subjunctive, except occasionally after *saber*: *no sé si **sea** cierto* 'I do not know whether it be true' for *no sé si es cierto, no sé si en este estado **pueda** continuar* (L. Rafael Sánchez, Puerto Rico, dialogue) 'I don't know if

I can go on in this condition'. *Ser* cannot be deleted after *si*: *si es urgente* 'if urgent', *ven antes si es posible* 'come earlier if possible'; compare also French *si nécessaire* 'if necessary', *si es/fuera/fuese necesario*. *Si* sometimes has a merely emphatic function: *pero, ¡si tiene más de cincuenta años!* 'but he's more than fifty years old!' See 31.4.8 for details. In the phrase *apenas si* it has no function: *apenas (si) la conocía* 'I/he/she/you barely knew her'.

25.8.2 Replacement of *si* by *como*

In informal language in type 1 (open) conditions, *como* with the present or imperfect subjunctive may replace *si*. This is usually confined to threats and warnings and is found on both continents, as the Cuban example shows (but Lope Blanch, 1991, 146, says that *como* + subjunctive is unknown in Mexican Spanish):

Como vuelvas a hablarme de mala manera, me voy	If you talk to me in a nasty way again, I'm going
Como no me lo pagues, me lo llevo	If you don't pay me for it, I'll take it away
Me dijo que como no se lo pagara/pagase, se lo llevaba/ llevaría	She told me that if I didn't pay her for it, she would take it away
—¿Está enfermo su hijo? —Enferma me pondrá a mí como lo deje (A. Arrufat, Cuba, dialogue)	'Is your son sick?' 'He'll make *me* sick if I let him'

Como with the indicative = 'since' is discussed at 33.5.2, e.g. *como no me lo has pagado, me lo llevo* 'since you've not paid me for it, I'm taking it away'.

25.8.3 Replacement of *si* by *de*

De plus an infinitive may replace *si* and a finite verb in an if-clause. This is only possible if the verb in the if-clause and the verb in the subordinate clause are in the same person: one can say *de haberlo sabido, me hubiera quedado en casa* 'had I known, I'd have stayed at home' (both first-person), but not **de llover, me quedo en casa* 'if it rains I'm staying at home' (*si llueve me quedo/quedaré en casa*):

Se me ocurrió que, de estar viva, la mujer me habría parecido más vieja y más digna (A. Martín, Spain, dialogue)	It occurred to me that, if she had been alive, the woman would have seemed older and more dignified to me
De no haberse hecho la cirugía estética en ese instante a Márgara, se le arrugaría la nariz (J. Asís, Argentina; Spain *se le habría arrugado*)	If Márgara hadn't had plastic surgery at that moment, her nose would have become wrinkled

When used thus *de* must have a hypothetical or future reference. One can say *de llover, lloverá mucho* 'if it rains it'll rain a lot', but not **de ser guapa, es mi novia* 'if she's beautiful, she's my girlfriend' (timeless statement). *De* cannot therefore be used in type 4 (fulfilled) conditional sentences (25.7).

25.9 Other ways of expressing conditions

(a) The gerund may sometimes have a conditional force: *hablando de esa manera no consigues nada* 'you'll get nowhere by talking like that' = *si hablas de esa manera ...* 'if you talk like that'. See note to 20.4.2 for more examples.

(b) A negative if-clause may be introduced by some phrase meaning 'unless', e.g. *a menos que, a no ser que* (see 16.12.8b):

Debe estar en casa, a no ser que/a menos que haya ido al bar con sus amigos	He must be at home, unless he's gone to the bar with his friends

(c) 'If' may be expressed by some phrase meaning 'on condition that', e.g. *con tal (de) que, a condición de que* (see 16.12.8a):

Compraré los riñones, con tal (de) que estén frescos	I'll buy the kidneys provided they're fresh

(d) *Al* + infinitive (see 18.7a) properly means 'on . . . -ing', but is sometimes seen with a conditional meaning:

?Al ser verdad esta afirmación se tendrá que repensar todo	If this claim is true, everything will have to be re-thought

This is not acceptable in Spain and is probably a Latin-American regionalism. It is stylistically dubious.

(e) *A* + infinitive can have a conditional meaning in a few cases:

A no ser por mí, le hubieran matado	Had it not been for me, they'd have killed him
a juzgar por lo que dicen . . . (= *si se juzga por lo que dicen . . .*)	to judge by what they say . . .
A decir verdad, no me cae bien (=*si digo la verdad . . .*)	To tell the truth, I don't like it/him/her/you

(f) *Por si . . .* forms conditionals of the sort translated by 'in case . . . ' or some similar phrase:

Me asomé a la ventana por si venía	I looked out of the window in case he was coming
Compramos otra botella por si acaso	We'll buy another bottle just in case
Por si esto fuera poco, también me han robado el reloj	As if that weren't enough, they've stolen my watch too

Note the phrase, much used in familiar European Spanish, *por si las moscas* 'just in case'.

25.10 Miscellaneous examples of conditional sentences

The following are translations of typical English conditionals (some taken from Quirk et al., 1972):

Had he known, he wouldn't have protested	*Si lo hubiese/hubiera sabido no habría/hubiera protestado* or *De haberlo sabido . . .*
Were that the only reason, there'd be no problem	*Si ésa fuera/fuese la única razón, no habría problema*
If possible, come earlier (not *si posible . . .*)	*Si es posible, ven antes*
I won't compromise, even if he offers/were to offer me money	*No transijo, incluso/aun si me ofrece/ofreciera/ofreciese dinero*
It'll be impossible unless you change your attitude	*Será imposible, a menos que/salvo que/a no ser que cambies de actitud*
Provided no objection is raised, the meeting will be held here	*Con tal (de) que no haya ninguna objeción, la reunión se celebrará aquí*

Should it turn out to be true, things will be different	*Si resulta ser verdad, las cosas serán distintas*

25.11 Translating 'if I were you . . .'

If I were you, I'd keep quiet	*Yo de usted/Yo que usted/Si yo fuera usted, me callaría/callaba*

Yo que tú/usted is the older Peninsular formula. *Yo de ti/usted* is a Catalanism which is now widespread in Spain, although it is censured by manuals of good usage (e.g. Santamaría et al. 1989, 309): *yo de ti lo dejaba* 'if I were you I would leave it', *yo de Ana no lo haría* 'if I were Ana I wouldn't do it'.

26

Pronominal verbs

26.1 General

Pronominal verbs (called 'reflexive' verbs in most traditional grammar books) are those which are accompanied by an object pronoun (i.e. *me, te, se, nos, os* or *se*) which is of the same person and number as the verb's subject: *yo* **me** *lavo* 'I'm washing (myself)', ***vais** a cansar**os*** 'you're going to tire yourselves/get tired', *(él)* **se** *ha marchado* 'he's gone/left'. The usual object pronouns are used with such verbs except in the third person (*usted, ustedes* included), which uses the invariable pronoun *se* for both singular and plural. Common forms of a typical pronominal verb are:

Infinitive *sentarse* 'to sit down'   **Gerund** *sentándose*

Imperative (*tú*) *siéntate*, (*vosotros/as*) *sentaos*, (*usted*) *siéntese*, (*ustedes*) *siéntense*

Present indicative   (*yo*) *me siento*   (*nosotros/nosotras*) *nos sentamos*
                        (*tú*) *te sientas*   (*vosotros/vosotras*) *os sentáis*
                        (*él/ella/usted*) *se sienta*   (*ellos/ellas/ustedes*) *se sientan*
                        etc.

A very large number of Spanish verbs can be pronominalized, even intransitive verbs like 'to be' and 'to die'. It is very misleading to give the name 'reflexive' to forms like *me voy* 'I'm going', *se cayó* '(s)he/it/you fell down', *no me lo creo* 'I don't believe it', *se venden* 'they are sold'. 'Reflexive' refers to just one of the *meanings* that the pronominal form of a verb can have: it shows that the subject performs an action on or for him/herself, as in 'I'm washing myself', 'he praises himself', 'they give themselves airs', etc. The range of meanings associated with pronominal verbs is in fact very wide and the relationship between them is sometimes subtle. The following chart lists these possible meanings and some of their distinctive formal characteristics:

Possible meanings of Spanish pronominal ('reflexive') verb forms[1]

Name	Example	Singular or plural verb	Person of verb	Animate or inanimate subject	Where discussed
1. Reflexive	*me lavo, me calzo*	either	any	animate	26.2

---

[1] Based on Moreira Rodríguez and Butt (1996), 3.

2. Reciprocal	*nos queremos, os habláis*	plural only	any	animate	26.3
3. Intransitive	*me irrito, se abrió*	either	any, if animate; third if inanimate	either	26.4
4. *Se de matización*	*se fue, se murió, te bajaste, me lo esperaba, se lo cree*, etc.	either	any	either	26.5–26.7
5. 'Total consumption'	*se bebió un litro de vino*	either	any	animate	26.9
6. Passive *se*	*se construyó el puente*	either	third only	inanimate with rare exceptions	Ch. 28
7. 'Special construction'	*se arrestó a tres personas*	always singular	third only	human	Ch. 28
8. Impersonal *se*	*en España se vive bien, en general se come demasiado*	always singular	third only	human	Ch. 28

Constructions 6, 7 and 8 are more appropriately included under the heading 'Passive and impersonal sentences' and are therefore discussed in Chapter 28.

Throughout the following discussion it must be remembered that the meaning of a pronominal verb is often ambiguous: *se critican* could mean 'they criticize themselves', 'they criticize one another', or 'they are criticized' (passive *se*: see Chapter 28). Such ambiguities are almost always resolved by reference to the background of the sentence or, often, by the meaning of the verb.

26.2 Reflexive meaning of pronominal verbs

This meaning is constantly encountered but it is not the most common, although for historical reasons it is usually the first one to be studied.[2] It indicates that an action is done by the subject to or for him/herself: *se está duchando* '(s)he's having a shower', *os alabáis mucho* 'you praise yourselves a lot' (or 'you praise one another a lot'; see next section), *me voy a comprar otro traje* 'I'm going to buy (myself) another suit'. Four important features of this reflexive meaning are:

(a) The subject is always animate (since a door or a stone doesn't usually do things to itself).
(b) The pronoun may stand for the direct or the indirect object: *se está afeitando* 'he's shaving' (*se* = direct object), *me estoy quitando la camisa* 'I'm taking my shirt off' (*me* = indirect object).
(c) The action can be deliberate or accidental and in a few common cases may actually be done by someone else to the subject (see note iii).

---

[2] It was virtually the only meaning given to pronominal verbs in Classical Latin.

(d) The original verb is always transitive. If the original verb is intransitive then the pronominal form cannot have a reflexive meaning, cf. *dormir* 'to sleep'>*se durmió* 'he went to sleep' (*se de matización*, not 'reflexive'). Examples:

Se está lavando	(S)he's washing
Me corté con una lata	I cut myself on a tin
Se ha roto una pierna	He's broken a leg
¡Qué bien te peinas!	How well you do your hair!
¡Cuidado, que te vas a salpicar!	Careful, you're going to get splashed!
Se daban crema para el sol	They were putting sun-cream on (or reciprocal 'they were putting sun-cream on each other')
Esto me lo pido, esto me lo pido . . . (little children overheard in a toy shop at Christmas deciding what to ask for in letters to the Three Kings; the *me* is a reflexive indirect object)	I'm asking for this . . . and this
Se mató en un accidente	He got killed in an accident[3]

Notes

(i) The subject in these constructions may be emphasized by use of the subject pronoun, sometimes reinforced by the appropriate form of *solo* 'alone' or *mismo*: this construction also makes it unambiguously clear that the meaning is reflexive: *primero vistió a la niña y luego se vistió ella* 'first she dressed the child, then she dressed herself', *no eches la culpa a nadie, te has perjudicado tú solo/mismo* 'don't blame anyone else, you did harm to yourself' , *la niña se pone los zapatos ella sola* 'the little girl puts on her shoes all by herself'.

If a preposition is used (including personal *a*), emphasis is obtained by using the appropriate prepositional form of the personal pronoun (*mí/ti/sí/nosotros/vosotros/sí*) plus the correct number and gender of *mismo*: *se decía a sí misma que no servía para nada* 'she told herself she was good for nothing' *me odio a mí mismo/misma* 'I hate myself', *nos mentimos a nosotros mismos con frecuencia* 'we lie to ourselves frequently'. *Mismo* is not used if the preposition is *para*: *se decía para sí que no valía la pena* 'she told herself that it wasn't worthwhile'.

(ii) Verbs expressing hurt take either the prepositional or non-prepositional form: *se hace daño él mismo/a sí mismo* 'he's hurting himself', *te perjudicas tú mismo/a ti mismo* 'you (masc.) are damaging yourself'.

(iii) With a few common verbs the reflexive meaning of the pronominal form may be extended to include 'to get or have something done for oneself'. This construction is not possible in all Latin-American varieties of Spanish, in which cases *mandar* or *hacer* are used, e.g. *mandó construir un palacio* or *hizo construir un palacio* 'he had a palace built'; both of these latter constructions are also used in Spain. Further examples: *se va a hacer un abrigo rojo* 'she's going to make herself a red coat'/'she's going to get a red coat made', *se ha construido un chalet* 'he has built himself a house (either himself or to his specifications)', *me voy a cortar el pelo* 'I'm going to get/have my hair cut', *¿dónde te vistes?* 'where do you get your clothes from?' (also 'where do you get dressed?'). Ambiguity can be removed by the appropriate use of the personal pronoun followed by *mismo* or *solo*, e.g. *me voy a cortar yo mismo el pelo* 'I'm going to cut my hair' (myself). See also note (i).

In a few cases it is unlikely or impossible that the action will actually be performed by the subject: *me voy a operar de cataratas* 'I'm going to have an operation for cataracts', *si te duele esa muela, debías sacártela* 'if that tooth's aching you ought to have it out' (or, less likely, 'you ought to take it out'), *no me gusta nada ese corte que tienes en la mano. Debes ir a vértelo* (colloquial, Spain) 'I don't like the look of that cut you've got on your hand. You ought to go and get it looked at.'

(iv) In colloquial language in Spain, but not in Latin America, the reflexive meaning of a few verbs may imply that the action concerns or is meaningful to the subject and to no one else: *tú sabrás*

---

[3] Not 'he committed suicide', even though it could mean this in other contexts; merely that he himself was performing the action that killed him. One could not say **se mató en una riña* *'he killed himself in a fight': *le mataron en una riña.*

*lo que **te** dices* 'I guess *you* know what you're talking about', *yo **me** entiendo* '**I** know what I'm referring to'/'I know what I'm talking about', *yo sé lo que **me** hago* 'I know what I'm doing' (i.e. even if you don't).

26.3 Reciprocal meaning of pronominal verbs

A plural pronominal verb can have a reciprocal meaning, i.e. it may show that an action is done to or for one another. *El uno al otro/los unos a los otros* can be added to make clear that the reciprocal meaning is intended: compare *se entristecen* 'they grow sad'/'they make themselves sad'/'they make one another sad', and *se entristecen los unos a los otros* 'they make one another sad':

Nos escribimos periódicamente	We write to one another regularly
Hace años que no se hablan	They haven't been talking to one another for years
Pasó mucho tiempo sin que nos viésemos/viéramos	We didn't see one another for a long time
Os conocisteis en Córdoba	You met in Cordoba
Se hacen la compra los unos a los otros	They do one another's shopping
Siempre se ponen pegas	They're always finding fault with one another

If one subject is feminine and the other masculine, masculine pronouns are used: *Pedro y María se quieren mucho el uno al otro* 'Pedro and María love one another a lot.'

26.4 Pronominalization and intransitivity

26.4.1 General remarks on pronominal verbs and intransitivity

One important function of the pronominal form is to show that a verb is intransitive. English does not systematically differentiate between transitive and intransitive verbs: 'I've finished the dinner'/'the dinner has finished', 'I boiled it'/'it boiled'. With a few important exceptions, Spanish specifies the intransitive meaning of a verb by using the pronominal form. A large number of transitive verbs therefore have pronominal intransitive counterparts. Compare:

Transitive	**Intransitive**
abrir to open[4]	*abrirse* to open (intransitive)
acabar to finish (transitive and intransitive)	*acabarse* to end (intransitive)
acostar to put someone to bed	*acostarse* to go to bed
casar to marry someone off (also intransitive in archaic or regional styles)	*casarse* to get married
cerrar to close	*cerrarse* to close (intransitive)
despertar to wake someone up (also intransitive)	*despertarse* to wake up
divorciar to divorce	*divorciarse* to get divorced
dormir to put somebody to sleep (also 'to sleep')	*dormirse* to go to sleep
enamorar to make someone fall in love	*enamorarse de* to fall in love with

---

[4] But see 26.7.1 for remarks on a possible intransitive use of *abrir* and *cerrar*.

involucrar to implicate	*involucrarse* to be implicated
meter to put in	*meterse* to get in, to interfere
perder to lose	*perderse* to get lost
preocupar to worry somebody	*preocuparse* to worry
presentar to introduce people	*presentarse* to appear unexpectedly
terminar (see *acabar*)	*terminarse* (see *acabarse*)
tirar to throw/pull	*tirarse* to jump

Intransitive pronominal verbs are so numerous that beginners sometimes conclude that all intransitive counterparts of Spanish transitive verbs must be pronominal in form. But a number of non-pronominal verbs have both a transitive and an intransitive meaning, Thus we can say *lo/le suspendieron en francés* 'they failed him in French' and *suspendió en francés* 'he failed in French',[5] *su cabeza asomaba por la ventana* 'his/her head was sticking out of the window' and *asomaba la cabeza por la ventana* '(s)he was sticking his/her head out of the window', *desconectó la radio* 'he disconnected the radio' and *en clase siempre desconecta* 'in class she always "switches off"' (i.e. 'daydreams'), *lo empezó* '(s)he/you began it' and *empezó* '(s)he/it/you began'.

The following are common examples (there is also a list of non-pronominal intransitive verbs denoting change of state at 27.2):

acabar to end (see 26.7.2)	*empezar* to begin
aflojar to loosen	*enfermar* to get ill/to make ill (*enfermarse* =
aprobar to approve/to pass (an exam)	'to get ill/sick' in Latin America)
aumentar to grow bigger/to make bigger	*mejorar* to improve (see 26.7.23)
	oscurecer to darken
bajar to go down/to lift down	*resucitar* to resuscitate
comenzar to begin	*sangrar* to bleed
conectar to connect	*subir* to go up/to lift up
desconectar to disconnect	*suspender* to fail (e.g. an exam)
despertar to wake up	*terminar* to end
empeorar to worsen	*vestir* to wear

Sometimes the pronominal form of the verb is radically different in meaning:

cambiar to change	*cambiarse de* to change clothes/house
correr to run	*correrse* to be ashamed/to 'come'
desenvolver to unwrap	*desenvolverse* to get ahead, to be good at something
despedir to see someone off/ to fire/sack	*despedirse de* to take one's leave/say goodbye
empeñar to pawn/pledge	*empeñarse en* to insist on doing something
gastar to spend	*gastarse* to wear out
llevar to take/to wear	*llevarse* to take with one/to steal
mudar to change bedclothes	*mudarse* to move house/to change one's clothes
negar to deny	*negarse a* to refuse to do something
oponer to contrast two views	*oponerse* to oppose

Some pronominal intransitive verbs have no transitive counterparts, at least in normal language; compare *acatarrarse/constiparse* 'to catch a cold', *arrepentirse* 'to

---

[5] This intransitive use of *suspender*, and also of *aprobar* 'to pass an exam', seems to be a recent development in the language.

repent', *abstenerse* 'to abstain', *apropiarse de* 'to take possession of', *atenerse a* 'to limit oneself to', *atragantarse* 'to choke', *atreverse a* 'to dare', *comportarse* 'to behave', *dignarse* 'to deign to', *equivocarse* 'to make a mistake', *inmiscuirse* 'to interfere', *quejarse* 'to complain', *suicidarse* 'to commit suicide', etc. All of these appear only in the pronominal form. Some pronominal verbs may also be transitive, as in *se bebió un litro de vino* 'he drank a litre/(US 'liter') of wine', or *me la conozco* 'I know her only too well'. See 26.9 for examples.

Note

Some pronominal verbs are being replaced by the non-pronominal form, as in the case of *entrenar* for *entrenarse* 'to train', which has become common in recent years in spite of grammarians' complaints, or *encarar* for *encararse con* 'to face up to (a problem)': *entreno mañana en el gimnasio* 'I'm training tomorrow at the gymnasium', *Arco 93 trata de encarar la crisis del mercado de arte* (*El País*, Spain), Arco 93 is trying to face up to the economic crisis in the art market.'

26.4.2 Pronominal and non-pronominal verbs denoting emotional reactions

A word is necessary about the existence of two different types of impersonal verbs and phrases denoting emotional reactions. The non-pronominal verbs and non-verbal expressions in List A (not exhaustive) are followed only by *que*, e.g. *le enfada* **que** *el perro no deje de ladrar* 'it annoys him that the dog won't stop barking'. These verbs do not appear – at least in educated usage – in the pronominal form with *de que*: one says *le irrita que* + subjunctive, not ?*se irrita de que . . .* If they are used pronominally *porque* should follow: *se irritaba porque . . .* + indicative 'he got irritated because . . .'.

The verbs in List B (also not exhaustive) have pronominal counterparts followed by *de que*. In these cases one can either say *le aburre que* + subjunctive 'it bores him that . . .' or *se aburre de que* + subjunctive 'he is bored by the fact that . . .'.

List A Emotional reactions and value judg(e)ments followed by *que* (and **not** by *de que*)

apenarle a alguien que	to pain someone that . . .
darle lástima a alguien que	to fill someone with pity that . . .
deprimirle a alguien que	to depress someone that . . .
encantarle a alguien que	to enchant someone that . . .
enfadarle/enojarle a alguien que	to anger someone that . . .
extrañarle a alguien que	to puzzle someone that . . .
fastidiarle a alguien que	to bother someone that . . .
gustarle a alguien que	to like: *me gusta que canten* 'I like them to sing'
importarle a alguien que	to matter to someone that . . .
irritarle a alguien que	to irritate someone that . . .
parecerle bien/mal a alguien que	to seem good/bad to someone that . . .
satisfacerle a alguien que	to satisfy someone that . . .

List B Emotional reactions followed by *de que*

The verbs in this list may appear either with *que* and a direct object (as in list **A**) or as pronominal verbs followed by *de que* (see also 16.6.2 for further remarks on these verbs):

aburrirle a alguien que/aburrirse de que	to bore someone that/to be bored by the fact that . . .
alegrarle a alguien que/alegrarse de que	to cheer someone that/to be happy that . . .
asustarle a alguien que/asustarse de que	to frighten someone that/to be frightened that . . .
avergonzarle a alguien que/avergonzarse de que	to shame someone that/to be ashamed that . . .
dolerle a alguien que/dolerse de que	to hurt someone that/to be hurt that . . .
emocionarle a alguien que/emocionarse de que	to excite someone that/to get excited by the fact that . . .
entristecerle a alguien que/entristecerse de que	to sadden someone that/to be saddened that . . .
entusiasmarle a alguien que/entusiasmarse de que	to make someone enthusiastic that/to be enthusiastic that . . .
horrorizarle a alguien que/horrorizarse de que	to horrify someone that/to be horrified that . . .
indignarle a alguien que/indignarse de que	to make someone indignant that/to be indignant that . . .
sorprenderle a alguien que/sorprenderse de que	to surprise someone that/to be surprised that . . .

Further examples of both types of construction:

Me molesta que te quejes tanto	It annoys me that you complain so much
Sólo/Solo faltaba que tú dijeras/dijeses eso	All it needed was for you to say that
Me importa un bledo que se celebre o no se celebre	I couldn't care less whether it takes place or not
Se aburre de que Gene Kelly baile siempre con Cyd Charisse (G. Cabrera Infante, Cuba, dialogue)	He gets bored with the fact that Gene Kelly always dances with Cyd Charisse
Les sorprendió que no lo supiera/supiese/ Se sorprendieron de que no lo supiera/ supiese	It surprised them/They were surprised that she didn't know
El catedrático de portugués se sorprendió mucho de que yo me sorprendiera cuando me contó que este año sólo tenía un estudiante (M. Vargas Llosa, Peru)	The professor of Portuguese was very surprised that I was surprised when he told me that he only had one student this year

26.5 Se de matización: general

Se de matización (lit. '*se* that adds a shade of meaning'[6]) refers to the use of the pronominal form to add a nuance to the meaning of the original verb, these nuances often being unpredictable in meaning. Compare *bajó del árbol* and *se bajó del árbol* 'he came down from the tree' (the difference between the two is barely

---

[6] Sections 26.5–26.7 are much indebted to Moreira and Butt (1996), from which the term *se de matización* is also taken. The term is, however, inaccurate in the sense that such verbs can appear in any person and number, e.g. *me voy, te duermes, nos trajimos, os creéis*, etc.

translatable), or *salió del cine* 'he left the cinema' and *se salió del cine* 'he walked out of the cinema'. Several points must be made about this construction:

(a) It is confined to a finite and apparently closed series of common transitive and intransitive verbs. The fact, for example, that *volver* 'to return' has a pronominal counterpart *volverse* 'to return before time'/'to turn back'[7] does not mean that *regresar* 'to return' also has a pronominal counterpart *regresarse* (the latter form is, however, much used in Latin America); nor does *descender* 'to descend' have a form **descenderse*, despite the fact that *bajar* has the form *bajarse*. For this reason these verbs must be learnt separately. The most common verbs that take *se de matización* are:

abrir	*correr*	*entrar*	*llevar*	*pasear*	*sonreír*
acabar	*crecer*	*envejecer*	*marchar*	*pensar*	*subir*
aguantar	*creer*	*escapar*	*mejorar*	*probar*	*suponer*
aparecer	*decidir*	*esperar*	*merecer*	*quedar*	*temer*
bajar	*dejar*	*estar*	*montar*	*regresar*	*traer*
caer	*desayunar*	*figurar*	*morir*	*reír*	*venir*
callar	*despertar*	*guardar*	*olvidar*	*resbalar*	*ver*
cambiar	*devolver*	*imaginar*	*oscurecer*	*resistir*	*volar*
cerrar	*empeorar*	*ir*	*parar*	*salir*	*volver*
coger	*encontrar*	*leer*	*parecer*	*saltar*	
conocer	*enfermar*	*llegar*	*pasar*	*sentir*	

Only a selection of the commonest of these verbs is discussed in detail below. The rest should be sought in a good dictionary.

(b) Some of the pronominalized forms described below are more characteristic of spoken language and may be replaced by the simple form in formal styles. Thus only *morir* 'to die' is used in formal written Spanish, whereas both *morir* and *morirse* are heard in colloquial speech, with a subtle difference of meaning.

(c) It is not guaranteed that all of the examples given below are used in Latin America, although the immense majority certainly are. There are some pronominal verbs of this type of verbs, e.g. *regresarse/devolverse* 'to return', *robarse* 'to steal', that are current in all or parts of Latin America but are not used in Spain (see 26.8 for examples).

(d) The nuance added by pronominalization is sometimes very subtle. The ability to distinguish correctly between pairs like *bajar/bajarse* 'to descend'/'to get down/out', *llegar/llegarse* 'to arrive'/'to approach' or *traer/traerse* 'to bring' is the mark of the true master of idiomatic Spanish.

(e) The existence of a pronominal form does not eliminate the possibility that the verb can be pronominalized for one of the reasons discussed elsewhere in this chapter. Out of context a form like *se encontraban* can therefore mean 'they found by chance', 'they found themselves', 'they found one another' or 'they were found'; context almost always clarifies the meaning. Pronominalized verbs of motion tend to share common features of meaning, so they are discussed separately at 26.6. Other examples of *se de matización* are discussed at 26.7.

---

[7] Not to be confused with *volverse* 'to become' or *volverse* 'to turn round'.

26.6 Verbs of motion and *se de matización*

Many common verbs of motion acquire an extra nuance in the pronominal form. The pronominal form may:

(a) draw attention to the point of departure as opposed to the destination; compare *ir* 'to go somewhere', *irse* 'to go *away from* somewhere'; or
(b) suggest that an action is untimely, accidental or unplanned, e.g. *caer* 'to fall', *caerse* 'to fall over/down'; *salir* 'to leave'/'to come out', *salirse* 'to leave unexpectedly'/'to leak' (liquids, gases). Sometimes both nuances are combined.

The commonest examples are listed hereafter in alphabetical order.

26.6.1 *Bajar/Bajarse* 'to go down'; *Subir/Subirse* 'to go up'

The difference between the two verbs is sometimes difficult to explain. As far as 'getting on/into' and 'getting off/out of' some kind of vehicle is concerned, it seems that the forms are usually interchangeable, although informal language strongly prefers the pronominal form, especially if unplanned exit/entry is involved:

Iba a bajar(me) en la Plaza de la Revolución, pero me voy a bajar aquí	I was getting out at Revolution Square, but I'm going to get out here
Vino hacia ellos sonriente tan pronto se bajaron del coche (M. Delibes, Spain)	He came towards them, smiling, as soon as they got out of the car

In both these examples the non-pronominal form could have also been used, but it is less often heard on both continents. Ordinary going up and down (e.g. stairs, lifts) requires the non-pronominal form unless reference is made to a whole set of stairs. (See 26.9. for a more detailed discussion of the latter construction):

Espérame abajo/arriba que bajo/subo enseguida	Wait for me downstairs/upstairs: I'll be down/up in a minute
Subía siempre las escaleras lentamente	He always used to go upstairs slowly
(Se) subió las escaleras de un tirón (the whole flight of stairs; see 26.9)	She rushed upstairs without stopping

Other meanings require the pronominal form:

Se subieron a la tapia de un salto	They **jumped** on top of the garden wall
—Bájate de ahí, papacito —le decía—. Es peligrosísimo. No te vayas a caer y te lastimes (A. Mastretta, Mexico, dialogue)	'Get down from there, papa', she was telling him. 'It's dangerous. Don't fall and hurt yourself.'
Se subía por las paredes	She was **climbing** the walls (with rage, not literally)

Notes

(i) *Bajar(se)/subir(se)* can also be used colloquially as transitive verbs meaning 'to take up', and 'to take down': *bája(te) estos tiestos al jardín* 'take these flowerpots down to the garden'.
(ii) The non-pronominal form is used for the meanings 'to increase', 'to diminish': *los precios suben/bajan* 'prices go up/down'.

26.6.2 *Caer/Caerse*

The non-pronominal form can stress either point of departure or arrival: *el meteoro cayó del cielo* 'the meteor fell from the sky', *el tigre cayó sobre su presa* 'the tiger fell on its prey', *el avión cayó aquí* 'the plane fell here'. It is also used when the point of departure is taken for granted: *caía una lluvia fuerte* 'heavy rain was falling'. The non-pronominal form is also reserved for the following figurative meanings:

Cayó en la guerra	He fell (was killed) in the war
El Gobierno ha caído	The government has fallen / has been toppled
Esa calle cae lejos de aquí	That street lies far from here
caer en la tentación	to fall into temptation
Ya caigo	I get it / I understand

Caerse suggests accidental falling ('falling over', 'falling down'):

(Se) cayó de la mesa	It fell off the table (accidentally)
Me caí por unas escaleras	I fell down a flight of stairs
¡Que no se te caiga el paquete!	Don't drop the parcel!
No tiene donde caerse muerto (figurative)	He hasn't got a cent (lit. 'he has nowhere to drop dead on')
Se le cayó el alma a los pies (figurative)	He suddenly became intensely depressed (lit. 'his soul dropped to his feet')

26.6.3 *Entrar/Entrarse*

Entrar 'to enter' is by far the more common form. The status of *entrarse* is problematic: most Peninsular speakers reject it altogether, although it is sometimes heard in popular speech and is quite common in Latin America to emphasize point of departure:

Salió al balcón pero volvió a entrar(se) porque hacía frío (many Peninsular speakers reject *entrarse* as substandard)	She went out on to the balcony but came in again because it was cold

26.6.4 *Escapar/Escaparse*

The pronominal form is the more usual. The non-pronominal form is used only for figurative meanings: *escapar con vida* 'to escape with one's life', *escapar del peligro* 'to escape danger', *escapar a la justicia* 'to escape justice', *escapar a la calle* 'to take to the street'. But *los prisioneros se escaparon* 'the prisoners escaped'.

26.6.5 *Ir/Irse*

The difference between the two generally coincides with the difference between 'to go' and 'to go away', French *aller/s'en aller*, Italian *andare/andarsene*:

Vamos a casa de Pepe (destination stressed)	We're going to Pepe's house
Me voy a casa de Pepe (departure stressed)	I'm off to Pepe's house
Vete (point of departure stressed)	Go away
Este avión va a Caracas (destination stressed)	This plane's going to Caracas
¡Voy! (destination stressed)	I'm coming! / I'll be right there!

26.6.6 *Llegar/Llegarse*

Llegar means 'to arrive' and is by far the more common form. *Llegarse* means 'to approach' or 'to pop over to':

Llegamos a Madrid	We arrived in Madrid

Llégate/Acércate a la tienda de enfrente	Go over to the shop/(US 'store') opposite
Se llegó a la reina	He approached the queen

26.6.7 *Marchar/Marcharse*

Marchar means 'to march' and *marcharse* means 'to leave a place', but in León and in much of western Spain *marchar* may have the same meaning as *marcharse*:

¡Mira cómo marchan los soldados!	Look at the soldiers marching!
Me marcho/Me voy	I'm leaving
El tren ya se marchó/ya salió	The train's already left

26.6.8 *Pasar/Pasarse*

As a verb of motion, both forms mean 'to pass'/'to pass by'/'to pass over'. (For *pasar* as a transitive verb meaning 'to pass time', see 26.7.30.) *Pasar* suggests normal motion (it is also used during card games: *paso* 'I pass'):

Cuando pasó la frontera	When he crossed the frontier
La carretera pasa por el pueblo	The road goes through the village

Pasarse suggests unwanted passage:

Se pasó de la raya	He went beyond the mark/overdid it
No te pases	Don't go too far/Don't overdo it

Pasárselo bien/mal is 'to have a good/bad time, e.g. *pásatelo bien* 'have a good time'. Compare also the non-pronominal form in *no les pasa ni una* '(s)he doesn't let them get away with anything', *pasa de todo* '(s)he doesn't care about anything'.

26.6.9 *Salir/Salirse*

Salir means 'to go out'/'to leave' without further implications. *Salirse* implies untimely or unexpected departure or, applied to inanimates, accidental leakages or escapes:

Salimos del cine cuando terminó la película (intentional)	We left the cinema when the film ended
Nos salimos del cine porque la película era muy violenta (unexpected)	We left the cinema (before the end) because the film was very violent
Salió del convento a las cinco (intended)	She left the convent at 5 o'clock
Se salió del convento a los treinta años (unexpected)	She left the convent at the age of thirty
El agua sale por aquí (intended)	The water comes out here (where it should)
El grifo se sale (accidental)	The tap's leaking
El tren se salió de la vía (accidental)	The train ran off the tracks

26.6.10 *Saltar/Saltarse*

Saltar is the normal word for 'to jump'. It can also mean 'jump over', but *saltarse* is replacing it in informal language in this last meaning. *Saltarse* is used for illegal or excessive jumps, e.g. jumping traffic lights or starting-signals:

Saltaban de alegría	They were jumping for joy
Se saltaban los semáforos	They were jumping the traffic lights
Te saltaste la pistola de salida	You jumped the starting pistol
(Se) saltó la hoguera	He jumped over the bonfire

26.6.11 *Subir/Subirse* (see *bajar/bajarse*)

26.6.12 *Venir/Venirse*

Venirse suggests 'to come away from somewhere' either permanently or for a long time. Applied to inanimates it implies accidental or unexpected coming. *Venir* simply means 'to come to a place':

Ha venido de París a pasar unos días (destination stressed)	She's come from Paris to spend a few days
Se ha venido de París porque no aguanta la contaminación (point of departure stressed)	He's come here from Paris because he can't stand the pollution
Dijiste sus nombres cuando te viniste (J. Cortázar, Argentina, dialogue; probably emphasizes permanent departure from somewhere else)	You mentioned their names when you came here
¿Por qué no vienes conmigo? (destination stressed)	Why don't you come with me?
¿Por qué no te vienes conmigo? (point of departure stressed)	Why don't you (leave him/her/this place and) come with me?[8]
¿(Te) vienes o no?	Are you coming or aren't you?
El edificio se vino abajo (accidental)	The building collapsed
Mira la tormenta que se nos viene encima (accidental)	Look at the storm that's going to hit us (lit. 'that's coming down on us')

Note

In Latin America *venirse* has the same taboo sexual meaning as 'to come'.

26.6.13 *Volver/Volverse;* Latin-America *Regresar/Regresarse,* also *Devolverse*

Volver means 'to return'. It is also used for intangible things, e.g. happiness, summer, fine weather. *Volver a* + infinitive is the most usual way of saying 'to do something again'. It is discussed at 32.6a.

Nunca volveré a aquella casa	I'll never return to that house
Has vuelto muy moreno	You've come back very suntanned
No vuelvas tarde	Don't come back late
Fue a París, se entrevistó con el presidente, y volvió a Londres	He went to Paris, talked to the president and returned to London
Vuelve la primavera	Spring returns

Volverse may mean 'to turn round', 'to turn back halfway', 'to return before time' (unplanned return):

Se volvió hacia ella	He turned to (to face) her
Me volví antes de llegar	I turned back before arriving
Nos hemos vuelto porque no paraba de llover	We've come back (ahead of time) because it didn't stop raining

Notes

(i) In Latin America, *regresar/regresarse* is used in the same way: *Helen se había regresado a Puebla* (A. Mastretta, Mexico, dialogue; Spain *se había vuelto* or *había regresado*). Some countries, e.g.

---

[8] One could also say *¿por qué no te vienes conmigo a pasar unos días?* 'why don't you come and spend a few days with me?', with the implication 'rather than stay here'. Also *¿(te) vienes al cine con nosotros?* 'are you coming to the cinema with us?'

Colombia, also use *devolverse* for 'to return': *. . . pero se había devuelto del Camino Real . . .* (G. García Márquez, Colombia) ' *. . . but he'd turned back on the highway . . .*'. *Devolver* (transitive) means 'to give back' or 'to vomit' in Peninsular Spanish and in many Latin-American countries.

(ii) *Volverse* has other meanings, e.g. 'to become' (see 27.3.2) or 'to turn round' as in *se volvió hacia ella* 'he turned towards her'. 'To turn round', i.e. 'make a U-turn' in a vehicle is *dar la vuelta*.

26.7 *Se de matización* with miscellaneous verbs

Pronominalization adds nuances to a number of other verbs, of which the following are frequently encountered.

26.7.1 *Abrir/Abrirse and Cerrar/Cerrarse*

Abrir 'to open' is the only form used when the verb is transitive, as in *abrimos la puerta* 'we opened the door'. *Abrirse* is used when the verb is intransitive: *la puerta se abrió* 'the door opened'. However, *abrir* is also used intransitively of the scheduled opening of establishments: *¿cuándo abre el restaurante?* 'when is the restaurant opening?', *el museo abre a las diez* 'the museum opens at ten'.

    Cerrar 'to close' behaves in the same way: *la puerta se cerró* 'the door closed' (on its own) but *el único cine del pueblo ha cerrado* 'the only cinema in the village/town has closed'.

26.7.2 *Acabar/Acabarse*

Acabar can be used transitively and intransitively, like its English translation 'to finish': *han acabado el proyecto* 'they've finished the project', *el proyecto ha acabado* 'the project's finished'. *Acabarse* is common in informal styles for the intransitive meaning. It is also much used to mean 'to run out': *se ha acabado la cerveza* 'the beer's run out', *¡bueno, esto se ha acabado!* 'well this is the last straw!'/'this is the end!'

26.7.3 *Aguantar/Aguantarse*

The basic meaning of *aguantar* is 'to tolerate'/'to bear': *este puente aguanta pesos muy fuertes* 'this bridge supports very heavy weights', *no puedo aguantarlos* 'I can't stand them'. *Aguantarse* is intransitive and means 'to stand upright' – *la abuela ya no se aguanta sola* 'grandmother can't stand on her own any more' – or 'to put up with something': *si te duele esa muela tendrás que aguantarte hasta el lunes* 'if that tooth aches, you'll have to put up with it until Monday'; *bueno, a aguantarse* 'oh well, we'll just have to put up with it'.

26.7.4 *Aparecer/Aparecerse*

Aparecer means 'to appear' without further nuances. *Aparecerse* is used of apparitions:

La revista aparece todos los días	The journal appears every day
Se le apareció la Virgen	The Virgin appeared before him

    However, in Latin America *aparecerse* is often used of people turning up unexpectedly: *se apareció en casa un martes por la mañana* '(s)he turned up at home suddenly one Tuesday morning' (non-pronominal form in Spain).

26.7.5 Callar/Callarse

Callar/Callarse are in theory interchangeable except when the subject is inanimate, in which case the pronominal form is less usual: *la música calló de repente* 'the music suddenly stopped'. When the subject is animate either form can be used, the pronominal form being more colloquial and informal: *el niño (se) calló en cuanto le dieron el biberón* 'the little boy stopped crying as soon as he was given a bottle'. There is a special nuance in the imperative: *¡calla!* can often mean 'quiet!' while *¡cállate!* can mean a curt 'shut up'. Nevertheless the preferred reply in both cases would be with the pronominal form: *ya me callo/no quiero callarme* 'I'm being quiet' / 'I don't want to be quiet/to shut up'.

26.7.6 Cambiar/Cambiarse

Cambiar means 'to change' in the sense of 'to alter': *la situación ha cambiado* 'the situation has changed', *Ángela ha cambiado desde que va a la universidad* 'Angela has changed since she's been going to university'. The most usual meaning of *cambiarse* is 'to get changed': *tengo la ropa mojada: me voy a cambiar* 'my clothes are wet – I'm going to get changed'.

26.7.7 Coger/Cogerse

Coger is used for physical catching or grasping hold of: *coger un tren/autobús/una pelota/un ladrón/una flor* 'to catch a train/bus/ball/thief', 'to pick a flower', etc. The pronominal form is rare (at least in standard Peninsular language), but it is found in colloquial phrases involving drunkenness: contrast *coger un catarro* 'to catch a cold' and *cogerse una borrachera* 'to get drunk'. *Coger* is universally used in Latin America as a taboo word for the sex act, to the extent that some regions prefer *agarrar* for 'to catch' (in Spain 'to clutch', 'to seize, but also used for emphasis, as in *he agarrado una gripe de cuidado* 'I've got a terrible bout of flu').

26.7.8 Conocer/Conocerse

Conocer covers all meanings of the French *connaître* 'to know a person/place' (cf. *saber* 'to know a fact/the truth/a language', etc.). It can also mean 'to meet for the first time': *la conocí en Madrid* 'I met her in Madrid'. The pronominal form implies total knowledge and may add an ironic tone: *se conoce todo Madrid* 'he knows the whole of Madrid' (but not just **se conoce Madrid*), *me la conozco . . .* 'I know her (and her little tricks . . .)'.

26.7.9 Correr/Correrse

Correr is overwhelmingly the more frequent form and is used for meanings including 'to run', 'to flow', 'to hurry' (in the latter case it can be used of a driver of a vehicle: *no corras tanto* 'don't go so fast'). The only use of the pronominal form in respectable language is to mean 'to shift over', 'to move over' (intransitive): *córrete hacia acá para que el señor pueda sentarse* 'move over this way so the gentleman can sit down'. Foreigners should be careful since it is used in popular language in Spain in the taboo sexual meaning of 'to come' (Latin America *venirse*).

26.7.10 *Crecer/Crecerse*

Crecer means to grow in size. *Crecerse* means to grow in worth or value:

La hierba crece mucho con tanta lluvia	The grass grows quickly with so much rain
¡Ya crezcan idiotas! (graffiti on a PRI propaganda poster in Mexico City. In Spain *crecer* usually implies only physical growth)	Grow up, you idiots!
Hay personas que se crecen con el peligro	There are people who grow stronger/more confident when they are in danger

In parts of Latin America *crecerse* means 'to be brought up': *yo me crecí* (Spain *me crié*) *en Bolivia*, 'I was raised in Bolivia'.

26.7.11 *Creer/Creerse*

The non-pronominal form translates most meanings of 'to believe'/'to think that . . .'. *Creer en* 'to believe in' appears only in the non-pronominal form. The pronominal form usually implies unfounded belief:

Creo que han llegado	I think they've arrived
Creo en ella	I believe in her
Ése/Ese se cree que habla francés	He thinks he speaks French
Se cree todo lo que le dicen	She believes everything they tell her
Yo (me) creía que él había llegado	I thought he had arrived

Creerse can also emphasize incredulity: *no me creo todavía que se haya muerto* 'I still can't believe that (s)he's dead'.

Notes

(i) idiom: *se lo tiene creído* 'he has a high opinion of himself', (British) 'he fancies himself'.
(ii) *Pensar/pensarse* 'to think' is used colloquially in the same way, although good style observes the difference between *creer* 'to believe'/'to have an opinion' and *pensar* 'to think', i.e. indulge in thinking activity, as in *es un escritor que piensa mucho* 'he's a writer who thinks a lot'. *Pensarse algo* means 'to think something through carefully'.

26.7.12 *Decidir/Decidirse*

Decidir can be used transitively in the sense of 'to make up someone's mind'/'to decide the outcome': *lo que me decidió fue el estado del presupuesto* 'what made up my mind was the state of the budget', *lo que decidió el resultado del partido . . .* 'what decided the outcome of the game . . .'. Used with an animate subject, the verb means 'to decide': *ha decidido dejar el trabajo* 'he's decided to leave work'. The pronominal form implies a decision taken after hesitation and effort, compare 'to make up one's mind': *a ver si te decides de una vez* 'make up your mind, for Heaven's sake!', *¿te has decidido a hacerlo?* 'have you made up your mind to do it?'

26.7.13 *Dejar/Dejarse*

Dejar translates 'to let' and 'to leave' (in the sense of 'abandon'). *Dejarse* emphasizes accidental leaving behind, but it can also have the reflexive meaning 'to let oneself go' (i.e. physically, morally):

Deja tu maleta aquí	Leave your suitcase here
cuando dejó el ejército . . .	when (s)he left the army . . .
Me he dejado el dinero en casa	I've left my money at home

Note

This use of *dejarse* is apparently confined to Spain. Latin-Americans informants said *dejé la plata . . .* 'I left my money . . .',[9] which in Spain would imply deliberate leaving.

26.7.14 Desayunar/Desayunarse

Desayunar is nowadays overwhelmingly the more common form in Spain and may be intransitive or transitive: *desayuno fruta y cereales* 'I have fruit and cereals for breakfast', *¿a qué hora desayunaste?* 'what time did you have breakfast?' The older form *desayunarse con* does, however, occur in Spain: *me desayuno con fruta* 'I have fruit for breakfast', and it is widespread in Latin America: *me desayuno temprano* 'I have breakfast early'.

26.7.15 Despertar/Despertarse

Despertar is used transitively: *me despertó la tormenta* 'the storm woke me up'. When the subject is human, either form can be used intransitively, the non-pronominal form being rather more formal: *(me) desperté a las cinco* 'I woke up at five o'clock'. The imperatives *despierta* and *despiértate* are used interchangeably.

26.7.16 Encontrar/Encontrarse

The transitive form means 'to find', the pronominal form 'to find something by chance' (but the reflexive meaning of *encontrarse*, 'to be found'/'to be located', is also very common):

Encontré el libro que buscaba	I found the book I was searching for
Me encontré una moneda de oro	I found a gold coin
Me encontré a Pepe	I ran into Pepe (by chance)
Me encontré con que no me quedaba nada de sal	I found that I didn't have any salt left
Todo el dinero es igual. Yo lo agarro de donde me lo encuentro (A. Mastretta, Mexico, dialogue; Spain *yo lo cojo/agarro donde lo encuentro*)	All money's the same. I grab it where I find it

26.7.17 Enfermar/Enfermarse

Enfermar is used intransitively in Spain, where one says *enfermó de bronquitis* '(s)he fell ill with bronchitis', the pronominal form being substandard or popular. In Latin America the pronominal form is universally used: *se enfermó de bronquitis*.

26.7.18 Esperar/Esperarse

Esperar translates 'to wait for'. Both *esperar* and *esperarse* are used for 'to expect' and 'to wait':

¿(A) qué estás esperando?	What are you waiting for?
Te estamos esperando	We're waiting for you
Eso no (me) lo esperaba yo	I wasn't expecting this
Hay que esperar(se) a que te atiendan	One has to wait to be served

Espera/espere and *espérate/espérese* seem to be interchangeable in the imperative.

---

[9] In Spain *la plata* = 'silver' and *el dinero* = 'money'.

26.7.19 *Estar/Estarse*

Estar means 'to be', and its use is discussed in Chapter 29. The pronominal form *estarse* is used:

(a) To form the imperative of *estar* (see 17.2.6 for details):

¡Estate quieto!	Sit still!
¡Estese tranquilo!	Stay calm!/Don't worry!

(b) To express obligatory or deliberate being in a place. The translation is usually 'to stay':

Se tuvo que estar en casa porque vinieron sus tíos	He had to stay at home because his aunt and uncle came
Me estuve estudiando toda la noche (from María Moliner)	I stayed up all night studying
He tenido que estar(me) a la cola todo el día	I had to queue all day/(US) I had to stand in line all day
. . . y aquí que se esté para lo que se ofrezca (A. Mastretta, Mexico, dialogue)	. . . and let him remain here in case anything turns up

Quedarse would have been possible in all these examples.

26.7.20 *Ganar/Ganarse*

Ganar is used in the phrase *ganar mucho/poco dinero* 'to earn a lot'/'very little money', *¿cuánto ganas?* 'how much do you earn?'. It also means 'to win'. *Ganarse* can sometimes add more emphasis to the amount earned. It is also used for metaphorical meanings or when the way of earning one's living is mentioned:

(Se) gana un millón de pesetas todos los meses	She earns a million pesetas every month
Se gana la vida bailando	He earns his living by dancing
Se gana el cariño de todos	She gains/wins everybody's affection
Siempre gano	I always win
Nos ganó cien mil pesos al póker	He won 100,000 pesos off us at poker
Me ganas en fuerza pero no en inteligencia	You are stronger than me but not more intelligent

26.7.21 *Imaginar/Imaginarse*

Imaginar is a transitive verb meaning 'to conceive of'/'to invent a new idea'. *Imaginarse* means 'imagine' in the sense of 'suppose', 'guess' or 'picture':

Imaginó un nuevo modo de hacerlo	He conceived/invented a new way of doing it
Te puedes imaginar lo que yo estaba pensando	You can imagine what I was thinking
Me los imagino divirtiéndose	I imagine them amusing themselves

Figurarse means the same as *imaginarse*: *me figuro que ya se ha marchado* 'I guess he must have gone already'. The non-pronominal form means 'to figure as an item': *no figura en el índice* 'it doesn't appear in the index'.

26.7.22 *Llevar/Llevarse*

Llevar means 'to wear', 'to take' or 'to carry'. *Llevarse* means 'to take away':

Voy a llevar el traje al tinte	I'm going to take my suit to the cleaner's

No se te olvide llevarte los libros Don't forget to take the books with you
Llevaba un abrigo negro She was wearing a black coat
Trae que te lleve ese paquete (the *trae* is Here, let me carry that parcel for you
 a colloquial Peninsular interjection)

26.7.23 Mejorar/Mejorarse

Mejorar as a transitive verb means 'to make better'; as an intransitive verb it means 'to improve'. *Mejorarse* means 'to get better' from an illness and is not used everywhere in Spain:

La situación ha mejorado The situation has improved
(Se) ha mejorado mucho/Está mucho He's a lot better (in health)
 mejor (but only *ha mejorado mucho en*
 español 'he's improved a lot in Spanish')

26.7.24 Morir/Morirse

Both translate 'to die', but the pronominal form denotes natural death, especially (but not exclusively) a gradual death: *su madre se murió de cáncer* 'his mother died of cancer'. *Morir* is generally used for accidental or deliberate death: *(se) murió de un ataque al corazón* 'she died from a heart attack', *murió en un accidente de avión* 'he died in a plane accident' (not *se murió . . .*). In formal written Spanish *morir* is used for all kinds of death. In colloquial Spanish, *morirse* is especially used for the death of relatives and friends:

Ha muerto el primer ministro The prime minister has died
La propia Tránsito Arias se murió Tránsito Arias herself died convinced that . . .
 convencida de que . . . (G. García
 Márquez, Colombia)
Yo lloré al contarle que casi se nos había I cried when I told him how he had nearly
 muerto esa noche (M. Puig, Argentina, died that night
 dialogue)

26.7.25 Ocurrir/Ocurrirse

Ocurrir means 'to happen'. *Occurírsele a alguien algo* means 'to occur to one', 'to have a sudden idea':

Esto lleva ocurriendo desde hace algún This has been happening for some time
 tiempo
Se me ha ocurrido una idea genial I've had a brilliant idea

26.7.26 Olvidar/Olvidarse(de)/Olvidársele algo a uno

The verb means 'to forget'. There are four forms in use: *olvidar algo*, *olvidarse algo*, *olvidarse de algo* and *olvidársele algo a alguien*, as in *se me olvidó algo* 'I forgot something'. When deliberate forgetting is implied, the first form is rather formal and is usually replaced in colloquial styles by *olvidarse de*: *no puedo olvidarla/no puedo olvidarme de ella* 'I can't forget her'. For absent-minded forgetting *olvidar* and *olvidársele* can be used, the former again being rather formal: *he olvidado mi agenda/se me olvidó la agenda* 'I've forgotten my diary'. In the latter construction the thing forgotten is the subject of the verb: *se me olvid**aron** las flores* 'I forgot the flowers' (lit. 'the flowers forgot themselves "on" me').

The form *olvidarse* (without the *de*) is colloquial and is censured by some grammarians, including Manuel Seco. Foreigners should probably say *me he olvidado de ella* or *la he olvidado* and not *?me la he olvidado*. It can, however, be used collo-quially for accidental forgetting of objects: *me he olvidado el libro/se me olvidó el libro* 'I've forgotten the book' (but, since absent-minded forgetting is implied, not *me he olvidado **del** libro*).

26.7.27 Oscurecer/Oscurecerse

The pronominal form means 'to get darker' (e.g. colo(u)rs): *este amarillo se ha oscurecido* 'this yellow has got darker', *el cielo se oscureció* 'the sky got darker'. The non-pronominal form may be transitive – 'to make darker' – or it may have the special meaning of 'to grow dark' (i.e. at dusk): *está oscureciendo* 'night is falling'.

26.7.28 Parar/Pararse

Both verbs translate 'to stop', but they are not usually interchangeable. The non-pronominal form indicates scheduled or planned halts, e.g. buses at bus-stops, trains in stations: *el tren expreso para en Montera* 'the express train stops at Montera'. The pronominal form suggests unexpected stops, i.e. at traffic lights or because of breakdown: *el motor se ha parado* 'the motor's stopped', *me tuve que parar en un semáforo* 'I had to stop at the lights'. When the subject is human, the pronominal form often suggests that the subject is personally moving, i.e. walking or running, and the non-pronominal form that (s)he is driving a car, *me paré delante de la tienda* 'I paused in front of the shop', *paré delante de la tienda* 'I stopped (the car) in front of/outside the shop'. *Parar* can also be used as a transitive verb: *¡para esa máquina!* 'stop that machine!'

26.7.29 Parecer/Parecerse

Parecer means 'to seem'; *parecerse a* means 'to look like':

Parece cansada	She seems/looks tired
Se parecen a su madre	They look like their mother

26.7.30 Pasar/Pasarse

For the use of these two as verbs of motion, see 26.6.8.
  Pasar means 'to spend time somewhere' or 'to pass' applied to time:

Pasó la noche en casa de su hermano	He spent the night in his brother's house
Pasaron tres horas	Three hours passed

  Pasarse means 'to spend time doing something':

Se pasa horas mirando por la ventana	He spends hours gazing out of the window
Podíamos pasarnos la vida sin verlos	We could spend our lives without seeing
(A. Mastretta, Mexico, dialogue)	them

26.7.31 Probar/Probarse

Probar means 'to prove', 'to test', 'to sample': *prueba este vino* 'try this wine', *eso no prueba nada* 'that proves nothing'. The pronominal form is used for the special meaning 'to try on': *se pasa horas en las tiendas probándose todo* '(s)he spends hours in the shops trying on everything'.

26.7.32 Quedar and Quedarse

Quedar basically means 'to remain'. With participles, adjectives and a few adverbs, therefore, it tends to indicate a more or less permanent outcome of some action:

Queda por ver si lo hará	It remains to be seen whether she'll do it
Queda bien/mejor/mal/feo	It looks nice/better/bad/ugly
La casa os ha quedado bien (more or less permanent result)	You've decorated the house very nicely
Tuvo un accidente y quedó cojo	He had an accident and became lame as a result

Quedar en means 'to agree to do something'. Compare also *he quedado con él a las siete* 'I've agreed to see him at seven'.

The basic meaning of *quedarse* is 'to stay', but with adjectives and participles it often means 'to become', and usually focuses on the change itself rather than on the state arising from it: compare *la casa se quedó vacía* 'the house emptied' and *la casa quedó vacía*, which suggests 'the house remained empty':

Me quedaré unos días contigo	I'll spend a few days with you
. . . y yo me quedé de pie ante él (C. Martín Gaite, Spain)	. . . and I remained (i.e. stayed) standing in front of him
Se quedó embarazada[10]	She became pregnant

Quedarse (con) algo 'to keep something' (e.g. change, a book; the preposition is often dropped in modern speech: *quédatelo* 'keep it'). For other meanings of *quedar(se)* see 27.3.6 (= 'to become') and 28.2.6a.

26.7.33 Reír/Reírse

Both mean 'to laugh'. *Reírse* is the more common form; *reír* is rather literary. However, *reírse* implies spontaneous laughter (the more usual kind), so it cannot be used when the cause of merriment comes from outside, as in *el gas me hizo reír* 'the gas made me laugh', *ya los haré reír* 'I'll make them laugh'. 'To laugh at' is *reírse de*:

Se rió de su propia risa (G. García Márquez, Colombia)	She laughed at her own laughter
Todos se reían de él	They all made fun of him

26.7.34 Temer/Temerse

Temer usually means 'to be afraid' in the literal sense of 'to fear', especially with a direct object; *temer/temerse* are interchangeable only in the sense of 'to suspect', 'to be worried that':

Teme a su padre	He's afraid of his father
(Me) temo que va a llegar tarde	I'm afraid she's going to be late

See 16.9 for further discussion of *temer/temerse*.

26.7.35 Traer/Traerse

Both translate 'to bring', but *traerse* is used to emphasize something bought, especially with someone else in mind, or to indicate that the thing brought belongs to at least one of the speakers. Some native speakers see a difference between

---

[10] Also *quedó embarazada* in northern Spain and perhaps elsewhere.

¿Qué quieres que te traiga?	What do you want me to bring you? (meaning something bought)
Si vas al supermercado no se te olvide traer la leche	If you go to the supermarket, don't forget to bring the milk

and

¿Qué quieres que me traiga?	What do you want me to bring back? (meaning something belonging to one or both of the speakers)
Cuando vayas al garaje tráete las herramientas	When you go to the garage bring back the tools with you

However, it seems to us that in modern Peninsular spoken usage *traerse* is used ever more commonly with the same meaning as *traer*, cf. *trae a tu marido/tráete a tu marido* 'bring your husband with you'.

Traer can also mean 'to wear': *traía un traje precioso* 'she was wearing a lovely suit/dress'. *Traerse* is used in phrases implying shady business: *yo creo que no es por ella, sino por su tío y los asuntos que os traéis entre manos* (J. Marsé, Spain, dialogue)'I think it has nothing to do with her but with her uncle and the things you're getting up to between you'.

26.8 *Se de matización in* Latin America

Most of the uses of *se de matización* heard in Spain are also normal in Latin America, but a few constructions accepted in Latin America sound quaint, rustic or plain wrong to Spaniards. The following selection (not exhaustive) includes verbs discussed elsewhere, and not all the forms are current in educated speech in all countries (the Peninsular equivalent is given in brackets):

crecerse to be brought up (*criarse*)	*prestarse* to borrow (*pedir prestado*): see note (ii)
desayunarse to have breakfast (*desayunar*)	*recordarse* remember (*recordar, acordarse*; see 18.2.3 note iv)
devolverse to return (particularly in Colombia; elsewhere *volver, regresar*)	*regresarse* to return (*volver, regresar*)
enfermarse to get ill/(US) 'sick' (*enfermar*)	*robarse* to steal (*robar*)
heredarse to inherit (*heredar*): see note (i)	*soñarse con* to dream of (*soñarse con*)
lloverse to leak (of roofs: rural Argentina)	*verse* to look (i.e. *parecer*)/to seem: see note (iii)
	vomitarse to vomit (*vomitar, devolver*)

Notes

(i) In some parts of Latin America, e.g. Mexico, the non-pronominal form can mean 'to leave to someone in a will' (Spain *dejar*): *estaba seguro de su alcurnia y pudo heredársela entera a su hija* (A. Mastretta, Mexico) 'he was sure of his pedigree and managed to bequeath it to his daughter'.
(ii) In Argentina the popular word for 'to borrow' is *emprestar*. This verb is heard in Spain and elsewhere, but is considered substandard.
(iii) In Latin America *verse* is used to refer to personal appearance: *te ves muy guapa* (A. Mastretta, Mexico, dialogue; Spain *qué guapa estás . . .*) 'you look very pretty', *y tú no te ves nada mal con esa tenida* (S. Vodanovic, Chile, dialogue: *no estás nada mal*) 'and you don't look at all bad in that outfit'.

26.9 Pronominal verbs of consumption, perception, knowledge

A curious optional function of the pronominal form of these transitive verbs is to emphasize the totality of an act of consuming, perceiving or knowing. Thus one says *como pizza* (no quantity specified), but, optionally (though usually), *me comí una pizza* 'I ate a (whole) pizza'.[11] The verb must have a direct object which must refer to a specific item or quantity:

Bebe mucho vino	He drinks a lot of wine
Se bebió un litro de vino	He drank a litre/(US 'liter') of wine
Pero aquella noche se sintió tan humillado que se tomó el brandy de un golpe (G. García Márquez, Colombia)	But that night he felt so humiliated that he drank his brandy down in one go
*Nos liquidamos las dos un par de Viña Tondonias y **nos** comimos un par de bolsas King size de patatas fritas* (C. Rico-Godoy, Spain)	The two of us (women) finished off a couple of bottles of Viña Tondonia and ate a couple of king-size bags of crisps/(US 'chips')
No deberías fumar	You shouldn't smoke
(Se) fuma tres paquetes al día	He smokes three packets a day
Ando mucho	I walk a lot
(Me) anduve cincuenta kilómetros	I walked 50 km
Aprendo francés	I'm learning French
(Me) aprendí todo el capítulo en una hora	I learnt the whole chapter in an hour
Sabe mucho	She knows a lot
¿(Te) sabes los verbos irregulares?	Do you know the irregular verbs?
Conozco Valencia	I know Valencia
(Me) conozco Valencia de cabo a rabo	I know Valencia inside out
Toma somníferos para dormir	He takes sleeping pills to sleep
Tóma(te) un somnífero	Take a sleeping pill
Trago mal	I can't swallow properly
(Se) lo ha tragado	He's swallowed it
Vi a tu cuñada	I saw your sister-in-law
(Se) vio todo el museo en diez minutos	He saw the whole museum in ten minutes
Lee muchas novelas	She reads a lot of novels
Vas a tener que releerte las obras completas [de Shakespeare] para que nos entendamos (C. Fuentes, Mexico, dialogue)	You're going to have to re-read the complete works of [Shakespeare] so that we can understand one another
Piénsalo	Think about it
Piénsatelo	Think it through (completely)
Tómate tus vacaciones y pásatelo bien (S. Puértolas, Spain, dialogue)	Go ahead and have your holiday and have a good time

26.10 Interpretation of pronominal verbs with inanimate subjects

A third-person pronominal verb may also be interpreted as a passive: *se construyó en España* means the same as *fue construido en España* 'it was built in Spain' (see 28.4 for more details).

---

[11] The construction is also heard in colloquial Italian – *mi sono mangiato una pizza* – and in Southern dialects of French – *?je me suis mangé une pizza* – but not in standard French. It is not used in Portuguese.

An occasional difficulty with sentences containing pronominal verbs, for example *se abrió la puerta*, is therefore that of deciding whether they are to be interpreted as intransitive, i.e. 'the door opened', or passive, 'the door **was** opened'. This problem only arises with certain verbs which have well-established pronominal intransitive forms, e.g. *abrir/abrirse* 'to open', *cerrar/cerrarse* 'to close', *encontrar/encontrarse* 'to find'/'to be located', *esconder/ esconderse* 'to hide' and others which will be found listed in good dictionaries. Most transitive verbs, e.g. *construir* 'to build', *derribar* 'to fell', *operar* 'to operate' do not have intransitive counterparts, so confusion is hardly possible.

The general rule for clarifying which sense is intended is as follows: if a pronominal verb has an established intransitive meaning, e.g. *abrirse* 'to open', *encenderse* 'to light up'/'to switch on', it will usually precede the subject if the passive meaning is intended, although this position does not preclude a pronominal interpretation. Thus *la puerta se abrió* usually means 'the door opened', but *se abrió la puerta* may mean either 'the door opened' or 'the door was opened'. Similarly:

Las luces se encienden a las nueve	The lights come on at nine
Se encienden las luces a las nueve	The lights are lit/come on at nine
Tres ventanas se rompieron durante la tormenta	Three windows broke in the storm
Se rompieron tres ventanas durante la manifestación	Three windows were broken in the demonstration

In the second of each of the foregoing examples the passive is the more likely meaning. If the verb has no intransitive possibility, then only a passive meaning is possible:

Se derribaron tres árboles/Tres árboles se derribaron	Three trees were felled
Los motivos se ignoran/Se ignoran los motivos	The motives are unknown

The foregoing points hardly constitute a hard and fast rule, and it must be remembered that complex word-order rules, discussed in Chapter 37, affect the choice between sentences like *los motivos se ignoran* and *se ignoran los motivos* 'the motives are unknown'.

26.11 Obligatory use of *uno* as impersonal pronoun with pronominal verbs

Uno/una must be used to give an impersonal meaning to a pronominal verb since two *ses* cannot occur with the same verb:

Se muere de frío en esta casa	He/She/It's/You're dying from cold in this house
*Se muere **uno** de frío en esta casa*	One dies from cold in this house/You die of the cold in this house
Cuando está así, se irrita fácilmente por cualquier cosa	When he's like that, he gets easily irritated over anything
*Cuando se está así, se irrita **uno** fácilmente por cualquier cosa*	When one is like that, one gets easily irritated over anything
Con estas cosas se cansa mucho	(S)he gets very tired with these things
*Con estas cosas se cansa **uno** mucho*	One gets very tired with these things

For more details about the pronoun *uno* see 28.7.1

27

Verbs of becoming

27.1 General

Spanish has no single word for the English 'become'. There are basically two ways in Spanish of expressing the idea: either use one of the many verbs derived from adjectives to indicate a change of state, e.g. *enfermó* (Lat. Am. *se enfermó*) *de bronquitis* 'he became ill/sick with bronchitis', *se entristeció* 'she became sad'; or use one of the verbs, e.g. *ponerse, volverse, hacerse, llegar a ser, convertirse, quedarse*, that translate 'to become'. One can therefore also say *se puso enfermo* 'he became ill/sick', *se puso/quedó triste* 'she became sad'. The tendency in everyday spoken Spanish is to prefer the latter type of construction.

Students of French are sometimes tempted to use the verb *devenir* to translate the English 'to become', but this word is virtually never used outside academic or philosophical texts. The infinitive means 'the process of becoming'.

27.2 Special verbs denoting change of state

These are numerous in Spanish. Many of them are pronominal verbs (i.e. 'reflexive' verbs: the term is explained in Chapter 26). The following is only a small selection:

aburrirse (de) to get bored	*enredarse* to get entangled
alegrarse (de) to cheer up/to be happy about something	*extrañarse (de)* to be puzzled at
	fastidiarse to get annoyed
asustarse (de) to get frightened	*indignarse* to get indignant
cansarse (de) to get tired	*irritarse (por)* to get irritated
deprimirse to get depressed	*marearse* to feel sick
divertirse to be amused	*molestarse (por)* to be bothered
endurecerse to grow hard/to harden	*vaciarse* to become empty
enfadarse (Lat. Am. *enojarse*) to get angry	

Notes

(i) Not all verbs denoting change of state are pronominal. 'To go mad' is *enloquecer* (also 'to send mad') and not **enloquecerse*, which is not used. Some other common cases of intransitive, **non-pronominal** verbs denoting 'to become …' 'to get …' are:

agonizar to be dying	*(cambiarse* to change clothes)
adelgazar to lose weight	*clarear* to grow bright
amanecer to dawn	*crecer* (for *crecerse* see 26.7.10) to grow
anochecer: anochece 'night is falling'	*disminuir* to diminish
aumentar to increase	*empeorar* (Lat. Am. *empeorarse*) to get worse
cambiar to change	*enfermar* (Lat. Am. *enfermarse*) to get ill

enflaquecer to lose weight
engordar to get fat
enmudecer to be silent/to lose one's voice
enrojecer to go red
ensordecer to go deaf
envejecer (also *envejecerse*) 'to age', but
  compare *rejuvenecerse* 'to grow young again'

mejorar§ to improve
nacer to be born
oscurecer to get dark (but *el cielo se*
  oscurece 'the sky grows dark')
palidecer to grow pale
resucitar to come back to life

§The pronominal verb *mejorarse* is reserved for the meaning 'to recover' (from an illness), e.g. *¡que te mejores!* 'get better soon!'

(ii) *Amanecer* can also be used with animate subjects and objects: *amanecí detestando mi color de pelo, mis ojeras, mi estatura* (A. Mastretta, Mexico) 'I woke up (lit. 'I dawned') hating the colour of my hair, the bags under my eyes, my height', *amaneció lloviendo* 'the day started with rain'. *Anochecer* and *amanecer* can also be used impersonally with object pronouns, as in **me** *anocheció/amaneció en medio de la carretera* 'night/morning found me on the road'.

27.3 Special verbs meaning 'to become'

Apart from the use of the pronominal forms discussed in the previous section, the following verbs (most, but not all, themselves pronominal verbs) are also used with various shades of meaning.

27.3.1 *Ponerse* 'to become', 'to get'

Ponerse is used to indicate change of mood, physical condition and appearance. The changes are usually short-lived, e.g. *ponerse enfermo/frenético/cabizbajo* 'to get ill/frantic/preoccupied', *ponerse contento* 'to become pleased', although there are exceptions. Thus there is a contrast between *se ha puesto muy pesado* 'he's become boring' (temporarily) and *se ha vuelto muy pesado* 'he's become a bore'. There is sometimes some overlap with *quedarse*, e.g. *quedarse delgado* 'to become thin', 'to lose weight'; see 27.3.6, and with *volverse* (see the examples). As mentioned earlier in the chapter, there are often equivalent pronominal verbs, i.e. *alegrarse* for *ponerse alegre*, *entristecerse* for *ponerse triste*; or non-pronominal ones, i.e. *engordar* for *ponerse gordo*, *enfermar* for *ponerse enfermo*, *envejecer* for *ponerse viejo* 'to get old'/'to age'.

Ponerse can have animate (animal and human) subjects and also certain kinds of inanimate subject, e.g. prices, foodstuffs, situations generally and, in some cases, weather conditions.

Cuando se enteró se puso muy contenta/triste/ de mal humor/enfadada (se entristeció, se enfadó could also be used)	When she heard about it she became very happy/sad/bad-tempered/ cross
Se puso/Se quedó ronco/Enronqueció de tanto hablar	He got hoarse from talking so much
Con tanto como comes te vas a poner gordo (for *delgado* 'thin' see *quedarse*, 27.3.6; *vas a engordar* could be used instead of *vas a ponerte gorda*, but *adelgazar* is reserved for the meaning 'to lose weight')	You are going to get fat from eating so much
En poco tiempo se ha puesto muy viejo/se ha aviejado mucho	He's got very old in a short time
Se puso muy elegante para ir a la boda	(S)he dressed up to go to the wedding

Se puso/Está mejor/Mejoró de su enfermedad (but not **la enfermedad se puso mejor)*	(S)he's better from his/her illness
En estos últimos años se me ha puesto el pelo rizado	My hair has got curly in recent years
La situación se ha puesto/vuelto insoportable	The situation has become unbearable
El día se ha puesto gris	It's turned grey/(US 'gray') (i.e. the weather)
El tiempo se está poniendo/volviendo frío	The weather is getting cold
El pescado se ha puesto malo	The fish has gone bad
Esto se está poniendo color de hormiga (M. Vargas Llosa, Peru, dialogue; the phrase is also common in Madrid)	Things are looking bad (lit 'things are turning ant-coloured')
Cuando hagas la salsa, no dejes que se ponga muy espesa/que espese mucho (also, less commonly, *se vuelva muy espesa*)	When you make the sauce don't let it get too thick

Notes

(i) *Ponerse* is often used with children to indicate that they are looking bigger or handsomer than ever: *¡pero qué guapo/grande se ha puesto este niño!* 'hasn't this child got handsome/big!'
(ii) *Ponerse a* + infinitive means to begin, i.e.: *se puso a llorar/correr/trabajar/escribir*, etc. '(s)he began to cry/started running/working/writing' etc., *nos pusimos a hablar de la muerte* (C. Rico-Godoy, Spain) 'we started talking about death'.

27.3.2 *Volverse*

This usually translates 'to become'/'to go', as in 'to go mad', and implies involuntary mental or psychological change when applied to animate subjects. It can also be used with some inanimate subjects, but not as often as *ponerse* since *volverse* tends to suggest changes in personal qualities. The change is felt to be more permanent than with *ponerse*:

¡Qué orgullosa te has vuelto!	You've become very proud
Con la edad nos vamos volviendo más de derechas	We get more right-wing with age
A raíz de su enfermedad se volvió viejo y desagradable	After his illness he became old and disagreeable
Últimamente todo se vuelven complicaciones, dificultades y disgustos (see 2.3.3 for agreement of *vuelven*)	Recently everything has become complications, difficulties and upsets
¿Dónde se volvió asesino ese chico? (M. Puig, Argentina, dialogue)	Where did that boy learn to be a murderer?
Esta zona se ha vuelto muy elegante	This district has become very smart
Todas sus alegrías se le habían vuelto tristezas	All his joys had turned to sadness
La vida se ha vuelto/puesto más complicada que antes	Life has become more complicated than it was before
. . . de modo que aquella casa se había vuelto peligrosa para ellos (G. García Márquez, Colombia)	. . . so that house had become dangerous for them
Durante un rato el cielo se volvió anaranjado (A. Mastretta, Mexico)	The sky turned orange for a while

See 26.6.13 for other meanings of *volver(se)*.

27.3.3 *Hacerse* 'to become'

This often implies voluntary or deliberate changes and it is usual for religious, professional or political changes. It can also occasionally be used of circumstances:

Se hizo católico/Se convirtió al catolicismo	He became a Catholic
Para hacerte arquitecto necesitas saber dibujo	You need to know how to draw to become an architect
Me hice amiga de todo el mundo	I became friendly with everybody
Emigró a México, se hizo inmensamente rico (A. Grandes, Spain)	He emigrated to Mexico and became immensely rich
La situación se está haciendo/poniendo/ volviendo difícil	The situation is getting difficult
. . . como volutas de humo que se hace progresivamente más espeso (C. Martín Gaite, Spain)	. . . like columns of smoke (that is) growing progressively thicker
Siempre llega un momento en la vida en el que los sueños se hacen realidad (*El Mundo*, Spain; or *se vuelven*)	A moment always comes in life when dreams become reality
Se me hace cuesta arriba tener que levantarme temprano	It's turning into a chore (lit 'uphill') for me to have to get up early

Notes

(i) There is no difference between sentences like *se está haciendo cada vez más vago* and *se está volviendo cada vez más vago* 'he's getting lazier and lazier'.

(ii) Idioms: *hacerse tarde* 'to get late', *hacerse de miel* 'to become so soft that people can take advantage of one'.

(iii) 'To become' with the meaning of 'to be appointed' is translated into Spanish as *nombrar* or *hacer*: *le/lo han nombrado/hecho ministro* 'he's become a minister'.

27.3.4 *Llegar a ser, pasar a ser*

Llegar a ser is used to indicate the result of a slow and sometimes difficult change, i.e. 'to manage to become'/'to become eventually'. It is only occasionally used with inanimate nouns, as in *la situación llegó a ser imposible* 'the situation (eventually) became impossible'.

Trabajó mucho y con el tiempo llegó a ser alguien/ director general/una persona importante	He worked hard and in due time he became someone/general manager/an important person

Pasar a (ser) means 'to go on to be' but it does not imply difficulty or lapse of time:

De secretario pasó a (ser) jefe	From being a secretary he went on to become the boss
Hay veces en que lo normal pasa a ser extraordinario (C. Martín Gaite, Spain)	There are times when what's normal becomes extraordinary
De hija pasé a ser esposa (C. Rico-Godoy, Spain)	From being a daughter I went on to being a wife

27.3.5 *Convertirse en* 'to become/change/turn into'

This verb precedes noun phrases but not adjectives. The change can be due to external circumstances:

Nada más tocarlo/le el hada con la varita el príncipe se convirtió en rana	As soon as the fairy touched him with her wand, the prince turned into a frog
Se ha convertido en un drogadicto/un criminal	He's become a drug addict/a criminal
El transporte se ha convertido en un problema para todos	Transport has become a problem for everybody
La silla se convierte fácilmente en una escalera	The chair turns easily into a stepladder

Note

'To convert to' a new belief is *convertirse a*; see also *hacerse*, 27.3.3: *no todos los que se convierten a una religión se vuelven buenos* 'not everybody who is converted to a religion becomes good'.

27.3.6 *Quedarse* and *quedar*

The relationship between *quedarse* and *quedar* (when they are used as verbs of becoming, i.e. are followed by an adjective or participle[1]) is affected by regional considerations that make it difficult to be precise about usage. In general, it seems to us that *quedarse* as a verb of becoming is much more common in Madrid, while *quedar* has a literary or regional character.

(a) In many cases, *quedarse* implies loss, incapacity or disadvantage:

Se quedó ciego/mudo/impedido/sordo	He became blind/dumb/disabled/deaf
Se quedó soltera/viuda	She never married/She became a widow
Se quedó solo en el mundo	He was left alone in the world
¡Qué delgado te has quedado!	Haven't you got thin!
Me he quedado helado esperándote	I've got frozen waiting for you
El mundo se me ha quedado pequeño	The world has got too small for me
El gerente se quedó fastidiado (C. Fuentes, Mexico)	The manager became irritated

(b) In a few other cases it does not imply loss or disadvantage See 26.7.32 and 28.2.6a for more remarks about *quedar(se)*:

¿Te has quedado contento?	Are you satisfied now?
Me quedé convencido de que era verdad	I became convinced that it was true
Se quedó embarazada	She became pregnant

Notes

(i) *Quedarse helado* can also apply to shock: *cuando se lo dijeron se quedó helado/de piedra/de una pieza* 'he had a terrible shock when they told him'/ 'he froze when they told him'.
(ii) In some Spanish regions *quedar* can be used instead of *quedarse* in the first four examples of **(a)** and also in *quedarse embarazada*. *Quedar embarazada* is not accepted in Madrid.

---

[1] Both verbs have other meanings not discussed here: *quedarse* = 'to stay'; *quedar* can mean 'to agree' or 'to be situated' (as in *queda lejos* 'it's a long way away').

28

Passive and impersonal sentences

28.1 General

This chapter discusses four constructions. Students who know French may find comparison with this language instructive:

(a) Passive with *ser* (28.2):

Fue construido	It was built	*Il a été construit*

(b) Passive *se* (28.4):

Eso no se dice	That isn't said/One doesn't say that	*Cela ne se dit pas/ On ne dit pas cela*
Se come mucho	A lot **of it** is eaten	*On **en** mange beaucoup*

(c) The 'mixed' construction with *se* and personal *a* (28.5):

*Se recibió **a** los embajadores*	The ambassadors were received	*Les ambassadeurs ont été reçus/On a reçu les ambassadeurs*
Se les recibió	They (i.e. the ambassadors) were received	*On les a reçus/Ils ont été reçus*

(d) Impersonal *se* (28.6):

Se entra	One enters	*On entre*
Se come mucho	People eat a lot	*On mange beaucoup*

These four constructions are all used to form impersonal sentences, i.e. those in which the agent of the action is unknown or irrelevant, as in *fue demolido el año pasado* 'it was demolished last year', *se dice que las zanahorias son buenas para los ojos* 'they say/it's said that carrots are good for the eyes', *se vive mejor en España que aquí* 'people live/one lives better in Spain than here'.

Passive with *ser* differs from the constructions with *se* in that the agent of the action can optionally be mentioned: *el puente fue construido **por** los militares* 'the bridge was built by the military'. In this case it is no longer an impersonal construction.

The first example under **(d)** shows that Spanish differs from French in allowing the use of *se* with intransitive verbs to form an impersonal sentence, as in *se es/se está . . .* (Fr. *on est . . .*), *se vive . . .* (Fr. *on vit . . .*), *se avanza* (Fr. *on avance*). In such cases *se* can be thought of as equivalent to the French impersonal subject pronoun *on*, German *man*, Catalan *hom*.

The example under **(c)** and the second example under **(d)** show how Spanish also differs from French in using *se* as an impersonal subject pronoun, even with transitive verbs. The reason for this use of *se* is historical. Medieval Spanish resembled French in that the word *hombre* could function like *on* or the English 'one', cf. *como hombre es mujer y vieja, no hacen caso de hombre* 'since one's a woman and old, they don't pay any attention to one', from G. Correas, *Vocabulario de refranes y frases populares*, 2nd edition, quoted Kany (1970), 179. When this useful construction became extinct its functions were transferred to the already heavily overburdened pronoun *se*.

As in English, second-person singular and third-person plural pronouns are often used in everyday speech as impersonal pronouns, i.e. to refer to no one in particular: *en algunos países no toman en serio a las mujeres* 'in some countries they don't take women seriously', *supongo que cuando te casas tienes que pensártelo antes* 'I guess that when you get/one gets married you/one ought to think it over beforehand'. This is discussed at 28.7.2 and 28.7.3.

28.2 Passive with *ser*

28.2.1 General

The passive with *ser* is formed from the appropriate tense and person of *ser* 'to be' and the past participle, which agrees in number and gender with the subject of *ser*:

Active	**Passive**
Solucionaron los problemas	*Los problemas fueron solucionados*
They solved the problems	The problems were solved
Manuel escribió la respuesta	*La respuesta fue escrita por Manuel*
Manuel wrote the reply	The reply was written by Manuel

There are several points to be made about this construction:

(a) English is unusual in allowing indirect objects to become the subject of the verb in a passive construction: '**she** was given twenty dollars', '**they** were told a tall story' – *se le dieron veinte dólares, se les contó un cuento chino*. **Ella fue enviada una carta* is unintelligible in Spanish for *se le envió una carta/le fue enviada una carta* 'she was sent a letter', and *fue enviada una carta* can only mean 'a letter was sent'.
(b) Whereas passive and impersonal *se* constructions occur in ordinary speech as an impersonal form or as a substitute for the passive, the passive with *ser* is more characteristic of written or non-spontaneous language, especially newspaper language. In informal speech the passive is usually replaced by impersonal 'they': *tres manifestantes fueron arrestados* = *arrestaron a tres manifestantes* 'they arrested three demonstrators', *fue entrevistado ayer* = *lo/le entrevistaron ayer* 'they interviewed him yesterday'. In fact, some grammarians assert that the passive with *ser* is not found in spontaneous speech, but this is not completely true, assuming that the following extracts really do reflect spontaneous speech:

| *Ese jardín es alemán, y la película se ve que* **fue hecha** *en Alemania* (M. Puig, Argentina, dialogue) | That garden's German, and you can see the film was made in Germany |
| *. . . la mujer "esposa de" que llevas dentro de ti y para lo que* **fuiste educada** *(Rosa Montero, Spain, dialogue)* | . . . the 'wife-woman' that you carry inside you and you were brought up to be |

Se trata de los papeles de mi marido	It's about my husband's papers . . .
*. . . Deben **ser ordenados** antes de que*	They have to be sorted before I die.
*muera. Deben **ser publicados*** (C. Fuentes,	They have to be published
Mexico, dialogue)	
Los derechos de filmación del fin del mundo	Film rights for the end of the world
*ya **fueron vendidos** a la televisión*	have already been sold to US
norteamericana (L. Rafael Sánchez,	television
Puerto Rico, dialogue. Spain . . . *ya han*	
sido vendidos)	

However, such examples are noticeably more common in the dialogue of Latin-American novels. The passive with *ser* is very rare in spontaneous Peninsular speech.

(c) The passive with *ser* is, however, very common in written Spanish everywhere and probably more so in the Americas. It abounds in newspapers, and this may indicate rushed translations of faxes from English-language press agencies, although it more probably reflects the need to produce a detached and 'objective' style. It should also be remembered that the passive with *ser* is not a modern invention: it appears frequently in medieval and Golden-Age Spanish, e.g. in *Don Quixote*, even in the dialogues: *nunca fui desdeñado de mi señora —respondió don Quijote* '"never was I spurned by my lady," Don Quixote replied.'

However, sentences like *estos ejemplos **son vistos** como logros enormes* (C. Fuentes, Mexico) 'these examples are seen as enormous successes' would almost certainly have been written . . . *se ven como logros enormes* in the recent past, and may still surprise Peninsular speakers. But the advance of this 'Anglicized' passive seems unstoppable, and it may eventually become a pervasive feature of Spanish. Until that day arrives, English speakers should beware of a tendency to over-use it, especially in speech.

(d) If no agent is mentioned, the passive with *ser* is often identical in meaning with passive *se* (explained at 28.4): *encontraron dos cargas explosivas que fueron desactivadas* and *encontraron dos cargas explosivas que se desactivaron* both mean 'they found two explosive charges which were deactivated', although the first is unambiguous whereas the second could conceivably be read as ' . . . which deactivated themselves'. But often there is a difference of nuance which may become crucial. The passive with *ser* is less impersonal than the *se* construction in the sense that the latter completely eliminates information about the agent from the message, whereas the former does not.[1] Thus it is probably more usual to say *el acusado fue sentenciado* 'the accused was sentenced' than *se sentenció al acusado*, since the agent (the judge) is obviously implicitly present in the message: *se sentenció . . .* almost implies 'someone sentenced the accused'. But *en el siglo II todavía se hablaba latín* 'Latin was still spoken in the second century' is more normal than . . . *el latín era hablado todavía* because the agent, in this case 'people', is too obvious or vague to be worth mentioning.

Por should not be used with passive *se*: **el latín se hablaba por los romanos* is generally considered to be bad Spanish for *los romanos hablaban latín*. This constraint

---

[1] For this reason there is a tendency in written Spanish to use passive with *ser* for actions that the writer prefers to attribute to someone else, and passive or impersonal *se* for actions that are normal and would be done by anyone. See 28.2.7 for discussion.

reflects the impersonality of *se* and may partly explain the increasing popularity of the passive with *ser*: see 28.4.1, note (iii) for more on this point. See also 28.2.7 for further remarks on the relationship between passive *se* and passive with *ser*. **(e)** The passive with *se* is more common with the preterite, future, perfect and pluperfect tenses and with the infinitive than with the imperfect, present and continuous tenses: *fue entrevistado ayer* is normal for 'he was interviewed yesterday', but a sentence like *Mario es entrevistado con frecuencia por periodistas de la prensa amarilla* 'Mario is frequently interviewed by journalists from the gutter press/(US yellow press)' is less usual. However, passive sentences in which the verb is timeless or habitual are nowadays increasingly common in writing and non-spontaneous speech, and more so in Latin America than Spain:

Los mismos ascensores son usados para el transporte de enfermos (*Cambio16*, Spain)	The same lifts are used for carrying patients
. . . *mientras Cabinda era defendida heroicamente por los combatientes del MPLA* (Fidel Castro, speech on Angola)	. . . while Cabinda was being heroically defended by fighters of the MPLA
Basta saber que un hombre es buscado para que todos lo vean de manera distinta (C. Fuentes, Mexico, dialogue)	It's enough to know a man's being sought for everyone to look at him in a different way
Algunos de ellos recuerdan que no hace mucho eran corridos por la Policía (*Cambio16*, Spain)	Some of them remember that not so long ago they were being chased by the police
El parlamento gibraltareño tiene 17 miembros, de los que 2 son puestos por el Gobierno inglés (*El País*, Spain)	The Gibraltarian parliament has 17 members, two of which are appointed by the British government

Most Peninsular informants found these sentences unnatural and preferred a *se* construction or, where the agent is mentioned, an active sentence, e.g. *al viajero le sorprende . . .* , *los mismos ascensores se usan . . .* , *basta saber que a un hombre se le busca . . .* , *recuerdan que no hace mucho la Policía les corría . . .* , *dos de los cuales los pone . . .* , although they were prepared to tolerate the third example *era defendida heroicamente*. The fact that the example mentioning Gibraltar sounds more natural if one substitutes *impuestos* 'imposed' for *puestos* is an indication of the difficulties surrounding the whole question of when use of the passive with *ser* is possible. Further examples of the passive with *ser* (active alternatives are shown in the unattributed examples):

Fue alcanzado por una bala (or *le alcanzó una bala*)	He was hit by a bullet
La conferencia será pronunciada por el decano (or *la conferencia la pronunciará el decano*)	The lecture will be given by the Dean
Han sido detenidos por la Guardia Civil (or *los ha detenido la Guardia Civil*)	They've been arrested by the Civil Guard
Las muestras les serán devueltas (or *se les devolverán las muestras*)	The samples will be returned to you
El hijo de Pilar Ternera fue llevado a casa de sus abuelos (G. García Márquez, Colombia; *llevar* cannot form a passive with *ser* if it means 'to wear' or 'to hold')	Pilar Ternera's son was taken (i.e. carried) to his grandparents' house

Note

The difference between the true passive *la ciudad **fue** destruida* 'the city was destroyed' (action) and *la ciudad **estaba** destruida* 'the city was in a state of destruction' is discussed at 28.2.5.

28.2.2 Constraints on the passive with *ser*

Students should observe the following rules about the use of the Spanish passive with *ser*:

(a) The passive must not be used when the subject of the passive sentence would be an indirect object: *le dieron dos regalos* 'he was given two presents', **never** **fue dado dos regalos*.

This is also true when the object of the verb in the active sentence takes the third-person pronoun *le/les*. One can transform *su marido la abandonó* into *fue abandonada por su marido* 'she was abandoned by her husband', but *su marido **le** pegó* 'her husband beat her' cannot be transformed into **fue pegada por su marido*. 12.6.4 includes a list of verbs similar to *pegar*. There are a few apparent exceptions to this rule, namely the verbs *pagar*, *preguntar* and *obedecer*:

*Los ministros **fueron preguntados** . . .* (El País, Spain)	The ministers were asked . . .
*Serás **pagado** por la Secretaría del Trabajo* (J. Marías, Spain, dialogue)	You'll be paid by the Labour (US 'Labor') Ministry
*Por la contundencia de su voz deduje que estaba acostumbrada a **ser obedecida*** (A. Gala, Spain, dialogue)	From her no-nonsense voice I inferred that she was used to being obeyed

But it is nevertheless impossible to include another object in such sentences: one cannot say **fui preguntado una pregunta* for 'I was asked a question' (*se me preguntó*) or **fui pagado el dinero* for 'I was paid the money' (*el dinero me fue pagado, se me pagó el dinero*).

(b) The passive is not usually used when the subject of *ser* is partitive, i.e. has no article: *se venden naranjas aquí* 'oranges for sale' but not **naranjas son vendidas aquí* 'oranges are sold here'. However, sentences like *en el mercado antiguo eran vendidas manzanas y otras frutas* 'in the old market apples and other fruits were sold' may be found, especially in literary Latin-American Spanish. *Se vendían manzanas y otras frutas* is more normal.

(c) The passive is very rarely used with a present or imperfect tense to denote a single action. The Academy (*Esbozo* . . ., 3.12.9c) says that *la puerta es/era abierta por el portero* 'the door is/was opened by the doorman' can only refer to a habitual or timeless event. This rule does not apply to all styles. Journalists sometimes use the imperfect for single events – *momentos después **era** asesinado por un terrorista* 'seconds later he was murdered by a terrorist' (see 28.2.1e and 14.5.8 for discussion) – and the historic present may denote a single past action, as in *el 22 de junio de 1941 la Unión Soviética **es** invadida por ejércitos alemanes* 'on 22 June 1941, the Soviet Union was (lit. 'is') invaded by German armies'.

(d) The passive is not used in reciprocal constructions. One can say *se vieron el uno al otro* 'they saw one another', but never **fueron vistos el uno por el otro* *'they were seen by one another'. This explains why, in both languages, *ver* and 'to see' can only be used in the passive with a non-reciprocal meaning. *Fue vista por Bill cuando salía del restaurante* 'she was seen by Bill when she was leaving the restaurant' is possible since she didn't know Bill was watching; but one can only say *Bill la vio anoche – fueron juntos a un restaurante* 'Bill saw her last night (i.e. they saw one another) – they went to a restaurant.'

(e) A phrase consisting of preposition + noun or pronoun cannot become the subject of a Spanish passive sentence. In this respect Spanish differs totally from English: one can only translate 'this bed has been slept **in**' by *alguien ha dormido en esta cama*, never by the incomprehensible **esta cama ha sido dormido en*. Spanish sentences cannot end with prepositions.

(f) Unattributed beliefs or opinions of the sort 'it is said that . . . ', 'it is believed that . . . ', 'people thought that . . .' are translated by a *se* construction: *se dice que, se cree que, se pensaba que.*

(g) The passive is not used with a large number of verbs, and for no obvious reason. These are more numerous than in English, which has similar constraints, e.g. 'the window was broken by Jill' but not ***'the stairs were descended by Jill'. Only familiarity with the language will eliminate such malformations as **fueron esperados por sus padres* 'they were expected by their parents', **fue permitido hacerlo* (but *le fue permitido hacerlo* is correct) 'he was allowed to do it', both of them sentences which should be expressed in active form or, in the second example, by impersonal *se*: *se le permitió hacerlo*. Likewise, one can say *la casa fue destruida por una bomba* 'the house was destroyed by a bomb', but not **la ventana fue rota por una piedra* 'the window was broken by a stone', which, curiously, is difficult to translate into Spanish: *esta ventana la han roto de una pedrada.*

Sometimes the passive is wrong with a personal pronoun, but acceptable with other types of agent: *él era admirado por todos* 'he was admired by everybody', but not ?*él era admirado por mí* 'he was admired by me' (*yo lo/le admiraba*).

In the following sentences passive with *ser* is not used (at least in normal styles), for no very obvious reason – other, perhaps, than the fact that they are all fairly relaxed, colloquial sentences:

Me arañó un gato	A cat scratched me
Me dio un periódico	He/She/You gave me a newspaper
A la niña la lavó la madre	The mother washed the little girl
Me irritó el humo	The smoke irritated me
La despertaron temprano	She was woken up early
La invitan a cenar con frecuencia	She's often invited out to dinner

It would be beyond the scope of this grammar to establish a comprehensive list of verbs which do not allow the passive with *ser*. As a general rule it seems that verbs commonly used in everyday conversation are less likely to appear in the passive form than verbs usually associated with formal or written language.

28.2.3 Avoiding the passive

English-speaking students constantly over-use the Spanish passive. It can be avoided by the following stratagems:

(a) Make the sentence active – the simplest solution, but stylistically tedious if overdone:

Los críticos lo/le alabaron (= *fue alabado por los críticos*)	The critics praised him
Suspendieron la sesión (= *la sesión fue suspendida*)	The session was suspended

(b) Use passive *se* (discussed at 28.4):

The following typical piece of journalese ... *su bufete privado es utilizado con frecuencia para asuntos propios del Gobierno* (*El País*, Spain) 'his private office is often used for Government business' could be equally well expressed by ... *su bufete privado se utiliza con frecuencia para asuntos propios del Gobierno*. This device should only be used if the agent of the action is not included in the sentence: *el fenómeno fue observado por un astrónomo japonés* 'the phenomenon was observed by a Japanese astronomer' should not be recast using *se*. See 28.4.1 note (ii) for details.

(c) Since one function of the passive is to turn the object of the active sentence into the topic of a sentence – compare 'he preferred Jane' and '**Jane** was preferred by him' – the effect of an English passive can often be reproduced in Spanish by putting the direct object before the verb. A redundant object pronoun then usually becomes necessary (see 11.16.1 for details):

La explicación hay que buscarla en otra parte	The explanation must be sought elsewhere
Las puertas las cierran los porteros a las diez	The doors are shut by the doormen at ten o'clock

28.2.4 Passive meaning of the infinitive

The distinction between active and passive is often blurred in infinitive constructions:

un partido heterogéneo y sin estructurar	a heterogeneous and unstructured political party (lit. 'without structuring')
Eso ya era de prever	That could be foreseen
Vi matar a dos personas	I saw two persons kill**ed**

The last of these sentences is in fact ambiguous: it could mean 'I saw two persons kill' or 'I saw two persons killed', the latter reading being more likely. See 18.2.5 and 18.5 for further examples.

28.2.5 Comparison between *fue convencido* and *estaba convencido* (the subject is also raised at 19.1)

The passive with *ser* denotes an action; the participle with *estar* usually describes a state arising from an action – i.e. it is not dynamic. Compare *la puerta fue abierta* 'the door was open**ed**' and *la puerta estaba abierta* 'the door was **open**'. The possibility of making this contrast is normally confined to verbs with a dynamic meaning, i.e. ones that describe actions, not states. The participle of a non-dynamic verb will probably denote only a state and therefore may only admit *estar*, cf. *estoy acostumbrado* 'I'm used to', *estás deprimido* 'you're depressed' (*ser* impossible).

In some cases a special participle is used with *estar*: cf. *estaba **despierto** porque había sido **despertado** por una voz de hombre* 'he was awake because he had been woken by a man's voice'. See 19.2.1 for a list of these participles. Examples:

La ciudad fue destruida	The city was destroyed
La ciudad estaba destruida	The city was in ruins
Fui detenido	I was arrested
Yo estaba detenido	I was under arrest
La reunión fue aplazada por decisión del presidente (action)	The meeting was postponed by a decision of the president

Cuando llegué me encontré con que la reunión estaba aplazada (state)	When I arrived I found the meeting was postponed
Este sitio **fue** *elegido porque abunda el agua, y* **estaba** *muy bien elegido porque había también una buena carretera*	This place was chosen because there is abundant water and it was very well chosen because there was a good road as well
Vino aquí . . . convencido de que iba a ser el mandamás. Y se encontró con que todo estaba hecho y muy bien hecho (M. Vargas Llosa, Peru, dialogue)	He came here convinced he was going to run the show. And he found everything was done and done properly
[El libro] estaba muy leído, subrayado en algunos pasajes, e incluso con notas al margen (C. Martín Gaite, Spain)	It [the book] had been read a lot, underlined in some places and it even had notes in the margins
Los hechos históricos no están gobernados por leyes (O. Paz, Mexico[2])	Historical facts are not governed by laws

28.2.6 Alternatives to *ser* to express passive meaning

Several other verbs may replace *ser* in the passive. They usually add nuances which can barely be translated into normal English:

(a) *Quedar*
When it is used to form the passive, *quedar* emphasizes a condition that has arisen from some event, rather like the popular English 'ended up':

Quedó herido	He was injured (as a result)
La Escuela de Periodismo informa que el plazo de inscripción quedará abierto en el mes de octubre (advertisement in *El País*, Spain)	The School of Journalism announces that the registration period will commence (lit. 'be opened') in October
Queda dicho al principio de este párrafo que . . . (Royal Academy, *Esbozo . . .*)	It was stated at the beginning of this paragraph that . . .

The use of *quedar/quedarse* with adjectives and participles is further discussed at 26.7.32 and 27.3.6.

(b) *Resultar*
Resultar also emphasizes the idea of a condition arising from an event:

Una veintena de personas resultaron heridas	About twenty people were injured (as a result)

(c) *Verse*
Verse is quite often used with a participle in literary styles, even with inanimate subjects:

Mis ingresos eran reducidos, ya que se veían afectados por la piratería informática (letter in *El País*, Spain)	My earnings were low as they were affected by software piracy
. . . esos individuos que se ven proyectados de golpe a la condición de clase dominante (E. Lynch, Argentina)	. . . those individuals who are suddenly catapulted into the ruling classes

---

[2] Since literary Latin-American Spanish often uses the passive with *ser* to express habitual actions, this sentence might well have been expressed as *son gobernados. Están gobernados* would be more normal in European Spanish.

(d) *Venir*

Use of *venir* emphasizes that a condition has arisen from some previous event. Again, it is confined to literary styles and it is particularly commonly used when quoting some previous statement:

. . . *como viene dicho en el párrafo anterior* . . .	. . . as was stated in the previous paragraph . . .
En el caso de producirse omisiones y errores en la guía, la Compañía Telefónica vendrá obligada a corregirlos en la siguiente edición (Spanish phone book)	If omissions or errors should appear in the directory, the Telephone Company shall be obliged to correct them in the next edition

28.2.7 *Fue arrestado* or *se le arrestó?*

Learners are often obliged to choose between the passive with *ser* and one of the *se* constructions described at 28.3–28.6, a choice that normally only arises in writing since the passive with *ser* is generally avoided in spontaneous speech.

The passive with *ser* seems to be preferred in newspaper or other impersonal, formal written styles. It is certainly much more common in such styles than the construction *se* + *a* + human direct object described at 28.5: *varias personas fueron arrestadas* is more usual in newspapers than *se arrestó a varias personas*. It seems that this popularity of the passive in news reports in the media is due to the fact that it tends to ascribe an action to some named or unnamed agent, whereas constructions with *se* can suggest that anyone might do the same. Compare *las patatas se fríen en aceite* '(the) potatoes are fried in oil' (the usual thing to do, so the sentence would sound normal in a cookery book) and *las patas habían sido fritas en margarina* 'the potatoes had been fried (by someone or other) in margarine' (which most people would not do). Compare also *se aplaudió mucho a las niñas* 'the girls were applauded warmly' but *las niñas fueron asesinadas* 'the girls were murdered', a repulsive action which we wish to ascribe to some specific even though unnamed individual.

The fact that, in the view of most grammarians, *por* should not be used with passive *se* also accounts for the frequent use in written language of the passive with *ser*: *varias personas fueron arrestadas por la policía* is the only possible passive rendering of *la policía arrestó a varias personas* 'the police arrested several people', not **se arrestó a varias personas por la policía*, which is generally considered to be incorrect.

28.3 General remarks about passive and impersonal *se*

There are three types of passive and impersonal construction that use *se*, discussed in Chapter 26:

(a) *Se pasivo* or 'passive *se*' (28.4). This is found only with transitive verbs in the third person, singular or plural. The verb agrees in number with the word that would have been the direct object in the equivalent active sentence, e.g. *se debatieron varios problemas* 'several problems were discussed', *se vacunaron las vacas* 'the cows were vaccinated', *se vendieron tres toneladas* 'three tons were sold', *la amigdalitis se cura con antibióticos* 'tonsillitis is cured with antibiotics'. The noun or pronoun in the original active sentence normally refers to something inanimate or non-rational (i.e. something which cannot perform the action on itself), otherwise the construction described under **(b)** is used.

(b) The 'mixed' construction *se* + transitive verb + *a* (28.5). This construction can be considered impersonal or passive according to one's point of view: it is in fact impersonal in form and passive in meaning. The verb is always singular: *se detuvo a tres narcotraficantes* 'three drug-dealers were arrested', *se advirtió a España del peligro* 'Spain was warned about the danger', *se llama a los perros con un silbido* 'dogs are called by whistling'.

(c) *Se impersonal* or 'impersonal *se*' (28.6). This is found with intransitive verbs, e.g. *se vive mejor aquí* 'one lives better here', and also with 'objectless' transitive verbs, as in *en España se come mucho* 'people eat a lot in Spain' (but if there is an implied object, e.g. 'meat', 'garlic', the construction is interpreted as passive *se*: 'a lot **of it** is eaten in Spain').

28.4 Passive *se*

28.4.1 Basic rules

Passive *se* can only be used with transitive verbs and in the third person, normally only with non-human nouns and pronouns so as to avoid clashes of meaning with other uses of *se* (see 28.5 for discussion). It is usually equivalent in meaning to passive with *ser*, but it is common in ordinary speech, more 'impersonal' than the passive with *ser* (see 28.2.1 and 28.2.7 for discussion) and it cannot be used when the agent of the action is mentioned; see note (iii):

Los cangrejos se cuecen en vino blanco	(The) crabs are boiled in white wine
El vino se le sirvió en copas de cristal (M. Vázquez Montalbán, Spain)	The wine was served to him in crystal glasses
Nunca se oyeron y leyeron en el Perú tantas definiciones de la libertad de información (M. Vargas Llosa, Peru)	Never were there heard and read in Peru so many definitions of freedom of information
Es una zona de mucha sequía, así que no se ven muchos árboles (M. Puig, Argentina, dialogue)	It's a very drought-ridden area, so you don't see many trees/not many trees are to be seen
No se han traído a la Tierra suelo y muestras de minerales del planeta Marte	Soil and mineral samples from the planet Mars have not been brought to Earth
Se reparan relojes	Watches mended
Estos errores podrían deberse a . . .	These errors could be due to . . .
Se acababan de promulgar varias leyes	Several laws had just been published
Que se sepa	As far as is known
Eso no se hace	That sort of thing isn't done
Se dice que va a dimitir[3]	They say/It's said that she's going to resign

---

[3] This can be interpreted either as passive *se* or as impersonal *se*; see 28.6. The old-fashioned form *dícese que* is probably the origin of a colloquial form, very widespread in Latin America in various guises, e.g. *isque, dizque*. It often implies scepticism: *a los seis años de andar dizque* (Spain *según dicen*) *gobernando se puso enfermo* (A. Mastretta, Mexico) 'after six year of "governing" (so they say) he fell ill'.

Notes

(i) For a comparison of this construction with the true passive – *el problema se solucionó/el problema fue solucionado* 'the problem was solved' – see 28.2.1(d) and 28.2.7.

(ii) In a passive *se* construction it helps to think of the word *se* as the direct object pronoun, for which reason a second direct object pronoun cannot appear: Spanish verbs cannot have two direct object personal pronouns (as explained at 11.7.4). Thus *vendieron los libros* 'they sold the books' can be transformed into the sentence *se vendieron* 'they were sold', but not into *se los vendieron*, which is good Spanish only if the *se* is an indirect object pronoun (i.e. derives from *le* or *les*) and the sentence means: 'they sold the books to him/her/you/them'.

(iii) Passive *se* should not be followed by *por* and the real agent of the verb: **la decisión se tomó por el presidente* is bad Spanish for *la decisión fue tomada por el presidente* 'the decision was taken by the president'. This rule is constantly broken in speech and not infrequently in writing, but this is considered incorrect: **la decisión de irnos se tomó conjuntamente y por personas de la misma línea política* (F. Ordóñez in *Cambio 16*, Spain) 'the decision to leave was taken jointly and by persons sharing the same political line', **el terrorismo no debe atacarse aisladamente por las naciones que lo padecen* (Felipe González in *El País*, Spain) 'terrorism must not be combated individually by those nations that suffer from it'.

These blunders could have been avoided either by use of passive with *ser*, or by a simple active construction. This misuse of *se*, it must be admitted, is fairly often seen in modern written texts (at least in carelessly edited ones), and it was also common in Golden-Age writing (sixteenth and seventeenth centuries). However, the fact remains that sentences like *?*se construyó el puente por los militares* are vehemently rejected by most literate Spanish speakers in favour of *el puente fue construido por los militares*.

(iv) Passive *se* may be used to form a passive imperative, useful for footnotes, written instructions and so on: *no se crea que* 'let it not be believed that', *téngase presente que* 'let it be borne in mind that', *desarróllese en castellano el siguiente tema* 'develop the following topic in Spanish'; see 17.8.

(v) It must be remembered that as far as form is concerned, there is no difference between this passive *se* construction and reflexive or reciprocal *se*. In other words, only common sense tells us that the first example does not mean 'the crabs cook themselves in white wine' or 'cook one another . . .'.

(vi) French passive *se*, as in *cela ne se dit pas* (= *eso no se dice* 'that isn't said'/'one doesn't say that') is more restricted in use and tends to be reserved for timeless statements.

28.4.2 Agreement of the verb with passive *se*

In theory, any verb used with *se* must agree with the logical subject. This is true for all constructions with reflexive, reciprocal or passive *se*. In other words, there is no formal distinction between passive *se* and the other two kinds of *se*. Compare *los niños se están lavando* (reflexive) 'the children are washing', *no se hablan* (reciprocal) 'they don't talk to one another', and *las tuercas se quitan con llave, no con martillo* (passive *se*) 'bolts are removed with a spanner, not with a hammer'. Further examples of the agreement of the verb with passive *se*:

*Se **mezclan** en el turmix los tomates sin pepitas y sin piel*	The tomatoes, with skins and pips removed, are mixed in the liquidizer
*Se **enviaron** los hombres y las armas necesarios para concluirla* (i.e. *la lucha*: Fidel Castro, Cuba, speech)	The men and weapons necessary to finish it [the fight] were sent
*. . . aquellos reportajes en que se **veían** los fusilamientos de los campesinos* (R. Arenas, Cuba)	. . . those documentaries in which one could see the executions of the the peasants

When passive *se* is used, the rules of agreement are always respected when a plural noun precedes the verb: *los libros se vendían a mil pesetas* 'the books were sold at 1,000 pesetas', never **los libros se vendía a mil pesetas*. But when the verb precedes a plural noun, popular language sometimes breaks the rules of agreement: *?se compra objetos usados* 'used articles bought' for *se compran objetos usados*. This phenomenon, which is probably less common than is sometimes imagined,[4] should not be imitated and it may sound quite illiterate in spite of the fact that there is much disagreement among native speakers about the issue, and some grammarians[5] accept the use of the singular on the grounds that this is really an impersonal construction (which is doubtful). Foreigners should make the verb agree, but it should be noted that in some contexts, especially advertisements of the type *se necesita camareros* 'waiters needed', singular agreement is more tolerated. The following forms may be unacceptable to many speakers:

*?Y nunca más se **ha** tenido noticias de su paradero* (*Abc*, Spain; for *se han tenido* . . .)
No further news has been received of his whereabouts

*?Se necesit**a** agallas para hacer eso* (Spanish informant overheard: *se necesitan agallas*)
You need 'guts' to do that

*?Se **les** dio varios premios* (for *se les dieron* . . .)
Several prizes were given to them

?Se vende máquinas de coser usadas (street sign in Mexico D.F.)
Used sewing machines sold

Notes

(i) The last example must be exceptional, if we are to believe the claim of Lope Blanch (1991), 12, that Mexican Spanish preserves, 'casi con exclusividad, la construcción pasiva refleja del tipo "se rentan departamentos", sin dar entrada a la construcción activa impersonal del tipo "se vende botellas", relativamente frecuente en el habla española'.

(ii) When passive *se* is followed by the interrogative words *cuánto, qué, cuál* or *quién* the verb is singular: *se calculó cuántos kilos había* 'it was calculated how many kilos there were', *se averiguó qué existencias quedaban* 'a check was made of what stocks remained', *no se sabe quiénes son* 'it is not known who they are'.

(iii) When a verb which is not a modal verb (see next section) precedes an infinitive whose direct object is plural, agreement is in the singular: *se intentó solucionar varios problemas* 'an attempt was made to solve several problems', *se decidió tomar estas medidas* . . . 'it was decided to take these measures . . . '. Other verbs that are not modal verbs and therefore have singular agreement with *se pasivo* when an infinitive follows them are: *tratar de* 'to try', *necesitar* 'to need', *esperar* 'to hope'. Incorrect plural agreement is, in fact, quite often seen: see 28.4.3, note (ii).

(iv) The verb *tardar* is a special case. It is always singular in this construction: *se tardó varias horas en llegar a un acuerdo* 'it took several hours to reach an agreement' (lit. 'several hours were taken to reach . . . ').

28.4.3 Agreement of passive *se* with modal verbs

Agreement with plural nouns is required with modal verbs (*poder, saber, tener que, haber de, querer, soler*) when they precede the infinitive of a transitive verb. In this case *se* can be suffixed to the infinitive or it can precede the modal verb:

Se tienen que resolver varios problemas/Tienen que resolverse varios problemas
Several problems must be solved

Se deben limpiar bien las verduras antes de cocerlas (= *deben limpiarse*)
Vegetables should be washed well before boiling

---

[4] DeMello (1995) reports in his survey of educated spoken Spanish in eleven major cities that agreement of the verb with a plural noun is in fact overwhelmingly the norm, being heard in 65% to 94% of cases, according to region.

[5] e.g. Molina Redondo (1974), 23–5 and the Chilean Academy, which tolerates sentences like *?se vende artículos de tocador* (*Notas*, 6, 1966, quoted in Seco 1998, 410). Seco considers such failures of agreement 'abnormal'.

. . . *cosas que no se quieren hacer/cosas que* *no quieren hacerse*	. . . things one doesn't want to do
En Londres por la calle se pueden observar *los tipos de personas más extrañas* (*Cosmopolitan*, Spain; = *pueden observarse*)	In London one can observe the strangest sorts of people in the streets

See 11.14.4 for further discussion of the position of pronouns with the infinitive.

Notes

(i) Singular agreement with modal auxiliary verbs is generally considered to be incorrect but it is very commonly seen and heard: compare *?se puede imprimir textos con más rapidez con un proce-sador de textos* (*Ordenador Personal*, Spain, for *se pueden*) 'texts can be printed more rapidly with a wordprocessor', *?la ley prohíbe que se pueda transferir fondos de un programa a otro* (*La Prensa*, Panama) 'the law prohibits the transfer of funds from one programme to another' (for *se puedan transferir*).

(ii) There is, however, a contrary tendency, deplored by grammarians and to be avoided by foreign learners, to give non-modal verbs preceding a transitive verb plural agreement; compare *se nece-sitan resolver muchos problemas para conseguirlo* 'many problems have to be resolved in order to achieve it', *cuando se tratan de estudiar los hallazgos de tiempos pasados* (*ABC*, Spain) 'when an attempt is made to study the discoveries of the past', *y en el ministerio de Obras Públicas (MOP) tam-bién se esperan firmar otros contratos* (*El Comercio*, Ecuador) 'and in the Ministry of Public Works it is also hoped that other contracts will be signed'.

28.5 *Se* + transitive verb + personal *a*

28.5.1 General

This special type of construction has evolved to eliminate some of the ambigu-ities surrounding the overworked pronoun *se*. Passive *se* as described at 28.4 is usually unambiguous if there is no noun in the sentence that could be under-stood to be the subject, as is usually the case when the subject is inanimate: *los platos se lavan* 'the plates are washed' is unlikely to mean 'the plates wash them-selves', which could be said *los platos se lavan a sí mismos/los platos se lavan solos.* However, the burden of ambiguity of *se* may be intolerable with animate or per-sonified nouns, particularly those referring to humans, since *se mataron dos ingle-ses* may mean 'two Englishmen killed themselves' as well as 'killed one another'. The language has developed a device for avoiding this ambiguity by marking the object by the preposition *a*: *se mató a dos ingleses*. Four points must be remem-bered about this construction:

(a) The verb is **always** singular: **se mataron a dos ingleses* for *se mató a . . .* is a bad mistake.

(b) In this construction the word *se* always implies an unidentified *human* agent, in which respect it resembles English 'one', French *on*, German *man*. In other words, one could not say *se mató a dos ingleses* if the Englishmen were killed by a falling tree or a bolt of lightning, in which case one would say *murieron dos ingle-ses* or *dos ingleses resultaron muertos*.

(c) The noun can be replaced by an object pronoun: *se me había reconocido* 'I'd been recognized', *se les reconoció* 'they were recognized'.

Examples of *se* + verb + personal *a*:

Se persiguió y encarceló a millares de creyentes (*El País*, Spain)	Thousands of believers were persecuted and jailed
Se incitaba a las muchachas a trabajar más que los muchachos	The girls were encouraged to work harder than the boys
¿Se puede destrozar a una persona de esa manera porque se la ama de esa manera . . . ? (A. Bryce Echenique, Peru)	Can one destroy a person in that way because one loves him/her in that way?
No se te paga tan mal, entonces, si puedes comprarte tus revistas (S. Vodanovic, Chile, dialogue)	You're not that badly paid if you can (afford to) buy your magazines

Notes

(i) When a pronoun replaces the noun in this type of sentence, many speakers, including Latin Americans, prefer to use *le/les* rather than *lo/la/los/las*, despite the fact that the pronouns are (presumably) the direct object of the verb and may also be feminine: . . . *hasta que se **les** pueda evacuar* (M. González in *El País*, Spain) ' . . . until they can be evacuated', *se **le** veía nerviosa* 'one could see she was nervous'. This is discussed in more detail at 12.6.3.

(ii) A sentence like *se mató a dos ingleses* exemplifies the peculiarities of *se*. *Se* is traditionally thought of as an 'object' pronoun, but in the above example *dos ingleses* is clearly the direct object of *matar*, in which case *se* is functioning as a subject. That *se* acts as a subject pronoun in this kind of sentence is further demonstrated by the fact that a direct object pronoun can appear in such sentences: *se **le/la** nota pálida*. If *se* were functioning as a direct object pronoun (as it does in passive *se* constructions: see 28.4.1 note ii), no second direct object pronoun could appear because a Spanish verb cannot have more than one direct object personal pronoun.

(iii) As was mentioned, the verb must be singular in this construction. **Se les notaban cansados* is an error sometimes heard in Spain and rather more often in Latin America (see 28.4 for examples like *se pueden ver los árboles desde aquí*, which is passive *se*).

(iv) The construction discussed in this section seems to be a relatively recent innovation. Before the eighteenth century, a sentence like *Juan y Antonio se vieron* could also mean 'Juan and Antonio were seen.' Nowadays it is taken to mean 'saw one another' or 'saw themselves', and *se vio a Antonio y Juan* (or, in written styles, *Antonio y Juan fueron vistos*) would be used for the passive meaning. In present-day formal written Spanish, passive with *ser* is in fact increasingly preferred to the construction with *se* + *a*, above all in journalism. See 28.2.7.

28.5.2 Difference between the construction *se* + verb + *a* and passive *se*

Foreign students often have difficulty distinguishing this construction from passive *se*, especially when pronouns replace nouns in the special construction. It should be emphasized that, at least in theory (and also in practice as far as most careful speakers and writers are concerned), passive *se* is used when the direct object of the equivalent active sentence refers to something inanimate, and *se* + *a* is reserved for cases in which it refers to an identified human or animal. This should be clear from the difference between the following sentences:

*A Eugenio d'Ors se **lo/le** lee poco* (special construction)	Eugenio d'Ors isn't read much
Los libros de Eugenio d'Ors se leen poco (*se pasivo*)	Eugenio d'Ors's books aren't read much
*Se **lo/le** lee poco* (refers to a male author; special construction)	**He** isn't read much/People don't read him much
Se lee poco (refers to a book: *se pasivo*)	**It** isn't read much
*Se **le/la** admira mucho* (i.e. a woman: special construction)	**She**'s admired a lot
Se admira mucho (e.g. a statue or some other work of art: *se pasivo*)	**It**'s admired a lot

Se las/les criticó duramente (i.e. some women: special construction)	They were strongly criticized
Se criticaron duramente (i.e. some books, attitudes, arguments or some other inanimate noun: *se pasivo*)	They were strongly criticized

These examples show that a true passive *se* construction cannot contain a direct object pronoun other than *se* itself. *Se los envió* can therefore either mean '(s)he sent them to her/him/you' (active sentence, *se* stands for *le* or *les*, the most likely meaning), or it could possibly be a transformation of some sentence like *envió a los estudiantes al director* 'he sent the students to the head/principal' > *se los envió (a él)*, preferably *se les envió* to make clear that the direct object is human. It cannot mean 'they were sent' if 'they' refers to something inanimate like 'books'. The latter can only be *se enviaron* (or *fueron enviados*).

The passive *se* construction is, however, allowed with human beings when the latter are unidentified, as in *se ven muchos turistas en la playa* 'a lot of tourists are seen on the beach': compare *desde aquí se ve a muchos turistas alemanes durmiendo en la playa* 'from here you can see a lot of German tourists sleeping on the beach' (identified or specified as German tourists).

Sometimes one finds sentences like *se ha comparado a los ordenadores con el cerebro humano* 'computers have been compared with the human brain', *se debe amar más a la verdad que a la fama* 'one must love truth more than fame', in spite of the fact that the logical object is inanimate. This is done with personified nouns to avoid all possibility of a reflexive meaning; see 22.10c for further comments.

Note

It must be acknowledged that impersonal *se* does occasionally appear with an inanimate direct object when the context makes it absolutely clear that an inanimate is involved, as in *el ascensor subía por dentro de las barandillas y se le oía chirriar desde todas las habitaciones de la casa* (C. Martín Gaite, Spain) 'the lift went up on the inside of the banisters, and one could hear it squeaking from every room in the house'. Foreigners should, however, avoid this tendency.

28.6 Impersonal *se*

28.6.1 General

Spanish also uses *se* with third-person verbs as an equivalent of the English 'one'/'people', French *on*, German *man*.[6] Impersonal *se*, like English 'one' and French *on*, refers to an unidentified human agent: this is demonstrated by the peculiarity of a sentence like ?*es difícil dormir por las noches porque se ladra mucho ?*'it's difficult to sleep at night because one barks a lot'. Impersonal *se* most commonly occurs with intransitive verbs: *se está mejor aquí* 'one's better off here' (French *on est mieux ici*), *se entra por aquí* (French *on entre par ici*), etc. But impersonal *se* can also be used with transitive verbs, as in *en este país se lee poco* 'in this country people don't read much'. See 28.6.3.

---

[6] This use of *se* with intransitive verbs has no counterpart in French, which uses *on*. Italian impersonal *si* is constructed differently from its Spanish equivalent; cf. *si è contenti* and *se está contento* 'one's content'/'people are content' (adjective always singular in Spanish).

28.6.2 Impersonal *se* with intransitive verbs

The following examples show the use of impersonal *se* with intransitive verbs. In some cases (explained in note iii), *uno* could be used instead of *se*:

No se puede entrar	Entrance forbidden
No se debe ir con prisas (or *uno no debe*)	One mustn't rush
Siempre se vuelve a los sitios a los que se pertenece (Antonio Gala, Spain, dialogue; or *uno vuelve . . . uno pertenece*)	One always returns to the places one belongs to
O se va a referéndum, o habrá guerra civil	Either a referendum is held, or there will be a civil war
¿Quién puede pensar en nada cuándo se está rodeado de idiotas? (C. Solórzano, Mexico)	Who can think of anything when one's/ they're surrounded by idiots?
Que un día cualquiera, uno sepa que es otra persona, que en vez de ser pobre, se es rica; que en vez de ser nadie, se es alguien . . . (S. Vodanovic, Chile, dialogue)	[To think that] some day one finds out that one's someone else; that instead of being poor one's rich, that instead of being nobody one's somebody . . .
En este país se duerme mucho (M. Benedetti, Uruguay, dialogue)	People sleep a lot in this country
A las tres de la madrugada pareció llegarse a un acuerdo tácito para descansar (J. Cortázar, Argentina)	At three in the morning it appeared that a tacit agreement was reached to get some rest
Se cruza si el semáforo está en verde y se espera si está en rojo (*El País*, Spain; or *uno cruza . . . uno espera*)	One crosses if the lights are green and one waits if they are red
No escuchaba cuando se le hablaba (*El País*, Spain; or *uno le hablaba*)	He didn't listen when somebody talked to him

Notes

(i) Impersonal *se* cannot be used with a verb that already has *se* or some other reflexive pronoun attached to it: one cannot say *se lava mucho for 'people wash themselves a lot': *la gente se lava mucho*. See 26.11.

(ii) As with most sentences involving *se*, common sense and context often clarify the meaning. Thus *se iba al teatro* may mean '(s)he was going to the theatre' (*irse* is also a pronominal verb meaning 'to go away') or 'people used to go to the theatre' (impersonal *se*).

(iii) In some cases impersonal *se* is an equivalent of *uno* and the latter could replace it. This happens when *se* includes the speaker, as in *nunca escuchaba cuando se le hablaba/cuando* **uno** *le hablaba* 'he never listened when one spoke to him/when he was spoken to'. But when the speaker is not included, *uno* is not possible, as in *éste/este es un país donde se fuma y se bebe mucho* 'this is a country where people smoke and drink a lot'.

(iv) Impersonal *se* may even appear in combination with passive with *ser*, although this is rare: *no se debe hablar más que con personas a las que* **se ha sido ya presentado** 'one must only talk to people one has been introduced to' (C. Rico-Godoy, Spain).

(v) For agreement of *se* with modal verbs preceding the infinitive of a transitive verb see 28.4.3.

28.6.3 Impersonal *se* with transitive verbs

Impersonal *se* can also be used with transitive verbs, in which case the verb is always singular and no direct object appears:

En España se come mucho	People eat a lot in Spain (in general; does not refer to any specific food)
Sí, se habla, se habla . . .	Yes, people talk and talk . . .

Es difícil vender periódicos en un país donde se lee poco (cf. *se leen poco*, passive *se*: 'they aren't read much')	It's difficult to sell newspapers in a where people don't read much
Se critica mucho pero se alaba poco	People criticize a lot but don't praise much

Students (and not a few native speakers) find it difficult to distinguish between this construction and passive *se*. The distinction depends on whether the context refers to a direct object, explicit or implicit: if it does, then the construction is passive *se*; if not, it is impersonal *se*. Thus if we are talking about garlic, the sentence *en España se come mucho* is assumed to mean 'a lot **of it** is eaten in Spain' (passive *se*, underlying object 'garlic'/*ajo*). If the conversation is simply about general eating habits, the same sentence means 'people eat a lot in Spain' (no underlying object) and the *se* is impersonal *se*.

Notes

(i) If a direct object pronoun appears in this construction it can only refer to a human being: *se le considera útil* 'he/she is considered useful/you're considered useful', but not 'it is considered useful', which is *se considera útil* (passive *se*): see 28.5, note (i).

If the object pronoun is an indirect object, the construction is likely to be impersonal *se* with an intransitive verb, as in *se le rompió la taza* 'the cup "broke itself" on him' (i.e. he accidentally broke the cup, intransitive verb *romperse* 'to break'), or passive *se* with an inanimate underlying object: *se le dio un regalo* (passive *se*) 'a present was given to him'/'he was given a present'.

(ii) How does one parse sentences like *se dice que está enferma* 'it's said that she's sick'/ 'they say that she's sick'? Are these instances of passive *se* or impersonal *se*? If we analyse the 'direct object' of this sentence as '. . . that she is ill' (i.e. the direct object is a clause), then the sentence is an example of passive *se*. If, however, we analyse this sentence as being 'objectless', then it is presumably impersonal *se*. But the question is academic, since the verb is singular in either case.

28.7 Other impersonal constructions

28.7.1 *Uno/una* as a pronoun

This is similar to the English 'one' in that it is often an oblique or modest way of saying 'I' or 'we'. A woman uses *una* if the pronoun refers to herself, but *uno* if no self-reference is intended. Its object forms are *lo/la/le*. For many Latin Americans *uno* is the only form used, even by women, but the examples from Vargas Llosa, A. Arrufat and M. Benedetti suggest that this may not be universal. This construction is often interchangeable with impersonal *se*:

Bueno, si no le dicen a una como hay que hacerlo . . . (woman speaking, or *si no se le dice a una*)	Well, if they don't tell one how to do it . . .
. . . como los pájaros que comen las migas que uno les tira (J. Cortázar, Argentina dialogue, woman speaking, or *que se les tiran*)	. . . like birds eating the crumbs one throws to them
Se puso a canturrear, ya que siempre olvidaba lo que uno le decía or *lo que se le decía*	He started humming, since he always forgot what one said to to him
Uno no hace mal a la gente que le es indiferente (E. Sábato, Argentina, dialogue, woman speaking; or *no se hace mal a . . .*)	One doesn't do harm to people one is indifferent to

En ese tiempo una no hablaba de eso con las amigas
(M. Vargas Llosa, Peru, dialogue, woman
speaking; or *no se hablaba de eso*)

In those days one didn't talk
about those things with one's
women friends

Con tal de salirse con la suya, la llevan a una
a la tumba (A. Arrufat, Cuba, dialogue;
mother complaining about her children)

As long as they get their own
way, they'll put you in your
grave

Cuando una se lava las manos en los aeropuertos
quedan bastante más limpias pero arrugaditas
(M. Benedetti, Uruguay, dialogue;
little girl speaking)

When one washes one's hands
at airports they come out
quite a lot cleaner but all
wrinkly

Notes

(i) *Uno* must be used to make an impersonal expression from a verb which already has *se* (since two *ses* cannot occur with the same verb): *en este pueblo* **se** *aburre* **uno** *mucho* 'in this village one gets bored a lot', *se empieza fumando unos cigarrillos y poco a poco* **se** *convierte* **uno** *en un fumador empedernido* 'one starts by smoking a few cigarettes and gradually one becomes a heavy smoker'. See 26.11 for discussion.

(ii) Colloquially *uno/una* may mean 'someone'. See 9.3, note (iv).

28.7.2 Impersonal *tú*

The second-person singular can be used impersonally, much the same as in English. *Uno* or *se* may be used when one is on very formal terms with the hearer:

Yo nunca voy allí porque te cobran más que
en otra parte (le cobran a uno más)
Es increíble, si lo piensas (si uno lo piensa)

I never go there because they
charge you more than elsewhere
It's incredible if you think of it

In theory the second-person singular cannot coexist in the same sentence with impersonal or passive *se*, but it appears in informal speech, just as pronouns are mixed in familiar English: *es que no* **se** *tiene conciencia de que pasa el tiempo cuando* **eres** *joven* (Queen Sofía, interview in *El País*, Spain) 'it's that **one** isn't conscious of time passing when **you**'re young'.

28.7.3 Impersonal third-person plural

As in English, the third-person plural is constantly used impersonally when the speaker does not include him/herself or the hearer in the reference:

Dicen que el ejercicio es bueno para el corazón

They say exercise is good for the
heart

Parece que hablan más despacio en Estados
Unidos que en Inglaterra

It seems that they speak more
slowly in the USA than in
England

29

Ser *and* estar

29.1 General

For the conjugation of *ser* see 13.3.45, and of *estar* see 13.3.21.

Ser and *estar* both translate the English 'to be', but the difference between the two Spanish words is fundamental and sometimes subtle.

Basically *ser* denotes being as opposed to non-being (one says *ser o no ser* 'to be or not to be') or nature or identity, while *estar* denotes condition, state or place: *soy español, pero estoy en Londres* 'I'm Spanish, but I'm in London'; *es callado* 'he's the quiet type', *está callado* 'he's keeping silent (at the moment)'; *puede que sea así* 'perhaps he/she/it is like that', *puede que esté así* 'perhaps that's the condition/situation he/she/it's in'.

It is misleading to imagine that *estar* always refers to temporary states while *ser* indicates permanence. This is usually true, but it is contradicted by sentences like *está muerto* 'he's dead' or by the fact that one can say either *soy calvo* or *estoy calvo* 'I'm bald'. Nor is a characteristic expressed by *ser* necessarily permanent. A brunette can change the colour of her hair and then say *antes era morena pero ahora soy rubia* 'I was a brunette before, but now I'm a blonde', the point being that each colour is nevertheless considered, at the time, to be a characteristic feature of the woman, not a passing state.

Ser is also often used with a few adjectives that indicate what can be thought of as states, e.g. *feliz* 'happy', *desgraciado* 'unhappy', *pobre* 'poor', *rico* 'rich', *consciente* 'conscious'; but these are probably best treated as exceptions: compare *está deprimido* 'he's depressed', *está contento* 'he's happy'/'content', *está animado* 'he's full of life' (*estar* obligatory).

Some adjectives, e.g. *gordo* 'fat', *divorciado* 'divorced', *casado* 'married', may be used with either *ser* or *estar* with hardly any significant change of meaning.

Estar before a noun phrase can normally only denote location: compare *¿es el jefe?* 'is (s)he/are you the boss?' with *¿está el jefe?* 'is the boss **in**?'

Learners constantly forget that *ser* must be used for the location of events as opposed to people or things: *¿dónde es la fiesta?* 'where's the party?', but *¿dónde está el libro?* 'where's the book?'

Ser is used to form the passive: *fue criticado* 'he was criticized'; see Chapter 28. *Estar* is used to form the continuous aspect of verbs: *está hablando* 'he's talking'; see Chapter 15.

29.2 Uses of *ser*

29.2.1 In equational sentences of the sort A = B

Ser is used to link elements in statements of the type 'A = B', where A and B are nouns or pronouns:

París es la capital de Francia	Paris is the French capital
Soy hombre que odia las medias tintas, el agua turbia, el café flojo (M. Vargas Llosa, Peru)	I'm a man who hates things that are not clearly defined, cloudy water, weak coffee
Es médico/abogado/bibliotecario	He's a doctor/lawyer/librarian
Es un estafador/Esto es una estafa	He's a swindler/This is a swindle
Miguel es el jefe	Miguel's the boss
Somos budistas	We're Buddhists
Es mi suegra	She's my mother-in-law
Es la una/Son las doce	It's one o'clock/twelve o'clock
Dos y dos son cuatro	Two and two are four
Ha sido un año/verano frío	It's been a cold year/summer
Esto es lo que me fastidia	This is what I find annoying
Esto es decir las cosas como son	This is calling a spade a spade
Es un tipo simpático	He's a likeable fellow
La confrontación de culturas en el siglo XXI puede ser sangrienta, vaticina Umberto Eco (*El Mundo*, Spain)	Umberto Eco predicts that clashes between cultures in the 21st century may be bloody

Note

Exceptions to this rule in colloquial speech are weather expressions like *está un día magnífico* 'it's a lovely day' (or *es un día . . . /hace un día*), and *estar pez*, e.g. *estoy pez en historia* 'I'm a complete dunce in history' (Spain only?). However, use of *estar* followed by a noun phrase in these weather expressions is not accepted by all speakers: many say only *hace un día magnífico* or *es un día magnífico*, etc. On the other hand, all Spanish informants questioned accepted *está un día que da gusto salir a la calle* 'it's one of those days when you like going out into the streets'. With an adjective *estar* is used in weather expressions: *está lluvioso* 'it's rainy'.

29.2.2 *Ser* with adjectives

Ser is used with adjectives or adjectival phrases referring to identity or nature, i.e. physical, moral and mental characteristics as opposed to conditions or states:

—¿Quién eres? —Soy Carlos	'Who are you?' 'I'm Carlos'
—¿Cómo eres? —Soy, alto, moreno y delgado	'What are you like?' 'I'm tall, dark and slim'
Las mariposas son diferentes de las polillas	Butterflies are different from moths
El marxismo es materialista	Marxism is materialist
El cobre es ideal para los cables	Copper is ideal for cables
Esa chaqueta es bien bonita	That jacket is very nice
Comer demasiado es malo	Eating too much is not good
Así soy de testarudo (G. Cabrera Infante, Cuba, dialogue)	That's how stubborn I am

Note

Hacer is used with many adjectives in statements about the weather: *hace frío/calor* 'it's cold/hot', etc.

29.2.3 *Ser* with certain adjectives apparently denoting states

Ser is normally used with *pobre* 'poor', *feliz* 'happy', *desgraciado* 'unhappy', *inocente* 'innocent', *culpable* 'guilty', *consciente* 'aware', despite the fact that they may be thought of as conditions:

Ahora que el precio del petróleo ha bajado, este país es pobre	Now that the price of oil has gone down, this country is poor
El acusado dijo que era inocente	The accused said he was innocent
Hay muchos que no se sienten culpables aunque lo sean	There are many people who don't feel guilty even though they are
Soy consciente de mis limitaciones	I'm conscious of my limitations
La gente así no suele ser feliz en la vida, señora (M. Vargas Llosa, Peru)	People like that are not usually happy in life, Señora
Pocas veces fue tan feliz como en las horas que precedieron a la entrevista con Bordenave (E. Sábato, Argentina)	He was seldom so happy as during the hours before his interview with Bordenave
Yo sólo quiero que sea feliz (A. Mastretta, dialogue, Mexico)	I only want her to be happy
—Soy tan desgraciada —me dijo (G. Cabrera Infante, Cuba)	'I'm so unhappy,' she told me
Ella me dijo soy pobre, pero honrada, tan sólo bailo para ganarme el pan (Argentinian tango)	She told me I'm poor but honest, I only dance to earn my living

Notes

(i) *Estar rico/pobre/feliz* is sometimes heard in Spain when describing a transitory state, although many Spaniards reject *estar* with these adjectives. Latin Americans frequently use *estar* with *feliz*: *estoy más pobre que una rata* 'I'm as poor as a church mouse' (lit. 'poorer than a rat'), *ahora estoy feliz y contento* 'now I'm happy and satisfied' (*contento* also means 'happy'), *estaban tan felices que me dieron envidia* (A. Mastretta, Mexico) 'they were so happy that they filled me with envy', *acaban de ganar las elecciones y están felices* (A. Bryce Echenique, dialogue, Peru) 'they've just won the elections and they're happy'.

    Estar rico generally means 'to be tasty'/'to taste nice' in Spain see (29.4.4), but not necessarily in Latin America: *Andrés acompañó al padre José que **estaba** riquísimo y lo oyó jurar por la Virgen de Covadonga que no tenía un centavo* (A. Mastretta, Mexico) 'Andrés accompanied Father José, who was extremely rich, and he heard him swear by the Virgin of Covadonga that he didn't have a cent.'

(ii) Peninsular usage normally differentiates *ser consciente* (*de*) 'to be aware/conscious of' and *estar consciente* 'to be conscious' (i.e. not asleep or knocked-out). Latin-American language seems to have retained the older usage: *estamos conscientes de que el debate y la discusión en la libertad son demandas de los jóvenes del país* (Unomásuno, Mexico) 'we're aware that debate and argument in (an atmosphere of) freedom are demands of the young people of the country', *Ballesca estaba consciente de que la antipatía que le profesaba ... podía trocarse en franca enemistad* (S. Galindo, Mexico) 'Ballesca was aware that the dislike she felt towards him ... could turn into open hostility.'

29.2.4 *Ser de*

Ser can be followed by *de* + noun or by *de* + *un* + adjective to denote identity, nature, origin or the material something is made of:

—¿De dónde eres?—De Londres	'Where do you come from?' 'London'
La situación era de risa	The situation was extremely funny
Es de día/noche	It's day/night
—¿De qué es la mesa?—Es de madera	'What's the table made of?' 'Wood'
Soy de carne y hueso como tú	I'm made of flesh and blood like you
Esa chica es de miedo	That girl is tremendous
Era una película de guerra	It was a war film/movie

Oye, que es de verdad	Listen, it's true
Es de un pesado . . .	(S)he's such a bore . . .
Tú eres de prontos impetuosos	You're given to hasty decisions
(C. Martín Gaite, Spain)	

29.2.5 *Ser* and *estar* in impersonal statements

As stated at 29.2.1, *ser* is used before nouns and noun phrases:

Es verdad/mentira/una tontería/una pena/una lata	It's true/a lie/nonsense/a pity/a bore, etc.

Impersonal phrases based on adverbs take *estar*:

Está fatal/bien/mal/estupendamente . . .	It's dreadful/fine/bad/great . . .

With adjectives, *ser* is the usual verb, but there are apparent exceptions:

Es triste/trágico/increíble que haya muerto tan joven	It's sad/tragic/incredible that (s)he died so young
es evidente/obvio que . . .	it's clear that . . .
es necesario/imposible/probable/dudoso, etc.	it's necessary/impossible/probable/doubtful . . .
está visto que . . .	it's evident that . . .
claro está . . .	clearly . . . /of course . . .

Note

Está claro 'it's clear/obvious' is usual in Spain, but *es claro* is common in Latin America: *es claro que, cuando eso acaba . . . debe quedarle a uno un sentimiento de dignidad* (M. Benedetti, Uruguay, dialogue) 'it's obvious that when that sort of thing ends . . . one must be left with a feeling of dignity'.

29.2.6 *Ser* to denote possession

Todo esto es mío, el día de mañana será tuyo	All this is mine; tomorrow it'll be yours
El piso es de mi yerno	The flat/apartment belongs to my son-in-law

29.2.7 *Ser* to denote impressions

Me es/resulta simpática	I find her likeable
Esto me es/resulta molesto	This is uncomfortable for me
Todo le era distinto (A. Carpentier, Cuba)	Everything seemed different to her

29.2.8 *Ser* of events

If 'to be' means 'to be held' or 'to happen' it must be translated by *ser*:

La fiesta es/se celebra en su casa	The party is at his place
Hay un incendio en el edificio pero no sé en qué piso es	There's a fire in the building but I don't know which floor it's on
¿Dónde es la manifestación?	Where is the demonstration?
El entierro sería a las cinco (G. García Márquez, Colombia)	The funeral was to be at five

Use of *estar* may imply a physical object. Compare:

¿Dónde es la conferencia?	Where's the lecture (being held)?
¿Dónde está la conferencia?	Where's the lecture? (i.e. the lecture notes or typescript)

Note

Also *el jarro es/va encima del aparador* 'the vase belongs/goes on top of the sideboard', as opposed to ... *está* ... 'is on ...'.

29.3 Uses of *estar*

29.3.1 *Estar* to describe state as opposed to identity or nature

Estar is used with adjectives that indicate mood, physical condition, temporary physical appearance or other non-characteristic features in general. Note the difference between *es guapa* 'she's good-looking' and *está guapa* 'she's looking good/attractive':

Está más bien triste	He's rather sad
Estuvo enfermo una temporada	He was ill/(US 'sick') for a time
Hoy no estoy muy católico	I don't feel very well today
Estoy segura de lo que te digo	I'm certain of what I'm telling you
Estaba rojo de vergüenza	He was red with shame
El agua que se añada tiene que estar caliente	The water to be added has to be hot
El televisor está estropeado	The television doesn't work
Está parado desde febrero	He's been out of work since February
Estuvo callado todo el tiempo	He was silent all the time
Nueva York está llena de ventanas (J. Aldecoa, Spain)	New York is full of windows

Notes

(i) The pervasive use of the passive with *ser* in written Latin-American Spanish, especially to denote habitual or continuous actions, may produce sentences which require *estar* in Spain. This seems to be particularly frequent in Mexico: *una de las mesas **era** ocupada por el doctor Bernstein* (C. Fuentes, Mexico, Spain *estaba ocupada*) 'one of the tables was occupied by Doctor Bernstein'.
(ii) *Ser hecho de* for *estar hecho de* sounds poetic or archaic: *¡y cuán frágil el barro de que somos hechos!* (R. del Valle-Inclán, Spain, written in the 1890s) 'and how fragile the clay of which we are made!'

29.3.2 *Estar de*

Estar de + adjective or noun to indicate mood, temporary employment or situation:

Está de buen/mal humor	He's in a good/bad mood
Está de camarero en Inglaterra	He's working as a waiter in England
Está de veraneo	He's taking his summer holidays/vacation
Está de viaje	He's travelling
Estamos de charla	We're having a chat
¿Estás de permiso?	Are you on leave?
Están de broma	They're fooling about

Colloquially:

Estás de un guapo subido	You look especially handsome
Estaba de un antipático ...	He was in such a bad mood ...

29.3.3 *Estar con*

Estar followed by *con* + noun:

Está con gripe	He's got the flu

Estaba con una cara malísima	He looked terrible
Estaba con un traje de chaqueta muy bonito	She was wearing a beautiful suit

29.3.4 *Estar* + adverb

Estar followed by an adverb or an adjective used as an adverb:

—¿Cómo estás?—Estoy bien/mal	'How are you?' 'I'm well/not well'
El nombre está mal. Se llamaba Luis José (*Cambio16*, Spain)	The name is wrong. His name was Luis José
Estamos fatal	We're feeling rotten

Adjectives used as adverbs are invariable in form, e.g. *estamos mal* 'we're in trouble'/'we're in a bad way'.

29.3.5 *Estar que*

Está que muerde	He's in an exceedingly bad mood (lit. ' he's ready to bite')
Hoy estás que no hay quien te aguante	You're unbearable today

29.3.6 *Estar* to indicate location

(For *ser* used for the location of events see 29.2.8.)

Segovia está en España	Segovia is in Spain
El cerezo está en el centro	The cherry tree is in the middle
No está (en casa)	He's not at home
Está encima de todo	It's on top of everything

But with nouns that are permanent fixtures or features there is a colloquial tendency to use *ser*:

*¿Dónde **es** la casa de tu amigo?*	Where's your friend's house?
*Aquí **era** la plaza de las Carretas* (J. L. Borges, Argentina, dialogue)	This is where Carretas Square used to be
*Turku **es** en Finlandia, ¿no?*	Turku's in Finland, isn't it?

Estar would also be correct in these three sentences.

29.3.7 *Estar* meaning 'to suit', or 'to fit'

Este traje te está muy bien	This dress suits you
El abrigo te está corto	The coat is too short for you
El puesto de ministro le está grande	The ministerial job is too big for him

For *estar* with *por* and *para* see 34.14.8.

29.3.8 Idiomatic use of *andar*, *encontrarse* and *hallarse* for *estar*

Andar 'to walk' is sometimes used in colloquial language instead of *estar* when the subject is human and the verb is followed by an adjective or participle. This is only possible when the phrase refers to some kind of activity or to dress or attitude. One could not say **ando calvo* for *estoy calvo* 'I'm bald':

Miguel dice que andan recelosos y no le falta razón (M. Delibes, Spain, dialogue)	Miguel says they're suspicious, and he's right
Andan muy atareados estos días	They've got a lot of work these days

Andar is also sometimes used colloquially (at least in Spain) to refer to objects that can easily move about, e.g. *Dios sabe dónde andarán mis gafas* 'God knows where my glasses have got to', *¿dónde anda el coche, tú?* (M. Delibes, Spain, dialogue) 'hey, whereabouts is the car?'

Encontrarse can mean the same as *estar*: *¿dónde se encuentra el museo?* 'where's the museum?', *¿qué tal te encuentras?* 'how are you'/'how do you feel?', *no me encuentro con fuerzas para seguir* 'I'm not strong enough to go on'. *Hallarse* is used in formal or literary language: *me hallo enfermo y fatigado* 'I'm feeling ill and tired'.

29.4 *Ser or estar?*

29.4.1 *Ser* and *estar* more or less interchangeable

(a) With words indicating marital status:

Sale con una chica que es/está divorciada	He's going out with a girl who's divorced
Tiene que mantener a su madre que es/está viuda	He has to keep his widowed mother
Le pregunté si era/estaba casado	I asked him whether he was married
Pero si es casado debe estar cenando en casa a estas horas (M. Puig, Argentina, dialogue)	But if he's married (i.e. 'a married man') he must be at home having his supper at this time of day

The tendency is to use *ser* for a stranger, although *estar* is not wrong. One would usually ask *¿es usted casado?* 'are you married?', but two friends meeting again after some time would say *¿estás casado?* or *¿todavía estás soltero?* 'are you married?' or 'are you still single?'

(b) With *calvo, gordo* and *delgado*, *estar* is always used when there has been a change of state. Elsewhere the two verbs are practically interchangeable except in generalizations, when *ser* is required:

¡Mujer, pero qué delgada estás!	Good heavens, haven't you lost weight!
*Siempre **ha sido** calvo/gordo, pero ahora **está** más calvo/gordo que nunca*	He's always been bald/thin but now he's balder/thinner than ever
Dentro de cien años todos seremos calvos (L. Rafael Sánchez, dialogue, Puerto Rico)	We'll all be bald in a hundred years
Ayer conocí a la novia de mi primo. Parece simpática pero está/es muy delgada	Yesterday I met my cousin's girlfriend. She seems nice but she's very thin
*Las mujeres de esa tribu **son** muy gordas* (generalization)	The women of that tribe are very fat

(c) With adjectives describing social manner when 'to be' = 'to behave':

Estuvo/Fue muy cortés conmigo	She behaved very courteously towards me
Siempre está/es cariñosa	She's always affectionate
Tienes que estar/ser más amable con él	You must be kinder to him

But *hoy has **sido** bueno* 'you've behaved well today' because *estar bueno* means 'tasty', 'appetising' and therefore also sexually attractive. Note, however

¡Hoy has estado bueno!	You had a good day today! (ironical, i.e. 'I don't think . . . ')

Estar cannot be used for general statements about behaviour: *antiguamente los ingleses **eran** muy corteses* 'formerly the English were very courteous'.

(d) With adjectives applied to events and with *vida* and *situación*:

La conferencia fue/estuvo muy interesante	The lecture was very interesting

La situación es/está caótica	The situation is chaotic
La fiesta fue/estuvo muy animada	The party was very lively
La vida es/está cara hoy día	Life is expensive nowadays

But *la vida es difícil/maravillosa/amarga* 'life is difficult/wonderful/bitter' can only be general comments on life. *La vida está difícil* means 'life is difficult **now**'.

(e) With adjectives referring to weather applied to *día* and *tiempo*:

El día es/está bueno	The weather is nice today
Es/Está un tiempo soleado, agradable	The weather is sunny and pleasant

(but see 29.2.1, note (i) for *estar* before noun phrases)

29.4.2 *Ser* and *estar* with prices and quantities

*¿Cuánto/A cuánto/A cómo **son** las uvas?*	How much are the grapes?
Son a cincuenta pesetas el kilo	Fifty pesetas a kilo
¿Cuánto (es lo que) le debo?	How much do I owe you?
¿Cuántos somos hoy para comer?	How many are we for lunch today?
Somos doce en mi familia	There are twelve of us in my family
Los sobrevivientes fueron pocos	Few people survived

Also:

*¿A cuánto/A cómo **están** las uvas?*	How much are the grapes (at this moment)?
*¿A cuánto/A cómo **están** esas acciones?*	What's the price of those shares?

29.4.3 *Estar* implying impression or change of condition

When *estar* denotes impression, sensation or appearance, it often calls for translation by a special verb in English, e.g. 'to look', 'to taste', 'to feel' or 'to get'. Use of *estar* rather than *ser* often shows there has been a change of condition. Compare:

Es muy guapa	She's very good-looking
Está muy guapa	She's looking very attractive
Este niño es muy alto	This child is very tall
Este niño está muy alto	This child has grown very tall
¡Qué fuerte eres!	How strong you are!/Aren't you strong!
Qué fuerte estás!	How strong you are! (these days)
Este sillón es ya viejo	This armchair is old
Este sillón está ya viejo	This armchair is getting old
*El pollo es riquísimo**	[The] chicken is very good
El pollo está riquísimo	The chicken tastes delicious
*El café es horrible**	(The) coffee is horrible
El café está horrible	The coffee tastes horrible
Tráelo como sea	Bring it any way you can
Tráelo como esté	Bring it as it is
Eres muy española	You're very Spanish
Estás muy española	You're looking very Spanish (or behaving like a typical Spanish woman)

The examples marked with an asterisk are ambiguous: *el pollo es riquísimo* is either a general statement about chicken or it could mean 'the chicken (uncooked) is very good quality'. *Estar* could only mean 'to taste'.

Note

Tú eres/Tú estás viejo para estas cosas 'you're old/getting old for these things' (there is a slight difference of meaning in both languages). But one says *tú eres demasiado joven para estas cosas.*

29.4.4 *Ser* and *estar* involving change of meaning

There are some words whose meaning is radically affected by choice of *ser* or *estar*. The following list is not exhaustive:

ser aburrido	boring	*estar aburrido*	to be bored
ser atento	courteous	*estar atento*	attentive
ser bueno	good	*estar bueno*	tasty
ser cansado	tiresome	*estar cansado*	tired
ser católico	catholic	*no estar católico*	unwell
ser decidido	resolute	*estar decidido*	decided
ser consciente	aware	*estar consciente*	conscious (not asleep or knocked out)
ser despierto	sharp/alert	*estar despierto*	awake
ser un enfermo	be an invalid	*estar enfermo*	be ill
ser interesado	self-seeking	*estar interesado*	interested
ser listo	clever	*estar listo*	to be ready
ser (un) loco	scatterbrained	*estar loco*	mad
ser malo	bad	*estar malo*	ill
ser negro	black	*estar negro*	very irritated
ser orgulloso	proud (pejorative)	*estar orgulloso*	proud (of something/ someone)
ser rico	rich	*estar rico*	delicious
ser torpe	slow-witted	*estar torpe*	clumsy, moving with difficulty
ser verde	green/smutty	*estar verde*	unripe
ser violento	violent/ embarrassing	*estar violento*	embarrassed
ser vivo (*ser un vivo*	sharp/alert be unscrupulous)	*estar vivo*	alive

30

Existential sentences

30.1 General

'Existential sentences' are sentences that refer to the existence of things: 'there's bread', 'there's no time', 'there is a planet called Pluto', 'God exists'/'there is a God', etc. In Spanish such sentences usually involve the special verb *haber* (present indicative *hay*), which means 'there is/are'. However, the picture is complicated for foreign students because of the existence of another verb, *estar*, which often means 'to be located'/'to be there'.

30.2 *Haber (hay)*

For the conjugation of *haber* see 13.3.22.

30.2.1 Basic uses

Haber has two uses: **(a)** as an auxiliary used to form perfect tenses, e.g. *han dicho* 'they've said' (discussed at 14.8); **(b)** as a verb meaning 'there is'/'there are', cf. French *il y a*, German *es gibt*.

In the latter sense the verb occurs only in the third-person singular (see notes (i) and (ii) for popular or colloquial exceptions). It is conjugated exactly as the third-person singular of the auxiliary *haber*, except that its present indicative is *hay*, not *ha*. In this chapter, *haber* in the sense of 'there is/are' is referred to as '*hay*' to avoid confusion with the auxiliary verb.

Hay can occur in any non-continuous tense with the meanings 'there is/are/were/will be/have been', etc. However, it does not mean ' . . . is/are/ were **there**' = *está/están/estaban* (*ahí/allí*). The relationship between *hay* and *estar* is discussed further at 30.3. Examples of *hay*:

Había muchas chicas de mi edad y más jóvenes (J. Marías, Spain)	There were many girls of my age and younger
Hay casos peores, hay quienes no pueden volver del exilio (A. Mastretta, Mexico)	There are worse cases, there are people who can't return from exile
—*¿Qué hay?* —*Lo que hay es que estoy harto*	'What's happening/How're things?' 'I'm fed up – that's what's happening!'
Hubo muchas noches que salíamos a recorrer su barrio (G. Cabrera Infante, Cuba, dialogue)	There were many nights when we went out for a walk round her part of town
¿Qué hubo?/¿Quiubo? (Colombia and surrounding areas only)	How're things?
había una vez . . ./érase una vez . . . (*érase* is here a grammatically anomalous set formula)	once upon a time there was . . .

Notes

(i) *Hay* must not be made plural: **había** *tres chicas* 'there were three girls', not **habían tres chicas*; **hubo** *clases de italiano el año pasado* 'there were Italian classes last year', not **hubieron clases de italiano* ... In Castilian-speaking Spain the plural construction is stigmatized as uneducated, but it is a common feature of everyday Castilian spoken in Catalonia, even among educated speakers. In Latin America it is universally common in everyday, even educated speech, and it quite frequently appears in informal writing, e.g. in letters and newspapers; but it is not accepted in careful styles.
(ii) It is used only in the third person: *hay cinco* 'there are five', but **somos** *cinco* 'there are five **of us**', *ustedes* **son** *cinco* 'there are five **of you**', also *son cinco* 'there are five **of them**'.

A first-person plural construction *?habemos cinco* 'there are five of us' (note not the usual form *hemos*) occurs in rustic speech in Spain for the more usual *somos cinco* and is rather more prevalent in popular speech in Latin America, although it is rejected by educated speakers.
(iii) *Hay* is not followed by the definite article, except when it means 'to exist', in which case *existir* is more commonly used: *ha venido el médico* (not **hay el médico*) 'there's the doctor! (i.e. he's arrived)', but *también hay/existe la posibilidad de* ... 'the possibility also exists of ...' Constructions like *?hay el cartero* for *ha venido el cartero* 'the postman's there'/'the postman's come' are typical Catalanisms.
(iv) For *hay que* 'it is necessary to' see 21.4.2.

30.2.2 Direct object pronouns and *hay*

Hay functions like an impersonal transitive verb. Since transitive verbs in Spanish must normally have a direct object, an object pronoun is often used to indicate the presence of a deleted noun. However, if this direct object pronoun echoes or resumes a noun already present in the sentence, it can usually optionally be omitted – as in all but the last of these examples:

*Parece que no hay huevos, pero si (**los**) hay, tráelos* (the *los* is not obligatory)	If looks like there are no eggs, but if there are, bring them
*Cada vez que espero una respuesta me horroriza la idea de que no **la** haya* (J. Marías, Spain, dialogue; the *la* is deletable at a pinch)	Every time I expect a reply I'm horrified by the idea that there may not be one
No hubo presiones, ni las hay, ni las habrá (Felipe González in *El País*; again, the *las* could be omitted)	There wasn't any pressure, there isn't any and there won't be
Es difícil encontrar las palabras, si las hay, para expresar un sentimiento tal como lo experimentamos (interview in *Granma*, Cuba; the *las* could be deleted)	In circumstances like these it is difficult to find words-if they exist-to express a sentiment such as we are experiencing
El cochero quiso asegurarse de que no había ningún error. No lo había (G. García Márquez, Colombia; the *lo* could be deleted)	The coach driver sought reassurance that there was no mistake. There wasn't
Incluso los hay que tienen la desfachatez de retratarse en sus propios anuncios (E. Lynch, Argentina; the *los* is required because it does not echo a noun present in the sentence)	There are even some people who have the nerve to put portraits of themselves in their own advertisements

The pronoun is not used when answering questions about the existence of non-countable things (bread, water, justice, etc.): *—¿Hay azúcar? —Sí, hay* '"Is there any sugar?" "Yes, there is"', *—¿Hay mucho que hacer? —Sí hay, sí.* '"Is there a lot to do?" "Yes, there is."' Compare this reference to countable items: *—¿Hay problemas? —Los hay y muchos* '"Are there any problems?" "There are. Plenty".' See 7.4 for resumptive pronoun with *ser, estar, parecer*.

30.3 *Hay* and *estar* in existential sentences

Estar has many other uses, discussed in detail in Chapter 29.

As far as its relationship with *hay* is concerned, *está* basically means ' . . . is **there**' and *hay* means 'there **is/are** . . . '. In other words, *hay* states that something exists; *estar* indicates that it is located somewhere. In certain cases the meanings overlap, as in —*¿El Sr. Ramírez?. —No está. —¿Y su mujer? —No está nadie/No hay nadie* '"Mr Ramírez?" "He's not in." "And his wife?" "There's no one in."' However, if one enters an empty building, one shouts *¿hay alguien?* 'is there anyone around?', and might comment *no hay nadie* 'there's no one there/here'.

30.3.1 Uses of *estar* and *hay* with defined nouns

Nouns accompanied by the definite article, by a possessive adjective or by a demonstrative (*ese, este, aquel*) normally require *estar*. *Hay* used with such noun phrases is restricted in its meaning to 'exists', as explained at 30.2.1 note (iii). *Estar* presupposes the subject exists and gives information about its location or availability:

*Hay **un** gerente en la compañía*	There's a manager in the company (i.e. 'a manager exists')
*Está **el** gerente*	The manager's there/here/in
No hay dinero	There's no money (anywhere)
*No está **el** dinero/**El** dinero no está*	The money isn't here/there
No hay	There isn't any (anywhere)
No está	(S)he/it isn't in/here/there/at home
¿Hay tortilla española?	Do you have Spanish omelette/(US 'omelet')?
*¿Está **la** tortilla española?*	Is the Spanish omelette/omelet on the list?/Is the Spanish omelette ready?
*Por un lado hay **las** grandes fiestas, y por el otro, **las** distracciones institucionales (Cambio16*, Spain; *= existen)*	On the one hand there are the major fiestas, and on the other hand institutionalized amusements
—¿Qué hay en este pueblo? —Hay la iglesia . . .[1]	'What is there in this village?' 'There's the church . . .'
—¿Había alguien? —Estaban ellos y sus padres (does not mean *existían*)	'Was there anyone there?' 'They and their parents were there'
*Al ascensor sólo tienen acceso los seres humanos, es decir no se pueden subir ni perros ni cosas . . . para eso **está** el montacargas* (E. Arenas, Spain, dialogue)	Only people have access to the lifts/ elevators, in other words dogs and things can't be taken up in them . . . the service lift is there for that
Las mujeres no estaban para hablar de temas que no fueran domésticos (A. Mastretta, Mexico)	Women weren't there to discuss non-domestic subjects (i.e. they existed, but that wasn't what they were there for)
Las columnas del periodismo no están para que el redactor desahogue sus humores (*Libro de estilo de El País*, Spain)	In journalism, columns aren't there for the writer to air his/her grievances

In this last example, *no hay columnas en el periodismo para que . . .* would have meant 'there are no columns in journalism for writers to air their grievances'. This is not true: columns **exist**, but they are not **there** for airing grievances.

---

[1] *Haber* is possible here with the definite article because it answers the question 'what things exist?' However, use of *haber* in this sentence may not be acceptable to Latin Americans.

Note

In relative clauses, *hay* and *estar* seem to be interchangeable: *reconocí al señor que* **estaba/había** *en la puerta* 'I recognized the gentleman who was at the door', *tropecé con la silla que* **estaba/había** *en el dormitorio* 'I tripped over the chair that was in the bedroom', . . . *del espejo que había sobre la chimenea* (C. Martín Gaite, Spain; *estaba* possible) '. . . from the mirror hanging over the fireplace', *el sitio estratégico es la mesa que* **hay** *al lado de la cristalera que da a la calle* (E. Arenas, Spain, dialogue; *está* possible) 'the strategic place is the table that's next to the window looking out on the street'.

30.3.2 *Estar* for mobile things

Estar implies that a thing is located in a specific spot, *hay* merely that it exists. For this reason, words like 'problem', 'question', 'atmosphere', 'accident' can only appear with *hay* since they are not locatable or mobile things:

Ha **habido** *un accidente*	There's been an accident
Ha **habido** *aquí tres presidentes*	There have been three presidents here/We've had three presidents (in this country)
Han **estado** *aquí tres presidentes*	Three presidents have been here/have visited here

30.3.3 *Hay* used before partitive nouns and numbers

Before partitive nouns (quantities, parts of a whole), only *hay* can be used:

Hay leche	There's (some) milk
Había gente	There were (some) people

Since *hay* can be used only in the third person (see 30.2.1, note ii), *ser* or *estar* must be used for other persons. This construction occurs with numbers:

Había *cuarenta personas en la fiesta*	There were forty people at the party
Éramos *cuarenta en la fiesta*	There were forty of us at the party
Vais (Lat. Am. *van*) *a* **ser** *cuarenta en la fiesta*	There will be forty of you at the party
Estábamos *más de quince personas encerradas en el ascensor*	There were more than fifteen of us shut in the lift

Very popular speech sometimes uses *haber* in the first or second persons: see 30.2.1 note (ii).

30.4 Miscellaneous English sentences whose translation requires *hay* or *estar*

If there hadn't been a doctor (available), he'd have died	*Si no hubiera habido (un) médico, él habría muerto/De no haber habido (un) médico, él habría muerto*
If the doctor hadn't been **there**, he'd have died	*Si no hubiera* **estado** *el médico, él habría muerto*
There's no such thing as fairies	*Las hadas no existen/No hay hadas/No existen las hadas*
There have always been economic crises	*Siempre ha habido crisis económicas*

Horchata available/*Horchata*[2] sold here	*Hay horchata*
There are rattlesnakes in Mexico	*Hay serpientes de cascabel*[3] *en México*
There's a book on the table	*Hay un libro encima de la mesa*
The book isn't there any more	*El libro ya no está ahí*

---

[2] A refreshing chilled drink made from crushed tiger nuts (*chufas*).
[3] *Yarará, crótalo* and other local words are used for rattlesnake in Latin America.

31

Adverbs

31.1 General

Spanish adverbials (i.e. adverbs and adverb phrases) can be divided into two large classes: (1) invariable words and phrases, and (2) adverbs formed from adjectives by adding the suffix -*mente* to an adjective. Examples of the first type are *mal* 'badly', *ayer* 'yesterday', *adrede* (familiar *aposta*) 'on purpose', *en serio* 'seriously' (i.e. not jokingly). Examples of the latter are *tranquilamente* 'tranquilly', *violentamente* 'violently', *naturalmente* 'naturally'. Although the suffix -*mente* is very productive there are severe and apparently arbitrary constraints on its use.

A few adjectives also function as adverbs: *hablaban fuerte* 'they were talking loudly'; see 31.3.3. More common in Spanish than in English is the use of an adjective where English uses an adverb: *el rey los recibió agradecido* 'the king received them gratefully', *vivían felices* 'they lived happily'; see 31.3.4.

31.2 Adverbs in *-mente*

Adverbs formed by adding -*mente* to an adjective are very numerous:

. . . *porque lo del médico había sido sencillamente horrible* (A. Grandes, Spain)	. . . because the business with the doctor had been simply dreadful
Sabía exactamente cómo quería sus estanterías (J. Marías, Spain)	He knew exactly how he wanted his shelving
Pero en el futuro no estamos solamente vos y yo (M. Benedetti, Uruguay, dialogue; Spain . . . *tú y yo*)	But it won't be just you and me in the future
. . . *muy inteligente, buen abogado, pero sumamente peligroso* (G. García Márquez, Colombia, dialogue)	. . . very intelligent, a good lawyer, but extremely dangerous

31.2.1 Formation

If the adjective has a separate feminine form, -*mente* is added to it. Otherwise it is added to the invariable singular form:

Masculine singular	Feminine singular	Adverbial form	
absoluto	*absoluta*	*absolutamente*	absolutely
cansado	*cansada*	*cansadamente*	in a tired way
evidente	*evidente*	*evidentemente*	evidently
leal	*leal*	*lealmente*	loyally
tenaz	*tenaz*	*tenazmente*	tenaciously

31.2.2 Accent rules for adverbs in *-mente*

The original stress should be preserved in pronunciation. As a result, adjectives that are irregularly stressed form adverbs in *-mente* that have two stress accents, one on the vowel that carries the written accent, another on the penultimate syllable: *crítico/críticamente* 'critical'/'critically', *electrónico/ electrónicamente* 'electronic'/'electronically', *hábil/hábilmente* 'skilful'/'skilfully', *sarcástico/sarcástica-mente* 'sarcastically'. Pronunciation of such words with a single penultimate stress should be avoided.

31.2.3 Consecutive adverbs in *-mente*

If more than one adverb in *-mente* is joined by a conjunction (e.g. *y, ni, pero*, etc.), *-mente* is dropped from all but the last:

Se lo dije sincera y llanamente	I told him sincerely and plainly
. . . lo que tradicional y ridículamente se ha considerado un comportamiento femenino (J. Marías, Spain)	. . . what has traditionally and ridiculously been considered feminine behaviour
Esto presenta un problema político mayor, y ni intelectual, ni política, ni económicamente se puede mantener tal postura (El País, Spain)	This presents a major political problem, and neither intellectually, nor politically nor economically can such a position be sustained
Tuvo la desvergüenza de decirme que era poco serio, que ni social ni literariamente era interesante (S. Pitol, Mexico, dialogue)	She had the nerve to tell me that it wasn't serious, that it was neither socially nor artistically (lit. 'literarily') interesting

This is an important rule of written Spanish, although rarely applied in spontaneous speech. But it is not normal when no conjunction is present: *y así, separados por el muro de vidrio, habíamos vivido ansiosamente, melancólicamente* (E. Sábato, Argentina) 'and thus, separated by the wall of glass, we had lived anxiously, melancholically'.

31.2.4 Limits on the use of the suffix *-mente*

-mente cannot be added to all adjectives, although there is no accounting for experiments, as when Julio Cortázar coins *pelirrojamente* 'red-hairedly' in his novel *Rayuela*.

In general, although with important exceptions (cf. *difícil/ difícilmente* 'difficult'/'with difficulty', *lleno* 'full', but 'fully' = *plenamente*; *inclusive* 'including'[1]), the set of Spanish adjectives that take *-mente* corresponds to the set of English adjectives that allow the adverbial suffix *-ly*. These are chiefly adverbs of manner or behaviour, so the following do **not** take *-mente* (at least in normal styles):

(a) Adjectives denoting physical appearance: *rojo* 'red', *negro* 'black', *calvo* 'bald', *gordo* 'fat', *cojo* 'lame', *viejo* 'old'/'aged', etc.

(b) Adjectives denoting origin, nationality, religion: *cordobés* 'Cordoban', *argentino* 'Argentinian', *protestante* 'Protestant', *musulmán* 'Muslim', etc. Two

---

[1] *Te mando las revistas el último número inclusive* (*inclusive* follows the noun) 'I'm sending you the magazines, including the latest number'; *inclusivamente* is hardly ever used. For the Latin-American use of *inclusive* for *incluso* 'even', as in 'he even gave me some money', see 31.7.4.

exceptions are *católicamente* and *cristianamente*: *tienes que educar a tus hijos católi-camente* 'you must bring up your children in the Catholic manner'.

(c) Ordinal numbers, e.g. *segundo* 'second', *quinto* 'fifth', *vigésimo* 'twentieth'. Exceptions: *primeramente* 'chiefly'/'firstly' and *últimamente* 'lately'/'lastly'. *En segundo lugar* = 'secondly'.

(d) Some adjectives, for no obvious reason, e.g. *vacío* 'empty', *lleno* 'full' (*plena-mente* = 'fully'), *importante* 'important', and most adjectives in *-ón*, cf. *mandón* 'bossy', *peleón* 'aggressive'/'prone to start fights'.

(e) Many verbal participles which cannot, by virtue of their meaning, function as adverbs, e.g. *roto* 'broken', which has no corresponding adverb *rotamente* ? 'brokenly'.

However, some Spanish participles take *-mente*: the following are some of the many examples. They all refer to behaviour or manner:

abatido: abatidamente downcast	*exagerado: exageradamente*
abierto: abiertamente open(ly)	exaggerated(ly)
acentuado: acentuadamente marked(ly)	*irritado: irritadamente* irritated(ly)
atrevido: atrevidamente daring(ly)	*perdido:* ('lost') *perdidamente*
debido: debidamente due/duly	hopeless(ly) (e.g. in love)
decidido: decididamente decided(ly)	*reiterado: reiteradamente* repeated(ly)
deliberado: deliberadamente deliberate(ly)	*resuelto: resueltamente* resolute(ly)
equivocado: equivocadamente mistaken(ly)	

31.2.5 Popular forms

Popular forms like *buenamente* and *malamente* are occasionally heard in familiar speech with specialized meanings:

Lo terminamos, pero malamente	We finished it, but it was rushed
Hazlo buenamente cuando puedas	Do it in your own time when you can

The forms ?*mayormente* 'especially' (very common in Latin America), *otramente* 'otherwise' (= *de otra manera*) and ?*mismamente*, cf. ?*mismamente el cura* 'the priest himself', are considered substandard or popular.

31.2.6 Equivalents of adverbs in *-mente*

The existence of a derived adverb in *-mente* does not mean that the adjective cannot itself function as an adverb or that there does not exist an adverbial phrase with or without the same meaning. Constant reading and dictionary work are the only solution to this problem, e.g.:

en vano/vanamente	in vain
de inmediato/inmediatamente	immediately
directo/directamente	directly
Siempre obra locamente/a lo loco	He always acts wildly/in a mad fashion

But only *locamente* is used as an intensifier: *no le sería difícil, con el tiempo, ena-morarse locamente de él* (L. Esquivel, Mexico) 'given time, she wouldn't find it difficult to fall madly in love with him'.

31.2.7 Too many adverbs in *-mente*

It is bad style to include too many adverbs in *-mente* in a single paragraph: the final syllables set off ugly rhymes. The barbarous sentence *evidentemente, todas las* *lenguas evolucionan constantemente, y sería totalmente absurdo pretender detener arbi-trariamente su crecimiento* makes passable English in literal translation – 'clearly, all languages evolve constantly, and it would be totally absurd to attempt to arrest their growth arbitrarily' – but must be recast in Spanish along the lines of *es evidente que todas las lenguas están en constante evolución, y sería totalmente absurdo pretender detener de manera arbitraria su crecimiento.*

A form in *-mente* can usually be replaced by *con* + an abstract noun or by some other adverbial phrase, e.g. *alegremente = con alegría* or *de un modo* (or *manera*) *ale-gre, rabiosamente = con rabia* or *de un modo rabioso, ferozmente = con ferocidad* or *de un modo feroz.* The sentence *vivían de un modo tranquilo, feliz y libre* 'they lived qui-etly, happy and free' is much better Spanish than *vivían tranquila, feliz y libre-mente.* For a selection of adverbial phrases, see 31.3.2.

31.2.8 *-ísimamente*

The suffix *-ísimo* (see 4.9) may be added (judiciously) to adverbs of manner and time. The result is very emphatic:

claramente	*clarísimamente*	extremely clearly
intensamente	*intensísimamente*	extremely intensely
recientemente	*recientísimamente*	extremely recently
tiernamente	*tiernísimamente*	extremely tenderly
urgentemente	*urgentísimamente*	extremely urgently

More common alternatives exist, e.g. *con gran claridad, con enorme intensidad, con gran urgencia,* etc.

Note

Lejos and cerca can also have *-ísimo* added to them: *lejísimos* (note the final s) and *cerquísima.* Col-loquially *lejotes* can be used to denote uncomfortable distance, often preceded by *allá/allí*: *esa casa está allí lejotes* 'that house is miles off/away'.

31.2.9 Adverbs in *-mente* to mean 'from a . . . point of view'

Adverbs in *-mente* are freely used to indicate point of view. This construction is much favoured in journalistic styles:

Económicamente, este país va a la ruina	Economically, this country is on the road to ruin
Personalmente, lo dudo	Personally, I doubt it
Editorialmente, no lo apruebo	From a publishing point , view of I don't approve of it

31.3 Other adverbs of manner

31.3.1 General

Adverbs of manner include words like *bien* 'well', *mal* 'badly', *despacio* 'slowly', *pronto* 'quickly', *adrede/aposta* 'on purpose', *igual* 'the same', as well as most of the adverbs formed with *-mente*, discussed earlier. There are regional differ-ences of usage, e.g. *deprisa* 'quickly' in Spain and *aprisa* in Latin America. The latter is considered popular or substandard in Spain: *quiero ir muy aprisa* (A. Mastretta, Mexico, dialogue, Spain *deprisa*) 'I want to go very fast'.

There are countless adverbial phrases: *a propósito* 'deliberately', *en balde* 'in vain', *a contrapelo* 'unwillingly', *en serio* 'seriously'. A selection appears at 31.3.2. Adverbs of manner can modify verbs, participles, adjectives or other adverbs:

Hable despacio	Speak slowly
Lo quieren así	They want it that way
Esto está mal hecho	This is badly made/This is the wrong thing to do
Está bien	It/He/She's OK/You're OK
Me da igual	It's all the same to me
Aquí estamos mejor/peor	We're better/worse (off) here
Infórmese gratis (advertisement Spain)	Get information free

A few can even modify nouns:

*Hace mucho tiempo que una cosa **así** no ocurría en la ONU* (El País, Spain)	It has been a long time since something like this happened in the UN
*¿No te das cuenta que una mujer **así** no puede ser aristócrata?* (S. Vodanovic, Chile, dialogue)	Don't you realize that a woman like that can't be an aristocrat?
una niña bien	a 'nice' girl/a girl from a 'respectable' family (pejorative)
Dos coñacs con hielo, y dos cafés igual	Two cognacs with ice, and two coffees the same way

Bien and *así de* can intensify adjectives:

Es bien lista (see 31.4.2)	She's pretty clever
Bien bueno que está, ¿eh?	It tastes great!
¿Adónde vas así de guapa? or *. . . vas tan guapa*	Where are you off to looking so pretty?

31.3.2 Adverbial phrases of manner

These are numerous, and they often provide an elegant alternative to an unwieldy adverb in *-mente*. The following is a small sample:

a buen paso at a smart pace
a caballo on horseback
a ciegas in the dark
a conciencia conscientiously
El agua sale a chorros The water is pouring out
a destiempo inopportunely
entrar a empujones to push one's way in
a escondidas secretly/clandestinely
a fuego lento on a low flame
a hurtadillas by stealth
al alimón together by turns/jointly
a la carrera at full speed
a la fuerza by force/under obligation
a la ligera hastily/without proper thought
a las claras clearly (i.e. without beating about the bush)
(llorar) a lágrima viva to shed floods of tears
a mano by hand

a máquina machine-made/by machine
a matacaballo at breakneck speed
a medias by halves
a oscuras in the dark
a quemarropa point-blank
a regañadientes reluctantly/unwillingly
a sabiendas de que . . . fully aware that . . .
a tiempo in time (e.g. for the train)
a tientas by touch/by feel
a traición treacherously
al raso in the open/out of doors
al sereno in the open/'under the stars'
bajo cuerda on the sly/in an underhand way
con delirio/locura madly/passionately
con frecuencia/a menudo frequently
de balde free (= without paying, i.e. gratis)
de continuo continuously
de corrido at one go/straight off

de costumbre usually	*de verdad* really / genuinely
de golpe suddenly	*en balde* in vain / pointlessly
de improviso unexpectedly	*en cambio* on the other hand
(saberse/aprenderse) de memoria (learn) by heart	*en confianza* confidentially
de ordinario normally / usually	*en cueros (vivos)/en pelota* stark naked
de puntillas on tiptoe	*en el acto* on the spot
de rodillas kneeling	*en lo sucesivo* from now on / hereafter
de seguro for certain / sure	*(hablar) por los codos* to talk too much
de sobra in excess / more than enough	(lit. 'through the elbows')
(leer algo) de un tirón to read something in one sitting / straight through	*sin empacho* coolly / unconcernedly
	sin reserva unreservedly
	sin ton ni son willy-nilly / thoughtlessly

31.3.3 Adjectives and participles as adverbs of manner

The masculine singular of a few adjectives may be used as an adverb, but only in certain phrases, e.g. *hablar claro* 'to speak clearly' but only *expresarse claramente/con claridad* 'to express oneself clearly':

Hablan alto/bajo	They talk loudly / softly
Lo hemos comprado barato/caro	We've bought it cheap / dear
El tren va directo a Tuy	The train goes direct to Tuy
Hay que tirar fuerte	You have to pull hard
Se me apiló firme (J. Cortázar, Argentina, dialogue; Spain: *se me arrimó*)	He pushed himself tight up against me
Anda rápido que vamos a llegar tarde (see 31.3.6 for *rápido*)	Walk fast or we'll arrive late
Respiraba hondo como si le costara trabajo	He was breathing deeply, as if with difficulty
Me sienta fatal	It doesn't suit me / agree with me at all
Él no juega limpio	He doesn't play fair
Me casé enamorada (J. Madrid, Spain, dialogue)	I was in love when I married

The following are typical of familiar speech and are not to everyone's taste:

Lo hemos pasado estupendo/fantástico/bárbaro	We had a tremendous / fantastic time
La chaqueta le sienta bárbaro a Mariluz	The jacket looks terrific on Mariluz
Eso se hace fácil	That's dead easy / That's a cinch

Note

Colloquial Latin American Spanish provides numerous examples unacceptable in Spain but admitted in informal styles in the Americas: *qué lindo canta* 'doesn't (s)he sing prettily', *pero toca muy bonito* 'but (s)he plays really well' (both examples from Kany, 1970, 53–5) . . . *un gran número de mexicanos que piensan distinto que el PRI* (*Excelsior*, Mexico) ' . . . a large number of Mexicans who think differently from the PRI', *inicialmente pensé que podíamos haber conseguido unos dólares fácil, sin problemas para la revolución* (*Vindicación de Cuba*, Cuba) 'initially I thought we could easily have got a few dollars, without any problems for the Revolution', *¡qué bonito baila!* (A. Mastretta, Mexico; Spain *¡qué bien baila!*) 'how beautifully she dances!'

31.3.4 Adjectives used to modify both subject and verb

Very common in Spanish is the use of an adjective in combination with a verb to produce an effect more easily created by an adverb in English. This is not a true adverbial use of the adjective, since the adjective agrees with the number and gender of the subject. This construction is restricted in the spoken language to a limited range of verbs and adjectives. The effect is to make the adjective act both as an adverb and an adjective, i.e. to make it modify both the verb and the subject of the verb. Sometimes the construction is obligatory: *las niñas cansadas dormían* 'the tired girls were sleeping' is not the same as *las niñas dormían cansadas*, which is most nearly translated as 'the girls were tired and asleep' or 'sleeping in their tiredness'. But one could hardly say ?*las niñas dormían cansadamente* 'the girls were sleeping tiredly' which modifies the verb but not its subject!

Obviously, this construction is confined to those adjectives that can equally well modify a noun or a verb, e.g. *inocente* 'innocent', *confuso* 'confused', *feliz* 'happy', but not adjectives like *harapiento* 'ragged' or *azul* 'blue', which can hardly describe an action:

Sonrió tranquila (J. Marsé, Spain)	She smiled gently
Se desvistió mientras se miraba distraído en el espejo del armario (J. Cortázar, Argentina; or *distraídamente*)	He got undressed as he gazed absent-mindedly at himself in the wardrobe mirror
Las mujeres protestaban indignadas (or *indignadamente*)	The women were protesting indignantly
Las máquinas de escribir tecleaban incansables (or *incansablemente*)	The typewriters were clattering tirelessly
Javier miraba atónito desde el vagón vacío (M. Benedetti, Uruguay)	Javier gazed in surprise from the empty carriage
Me extendió un papel que leí asombrado (A. Bryce Echenique, Peru; same as . . . *leí con asombro*)	He handed me a paper that I read with surprise
Viven felices (normal style)	They live happily

31.3.5 Nouns used adverbially

For familiar constructions like *llover cantidad, divertirse horrores*, see 31.4.7.

31.3.6 *Rápido*

Rápido is an adjective, and is correctly used in phrases like *tren rápido* 'fast train', *comidas rápidas* 'fast food', etc. As an adverb it is, like 'quick', familiar; *con prisa*, *deprisa* (*aprisa* is considered substandard in Spain), *rápidamente*, *pronto* are correct adverbial forms: *¡rápido (deprisa/pronto), que se va el tren!* 'quick, the train's going!', *¡fuera! ¡Rápido!* 'get out! Quick!' *Rápido* sounds too colloquial to Peninsular ears in the following extract from an editorial in *El Tiempo*, Colombia: *que juzguen rápido a los narcotraficantes* 'let them bring the drug-traders to justice quickly'. Spaniards would probably write *rápidamente*.

31.3.7 *A la* and *a lo*

Both may form adverbial phrases of manner, but *a la* followed by a feminine adjective is much more common than *a lo*, which is probably nowadays confined to set phrases:

tortilla a la francesa	plain omelette
lenguado a la normanda	sole à la normande
despedirse a la francesa	to leave without saying goodbye
divorcio a la italiana	divorce Italian-style
Viven todavía a la antigua	They still live in the old style

Siempre viste a la inglesa	He always dresses English-style
a lo loco	crazily/without stopping to think
Ando un poco a la defensiva	I'm feeling a bit on the defensive
(C. Martín Gaite, Spain, dialogue)	

Note

En plan . . . is rather colloquial, like '-style': *viajar en plan turista* 'to travel tourist-style', *hablar en plan Tarzan* 'to talk Tarzan-style'.

31.3.8 Note on position of adverbs of manner (see also 37.2.6 and 37.4)

An adverb of manner usually follows an intransitive verb:

Trabaja intensivamente en una segunda novela	He is working very hard on a second novel
Este problema está íntimamente ligado al problema del paro	This problem is intimately linked to the problem of unemployment
Esa cara de asco que parece ser habitualmente la suya	That look of disgust which seems habitually to be his

But an adverb may precede the verb to add emphasis:

Tu vida inevitablemente se dispone a recorrer el tramo final de la parábola (J. Marías, Spain)	Your life is inevitably getting itself ready for the last lap (lit. 'to run the last section of the parabola')

In a transitive sentence, an adverb may follow the object – *habla griego correctamente* – or the verb – *habla correctamente el griego* 'he speaks Greek perfectly/ without making mistakes'; there is no noticeable change of meaning here. The difference can be almost imperceptible in many cases, but strictly speaking an adverb that follows the object modifies the whole verb phrase, whereas an adverb that precedes the object modifies only the verb. Thus *robaba dinero con frecuencia* 'he frequently stole money', but *robaba con frecuencia dinero . . .* 'he frequently stole money . . . ' is the appropriate order if further items, e.g. jewellery, are to follow.

31.4 Intensifiers and moderators

31.4.1 General

Intensifiers and moderators strengthen or weaken the force of a verb, adverb, adjective and, occasionally, noun. Typical intensifiers are *muy* 'very', *mucho/poco* 'much'/'little', *intensamente* 'intensely', *extremadamente* 'extremely', *algo/más bien* 'rather', *increíblemente* 'incredibly', *sobremanera* (literary) 'exceedingly'. Many intensifiers have other functions, and are dealt with elsewhere, e.g. *algo* and *más bien* see 9.2, *demasiado* see 9.9, *mucho* and *poco* see 9.12.

New colloquial intensifiers appear and vanish as fashion dictates. *Requete-* used to be a popular prefix and has created permanent expressions in Spain like *requeteguapo/a* 'very good-looking' and *requetebién* 'extremely well done'. *Archi-* can still be found in *archiconocido/archisabido* 'very well known'. Nowadays, at least in Spain, any adjective can be reinforced in colloquial styles by *super-*: *supertonto/superinteligente* 'extremely silly'/'extremely intelligent'.

31.4.2 *Muy*

Muy 'very' is originally an abbreviated form of *mucho*, and the full form must be used in isolation:

Es muy inteligente	He's very intelligent
—¿Es inteligente? —Sí, mucho	'Is she intelligent?' 'Yes, very'

Note

Bien is sometimes used in Spain in the sense of 'very': *me voy a dar una ducha bien caliente* 'I'm going to have a very hot shower'. This usage is more common in Latin America: *es bien simpático* (Chilean informant) 'he's very likeable', *¡si está bien viejo para ti!* (popular Mexican, quoted Arjona Iglesias, 1991, 78) 'he's really/pretty old for you!'

31.4.3 Intensifiers in *-mente*

There are numerous intensifiers ending in *-mente*, e.g. *sumamente* 'exceedingly', *increíblemente* 'incredibly', *tremendamente* 'tremendously', *fenomenalmente* 'phenomenally', etc. These cannot modify another adverb in *-mente*, i.e. 'he speaks English incredibly fluently' cannot be translated **habla inglés increíblemente corrientemente* but must be recast, e.g. *habla inglés increíblemente bien/con una soltura/facilidad increíble*:

Ha actuado con admirable honradez	He's acted admirably honestly/with admirable honesty
Lo hicieron con una prisa absurda	They did it absurdly quickly/with absurd haste
Le voy a hablar con una franqueza total	I'm going to talk to you totally frankly

31.4.4 *Más* and *menos*

(For the use of *más* and *menos* in comparisons, see Chapter 5.) *Más* is used as an intensifier in familiar speech, without any comparative meaning:

Es que eres más tonto . . .	Heavens, are you stupid!
Está más borracho . . .	Is he drunk!

31.4.5 *Lo* as an intensifier

For *lo* in sentences like *cuéntale lo bien que canta* 'tell her/him how well he/she sings', *camina lo más lentamente que puedas* 'walk as slowly as possible' see 7.2.2.

31.4.6 *Qué* and *cuán* as intensifiers

Exclamatory *qué* is discussed at 24.4, *cuán(to)* at 24.6. For *no recordaba lo guapa que eres* 'I didn't remember how attractive you are', etc., see 7.2.2.

31.4.7 Nouns used as intensifiers

Familiar speech uses some nouns as intensifiers – not to every taste, as the translations show:

Lo pasamos bomba (already old-fashioned?)	We had a terrific time (lit. 'we had a bomb of a time')
Canta fenómeno	(S)he's a smashing singer
Para los setenta y cinco años que traía a cuestas . . . ¡estaba fenómeno! (S. Galindo, Mexico, dialogue)	For her seventy-five years (lit. 'for the seventy-five years she was carrying on her back'), she looked great!

Nos aburrimos cantidad	We were bored stiff/bored to death
Nos hemos reído cantidad	Did we have a laugh!

31.4.8 *Sí* and *si* as intensifiers

Sí, which means 'yes', and *si*, which usually means 'if', can both also be used as intensifiers.

Sí (with an accent) is used to assert a fact that the speaker thinks has been contradicted or doubted, or for purposes of contrast: —*María no vendrá.* —*Sí que vendrá. Me lo prometió* ' "María won't come." "She *will* come. She promised me." ', *una respuesta que esta vez sí me irritó* 'a reply that *did* annoy me this time', *entonces me entró cierta impaciencia por conocer un país que sí pudo llevar a cabo su cambio* (M. Benedetti, Uruguay, dialogue) 'then I felt a certain impatience to get to know a country that actually did complete its process of change'.

Si (no accent) may be used as an intensifier in spoken language, usually preceded by *pero*. It emphasizes the following statement, often with an indignant or insistent tone: *¡(pero) si te oí la primera vez!* 'but I heard you first time!', *pero si vivimos muy bien. No necesitamos nada* (Soledad Puértolas, Spain, dialogue) 'but we really do live well. We don't need anything', —*¿Ahorita?* —*Sí.* —*Pero si son las diez* (E. Poniatowska, Mexico, dialogue; *ahorita* = *ahora mismo* in Spain) "This very minute?" "Yes." "But it's ten o'clock!" ', *pero si mañana me voy al Perú y no vuelvo más* (A. Bryce Echenique, Peru, dialogue) 'but tomorrow I'm going to Peru and I'm not coming back'.

For *apenas si* 'scarcely' see 23.5.7.

31.5 Adverbs of doubt

Words meaning 'perhaps', 'probably', 'possibly' may call for the subjunctive and are discussed under 16.3.

31.6 Adverbs of place

31.6.1 *Aquí, ahí, allí*

It is important to distinguish carefully between *ahí* and *allí*: to the untrained ear they tend to sound similar, at least in some varieties of Spanish. These adverbs are closely linked in meaning to the demonstratives:

este this near me/us	*aquí* here near me/us
ese that	*ahí* (just) there
aquel that further away	*allí* there further away

In other words, *ahí* points to space near the hearer: one can say on the telephone to someone far away *¿qué tal tiempo hace ahí?* 'what's the weather like there?' However, misuse of *ahí* to refer to something distant from the hearer produces a bizarre effect: Carnicer (1972) 24, remarks that to ask people from another country *¿qué tal se vive ahí?* 'what's it like living just there?' instead of *allí* prompts them to look under their chairs.

Vente aquí a pasar unos días con nosotros	Come here and spend a few days with us
Pero otras veces me siento aquí también un exiliado (M. Benedetti, Uruguay, dialogue)	But some times I feel like an exile here too

Aquí construiremos la casa, ahí el garaje, *y allí al final del jardín, la piscina*	We'll build the house here, the garage there, and the swimming pool there at the bottom of the garden
Deja la linterna ahí a tu lado	Leave the torch there next to you
Sería interesante visitar Groenlandia, *pero no quisiera vivir allí*	It would be interesting to visit Greenland, but I wouldn't like to live there

If the place referred to is out of sight, *ahí* is generally used if it is near by or in the same town, *allí* for more remote places:

—*Lo he comprado en esa tienda.* —*Ah, sí,* *yo compro siempre ahí*	'I bought it in that shop. ' 'Oh yes, I always shop there'
Ya están ahí monsieur Fréjus y monsieur *Bebé, y quieren cocktails* (J. Cortázar, Argentina. dialogue; note *están* *ahí* = 'have arrived')	Monsieur Fréjus and Monsieur Bebé are here, and they want cocktails
Ismael detestaba la canción española. *Ahí es donde le traicionaba* (Maruja Torres, Spain)	Ismael hated Spanish songs. There's where I had to let him down
Mi hermana nació en Caracas, y yo *también nací allí*	My sister was born in Caracas, and I was born there too
El rock les entra por un oído, les deteriora *un poco el tímpano pertinente y se les* *queda allí, en el cerebro* (M. Benedetti, Uruguay; *ahí* could have been used instead)	Rock goes in one of their ears, does a bit of damage to the affected eardrum and stays there, in their brains

When there is more than one verb it is important to place *allí* and *ahí* near the verb it qualifies:

Allí/Ahí me dijo que nos casaríamos	She told me there that we would get married
Me dijo que nos casaríamos allí/ahí	She told me we would get married there

Note

Native speakers may use *ahí* for *allí* (but not vice versa) if they feel emotionally close to the place they are talking about: *¿conoces la iglesia a la entrada del pueblo? Pues ahí/allí se casaron mis padres* 'do you know the church on the way in to the village? Well, that's where my parents got married', —*Y al fin llegué a Manaos. De ahí era fácil pasar a Iquitos.* —*Y ¿ahí fue donde conociste al señor Julio Reátegui?* (M. Vargas Llosa, Peru, dialogue) '"And I eventually got to Manaos. From there it was easy to cross to Iquitos." "And was that where you met Sr Julio Reátegui?"', *ahí está, dijo, y ahí estaba porque él lo conocía* . . . (G. García Márquez, Colombia, dialogue, pointing to a comet in the sky; or *allí*) '"There it is," he said, and there it was because he was familiar with it.'

31.6.2 Acá, allá

In the Southern Cone and in many other parts of Latin America, *acá* has more or less replaced *aquí*, even in good writing: *acá en la Argentina si querés una taza de té, tenés que beber mate* = in Peninsular Spanish *aquí en Argentina, si quieres una taza de té, tienes que beber mate* 'here in Argentina if you feel like a cup of tea you have to drink *mate*'.

In Spain, *acá* and *allá* are much less common than *aquí*, *ahí*, *allí* and denote vague or non-specific location or, most commonly, movement (often with the preposition *para*):

Ven acá/aquí, que te voy a contar una cosa	Come here, I'm going to tell you something
Íbamos allá/hacia allí cuando nos lo/le *encontramos*	We were on the way there when we ran into him

Que se venga para acá en cuanto pueda   (S)he must come here as soon as (s)he can

Notes

(i) *Allá* is often used of large distances in Latin America and occasionally in Spain. It can also in both regions express vague yearnings. In time phrases it emphasizes remoteness and may be obligatory: *allá/allí en (la) Argentina tenemos mucha familia* (*allí* in Spain) 'we have a lot of family out there in Argentina', *nos casamos allá en los años veinte* (not *allí*) 'we got married some time in the twenties', *el sur era y es acentuadamente indio; allá la cultura tradicional está todavía viva* (O. Paz, Mexico) 'the south was and is markedly Amerindian; (down) there traditional culture is still alive', *al otro lado de las lágrimas, allá arriba en lo alto de su rabia, más allá de las ramas del almendro y de las palmeras . . .* (J. Marsé, Spain) 'on the other side of her tears, up there high in her rage, beyond the branches of the almond trees and the palms . . .'.

(ii) *Acá* and *allá* can take an intensifier, unlike *aquí, ahí, allí*: *más allá del sistema solar* 'beyond the solar system', *más allá de la realidad y el sueño* (L. Mateo Díaz, Spain) 'beyond reality and dreams', *más acá de la frontera* 'on this side of the frontier', *muévelo un poco más acá/hacia aquí* 'move it this way a bit', *un poco más acá del horizonte* (M. Benedetti, Uruguay) 'just on this side of the horizon', *¡un poquito más acá!* 'this way a bit!', *lo más acá/allá posible* 'as far over here/there as possible'. *El más allá* is 'the beyond' of science fiction and the occult'.

(iii) *Allá* with a pronoun translates 'let him/her get on with it', 'it's your look-out', etc.: *allá él si hace tonterías* 'if he wants to fool about, that's his affair', *bueno, allá tú si no me haces caso* 'well, if you don't pay any attention to me, it's your problem'.

(iv) *Acá* is sometimes used in time expressions in informal language, though it sounds a little old-fashioned (at least in Spain), and *desde* on its own is normally used: *¿de cuándo acá no se dice hola a los amigos?* (*desde cuándo . . .*) 'since when have people not been saying "hello" to their friends?', *desde las elecciones (acá), este país ya no tiene remedio* 'since the elections, this country's been beyond hope', *de un tiempo acá se le nota cansada* (*desde un tiempo a esta parte . . .*) 'she's been looking tired for some time now'.

31.6.3 Use of adverbs of place as pronouns

One hears uneducated speakers use *aquí/ahí/allí* for *éste/ése/aquél*: *aquí me dice* = *éste me dice* 'this one here says to me'(itself very familiar). The same phenomenon occurs in Latin America, and also with *acá/allá*.

31.6.4 Adverbs of place with prepositions

All the adverbs of place can be preceded by *de, desde, hacia, hasta, por* and, less commonly, *para* (for which see *acá/allá*):

Los melocotones de aquí son mejores que los de Estados Unidos	The peaches (from) here are better than the ones from America
Mira el sombrero que lleva la señora de allí	Look at the hat that lady over there is wearing
Hasta aquí hemos llegado y de aquí no paso	We've got this far and I'm going no further
Desde aquí se ve el mar	You can see the sea from here
Se sale por aquí	This is the way out

31.6.5 *Dentro/adentro, fuera/afuera*

'Inside' and 'outside' respectively. In Spain *dentro* and *fuera* are preferred after prepositions (except perhaps *para*) and also to form prepositional phrases when followed by *de. Afuera* and *adentro* strictly speaking denote motion *towards* and should be used only in this sense, although they are occasionally found in isolation with the meaning of *fuera, dentro*. European Spanish:

Por dentro era negro, y por fuera blanco	On the inside it was black, on the outside white

Dentro había flores en macetas	Inside there were flowers in pots
Dentro de la caja había otra	Inside the box was another
Ven (a)dentro y te lo explicaré	Come inside and I'll explain it to you
Vamos a cenar fuera	We're eating out (tonight)/We're having dinner outside
El gas tiende a escaparse hacia fuera	Gas tends to escape outwards
He estado fuera unos días	I've been away for a couple of days
Al acabar el discurso se oyeron gritos de ¡fuera! ¡fuera!	When the speech ended shouts of 'out! out!' were heard
¡Las manos fuera de Cuba!	Hands off Cuba!
Su ocurrencia ha estado fuera de lugar	His witty remark was out of place
Las luces de fuera (C. Martín Gaite, Spain)	The lights outside
Afuera quedaba el domingo de verano, despoblado y soso (F. Umbral, Spain. Poetic: *fuera* is more normal in Spain)	Outside was the summer Sunday, empty (lit. 'depopulated') and lifeless

Latin-American usage:

Afuera and *adentro* tend to be used in all circumstances. *Adentro de* and *afuera de* are also used as prepositional phrases, this usage being considered normal in Argentina and colloquial in most other Latin-American countries. Only *fuera de* and *dentro de* are allowed in Spain:

Afuera hacía calor porque empezaba enero (J. Cortázar, Argentina; Spain *fuera*)	Outside it was hot because January was beginning (Argentina is in the southern hemisphere)
Afuera en el parque, y adentro, por la casa entera seguían los disparos (José Donoso, Chile; Spain *fuera, dentro*)	Outside in the park, and inside, throughout the house, the shooting continued
Cuando uno está afuera e imagina que puede pasar varios años entre cuatro paredes, piensa que no aguantaría (M. Benedetti, Uruguay, dialogue)	When one's outside (or 'out in the open') and imagines that one may spend several years between four walls, one thinks one couldn't stand it
Adentro de Aqueronte hay lágrimas, tinieblas, crujir de dientes (J. L. Borges, Argentina; Spain *dentro de*)	Within Acheron there are tears, darkness, gnashing of teeth
. . . nuestros treinta años adentro de Abc Color (*Abc Color*, Paraguay)	. . . our thirty years (working) at *Abc Color*

However, *dentro de* is used in Latin America, as in Spain, in time phrases of the sort *dentro de una semana* 'in a week's time' (often *en una semana* in Latin America).

31.6.6 *Abajo, debajo de, arriba, encima*

For the prepositions *bajo, debajo de* see 34.3. For *encima de* see 34.9 and 34.17.

Abajo means 'down' or 'downstairs', and *arriba* means 'up' or 'upstairs':

Te espero abajo/arriba	I'll wait downstairs/upstairs
Caminaba calle abajo/arriba	She walked downhill/uphill

Abajo de is often used in Latin America for the prepositional phrase *debajo de* 'underneath':

¿Chofi guarda las quincenas abajo del colchón? (A. Mastretta, Mexico; *debajo de* in Spain. *Quincenas* are wages paid every two weeks)	Does Chofi keep her wages under the mattress?

La nevera está abajo del bar (C. Fuentes,   The fridge is under the bar
   Mexico, dialogue; *debajo de* in Spain)

The difference between *arriba* and *encima* is basically the same as between 'up'
and 'on top':

Ponlo encima de la mesa	Put it on (top of) the table
Ponlo ahí encima	Put it there on top
Ponlo ahí arriba	Put it up there
El avión pasó por encima del pueblo	The plane flew over the village

Encima can also be used figuratively:

Le dije que se lo daría y encima se	I told her I would give it to her and on top
queja	of that/even then she complains

31.6.7 *Detrás, detrás de* and *atrás*

Atrás 'behind'/'backwards' denotes motion backwards whereas *detrás* and the
prepositional phrase *detrás de* 'behind' denote place:

dar un paso atrás	to move a step backwards
Miré hacia atrás (J. Madrid, Spain)	I looked back
Ella subió las escaleras sin siquiera mirar	She went up the stairs without even looking
hacia atrás (G. Cabrera Infante, Cuba)	back
Ponte detrás	Stand behind
detrás de mí/detrás de la mesa	behind me/the table

In Latin America *atrás de* often means *detrás de*:

Las demás me veían desde atrás de la	The others looked at me from behind the
mesa (A. Mastretta, Mexico; *me*	table
miraban . . . desde **detrás** *de la mesa*	
in Spain)	

31.6.8 *Delante, delante de* and *adelante*

In Spain *delante* 'in front' and the prepositional phrase *delante de* 'in front of'
denote place; *adelante* 'forward(s)'/'onward(s)' denotes motion forward:

Yo iba delante	I was walking ahead
Delante de ti no hablará	She won't say anything in front of you
Sigue adelante que yo te alcanzaré	Go on ahead. I'll catch up with you

Alante is a popular variant for *adelante*. In colloquial Latin-American Spanish
adelante de is often used for *delante de*, but this is not accepted in Spain: *vio a Fede-*
rico que, unos cuantos pasos adelante de él, se detenía y agachaba a tomar una piedra (S.
Galindo, Mexico; Spain *delante de él*) 'he saw Federico, who was stopping and
bending down to pick up a stone a few paces in front of him'.

Notes

(i) Only *adentro, afuera, abajo, arriba, atrás, delante* and *adelante* should be intensified: *más aden-*
tro/abajo/arriba/atrás 'further inside/down/up/back', *más afuera* or *más hacia fuera* 'more to the outside', *más hacia delante* 'further forwards'. *Más adelante* means 'later on', e.g. *ya hablaremos más*
adelante 'we'll talk later on'.
(ii) Omission of *de* in the prepositional phrase, common in Latin America, occasionally heard in
Spain, is considered incorrect in careful language everywhere: *dentro* **de** *mi corazón, fuera* **de** *la casa*.
(iii) *Fuera de* can mean *aparte de*, 'apart from' but is rather colloquial: *fuera de él no hay nadie en que*
yo pueda confiar 'apart from him, there's no one I can trust' (some grammarians prefer *excepto él*).

(iv) *Atrás* is also used in the time phrases *años/meses/días atrás* 'some years/months/days ago'.

(v) *En adelante* can also be used in time phrases and in quantities: *para esto necesitas de un millón en adelante* 'for this you'll need a million or more', *de ahora en adelante no lo vuelvo a hacer* 'from now on I won't do it again'.

31.7 Adverbs of time

31.7.1 *Ya, ya no*

Ya has a wide variety of uses. In many common constructions its meaning is determined by the time of the verb that it modifies:

Vienen ya	They're coming right now
Ya llegarán	They'll arrive, for sure
Ya han llegado	They've already arrived
Ya llegaron (Latin America)	They already arrived (US)
Ya no vienen	They're not coming any more
Ya no llegarán	They won't be arriving any more
(but only *aún/todavía no han llegado*	they haven't arrived yet)

Further examples:

Los autores que aportaron nuevos recursos estilísticos al ya idioma castellano (or *al que ya era idioma . . .*)	The authors who contributed new stylistic resources to what was already the Castilian language
Eres hombre ya/Ahora eres ya un hombre	You're a man now
¿Quién se acuerda ya de lo que era el Charleston?	Who can remember any more what the Charleston was?
Ya no tengo edad para trabajar (J. Madrid, Spain, dialogue)	I'm no longer of an age to be working/I'm too old to work
Estaba perdido, extraviado en una casa ajena donde ya ni nada ni nadie le suscitaba el menor vestigio de afecto (G. García Márquez, Colombia)	He was lost, adrift in a strange house where nothing and nobody aroused the slightest trace of affection in him any more
Ya desde mucho antes, Amaranta había renunciado a toda tentativa de convertirla en una mujer útil (ibid.)	Long before this (already), Amaranta had abandoned all attempts to change her into a useful woman

But *ya* has many idiomatic uses. It can indicate impatience, accumulating frustration, fulfilled expectations, resignation, certainty about the future, incredulity or, in negative sentences, denial of something expected:

Iros, iros a la playa, que ya me quedo yo aquí a lavar la ropa (Carmen Rico-Godoy in *Cambio16; iros* is familiar Peninsular usage for *idos*. See 17.2.4 for discussion)	Go on, off you go to the beach while I stay here washing the clothes (martyred tone)
Lleva seis meses en la cama. Si eso no es grave, pues ya me dirás	He's been in bed six months. If that's not serious, then you tell me what is
Porque la tarea que tenemos planteada es casi una tarea de titanes. Pero el país puede resolverla. Ya verán (*Cambio16*, Spain)	Because the task confronting us is almost a task for Titans. But the country can solve it. You'll see
Sirve ya la cena, que hemos esperado bastante	Serve supper now, we've waited long enough
Por mí, que se vaya ya	He can go right now, as far as I'm concerned

el estudiante de nuestros días – ya no pensaré en el estudiante del año 2000 o 2500 (Peru, in *Variedades*, 174)	The student of our day – I shan't even consider the student of the year 2000 or or 2500
Ya le pasaré la cuenta cuando gane el gallo (G. García Márquez, Colombia, dialogue: *ya* here makes a promise more certain)	I'll send you the bill when your cockerel wins
¡Basta ya! ¡Calla ya!	That's enough! Not another word!
¡Ya está bien!	That's enough!
Bueno, eso es el colmo ya	Well, that *is* the limit!
Ya puedes tener buen olfato con la nariz que tú tienes	You can well have a good sense of smell with the nose you've got
Ya puedes invitarnos con el dinero que tú tienes	I should think you *could* pay for us with the money you've got
Ya quisiera la Diana Ross para sus días festivos ser tan linda como tú (L. Rafael Sánchez, Puerto Rico, dialogue; Spain *para sus días de fiesta*)	Diana Ross on a good day (lit. 'on her holidays') wouldn't mind being as pretty as you
Por mí, ya puede llover, que tenemos tienda de campaña	As far as I'm concerned, it can go ahead and rain – we've got a tent
Hitler habría sido todavía peor – y ya es decir – si a su criminal racismo hubiera juntado un fanatismo religioso (*Abc*, Spain)	Hitler would have been even worse – and that's saying something – if he had added religious fanaticism to his criminal racism
cuando ya acabemos de limpiar la casa . . .	when we finally finish cleaning the house . . .
No, no, ya te digo que él no sabía nada de todo aquello	No, no, I'm *telling* you he knew nothing about all that
¡Ya tuviste que contarme el final!	You *would* have to tell me the ending!
Ya lo sé	I already know/I *know*
Ya empezamos . . .	(Oh dear) here we go again . . .
Ya era hora	It's about time . . .
Ya siéntate y deja de interrumpir (A. Mastretta, Mexico, dialogue, impatient tone[2])	Sit down and stop interrupting
—*¿No ves lo inteligente que soy?* —*Ya, ya . . .*	'Don't you see how intelligent I am?' 'Sure, sure . . . ' (ironic)
—*El jefe quiere hablar conmigo. Está muy enfadado.* —*Ya será menos*	'The boss wants to talk to me. He's very angry'. 'Come on, it won't be that bad'.
Ya ves	There you are/Didn't I say so?

Notes

(i) *Ya . . . ya* is a literary alternative for *o . . . o* 'either . . . or': *ya porque la idea del matrimonio acabara por asustarle, ya porque no pudiera olvidar a María, no apareció en la iglesia* 'either because the idea of marriage eventually frightened him or because he couldn't forget Maria, he didn't appear at the church'.

(ii) *Ya* may be an abbreviation of *ya lo sé* 'I know', or *ya entiendo* 'I understand': —*Cuando veas la luz verde pulsa el botón rojo.* —*Ya* '"When you see the green light, push the red button." "Right/OK."'

(iii) *Desde ya* 'straightaway' is an expression from the Southern Cone which is sometimes now heard in Spain.

31.7.2 Recién

In Spain *recién* can only appear before participles, e.g. *recién pintado* 'newly painted', *recién casado* 'newly wed', *recién divorciado* 'recently divorced', *un chico*

---

[2] In Spain the *ya* is placed after the imperative: *siéntate ya* 'sit down, now!'

recién salido del colegio 'a boy who has recently left school'. Its use before other parts of speech is very rare.

The use of *recién* as a free-standing adverb of time is one hallmark of Latin-American Spanish everywhere. It is very common in speech and also appears even in quite formal written language. It has two basic meanings:

(a) 'Right now' or 'just now':

Recién lo vi (Spain *le acabo de ver*)	I've just seen him
—¿Cuándo lo dijo? —Recién (Spain *ahora mismo*)	'When did he say it?' 'Just now'

(b) 'Only', as in 'only now', 'only this year'. This usage is colloquial in some regions:

Pero recién en los últimos siete años la desesperada ciencia se ha aferrado a una hipótesis: la del movimiento de placas o bloques (*Tiempo*, Chile, quoted in *Variedades* 39; *sólo* in Spain)	But only in the last seven years has science, in despair, seized hold of a hypothesis: the movement of (continental) plates or blocks
Recién entonces me di cuenta (Spain *sólo entonces*)	Only then did I realize
Recién mañana llegará (Spain *no llegará hasta mañana*)	He won't be here till tomorrow
—Y él recién entonces se da cuenta de que está herida porque las manos se le están manchando de la sangre de ella (M. Puig, Argentina dialogue; Spain: *. . . sólo entonces se da cuenta . . .*)	And only then he realizes that she's injured because his hands are being stained with her blood
Por eso es que recién ahora se descorre el velo sobre el déficit real de la administración Vázquez (editorial in *El País*, Uruguay: Spain *por eso es por lo que, . . . sólo ahora*)	This is why the veil concealing the real deficit accrued by Vázquez's administration is being lifted only now

Used thus, *recién* precedes the word or phrase it modifies. There is a colloquial diminutive *reciencito*.

31.7.3 *Todavía, aún, ya no*

Todavía and *aún* both mean 'still'/'yet' and are synonymous. With words like *menos, más, menor* and *mayor* they are translated as 'even'. *Aún* 'still' must be distinguished from *aun* meaning 'even'; the latter discussed at 31.7.4. Before or after comparative adjectives and adverbs (including *más* and *menos*), 'even' is translated by *todavía, aún* or *incluso* (not by *aun*):

Todavía/Aún están aquí	They are still here
No han venido aún/todavía	They haven't come yet
Su cara puede verse menos bonita aún, se lo aseguro (C. Fuentes, Mexico, dialogue; or *todavía menos/menos bonita todavía*)	I can assure you, your face can look even less pretty
Es todavía/aún/incluso/hasta más difícil de lo que yo pensaba	It's even more difficult than I thought

31.7.4 *Incluso (inclusive), hasta, aun, siquiera*

All these words may translate the English 'even' in such sentences as 'he even speaks Russian and Greek', 'even in England the sun shines sometimes'. *Incluso* and *aun* are synonyms, but nowadays *incluso* is more often used:

Incluso/Aun hoy día algunas personas siguen creyendo en las hadas	Even today some people still believe in fairies
Incluso/Aun si le das dinero, no lo hará	Even if you give him money he won't do it

Inclusive is much used in Latin America where Peninsular Spanish uses *incluso*:

Para que una persona con un malestar llegue a un bienestar, debe pasar inclusive por un malestar peor que el que ya tenía (Interview in *Cuba Internacional*; Spain *malestar* = 'discomfort', 'indisposition', 'economic embarrassment')	For people with troubles to get out of them (lit. 'to arrive at well-being'), they have to pass through even worse troubles than they already had
Contrasta violentamente con el anuncio en la campaña electoral de que dejarían las finanzas equilibradas, e inclusive con un pequeño superávit (*El País*, Uruguay)	It contrasts violently with the announcement in the electoral campaign that they would leave the books balanced, and even with a slight surplus

Grammarians condemn this because *inclusive* is properly an adverb which follows any noun it refers to and means 'including'/'inclusive', cf. *hasta el domingo inclusive* 'up to and including Sunday'. But the Latin-American variant is deeply rooted, even in educated speech and in writing.

Hasta, literally 'until', may also mean 'even':

Ha llovido tanto que hasta/incluso/aun los patos están hartos	It's rained so much that even the ducks have had enough/are sick of it
. . . y un día hasta me dijeron que usara el teléfono cuando quisiera (A. Bryce Echenique, Peru, dialogue)	. . . and one day they even told me to use the phone whenever I liked

Siquiera means 'at least':

Dame siquiera mil pesetas	Give me one thousand pesetas at least/if nothing else
Yo creo que si se mete uno a eso de las caridades, tiene que ser a lo grande, siquiera quedar como San Francisco (A. Mastretta, Mexico, dialogue)	I think that if one's going to go into charity work, one's got to do it in a big way, at least be like Saint Francis
Siquiera el General es generoso. Mira el coche que me regaló (idem)	At least the general is generous. Look at the car he gave me

Ni siquiera translates 'not even':

Bueno, los ingleses . . . los autos por la izquierda . . . ni siquiera han aceptado el sistema métrico (C. Catania, Argentina, interview; *los autos* = *los coches* in Spain)	Well, the English . . . cars on the left-hand side of the road . . . they haven't even accepted the metric system

31.7.5 *Luego* and *entonces*

Both words are translatable as 'then', but they usually mean different things.

(a) As time words, *entonces* means 'then'/'at that moment' whereas *luego* means 'afterwards'/'later on'. *Luego* in this sense is stressed: **luego** *viene/viene* **luego** 'he's coming later'. If the *luego* is not stressed here, it means 'so'/'in that case':

Abrí la puerta, y entonces me di cuenta de lo que había pasado (*luego* here would mean *después* 'afterwards')	I opened the door, and then realized what had happened
Entonces supe que Mario había mentido (*luego* would mean 'later on')	I realized then that Mario had lied
Desde entonces soy feliz	From that time on I have been happy
Recuerdo que los cines de entonces siempre apestaban a agua de colonia	I remember that cinemas at that time always stank of eau de Cologne
el entonces catedrático de griego	the professor of Greek at that time/the then professor of Greek
Gary Hart derrotó al hasta entonces favorito demócrata Walter Mondale	Gary Hart defeated the until then democrat favourite Walter Mondale
—¿Quién es? —Te lo diré luego	'Who is it?' 'I'll tell you later'
Lo haré luego	I'll do it later
hasta luego (cf. *hasta ahora*, 'see you in a minute')	see you later/goodbye
Según dice mamá, que luego estuvo seis años liada con Tey . . . (J. Marsé, Spain)	According to mother, who later on was involved with Tey for six years

Note

Luego de hacerlo (literary) = *después de hacerlo* 'after doing it'.

(b) Both *entonces* and *luego* may mean 'in that case'. In this meaning *luego* is not stressed:

—En Madrid hace 40 grados, en Sevilla 38. —Entonces hace más calor en Madrid que en Sevilla (or *Luego, hace . . .*)	'In Madrid it's 40 degrees, in Seville 38.' 'In that case it's hotter in Madrid than in Seville'
Es mi secreto. Entonces ya me lo contarás. Los secretos siempre se cuentan (A. Buero Vallejo, Spain, dialogue; *luego* not possible in conjunction with *ya*)	'It's my secret.' 'Then you'll soon tell me. Secrets always get told'
Pienso luego existo (set phrase)	I think, therefore I am

Notes

(i) Use of *luego* to mean 'straightaway'/'immediately' is a regionalism in Spain, but it is common in certain Latin-American countries.

(ii) The following words also convey the idea of 'then': *después*, 'after', *acto seguido* 'next/immediately after', *a continuación* 'next/immediately after', *en seguida/enseguida* 'immediately'/'straightaway'.

31.7.6 *Antes* 'before', *después* 'afterwards'

Antes must be distinguished from the entirely separate word *ante* 'in the presence of'/'in front of', discussed at 34.2:

Antes prefería hablar contigo	First I'd like to talk to you
Ella llegó mucho antes	She arrived much earlier/long before
Después Dios dirá	In the long run (lit 'afterwards') only God knows (lit. 'will say')

For the subordinators *antes de que* and *después de que* see 16.12.7 and 18.3.

32

Expressions of time

32.1 General

This chapter is divided into two parts. Sections 32.2–32.8 cover such matters as the expression of duration, e.g. 'for *n* days', 'since . . . ', 'during . . . ', 'still'. Sections 32.9–32.10 contain translations of a number of useful expressions connected with the clock, dates and similar matters.

32.2 General remarks on tenses used in expressions of duration and other expressions of time

English-speaking learners of Spanish constantly use the wrong tense in sentences meaning such things as 'I have been learning Spanish for three years', 'it's the first time I've seen her for months', etc. It is difficult to lay down hard and fast rules because of differences between European and Latin-American usage, but unlike English, European Spanish often uses – and Latin-American Spanish normally uses – the present tense to indicate events that are still in progress or are likely to recur: *estudio español desde hace tres años* 'I've been learning Spanish for three years' (not *he estudiado . . .*), *es la tercera vez que **pierdo** la misa del domingo desde que **tengo** uso de razón* (G. García Márquez, Colombia, dialogue; Spain . . . *que me **pierdo**/que me **he perdido** la misa . . .*). English uses past tenses in the same kind of sentence: 'it's the third time **I've missed** Sunday Mass since **I've been able** to reason'.

If the event was continuing in the past, European Spanish often uses – and Latin-American normally uses – the imperfect tense where English uses the pluperfect: *estudiaba español desde hacía tres años* 'I/(s)he had been learning Spanish for three years', *desde que llegó a Europa por primera vez **andaba** en el landó familiar* (G. García Márquez; Spain *iba* a todas partes/*había ido* a todas partes . . .) 'since he'd first arrived from Europe **he had been driving** around in the family landau'.

English speakers constantly forget these rules and use the compound tenses (perfect and pluperfect) for both completed and incomplete events. Since the Spanish perfect tense is a past tense, *¿cuánto tiempo **has estado** en Nueva York?* implies that the hearer's stay in New York is over: it means much the same as *¿cuánto tiempo **estuviste** en Nueva York?* 'how long **were** you/**did you stay** in New York?' The present tense would be used if the hearer is still there: *¿cuánto tiempo hace que **estás** en Nueva York?* or *¿cuánto tiempo **llevas** en Nueva York?* French and Italian have similar rules: *vous êtes ici depuis combien de temps?* 'how long have you been here?', *da quando sei a Roma*? 'how long have you been in Rome?'

32.3 Duration

There are various possibilities, not all of them interchangeable, e.g. *llevar . . . , hace . . . , desde hace . . . , desde, durante, en, por, para.*

32.3.1 *Llevar*

This common verb provides the best idiomatic translation of sentences like 'I've been doing something **for** *n* hours/days/months/years', but it can only be used when the event is or was still in progress: one cannot say *llevo seis meses en España* 'I've been in Spain for six months' after one has left the country for good; one would say *he estado/estuve seis meses en España*. A following verb appears in the gerund form, but the gerund cannot be negated: **llevo años no fumando* is not a possible translation of 'I haven't been smoking for years': *hace años que **no** fumo/llevo años **sin fumar**/no fumo **desde hace** años*:

Llevo años diciendo que acabarían casándose	I've been saying for years that they'd eventually get married
Llevamos cinco años viviendo juntos (C. Rico-Godoy, Spain)	We've been living together for five years
¿Cuánto (tiempo) llevas en este trabajo?	How long have you been in this job?
El ascensor lleva estropeado dos meses (C. Rico-Godoy, Spain)	The lift/elevator has been broken for two months
Lleva veinte años peleando y está como un gallo nuevo (interview in *Granma*, Cuba)	He's been fighting (i.e. boxing) for twenty years, and he's like a fresh fighting cock
Llevo siete días aquí contigo (C. Fuentes, Mexico, dialogue)	I've been here with you for seven days
Se comprende que llevan un buen tiempo apostados allí (E. Lynch, Argentina)	As one can see, they've been waiting there for some time (*apostar* = 'to post a sentry'/'set up a guard')

If the event or state *was* still in progress at the time, the imperfect of *llevar* is used (*he llevado . . .* is not possible in this construction):

Llevábamos dos años en Madrid cuando me puse enfermo	We'd been in Madrid for two years when I fell ill
Llevabas años diciéndolo	You had been saying it for years
Ya llevaba varios meses en Montevideo (M. Benedetti, Uruguay)	He had already been in Montevideo for several months

Notes

(i) *Llevar*, whose original meaning is to carry some kind of burden, definitely implies a significant period of time. One would not say **sólo/solo llevo unos segundos aquí* for *sólo/solo he estado aquí unos segundos* 'I've only been here for a few seconds'.

(ii) This construction with *llevar* is very common in Peninsular speech, but less common in written language than the construction using *hace . . . /hacía . . .* described in the next section.

In Latin America it is often replaced by *tener*: **tengo** *dos años aquí*, 'I've been here for two years', **tenía** *pocos meses de gobernar cuando logró el cambio* (A. Mastretta, Mexico, dialogue) 'he'd only been acting as Governor for a few months when he managed to bring about the change'; Kany (1970), 273–4, cites examples from all parts of the continent. This construction is also found in formal Latin-American writing: *aunque **tengan** muchos años de vivir allí . . . nadie los confundiría con*

los norteamericanos auténticos (Octavio Paz, Mexico) 'although they've been living there for years, no one would take them for true North Americans'.
(iii) The following idioms with *llevar* are noteworthy: *esto me va a llevar mucho tiempo* 'this is going to take me a long time', *Ana me lleva tres años* 'Ana's three years older than me.'

32.3.2 *Hace/hacía/hará ... que ...*

Hace dos años que estoy en Madrid means the same as *llevo dos años en Madrid* 'I've been in Madrid for two years' (and I'm still there). *Hace* in this construction is followed by a simple present tense when the following verb indicates an action that started in the past and is still in progress: *hace años que me veo con ella todos los días* 'I've been seeing her every day for years'. If the sentence is negative, the perfect tense is, however, also often found in Spain, but not usually in Latin America, to indicate an event that has **not** been in progress for a period of time e.g. *hace años que no la he visto/no la veo* 'I haven't seen her for years', *¿cuántos años hace que no le has visto?* (J. Marsé, Spain, dialogue) 'how long has it been since you last saw him?' (lit. 'since you haven't seen him'). Use of the perfect tense instead of the present in this type of sentence is rejected by many Latin Americans (and by some Spaniards, particularly northerners) and should probably be avoided by learners of American varieties of Spanish, aversion to the compound tenses apparently being stronger in the speech of the Southern Cone than elsewhere (but there is much regional variation in this matter).

Hacía + the imperfect + *que* translates 'for' in past time and is followed by the imperfect to denote an action that was still in progress: *hacía tiempo que nos veíamos* 'we had been seeing one another for some time'. In this case the pluperfect changes the meaning: *hacía tiempo que nos habíamos visto* 'it had been some time since we had seen one another', But Peninsular Spanish often uses the pluperfect in negative sentences in the same way as English: *hacía siete años que Juan de Dios no había visto a su hijo mayor* (M. Vázquez Montalbán) 'Juan de Dios hadn't seen his eldest son for seven years'. Some northern Peninsular informants thought this should have been expressed . . . *que no veía a su hijo mayor*, use of the perfect tense being less prevalent in north and north-west Spain than in the rest of the country (see, for example, footnote to 14.9.3).

Hará ... que + the present tense is commonly used in suppositions or approximations: *hará dos años que no la veo* (Spain also . . . *no la he visto*) 'it must be two years since I've seen her'.

Further examples (affirmative sentences):

Hace tiempo que pienso/tengo pensado ir a verla	For some time now I've been thinking of going to see her
¿Hace cuánto tiempo que es usted el amor de Joaquín? (M. Vargas Llosa, Peru, dialogue; Spain *¿Cuánto tiempo hace que es usted la amante de Joaquín?*)	How long have you been Joaquín's lover?
Me dijo que la señorita Brines hacía más de un mes que venía merodeando por el edificio (A. Bryce Echenique, Peru, dialogue)	She told me that Ms Brines had been lurking around the building for more than a month
Hacía tiempo que la cosa andaba mal (M. Benedetti, Montevideo)	Things had been going wrong for some time

Negative sentences:

Hacía años que no veía a David (J. Aldecoa, Spain, dialogue)	I hadn't seen David for years

Hace dos días que no la veo (L. Spota, Mexico, dialogue)	I haven't seen her for two days
No los veo hace mil años (A. Bryce Echenique, Peru, dialogue)	I haven't seen them in a thousand years
. . . como no bebo hace tiempo . . . (M. Vargas for Llosa, Peru, dialogue)	. . . since I haven't been drinking some time . . .

Notes

(i) One cannot use the present tense if no preposition is used. One can say **he estado** *tres horas aquí* 'I've been here three hours', but not **estoy tres horas aquí*. If one intends to remain one must say **llevo** *tres horas aquí*/**hace** *tres horas que* **estoy** *aquí*/**estoy** *aquí* **desde hace** *tres horas*.

(ii) The verb *hacer* does not appear in the plural in this construction: **hacían años que no hablaban de otra cosa* 'they hadn't talked of anything else for years' is bad Spanish for **hacía** *años que . . .* This is a common error of popular speech.

(iii) The imperfect tense may be used in negative sentences with a change of meaning. *Hace años que no* **tomábamos** *café juntos* 'we haven't had coffee together for years' differs from *hace años que no* **tomamos** *café juntos* in that the former would be said while one is actually drinking coffee with the friend, whereas the latter implies that it would be a good idea to have coffee together.

(iv) *En* may be used in the same way as the English 'in' in negative sentences, e.g. 'I hadn't seen her in/for three days'; see 32.5.

32.3.3 Translating 'for' when the event is no longer in progress

Verb in a past tense and no preposition:

Estuvo una temporada en Guatemala, y luego se volvió a California	He was in Guatemala for a while and then he returned to California
Trabajé varios años en Madrid	I worked in Madrid for several years
Trabajábamos sin pausa tres o cuatro horas	We used to work non-stop for three or four hours
Esperamos cinco minutos en la parada	We waited at the stop for five minutes
¿Cuánto tiempo **ha estado** *usted/* **estuvo** *en Madrid?* (addressed to someone whose stay is over)	How long **were** you in Madrid?
. . . la clase de clínica, que **dictó** *todos los días hasta el día de su muerte* (G. García Márquez, Colombia)	. . . the class in clinical techniques he gave every day until the day of his death

Sentences like '**I haven't** seen him for years', 'she **hasn't** smoked for years' can be thought of as 'non-events' that are still in progress. For this reason they are discussed at 32.3.2. *Hace . . . que* with a preterite tense means 'ago' and is discussed at 32.4.

32.3.4 *Durante*

The basic meaning of *durante* is 'during': *durante el siglo veinte* 'during the twentieth century', *durante los tres meses que estuvo aquí* 'in the three months he was here'. Unlike 'during' it is regularly used before plural nouns to mean 'for' a specific period of time: *durante años* 'in years', *durante muchos siglos* 'for/in many centuries'. When the event lasted throughout the whole of the period mentioned, the verb is in the preterite tense. See 14.4.1 for a detailed discussion: *durante años nunca* **supe** *si me contaban fantasías o verdades* (A. Mastretta, Mexico, dialogue) 'for years I never knew whether they were telling me truths or fantasies'.

Notes

(i) Spanish uses the preterite continuous (**estuve** *hablando,* **estuvo** *leyendo,* etc.) to emphasize that an event continued uninterrupted throughout a period of time: *estuve leyendo durante tres horas* 'I read/was reading for three hours', *durante un cuarto de hora* **estuvo** *mirándote* (L. Spota, Mexico, dialogue) 'he was gazing at you for a quarter of an hour'.

(ii) *En* may be used for *durante* in Latin America: *Olga no habló* **en** *varios minutos* (L. Spota, Mexico) 'Olga didn't speak for several minutes.'

(iii) Use of *en* may, on both continents, also correspond to English in negative sentences like 'I haven't smoked in/for years'; see 32.5.

(iv) *En* may also, especially in Latin America, be an alternative for *dentro de* in sentences like *tienes que bajar dentro de/en 5 minutos* 'you've got to be down in five minutes'. See 32.5 for discussion.

32.3.5 *Por* meaning 'for' in time phrases

Por is used for 'for' when referring to brief moments of time (seconds, minutes, etc.), when the speaker emphasizes the shortness of the period. The preposition may in some cases be omitted altogether:

Entraré sólo/solo **(por)** *un momento*	I'll come in just for a moment
Me he matriculado sólo/solo **(por)** *un trimestre*	I've signed on for only one term
Me ha prestado el coche sólo/solo **(por)** *tres días*	He lent me the car for three days only
Por un momento, Bernardo estuvo a punto de ocultar los motivos de la visita . . . (J.-M. Merino, Spain; set phrase)	For a moment Bernardo was about to conceal the reasons for his visit . . .
Por un instante, Félix sintió que una pantalla plateada los separaba a él y a Mary (C. Fuentes, Mexico)	For a moment Félix felt that a silver screen was separating him and Mary

Notes

(i) *Por* and *para* are interchangeable in time expressions fixing the duration of some future need (see also 32.3.6 for *para* in time phrases): *sólo/solo queremos la habitación por/para unos días* 'we only want the room for a few days'.

(ii) When longer periods are involved, Latin Americans may use *por* where Peninsular speakers use nothing or *durante*: *por cuatro o cinco años nos tuvieron acorralados* (M. Vargas Llosa, Peru, dialogue; Spain *durante . . .*) 'they had us cornered for four or five years', *tuve que sustituirlo por mi viejo sombrero, que ha soportado soles y lluvias por más de tres años* (J. J. Arreola, Mexico, dialogue; Spain *durante*) 'I had to replace it with my old hat that has put up with rain and sun for more than three years', *ahí permaneció por casi dos semanas* (L. Sepúlveda, Chile; Spain *durante . . .* or no preposition) 'there he stayed for nearly two months'.

32.3.6 *Para* in expressions of duration

Para is used to translate the idea of 'for' a specified period of time in the future:

Tenemos agua para tres días	We've enough water for three days
Vamos a tener lluvia para rato	We're going to have rain for some time

Note

Ir para is a colloquial translation of 'for nearly . . .': *va para cinco años que trabajo aquí* 'I've been working here for nearly five years'/'it's getting on for five years that I've been working here'.

32.3.7 *Desde*

Desde translates 'since' or, sometimes, 'for'. *Desde que* is used before verb phrases, *desde* before singular noun phrases, and *desde hace/hacía* before plural or numbered nouns to translate 'since . . . ago'. *Desde* can appear before nouns: *desde niña hablo catalán* 'I've spoken Catalan since I was a girl'.

Desde que se casó con el millonario ese, ya no se habla con los amigos	Since she married that millionaire she doesn't talk to her friends any more
No viene/No ha venido desde marzo	She hasn't come since March
Estudio castellano desde hace un año/tres años	I've been studying Spanish for one year/three years (lit. 'from since one/three years ago')

Correct choice of the tense is important, especially in Latin-American Spanish. Events that are still in progress require the present tense; events that were still in progress require the imperfect. However, European Spanish optionally uses the perfect tense with *desde* even when the action is or was still in progress:

Te he estado esperando desde antes de la una	I've been waiting for you since before one o'clock
He estado aquí desde marzo	I've been here since March
La administración de la televisión pública ha sido un desastre desde siempre, desde su fundación (Tribuna, Spain)	The administration of public television has been a disaster from the start (lit. 'since always'), from its foundation
Desde niño Franco ha sido una sombra que ha modificado mi vida (M. Vázquez Montalbán, Spain, dialogue)	Since I was a child (General) Franco has been a shadow that has altered my life
Desde entonces nada le ha durado mucho (J. Marías, Spain; Lat. Am. . . . nada le dura)	Since then nothing has lasted long for him

Use of a past tense in the foregoing sentences is rejected by many Latin Americans. In the following examples the variant with the compound tense is optionally possible in Spain:

Desde pequeño tengo miedo de las arañas (he tenido . . .)	I've been scared of spiders since I was little
¿Desde cuándo se hace eso? (se ha hecho eso)	Since when have people been doing that?
Lo sé desde que te vi en el hospital (G. García Márquez, Colombia, dialogue; Spain lo he sabido)	I've known it since I saw you in the hospital
Preo es periodista desde la época de la famosa revista Marcha (ha sido periodista . . .)	Preo has been a journalist since the period of the well-known periodical *Marcha*
. . . pese a la cortina de silencio tendida deliberadamente sobre lo que está pasando desde julio del pasado año (Granma, Cuba; Spain ha estado pasando)	. . . despite the curtain of silence deliberately drawn over what has been happening since July last year
Desde la gran crisis dormían en habitaciones separadas (S. Pitol, Mexico; Spain also habían dormido)	Since the great crisis they had been sleeping in separate rooms

Events that are or were no longer in progress require a past tense, normally the compound tense (perfect, pluperfect) in Spain and the preterite in much of Latin America:

He fumado tres veces desde octubre/Había fumado tres veces desde entonces	I have smoked three times since October/I had smoked three times since then

Claro que he vuelto a hacerlo/volví a hacerlo desde entonces (the preterite may be preferred in Latin America)	Obviously I've done it again since then
Ayer te estuve esperando desde antes de la una	I was waiting for you yesterday from before one o'clock

Desde hace/desde hacía are required before plural nouns, before specified periods of time and before numbers. The compound tenses are possible in Peninsular Spanish:

Me tranquilizo pensando que todos los adolescentes se han comportado exactamente igual desde hace tres mil años (C. Rico-, Godoy, Spain; *se comportan* possible in Spain, normal in Latin America)	I console myself with by thinking that all adolescents have been acting the same way for three thousand years
. . . la rememoración de quienes permanecían desde hacía años en su memoria (J.-M Merino, Spain; or *habían permanecido*)	. . . recollection of people who'd been in his memory for years
Desde hacía tiempo sospechaba que Tita deseaba que ella desapareciera de este mundo (L. Esquivel, Mexico)	She had been suspecting for a long time that Tita wanted her to disappear from this world
Eso es un campo de batalla desde hace un año (M. Vargas Llosa, Peru, dialogue; Spain also *ha sido*)	That's been a battlefield for a year now

Notes

(i) Literary styles (especially in Spain) often use a *-ra* or *-se* form of the verb after *desde* where one would expect the preterite: *ésta/esta es la primera vez que menciona el asunto desde que ingresara/ingresase/ingresó en la cárcel* 'this is the first time he has mentioned the matter since he entered prison'. This phenomenon is discussed further at 14.10.3.

(ii) This Mexican example shows that other tenses may be used for events that are still in progress: *desde que tenía diez años soñé con ser estrella de cine* (L. Spota, dialogue) 'since I was ten I've dreamt of being a film-star'.

(iii) 'Since' may sometimes need to be translated by *hace que . . ./hacía . . . que* with a past tense. *Hace ya ocho años que nos casamos* 'it's eight years since we married/got married'/'we got married eight years ago.'

(iv) *Desde* is sometimes used in Mexico and elsewhere in Latin America simply to emphasize the moment at which something was done: *desde el martes llegó mi hermano* 'my brother arrived on Tuesday (already)'.

(v) As was mentioned, *desde hace . . .* is used before plural or numbered nouns: *desde hace un año* 'since a year ago', *desde hace varias semanas* 'since several weeks ago'. Colloquial speech sometimes omits the *desde*, e.g. *trabajo aquí (desde) hace varios años* 'I've been working here for a few years', but this is considered careless by many speakers. It may be more acceptable in colloquial Latin-American usage, cf. *hace treinta años estoy sentado frente a una máquina de escribir ahora convertida en una pantalla de computadora* (Abc Color, Paraguay; 'computer' = *el ordenador* in Spain) 'for thirty years I've been sitting in front of a typewriter, which has now become a computer screen'.

32.4 Translating 'ago'

Hace/hacía with a preterite or pluperfect (or, in Spain, a perfect of recency, see 14.9.3) is the usual formula:

Lo/Le vi hace años	I saw him years ago
Lo/Le habíamos visto hacía años	We'd seen him years ago/before then
Hace ya algún tiempo dijiste que . . .	Some time ago you said that . . .

La vi hace cosa de dos meses	I saw her a couple of months ago
La he visto (Lat. Am. *la vi*) *hace un momento*	I saw her a moment ago
(European Spanish perfect of recency)	

Atrás is sometimes used in literary styles: *lo repararon tiempo atrás* 'they mended it/fixed it some time ago', *lo/le conocí días atrás* 'I met him some days ago'.

Use of the verb *haber* for *hacer* in this construction is now archaic in Spain, but apparently survives in colloquial Latin-American varieties: *ha mucho que él perdió a su madre* (M. Puig, Argentina, dialogue) 'he lost his mother a long time ago'.

32.5 'In n days/weeks', etc.

Foreign students often misuse *dentro de* when translating the English 'in'. *Dentro de* can only refer to the future. One cannot say **lo hice dentro de un año* 'I did it in one year' (*lo hice en un año*):

—*¿Cuándo empieza?* —*Dentro de tres días*	'When does it start?' 'In three days' time'
Lo haré dentro de un momento	I'll do it in a moment
Me dijo que dentro de un año estaríamos casados	(S)he told me that in a year's time we would be married
de hoy en ocho días	in eight days' time
Me faltan/quedan tres días para irme	I'm going in three days' time

Notes

(i) Use of *en* to mean *dentro de* is common in Latin America, much less common in Spain: *no te preocupes, vuelvo en un rato* (A. Mastretta, Mexico, dialogue) 'don't worry, I'll be back in a minute'. Seco (1998), 186, says that this use of *en* for *dentro de* is an Anglicism that should be avoided as ambiguous since it can also mean 'in the space of': *lo haré en un momento* also means 'it'll only take me a moment to do it'.

(ii) *En* can mean the same as the English 'in' in negative sentences like 'I've not been there in/for years': *sabe usted que no nos hemos visto en doce años* (C. Fuentes, Mexico, dialogue) 'you know that we haven't seen one another in/for twelve years'.

32.6 'Again'

There are numerous ways of translating 'again':

(a) *Volver a* . . . :

This is probably the most usual construction before a verb:

Han vuelto a hacerlo	They've done it again
Cuando cerró la puerta volví a llorar	When he shut the door, I started
(A. Mastretta, Mexico, dialogue)	crying again
Como me vuelvas a hablar de esa manera . . .	If you talk to me like that again . . .
(this use of *como* is discussed at 25.8.2)	

(b) *Otra vez:*

Hazlo otra vez/Vuelve a hacerlo/Hazlo de nuevo	Do it again
No te lo digo otra vez/No te lo vuelvo a decir/No vuelvo a decírtelo	I won't tell you again
Otra vez no te lo digo	Another time I won't tell you/The next time I won't tell you

(c) *De nuevo* is more literary than *otra vez:*

De nuevo volvieron las suspicacias y los recelos	Once again suspicion and distrust returned

32.7 *Tardar*

Tardar, as well as meaning 'to be late' (*no tardes* 'don't be late') may translate 'to take' in expressions of time:

Tardó un año en escribirnos	He took a year to write to us/He didn't write to us for a year
Tardará casi tres horas en acabarlo	She'll take nearly three hours to do it
Se tarda media hora andando	It takes an hour to walk it

Note

Llevar may also be used in certain expressions: *eso te llevará horas* 'that'll take you hours', *me llevó días* 'it took me days'; but *el viaje duró varias horas* 'the journey took several hours'.

32.8 'Still'

(*Todavía* and *aún* are discussed at 31.7.3.) A very frequent construction is *continuar* or, more commonly, *seguir* followed by the gerund (**continuar a hacer algo*, 'to continue to do something' is not Spanish). *Seguir* is used before adjectives and participles, i.e. one says *sigue enfermo* 'he's still ill' rather than *continúa enfermo*.

Te has dado cuenta de que sigues llevando puesta la chaqueta del pijama (J.-M. Merino, Spain, dialogue)	You've realized that you've still got your pyjama/(US 'pajama') jacket on
Continuaban/Seguían viéndose	They went on seeing one another
Pero yo seguía preguntándome cómo demonios podía vivir una familia así (A. Bryce Echenique, Peru)	But I went on wondering how the devil a family like this could live
Pero ella sigue soltera (C. Fuentes, Mexico, dialogue)	But she's still unmarried

32.9 Dates

32.9.1 Saying and writing dates

Months are not written with a capital letter in Spanish. The usual way of saying dates is *quince de mayo de 1999* 'fifteenth of May nineteen-ninety-nine', *dos de abril de dos mil dos* 'May second two thousand and two', i.e. the cardinal number and not the ordinal is used. The only exception is *primero de . . .* 'the first of', but the form *el uno de . . .* is increasingly common, and although purists censure it, Manuel Seco has no objection to it.

The format used for dates in Spain is the same as in Great Britain, dd-mm-yy: *17 de junio de 1999*. In Latin America the American format mm-dd-yy may appear, as in *junio 17 de 1999*. When dates are written as numbers, the European order – dd-mm-yy – is standard: *23-IV-2010* = British 23/4/2010, US 4/23/2010. Note the common use of Roman numerals for the month in Spanish.

Typists often use a point after the thousands when writing years, e.g. 1.999, but grammarians, including Manuel Seco and *El País*, condemn this.

32.9.2 Decades

La década is the normal word for a decade, which can only start in a year that is a multiple of ten. *El decenio* means any period of ten years, which could, for example, start in 2002 or 2031. The most common way of referring to decades is *los años cincuenta* 'the fifties', *los años noventa* 'the nineties'. One can also say *la década de los cincuenta*, but Seco (1998), 50, considers it long-winded. *El decenio 1950–1960* is another, rather literary, possibility, and the formula *los cincuentas* 'the fifties', *los noventas* 'the nineties' is also found, but condemned as an Anglicism by Seco.

32.10 Miscellaneous time expressions

32.10.1 Telling the time

The verb is singular only for one o'clock: *es la una* 'it's one o'clock', but *son las dos* 'it's two o'clock'. Minutes, quarter-hours and half-hours after the hour are joined to the hour by *y*. Minutes before the hour are joined by *menos*. The 24-hour clock is used in the same way as in English.

Except where specified, the following examples reflect Peninsular usage. Several variations may be heard in the various Latin-American republics. Some of the English translations ('half-past', 'a quarter to', etc.) reflect British usage and will be unfamiliar to North Americans, and some US forms in the translations will be unfamiliar to British readers:

(a) Asking the time (12-hour clock):

¿Qué hora es? (Lat. Am. *¿Qué horas son?*)	What time is it?
¿Qué hora tiene?	What time do you make it?
¿Qué hora será?	I wonder what time it is
¿A qué hora viene/empieza?	What time is (s)he coming/does it start?

(b) Telling the exact time:

Es la una (*en punto*)	It's one o'clock (exactly)
Son las dos, las tres, etc.	It's two o'clock, three o'clock, etc.
Es la una de la mañana	It's one in the morning
Son las tres de la tarde	It's three o'clock in the afternoon
Son las cuatro y cinco (also *son las cuatro con cinco minutos* in Mexico)	It's five (minutes) past/after four
Son las cinco y cuarto	It's a quarter past five/five fifteen
Son las seis y media	It's six-thirty
Son las siete y veinticinco	It's seven twenty-five/twenty-five past seven
Son las ocho menos cuarto (also *un cuarto para las ocho* in parts of Latin America)	It's a quarter to eight/seven forty-five
Son las nueve menos diez	It's ten to nine
Son y media	It's half-past/thirty minutes past
Son y cuarto	It's a quarter past/fifteen minutes past
Son menos diez/y cinco	It's ten to/five past
Empezará a las diez de la noche	It'll begin at ten at night
Falta mucho para las cuatro (A. Mastretta, Mexico, dialogue)	It's a long time until four o'clock
Los autobuses salen a menos veinte	The buses leave at twenty to
Van a dar las doce	It's just coming up to twelve
Acaba de dar la una	The clock has just struck one/It's just turned one

Acaban de dar las dos	The clock has just struck two
Llegó cuando daban las tres	He arrived on the stroke of three
Cuando daba la última campanada de las cuatro	On the last stroke of four
La consulta es de nueve a once/desde las nueve hasta las once	The doctor's surgery is from nine to eleven
La conferencia es a las cinco	The lecture is at five
Al filo de la medianoche (poetic)	At exactly midnight

(c) Approximate time:

(Ya) han dado las siete	It's already gone seven
Son las ocho más o menos	It's about eight o'clock
Son pasadas las ocho (not **después de las ocho*)	It's gone eight/past eight
Son cerca de las nueve	It's nearly nine o'clock
Deben de ser las/cerca de las nueve (or *serán las nueve*)	It must be nine o'clock/nearly nine o'clock
Llegaré a eso de/aproximadamente a las dos de la mañana (or *sobre las dos*)	I'll be there around two
Serían las siete de la tarde cuando llegó	It must have been seven o'clock when she arrived
No acabaré hasta después de las tres/hasta pasadas las tres	I won't finish until after three

32.10.2 The 24-hour clock

El tren sale a las quince horas	The train leaves at fifteen hundred
El avión llegó a las diecisiete (horas) quince minutos/y quince	The plane arrived at seventeen fifteen

32.10.3 Times of the day

a primera hora de la mañana/por la mañana temprano	early in the morning
por la mañana (Lat. Am. *a/en la mañana*)	in the morning
a media mañana	in the middle of the morning
a mediodía	at noon
a la hora de comer/almorzar	at lunchtime (2–4 p.m. in Spain)
a la hora de la merienda	at teatime (i.e. around 4 p.m.)
a la hora de cenar	at dinnertime (9–11 p.m. in Spain)
después de comer/cenar; 'to have lunch' = *almorzar* in Latin America)	after lunch/dinner
por la tarde	in the afternoon (from lunchtime until about 8 p.m.)
al atardecer/anochecer	in the evening
por la noche	at night
a (la) medianoche	at midnight
al amanecer/de madrugada	at dawn
Ven esta noche/a la noche	Come tonight
Ven por la noche	Come during the night/by night

32.10.4 Greetings associated with different times of the day

buenos días	good morning
buenas tardes (used between about 1 p.m. and about 8 p.m.)	good afternoon/evening
buenas noches	good evening/good night (greeting and goodbye; used after about 8 p.m.)

32.10.5 Miscellaneous expressions

dos veces a la semana/al día	twice a week/a day
cada media hora/dos o tres días	every half-hour/every two or three days
todos los días	every day
Cada día que amanece nos trae más problemas	Each day that dawns brings us more problems
El sábado/Los sábados no trabajo	I don't work on Saturdays
todos los días entre semana	every day from Monday to Friday

Note

For *cada día* and *todos los días* see 9.6.

—¿Qué (día) es hoy? —Domingo	'What day is it today?' 'Sunday'
Hoy es lunes, martes, etc.	Today's Monday, Tuesday, etc.
Hoy es el/estamos a 28 de marzo	Today it's the 28th of March
¿A cuántos estamos? (¿Qué fecha es hoy?)	What's the date today?
a 17 de enero de 1999 (el 17 de enero de 1999)	the 17th of January, 1999
Estamos a mediados/principios/finales/últimos/ de este mes	We're at the middle/beginning/end of this month
el 5 del corriente (business language)	the 5th of this month/'the fifth inst.'
Saldremos el viernes 28 (veintiocho) al mediodía	We'll leave on Friday the 28th at midday
la semana/el mes/el año pasado	last week, month, year
Se casaron el 20 de julio pasado	They got married on the 20th of last July
Nació en (el mes de) abril del año pasado	He was born in February last year
al cabo de un año	a year later
a los 5 minutos quería salirse	after 5 minutes she wanted to leave
al día siguiente	the following/next day
de hoy en ocho días	a week today
ayer/anteayer	yesterday/the day before yesterday

32.10.6 Translating 'next'

El próximo lunes hablaremos	We'll talk next Monday
Vendrá al/el año próximo	He'll come next year
el/al año/mes/la semana que viene (but *que viene* is not used with the names of months: *el próximo julio* 'next July')	next year/month/week
la próxima vez que lo hagan	the next time they do it

32.10.7 Age

The word *años* cannot usually be omitted when talking about age, at least on the first mention of the topic: *al año andaba, a los dos hablaba dos idiomas, a los tres leía* '(s)he was walking by the time (s)he was one, speaking two languages at two and reading at three'.

A los 15 años se mudó a La Habana (Latina, New York)	At fifteen she moved to Havana
—¿Cuántos años tienes? —Veinte (the word *años* can be omitted only when answering this question)	'How old are you?' 'I'm twenty'
Mi hermano tiene quince años	My brother is fifteen

¿A qué edad andan los niños?	At what age do children walk?
Acaba de cumplir los cincuenta años	(S)he has just turned fifty
Andará por los cuarenta	(S)he must be around forty
a los cuarenta años	at the age of forty

32.10.8 Omission of preposition before certain expressions of time

There is no preposition before some words and expressions. These are:

(a) Days of the week:

Nos vemos el lunes/el viernes	We're meeting on Monday/Friday

(b) With a demonstrative + *año/día/mañana/tarde/noche/vez:*

Aquel día/año llovió mucho	It rained a lot that day/year
Lo/Le vi esta mañana	I saw him this morning

In informal Latin-American Spanish the preposition may also be omitted before some other words, as in *la ocasión que te vi* (Spain . . . *en que te vi*) 'the occasion I saw you', . . . *cuando la mañana siguiente me anunció que* . . . (A. Mastretta, Mexico; Spain *a la mañana siguiente*) 'when the following morning he announced to me that . . . ', . . . *los funcionarios destituidos injustamente los últimos 18 meses* (*La Prensa*, Panama) 'State employees unfairly dismissed during the last 18 months' (normally *durante/en los últimos 18 meses*).

33

Conjunctions and connectors

This chapter discusses the following words:

pero, sino, mas but 33.1
o/u or 33.2
y/e and 33.3
    que, de que that 33.4
porque/pues/como and other words
    meaning 'because', 'since . . . ' 33.5.1
ya que/puesto que/como and other words
    meaning 'since'/'seeing that' 33.5.2
aunque, y eso que and other words
    meaning 'although' 33.6

con tal de que, a menos que and other
    expressions of condition and
    exception 33.7
words indicating purpose 33.8
    de modo/manera que and other words
    expressing result 33.9
connectors (e.g. 'however',
    'nevertheless', 'on the other hand')
    33.11

A large number of Spanish subordinating conjunctions, e.g. *cuando, sin que, después de que*, are associated with the subjunctive and are also discussed in Chapter 16. They are merely noted in the appropriate section of this chapter.

33.1 *Pero, sino, mas*

All of these translate 'but'. *Mas* (no accent) is virtually extinct, but it is occasionally found in flowery written language and in the bad Spanish of students influenced by French or Portuguese. The distinction between *pero* and *sino* is crucial:

(a) *Sino* is used in statements of the sort 'not A but B . . . '. It is almost always preceded by a negative statement and is very common in the construction *no sólo/solo . . . sino (que) . . .* 'not only . . . but . . . '. Before a verb phrase *sino **que*** must be used. Examples:

No quiero pan, sino vino	I don't want bread, but wine
no tú, sino él	not you, but him
no éste/este, sino ése/ese	not this one, but that
No sólo/solo van a misa todos los días, sino ***que*** *rezan en sus cuartos también*	They not only go to Mass daily but they pray in their rooms as well
*. . . mientras no ponía, sino **que** arrojaba las tazas sobre la bandeja* (C. Rico-Godoy, Spain)	. . . while she was not so much putting as flinging the cups on the tray
*Yo no dije que fuera mentira, sino **que** no lo creía*	I didn't say it was a lie, but that I didn't believe it

Pero is not possible in any of the above examples, but it translates the English word 'but' in all other cases:

Habla francés, pero mal	He speaks French, but badly

No van a misa todos los días, pero rezan en sus cuartos
Pero ¿es posible?

They don't go to Mass every day, but they **do** pray in their rooms
But can it (really) be possible?

Notes

(i) *Sino* may sometimes be translated by 'except': *¿qué puedo decir sino que lo siento?* 'what can I say but/except that I'm sorry?', *¿por quién sino por ti habría subido las escaleras cantando a gritos aprendimos a quererte?* (A. Bryce Echenique, Peru) 'for whom except you would I have gone up the stairs singing "we learnt to love you" at the top of my voice?', *ni él pudo entenderlo sino como un milagro del amor* (G. García Márquez, Colombia) 'even he couldn't understand it except as a miracle of love'.

(ii) *No . . . sino* may translate 'only' or 'just': *yo no podía sino dar gracias a Dios . . .* 'I could only thank God', *no pensaba sino en ella/no pensaba más que en ella* 'he thought only of her', *el pueblo mexicano . . . no cree ya sino en la Virgen de Guadalupe y en la Lotería Nacional* (O. Paz, Mexico) 'the Mexican people now believe in nothing but the Virgin of Guadalupe and the National Lottery', *pero esa sabiduría no te tranquiliza ni reconforta sino todo lo contrario* (E. Lynch, Argentina) 'but that wisdom doesn't calm you down or comfort you – just the opposite'.

(iii) *Sino* must not be confused (as it sometimes is in older or badly written texts) with *si no* 'if not'.

33.2 O

'Or'. It is written and pronounced *u* before a word beginning with *o-* or *ho-*: *hombres o mujeres* 'men or women', but *mujeres u hombres* 'women or men'. Spoken language often neglects to use *u*, and *o* is also sometimes retained if it is the first word in a sentence.

O . . . o translates 'either . . . or': *o lo sabe o no lo sabe* 'either he knows it or he doesn't':

Os digo que u os apartáis, u os araño (dialogue in a popular novel, Spain; *o os . . .* is more likely in spontaneous speech)

I'm telling you, either you get out of my way, or I'll scratch you

Note

O is often written with an accent when it appears alongside a number to avoid confusion with zero: *6 ó 5* '6 or 5'. However, *El País* insists on *6 o 5* on the grounds that no confusion is likely with *605* (which may be true in print, but not in handwriting).

33.3 Y

'And'; used much like its English equivalent. It is written and pronounced *e* before a word beginning with a pure *i* sound, e.g. *Miguel e Ignacio, padre e hijos*, but not before words beginning with a *y* sound – *carbón y hierro* 'coal and iron' – and not when it means 'what about?': *¿Y Ignacio?* 'what about Ignacio?' Substitution of *e* for *y* is not always made in spontaneous speech. The use of *y* differs from the English 'and' in a few respects:

(a) It is occasionally translatable as 'after' in sentences like:

Transcurrieron días y días sin tener más noticias de lo ocurrido

Day after day passed without any further news of what had happened (lit. 'without having news of')

(b) As mentioned earlier, it often means 'what about?':

¿Y el perro?	What about the dog?
¿Y la democracia?	What about democracy?
¿Y qué?	So what?/Who cares?

33.4 Que

Que is an overworked word: it has at least four separate uses in Spanish:

(a) As the most common relative pronoun: *la mujer que vi* 'the woman that/whom I saw', *el año en que nací* 'the year I was born in'. This use is discussed in Chapter 35.

(b) *Qué* with an accent means 'what' and is best thought of as an entirely different word. It is discussed at 24.4.

(c) *Que* may mean 'than' in comparisons: see Chapter 5.

(d) As a subordinating conjunction: see the next section.

33.4.1 *Que* as a subordinating conjunction

Que introduces clauses in the same way as the English conjunction 'that'. It differs from the latter in that it cannot be omitted (see 33.4.6 for rare exceptions):

Dice que viene	He says (that) he's coming
Cree que no ha pagado	She thinks (that) he hasn't paid
Parece que va a llover	It seems (that) it's going to rain

However, the absence of a personal infinitive construction in Spanish makes this use of *que* much more common than the English 'that':

*Te aconsejo **que** no lo hagas*	I advise you not **to do** it
*Quiero **que** vengas*	I want you **to come**
*Les pidió **que** no firmasen/firmaran*	He asked them not **to sign**

Statements followed by *que* that require the subjunctive, for example *quiero que* . . . 'I want . . . ', *es necesario que* . . . 'it's necessary that . . . ', are discussed in Chapter 16.

33.4.2 De before que

In certain circumstances a subordinate clause must be introduced by *de que*. This is necessary:

(a) After noun phrases:
This happens when *que* is a conjunction and not a relative pronoun. English does not clearly differentiate between the relative pronoun 'that' and the subordinating conjunction 'that': the phrase 'the idea **that** he liked . . . ' is therefore ambiguous out of context. If 'that' can be replaced by 'which', *que* alone is possible in the Spanish translation. Compare:

the idea that/which he liked	*la idea **que** le gustaba* . . . (relative pronoun; *de que* impossible)
The idea that he likes mustard is absurd ('that' not replaceable by 'which')	*La idea **de que** le gusta la mostaza es absurda* (subordinating conjunction)

Further examples:

*Se dio cuenta **de que** ya no llovía*	He realized that it was no longer raining

*Cuando yo era chico y me desesperaba ante la idea **de que** mi madre debía morirse un día ...* (E. Sábato, Argentina)	When I was a little boy and I despaired at the idea that my mother would have to die one day ...
tengo ganas de que ...	I feel like ...
tengo la certeza de que ...	I'm certain that ...
tenía miedo de que ...	he was afraid that ...
soy partidario de que ...	I'm in favour of ...
el argumento de que ...	the argument that ...
la creencia de que ...	the belief that ...
la causa de que no llegara a tiempo	the cause of his not arriving on time

(b) After a number of common verbs that require the preposition *de*:

me acuerdo de que ...	I remember that ...
me olvidaba de que ...	I was forgetting that ...
se convenció de que ...	(s)he became convinced that ...
se lamentaba/quejaba de que ...	(s)he was bewailing the fact that .../ complaining that ...
se trata de que ...	it's about .../it's a question of ...

and similarly after a number of verbs denoting mental or emotional states such as *aburrirse de que* 'to be bored that', *cansarse de que* 'to get tired of. . .', etc. For a selection of these verbs see 26.4.2.

(c) After certain adjectives and adverbial phrases that are normally followed by *de*:

estoy seguro/convencido de que ...	I'm sure/convinced that ...
estamos contentos de que ...	we're pleased that ...
estoy cansado/harto de que ...	I'm tired/fed up with ...
soy consciente de que ...	I'm aware that ...
estoy hasta la coronilla de que ...	I'm sick to death with ...

(d) After subordinators that include *de*:

antes de que llegase	before he arrived
después de que se fueron	after they went
a condición de que ...	on condition that ...
a cambio de que ...	in exchange for ...

and also *a pesar de que* 'despite the fact that', *con tal de que* 'provided that', *en lugar de que* 'instead of', *con el objeto de que* 'with the object of . . .'.

Notes

(i) There is, however, a colloquial tendency, much stronger in Latin America than in Spain, to drop the *de* in the more common of these constructions: *Wenceslao se había dado cuenta **que** la maniobra de Juvenal era extraviar a sus primos* (J. Donoso, Chile) 'Wenceslao had realized that Juvenal's manoeuvre was (designed) to lead his cousins astray', *pero estoy segura **que** es lo que haces* (L. Goytisolo, Spain, dialogue) 'but I'm sure that that is what you're doing', *aun en el supuesto **que** se tratara de complots ...* (*Caretas*, Peru) 'even on the assumption that plots were involved ...', *para que te convenzas **que** la dignidad no se come* (G. García Márquez, Colombia, dialogue) 'to convince you that (lit. 'so you convince yourself') that one can't eat dignity'.

In general, omission of *de* in such cases may be rejected as substandard by Peninsular speakers, but it is very common in informal and journalistic Latin-American Spanish, although much rarer in formal written styles.

(ii) *Antes que* 'before' may be used instead of *antes de que* in many regions, cf. *venda ese gallo antes **que** sea demasiado tarde* (G. García Márquez, Colombia, dialogue) 'sell that cockerel before it's too late', *lo conozco desde antes **que** tú nacieras* (M. Vargas Llosa, Peru, dialogue) 'I've known him since before you were born', *antes que te cases, mira lo que haces* (Spanish proverb) 'before you marry, look what you're doing'. *Antes que* is more common in Latin America, though *antes de que* is frequent, especially in writing. Peninsular informants found *antes que* acceptable in the previous examples but it is generally much less common in Spain than *antes **de** que*.

Antes que also means 'rather than' everywhere: *cualquier cosa antes que eso* 'anything but/rather than that', ... *debe ser tratado con pragmatismo para evitar que resulte un nuevo problema antes que la solución deseada* (*El Comercio*, Ecuador) ' ... it should be treated pragmatically so as to avoid it becoming a another problem rather than the desired solution', ... *el aprecio por las cosas bellas antes que por las que tienen éxito* (A. Mastretta, Mexico) '... the appreciation of beautiful things rather than successful ones'.

33.4.3 Dequeísmo

There is a growing tendency on both continents to insert *de* before *que* after verbs denoting opinions or states of mind other than those mentioned above, e.g. *decir* 'say', *afirmar* 'claim', *creer* 'believe', *sostener* 'maintain', *negar* 'deny', *pensar* 'think', *confesar* 'confess', *argüir* 'argue', etc. Example:

> *?Dice **de que** no viene* (for *dice que no viene*) '(S)he says (s)he's not coming'
> *?Creo **de que** no es verdad* (for *creo que es verdad*) 'I think it isn't true'

This use of *de que* for *que* is vehemently rejected by educated speakers everywhere and should be avoided at all costs. It is especially frequent in some regions, notoriously Peru, where it is constantly heard on radio and TV.

Notes

(i) *Hablar de que* is correctly used for 'to talk about ...' in such sentences as *habló **de que** Miguel estaba enfermo* 'he talked about Miguel being ill'.

(ii) *Dudar de que* is a permitted variant of *dudar que* 'to doubt': *nadie dudó **(de) que** dijera la verdad* 'no one doubted that he told the truth', *ni a nosotros se nos ocurría dudar de que él abandonase su camino* (S. Puértolas, Spain) 'it didn't even occur to **us** to doubt that he would abandon his vocation (lit. 'way')'.

(iii) The construction with *informar* is *informar a alguien de algo* 'to inform someone of something', so *les informó **de que** no era cierto* is correct for 'he informed them it was not true'. However, *informar que* is also commonly heard, presumably because people are anxious to avoid any accusation of *dequeísmo*.

33.4.4 Que at the head of a phrase

Que may appear at the head of a sentence or clause, especially in speech. Its main functions are:

(a) To reinforce the idea that what follows expresses something expected, something repeated or something that is being insisted on. In this case some verb like *decir* or *preguntar* may have been omitted:

*¿**Que** cómo se llama mi película?*	(did you ask) What's my film called?
¿Que si me gustó?	(did you ask me) Did I like it?
¿Que por qué no van obreros al teatro?	(you're asking me) Why don't workers go to the theatre/(US 'theater')?
Que no quiero verla	(I said that) I don't want to see her/it
Oye, que aquí pone que no hay que abrirlo	Listen, it says here that it mustn't be opened
¡Que sí! ¡Que no!	Yes! No! (impatient repetition)
¡Socorro! ¡Que me ahogo!	Help! I'm drowning!

(b) As a colloquial subordinator of cause. It is often inserted to connect one idea to another where English uses a pause represented in writing by a dash:

*¡Rápido! ¡Rápido! ¡**Que** se va!*	Hurry! Hurry! It's going! (e.g. the train)
Eso dijo, que lo oí yo con mis propios oídos	That's what he said – I heard it with my own ears
¡¿Dónde está mi marido que lo degüello?!	Where's my husband – I'm going to slaughter him!
No me des la lata con lo que dicen los lectores, que tengo cosas más importantes de que ocuparme (C. Rico-Godoy in *Cambio16*, Spain)	Don't pester me with what the readers are saying – I've more important things to bother about
No te cases con tu novio, que ése va a por tu dinero (A. Grandes, Spain, dialogue)	Don't marry your boyfriend. He's after your money
No lo inclines tanto, que se caen los papeles (J. de Jesús Martínez, Panama, dialogue)	Don't tilt it so much – the papers will fall off

(c) Colloquially, to show that the truth has dawned after some doubt:

¡Ah! Que usted es el fontanero (Lat. Am. *plomero*)	Ah – so you're the plumber, then
Que tú eres entonces el que lo hizo	So you're the one who did it, then
¿Que no quieres ir conmigo?	You mean you don't want to go with me?

(d) To translate 'that' in colloquial sentences meaning 'it was so . . . that . . . ':

Tengo un sueño que no veo	I'm so tired I could drop (lit. 'that I can't see')
Estaba la habitación que no cabía un alfiler	The room was so crowded that a pin wouldn't fit/you couldn't get a pin in it
Ya no sabíamos ni donde poner la plata, que nos faltaban muebles para guardarla, de tantísima que teníamos (A. Grandes, Spain)	We didn't know where to put the silver any more, we had so much that we were short of furniture to keep it in.

(e) With the subjunctive in commands, exhortations and wishes, e.g. *que venga en seguida* 'tell him/her to come/have him/her come immediately', *que te acuerdes de escribirnos* 'remember to write to us'. See 17.6 for details.

(f) To mean 'the fact that', in which case it is likely to take the subjunctive. See 16.10.1 for further discussion.

(g) Occasionally in very colloquial (never in written) Peninsular Spanish, as a substitute for *si* 'if': *que no quiere venir, me lo dices* (better *si no quiere venir . . .*) 'if he doesn't want to come, tell me'.

33.4.5 *Que* in indirect questions

Decir que may mean 'to ask'. *Que* is also used optionally after *preguntar* 'to ask':

—*¿Sabes lo que me dijo este animal de bellota?*	'Do you know what this pig (lit. 'acorn animal') said to/asked me?'
—*Te dijo **que** si estaba la cena lista* (C. Rico-Godoy, Spain, dialogue complaining about husbands)	'He asked you if dinner/supper was ready'
Yo me pregunto (que) dónde estará ella estudiando	I wonder where she's studying
Le pregunté (que) qué hacía allí	I asked him/her what (s)he was doing there

33.4.6 Omission of conjunction *que*

Que is occasionally omitted, but much less so than the English 'that':

(a) if the following verb is in the subjunctive, and especially with the verb *rogar que* 'to request'. This construction is practically confined to business letters and other official language. It is also found in substandard language:

Les ruego envíen más información sobre la máquina de escribir ES 3 (advertisement in *Cambio16*, Spain)	Please send more information about the ES 3 typewriter
No importa le tilden de bufón (Popular press, Spain; substandard for *no importa* **que** *le tilden . . .*)	It doesn't matter if they dub him a clown
Por otro lado, solicitan se les solucione la deuda que mantiene el Estado con ellos relativa a seis partidas del decimotercer mes (*La Prensa*, Panama)	As well as this, they are requesting settlement of the debt the State has contracted vis-à-vis them with respect to six 'thirteenth month' payments (i.e. bonuses)

Such omission is best avoided by foreign students.

(b) In relative clauses introduced by *que* so as to avoid excessive use of *que*. This is probably confined to written language (# marks the point of omission):

desde este punto de vista, que pienso # comparten muchos españoles	from this point of view, which I think many Spaniards share
Me contestó con una serie de argumentos que supongo # están de moda hoy día	She replied with a series of arguments which I suppose are fashionable nowadays

33.4.7 Replacement of subordinating *que* by an infinitive

For a discussion of sentences like *dice estar enferma* 'she says she's ill' (for *dice que está enferma*) see 18.2.2.

33.4.8 Miscellaneous examples of *que*

The bracket indicates that the *que* is optional:

Qué bien (que) lo hemos pasado (the redundant *que* sounds uneducated)	What a nice time we've had
. . . y él habla **que** *habla* (colloquial)	. . . and he kept talking on and on . . .
Yo venga a pedirle el divorcio y él **que** *no* (*venga a* is a colloquial Peninsular form suggesting constant repetition)	I kept on asking him for a divorce and he wouldn't have it/kept saying no
Lucho por conseguir comprensión, **(que)** *no amor*	I'm struggling to get understanding, not love
¡Tonto! Eran monos, **(que)** *no seres extraterrestres*	You fool! They were monkeys, not creatures from another planet
¡Cuidado **que** *sois pesados!*	Heavens, are you a nuisance!

33.5 Causal conjunctions

The most common are:

porque because	*pues* for (= 'because')	*puesto que* since
como since, as	*ya que* since	*en vista de que* in view of the fact that

33.5.1 *Porque*

Porque means 'because'; *por qué*, spelt and pronounced differently (the *qué* is stressed), means 'why'. The noun *el porqué* means 'the reason why'. *Porque* may occasionally require the subjunctive. See 16.12.4b. The difference between *porque* 'because' and *por qué* 'why' is crucial:

No sabe, porque es tan ignorante	He doesn't know because he's so ignorant
No sabe por qué es tan ignorante	He doesn't know **why** he's so ignorant

Notes

(i) *Porque* may also be found as an optional alternative to *para que* after those words which allow *por*, e.g. *esforzarse por* 'to make an effort to . . . ', *tener prisa por. . .* 'to be in a hurry to. . .' (see the section on *por* and *para* 34.14). For the difference between *por qué* and *para qué* 'why' see 24.10.
(ii) *Por* is intimately associated with the idea of cause, e.g. *te lo mereces, **por** tonto* 'serves you right for being stupid', *se perdieron **por** no haber comprado un mapa* 'they got lost as a result of not having bought a map'. See 34.14.4 for more examples.
(iii) *Porque* and *por qué* can never be used to translate 'that's why' or 'that's the reason why'; see 36.2.4.

33.5.2 *Como, ya que, puesto que, que, en vista de que*

All of these may translate 'since'. *Que* is discussed under 33.4.

Puesto/Ya que quieres que me vaya, me voy	Since you want me to go, I'm leaving
La reunión se aplazó en vista de que no vino casi nadie	The meeting was postponed in view of the fact that hardly anybody turned up

Care is required with the word *como* when it is used to mean 'since'/'because'. When used thus it can appear only at the head of the phrase it refers to. **Yo no comía como no tenía apetito* is not Spanish, but *como no tenía apetito, yo no comía* 'as I had no appetite, I didn't eat' is correct. Compare *no lo hice como me dijiste* 'I didn't do it the way you told me to', and *no lo hice, como me lo dijiste* (example from *Libro de estilo de El País*) 'I didn't do it, just as you told me' (i.e. 'because you told me not to'). Further examples:

Es de peor educación todavía insinuar que, como soy una mujer, se supone que no soy nadie (C. Rico-Godoy, Spain, dialogue)	It's even more ill-mannered to hint that, since I'm a woman, it's assumed that I'm nobody
Como se sentía cansado y no quería que le molestaran, les ordenó que escribieran una composición (S. Galindo, Mexico)	As he was feeling tired and didn't want them to bother him, he told them (the schoolchildren) to write an essay
luego, como veía que no llegaban . . .	then, since he could see that they weren't coming . . .
pero, como yo no sabía qué hacer . . .	but since I didn't know what to do . . .

Notes

(i) *Desde que* is found in Latin America with the meaning *ya que*. Its standard meaning is 'since' as in *desde que los vi* 'since (the moment when) I saw them'.
(ii) The form *como que* for *ya que* 'since'/'as', when placed before the main verb, should generally be avoided. Seco (1998), 118, censures it as a Catalanism that has spread to Aragon; *como* alone should be used: *ya que no es posible no podemos hacerlo*, 'since it is not possible, we cannot do it', not ?*como que no es posible . . .* Placed after the main verb it is, however, found on both continents

as an alternative to *como* = 'since': *ella lo siguió encontrando todo muy natural y como que empezó a tomarme afecto . . .* (A. Bryce Echenique, Peru) 'she continued to find everything very natural, and since she had started to grow fond of me . . .'. However, when used emphatically it may introduce a following explanatory sentence: *claro que está bien. ¡Como que lo he hecho yo!* 'of course it's well-made/right. *I* did it!'

(iii) *Como* with the subjunctive translates 'if' in conditional sentences; see 25.8.2. Occasionally *como* meaning 'since' occurs with a *-ra* verb form, as in *—Quizá —dijo Víctor. Y como Arturo no replicara, añadió—: Bueno, me subo* (M. Delibes, Spain) '"Perhaps," Víctor said. And as Arturo didn't reply, he added "OK, I'm getting in"' (i.e. *ya que . . ./puesto que . . .* + indicative).

33.5.3 *Pues*

Pues has numerous uses, but its basic function is probably to show that what follows is inspired by something said just before, or that the speaker has reflected a moment before continuing.

(a) *Pues* meaning 'because':

Pues should be employed very sparingly as a causal conjunction meaning 'because'. Gili y Gaya (1972), 15, remarks that 'discovery of causal *pues* as a way of adding a certain literary flourish to one's style is typical of writing between childhood and adolescence. This phase does not usually last long.' So whereas *pues* may be an elegant written variation on *porque* in the hands of a stylist, just as 'for' is an occasional flowery variant for 'because' in English ('it cannot be done, **for** there is no money'), non-natives should probably stick to *porque, ya que* or *puesto que*:

La voz no se sabe si es femenina o de hombre, ***pues*** *es aguda, verdaderamente penetrante* (J.-M. Arguedas, Peru)	One can't tell whether the voice is a woman's or a man's, for it's high-pitched truly piercing

(b) 'In that case . . . ' This use is very frequent in everyday speech:

*—No queremos comer ahora. —**Pues**, cuando ustedes quieran . . .* (or *entonces/en ese caso*)	'We don't want to eat now.' 'In that case, when you like . . . '
*—No quiero estar aquí. —**Pues** vete*	'I don't want to be here.' 'Go away then'

(c) Like the English 'well', it may downtone an answer to a question, adding a modest or tentative note or perhaps showing that the speaker has thought for a moment before answering:

—¿En qué situación se encuentran las negociaciones entre los dos gobiernos?	'What is the state of the negotiations between the two governments?'
*—**Pues**, el hecho es que no hay negociaciones* (interview, *Cambio16*, Spain)	'Well, the fact is there are no negotiations'
*—¿Quiénes estaban? —**Pues** . . . Manuel, Antonio, Mariluz . . .*	'Who was there?' 'Er . . . Manuel, Antonio, Mariluz . . . '

(d) It may add emphasis or a note of contradiction:

*—Yo creía que estaba enfermo. —**Pues** no*	'I thought he was ill.' 'Well he isn't'
*No, si ya me figuro dónde está ¡**Pues** me va a oír!* (A. Buero Vallejo, Spain, dialogue)	No, I can well imagine where she is. Well, she's going to hear what I've got to say!

Notes

(i) In some parts of Latin America and Northern Spain, conversation is sprinkled with *pues*: *oye pues, vámonos pues*, etc.

(ii) Students of French should not confuse *pues* with *puis* which means *después, entonces* or *luego*.

33.6 Concession

33.6.1 Phrases that introduce concessions ('although', etc.)

The main ways of introducing a concession are as follows (forms marked with a dagger are typical of literary language):

aunque/bien que/y eso que/así/ aun cuando/si bien	although/even though/even in the event that
a pesar de que/pese a que⁺/por más que/a despecho de que⁺	despite the fact that
por mucho que	however much

All of these, except *y eso que* and *si bien*, may appear with the subjunctive and are discussed at 16.12.9. *Por mucho que* is discussed at 16.13.2.

33.6.2 *Y eso que* and *si bien*

Y eso que is stylistically informal and does not take the subjunctive. It can only refer to events that are realities, i.e. it means 'despite **the fact** that': *no la reconocí,* ***y eso que*** *la había visto dos días antes* 'I didn't recognize her, although/despite the fact that I'd seen her two days before'. *Y eso que* has the peculiarity that it cannot appear at the beginning of a sentence or main clause: one could not begin the next example **Y eso que lo había visto saltar . . .* :

Lo primero que hice fue darme cuenta de que el terrón no estaba a la vista y eso que lo había visto saltar hasta los zapatos (J. Cortázar, Argentina, dialogue)	The first thing I did was realize the sugar lump was out of sight, even though I'd seen it bounce down to my shoes
. . . y eso que no leo novelas eróticas (A. Bryce Echenique, Peru)	. . . despite the fact that I don't read erotic novels
. . .y eso que devolvió de forma increíble varias bolas (El País)	. . .despite the fact that he made some incredible returns (in tennis)

Si bien is rather literary in style and is used like *y eso que* only to refer to an established fact (i.e. it cannot refer to the future). Unlike *y eso que*, *si bien* can, however, appear at the start of a sentence:

Si bien la lluvia es frecuente, el verano inglés es a menudo agradable	Despite the fact that rain is frequent, the English summer is often pleasant
Si bien el Programa de Riesgos Profesionales muestra un superávit de 150 millones de dólares . . . (La Prensa, Panama)	Despite the fact that the Professional Indemnities programme has 150 million dollars in reserve . . .

33.7 Condition and exception

(a) The main conjunctions of condition are (all can be translated as 'provided that'/'as long as'):

con tal (de) que	*bajo (la) condición de que*	*mientras (no)*
a condición de que	*siempre que*	*como*
	siempre y cuando	

All of these require the subjunctive and are discussed under 16.12.8a.
(b) The main conjunctions of exception are:

a menos que	*a no ser que*	*fuera de que*
excepto que/salvo que	*como no*	*si no* (if not)

All of these mean 'unless' and are discussed at 16.12.8b since they may require the subjunctive.

33.8 Subordinating conjunctions of purpose and aim

The most common are:

(a) 'in order that'/'so that':

para que	*de modo que†*	*a fin de que*
de manera que†	*a que*	*con el objeto de que*
porque	*de forma que†*	

(b) lest/in order that not. . . :

no sea que . . .	*no fuera que . . ./no fuese que . . .*

All conjunctions of purpose require the subjunctive and are discussed under 16.12.3. Those that have daggers may also indicate result and are then followed by the indicative. See 16.12.5 for discussion.

33.9 Subordinating conjunctions of result

Subordinators that express manner can denote either a result or an aim. In the latter case they take the subjunctive. *Conque* and *así que* indicate results: *conque ha sido ella* 'so it was her', *así que no he vuelto* 'so I haven't gone back'. *De modo que, de manera que, de forma que* can express results or intentions: in the latter case they take the subjunctive. All are discussed under 16.12.5, but it should be noted that the phrases *de **tal** modo que, de **tal** manera que, de **tal** forma que* can only express result, not purpose:

Gritó de tal modo/manera/forma que todos los vecinos se asomaron a la ventana	He shouted in such a way that all the neighbours leant out of their windows

33.10 Subordinating conjunctions of time

These include such words and phrases as:

a la vez que at the same time as	*al poco rato de que* shortly after	*en tanto que* as long as
a partir del momento en que from the moment that	*antes de que* before	*hasta que* until
	apenas scarcely	*mientras* while/as long as
	así que as soon as	*nada más que* as soon as
a poco de que shortly after	*cada vez que* every time that	*no bien (que)* scarcely
al mismo tiempo at the same time as	*cuando* when	*siempre que* whenever/as long as
	después de que after	*tan pronto como* as soon as
	en cuanto as soon as	*una vez que* once/as soon as

All subordinators of time require the subjunctive in certain circumstances (*antes de que* always takes the subjunctive). They are discussed at 16.12.7. For further remarks on *cuando* 'when' see 24.8.

33.11 Connectors

'Connectors' is the name we apply loosely to words used to link what has been said to what is going to be said. There are usually several possibilities, depending on style. The colloquial variants listed below reflect Peninsular usage. Many conjunctions mentioned in the first part of this chapter and in Chapter 16 could have been included here but are dealt with elsewhere. These are:

Conjunctions used as connectors

antes que rather than (16.12.7)
a pesar de, pese a in spite of (16.12.9)
aunque, y eso que, si bien although, even
 though (16.12.9 and 33.6.2)
como however (16.12.5c)
con tal de que, bajo la condición de que and
 similar phrases 'provided that' (33.7,
 16.12.8)
a menos que unless (16.12.8b, 25.9b)

conque so . . . (16.12.5a)
o/u or (33.2)
pero, sino, mas but (33.1)
porque, pues, como because (33.5.1,
 16.12.4b)
que/de que that (33.4)
y/e and (33.3)
ya que, puesto que since (33.5.2)

The old rule that sentences should not begin with conjunctions like the above is no longer strictly observed in either language. In fact, sentences beginning with 'and' and sentences consisting only of subordinate clauses are nowadays apparently more common in Spanish than in English: *Y aunque el esclarecimiento del caso se haya demorado largamente, su final demostraría que 'el criminal nunca gana'. Como corresponde a una historia tan de los años cincuenta* (*El País*, Spain) 'And although the solution of the crime has been long delayed, its conclusion tends to show that the 'criminal never wins'. As is appropriate for a story that is so typical of the 1950s.'

33.11.1 Afterthoughts

The standard ways of introducing an afterthought or some apparently unconnected remark are *a propósito* and *por cierto*, which both mean 'by the way'/'incidentally':

A propósito/Por cierto vi a tu madre ayer	By the way I saw your mother yesterday

Por cierto is slightly more colloquial than *a propósito*. It does not mean 'for certain'. *A propósito* can also mean *adrede* 'on purpose'.

33.11.2 Addition

There are several sentence-openers that indicate the speaker's intention of adding new information, e.g. *además, es más* 'moreover', *encima* 'moreover'/'on top of that', *por lo demás* 'apart from that':

Por lo demás no tengo más que decirte	Apart from that I haven't got anything else to tell you
Es más, también se lo dije a su hermano	Moreover I also told his brother
Además, mi mujer era mecanógrafa (G. Cabrera Infante, Cuba, dialogue)	Moreover, my wife was a typist
Encima no nos han dado el contrato	On top of everything we haven't got the contract

33.11.3 Qualification, reservation

There are a number of ways of indicating that what precedes is not the whole truth:

(a) *Sin embargo* 'nevertheless'/'still ... '/'however'/'in spite of that' occurs in speech and in writing. *No obstante* means the same thing, but is confined to writing. *Empero* also means 'nevertheless', but is highly literary, even archaic:

Sin embargo a los extranjeros, y especialmente a los españoles, les gusta Montevideo (M. Benedetti, Uruguay)	Nevertheless foreigners, and especially Spaniards, like Montevideo
Estaba muy cansado. Sin embargo/no obstante tenía que acabarlo	He was very tired. Nevertheless/in spite of that he had to finish it
Empero lo más importante es que se inicia un proceso para eliminar "la joroba de pagos", que por vencimiento de deudas se nos venía en los próximos tres años (*La Reforma*, Mexico)	However, the most important thing is that a process is being initiated to eliminate the debt burden (lit. 'payments hassle') which due to the expiry of debt deadlines was going to affect us in the next three years

(b) In colloquial language, the ubiquitous word *bueno* is much used to express scepticism when it is combined with a sceptical intonation, e.g. 'that's as may be, but ...':

—*Es que no pude venir a clase ayer porque tenía gripe.* —*Bueno, te has recuperado muy rápidamente*	'I couldn't come to class yesterday because I had the flu.' 'Well, you got over it pretty quickly'

(c) A colloquial way of saying 'however' is *pero, bueno* ... :

No tenemos mucho dinero, pero, bueno, tenemos que pagar nuestras deudas	We don't have a lot of money, but still, we have to pay our debts

(d) Colloquially, *mira que* can express the idea of 'nevertheless':

Las asistentas siempre se me van, y mira que las trato bien	My home-helps always walk out on me, despite the fact that I always treat them well

The phrase is quite strong: perhaps 'but I'm telling you', 'and mind you. . .' might be appropriate translations.

33.11.4 Dismissing or downgrading information

Words meaning 'anyway' essentially indicate that the speaker has chosen to disregard some aspect of the previous information: they express some variant on the theme 'it doesn't matter . . .'.

Phrases like *de todas formas/maneras, sea como sea,* are usual in all styles, including writing; *sea como fuere* is literary. Colloquially, 'anyway' can be expressed by *bueno,* which has numerous uses as a connector, most of them differentiated by intonation. *Nada,* sometimes combined with *bueno,* is also much used in spoken Peninsular Spanish to discount information previously received:

(Bueno,) De todos modos/De todas formas, llámame mañana	Anyway, ring me tomorrow
—*Es que nunca está aquí los viernes.* —*(Bueno,) nada, volveré el lunes*	'He's never here on Fridays.' 'It doesn't matter, I'll come on Monday'

33.11.5 Resumption

The effect of these words is to draw a conclusion from what has previously been said.

(a) The most common are *de modo que, de manera que, de forma que*, which all mean the same, and *así que, conque* (colloquial):

De modo/forma/manera que, como íbamos diciendo . . .	So, as we were saying . . .
De forma que lo extraordinario se ha convertido en ordinario (M. Fernández Álvarez, Spain)	So the ordinary has become extraordinary
Así que, en lugar de dejarlo allí, te lo llevaste	So, instead of leaving it there, you took it with you . . .
Conque lo que pasó fue eso . . .	So what happened was that . . .

(b) *Bueno*, without a sceptical intonation, is much used in spoken, not written Spanish, to show that the speaker has taken previous remarks into account before continuing. Its rough equivalent is 'right . . .'/'OK . . .'/'fine . . .':

Bueno, yo no sabía todo eso, y si las cosas están así, me voy . . .	Right/OK/Fine, I didn't know all that, and if that's the way things are, I'm going . . .
—Es que no he podido terminarlo. —Bueno, tendrás que dejarlo para mañana	'I wasn't able to finish it. . .' 'Right/OK, you'll have to leave it until tomorrow'

33.11.6 Emphasis and insistence

There are various ways of driving home a point.

(a) *En realidad, realmente* are like the English 'really' or 'actually': they indicate that the speaker is about to reveal what is 'really' true:

En realidad/Realmente este tipo de argumento no viene al caso	In fact/In reality/To tell the truth, this line of reasoning is irrelevant

(b) *De hecho* means 'the fact is':

De hecho es como si fuera mi padre	In fact it's just as if he were my father

(c) *Ahora bien* is like the English insistent 'now' used to hammer home on the following statement as something that may not yet have been fully taken into account. A typical construction is *ahora bien, hay que tener en cuenta* 'now, we must take into account . . .' It is used more than its English equivalent:

Ahora bien, hay que insistir en que los ejércitos de la Monarquía Católica estaban integrados por soldados de muy diversas nacionalidades (M. Fernández Álvarez, Spain)	Now, it must be stressed that the armies of the Catholic Monarch consisted of soldiers of different nationalities

(d) Colloquially, Spanish makes much use of the formula *es que* . . . which conveys the idea of 'the fact is . . .' but is used mainly in reponse to something said before':

—Te llamé pero no contestaste. —Es que/El hecho es que no dormí en casa	'I rang you but I couldn't get an answer'. 'The fact is that I didn't sleep at home'

33.11.7 Summing up

There are several ways of summarizing the previous information.

(a) *En resumen* and *en suma* are literary phrases meaning 'in short'/'to sum up . . .':

En suma, todo cuanto pueda hacerle ganar en prestigio, ... , lo cuidará al máximo (M. Fernández Álvarez, Spain)	In short, he'll be extremely careful about anything that can enhance his prestige, . . .
En resumen, las cifras de este año son marcadamente inferiores a las del año pasado	To sum up, this year's figures are markedly lower than last year's

(b) *Total* can be thought of as a colloquial equivalent of *en resumen*. It indicates that the speaker has decided to cut things short and come to the point. It does not have an obvious English equivalent, although a slightly impatient 'anyway' is also often used in a similar way:

Total, se levanta y se va	To cut a long story short/Anyway, he gets up and walks out
Total, has metido la pata	In a word, you've put your foot in it

(c) *En fin* is constantly used, but its meaning is, like *total*, rather indefinable. It means 'well' when this word is used to show that the speaker is about to introduce a conclusion arrived at after a certain amount of thought. There are several English possibilities:

En fin, a mí me sigue pareciendo que es como si Sherlock Holmes resolviera sus casos acudiendo a la Interpol (J. A. Marina, Spain, dialogue)	Well, it still seems to me like Sherlock Holmes solving his cases by calling in Interpol
En fin, lo que me estás diciendo es no que has perdido el dinero sino que te lo has gastado	OK/Right, what you're telling me is that you haven't lost the money but you've spent it

33.11.8 Contradiction

These words show that the speaker does not agree with the previous information:

(a) *Por el contrario, al contrario* are standard equivalents of 'on the contrary'. *Por el contrario* is rather literary:

—*¿Te encuentras mal?* —*Por el/Al contrario, estoy estupendamente*	'Are you feeling ill?' 'On the contrary, I feel great'

(b) *Qué va* is a colloquial phrase expressing strong disagreement:

—*Es que es riquísimo* —*Qué va, no tiene donde caerse muerto*	'He's really rich,' 'The heck he is. He hasn't got a cent' (lit. '. . . hasn't got anywhere to drop dead on')

(c) *De ninguna manera* expresses strong refusal, and is common in all styles. *De eso nada* is a colloquial phrase that conveys the same idea (cf. 'no way . . . '):

—*¿Puedo pagarte por/a plazos?* —*De ninguna manera/De eso nada*	'Can I pay you by instalments?' 'Certainly not.'

(d) *Oye* (*oiga* to a stranger or person held in special respect) is commonly used in colloquial language to reject an implication (but it may also simply mean 'listen!'):

Oye, si yo lo he pagado	(I'm telling you) I've already paid it

(e) The word *si*, which usually means 'if', is much used on both continents to disapprove of previous information (see also 31.4.8):

—*Te tienes que levantar.* —¡*Si sólo son las cinco y media!*	'You've got to get up.' 'It's only five-thirty, for God's sake!'

Note

The words *ca* or *quia* used to be used to mean 'certainly not' until the 1940s, but they now seem to be entirely extinct.

33.11.9 Contrast

Various words and phrases imply contrast, like the English 'on the other hand'.
Por otra parte is also an equivalent of 'on the other hand':

Por otra parte es posible pensar que tiene razón	On the other hand, it's possible to think that he's right

En cambio can have a similar meaning but is more often used to express difference or contrast:

Ella le adora, en cambio/sin embargo él no la puede ver	She adores him; on the other hand/ however, he can't stand her
En cambio, cabe suponer que nunca hubo vida en Marte	On the other hand, there is room to suppose that life never existed on Mars

33.11.10 Consequence and result.

These words and phrases show that what follows is the result of what preceded.

(a) *Por lo tanto, por consiguiente, en/como consecuencia* both mean 'as a result' and are all typical of rather formal styles:

Por lo tanto, estamos ante otro instrumento de la Monarquía de los Austrias (M. Fernández Álvarez, Spain)	Here we have, therefore, another of the tools used by the Austrias
La inflación sigue aumentando. Por lo tanto/Por consiguiente/Como consecuencia, habrá que pensar en un incremento de los tipos de interés	Inflation continues to rise. As a result, it will be necessary to think of an increase in the interest rate

(b) *Por ende* 'hence' is archaic, but is occasionally resurrected for stylistic effect. It could have replaced *por consiguiente* in the previous example, but the result would have sounded pompous.

(c) *De modo que, de forma que, así que, conque* can all also mean 'hence', 'as a result'. They are discussed above at 33.11.5.

(c) *Por eso . . .* 'that's why . . .' is much used in everyday language in all styles:

Por eso las generalizaciones no sólo son absurdas y peligrosas, sino indefectiblemente inexactas (J. Marías, Spain)	That's why generalizations are not only absurd and dangerous, they are also inevitably inaccurate

Por esta razón 'that's why' has the same meaning.

(d) *Entonces*, as well as meaning 'then' in the sense of 'just after', is much used to introduce a conclusion:

¿Te gusto entonces? (G. Cabrera Infante, Cuba, dialogue)	Do you like me, then?
Entonces ¿estamos de acuerdo?	So, are we in agreement?
Entonces, no puedo sino concluir que usted es el culpable	In that case, I can only conclude that you are the guilty person

(e) *Pues* is discussed elsewhere, and it can mean 'since' in literary language; see 33.5.3. It is constantly used in colloquial language to introduce conclusions:

—No me gusta el color. —Pues cámbialo.	'I don't like the colo(u)r.' 'Then change it.'
Pues eso mismo te iba a decir	That's just what I was going to tell you

33.11.11 Agreement

There are numerous ways of agreeing with the previous information or of asserting something as self-evident.

(a) *Claro* is probably the most common, and is found in all styles, although it is slightly colloquial:

Claro, no me avisaste con tiempo, no pude ir	Of course, you didn't warn me in time: I couldn't go
Claro que si no quieres venir, no vengas	Obviously if you don't want to come, don't come
Claro está que no quiero presionar a nadie	It's obvious I don't want to put pressure on anyone

Sometimes it makes *sí* 'yes' unnecessary:

—¿Puedo pasar unos días en tu casa?	'Can I stay a few days with you?' 'Yes, of course, any time you want'
—Hombre, claro, cuando quieras	

Está claro (Latin America *es claro*) is discussed in the note to 29.2.5.

(b) *Desde luego* means 'of course' and is in daily use, at least in Spain:

Desde luego, si quieres entrar tendrás que pagar	Obviously, if you want to go in you'll have to pay

(c) *En efecto* and *efectivamente* both signify agreement with what has preceded:

En efecto/Efectivamente todos estaban de acuerdo conmigo	They were indeed all in agreement with me
—Bueno, estamos fastidiados.	'Well, we've had it/we're in trouble.'
—Efectivamente/En efecto	'You're right'

(d) *Ya* has many uses, listed at 31.7.1. It is often used to indicate agreement with the previous statement, although uttered sarcastically it can mean the exact opposite:

—Es que hay que darle un nombre al fichero antes de guardarlo. —Ya	'You have to give the file a name before saving it.' 'Right/OK/I see'
—Es que soy más inteligente que tú —Ya, ya . . .	'I'm smarter than you' 'Yeah, sure . . .'

(e) *De verdad* insists on the truth of a statement, rather like *en serio* 'seriously':

De verdad te lo digo que estoy loca por él	I'm telling you I'm, really mad about him

A decir verdad 'to tell the truth . . . ' has a similar meaning.

34

Prepositions

Prepositional usage is more subject than other areas of syntax to the arbitrariness of linguistic change, and the whole subject is plagued with quibbles and doubts. In this chapter prepositions are treated in alphabetical order and special emphasis has been given to aspects of prepositional usage likely to be unfamiliar to English speakers.

a 'to', 'at' 34.1	*contra* 'against' 34.6	*hacia* 'towards' 34.11	*sin* 'without' 34.16
ante, delante de 'in front of', 'faced with' 34.2	*de* 'of', 'from' 34.7 *desde* 'from' 34.7.5	*hasta* 'until', 'as far as' 34.12	*sobre* 'over', 'on', 'about' 34.17
bajo, debajo de 'beneath', 'underneath' 34.3	*durante* 'during' 34.8	*mediante* 'by means of' 34.13	*tras, detrás de* 'after', 'behind' 34.18
cabe (archaic) 'next to' 34.4	*en* 'in', 'on', 'at' 34.9	*para* and *por* 'for', 'because of', etc. 34.14	
con 'with' 34.5	*entre* 'between', 'among' 34.10	*según* 'according to' 34.15	

Many of these can be combined with other words to form prepositional phrases such as *debajo de* 'underneath', *frente a* 'opposite', *a razón de* 'at the rate of', etc. A list of common prepositional phrases is included at 34.19.

English speakers should take literally the meaning of the Spanish word *preposición*, 'something placed in front', since Spanish prepositions appear only immediately before noun phrases. This makes the structure of English sentences like 'the house I'm talking **about**' impossible in Spanish: *la casa **de** la que estoy hablando*, **never** **la casa que estoy hablando de*.

For the same reason many grammarians, including the Academy, reject sentences like *?la cerámica es hecha por y para los mismos habitantes del pueblo* 'the pottery is made by and for the villagers themselves' since *por* here stands in front of a conjunction, *y*. They prefer . . . *es hecha por los habitantes del pueblo y para ellos mismos*. Similarly, 'I'll go with or without you' should be translated *iré contigo o sin ti*, not **iré con o sin ti*. But this 'rule' is constantly broken, and the linguist Valentín García Yebra[1] sees no objection to phrases like *el tráfico aéreo desde y hacia Berlín* 'air traffic to and from Berlin', *la imagen construida en y por el texto* 'the

---

[1] *Claudicación en el uso de las preposiciones* (Madrid: Gredos, 1988), 243 ff.

image constructed in and by the text'. The 'correct' constructions, *tráfico aéreo hacia Berlín y desde él, la imagen construida en el texto y por él* are long-winded.

On the other hand, omission of prepositions should be avoided: **personas acusadas de pertenecer y colaborar con el movimiento terrorista* 'persons accused of belonging and collaborating with the terrorist movement' sounds bad in both languages: . . . *acusadas de pertenecer al movimiento terrorista y de colaborar con él* is correct, . . . *pertenecer a y colaborar con el movimiento terrorista* is possible, but may offend purists. However, this rule can produce cumbersome sentences: *entraban y salían del edificio* 'they entered and left the building' is nowadays usual, even if purists theoretically require *entraban en el edificio y salían de él*. And, as García Yebra points out, no one would say **un billete de ida a Segovia y de vuelta de ella* for *un billete de ida y vuelta a Segovia* 'a round trip to Segovia'/'a return ticket to Segovia'.

The English language is precise in defining spatial location or movement; Spanish is often quite vague. The subtle differences between the colloquial English uses of spatial adverbs, as in 'I'm going to/across to/round to/down to/up to/over to the shops' are virtually untranslatable: *voy a las tiendas*. The Spanish word *en* can mean 'in', 'inside', 'at', 'on' according to context. Very often the meaning of English prepositions must be expressed by a suitable Spanish verb: 'he's in prison' = *está en la cárcel*, 'he's at the prison' = *ha ido a la cárcel*; 'he walked through the city' = *atravesó la ciudad/pasó por la ciudad*, 'he walked round the city' (*se*) *paseó por la ciudad/dio una vuelta por la ciudad/deambuló por la ciudad*.

34.1 A

This very common preposition has many uses. Apart from the problems they have with personal *a* before certain kinds of direct object (discussed in Chapter 22), English speakers tend to misuse it when translating phrases like 'at the dentist's', 'at Cambridge', 'at the station'. See (c) for discussion.

(a) Motion, **to**, **at**, **up**, **down**, etc.:
Almost any verb or noun indicating motion is likely to be followed by *a*. As a result its meaning includes 'on', 'into', 'onto', 'down', 'up', as well as 'to' and 'at':

Por fin llegaron a Managua	They finally got to Managua
Fui a/para que me diera hora	I went to make an appointment
Bajó al sótano	He went down to the basement
Se acercó al buzón	He approached the letter box
Me subí al coche/al tren	I got into the car/on the train
El gato se subió a un árbol	The cat ran up a tree
Salté a un autobús	I jumped on a bus
Lanzaban piedras a/contra las ventanas	They were throwing stones at the windows
Arrojó la espada al aire	He hurled the sword into the air
Entró a/para saludarnos	He came in to say hello to us
Salieron a/para dar batalla	They went out to do battle
Ha venido a/para/por hablar con usted	He's come to talk to you
Lo pegó al/en el sobre	She stuck it on the envelope
Cuélgaselo al cuello	Hang it round his neck
(cf. *cuélgalo en la pared*	hang it on the wall)
Cayó al suelo/al mar	It fell to the ground, into the sea
Se tiró al vacío	He threw himself into the void
una expedición a Marte	an expedition to Mars

salida a la calle	way out to the street
tiro al blanco	target shooting

Notes

(i) *A* is omitted after verbs of motion before *aquí, acá, ahí, allí, allá: ven aquí/ven acá/ven para acá* 'come here', *allá voy/voy para allá* 'I'm going there'.

(ii) Compare Spain *entrar en el cuarto*, Latin America *entró al cuarto* 'he entered the room' – *Chile ingresó a la Conferencia sobre Desarme* (*La Época*, Chile) 'Chile joins Disarmament Conference' – although *entrar a* is sometimes heard in Spain (and always before infinitives). The noun everywhere takes *a*: *entrada a la galería* 'entrance to the gallery'. Spain also prefers *en* with *penetrar* 'penetrate', *ingresar* 'to join (club, etc.)', *introducir* 'to insert', but the use of *a* is widespread in Latin America, cf. *ingresa como adepto laico **a** la orden* (J. L. Borges) 'he entered (historic present) the order as a lay follower'.

(iii) *Para* is also found colloquially after *ir: voy para Lugo* 'I'm heading for Lugo'.

(b) Direction, 'at':

Mira al techo y no te entrará agua	Look up at the ceiling and you won't get
en los ojos	water in your eyes
Apunta a la bombilla	Aim at the light bulb

Note

Spanish differentiates *mirar a* 'to look towards/in the direction of' and *mirar* 'to look at': compare *mira este cuadro con detenimiento* 'look at this painting attentively' and *mira a la derecha/a la izquierda* 'look to the right/to the left'.

(c) After verbs of giving, sending, informing, etc:

Dáselo a papá	Give it to father
Le envió cien dólares a su hijo	He sent his son $100
Le dejó su finca a su yerno	He left his country estate to his son-in-law
Comunicaremos los datos a los aseguradores	We will inform the insurers of the details

(d) Place (static):

The use of the preposition *a* to indicate 'at' or 'in' a place is limited in Spanish. English speakers – particularly those who know French, German or Italian – must not use *a* in sentences like *estoy haciendo mis estudios en Cambridge* 'I'm studying *at* Cambridge', *te esperaré en la estación* 'I'll wait for you *at* the station (cf. *à la gare, am Bahnhof, alla stazione*, etc.), *vive en Londres* '(s)he lives in London' (*il habite à Londres*), etc. Apart from set phrases like *al lado de* 'at the side of', *a la luz de* 'in the light of', *a* can only be used with a few nouns like *vuelta*, 'turn', 'return' (*a mi vuelta de* 'on my return from'), *salida* 'exit', *entrada* 'entrance' which denote actions or moments in time rather than places. *Os esperaré a la salida* is best thought of as 'I'll wait for you on the way out' rather than 'at the exit', which is *en la salida*.

In phrases like *estaba asomado a la ventana* 'he was leaning in/out of the window' *asomar* is a verb of motion: *estaba en la ventana* is, however, safer than *estaba a la ventana* 'he was at the window'. Similarly, *fue a estudiar a Salamanca* is only a variant of *fue a Salamanca a estudiar* 'he went to Salamanca to study': it does not mean 'he went to study *at* Salamanca University' – *... en Salamanca*.

A is used to translate 'at' in a number of situations involving close proximity to an object, e.g. *a la barra* 'at the bar', *a la mesa* 'at table' (i.e. 'at mealtime'); but note *se sienta en una mesa de la calle y pide una cerveza* 'he sits down *at* a table in the street and asks for a beer' (J. Cortázar, Argentina):

Vivo a la vuelta	I live round the corner
a orillas del mar	on the seashore
Oí pasos a mi espalda	I heard footsteps at my back
Se pasa horas sentado al ordenador	He spends hours sitting at the computer
Se arrodilló a los pies de la Virgen	He knelt at the feet of the Virgin
Está con el agua al cuello	He's up to his neck (in trouble: *hasta* implies real water)
a la izquierda/derecha de	to the left/right of (cf. *a diestro y siniestro* 'to right and left', i.e. 'on all sides')
a lo lejos/en la distancia	in the distance
Se sentaron al sol/a la luz/al calor del fuego/a la sombra/al amparo de un roble	They sat in the sun/light/warmth of the fire/shade/in the shelter of an oak

Compare:

Espérame en la parada del autobús	Wait for me at the bus stop
Estaba parado en un semáforo	He was waiting at a traffic light
Mario está en el banco	Mario is at/in the bank
Los niños están en el colegio	The children are in/at school
(cf. *mi hijo todavía no va al colegio*)	My son isn't at school yet, i.e. doesn't go yet
... *para que el coche no estuviera tanto tiempo estacionado en la puerta* (G. García Márquez, Colombia. *Coche* here refers to a horse-drawn carriage)	... so the carriage wouldn't be parked so long at the door
La vi en la puerta de la iglesia	I saw her at the church door

Notes

(i) *A la puerta* is also good Spanish for 'at the door', but we found that some American informants preferred *en* – but compare *Morelli habla del napolitano que se pasó años sentado a la puerta de su casa* (J. Cortázar, Argentina) 'Morelli speaks of the Neapolitan who spent years sitting at the door of his house.'

(ii) Spanish thus has no prepositions that can differentiate 'he's at the hospital' and 'he's in (the) hospital': verbs are used instead – *ha ido al hospital* and *está en el hospital.*

(e) Manner (adverbial phrases of manner with *a* are numerous):

a pie/a mano/a lápiz	on foot/by hand/in pencil
a golpes/a tiros/a patadas	with blows/by shooting/with kicks
Pedía socorro a gritos	He was shouting for help
un documento escrito a máquina	a typed document
El servicio es a voluntad del cliente	Service charge at the customer's discretion
Las patatas están a punto	The potatoes are done
Le cortaron el pelo al rape	They cropped his hair short
Estoy a dieta	I'm on a diet
a la buena de Dios	any old how/willy-nilly
a oscuras/a la luz del día	in the dark/by daylight
Las verduras se pueden guisar al vapor	Vegetables can be steamed
Estaba vestido a la inglesa	He was dressed English-style
a la manera de Dickens (M. Torres, Spain)	in the style of Dickens

Note

The curious construction with *a* found in the phrase *sois dos a ganar* 'there are two of you earning' may perhaps be included under this heading.

(f) In certain time phrases:

a las diez/a medianoche	at 10 o'clock/at midnight
Se cansa a los cinco minutos	He gets tired after five minutes

Bonos del Estado a diez años	ten-year Government Bonds
Se casaron a los veinte años	They got married at the age of twenty
(Se casaron con veinte años)	
al día siguiente/al otro día	on the following day
a la mañana siguiente	the following morning
a la caída de la noche/al alba	at nightfall/at dawn
al mismo tiempo	at the same time
A su recepción pagaré la cantidad	On receipt I shall pay the stipulated
estipulada	amount
a su regreso, a su llegada	on his return, on his arrival
Estamos a miércoles/a quince	it's Wednesday/the fifteenth
tres veces al/por día	three times a day
Se enfada a/por la menor provocación	He gets angry at the slightest provocation

A is particularly common in the construction *al* + infinitive where it means 'on . . . -ing', e.g. *al ver* 'on seeing', *al volverse* 'as he turned round/back'. See 18.3.3.

Notes

(i) One can say *a su muerte se dividió el reino en tres partes* 'at his death the kingdom was divided into three parts', but only *cuando nació . . .* 'at his birth . . .'.

(ii) Note the construction *ya deben estar al llegar* 'they must be about to arrive'.

(g) To translate 'of' or 'like' after verbs meaning 'smell', 'taste', 'sound', and also after the nouns derived from some of these:

Me suena a cuento chino	It sounds like a tall story to me
Esto sabe a pescado	This tastes of fish
En esta casa huele a quemado	There's a smell of burning in this house
La buena leche huele a fresca	Good milk smells fresh
Esta mantequilla apesta a ajo	This butter reeks of garlic
Había un leve olor a fritura y a crema	There was a faint smell of frying and suntan
bronceadora (F. Umbral, Spain)	cream
La ginebra tiene un sabor a agua de colonia	Gin has a taste like eau de Cologne

(h) 'Fitted with', 'propelled by':

Grammarians reject *a* as a Gallicism in the following constructions, but most of them are normal in everyday language:

olla a presión	pressure cooker
caldera a/de gas-oil	oil-fired boiler
motor a/de dos tiempos	two-stroke motor
un suplemento a color (El País; also	a colour supplement
en color)	
un avión a/de dos motores	a twin-engine plane
un coche que va a/por metanol	a methanol-powered car

Note

The use of *a* to denote an ingredient is occasionally seen in advertising language but it should not be imitated: *crema bronceadora a lanolina* 'suntan cream with lanolin' (better *con lanolina*).

(i) Rate, measure, speed, amount, distance:

Se vende a mil pesos el metro	It's on sale at 1,000 pesos a metre
¿A cómo están las peras?	How much are the pears?
Volaba a más de dos mil kilómetros	It was flying at more than 2,000 km per
por hora	hour

Compraba tebeos de segunda mano que luego revendía o cambiaba a razón de dos por uno (L. Goytisolo, Spain)	He used to buy second-hand comics which he then resold or swapped at the rate of two for one
Está a cinco manzanas (Latin America: *cuadras*) *de aquí*	It's five blocks from here
si Vd. tiene un 80386 a 20 Mhz y un módem a 28.800 bps . . . (computer manual, Spain)	if you have a 20–megaherz 80386 (computer) and a 28,800 bits-per-second modem . . .
a montones	in heaps
Trabaja a ratos/a veces	He works now and again/sometimes

(j) It translates 'from' after a number of words with such meanings as 'steal', 'confiscate', 'buy', and after *oír* 'to hear':

Le robaron una sortija a mi tía	They stole a ring from my aunt
Le compró un coche a su vecino	He bought a car from his neighbour
una banda de traficantes de drogas, a los que aprehendieron trece kilos de cocaína (*La Vanguardia*, Spain)	a gang of drug-peddlers, from whom thirteen kilos of cocaine were confiscated
Se lo oí decir a Amparo	I heard Amparo say it
Eso se lo has oído a tu padre	You've heard that from your father

And similarly verbs such as *quitar* 'take away', *sustraer* 'steal', *confiscar* 'confiscate', *llevarse* 'take away', *sacar* 'to take out/remove', etc. However, *recibir* 'to receive', *adquirir* 'to acquire' and *aceptar* 'to accept' take *de*: *aceptar algo de alguien* 'to accept something from someone'.

(k) Before certain types of direct object (the so-called 'personal *a*', e.g. *vi al gitano* 'I saw the gypsy'). See Chapter 22 for detailed discussion.

(l) After verbs meaning 'begin', 'start', 'get ready to . . . ':

Rompió a llorar	He burst into tears
Echó a correr	She broke into a run
El cielo empezaba a despejarse	The sky was beginning to clear

and similarly after *comenzar a* 'to begin', *ponerse a* 'to start to', *prepararse a* 'to get ready to', *disponerse a* 'to prepare oneself to', *meterse a* 'to take up . . . ' (usually with some implication of futility, as in *no te metas a (p)sicoterapeuta con él, porque solamente complicarás las cosas* 'don't get into being a psychotherapist with him, because you'll only complicate things'.

(m) After numerous verbs, adjectives and adverbs which must be learnt separately:

Aspiraba a hacerse médico	He was aiming to become a doctor
Acostumbraban a hacerlo	They habitually did it
Tienes que hacerte al trabajo	You have to get used to the work
Prefiero una vida mediocre a ser héroe	I prefer a mediocre life to being a hero
Te ayudaré a apretar las tuercas	I'll help you tighten the nuts
El viejo argumento de que la religión sirve de freno a los instintos	The old argument that religion serves as a curb on the instincts
Se ha convertido al budismo	He's converted to Buddhism
jugar al fútbol/al hockey	to play soccer/hockey
tocar algo al acordeón/a la guitarra	to play something on the accordion/guitar
Pudo salvarse agarrándose a/de un árbol	He managed to save himself by clinging to a tree
No hay otro igual a él	There is no other equal to him
Tenía el jersey liado en torno a la cintura	He had his jersey tied round his waist
Es muy parecido al de ayer	It's very much like the one from yesterday

Tendían emboscadas a las Ninfas	They laid ambushes for the Nymphs
(J. L. Borges, Argentina)	

(n) To link two nouns whenever ambiguity might arise from the use of *de*: *el amor de Dios* = 'God's love' and *el amor a Dios* 'love for God'. Often either preposition is possible. *A* is also often used to link two nouns when a common verbal phrase exists which also requires *a*, e.g. *les tiene miedo a los toros* 'he's afraid of bulls', *su miedo a los toros* 'his fear of bulls':

el abrazo de un padre a su hijo	the embrace that a father gives to his son
el amor a la patria	love for one's home country
el respeto a la autoridad	respect for authority
Lo denunciaron como traidor a/de su clase	They denounced him as a traitor to his class
La Casa Blanca confirmó el boicot a los Juegos de Moscú (*Cambio16*, Spain)	The White House confirmed the boycott of the Moscow Games
Insinué algo en el prólogo al libro de Lafaye . . . (O. Paz, Mexico; *del* possible)	I hinted something in the prologue to Lafaye's book . . .
Espero que no sea una referencia personal a mí	I hope it's not a personal reference to me
El culto al sol tendría sus ventajas	Sun-worship would have its advantages
El departamento se encargará de la protección a/de la carretera	The department will take over responsibility for protecting roads

Note

With words like *miedo* 'fear' or *amor* 'love' one can use *de* if no ambiguity arises: compare *así que tiene miedo de las cucarachas* (C. Martín Gaite, Spain, dialogue) 'so you're afraid of cockroaches . . .'

34.2 Ante

'Before' (i.e. 'in front of') or 'in the presence of' and, like the English 'before', it can in literary usage have a spatial meaning, 'facing'/'in front of'; compare *me eché en la cama ante la televisión* (J. Marías, Spain) 'I lay down on the bed in front of/before the television', *detuvo el coche ante la que parecía ser mansión de los Conesal* (M. Vázquez Montalbán, Spain) 'he stopped the car in front of/outside what seemed to be the Conesals' mansion', *ante el negro y el niño había dos tazas de chocolate* (J. L. Borges, Argentina) 'in front of/before the black man and the child were two cups of chocolate'. *Delante de* is used in everyday language for this spatial meaning. *Ante* is, however, very common in the figurative meaning of 'faced with', 'in the face of'. It must not be confused with the entirely separate word *antes* 'before' (in time). Examples:

Se sentía nervioso al comparecer ante el tribunal	He felt nervous on appearing before the court
Ante mí/Frente a mí/Delante de mí se elevaba una enorme torre	Before me there rose an enormous tower
. . . y ellas presumían de parienta famosa ante las otras viejas (M. Torres, Spain)	. . . and they boasted of having a famous female relative in front of/in the presence of the other old women
ante este dilema . . .	faced with this dilemma . . .
ante tamaño insulto . . .	in the face of such an insult . . .
Ante tantas posibilidades, no sabía cuál escoger	Faced with so many possibilities, he didn't know which to choose
Ante todo, quisiera agradecer al organizador	Above all, I would like to thank the organizer . . .

Notes

(i) *Delante de* makes it clear that physical location rather than figurative 'presence' is implied, cf. *justificarse ante Dios* 'to justify oneself before God', but *arrodillarse delante de la Virgen* 'to kneel before (a statue of) the Virgin'. For further details about *delante de*, see 31.6.8.

(ii) *Frente a* for *ante* in phrases like *frente a estos problemas* 'faced with these problems' is very widespread.

34.3 *Bajo*

Bajo means 'beneath' or 'under'. It may be a literary variant of *debajo de* 'underneath' (discussed at 31.6.6), but in this sense it is spatially less specific (cf. 'under' and 'underneath'): *se resguardaron bajo un haya* 'they sheltered under/beneath a beech tree' but *enterró el botín debajo de un roble* 'he buried the loot underneath (i.e. under the roots of) an oak tree'.

Carnicer notes that for those educated speakers who use *bajo* the difference is that it implies 'a good distance under' or 'under but not close to or touching' – *bajo una masa de nubes* 'under a mass of clouds', *no me quedo ni un minuto más bajo este techo* 'I'm not staying one more minute under this roof' – whereas *debajo de* implies 'underneath and close to whatever is on top': *hay mucho polvo debajo de la alfombra* 'there's a lot of dust underneath the carpet'. ?*El perro está bajo la silla* 'the dog's beneath the chair' sounds affected in both languages: . . . *debajo de la silla* 'under(neath) the chair'.

Bajo must be used in the figurative sense of 'under' in phrases like *bajo el gobierno de* 'under the government of', *bajo ciertas condiciones* 'under certain conditions', etc.:

No hay nada nuevo bajo el sol (cf. *sentarse al sol* 'to sit in the sun')	There's nothing new under the sun
bajo las estrellas/la lluvia/un cielo azul	beneath the stars/in the rain/beneath a blue sky
bajo tierra (or *debajo de la tierra*)	underground
bajo la monarquía/la república/el socialismo	under the monarchy/republic/socialism, etc.
La temperatura alcanzó treinta bajo cero	The temperature reached thirty below zero
bajo tantos golpes . . .	under so many blows . . .
bajo los efectos de la anestesia	under the effects of the anaesthetic
bajo juramento	under oath
Bajo la máscara se percibe el lento trabajo de la verdad (M. Torres, Spain)	Beneath the mask the slow workings of truth are visible

Note

Abajo de is often heard for *debajo de* in Latin America, but it is not accepted in Spain.

34.4 *Cabe*

An archaic or rustic equivalent of *junto a/cerca de* 'by'/ 'near' still occasionally found in Latin-American authors.

34.5 *Con*

(a) In many contexts it coincides with the English 'with', but it is used more widely than the latter.

Sentences like 'the boy with the blue Mercedes' require *de*: *el chico del Mercedes azul*. But if 'wearing' or 'carrying' are implied, *con* is usual unless the article is habitually associated with the person: compare *nunca te he visto con gafas* 'I've never seen you with glasses', but *¿te acuerdas del viejo del impermeable que venía todos los días?* 'do you remember the old man with/in the raincoat who used to come every day?'

Fui a la reunión con Niso	I went to the meeting with Niso
Llegaron dos policías con perros	Two policemen with dogs arrived
Yo sí te he visto con camisa de seda	I have seen you in a silk shirt
Está escrito con/a lápiz	It's written with a/in pencil
No podía quitarlo con una llave normal	I couldn't get it off with a normal spanner
con lo enferma que está . . .	and with her being so ill . . .
Nos trató con mucha cortesía	He treated us with much courtesy
té con miel/café con leche	tea with honey/coffee with milk
Se produjeron varios enfrentamientos con la policía	There were several clashes with the police
Se levantó con el sol	He got up with the sun
con la llegada del otoño	with the arrival of autumn

Notes

(i) *Con* cannot be used in combination with the nominalizer *el*: contrast *el chico con/de la americana blanca* 'the boy with the white jacket' and *el de la americana blanca* and 'the one (masc.) with/in the white jacket'. Phrases like **el con gafas* for 'the one with glasses' are not Spanish.

(ii) *Con* differs from *a* in phrases like *con la llegada de la primavera* 'with the arrival of spring' in that *a la llegada* implies 'at the moment of the arrival of', which is too punctual for the onset of a season. Compare *todos se marcharon a la llegada de la policía* 'they all left on the arrival of the police' and *con la llegada de Pepe, todo empezó a cambiar* 'with Pepe's arrival, everything began to change'.

(b) After phrases meaning 'to show an attitude towards' *con* alternates with *para con*, much as 'with' alternates with 'towards': *es muy cariñoso (para) con su mujer* 'he's very affectionate towards/with his wife', *su amabilidad es igual (para) con todos* 'her kindness is the same towards all'. But if the object of the attitude does not benefit by it, *para* is not used:

Es muy crítico con su hijo	He's very critical with/towards his son
Eres muy cruel con tu novia	You're very cruel to your girlfriend
Es poco confiado con sus colegas	He's not very trusting with his colleagues

(c) It may be used with expressions signifying meeting, encounter, collision, 'facing up to', 'struggle with', etc.:

Me encontré/Tropecé hoy con tu jefe	I ran into/met your boss today
Ha vuelto con su marido (ha vuelto a is not used in this sense)	She's gone back to her husband (or 'she's come back with her husband')
Tengo que vérmelas con el vecino	I'll have to have it out with the neighbour (i.e. have a frank talk with)
Iba en la moto y se dio un golpe con/contra un poste	He was on his motor bike and crashed into a post
Mi bicicleta chocó con un camión	My bicycle ran into a lorry
Se enfrentaron con los guerrilleros	They clashed with the guerrillas

Tendremos que enfrentarnos con el problema/enfrentar el problema	We'll have to face up to the problem
Los ingleses suelen dudar con el subjuntivo	English people usually hesitate over the subjunctive

(d) It may – strangely to English speakers – mean 'containing':

un vaso con/de agua, un saco con/de patatas	a glass of water/sack of potatoes
Llevaba una cesta con pan, huevos, uvas y vino (de is not possible here)	He was carrying a basket of bread, eggs, grapes and wine
una jeringa con morfina	a syringe full of morphine

Note

This use eliminates any ambiguity caused by *de*, which either means 'full of' – *una cesta de huevos* is 'a basketful of eggs' and it cannot contain anything else – or may denote the container but not the contents: compare *una botella de coñac* 'a bottle of cognac' or 'a cognac bottle', but *una botella con coñac* 'a bottle with cognac in it'.

(e) 'Despite' or some similar phrase (*a pesar de* is often an equivalent):

Con/A pesar de todos sus esfuerzos, nunca llegó a coronel	Despite/for all his efforts, he never made the rank of colonel
Con ser inteligente y rico nunca llegó a nada	Despite being intelligent and rich, he never came to anything
Con todo, la vida no es tan terrible	Despite everything, life isn't so awful
con lo guapa que estarías con el pelo recogido . . .	to think how attractive you'd look with your hair up . . .

(f) *Con* plus an infinitive may, like the gerund, have a conditional sense:

Con hacer (or *haciendo*) *lo que yo os digo, todo irá bien*	Provided you (pl.) do what I say everything will go well
Con tener un poco más de suerte me hubiera hecho rico	If I'd had a bit more luck I'd have got rich
Sólo/Solo con pulsar una tecla el ordenador almacena los datos	If you simply press a key the computer stores the data

A subjunctive may also follow *con* in this conditional meaning but *con que* must then be used. This must not be confused with the conjunction *conque* or with *con* plus a relative pronoun:

Con que me pagaran mis gastos me conformaba	I would be quite happy if they paid my expenses

(g) It may, like the gerund, mean 'as a result of':

Se nos ha ido la tarde con hablar/hablando	The afternoon's gone with all this talking
No conseguirás nada con tratarme/ tratándome de esa manera	You'll achieve nothing by treating me that way
Con cambiar/Cambiando de empleo no resuelves nada	You'll solve nothing by changing jobs

(h) It may indicate the cause or origin of a condition:

Estamos muy entusiasmados/ilusionados con la perspectiva de un nuevo gobierno	We're very excited about the prospect of a new government
Está muy preocupado con sus negocios	He's very taken up with his business affairs

Compare *me preocupo por ellos* 'I worry about them', and *me preocupo de hacer todo lo posible* 'I take care to do everything possible'.

Se puso enfermo (enfermó de, Lat. Am. *se enfermó de) paludismo*	He fell ill with/from malaria
Se mareó con el vaivén del tren	(S)he felt nauseous/(British 'sick') because of the swaying of the train
Me contento con lo que tengo	I content myself with what I have
Se alegró con/de la noticia del nacimiento de su nieto	(S)he cheered up at the news of his/her grandson's birth

Note

Miscellaneous examples of *con* used in ways unfamiliar to English speakers: *hace años que él se escribe con ella* 'he and she have been writing to one another for years', *murió con más de setenta años* 'she died aged more than seventy', *usted fue el último que lo vio con vida* 'you were the last one to see him alive', *voy a verme con ella esta noche* 'I'm seeing her tonight'.

34.6 *Contra*

A close equivalent of 'against', but it may mean 'at' after verbs meaning firing, throwing, launching, etc. *En contra de* is an equivalent of *contra* when the latter means 'in opposition to'. It becomes *en contra de que* before a verb:

El régimen ha organizado una campaña contra/en contra de la corrupción	The regime has organized a campaign against corruption
Contra lo que creen algunos, yo no soy pesimista	Despite/to the contrary of what some believe, I am not a pessimist
Apoya tu pala contra el árbol	Lean your spade against the tree
En ese caso optarían por lanzar un misil contra el enemigo	In that case they would opt for launching a missile at the enemy
Lanzó la piedra contra el árbol	He threw the stone at the tree (intending to strike it)
(cf. *se la lanzó al árbol*	He threw it up at the tree e.g. a lasso or rope)
Conviene inyectarse contra la hepatitis antes de viajar a esas regiones (not **inyectarse para . . .*)	It's a good idea to get immunized against/for hepatitis before travelling to those regions
¿Está usted en contra de que lo hagan ellos?	Are you against them doing it?

Notes

(i) For *contra mí, en contra tuya,* etc. 'against me'/'against you' see note to 8.7.
(ii) The use of *contra* for *cuanto* in such phrases as *cuanto más trabajas, más te dan* 'the more you work, the more they give you', heard in some Latin-American varieties and in substandard speech in Spain, should be avoided. See 5.11 for details.

34.7 De

34.7.1 General uses

Section (a) covers those uses of *de* which correspond to the English 'of' or to the genitive ending 's: these sentences should give English speakers no great problems. French speakers must resist the temptation to replace *de* by *a: c'est à vous?* = *¿es de usted?* 'is it yours?'

(a) 'Of', 'belonging to':

el primer ministro de Tailandia	The prime minister of Thailand

los discos de mi primo	my cousin's records
la matrícula del coche	the car number-plate
las bisagras de la puerta	the hinges of/on the door
el primero/uno de mayo	the first of May
Ese attaché es del profesor	That briefcase is the teacher's
¿De quién es esto?	Whose is this?

(b) To create 'compound' nouns, usually – but not always – expressed in English by the juxtaposition of nouns. Note that *de* in such cases is not followed by a definite article:

un traje de baño	a swimsuit
un reloj de pulsera	a wrist-watch
unos recortes de prensa	some press-cuttings

Note

This is the usual way of forming the equivalents of English compound nouns, but there are other methods, e.g. *un año luz* 'a light-year' or *la industria hotelera* 'the hotel industry' mentioned at 2.1.7b and 4.12 respectively.

(c) Origin (see 34.7.5 for the difference between *de* and *desde*):

Soy de México	I'm from Mexico
un ser de otro planeta	a being from another planet
un vino de solera	a vintage wine
Este manuscrito es de la Biblioteca Nacional	This manuscript is from the National Library
una oda del siglo quince	a fifteenth-century ode
un dolor de cabeza	a headache

Notes

(i) English speakers tend to use the preposition *en* to join two nouns to indicate belonging to or originating from a place. Spanish strongly prefers *de*: *los hombres **de** Grecia* 'the men in Greece' (= Greek men), *las flores **de** los Andes* 'the flowers in (= of) the Andes', *las colinas de tierra adentro son más verdes* 'the hills in the interior/inland are greener'. The temptation is particularly strong after a superlative: *éste es el mejor restaurante **de** Madrid* 'this is the best restaurant in Madrid', *el más antiguo monumento **del** Perú* 'the most ancient monument in Peru', *el mejor momento **de** mi vida* 'the best moment in/of my life'.

However, spoken and journalistic Mexican Spanish regularly uses *en*: *el plan más ambicioso en el mundo* (Mexican television) 'the most ambitious plan in the world', *el mejor surtido en México* 'the best range in Mexico' (advertisement).

(ii) *Viene de Toledo* normally only means 'he's coming from Toledo'; *es de Toledo* = 'he's **from** Toledo'.

(d) 'Made of', 'consisting of':

una estatua de oro macizo	a solid gold statue
un manuscrito de pergamino	a parchment manuscript
una novela de ciencia-ficción	a science-fiction novel
Tiene una voluntad de hierro	She has an iron will
Este yogur es de leche de oveja	This is ewe's-milk yoghurt

(e) 'About' in the sense of 'concerning':

It is doubtful whether *de* often means 'concerning', except after certain verbs like *hablar, quejarse de, protestar*: *una carta de amor* 'a love letter' is very different from *una carta sobre el amor* 'a letter about love'. When it is used to mean 'about', *de* implies something less formal than *sobre*, which is closer to 'on the subject of':

No quiero hablar de mis problemas personales	I don't want to talk about my personal problems
Esta noche va a hablar sobre problemas personales	Tonight he's talking on/about 'personal problems'
Es que yo quería hablar con usted de mi salario[2]	Actually I wanted to talk to you about my wages
No hace más que quejarse de que tiene demasiado trabajo	All he does is moan about having too much work
¿De qué va la cosa?	What's it all about?

(f) 'Costing':

Las naranjas de mil pesos son las mejores	The 1,000-peso oranges are the best
Han comprado una casa de un millón de libras	They've bought a million-pound house

(g) Emotions arising from something:

Tengo miedo del agua	I'm afraid of the water
el respeto de/a los derechos humanos	respect for human rights
Me da pena de él	I'm sorry for him
Yo también experimenté la obsesión de/por la forma literaria	I also experienced the obsession for literary form

And, similarly, *el horror de/a/hacia una cosa* 'horror towards/about a thing'.

However, after *sentir, experimentar* and similar verbs the following words take *por* or *hacia*: *compasión* 'pity', *simpatía* 'affection'/'liking', *admiración* 'admiration', *desprecio* 'contempt', *odio* 'hatred', etc.

Note also *le tengo miedo al agua, tengo miedo de/le tengo miedo a todo*. See 34.1.

(h) In certain adverbial phrases of manner:

Lo escribió de manera que nadie pudiera leerlo	She wrote it in such a way that no one could read it
Me puse a pensar de qué modo podría ayudarlos	I set about thinking how I could help them
Le ha venido de perlas	It suited him just right
Sólo/Solo he estado en Sevilla de paso	I've only been in Seville on the way to somewhere else
Intentaron entrar de balde	They tried to get in free/without paying
Sale todos los sábados de juerga	He goes out on the town every Saturday
Estuvimos de bromas hasta las tres de la mañana	We were up until three telling jokes/larking about

(i) Condition (English 'as', 'in'):
This construction is closely related to the previous one:

De niña me gustaba mucho coser (M. Arrafut, Cuba, dialogue)	As a child I really used to like sewing
Trabajó dos meses de camarero	He worked as a waiter for two months
—¿De qué vas al baile? —De pastora	'What are you going to the ball as?' 'As a shepherdess'
Tú aquí estás de más	You're not needed here
Vi a una criada de blanco paseando al niño	I saw a maid in white taking the child for a walk

---

[2] In Spain *el salario* = 'wages', *el sueldo* = 'salary', e.g. *salario de miseria* 'starvation wages'. *Salario* = 'salary' in Latin America.

una chica joven de vaqueros y chaqueta de hombre (C. Martín Gaite, Spain)	a young girl in jeans and a man's jacket

Note

De + an adjective is a common colloquial way of describing the condition something is in, especially when the condition is in some way extreme or surprising: *la cesta de costura casi no cierra de puro llena* (C. Martín Gaite, Spain) 'the sewing basket almost won't shut because it's so full', *no podía continuar de (lo) cansada que estaba* 'she couldn't carry on because she was so tired', *de puro ansioso, Javier había bostezado* (M. Benedetti, Uruguay) 'Javier was so anxious that he yawned'.

(j) To mean 'if':

For *de* plus the infinitive used for *si* in the if-clause of a conditional sentence, see 25.8.3.

(k) Age, measurements:

un hombre de cuarenta años	a man aged forty
un pan de tres días	a three-day-old loaf
Esta soga tiene tres metros de largo	This rope is three metres long
En algunos puntos el mar tiene más de seis kilómetros de profundo	In some places the sea is more than six kilometres deep

(l) *De* is used in certain circumstances with adjectives before an infinitive. Compare *su conducta es difícil **de** comprender* 'his behaviour is difficult to understand', and *es difícil comprender su conducta* 'it's difficult to understand his behaviour'. See 18.10 for further examples and discussion.

(m) *De* is used after *más* and *menos* before numerals and quantities: *ha comprado más de tres kilos* 'he's bought more than three kilos', *los cojinetes necesitan menos de medio litro de aceite* 'the bearings need less than half a litre of oil'. See 5.5 for further discussion.

(n) *De* replaces *que* in comparisons involving a clause: *es más listo de lo que parece* 'he's cleverer than he seems', *no uses más de los que necesites* 'don't use more than those you need'. See 5.6 for discussion.

(o) *De* alternates with *para* in sentences of the type 'his attitude is not to be copied', 'his stories aren't to be believed':

Sus excusas no son de/para creer	His excuses aren't to be believed
Su veracidad no es muy de recomendarse (J. J. Arreola, Mexico, dialogue; *para* is not used after *muy* in this kind of phrase)	One can't recommend its truth very much
Su habilidad no es de/para subestimar	His cleverness is not be underestimated

(p) After certain verbs meaning 'to take by', 'seize by', 'pull on', etc.:

La cogió de la mano	He took her by the hand
Me tiraba de la manga	She was pulling on my sleeve
El profesor lo/le asió de una oreja	The teacher took him by an ear

(q) To denote the agent in some types of passive construction and to indicate the author of a work or the main actor in a film or play:

acompañado de su esposa	accompanied by his wife
. . . un viejo acompañado de un perro (M. Benedetti, Uruguay)	an old man accompanied by a dog
una novela de Unamuno	a novel by Unamuno

un cuadro de Velázquez	a painting by Velázquez
una película de Clark Gable	a Clark Gable film

See 34.14 note (ii) for discussion of participle + *de*.

(r) In certain set time phrases:

de día/de noche	by day/by night
Se levantó muy de mañana	He got up very early in the morning

(s) In constructions of the type *pobre de ti* 'poor you', *ese tonto de John* 'that fool John', etc.:

Tendrás que habértelas con el gandul de Fulano	You'll have to tackle that layabout so-and-so
¿Sabes lo que ha hecho la pobre de su mujer?	Do you know what his poor wife has done?

(t) Partitive *de:*

De is occasionally used before adjectives – particularly demonstrative adjectives – to mean 'some of', 'one of': *hay de todo* 'there is a bit of everything':

Puedes comprar de todo	You can buy a little of everything
Tráiganos de ese vino que nos sirvió ayer	Bring us some of that wine you served us yesterday

34.7.2 Deber or deber de?

The traditional and soundest rule is that *deber* implies obligation and *deber de* assumptions: *debes comer menos* 'you must eat less', *deben **de** ser las cinco* 'it must be five o'clock'. Unfortunately, modern colloquial Spanish tends to use *deber* for both meanings, with a consequent loss of clarity. See 21.3 for details.

34.7.3 De before que

Some verbs, all verbal phrases involving a noun or adjective, and some adverbial phrases, must be followed by *de que* when they introduce a clause: *nos dimos cuenta de que ya no llovía* 'we realized that it was no longer raining'. See 33.4.2 for discussion.

34.7.4 Dequeísmo

For the popular and spreading tendency to use *de que* instead of *que* after verbs of belief and communication, e.g. *?dice de que no viene* for *dice que no viene* 'she says she isn't coming', see 33.4.3. This construction is vehemently repudiated by educated speakers everywhere.

34.7.5 Desde, and de with the meaning of 'from'

The existence of two Spanish words which both mean 'from' is a source of confusion; nor is the distinction always strictly observed by native speakers. *Desde* stresses the idea of movement or distance more than *de*. It is therefore appropriate when motion 'from' a place requires some unusual effort or when the point of origin is mentioned but not the destination, as in *os veo desde mi ventana* 'I can see you from my window'. It is also much used in time phrases to mean 'since'; see 32.3.7:

Desde nuestro balcón se divisa la cima de Mulhacén	From our balcony one can make out the summit of Mulhacén

Desde aquí el camino es muy bueno	From here the road is very good
Avanzó desde la puerta con un cuchillo en la mano	(S)he moved forward from the door with a knife in his/her hand
He venido andando desde el centro: el metro está en huelga	I've walked all the way from the centre: the Metro is on strike
Y entonces una soga lo atrapó desde atrás (J. Cortázar, Argentina)	Then he was caught from behind by a rope
Desde hoy/A partir de hoy tienen que llegar a tiempo	From today you must arrive on time
Los tenemos desde cincuenta centavos hasta cinco pesos	We have them from 50 centavos to 5 pesos
Desde siempre oí que ella era perfecta (A. Mastretta, Mexico, dialogue)	I had always heard that she was perfect

Notes

(i) If *a, hasta* or an adverb of place appears, *desde* is often interchangeable with *de*: *de/desde aquí a/hasta el centro las calles son muy estrechas* 'from here to the centre the roads are very narrow', *de/desde aquí a la cima mide diez mil metros* 'from here to the summit it measures 10,000 metres', *desde/de 1922 a 1942 estuve en Colombia* 'from 1922 to 1942 I was in Colombia'.

If no such prepositional phrase of destination occurs *desde* is usually the safer option, though usage is fickle: *las partículas subatómicas que llegan desde/de otras galaxias* 'subatomic particles arriving from other galaxies', *¿desde dónde hablas?* 'where are you talking from?', *desde entonces no lo/le he vuelto a ver* 'since then I haven't seen him'.

In the following types of sentence only *de* is possible: *yo soy de Madrid* 'I'm from Madrid', *las hojas caen ya de los abedules* 'the leaves are already falling from the birches', *sacó tres diamantes de la bolsa* 'he took three diamonds from the bag', *pasó de secretaria a jefe en tres meses* 'she went from secretary to boss in three months', *hizo un modelo de un trozo de madera* '(s)he made a model from a piece of wood', *del techo pendía una enorme araña de luces* 'from the ceiling hung an enormous chandelier', *se ha venido de España a vivir en Inglaterra* 'he's come from Spain to live in England', *sólo/solo la veo de Pascuas a Ramos* 'I only see her once in a blue moon' (lit. 'from Easter to Palm Sunday').

(ii) *Desde ya* is commonly found in the River Plate region (and increasingly in Spain, according to Manuel Seco) with the meaning of 'right away'. *Desde luego* means 'of course' on both continents.

34.8 *Durante*

This word, which means 'during', 'for . . . ' a period of time, and other ways of saying '*for* a period of time', is discussed at 32.2 and 32.3.4.

34.9 *En*

As a preposition of place *en* is disconcertingly vague since it combines the meanings of 'in' and 'on' (French *sur* and *dans*), as well as 'at', 'into', 'onto': *en la caja* 'in the box', *en la mesa* 'on/at the table', *está en la comisaría* 'he's in/at the police station'; Spanish-speaking learners of English have problems in differentiating 'in', 'on' and 'at'. For the relationship between *en* and 'at' in sentences like 'at the station', 'at Cambridge', see 34.1d.

When it means 'on a horizontal surface', it alternates with *sobre* (see 34.17) and also sometimes with *encima de* 'on top of'. Thus one can say *en/sobre/encima de la mesa* 'on the table', but *mi hijo duerme en mi cama* 'my son sleeps in my bed', since 'inside' is implied. *En* may be replaced by *dentro de* 'inside' if the idea of 'inside' needs to be stressed.

(a) As an equivalent of 'in', 'on' or 'at':

Tus camisas están en el cajón	Your shirts are in the drawer
Cuelga el cuadro en la pared	Hang the picture on the wall
Dio unos golpes discretos en la puerta	He tapped discreetly on the door
La llave está en la puerta	The key's in the door
Gasto mucho dinero en juegos de azar	I spend a lot of money on gambling (lit. 'games of chance')
... sentado a/en una mesa (see note i)	... sitting at a table
El agua ha penetrado en las vigas	The water has soaked into the joists
Uno de mis pendientes se me ha caído en el agua (see note ii)	One of my earrings fell off in the water (note translation)
La bruja lo/le transformó en rana	The witch turned him into a frog
Propusieron convertirlo en sanatorio	They suggested turning it into a sanatorium
en otoño/primavera/1924	in autumn/spring/1924
Todavía está en proyecto	It's still at the planning stage
Te da ciento y raya en latín	He's miles better than you in Latin

Notes

(i) Compare *se sentó **a** la mesa* 'he sat down at table' with *siempre se comporta mal **en** la mesa* 'he always misbehaves at table'. See 34.1d for discussion.

(ii) The example with the earrings suggests the wearer was already in the water, e.g. swimming. If trajectory down to the water is meant, *a* is more usual: *se tiró al río* 'he jumped into the river', *el avión cayó al mar* 'the plane fell into the sea'. A is the preposition of choice after verbs of motion: *llegaron a Madrid* 'they arrived in Madrid'.

(iii) *Entrar* and similar verbs take *en* (often *a* in Latin America, and occasionally in Spain): *entró en el cuarto* 'he entered the room'.

(b) To express the thing by or at which something else is judged or estimated:

Los daños se han calculado en diez millones de dólares	The damage has been calculated at ten million dollars
El tipo oficial quedó fijado en 151,93 por dólar (El País)	The official rate was fixed at 151.93 to the dollar
Lo vendieron en/por un millón de pesetas	They sold it for a million pesetas
Te tenía en más	I thought more highly of you
El progreso logrado en esta investigación es computable en cero	The progress achieved in this investigation can be reckoned as zero
Me lo presupuestaron en cien mil	They gave me an estimate of 100,000 for it
Se nota que es inglés en su manera de hablar	One can tell he's English by the way he talks
Lo/Le conocí en el andar	I recognized him from the way he walked

(c) In a number of adverbial phrases:

Lo tomaron en serio	They took it/him seriously
en mangas de camisa/en cueros/en broma/en balde	in shirtsleeves/naked/as a joke/pointlessly
en fila/en seguida (or *enseguida*)	in a row/straight away
Estoy en contra	I'm against

(d) To mean 'as':

Como is much more usual nowadays in the following sentences:

Hablar de esa manera, en/como ser superior, es absurdo	To talk like that, as a superior being, is absurd
Os hablo en/como perito	I'm talking to you as an expert

(e) After a number of common verbs, and in several miscellaneous constructions:

Pensé mucho en usted	I thought of you a lot
Quedamos en vernos a las siete	We agreed to meet at seven
Tardaron cinco semanas en reparar el coche	They took five weeks to mend the car
Vaciló en contestarme	He hesitated before answering me
No dudó en devolvérmelo	She didn't hesitate to give it back to me
No ayuda en nada	(S)he's/It's no help at all
La reina abdicó en su hijo	The queen abdicated in favour of her son
Se interesa mucho en/por la filatelia	She's very interested in stamp collecting
El fue el primero/último en hacerlo	·He was the first/last to do it
hablar en inglés	to speak in English

Notes

(i) See 18.2 for further remarks about prepositional usage with verbs. For the obsolete construction *en* + gerund see 20.5.

(ii) *En la mañana* may be used in Latin America for *por la mañana*: *en las mañanas salíamos a montar a caballo* (A. Mastretta, Mexico) 'in the mornings we used to go riding'.

34.10 *Entre*

Both 'between' and 'among'. *Entre* also has a number of uses unfamiliar to English speakers.

Prepositional pronoun forms are not nowadays used after *entre*: *entre Juan y tú recogeréis los papeles* 'you and John will pick up the pieces of paper between you' (not **entre Juan y ti*). But the prepositional form *sí*, from *se*, is used after *entre*. See section (c) below.

(a) 'Between':

Estábamos entre la espada y la pared	We were between the sword and the wall (i.e. 'we had our backs to the wall'/'we were between the Devil and the deep blue sea')
... constantemente entre la excitación y la depresión (M. Vázquez Montalbán, Spain)	... constantly between excitement and depression
Cuestan entre mil y dos mil	They cost between one and two thousand
entre tú/usted y yo . . .	between you and me . . .
Entre todos rehabilitaremos Madrid (poster)	Working together we'll modernize Madrid
Lo terminaron entre María y su hermana	Maria and her sister finished it between them

Note

The last example is typical of a construction unfamiliar to English speakers: *llenan el pantano entre cuatro ríos* (from Moliner (1998), I, 1146) 'four rivers combine to fill the reservoir', *trozos de una novela rosa que fuimos escribiendo entre las dos* (C. Martín Gaite, Spain) 'bits of a romantic novel the two of us were writing together'.

(b) 'Among':

It is used with a wider range of nouns than its English equivalent, e.g. *entre la niebla* 'in the mist', *encontraron la sortija entre la arena* 'they found the ring in the sand':

No pude encontrar el libro entre tantos tomos	I couldn't find the book among so many volumes
Vivió diez años entre los beduinos de Arabia	He lived for ten years among the Bedouins of Arabia
La perdí de vista entre la muchedumbre	I lost sight of her in the crowd
No podía decidir entre tantas posibilidades	I couldn't choose among so many possibilities
. . . y entre el ruido de la lluvia se escuchaba el ladrido de los perros (L. Sepúlveda, Chile)	. . . and through/above the noise of the rain the barking of the dogs was heard
Entre la niebla se percibía una masa inquieta (L. Mateo Díez, Spain)	A restless mass/shape could be seen in the fog

(c) 'Among themselves', 'one from the other':

In the second of these two meanings *entre* is used in a way unfamiliar to English speakers. It is especially liable to appear with the pronoun *sí* (discussed in detail at 11.5.3):

En casa hablan castellano entre sí (or *entre ellos*)	At home they speak Spanish among themselves
Es más fácil que dos personas vivan en armonía cuando se respetan entre sí	It's easier for two people to live in harmony when they respect one another
Los idiomas que se hablan en la India son muy diferentes entre sí	The languages spoken in India differ widely one from another
Enseguida notamos el recelo manifiesto que se dispensan entre sí (E. Lynch, Argentina; one can also write *en seguida*)	We immediately noticed the obvious distrust they felt for one another

(d) It can translate the English phrase 'what with':

Entre los niños y el ruido que hacen los albañiles, me estoy volviendo loca	What with the children and the noise the builders make, I'm going mad
Entre el problema de la inflación y la deuda exterior este país va cuesta abajo entre pitos y flautas . . .	What with the problem of inflation and the foreign debt, this country is going downhill what with one thing and another . . . (lit. 'what with whistles and flutes')

(e) In certain phrases, in a way strange to English speakers:

Van como ovejas al matadero, decía entre sí	They're going like lambs to the slaughter, he said to himself
Decía entre mí . . .	I said to myself . . .
El museo está abierto entre semana	The museum is open on weekdays and Saturdays

34.11 *Hacia*

(a) A close equivalent of 'towards', but rather wider in application since it also translates the English suffix *-ward/-wards*:

El satélite viaja hacia Venus	The satellite is travelling towards Venus
La muchedumbre se dirigía hacia el palacio presidencial	The crowd was making for the presidential palace
Señaló hacia el este	He pointed to the east
Hacia el oeste no había más que dunas	Towards the west there was nothing but dunes

La actitud de la ONU hacia tales problemas parece ambigua	The attitude of the UN towards such problems seems ambiguous
El incidente ocurrió hacia las tres de la tarde	The incident occurred towards three in the afternoon
El coche rodaba hacia atrás	The car was rolling backwards
Se apoyaba hacia delante en un bastón	He was leaning forwards on a stick

In time phrases *hacia* can less commonly be replaced by *sobre* – *sobre finales de agosto* 'around the end of August', *sobre las tres de la tarde*, 'around 3 p.m.' – or, with dates, by *para*: *para octubre* 'towards/around October'.

(b) Emotions, attitudes 'towards':

Por, con and *para con* are also possible, but not always interchangeable. Deep emotions such as love or hatred prefer *hacia* or *por*; attitudes (e.g. kindness, severity, irritability) prefer *hacia* or *con*. For *para con* see 34.5b.

mi profundo amor hacia/por/a todo lo andaluz	my deep love for everything Andalusian
Mostraba una indiferencia total hacia/por las críticas	He displayed total indifference towards criticisms
la simpatía de los insurgentes hacia/por el modelo cubano	the insurgents' sympathy for the Cuban model

34.12 *Hasta*

(a) 'As far as', 'until', 'up to':

hasta ahora	until now/up to now
Llegaron hasta el oasis, pero tuvieron que volverse	They got as far as the oasis, but had to turn back
No nos vamos hasta el día trece	We're not leaving until the thirteenth
Siguió leyendo hasta que no había luz	She kept reading until there was no light
Bailaron hasta no poder más	They danced until they were exhausted
Estoy de exámenes hasta la coronilla (or hasta las narices)	I've had enough of exams (I'm sick to death of exams)
hasta luego	goodbye/au revoir

(b) *Hasta que no:*

See 23.2.4d for this construction.

(c) As an equivalent of *incluso* 'even':

Hasta llegó a ofrecerles dinero	He even went as far as offering them money
Hasta en Inglaterra hace calor a veces	Even in England it's hot sometimes

Note

In Mexico, and in neighbouring countries, *hasta* has acquired the meaning of 'not until': *perdona que te llame hasta ahora* (C. Fuentes, dialogue), 'sorry for not ringing you before now', *bajamos hasta la Plaza de la Independencia* 'we're not getting off until Independence Square', *hasta entonces me di cuenta* 'I realized only then' or 'I didn't realize until then'.

34.13 *Mediante*

A close equivalent of 'by means of' some instrument, argument or device:

Es inútil intentar abolir el abuso de alcohol mediante/por decreto/con decretos	It is useless to try to abolish alcohol abuse by decree
Lograron abrir la caja mediante/con una antorcha de butano	They managed to open the safe by means of a butane torch

34.14 *Para* and *por*

34.14.1 The difference between them

The existence of two prepositions which both sometimes seem to mean 'for', French *pour*, is one of the stumbling blocks of the language. Although the difference is best learnt from examples, one basic distinction is that *para* expresses purpose or destination and *por* cause or motive, a difference clearly visible in the two sentences *hago esto para ti* 'I'm **making** this for you (to give to you)' and *hago esto por ti* 'I'm **doing** this because of you/on your behalf'. English speakers are usually confused by sentences like 'this fence is for the rabbits': since this obviously means 'because of the rabbits' rather than something given to them, one must say *esta valla es **por** los conejos*. The Spanish Civil Guards' motto *Todo por la Patria* 'Everything for the Home Country' exemplifies *por* at its most confusing. It means 'everything (we do is done) for our country', i.e. 'all our actions are inspired by our country', whereas *Todo para la Patria* would mean 'everything (we have is) **for** our country', i.e. 'we give all our belongings to our country'.

It is useful to recall that if 'for' can be replaced by 'out of' or 'because' then *por* may be the correct translation, but not *para*: *lo hizo por amor* 'he did it for (out of) love', *lo hago por el dinero* 'I do it for (because of) the money':

Llevo el abrigo por/a causa de mi madre	I'm wearing this coat because of my mother (she'll be cross/worried if I don't)
Llevo este abrigo para/a mi madre	I'm taking this coat for my mother (i.e. to give to her)
Han venido por ti	They've come to get you/come because of you/come instead of you
Han venido estos paquetes para ti	These parcels have come for you
Lo has conseguido por mí	You've got it as a result of me (i.e. I helped you)
Los has conseguido para mí	You've got it for me

Particularly troublesome is the fact that *por* and *para* can be almost identical in meaning in some sentences that state an intention: *ha venido **por/para** estar contigo* '(s)he's come to be with you', whereas in others only *para* is possible: *el carpintero ha venido **para** reparar la puerta*, 'the carpenter's come to mend the door'. This problem is discussed at 34.14.7.

Note

The form *pa* is substandard for *para* and should be avoided. It is accepted in a few humorous familiar expressions used in Spain (and possibly elsewhere), e.g. *es muy echao p'alante* 'he's very forward', *estoy p'al arrastre* 'I'm all in/exhausted', *p'al gato* 'worthless' (literally 'for the cat').

34.14.2 Uses of *para*

Para is used:

(a) To indicate purpose, object or destination, e.g. *¿para quién es esto?* 'who(m) is this for?', *¿para qué es esto?* 'what's this for?', *trabaja para ganar dinero* 'he works to earn money', etc. (but see 34.14.7 for the possible alternative use of *por* in some contexts):

Este dinero es para Oxfam	This money is for Oxfam
Una mesa para dos, por favor	A table for two, please

Se preparó para saltar	He got ready to jump
Lo hace para/con el fin de/por llamar la atención	She does it to attract attention
Un coche hecho para durar (advertisement, Spain)	A car made to last
Estudia para médico	(S)he's studying to become a doctor
Para manzanas, Asturias	For good apples – Asturias (i.e. if you want good apples go to Asturias)

Notes

(i) *Para* can also express ironic purpose, like the English 'only to': *se abstuvo durante años de fumar y beber, para luego morir en un accidente de coche* 'he refrained for years from smoking and drinking, only to die in a car accident', *corrió a casa para encontrarse con que ya se habían marchado* 'she hurried home only to find that they'd already left'.

(ii) The following construction may also be thought of as expressing the object or purpose of something: *sus historias no son para/de creer* 'his stories aren't to be believed' (lit. 'aren't for believing'), *no es para tanto* 'it's not that serious/it doesn't call for that much fuss'.

(iii) For the difference between *¿por qué?* 'why?' and *¿para qué?* 'what for?', see 24.10.

(b) Direction after verbs of motion:

Íbamos para casa cuando empezó a llover	We were on the way home when it started raining
La secretaria ya ha salido para Burgos	The secretary has already left for Burgos
Ya va para viejo	(S)he's getting old now
Va para ministro	He's on the way to becoming a minister

(c) To indicate advantage, disadvantage, usefulness, need:

Fumar es malo para la salud	Smoking is bad for the health
La paciencia es un requisito indispensable para los profesores	Patience is an indispensable requirement for teachers
Con esto tenemos para todos	With this we've enough for everybody
Tú eres para él lo más importante	You're the most important thing to/for him

(d) Reaction, response, mood:

Para mí eso no es justo	That doesn't seem fair to me
Esto para mí huele a vinagre/Esto a mí me huele a vinagre	This smells of vinegar to me
Yo no tengo amigos. Para mí, que mi mujer los espanta	I haven't got any friends. If you ask me, my wife scares them away
Para su padre es un genio	(S)he's a genius in his/her father's eyes

Notes

(i) For *para con* in sentences like *es muy atento para con los invitados* 'he's very courteous towards guests', see 34.5b.

(ii) *Para* can also translate 'not in the mood for': *no estoy para bromas* 'I'm not in the mood for jokes'.

(e) To translate 'for' when it means 'considering', 'in view of':

Está muy alto para su edad	He's very tall for his age
Estás muy viejo para esos trotes	You're very old for all that
Es poco dinero para tanto trabajo	It's not much money for so much work

(f) 'To' in certain reflexive expressions:

Me lo guardo para mí	I'm keeping it to/for myself

Esto acabará mal, me decía para mí/entre mí	This will end badly, I said to myself
Murmuraba para/entre sí	(S)he was muttering to himself/herself

(g) 'About' in the meaning of 'on the point of':

Ya deben estar para/al llegar	They must be about to arrive
La leche está para cocer	The milk's about to boil
Pues yo estoy para cumplir treinta y cinco la semana que viene (E. Arenas, Spain, dialogue)	Well, I'm going to be thirty-five next week

Note

In Latin America *estar por* is used: *está por llover* 'it's about to rain', *en 1942, cuando volvió definitivamente, estaba por cumplir veinte años* (S. Pitol, Mexico) 'in 1942, when he came back for good, he was on the verge of his twentieth birthday', *oye bien. Un pájaro está por cantar* (J. L. Borges, Argentina) 'listen. A bird is about to sing'. In Spain *estar por* means 'to be in favour of'/'to be thinking about doing something'.

34.14.3 *Para* in time phrases

(a) To translate 'by':

Lo tendré preparado para las cinco	I'll have it ready by/for five o'clock
Para entonces ya estaremos todos muertos	We'll all be dead by then
Si ensayamos fuerte durante todo el año, para el verano estaremos en condiciones de actuar (S. Puértolas, Spain, dialogue)	If we rehearse hard all year we'll be in a condition to perform by Summer

(b) 'For':

Para sometimes expresses the idea of 'for *n* days/weeks/years'. See 32.3.6 for further discussion.

(c) 'Around', 'towards':

El embalse estará terminado para finales de noviembre	The dam will be finished around the end of November
Volveremos para agosto	We'll return around August

Notes

(i) In the last example *para* is more precise than *hacia* and *por* and less precise than *en*.
(ii) *Ir para* is a colloquial translation of 'for nearly . . .' in time phrases: *va para cinco años que trabajo aquí* 'I've been working here for nearly five years'.

(d) 'Not enough to', 'considering how much':

No había tomado suficientes pastillas como para matarse (M. Vázquez Montalbán, Spain)	She hadn't taken enough pills to kill herself
. . . un matrimonio rápido, bastante rápido para lo mucho que siempre se dice que hay que pensárselo (J. Marías, Spain)	. . . a quick marriage, pretty quick considering how much they always say one ought to think it over

34.14.4 Main uses of *por*

(a) *Por* often means simply 'because of', as in *¿por qué?* (two words!) 'why?' (i.e. 'because of what?') and *porque* 'because':

No pudimos salir por/a causa de la nieve	We couldn't go out because of the snow
el índice de muertes por/a causa de infecciones pulmonares	the death rate from lung infections
Lo hice por dinero	I did it for money
la razón por la que me voy	the reason for my leaving
muchas gracias por el regalo	many thanks for the present
Me pusieron una multa por aparcar en el centro	They fined me for parking in the centre
Te ha pasado por tonto	It happened to you because you're a fool
Las críticas de la izquierda vienen por/a causa de tres temas	Criticism from the left arises on three grounds (lit. 'from three topics')
El profesor la calificó con un cero por no saber la lección (M. Puig, Argentina)	The teacher gave her a zero because she didn't know the lesson
Las empresas navieras sufren un descalabro importante por la situación actual del mercado (*Abc*, Spain)	Shipping firms have suffered significant losses due to the present state of the market

Por may thus indicate the origin or inspiration of an emotion or mental state:

No lo/le puedo ver por lo engreído que es	I can't stand him because of his conceitedness
Me fastidias por lo mal que cantas	You annoy me because of your bad singing
Lo/Le odio por su mal genio	I hate him for/because of his bad temper
Nuestro amor por/hacia/a nuestros hijos	our love for our children
su fascinación por los Estados Unidos	His/her fascination with the USA
Siento una enorme curiosidad por saber si ésta/esta es la única vida	I feel enormous curiosity to know whether this is the only life
Tuvo un recuerdo nostálgico por el Londres de su juventud	He had a nostalgic recollection of the London of his youth
No por previsible la foto anual dejaba de ser un acontecimiento excepcional (E. Lynch, Argentina)	Predictability did not stop the annual photograph from being an exceptional occasion

Note the idiom, common to Spain and Latin America, *darle a uno por* 'to take up', 'to get keen on', e.g. *no, a Carlos no le interesan estas cosas; le ha dado por el arte* (L. Otero, Cuba, dialogue) 'no, Carlos isn't interested in those things. He's taken up art/He's developed a passion for art.'
(b) *Por* = 'by' in passive constructions:

Sus novelas fueron elogiadas por los críticos	His novels were praised by the critics
La catedral fue diseñada por Gaudí	The cathedral was designed by Gaudí
Los campos estaban devastados por la sequía	The fields were devastated by drought
El suelo estaba cubierto por/de un lecho de hierba	The ground was covered by a bed of grass
Sociedad y economía aztecas por M. León-Portilla	*Aztec Society and Economy* by M. León-Portilla

Notes

(i) For *de* meaning 'by' to indicate the author of a work or the main actor in a film or play see 34.7.1q.
(ii) *De* is not nowadays used in passive sentences to mean 'by', except with certain verbs which are best learnt separately. Where there is a possibility of using either *por* or *de*, the former usually implies an active agent and the latter generally implies a state. *De* is therefore common when *estar* is used (see 28.2.5 for *estar convencido* contrasted with *ser convencido*): *me sentía tentado de tomar el atajo* 'I felt tempted to take the short cut', *Jesús fue tentado por el Diablo* 'Jesus was

tempted by the Devil', *María dijo algunas palabras en voz muy baja . . . seguidas de un ruido de sillas* (E. Sábato, Argentina) 'Maria said a few words in a very low voice, followed by a sound of chairs', *en todas partes era seguido por una muchedumbre de admiradores* (*le seguía una muchedumbre* is more natural) 'he was followed everywhere by a crowd of admirers', *el formulario debe estar acompañado de dos fotos* 'the form must be accompanied by two photos', *las zonas pantanosas suelen estar plagadas de mosquitos* 'marshy zones are usually plagued with mosquitoes', *en verano las vacas están atormentadas por las moscas* 'in summer the cows are tormented by flies'.

(c) 'Runs *on*', 'works *by*'; 'by means of':

El sistema de alarma funciona por rayos infrarrojos	The alarm system works by infra-red rays
El tratamiento por/con rayos X ha producido resultados animadores	Treatment by X-rays has produced encouraging results
un coche que marcha por/con/a gas-oil	a car which runs on diesel oil
Se puede pagar por/con cheque bancario	Payment by cheque/(US 'check') accepted
[el Buda] enseñaba la aniquilación del dolor por la aniquilación del deseo (J. L. Borges, Argentina)	[The Buddha] taught the extinction of suffering by the extinction of desire

(d) 'In support of', 'in favour of', 'on behalf of':

Yo voté por que tu libro fuera premiado (R. Arenas, Cuba)	I voted in favour of your book getting the prize
¿Estás tú por la violencia?	Do you support violence?
Encuentro de Escritores por la Paz	Conference of Writers for Peace (i.e. who support peace)

(e) Exchange *for*, substitute *for*, distribution *per*:

Llévelo al departamento de reclamaciones y se lo cambiarán por uno nuevo	Take it to the complaints department and they'll change it for a new one
Ahora daría lo que no tengo por oírla (C. Martín Gaite, Spain)	Now I'd give everything I haven't got (for the chance) to hear her (voice)
Te han dado gato por liebre	They've served you cat for hare (i.e. swindled you)
¿Por quién me toma usted?	Who do you take me for?
Lo doy por supuesto/sentado	I take it for granted
Él dará la clase por mí	He'll give the class instead of me
Comes por tres	You eat enough for three
tres raciones por persona	three helpings per person
cien kilómetros por hora	100 km an hour
40 horas a la/por semana (*a* is more usual)	40 hours a week
la media anual por español	the annual average per Spaniard
El dos por ciento es protestante/son protestantes	Two per cent are Protestants

(f) Prices, amounts of money:

un cheque por/de cien dólares	a cheque/(US 'check') for 100 dollars
Compró una casa por un millón de dólares	He bought a house for one million dollars

Note

Por is used with *pagar* only when the latter already has a direct object in the form of a quantity of money: *he pagado **mil libras** por este ordenador* (Lat. Am. *por esta computadora*) 'I paid £1,000 for this computer', *he pagado **mucho** por él* 'I paid a lot for it', but *yo **lo** pagué la semana pasada* 'I paid for it last week'. *Por* also appears in certain set phrases: *me pagan por horas* 'they pay me by the hour', *no te pago por no hacer nada* 'I'm not paying you to do nothing'.

(g) 'To judge *by*':

. . . por las señas que me ha dado . . .	. . . from the description she's given me . . .
por lo que tú dices . . .	from what you say . . .
por lo visto	apparently
Evidentemente, por su voz, por su aspecto, *por su ropa era una persona decente* (G. Cabrera Infante, Cuba)	Clearly, to judge by his voice, looks and clothes, he was a decent person

(h) 'In search *of*':

Peninsular speech prefers *a por*, a construction grudgingly admitted by grammarians and rejected by Latin Americans:

Ha ido (a) por agua	He's gone for water
Lo/Le enviaron (a) por el médico	They sent him for the doctor
Voy al baño a por Kleenex (C. Rico-Godoy, Spain; Lat. Am. *por Kleenex*)	I'm going/I go to the bathroom/toilet to fetch a tissue
Fui por mi abrigo (A. Mastretta, Mexico)	I went for my coat/I went to get my coat

(i) 'Through' (= 'by means of'):

Conseguí el empleo por/a través de mi tío	I got the job through my uncle
Me enteré por un amigo	I found out through/from a friend

(j) *Por* in adverbial phrases of manner:

una campaña por/en pro de/a favor de la libertad de la prensa	a campaign for freedom of the press
Él es senador por Massachusetts	He's senator for Massachusetts
Aprendió a tocar el piano por sí misma/ella sola	She learnt to play the piano by herself
por correo/avión/mar (but *en tren, en coche, en bicicleta, a pie*)	by mail/air/sea
Los denuncio por igual	I denounce both/all sides equally
por lo general/generalmente	generally
por lo corriente/corrientemente	usually
Me lo tendrás que decir por las buenas o por las malas	You'll have to tell me one way or another

(k) 'However . . . ' in concessions (see 16.13.2):

Por más inteligente que seas, no lo vas a resolver	However intelligent you may be, you won't solve it
Era la verdad por dura que me pareciera (M. Torres, Spain)	It was the truth however hard it seemed to me
Por mucho que protestes, te quedas aquí	However much you protest, you're staying here

(l) Miscellaneous examples:

Por mí haz lo que quieras	As far as I'm concerned, do what you like
¿Por quién pregunta?	Who are you asking for?
Es agrimensor, o algo por el estilo	He's a surveyor, or something like that
Siéntese por Dios (not brusque, i.e. not 'sit down for God's sake'!)	Do please sit down
Cinco por tres son quince	5 times 3 equals 15
Mide 7 por 5	It measures 7 by 5

(m) With numerous verbs, e.g.:

afanarse por to strive to
apurarse por§ get anxious about
asustarse por/de get frightened about
decidirse por to decide on
desvelarse por to be very concerned
   about
disculparse por to apologize for
interesarse por to be interested in

jurar por swear by/on
luchar por to struggle to
molestarse por to bother about
optar por to opt for
preguntar por to ask about/after
preocuparse por to worry about
tomar por to take for
votar por to vote for

§*Apurarse* means 'to hurry' in Latin America.

34.14.5 *Por* in time phrases

(a) *Por* = 'in', but less precise than *en* where the latter is also possible:

Debió ser por mayo
por aquellos días

It must have been some time in May
in those days/during those days

For 'just for', 'only for' and a more detailed discussion of *por* in time phrases
see 32.3.5.

Note

Latin Americans sometimes use *por* where Spaniards would use *durante*. See 32.3.5, note (ii).

34.14.6 *Por* as a preposition of place

(a) 'All over', 'throughout':

He viajado por Latinoamérica
Había muchos libros desparramados por
   el suelo
Oye,¿me das crema por/en la espalda?

I've travelled around Latin America
There were many books scattered over
   the floor
Could you please put cream on my back?

(b) 'In': less precise than *en* and often implying motion:

La vi por/en la calle
Creo que las mujeres andan por Europa
   (M. Benedetti, Uruguay, dialogue)
Debe estar por el jardín
Yo no sabía por dónde empezar
   (M. Torres, Spain)

I saw her in the street
I think the women are somewhere in
   Europe
it must be somewhere in the garden
I didn't know where to begin

(c) 'Up to':

El agua le llegaba por la cintura
Me llegas por los hombros

The water was up to his waist
You reach my shoulders (e.g. to a
   growing child)

(d) 'Through', 'out of', 'down':

Se tiró por la ventana
Entró por la puerta
Se cayó por la escalera
Salía agua por el/del grifo
El tren pasó por/a través del túnel

He threw himself out of the window
He came through the door
He fell down the stairs
Water was coming out of the tap
The train went through the tunnel

(e) In conjunction with adverbs of place, to denote direction or whereabouts:

por aquí

this way/around here

por allí	that way/around there
por delante	in front
por detrás	from behind/behind
por entre	in between
por Madrid	through/via Madrid

34.14.7 *He venido por hablarle* or *para hablarle?*

Both prepositions may translate 'to' or 'in order to' in sentences like 'I've come to talk to you'. In some cases they are virtually interchangeable:

¿Para qué has venido?	What have you come for?
¿Por qué has venido?	Why have you come?
Estoy aquí para/por verle	I've come to see him
. . . *todo cuanto ella hacía por hacerlo feliz* (G. García Márquez, Colombia; or *para*)	. . . everything she did to make him happy
. . . *el esfuerzo por conservarse bien y por vestirse como una vamp de película de Hollywood revival de los años 50* (M. Vázquez Montalbán, Spain; or *para*)	. . . the effort to look after herself and to dress like a revival 1950s Hollywood film vamp

A useful rule seems to be: if the English sentence can be rewritten using a phrase like 'out of a desire to' or 'from an urge to', then *por* can be used. If not, *para* is indicated; i.e. *por* refers to the mental state of the subject, *para* to the goal of his/her action.

Thus, *me dijeron que estabas en Madrid y he venido por verte de nuevo* 'I heard you were in Madrid and I've come to (out of an urge to) see you again' is possible (*para* could also be used). But **el fontanero ha venido por reparar el grifo* is as absurd as 'the plumber has come out of an urge to mend the tap'. Another example may clarify the point: —*¿Para qué salgo a cenar contigo?* —*Para comer* (not *por*) '"What am I going out to dinner with you for?" "(In order) to eat"'. —*¿Por qué salgo a cenar contigo?* —*Por/Para estar conmigo* '"Why am I going out to dinner with you?" "To be with me."'

Estuve toda la noche sin dormir por/para no perderme el eclipse	I spent the whole night without sleeping so as not to miss the eclipse
Llegó a las cinco de la mañana por/para cogerlos en la cama	(S)he arrived at five in the morning so as to catch them in bed
Ella le habría vendido el alma al Diablo por casarse con él (G. García Márquez Colombia)	She'd have sold her soul to the Devil to marry him
Dame una aspirina para calmar el dolor	Give me an aspirin to ease the pain
Incluso contrataron a un detective privado para buscarle/buscarlo	They even hired a private detective to look for him
Le prometo que haré lo posible por dar con él (A. Mastretta, Mexico, dialogue)	I promise you I'll do everything possible to find him

Note

After some words *por* is required: *teníamos prisa **por** verla* 'we were in a hurry to see her', *me esforzaba **por/para** llegar a tiempo* 'I used to make an effort to arrive on time', *el celo por la reforma* 'eagerness for reform', *el anhelo por la gloria* 'longing for glory'.

34.14.8 Some vital differences between *por* and *para*

Tengo muchas cosas por/sin hacer	I have a lot of things still to do
Tengo muchas cosas para hacer	I have many things to do
Estoy por hacerlo	I feel inclined to do it
Estoy (aquí) para hacerlo	I'm here in order to do it
Estaba para hacerlo (Lat. Am. *por*)	I was about to do it
Está por/sin acabar	It isn't finished yet
Está para acabar	This has to be finished
Está para (Lat. Am. *por*) *acabar de un momento a otro*	(S)he/It's about to finish at any moment

34.14.9 'For' not translated by *por* or *para*

la razón de mi queja	the reason for my complaining
Bebía porque no tenía otra cosa que hacer	She drank for want of something else to do
Los días eran cortos pues era ahora noviembre (see 33.5.3)	The days were short, for it was now November
el deseo de fama	the desire for fame
Lloró de alegría	She wept for joy
Es una buena secretaria a pesar de lo que gruñe	She's a good secretary, for all her grumbling
No dijo una palabra durante dos horas	He didn't say a word for two hours
No lo/le he visto desde hace meses	I haven't seen him for months
Llevamos tres semanas sin que recojan la basura	They haven't collected our rubbish/(US 'trash') for three weeks
Estuvimos horas esperando	We waited for hours
Se podía ver muy lejos	You could see for miles
ir a dar un paseo	to go for a walk
irse de vacaciones	to go for a holiday/vacation
Me voy a Madrid unos días	I'm going to Madrid for a few days

34.15 *Según*

'According to', 'depending on'. As with *entre*, a following pronoun appears in the subject form: *según tú* 'according to you', not **según ti*:

según el parte meteorológico	according to the weather report
Según tú, se debería abolir la televisión	According to you, television should be abolished
Iremos modificando el programa de estudios según el tipo de estudiante que se matricule	We'll modify the syllabus according to the type of student that signs on
Los precios varían según a qué dentista vayas (or *según el dentista al que vayas*)	The prices vary according to which dentist you go to
Me decidiré luego, según cómo salgan las cosas	I'll decide later, depending on how things turn out

Notes

(i) As the examples show, *según* often functions as an adverb: *—¿Vas tú también? —Según* '"Are you going too?" "It depends"', *la policía detenía a los manifestantes según iban saliendo del edificio* 'the police were arresting the demonstrators as they came out of the building', *lo haremos según llegue papá* (*en cuanto llegue* is more usual) 'we'll do it as soon as father arrives', *según llegábamos al aparcamiento . . . un automóvil abandonaba un lugar grande y espacioso* (C. Rico-Godoy, Spain) 'just as we were arriving at the parking lot a car was leaving a large and roomy parking space', *según dicen . . .* 'according to what they say . . .'.

(ii) The following are colloquial or dialect: *dirías que es un millonario según habla* (*por la manera en que habla*) 'you'd think he was a millionaire from the way he talks', *a mí, según qué cosas, no me gusta* *hacerlas* (regional for *ciertas cosas* . . .) 'there are certain kinds of things I don't like doing', the last example being typical of eastern Spain.

34.16 *Sin*

'Without'. *Sin* raises few problems for the English speaker, except when it appears before an infinitive, in which case it sometimes cannot be translated by the English verb form ending in -ing: compare *dos Coca-Colas sin abrir* 'two Coca-Colas, unopened' (or 'not opened'). See 28.2.4.

No subas al tren sin billete	Don't get on the train without a ticket
Como vuelva a verte por aquí te echo sin contemplaciones	If I see you around here again I'll throw you out on the spot (lit. 'without consideration for you')
Fumabas sin cesar	You were smoking ceaselessly
Estoy sin blanca	I haven't got a penny
¡Cuántos hay sin comer!	How many there are who have nothing to eat!
Está más guapa sin peinar	She's more attractive without her hair done

Sin can be used to create a new noun, e.g. *los sin hogar/los sin casa* 'the homeless'. *Sin* exists as a prefix in a few words, like *sinnúmero* 'vast abundance', *sinrazón* 'insanity'/'absurdity', *sinvergüenza* 'shameless person'.

34.17 *Sobre*

This preposition combines some of the meanings of the English words 'on', 'over', 'on top of' and 'above'.

(a) As a preposition of place:
It is an equivalent of *en* in the sense of 'on': *en/sobre la mesa* 'on the table', *en/sobre la pared* 'on the wall'. It is rather more literary than *en*. *Encima de* is also used of horizontal surfaces: *encima de la mesa* 'on (top of) the table'. However, where 'on top of' is impossible in English *encima de* is impossible in Spanish: *los hinchas se encuentran todavía en/sobre el terreno* 'the fans are still on the field,/(British 'pitch').

Querían edificar sobre estos terrenos un hotel nuevo	They wanted to build a new hotel on this land
Este neumático tiene poco agarre sobre mojado	This tyre has poor grip on wet surfaces
Los rebeldes marcharon sobre la capital	The rebels marched on the capital
El castillo está edificado sobre un pintoresco valle	The castle is built overlooking a picturesque valley
Dios vela sobre sus hijos	God watches over his children
Una mujer habla con un chico y un árbol agita unas hojas secas sobre sus cabezas (J. Cortázar, Argentina)	A woman is talking to a boy and a tree is waving a few dry leaves over their heads
Un sol de fuego caía sobre los campos	A fiery sun fell on the plains

Note

Compare *sobre*, *encima de* and *por encima de* in the following examples: *el rey está por encima de/sobre todos* (rest, not motion) 'the king is above everyone', *mi jefe siempre está encima de mí* 'my boss is always breathing down my neck', *la bala pasó por encima de su cabeza, rozándole el pelo* (motion) 'the bullet passed over his/her head, just touching his/her hair', *el avión voló por encima del/sobre la ciudad* (motion: *sobre* implies height and is often more literary than *encima de*) 'the plane flew over the city'.

(b) Approximation (more usually with time):

Llegaremos sobre las cinco de la tarde	We'll arrive around 5 p.m.
Tenía sobre cuarenta años (. . . *unos 40 años* is more usual)	He was around forty years old
Costó sobre cien mil (*unos/unas 100.000* . . . is more usual)	It cost around 100,000

(c) 'About':

In this sense, *sobre* implies formal discourse 'about', i.e. 'on the subject of' something. Informal discourse usually requires *de*, cf. *no he venido a hablar de tus problemas* 'I haven't come to talk about your problems' (not *sobre*):

Pronunció una conferencia sobre los problemas del Oriente Próximo	She delivered a lecture on the problems of the Near East
La OMS advierte sobre el peligro del uso de tranquilizantes sin receta médica	The WHO (World Health Organization) warns of use of tranquillizers without medical prescription

(d) Centre of rotation:

El mundo gira sobre su eje polar	The world spins about its polar axis
Las puertas se mueven sobre bisagras (from Luque Durán, 1973)	Doors turn on hinges
Dio media vuelta sobre el pie izquierdo (ibid.)	He did a half-turn on his left foot

(e) Superiority or precedence 'over':

El triunfo de los conservadores sobre la izquierda	The victory of the conservatives over the left
No tiene derecho a reclamar su superioridad sobre los demás	He has no right to claim superiority over others
Sobre todo, quisiera agradecer a mi mujer . . .	Above all, I would like to thank my wife . . .
Y, sobre cualquier escrúpulo, estaba mi hijo (A. Gala, Spain, dialogue)	And over and above any scruples there was my child (not 'son' here, since it was still in the womb)
El crecimiento, en términos reales, de las exportaciones en el primer mes de 1984 supera el 50% sobre enero de 1983 (*El País*)	In real terms, the growth in exports in the first month of 1984 is 50% higher than January 1983
impuestos sobre la renta	taxes on income

34.18 *Tras*

'Behind', 'after'. It is a close equivalent of the more usual *detrás de* 'behind' (location) and *después de* 'after' (time). Its brevity makes it popular with journalists, but it is very rare in everyday speech. *Tras de* is an equally literary variant.

Dos siluetas deformes se destacaron tras el vidrio esmerilado (L. Goytisolo, Spain)	Two distorted outlines loomed through/ behind the frosted glass (i.e. semi-opaque ground glass)

¿Quién sabe qué cosas pasan tras las cortinas de aquella casa?	Who knows what things happen behind the curtains of that house?
un generoso proyecto tras el cual se esconden intenciones menos altruistas	a generous project behind which less generous intentions lurk
Me oculté tras el marco de la puerta (G. Cabrera Infante, Cuba)	I hid behind the door frame
Una banda de gaviotas venía tras el barco	A flock of gulls was following the boat

Detrás de could be used in all the above examples.

Así, tras de los duros años de 1936 a 1939 . . . (popular press; *después de* possible)	So, after the hard years between 1936 and 1939
Los cazadores denuncian 'intereses políticos' tras las críticas de un grupo ecologista andaluz (El Mundo, Spain)	Hunters denounce 'political interests' after criticisms by an Andalusian ecological group
Tras de sus ojos se fue como imantado (M. de Unamuno, Spain)	He went off after her, drawn by her eyes, as though magnetized

Notes

(i) Occasionally *tras* is unavoidable: *siguieron el mismo ritmo de trabajo, año tras año/día tras día* 'they followed the same work-pace, year after year/day after day', . . . *una beca para primer año, que será renovada para segundo . . . y así año tras año* (M. Puig, Argentina, dialogue) ' . . . a grant for the first year, which will be renewed for the second . . . and so on, year after year', *han puesto un detective tras sus pasos* 'they've put a detective after him/on his trail'.

(ii) Note also the following construction: *tras de tener él la culpa, se enfada* (or *encima de tener él . . .*) 'not only is it his fault, he has the nerve to get angry'.

34.19 Prepositional phrases

The following is a list of common prepositional phrases. They can appear before nouns and, if their meaning is appropriate, before pronouns and infinitives:

a base de based on/consisting of
a bordo de on board (of)
a cambio de in exchange for
a cargo de in charge of
a causa de because of
a costa de at the cost of
a despecho de in spite of
a diferencia de unlike
a disposición de at the disposal of
a distinción de unlike
a espaldas de behind the back of
a excepción de with the exception of
a expensas de at the expense of
a falta de for lack of/for want of
a favor de in favour of
a fin de with the aim of
a finales/fines de towards the end of
a flor de flush with/at . . . level (used with *piel* 'skin', *agua* 'water', *tierra* 'ground')
a fuerza de by dint of
a guisa de (literary) = *a modo de*
a gusto de to the taste of

a juicio de in the opinion of
a la sombra de in the shadow of
a más de as well as
a mediados de towards the middle of
a modo de in the manner of
al nivel de at the level of
a partir de starting from
a pesar de despite
a por see 34.14.4h
a principios de towards the beginning of
a prueba de -proof, e.g. *a prueba de incendios* 'fireproof'
a punto de on the verge of
a raíz de immediately after/as an immediate result of
a razón de at the rate of
a riesgo de at the risk of
a sabiendas de with the knowledge of
a través de through/across
a vista de in the sight/presence of
a voluntad de at the discretion of
a vuelta de e.g. *a vuelta de correo* 'by return of post'

además de as well as
al alcance de within reach of
al amor de in the warmth of (e.g. a fire)
al cabo de at the end of
al contrario de contrary to
al corriente de 'au fait with'/informed
    about
al estilo de in the style of
al frente de at the head/forefront of
al lado de next to
abajo de (Lat. Am. only) underneath; see
    34.3 and 31.6.6
adentro de (Lat. Am. only) inside; see
    31.6.5
afuera de (Lat. Am. only) outside; see
    31.6.5
alrededor de around
atrás de (Lat. Am. only) behind; see
    31.6.7
al tanto de = *al corriente de*
a la hora de at the moment of/when it
    comes to . . .
a la vera de (literary) = *al lado de*
a lo largo de throughout/along
bajo (la) condición de que on condition of
bajo pena de on pain of
cerca de near
con arreglo a in accordance with
con miras a bearing in mind/with a
    view to
con motivo de on the occasion of (an
    anniversary, etc.)
con objeto de with the object of
con relación a in respect of/in relation to
con respecto a with respect/reference
    to/in comparison to
con rumbo a in the direction of (i.e.
    moving towards)
con vistas a with a view to/bearing in
    mind
de acuerdo con in accordance with
de regreso a on returning to
    debajo de see 34.3 and 31.6.6
    delante de see 34.2, 31.6.8
    dentro de see 31.6.5
después de after (time); see 14.10.3

detrás de behind; see 34.18, 31.6.7
en atención a in consideration of
en base a on the basis of (i.e. *sobre la base
    de*)
en busca de in search of
en caso de in case of
en concepto de as/by way of e.g. *este
    dinero es en concepto de ayuda* 'this
    money is by way of assistance'
en contra de against
en cuanto a as for . . . /concerning
en forma de in the shape of
enfrente de opposite
en honor de in honour of (but *en honor a
    la verdad* 'strictly speaking')
en lugar de instead of (+ noun or
    pronoun)
en medio de in the middle of
en pos de (literary) in search of/(also =
    tras de)
en pro de (literary) = *a favor de*
en torno a around (the subject of)/
    concerning
en vez de (+ infinitive) instead of . . .-ing
en vías de on the way to: *país en vías de
    desarrollo* 'developing countries'
en vísperas de on the eve of
en vista de in view of
encima de see 34.9 and 34.17
fuera de see 31.6.5
lejos de far from
luego de (Lat. Am.) after; see 14.10.3
más allá de beyond
no obstante (literary) notwithstanding
por causa de = *a causa de*
por cuenta de = *a mis/tus/sus/nuestras
    expensas* at the expense of
por encima de over the head of/against
    the will of
por parte de on the part of
por razón de = *a causa de*
sin embargo de (literary) notwithstanding
so pena de (literary) = *bajo pena de*
so pretexto de (literary) on the pretext of
tras de see 34.18

35

Relative clauses and pronouns

35.1 General

There are five relative pronouns in Spanish: *que, quien(es), el que, el cual* and *cuyo*. These perform the functions of the English pronouns 'that', 'who(m)', 'which' and 'whose' in such sentences as 'the book that I read', 'the woman that/who(m) we saw', 'the book that/which I'm talking about', 'the students whose books are on the table'. Spanish relative pronouns are not written with an accent.

35.1.1 Forms of relative pronouns

El que and *el cual* agree in number and gender with their antecedent[1] and can therefore take the forms:

	Singular	Plural
masculine	*el que/el cual*	*los que/los cuales*
feminine	*la que/la cual*	*las que/las cuales*

The plural of *quien* is *quienes*, but it has no separate feminine form.

When it is used as a relative pronoun, *el que* is found only after prepositions (it has other uses as a nominalizer, explained in Chapter 36). Foreign students tend to overuse *el cual* and neglect the more usual *el que* and *quien*. *El cual* tends nowadays to be confined to formal styles and it is discussed separately at 35.5.

Cuando, donde and *como* may also introduce relative clauses: e.g. *la calle donde/en la que la vi* 'the street I saw her in/where I saw her'. See 35.10–35.12 for discussion.

35.1.2 Restrictive and non-restrictive relative clauses

This chapter occasionally refers to a distinction between restrictive and non-restrictive clauses.

Restrictive clauses limit the scope of their antecedent: *dejamos las manzanas que estaban verdes* 'we left the apples that were unripe'. This refers only to those apples that were unripe.

Non-restrictive clauses or appositive clauses do not limit the scope of their antecedent: *dejamos las manzanas, que/las cuales estaban verdes* 'we left the apples,

---

[1] The antecedent of a relative pronoun is the noun or pronoun that it refers to: in 'the dog that I bought', 'dog' is the antecedent of 'that'.

which were unripe'. This sentence clearly claims that all the apples were unripe. In writing, non-restrictive clauses are typically marked in both languages by a comma, and in speech by a pause. Note that English does not allow the relative pronoun 'that' in such sentences, and Spanish allows *el cual* in such cases, at least in formal styles.

A relative clause which refers to the whole of a unique entity is bound to be non-restrictive:

La abadía de Westminster, que/la cual es uno de los monumentos más visitados por los turistas	Westminster Abbey, which is one of the monuments most visited by tourists

35.1.3 English and Spanish relative pronouns contrasted

Spanish relative clauses differ from English in four major respects:

(a) Prepositions must never be separated from a relative pronoun: 'the path (that/which) we were walking **along**' = *el camino **por el que** caminábamos*. Sentences like **el camino que caminábamos por*, occasionally heard in the Spanish of beginners, are virtually unintelligible.

(b) A relative pronoun can never be omitted in Spanish: 'the plane I saw' = *el avión **que** (yo) vi*.

(c) English and French constantly replace relative pronouns by a gerund or participle form: 'a box containing two books'/*une boîte contenant deux livres*. This is usually impossible in Spanish: *una caja **que contiene/contenía** dos libros*. The subject is discussed in detail at 20.3.

(d) Spanish does not allow a relative pronoun to be separated from its antecedent by a verb phrase. The type of sentence sporadically heard in English like ?'the man doesn't exist whom I'd want to marry', for the normal 'the man (whom/that) I'd want to marry doesn't exist', cannot be translated by **el hombre no existe con el que/con quien yo quisiera casarme*. The correct translations are *no existe el hombre con el que/con quien yo quisiera casarme* or *el hombre con el que/con quien yo quisiera casarme no existe*. The first of these two translations is preferable, which has important consequences for the word order of Spanish sentences containing relative clauses. See 37.2.1 for discussion. Further examples:

Acudieron corriendo los vecinos, que/quienes/los cuales no pudieron hacer nada (not **los vecinos acudieron corriendo, que . . .*)	The neighbours came running, but could do nothing (literally, 'who could . . . ')
Han vuelto las cigüeñas que hicieron su nido en el campanario el año pasado (not **las cigüeñas han vuelto que . . .*)	The storks that made their nest in the belfry last year have returned

35.2 The relative pronoun *que*

Que is by far the most frequent relative pronoun and may be used in the majority of cases to translate the English relative pronouns 'who', 'whom', 'which' or 'that'. However, there are certain cases in which *el que*, *quien* or *el cual* must be used, especially after prepositions. See 35.4 and 35.5 for further discussion. Examples of *que* as a relative pronoun:

los inversionistas que se quemaron los dedos	the investors who burnt their fingers
las hojas que caían de las ramas	the leaves (which were) falling from the branches

el libro que compré ayer	the book (that/which) I bought yesterday
*Las experiencias **que** se narran tampoco tuvieron lugar* (M. Torres, Spain)	The experiences described did not happen either
las enfermeras que despidieron el año pasado (see 22.4.2 for use of personal *a* in this type of sentence)	the nurses (that/whom) they fired/sacked last year
*Le decía a cada momento que era diferente a todos los hombres **que** había conocido* (S. Pitol, Mexico)	She told him constantly that he was different from all the men (whom/that) she had known

Notes

(i) The word *todo* requires the relative pronoun *el que*: *todos **los que** dicen eso* . . . 'all who say that . . .'/'everyone who says that . . .'

(ii) *Quien/quienes* are not used in restrictive clauses unless they follow a preposition (see the next two sections). Incorrect forms like **la chica quien viene*, **los hombres quienes dijeron eso* are common in the Spanish of English-speakers. *La chica **que** viene* . . . 'the girl who's/that's coming', *los hombres **que** dijeron eso*, 'the men who/that said that . . .', are the only possible construction in such cases.

35.3 Use of *que*, *quien*, *el cual* in non-restrictive relative clauses

When no preposition appears before the relative pronoun and the relative clause is **non-restrictive** (see 35.1.2 for definition), *que*, *quien* or *el cual* may be used. *Quien* is nowadays used only for human beings, and *el cual* is emphatic and tends to be restricted to formal language (see 35.5 for discussion):

Fueron a hablar con José, que/quien/el cual estaba de mal humor	They went to talk to José, who was in a bad mood
Tres cajas de ropa que/las cuales, no pudiendo olvidar a su difunto marido, se negaba a vender	Three chests of clothes which, being unable to forget her late husband, she refused to sell
el presidente, que/quien/el cual acababa de pronunciar un discurso	the president, who had just delivered a speech

El cual or *quien* is more likely to be used whenever the relative pronoun is separated from its antecedent or from the verb of which it is the subject or object, or after a heavy pause. *El cual* is discussed further at 35.5.

Notes

(i) Only *que* can be used after personal pronouns: *yo que me preocupo tanto por ti* . . . 'I who worry so much about you . . .' . . . *y ahora, hablando con ella, que tenía el sol de la tarde en el rostro* (F. Umbral, Spain) ' . . . and now, talking to her, who had the evening sun on her face', *él, que en el fondo es muy clase media, vive en una casita nada suntuosa de el Prado* (M. Benedetti, Uruguay) 'he, who is at heart very middle class, lives in a by no means sumptuous little house in the Prado'.

(ii) In 'cleft' sentences (discussed at 36.2) a nominalizer, e.g. *el que* or *quien*, must be used: *fue María quien/la que dijo la verdad* 'it was María who told the truth', *soy consciente de que tengo que ser yo misma la que/quien resuelva el problema* (female speaking) 'I'm aware that I must be the one to solve the problem myself'.

(iii) *El que* also translates 'the one who/which' and is discussed under nominalizers at 36.1: *aquella chica es Charo – la que lleva el chándal rojo* 'that girl over there is Charo – the one wearing the red tracksuit'. *El que* is rare as a subject relative pronoun, though the preceding construction is sometimes similar to a non-restrictive clause. Compare *hacia el final de los debates, comenzó a perfilarse una cuarta opción, **la que** reclamaba un "nuevo concepto de un nacionalismo pluralista"* (El País, Spain) 'towards the end of the discussions a fourth option began to take shape, one which demanded a "new concept of a pluralist nationalism"'.

35.4 Relative pronoun after prepositions

35.4.1 After prepositions *el que, quien* or *el cual* are used

The relative pronouns required are:

(a) non-human antecedents: *el que* (or *el cual*);
(b) human antecedents: *el que, quien* (or *el cual*). *Quien* is slightly more formal than *el que*.

However, *que* may occasionally be used on its own after a preposition in the special circumstances discussed at 35.4.2. Use of *el cual* is discussed separately at 35.5.

. . . *la misión a la que ha dedicado su vida* (J. L. Borges, Argentina)	. . . the mission to which he has dedicated his life
la amenaza de guerra bajo la que vivimos	the threat of war we're living under
la puerta tras la que se escondió	the door behind which she hid
la maniobra en virtud de la que consiguió un éxito inmerecido	the manoeuvre whereby he gained an undeserved success
. . . *comunicados en los que se recuerda la ilegalidad de las acciones propuestas* (*Abc*, Spain)	. . . communiqués in which attention is called to the illegality of the proposed actions
la calle desde la que/donde he venido andando	the street I've walked from
¿ . . . *y todas . . . ésas con quien has paseado?* (Buero Vallejo, Spain, dialogue; *quien* for *quienes* is popular style)	. . . and what about all those . . . women you've walked out with?
. . . *como se ayuda a alguna persona a quien se quiere* . . . (J. J. Arreola, Mexico)	. . . as one helps some person whom one loves . . .
Yo era para ella . . . *el ser supremo con el que se dialoga, el dios callado con quien creemos conversar* (F. Umbral, Spain; both relative pronouns used)	I was for her . . . the supreme being one talks with, the silent god we imagine we are conversing with
Hay veces que me rodean individuos con los que no tengo nada que ver (E. Lynch, Argentina)	There are times when I'm surrounded by individuals with whom I have nothing in common
. . . *y sin llegar al extremo de un Lezama Lima, para quien todo es metáfora de todo* . . . (M. Vargas Llosa, Peru)	. . . and without going to the extreme of a Lezama Lima, for whom everything is a metaphor for everything
Hay gente con la que la vida se ensaña (A. Mastretta, Mexico)	There are people whom life delights in tormenting

Notes

(i) If the gender of a human antecedent is not known or is not relevant, the genderless *quien* must be used: *no hay nadie con quien hablar* 'there's no one to talk to', *busca a alguien de quien te puedas fiar* 'look for someone you can trust'.

(ii) After neuter antecedents like *algo, nada* and *mucho, lo que* or *que* are used: *no hay nada con (lo) que puedas sacarle punta* 'there's nothing you can sharpen it with', *esto es algo sobre lo que tenemos que reflexionar* (J. Caro Baroja, Spain) 'this is something we have to reflect on', *iba a morir allí, no por algo en lo que creía, sino por respeto a su hermano mayor* (M. Vargas Llosa, Peru) 'he was going to die there, not for something he believed in, but out of respect for his elder brother'.

(iii) The use of personal *a* before relative pronouns is discussed at 22.4.2.

35.4.2 Relative pronoun *que* after a preposition

Que alone is preferred as a relative pronoun after prepositions in certain circumstances difficult to define:

(a) After *a* (when it is not personal *a*), after *con* and after *de* – unless the latter means 'from'. Use of *que* alone is especially common after abstract nouns:

la discriminación a que están sometidas nuestras frutas y hortalizas (El País)	the discrimination which our fruits and vegetables are subject to
la notoria buena fe con que Collazos expone sus dudas y sus convicciones (M. Vargas Llosa, Peru)	the well-known good faith with which Collazos expounds his doubts and convictions
ese conjunto de sutiles atributos con que el alma se revela a través de la carne (E. Sábato, Argentina)	that set of subtle attributes by which the soul reveals itself through the flesh
la aspereza con que la trataba (S. Pitol, Mexico)	the harshness with which he treated her
. . . el aire ausente y apenado con que vive (A. Bryce Echenique, Peru, dialogue)	. . . the absent, long-suffering look about him (lit. 'with which he lives')
las especies de escarabajo de que estoy hablando	the species of beetle I am talking about
Suspiraba con la misma compasión con que le habían oído en los sueños (L. Mateo Díez, Spain)	He sighed with the same compassion they had heard him sigh with in their dreams

El/la/los/las que would be possible, though less elegant, in the foregoing examples.

(b) Frequently after *en* when precise spatial location is not intended. Compare *la caja en la que encontré la llave* 'the box I found the key in', but *la casa en que/donde vivo* 'the house I live in', not *'the house **inside which** I live'. If precise spatial location is intended *el/la/los que* is needed: *trenzó primero su melena en la que se le habían multiplicado las canas* (A. Mastretta, Mexico) 'she first plaited her hair where grey/(US 'gray') hairs had multiplied':

el desierto humano en que ella estaba perdida (F. Umbral)	the human desert she was lost in
Me gustaría vivir en un sitio en que/donde no hubiera coches	I'd like to live in a place where there were no cars
las formas racionales en que se basa la vida social (M. Vargas Llosa, Peru)	the rational forms on which social life is based
la época en que todavía se hablaba latín	the period in which Latin was still spoken
el momento político en que salía (M. Vargas Llosa, Peru)	the political moment at which it appeared
. . . en aquel momento en que lo que vieron fue la luz apagada de la cocina (J. Marías, Spain)	. . . at that moment when what they saw was that the kitchen light was out (or 'the absence of light in . . . ')

En que is also preferred when the preceding noun is a period of time. After *día, semana, mes, año, momento* the *en* is also often omitted. In all the preceding examples so far *el que* is also possible, but not in the following:

una noche en que iba a buscarla (F. Umbral)	one night (when) I went to fetch her
el día que te vi	the day I saw you
el único día que se produjeron diferencias de importancia fue el jueves (La Nación, Argentina, quoted in *Variedades* 124)	the only day on which any important differences were recorded was Thursday
el año que nos casamos	the year we got married
el mes que llovió tanto	the month it rained so much
en los meses que estuvo Edwards en Cuba (M. Vargas Llosa, Peru)	during the months Edwards spent in Cuba
durante el año y medio que he estado en el cargo	in the year and a half I've been in the job

Note

If the antecedent is precise as to the number of units of time, *el que* may also be used:[2] *aquellos millones de años en (los) que el hombre aprendió a cazar y a servirse de sus herramientas* 'those millions of years in which man learnt to hunt and use his tools', *un tipo de genocidio que estará consumado dentro de treinta años, en los que las buenas intenciones de ciertas instituciones . . .* (A. Carpentier, Cuba) 'a type of genocide which will be complete within thirty years in which the good intentions of certain institutions . . .'.

35.5 *El cual*

In general *el cual* is more formal than *el que* or *quien* and is yielding ground to them: foreigners spoil much good Spanish by overusing it.[3] But it may be preferred or obligatory in the following contexts:

(a) After *según* when it means 'according to' rather than 'depending on', as it does in —*¿Qué precio tienen?* —*Según los que quiera* ' "What's their price?" "It depends on which ones you want" ':

el argumento según el cual . . .	the argument according to which . . .
José Carlos Mariátegui, según el cual	J. C. Mariátegui, according to whom
"*el marxismo leninismo es el sendero*	'Marxist Leninism is the shining
luminoso de la revolución" (M. Vargas	path to revolution'
Llosa, Peru)	

(b) It is often preferred after long prepositions, i.e. of more than one syllable, e.g. *para, contra, entre, mediante*, and after prepositional phrases, e.g. *a pesar de* 'despite', *debajo de* 'underneath', *delante de* 'in front of', *frente a* 'opposite', *en virtud de* 'by reason of', etc.:

. . . una formación profesional mediante la cual	. . . professional training whereby
los funcionarios de grado medio estén	middle-grade civil servants will be
capacitados para . . . (*Cambio16*, Spain)	equipped to . . .
Hay cuerpos, seres, con atmósfera propia, dentro	There are bodies, beings, with their
de la cual es bueno vivir (F. Umbral, Spain)	own atmosphere, within which it is
	good to live

However, *el que* is sometimes found even in these contexts.

El otro fue alcanzado por ocho balazos, a	The other one received eight bullet
*consecuencia **de los** que moriría minutos*	wounds, as a consequence of which
más tarde . . . (*El País*, Spain)	he was to die a few minutes later
*. . . la localización de la abadía, sobre **la***	. . . the location of the abbey, about
***que** Adso evita toda referencia concreta*	which Adso avoids all specific
(Umberto Eco, translated by R. Pochtar)	reference

---

[2] DeMello (1994, 3), reports that in the corpus of educated spoken Spanish *que* alone is overwhelmingly preferred here, while *el que* does not appear in this context.
[3] However, in a statistical survey of the corpus of educated spoken Spanish, DeMello (1994, 2), reports that *el cual* is still the most favoured form after prepositions in spontaneous speech in Buenos Aires, Santiago de Chile, Lima, Bogotá and Caracas, whereas *el que* was preferred in Mexico, Havana, Madrid and Seville.

(c) *El cual* is also especially favoured when the antecedent is separated from the relative pronoun by intervening words, or when the relative is separated from its verb:[4]

*Hay chequetrenes con los que usted puede viajar por un valor de 15.000 a 20.000 pesetas, pero por **los cuales** usted sólo paga 12.750 y 17.000 ptas. respectivamente* (advertisement, Spain)	There are 'Traincheques' with which you can travel to a value of 15,000–20,000 pesetas, but for which you only pay 12,750 and 17,000 pesetas respectively

(d) *El cual* is used after *algunos de . . . , todos . . . , la mayoría de . . . , parte de . . .* and similar phrases:

los jóvenes españoles, la mayoría de los cuales son partidarios del divorcio	young Spaniards, the majority of whom are in favour of divorce
. . . árboles, pocos de los cuales tenían hojas	. . . trees, few of which had leaves
. . . defender la revolución social, parte integrante de la cual era la emancipación de la mujer	. . . to defend the social revolution, of which an integral part was the emancipation of women
Corren por Madrid muchos rumores, algunos de los cuales vamos a recoger aquí	Many rumours are circulating in Madrid, some of which we shall report here

(e) As the subject of a verb, *el cual* seems to be obligatory after a heavy pause such as a sentence break, a construction not easily imitated in English and not particularly common in Spanish:

*Fueron a hablar con su tío, un setentón de bigote blanco y acento andaluz, que hacía alarde de ideas muy avanzadas. **El cual**, tras un largo silencio, contestó . . .*	They went to talk with his uncle, a seventy-year-old with a white moustache and an Andalusian accent who boasted of very advanced ideas. Who, after a long silence, replied . . .

35.6 *Lo cual* and *lo que*

These are used when the relative pronoun refers not to a noun or pronoun but to a whole sentence or to an idea, which, being neither masculine or feminine in gender, require a neuter pronoun. Since the clause is always non-restrictive, *lo cual* is common, especially in writing. Compare: *trajo una lista de cifras que explicaba su inquietud* 'he brought a list of figures which (i.e. the list) explained his anxiety', and *trajo una lista de cifras, lo cual/lo que explicaba su inquietud* 'he brought us a list of figures, which (i.e. the fact he brought it) explained his anxiety'. Further examples:

En un primer momento se anunció que los misiles eran americanos, lo cual fue desmentido en Washington (*El País*, Spain)	Initially it was stated that the missiles were American, which was denied in Washington
Llegué tarde, por lo que/lo cual no pude asistir a la reunión	I arrived late, which is why I couldn't attend the meeting
El año siguiente fue la exaltación de Amadeo de Saboya al trono de España, lo cual le tuvo vagando por Madrid hasta altas horas de la madrugada (J. M. Guelbenzu, Spain)	The following year there occurred the elevation of Amadeo of Savoy to the Spanish throne, which had him wandering round Madrid until the small hours

---

[4] DeMello (1994, 3) confirms this from a survey of spoken Spanish in eleven major cities.

35.7 *Cuyo*

This translates 'whose', and is often an elegant alternative for an otherwise tor-tuous relative clause. It agrees in number and gender with the following noun. If there is more than one noun, it agrees only with the first: *una mujer cuyas manos y pies estaban quemados por el sol* 'a woman whose hands and feet had been burnt by the sun', *una señora cuyo sombrero y guantes eran de seda* 'a lady whose hat and gloves were made of silk':

Hay que visitar las (pirámides) de Sakkara, en cuya necrópolis están representadas todas las épocas de la historia del Egipto faraónico (L. Carandell, Spain)	One must visit the Saqqara pyramids, in whose necropolis all the periods of the Egypt of the Pharaohs are represented
. . . la Asamblea Constituyente, cuyos miembros serían elegidos en diciembre (G. García Márquez, Colombia)	. . . the Constituent Assembly, whose members would be elected in December
un hombre de cuya honradez no dudo	a man whose honesty I don't doubt
una medida cuyos efectos son imprevisibles	a measure whose effects are unforeseeable

Notes

(i) Grammarians condemn such commonly heard sentences like *?se alojó en el Imperial, en cuyo hotel había conocido a su primera mujer* 'he stayed at the Imperial, in which hotel he had met his first wife', better . . . *el Imperial, hotel donde/hotel en el cual había conocido a su primera mujer*. But this construction is allowed with *caso: nos han alertado acerca de la posibilidad de que todos los hoteles estén completos, en cuyo caso la reunión será aplazada* 'they have warned us of the possibility that all the hotels may be full, in which case the meeting will be postponed'.

(ii) *Del que/de quien* occasionally replace *cuyo*, although this is censured by Seco (1998), 143: *un torero, de quien alabó el tesón y el valor a toda prueba* (i.e. *cuyo tesón y valor alabó . . .*) 'a bullfighter, whose indefatigable steadfastness and courage he praised', *Alidio era un preso del que nunca se supo con exactitud su delito* (L. Mateo Díez, Spain; i.e. *cuyo delito nunca se supo . . .*) 'Alidio was a prisoner whose crime was never precisely known'.

(iii) *Cuyo* is rare in spontaneous speech and virtually unheard in popular styles. See 35.8c for a discussion.

(iv) There used to exist an interrogative form *cúyo*, but it is not nowadays used, except in some local Latin-American dialects, e.g. rural Colombia: *¿de quién es esa mochila?* 'whose rucksack is that?', not **¿cúya mochila es ésa/esa?*

35.8 Relative clauses in familiar speech

Students will encounter a number of popular or familiar constructions that should probably be left to native speakers.

(a) There is a colloquial tendency, which may sound uneducated, to insert a redundant pronoun in relative clauses:

Los gramáticos aconsejan muchas cosas que nadie las dice (overheard)	Grammarians recommend many things that no one says
Sólo por ti dejaría para siempre a don Memo, a quien tanto le debo (C. Fuentes, Mexico, dialogue)	Only for you would I leave Don Memo for ever. I owe him so much

See 11.16.5 for more details.

(b) Popular and relaxed informal speech often avoids combining prepositions and relative pronouns by a type of construction banned from writing:

?*en casa de una mujer que yo vivía con ella . . .* (*con la que yo vivía*)	in the house of a woman I was living with
?*Te acuerdas del hotel que estuvimos el año pasado?* (*. . . en el que estuvimos . . .*)	Do you remember the hotel we stayed in last year?
?*Soy un emigrante que siempre me han preocupado los problemas de la emigración* (*. . . al que siempre han preocupado los problemas*) (reader's letter in *El País*)	I am an emigrant who has always been concerned with the problems of emigration

This construction is not uncommon in Golden-Age texts, but it should not be imitated by foreign learners.

(c) *Cuyo* is avoided in spontaneous speech, especially by less educated speakers. There are many correct alternatives, e.g. *las mujeres cuyo marido las ayuda en casa* 'women whose husbands help them in the house' can be recast as *las mujeres que tienen un marido que las ayuda en casa*. However, popular speech often uses a construction called *quesuismo* which is generally stigmatized:[5] *los alumnos que sus notas no están en la lista* (*cuyas notas no están . . .*) 'the students whose marks aren't on the list'.

35.9 *Cartas a contestar . . .* , etc.

The following construction is nowadays very common in journalism, official documents or business letters: *un libro y una tesis a tomar muy en serio por estudiosos y ciudadanos en general* (*Cambio16*, Spain, for *que deben ser tomados en serio . . .*) 'a book and a thesis to be taken very seriously by students and citizens in general'. For a discussion of this controversial construction see 18.12.

35.10 *Donde, adonde, en donde* as relatives

Donde is commonly used as a relative, especially after *hacia*, *a* (in the meaning of 'towards'), *desde*, *de* meaning 'from', *por* meaning 'along'/'through', *en* meaning 'place in', etc.

As a relative its use is rather wider than the English 'where':

Lo recogí en la calle donde te vi	I picked it up in the street where I saw you
Añoraba las playas donde se había paseado durante aquel verano	He longed for the beaches where he had strolled that summer
Ése/Ese es el baúl de donde sacó los papeles	That's the trunk from which she took the papers
la ciudad hacia donde avanzaban las tropas enemigas . . .	the city towards which enemy troops were advancing . . .
un balcón desde donde se podía ver el desfile	a balcony from which/where one could see the parade

In all the above restrictive clauses, *el que* or *el cual* could be used with the appropriate preposition. However, in the following non-restrictive clause only *donde* is possible:

Volvieron a encontrarse en París, donde se habían conocido veinte años antes	They met again in Paris, where they had met for the first time twenty years before

---

[5] But despite its universal condemnation by grammarians, this construction quite often slips into the speech of educated persons, as DeMello (1992, 5) shows.

Notes

(i) *Adonde* is not the same as *a donde* or *adónde*. The first is a relative used before verbs of motion and with an explicit antecedent. The second is an adverb found before verbs of motion but with no antecedent. The third form is found in direct or indirect questions. One says *el pueblo adonde yo iba* (relative) 'the village I was going to', *fueron a donde tú les dijiste* (no antecedent) 'they went where you told them to go', *no quería decirle a dónde iba yo* (indirect question, hence the accent) 'I didn't want to tell him/her where I was going (to)', *adónde va usted?* (direct question) 'where are you going?', *¿adónde habrán ido rodando las pastillas de Optalidón?* (C. Martín Gaite, Spain) 'where can the Optalidon tablets have rolled to?'

(ii) *En donde* is spatially more specific than *donde*, and is rather literary: *hay una tienda pequeña en Westwood en donde venden infinidad de camisetas con letreros increíbles* (C. Rico-Godoy, Spain) 'there's a little shop/(US store) in Westwood where they sell a vast range of T-shirts with fantastic things written on them' (. . . *Westwood donde venden* . . . would have come to the same thing), *los cajones en donde el tío guardaba sus útiles de trabajo* (M. Torres, Spain) 'the drawers where my uncle kept his tools'.

(iii) *Donde* is sometimes used colloquially in Mexico (and possibly elsewhere in northern Latin America) to mean an apprehensive 'what if?' In this context Peninsular Spanish uses *anda que si* + indicative or *anda que como* + subjunctive: *no digas, estoy muy espantada,* **donde** *a la pobre criatura le salga la nariz de este hombre* (A. Mastretta, Mexico, dialogue; Spain *anda que como le salga* . . .) 'don't even mention it, I'm really terrified. What if this poor little thing gets this man's nose?!', *no sé cómo se van a casar.* **Donde** *estén igual de ignorantes en lo demás* (ibid.: Spain *anda que como estén* . . . , *anda que si están* . . .) 'I don't know how they're going to get married. What if they're just as ignorant about all the other things?!'

(iv) For *donde* meaning 'at the house of', see 24.9.

35.11 *Como* as a relative

Como is officially recommended after *la manera* and *el modo*, although *en que* is used after *forma*, and usually after the other two as well:

La manera **como** *un país se fortalece y desarrolla su cultura es abriendo sus puertas y ventanas* (M. Vargas Llosa, Peru)	The way a country strengthens and develops its culture is by opening its doors and windows
. . . *y la manera en que nos adorábamos* (A. Bryce Echenique, Peru)	. . . and the way we adored one another
Me gusta la manera como/en que lo hace	I like the way she does it
Me gusta la forma en que lo hace	I like the way she does it

Note

Mismo plus a noun requires *que*: *lo dijo del mismo modo que lo dijo antes* 'he said it the same way as he said it before', *llevas la misma falda que yo* 'you're wearing the same skirt as me'.

35.12 *Cuando* as a relative

Cuando occurs only in non-restrictive clauses: *en agosto, cuando les den las vacaciones a los niños, nos iremos al campo* 'in August, when the children have their holidays/(US 'vacation'), we'll go to the countryside', *incluso en nuestros días, cuando nadie cree ya en las hadas* 'even in our day, when no one believes in fairies any more'; but *solamente puedo salir los días (en) que no trabajo* (restrictive) 'I can only go out on the days I'm not working'.

Notes

(i) *Cuando* is used with *apenas, aún, todavía, entonces, no, no bien*: *apenas había aparcado el coche cuando se acercó un policía* 'she had hardly parked the car when a policeman came up', *aún/todavía no había empezado a estudiar cuando le dieron un empleo* 'he hadn't yet started studying when they gave him a job'. Compare the following restrictive clauses: *en un momento en que* . . . 'at a moment when . . . ', *en una época en que* . . . 'in a period when . . . ', *en un año (en) que* . . . 'in a year when . . . ', etc.

(ii) *Que* is used in the following phrases: *ahora que usted sabe la verdad* 'now (that) you know the truth', *luego que haya terminado* 'as soon as (s)he's finished', *siempre que haya bastante* 'as long as there's enough', *cada vez que me mira* 'whenever (s)he looks at me', *de modo que/de manera que* 'so that'.

In cleft sentences *donde, como* or *cuando* may be obligatory and *que* disallowed (especially in Peninsular Spanish): *es así **como** hay que hacerlo* 'this is how it must be done', *fue entonces **cuando** lo notó* 'it was then that he noticed it'. See 36.2 for discussion.

35.13 Relative clauses after a nominalizer

A nominalizer (e.g. *el que* meaning 'the one who/which') cannot be followed by the relatives *el que* or *el cual*. The noun must be repeated or, in written language, *aquel* is used:

*Se imagina un nuevo don Julián, una versión moderna de **aquel** al que rinde homenaje el título del libro* (M. Vargas Llosa, Peru; not *el al que . . .)	He imagines a new Don Julian, a modern version of the one to whom the book's title pays homage
Traiga otro plato, que no me gusta comer en los platos en los que han comido otros (spoken language)	Bring another plate – I don't like eating off those that others have eaten off

35.14 Miscellaneous examples of relative clauses

Falta saber las condiciones en que está/en qué condiciones está/en las condiciones que está	We have yet to know what conditions he is in
según el cine a que vayas/Según al cine que vayas (both examples from M. Moliner)	depending on what cinema you go to
Era la habitación más pequeña en (la) que jamás he estado/de todas las que he estado (familiar spoken language)	It was the smallest room I've ever been in
¿Cómo se explica el fenómeno singular que fue la victoria de los liberales?	How does one explain the singular phenomenon of the liberals' victory?
el espectáculo conmovedor que son las ruinas de Machu Picchu	the moving spectacle of the Machu Picchu ruins

36

Nominalizers and cleft sentences

36.1 Nominalizers

36.1.1 General

'Nominalizers' are words or phrases that allow other words to be used as nouns or pronouns. This chapter discusses an important type of nominalizer: *el de, lo de, el que, lo que* and *quien* used as pronouns with such values as 'the one from', 'the one belonging to . . . ', 'the one who/that . . . ', 'the person who . . . ', etc.; compare French *celui de, celui qui, celle qui, ceux qui, ce qui,* etc. Some grammars discuss these under relative pronouns, but they are in fact devices for creating noun phrases: *los que interrogan* 'those who interrogate' is close in meaning to *los interrogadores* 'the interrogators', *la de antes* 'the one (fem.) from before' to *la anterior* 'the previous one', etc.

For the use of *el que* and *quien* as relative pronouns (*el hombre con el que/con quien hablaba, la mesa en la que escribo*) see Chapter 35, especially 35.3 and 35.4. For *quién* in questions, see 24.5.

36.1.2 *El de*

'The one(s) belonging to', 'that/those of', 'the one(s) from', etc. *El de* agrees in number and gender with the noun it replaces:

*Entre los problemas de España y **los de** Estados Unidos, creo que **los de** los EE.UU son más graves*	Between the problems of Spain and (those of) the USA, I think the USA's are more serious
El de Buenos Aires es mejor	The one (masc.) from Buenos Aires is better
—¿Quién ha venido? —Las de siempre	'Who's come?' 'The same women/ girls as usual'
La de los refugiados es la gran tragedia de nuestro siglo (El País)	The tragedy of our century is that of refugees
Ningún clima templado vería jamás una cortina de agua como la que esa tarde azotó los parabrisas del Chevrolet de Félix (C. Fuentes, Mexico)	No mild climate would ever see a sheet (lit. 'curtain') of rain like the one that lashed the windscreens of Félix's Chevrolet that afternoon

Translation by a Saxon genitive or by a compound noun is sometimes appropriate:

Quita los de ayer y pon los de la semana pasada	Take away yesterday's and put last week's
Tenía los ojos saltones como los de una rana	(S)he had bulging eyes like a frog's
la industria del petróleo y la del carbón	the oil and coal industries

Lo he hecho para aumentar la moral, sobre todo I've done it to raise morale, especially
 la de los escritores (J. M. Lara, *El País*) writers' (morale)

Note

La de can mean 'the amount of '/'how many' in colloquial language: *no sé la de temas que tengo apun-tados* (C. Martín Gaite, Spain) 'I don't know how many topics I've got jotted down', *¡la de veces que te lo habré dicho!* 'the number of times I must have told you!' See also 3.2.30.

36.1.3 *Lo de*

This is the neuter version of *el de*. Like all neuter pronouns, its use is obligatory if there is no noun to which it can refer. It is invariable in form. *Lo de* has limited uses, but it is a common equivalent of 'the . . . business/affair' in such phrases as *lo del dinero perdido* 'the affair of the lost money':

Siempre está a vueltas con lo de que cuándo nos (S)he's always coming back to/going
 vamos a casar on about the issue of when we're
  going to get married

Lo de que perdió el dinero no me convence That story about his/her losing the
 money doesn't convince me

De lo de la abuela poco les debe quedar They must have very little left of
 (C. Martín Gaite, Spain) grandma's (things, money)

Cedí en lo de dejar el piso a Chule por tres días I gave in about letting Chule have the
 más (I. Merlo, Spain, dialogue) flat for another three days

La primera vez que vi a Andrés furioso . . . The first time I saw Andrés furious
 fue cuando lo de la plaza de toros was at the time of the bullring
 (A. Mastretta, Mexico, dialogue; for the business
 prepositional use of *cuando* see 24.8)

Todo lo del maldito telegrama se me vino a la I recalled the whole business of the
 memoria (A. Bryce Echenique, Peru, dialogue) damned telegram

Note

It is common in Argentina and other parts of the Southern Cone in the meaning *en casa de* 'at . . .'s house'; compare *la semana pasada tuvimos una reunioncita en lo del viejo Leandro* (M. Benedetti, Uruguay, dialogue) 'last week we had a get-together at old Leandro's house'.

36.1.4 *El que*

This translates 'the one(s) who/which', 'that/those which', etc. (Fr. *celui/celle/ celles/ceux qui*). It agrees in number and gender with the noun it replaces:

la que está fuera the one (fem.) who/that is outside
el que llegó ayer the one (masc.) who/that arrived
 yesterday
los que dicen eso the ones/those (masc.) who say that
Vivo en la que está pintada de blanco I live in the one (i.e. *la casa*) painted
 white
. . . la que fue considerada doctrina alternativa . . . that which was considered the
 (*El País*) alternative doctrine
Yo no soy el que fui (J. Marías, Spain, I'm not the person I was
 dialogue)
Me atraían las que le tuvieron cariño, las que I felt attracted towards those women
 incluso le parieron hijos (A. Mastretta, who had been fond of him, even
 Mexico, dialogue) towards those who had given him
  children

Notes

(i) *El de* and *el que* can be combined: *la libertad de la televisión debería ser siempre la del que la contempla . . . no la del que la programa* (*El País*, Spain) 'freedom in television should always belong to the person watching it . . . not to the person programming it'.
(ii) For *el que* (invariable) + subjunctive meaning 'the fact that' (*el hecho de que*), see 16.10.1.
(iii) *La que* is often used instead of *lo que* in humorous warnings: *no sabes la que te espera* 'you don't know what's waiting for you . . .', *¡la que te tienen preparada! . .* 'what they've got in store for you! . . .'

36.1.5 *Lo que*

The invariable neuter version of the above: it refers to no specific noun. It can normally be translated by the phrase 'the thing that . . . ' or by the pronoun 'what' (cf. Fr. *ce qui/ce que*):

lo que más me irrita es . . .	what most irritates me is that . . .
Se asombró de lo que dijo el portavoz (Lat. Am. *el vocero*)	(S)he was amazed at what the spokesman said
La valla se prolonga todo lo que da de sí la vista	The fence stretches as far as the eye can see
Le pasa lo que a ti	The same thing happens to him as to you
Lo que más me gusta es cuando haces versos (C. Martín Gaite, Spain, dialogue)	What I like best is when you make up rhymes
Octavia, un hombre es lo que siente (A. Bryce Echenique, Peru, dialogue)	Octavia, a man is what he feels
. . . tuvo bien acordarse de un chiste tras otro en lo que quedó de cena (A. Mastretta, Mexico)	. . . he was obliging enough to remember joke after joke during what was left of dinner

Compare *por Rosario fue por la que se pelearon* 'Rosario was **the woman** they fought over', and *por Rosario fue por lo que se pelearon* 'Rosario was **what** (i.e. the issue/problem) they fought over'.

Note

Cuanto (invariable) can be used pronominally as an equivalent of *todo lo que* 'everything that . . . ': *se cree cuanto le dicen* = *se cree todo lo que le dicen* 'he believes everything they tell him'. This use of *cuanto* is rather literary nowadays.

36.1.6 *Quien* as an equivalent of 'the one who'

Quien/quienes can optionally replace *el que* in many contexts provided it refers to a human being. Since *quien* is not marked for gender it is not an exact equivalent of *el que* and must be used when reference to a specific gender is to be avoided. Only *quien* is possible in the meaning of 'no one':

El que diga eso es un cobarde	The person who says that is a coward
Quien diga eso es un cobarde	(same, but rather literary)
Quienes/Los que no estén de acuerdo, que se vayan	Anyone not in agreement should go
Que se lo diga al que/a quien quiera	Let him tell whomever he likes
Quien no es mala persona es el sargento	Someone who's not a bad fellow is the sergeant
El coronel no tiene quien le escriba (G. García Márquez, Colombia, title; *el que* impossible here)	*The Colonel Has No One to Write to Him*

Tú no eres quien[1] para decirme eso (colloquial; *el que* impossible)	You're no one to tell me that/Who are you to tell me that?
Escuchaba sin oír las conversaciones de quienes se cruzaban con nosotros (S. Puértolas,) Spain	He listened absent-mindedly (lit. 'without hearing') the conversations of the people walking by us
. . . como quien espera el alba (title, L. Cernuda, Spain)	. . . like someone waiting for dawn
Cada quien tiene sus ritos (A. Mastretta, Mexico; Spain *cada cual*)	Everyone has different rites/rituals

Note

Since it is indeterminate, *quien/quienes* cannot be used when the identity or sex of the person referred to is known and stressed: *lo/le vimos con la que vive al lado* (**lo/le vimos con quien vive al lado* = *'we saw him with whoever lives next door') 'we saw him with the girl who lives next door'.

36.2 'Cleft' sentences

36.2.1 General

A number of the examples given in 36.1 are in fact 'cleft' sentences. These are sentences in which an object, predicate or adverbial phrase is isolated and focused by using 'to be'. This can be done in one of two ways:

Simple sentence	*Cleft sentence*
The fire started here	It was here that the fire started
	Here was where the fire started
John said it	It was John who said it
	John was the one who said it
I cut it with this knife	It was this knife I cut it with
	This knife is the one I cut it with

The structure of such sentences differs in Spanish from its French and English counterparts, and there are important differences between Peninsular and Latin American usage with regard to cleft sentences containing a preposition.

Notes

(i) The following is not a cleft sentence: *éstas son las niñas **que** me lo dijeron* 'these are the girls who told me', but this is: *fueron estas niñas **las que/quienes** me lo dijeron* 'it was these girls who told me', and so is *estas niñas fueron **las que/quienes** me lo dijeron*. In other words, the English translation of the cleft sentence begins with 'it' or it contains the pronoun 'one', as in 'these girls are the ones who told me'.

(ii) In cleft sentences the tense of the two verbs should be the same: *fue aquí donde la **vi*** 'it was here that I saw her', *ha sido aquí donde la **he visto*** (same meaning, but perfect of recency), *era aquí donde la **veía*** 'it was here that I used to see her'. One should not, for example, say *?era aquí donde la vi*; compare English 'it is here that I saw her', although *es aquí donde la vi* 'it is here that I saw her' is heard.

When *ser* is in a future tense, the other verb is in the present subjunctive: *seré yo quien **tenga** que solucionarlo* 'it'll be me who has to solve it', *será el comité el que **decida** esto* 'it'll be the committee that decides this'.

---

[1] Since it is stressed in speech, *quien* is often written with an accent in this construction. But nominalizers do not have accents, so the unaccented word is presumably the correct form.

36.2.2 'She is the one who . . . ', etc.

English speakers, especially those who know French, are tempted to link this type of cleft sentence by the word *que*, but only a nominalizer (*el que* or *quien*) can be used:

Es este coche el que compré	It's this car I bought
Este coche es el que compré	This car's the one I bought
Fue esa chica la que/quien lo hizo	It's that girl who did it
Esa chica fue la que/quien lo hizo	That girl is the one who did it
Fue usted el que/quien lo dijo	It was you (masc.) who said it
Usted fue el que/quien lo dijo	You were the one who said it
Esto es lo que más rabia me da	This is what makes me most furious
Lo que más rabia me da es esto	What makes me most furious is this
Porque nunca es ella, doña Pilar, la que aporta el dinero (interview in *Cambio16*, Spain)	Because it's never Doña Pilar who brings in the money
Son los pequeños sacrificios los que le hacen sentirse a uno miserable (J. Marías, Spain)	Small sacrifices are the ones that make one feel wretched
El pelaje overo es el que prefieren los ángeles (J. L. Borges, Argentina)	Lamb's fleece is the one that angels prefer
Para entonces será la guerra mundial la que haya solucionado todo (*Cambio16*, Spain)	By then it'll be world war that will have solved everything
Fue probablemente su intuición la que le llevó a seguir aquella línea de conducta (S. Pitol, Mexico)	It was probably his intuition that made him follow that line of behaviour
Fui yo finalmente quien la convencí de que viniera para La Habana (G. Cabrera , Infante Cuba, dialogue)	It was I/me who eventually managed to convince her to come to Havana

Note

Foreign students tend to make the mistake of not using a nominalizer in a cleft sentence. This produces bad Spanish like **fue él que me dijo* for *fue él quien/el que me dijo* 'it was he who told me' **fue esto que* (or even **qué*) *descubrió Darwin* for the correct *fue esto lo que descubrió Darwin/esto fue lo que descubrió Darwin* 'this is what Darwin discovered'. The question-words *quién, qué, cuál, dónde, cómo*, are never used to join cleft sentences.

36.2.3 Cleft sentences involving prepositions or adverbs

(a) If the first half of a Spanish cleft sentence contains a preposition, the preposition must normally be repeated in the second half, i.e. Spanish says 'it's with her **with whom** you must speak', *es con ella **con la que/con quien** tienes que hablar*. A major difference exists here between European and Latin-American Spanish. The latter, especially spoken but also informal written language, regularly uses *que* alone in a way similar to French or to the English 'that', when the cleft sentence begins with *ser*. This 'Gallicism' is vehemently rejected by many native Spaniards (although it is heard increasingly among younger generations of Spaniards):[2]

---

[2] The standard construction with repeated pronouns is, however, quite often used in Latin America in formal styles, cf. *es por lo anterior por lo que nos gusta la idea de Ecopetrol* (*El Tiempo*, Colombia) 'it is because of the previous point that we like the idea of Ecopetrol'. The construction with *que* alone seems to be more acceptable in writing in Argentina than elsewhere.

Sp. *Es* **desde** *esta ventana desde* **donde** *se ve el mar* Lat. Am. *Es desde esta ventana* **que** *se ve el mar*	It's from this window that you can see the sea
Desde *esta ventana es desde* **donde** *se ve el mar* (avoided in Latin America?)	This balcony is where you can see the sea from
Sp. *Fue* **por** *este motivo* **por el que** *decidió cambiar de empleo* Lat. Am. *Fue por este motivo que decidió . . .*	It was for this reason that he decided to change jobs
Pero es con la Maga que hablo (J. Cortázar, Argentina, dialogue; Spain . . . *con la que/quien hablo*)	But it's Maga I'm talking to
No fue **por** *Pepita sino* **por** *Teresa* **por** *la que/quien se pelearon* (Spain)	It wasn't Pepita but Teresa they fought over
No fue por el champagne que vine aquí día tras día (S. Pitol, Mexico, Spain *por lo que*)	It wasn't because of the champagne that I came here day after day
Era **para** *esto* **para** *lo que he tenido que esperar tanto* (J. Madrid, Spain, dialogue)	It was for that that I had to wait so long

(b) If the first part of a cleft sentence contains an adverb or adverbial phrase of time, place or manner, it must be joined to the second part by *cuando*, *donde* or *como* respectively, although Latin Americans may use *que* if the cleft sentence begins with *ser*, especially in informal speech:

Sp. *Fue aquí* **donde** *ocurrió* Lat. Am. *Fue aquí* **que** *ocurrió*	It was here that it happened
Sp./Lat. Am. *Aquí fue* **donde** *ocurrió*	Here is where it happened
Es en esta última novela **donde** *se enfrentan los más verídicos tipos clericales trazados por Galdós* (Ínsula, Spain)	It is in this last novel where the most lifelike clerical figures drawn by Galdós confront one another
Fue en Pueblo Nuevo **que** *supimos que el novio de Petra no había vuelto más al pueblo* (G. Cabrera Infante, Cuban dialogue; Spain *donde*)	It was in Pueblo Nuevo that we found out that Petra's boyfriend had never returned to the village
Es en los ojos de los demás **que** *uno se ve reflejado por primera vez* (M. Puig, Argentina, dialogue; Spain *donde*)	It's in other people's eyes that one sees oneself reflected for the first time
La chica se acuerda de que es ahí **que** *está la guarida del brujo* (M. Puig, Argentina, dialogue; Spain *donde*)	The girl remembers that it is there where the wizard's lair is
Fue en casa de ella **que** *tuvo lugar aquel encuentro con Vallejos* (M. Vargas Llosa, Peru, Spain *donde*)	It was in her house that this meeting with Vallejos took place
Sp. *Es así como hay que hacerlo* Lat. Am. *Es así que hay que hacerlo.* Sp./Lat. Am. *Así es como hay que hacerlo*	This is how you have to do it
Fue entonces **cuando**, *podríamos decir, comenzó la historia del automóvil* (El País, Spain)	It was then, we might say, that the story of the car began
Naturalmente tenía que ser en ese momento . . . **que** *sonara el timbre* (J. Cortázar, Argentina; Spain *cuando*)	Of course it had to be at that moment . . . that the bell rang

Notes

(i) Care is required with cleft sentences involving *lo que*. The neuter pronoun must be retained; compare *lo que me sorprende es su timidez/es su timidez* **lo que** *me sorprende, es la inseguridad lo que le hace reaccionar de esa forma* 'it's insecurity that makes him react like that' (i.e. 'what makes him react thus is insecurity'), *ha hecho cine, teatro, televisión, pero es con la canción con lo que le gustaría triunfar* (*Cambio16*, Spain) 'he has worked in cinema, theatre and TV, but it is in singing that he would like to make a success', *era un traje negro lo que llevaba* 'it was a black suit that (s)he was wearing' (answers question 'what was (s)he wearing?'), but *el que llevaba era el traje negro/era el traje negro el que llevaba* 'the one (s)he was wearing was the black suit' (answer to 'which suit was (s)he wearing?').

(ii) English makes the verb 'to be' singular when it is shifted to the head of a cleft sentence: 'the mosquitoes are what annoys him'/'it's the mosquitoes that annoy him'. In Spanish *ser* normally remains plural in such cleft sentences: *tenían que ser los partidos socialistas quienes/los que implementaran esta política de austeridad* 'it had to be the socialist parties which implemented this austerity policy', *son los mosquitos lo que me irrita* 'the mosquitoes are what annoys me', *lo que me irrita son los mosquitos*[3] 'what annoys me is the mosquitoes'. But this construction is not universal: *en la terrible escasez que vive el país, lo único que no falta es cigarrillos* (M. Vargas Llosa, Peru) 'amid the terrible shortages the country is living through, the only thing that isn't lacking is cigarettes'.

(iii) Cleft sentences involving lengthy prepositional phrases may be connected by *que* in Latin American usage but are likely to be avoided by careful Peninsular speakers: *?fue bajo esta impresión que continuamos con el programa* (Spain *fue así, bajo esta impresión, como continuamos con el programa*) 'it was under this impression that we carried on with the programme', *teniendo en cuenta que es gracias al número de parados que podemos mantener la inflación a nivel europeo* (*Triunfo*, Spain, Argentine writer) 'bearing in mind that it is thanks to the number of unemployed that we are able to keep inflation at European levels', *fue a causa de eso que lo hizo* (Latin American) or *lo hizo a causa de eso* or *fue a causa de eso por lo que lo hizo* 'it was because of that that he did it'.

(iv) The complexities of cleft sentences can be avoided by not using *ser* (which is what usually happens in ordinary conversation): *por eso te digo . . . , desde esta ventana se ve el mar, se pelearon por Pepita, no por Teresa.*

(v) The use of *quien* for things was once normal: phrases like *la mesa en quien* for *la mesa en la que . . .* are found in Golden-Age Spanish. This is still occasionally found, although it should not be imitated: *no fueron las máquinas quienes desencadenaron el poder capitalista, sino el capitalismo financiero quien sometió la industria a su poderío* (E. Sábato, Argentina) 'it was not machines which unleashed capitalist power, but finance capitalism which subjected industry to their domination'.

36.2.4 Translating 'that's why'

Porque means 'because' and it cannot be used to translate sentences like 'she's got the flu, **that's why** she didn't come to work'. A construction with *por* is called for: *tiene gripe, por eso no ha venido al trabajo/por eso es por lo que no ha venido al trabajo*:

Por eso lo hice/Por eso es por lo que lo hice	That's why I did it
Fue por eso por lo que no te llamé antes/	That's why I didn't ring before
Por eso no te llamé antes; Lat. Am. *Fue por eso que no te llamé antes*	
Ésa/Esa es la razón por la que no lo compré	That's why I didn't buy it
Quizá fue sólo por eso por lo que fuimos presentados (J. Marías, Spain, dialogue; or *solo*, according to Seco and the Academy)	Perhaps that was the only reason why we were introduced
Es por eso que en el lenguaje deportivo abundan las hipérboles (*El Litoral*, Argentina, Spain *por eso es por lo que . . .*)	That's why hyperboles abound in sporting language
Es también por eso por lo que se traiciona a cualquiera (J. Marías, Spain)	That's also why one betrays anyone

36.2.5 Agreement in cleft sentences

The view of María Moliner, confirmed by native informants, is that in the singular either *tú fuiste el que lo/le mataste* or *tú fuiste el que lo/le mató* 'you're the

---

[3] But *los mosquitos son los que me irritan, no las polillas* 'it's the mosquitoes that are annoying me, not the moths', where the *los que* refers to some omitted noun like *insectos* or *bichos*.

one who killed him' is correct, with a preference for third-person agreement. But strict agreement seems to be the only possible construction in the plural: *vosotros fuisteis los que lo/le matasteis* 'you were the ones who killed him'. Further examples:

Yo fui la que se lo bebió	I was the one (fem.) who drank it
Yo fui la que me lo bebí	
No, eres tú el que no me entiende (J. Madrid, Spain, dialogue)	No, it's you who doesn't understand me
Soy yo quien no se soporta a sí misma (J. Madrid, Spain, dialogue)	It's me who can't stand myself
Vos sos el que no me aguanta. Vos sos el que no aguantás a Rocamadour (J. Cortázar, Argentina dialogue; both constructions used. Spain *tú eres* for *vos sos*, *aguantas* for *aguantás*.)	You're the one who can't stand me. You're the one who can't stand Rocamadour
El que lo sabe soy yo	I'm the one (masc.) who knows
El que lo sé soy yo	
Somos los únicos que no tenemos ni un centavo para apostar (G. García Márquez, Colombia, dialogue)	We're the only ones who haven't got a *centavo* to bet
Vosotros sois los que lo sabéis	You're the ones who know
Ellos son los que trabajan más	They're the ones who work hardest

37

Word order

37.1 General

Compared with English and French, word order in Spanish is free. Many adjectives may be placed before or after the noun that they modify: *en el pasado remoto/en el remoto pasado* 'in the remote past'; see 4.11 for discussion. A subject may follow or precede a verb: *Juan lo sabe/lo sabe Juan* 'Juan knows' (different focus). A direct object noun phrase may follow or precede the verb: *no tengo hambre/hambre no tengo* 'I'm not hungry'. As in English, adverbs and adverb phrases may occupy various positions in relation to the verb that they modify: *normalmente lo hace/lo hace normalmente* 'normally he does it'/'he does it normally', *a veces llueve/llueve a veces* 'sometimes it rains'/'it rains sometimes'.

Often the factors that call for a particular word order depend on considerations of style, context, emphasis and rhythm of the sort that few non-natives are sensitive to. In this respect word order can be as complex a question in Spanish as intonation and sentence stress is in English. Sections 37.2–37.4 deal with patterns of word order that can be explained in terms of more or less clearly definable rules. Sections 37.5 and 37.6 consider the more difficult questions of word order that depend on matters of topicalization and other semantic functions.

This chapter presumes that Subject-Verb order, e.g. *Mario llega hoy* 'Mario's arriving today', and Subject-Verb-Object order, e.g. *Juan come una manzana* 'John is eating an apple' are 'normal' and that other arrangements of Verb, Subject and Object are departures from the norm. It is worth repeating that we are here discussing only plain-style, late-twentieth-century Spanish. In poetic styles and in prose from earlier periods (when Classical Latin influenced style) word order was typically much freer than in modern Spanish.

37.2 General rules of word order

37.2.1 Verb-Subject order in sentences containing relative clauses

The two principles explained here account for one of the most commonly encountered differences between Spanish and English as far as the position of the verb in relation to its subject is concerned.

(a) When a sentence includes a relative clause, Verb-Subject order is very often preferred in the main clause to ensure that the relative pronoun is not separated from its antecedent by a verb phrase: *lo compró un señor que había estado en Venezuela* 'a man who had been in Venezuela bought it', not **un señor lo compró* *que había estado en Venezuela*. The latter incorrect sentence breaks the strong rule (also discussed at 35.1.3d) that a verb phrase (*lo compró*) cannot come between a noun phrase (*un señor*) and a relative pronoun that refers to it (*que*). Another example: *no existe todavía el coche que yo quiero comprar* 'the car that I want to buy doesn't exist yet', not **el coche no existe todavía que yo quiero comprar*? 'the car doesn't exist yet that I want to buy'. The second sentence is not Spanish and probably not English either.

In both cases another, more recognizably English order is also possible, e.g. *un señor que había estado en Venezuela lo compró* 'a gentleman who had been in Venezuela bought it', *el coche que yo quiero comprar no existe todavía* 'the car that I want to buy doesn't exist yet'. But this order is usually less elegant in Spanish, especially when the verb is separated from its subject by a long string of words. As a result, the verb in the main clause is usually put at the head of the utterance, as explained earlier:

Tienen suerte las mujeres cuyo marido siempre las ayuda en casa[1]	Women whose husbands always help them in the house are lucky

which is better than *las mujeres cuyo marido siempre las ayuda en casa tienen suerte*.

Me llama una chica que se llama América (C. Rico-Godoy, Spain, dialogue)	A girl called América rings me

is better than *una chica que se llama América me llama*. But there is no objection to this order provided the verb does not come last, as in *una chica que se llama América me llama para pedirme un favor*.

(b) Verb-Subject order is also strongly favoured in the relative clause to keep the verb close to the relative pronoun. Spanish dislikes sentences structured like 'that's the dog that my friend from Kansas City **bought**', best translated *ése/ese es el perro **que compró** mi amigo de Kansas City*, not *?ése/ese es el perro que mi amigo de Kansas City compró*. Examples:

Estas acciones han rendido más que las que compró tu madre	These shares have yielded more than the ones your mother bought
. . . el carnaval de invierno que organiza el Departamento de Turismo (*El Mercurio*, Chile, in *Variedades*, 182)	. . . the Winter Carnival that the Department of Tourism is organizing

When these rules **(a)** and **(b)** are combined, sentences are produced whose word order differs markedly from their English equivalents: *gana la que eligen los jueces* 'the winner is the girl/woman whom the judges select', literally: 'wins the one whom elect the judges'. Further examples of inversion in both main and relative clauses:

Así dice la carta que nos envió tu padre	That's what's in the letter your father sent (lit. 'thus says the letter that sent your father')
Son innumerables las dificultades que plantea la lucha contra el terrorismo (*La Vanguardia*, Spain)	The difficulties posed by the struggle against terrorism are innumerable

---

[1] In colloquial language *cuyo* is avoided: *tienen suerte las mujeres que tienen un marido que las ayuda en casa*.

Durante toda mi vida, ahí donde hubiese un duro, ahí estaba yo (interview in *Cambio16*, Spain)	Throughout my life, wherever you could find five pesetas you'd find me (lit. '... wherever there was a five-peseta coin, there was I')

However, set verb phrases like *tratar de, tener que*, are not divided unnaturally:

... la aldea abrasada por la sal del Caribe donde su madre había tratado de enterrarla en vida (G. García Márquez, Colombia; rather than *... donde había tratado su madre de enterrarla en vida*)	... the salt-caked Caribbean hamlet where her mother had tried to bury her alive
[Las maestras] no tienen la culpa: si no existiera la maldita instrucción primaria que ellas tienen que aplicar ... (J. Cortázar, Argentina; rather than *que tienen ellas que aplicar*)	[The school mistresses] aren't to blame: if the wretched primary education they have to administer didn't exist ...

37.2.2 Word order in questions (direct and indirect)

Verb-Subject order is required when a question word opens the sentence. Verb-Subject order is also required in indirect questions in the clause following the question word.

Question words are:

¿cómo?/¿qué tal? how?   *¿cuánto?* how much/many?   *¿qué?* what?/which? (see note i)
¿cuál (de)? which (of)?   *¿dónde?* where?   *¿a quién?* whom?
¿cuándo? when?   *¿por/para qué?* why?

Examples (subject in bold):

*¿Cómo va **una** a estar esperando y delgada?* (A. Mastretta, Mexico, dialogue)	How is one going to be expecting a baby and (be) thin?
*¿Qué tal va **tu nuevo trabajo**?*	How's your new job going?
*¿Cuál de los collares prefiere **tu novia**?*	Which of the necklaces does your girlfriend prefer?
*¿A quién arrestó **la policía**?*	Whom did the police arrest?
*No sé cuándo llegan **los demás***	I don't know when the rest are arriving
*Todo el mundo se pregunta por qué no se levanta **Ricardo** más temprano* (less likely *... Ricardo no se levanta más temprano*)	Everyone's wondering why Ricardo doesn't get up earlier
*No recuerdo dónde vive **tu hermano***	I don't remember where your brother lives
*No me imagino qué pensaría **tu mujer** de todo esto*	I can't imagine what your wife would think about all this

As the examples show, a direct object precedes the verb as in English: *¿qué consejos me das?* 'what advice do you give me?', *¿cuántas naranjas has comido?* 'how many oranges have you eaten?' Verb-Object order can occasionally be used colloquially to express shock or incredulity: *¿has comido **cuántos?** ...* (more usually *¿cuántos dices que has comido?*) 'you've eaten *how many* ...?'

When the sentence contains an object and a separate subject there are three possibilities:

(a) When the object is shorter than the subject Verb-Object-Subject order is usual. **(b)** when the subject noun phrase is shorter, Verb-Subject-Object order is preferred. **(c)** When subject and object are of equal length, either order may be used (object in bold):

*¿Dónde compran **drogas** los adolescentes?* (short object)	Where do young people buy drugs?
*¿Dónde compran los adolescentes **las drogas vendidas por los narcotraficantes?*** (long object)	Where do young people buy the sold drugs by drug-pushers?
*¿Dónde compra **pan** mamá?/¿Dónde compra mamá **pan?*** (equal length)	Where does mother buy bread?

Further examples (object in bold):

*¿A quién ha escrito **la carta** tu amigo Federico?* (short object)	To whom did your friend Federico write the letter?/Who(m) did your friend Federico write the letter to?
*¿Por qué ha tenido **tan mala prensa** Antena 3 en su primer año de emisiones?* (*Cambio16*, Spain) (short object)	Why has Antenna Three had such a bad press during its first year of broadcasting?
*¿Cómo ha afectado la guerra a **su empresa?***[2] (short subject)	How has the war affected your company?
*¿Cuándo va a incluir su revista **programas y artículos dedicados a ordenadores tales como los ya citados?*** (long object; reader's letter in *El Ordenador Personal*, Spain. Lat. Am. *la computadora = el ordenador*)	When is your magazine going to include programs and articles devoted to computers like the ones mentioned above?
*¿Cuándo piensan hacer**lo** ustedes?/¿Cuándo piensan ustedes hacer**lo?*** (equal length)	When are you thinking of doing it?

Notes

(i) A noun phrase introduced by *¿qué?* meaning 'which?' or by *¿cuál de?* 'which?' always appears before the verb: *¿qué programas han gustado más al público?* 'which programmes/(US 'programs') did the public like most?', *¿cuál de los aviones consume menos combustible?* 'which of the planes uses least fuel?', *¿qué frutas ha comprado Inés?* 'what fruits did Inés buy?', *¿cuál de los proyectos ha aceptado el comité?* 'which of the projects has the committee accepted?'

(ii) Cuban and other Caribbean varieties of Spanish are unusual in optionally retaining Subject-Verb order after question words (subject in bold): *¿cómo **usted** conoció que Tony tenía negocio de narcotráfico?* (*Vindicación de Cuba*; standard Spanish . . . *se enteró **usted** de que . . .*) 'how did you find out that Tony had a drug-peddling business?', *¿en qué fecha **usted** ingresó en la Corporación CIMEX?* (ibid., standard Spanish *ingresó **usted***) 'on what date did you join the CIMEX Corporation?', *¿qué **tú** crees del acto de hoy en el Teatro Oriente?* (L. Otero, Cuba, dialogue) 'what do you think of the meeting/event today at the Oriente Theatre?'

37.2.3 Word order in questions that do not contain a question word

When no question-word is included in a question, Subject-Verb-Object order can be used, in which case question marks or, in speech, interrogative (rising) intonation, are the only things that show that a question is intended:

¿Mamá ha comprado leche? (or *¿Ha comprado leche mamá?*; the unmodified form denotes surprise)	Has mother bought any milk?
¿Tú también notaste lo bonito que se ríe? (A. Mastretta, Mexico, dialogue)	Did you also notice how prettily she laughs?

---

[2] However, spontaneous speech is less careful about sentence balance and might produce a sentence like *¿cómo ha afectado la guerra esta tan terrible que tenemos a su empresa?* 'how has this terrible war we're having affected your company?'

¿El XIII [decimotercer] Congreso va a ser el de la desaparición de su partido? (interview with Communist leader in *Tribuna*, Spain)	Is the 13th Congress going to be the one at which your party disappears?

However, in such sentences Verb-Subject order is usual if there is no object: *¿ha llamado mi hermano?* 'has my brother called?'

If the sentence includes an object, Verb-Object-Subject order is usual if the object is shorter than the subject (object in bold): *¿ha traído **flores** el vecino de tu suegra?* 'has your mother-in-law's neighbour brought flowers?'

But if the object is longer than the subject, Verb-Subject-Object order is usual; and if they are of the same length, the order is optional (object in bold):

*¿Ha traído Miguel **las flores que encargamos ayer por la noche**?* (short subject, so not **¿Ha traído las flores que encargamos anoche Miguel?*)	Has Miguel brought the flowers we ordered last night?

but

*¿Ha traído **flores** Miguel?/¿Ha traído Miguel **flores**?* (same length)	Has Miguel brought (some) flowers?

Note

Words should not be inserted between the auxiliary *haber* and a past participle: never ***¿ha Miguel traído flores?* 'has Miguel brought flowers?'

37.2.4 Word order in exclamations

When one of the words listed at 37.2.2 introduces an exclamation, (Object-)Verb-Subject order is required:

¡Qué guapo es tu hermano!	Isn't your brother good-looking/My, your brother's good-looking!
¡Cómo se parece Ana a su madre!	Doesn't Anna look like her mother!/Anna really looks like her mother!
¡Cuántos piropos te echa el jefe!	What a lot of compliments you get from the boss!

37.2.5 Inversion in dialogue identifiers

Verb-Subject order is required in writing in dialogue identifiers of the sort 'Mary said', 'John replied', when they follow the words quoted. Inversion in this case is nowadays optional in English and is disappearing:

—*Está bien, dijo el presidente*	'Fine,' the president said/said the president
—*Lo dudo, contestó Armando*	'I doubt it,' Armando replied/replied Armando

37.2.6 Verb-Subject order required after adverbs

Verb-Subject is very common when certain adverbs and adverbial phrases precede the verb.

When the verb is intransitive, inversion is usual. Speakers of either language would probably prefer sentences **(a)** to **(b)** (subjects in bold):

(a) *Delante de ella se levantaba **un enorme edificio***	Before her stood an enormous building

*Delante de ella aparecieron **dos hombres chillando y gesticulando***	Before her there appeared two men screaming and gesticulating
(b) *?Delante de ella **un enorme edificio** se levantaba*	?Before her an enormous building stood
*?Delante de ella **dos hombres chillando y gesticulando** aparecieron*	?Before her two men screaming and gesticulating appeared

When the verb has an object it seems that either word order is possible in Spanish (subject in bold): *delante de ella **dos mujeres** voceaban sus mercancías* 'before her two women were calling out their wares', or *delante de ella voceaban sus mercancías **dos mujeres***.

In the following examples, Subject-Verb order is not always impossible, but it is usually awkward (subject in bold).[3]

*Siempre me dijeron **las brujas y echadoras de cartas** que mi número mágico era el tres* (C. Rico-Godoy, Spain)	Witches and card-readers always told me that my magic number was three
*Siempre fue altanera **la Sofía**[4]* (A. Mastretta, Mexico, dialogue)	Sofia was always haughty/arrogant
*Nunca me hablaban **los vecinos***	The neighbours (US 'neighbors') never spoke to me
*Apenas salían **sus padres**, ponía música rock*	He used to put on rock music as soon as his parents went out
*También decía **su madre** que . . .*	Her mother also used to say that . . .
*Bien saben **las autoridades** que . . .*	The authorities know very well that . . .
*Así dice **Platón***	This is what Plato says
*Todavía humeaban **algunos incendios***	Some fires were still smoking
*Solamente pueden usarse **las iniciales de la víctima** en este tipo de caso*	Only the victim's initials may be used in this type of case
*Para tales personas existen **las cárceles***	Prisons exist for such people

Adverbial phrases of place especially favour Verb-Subject order (subject in bold: see also 37.4 for further remarks about the position of adverbial phrases):

*Ahí vivo **yo***	That's where I live
*Aquí dejó la sangre **el muerto** (J. Ibargüengoitia, Mexico, dialogue)	The dead man left his blood here
*En su mirada veía **yo** con claridad que me estaba pasando de la raya* (C. Rico-Godoy, Spain)	I could see clearly by his expression (lit. 'in his gaze') that I was overdoing it
*Junto a la puerta colgaba **una deshilachada toalla*** (L. Sepúlveda, Chile)	Next to the door hung a frayed towel

37.3 Miscellaneous word order rules

This section includes a number of miscellaneous but important rules that explain various features of Spanish word order.

---

[3] It is difficult to be precise on this matter. Native speakers who have an ear for sentence structure will know when Subject-Verb order sounds right, as in *nunca los intereses publicitarios motivarán la publicación de un artículo o suplemento* (*Libro de estilo de El País*) 'the publication of an article or supplement will never be motivated by publicity interests', rather than *nunca motivarán los intereses publicitarios . . . .*

[4] See 3.2.21 for remarks on the use of the definite article with personal names.

37.3.1 The link between a preposition and the word it modifies

Spanish does not separate prepositions from the noun or pronoun that they modify. This rule is important in relative clauses: a typically English sentence like 'that's the hotel we're going **to**' must be expressed *ese/ese es el hotel al que vamos* 'that's the hotel to which we're going'. In general, only *no* should separate a preposition from its infinitive:

Su nombramiento se demoró por estar siempre la vacante ocupada (not **por la vacante estar*)	His appointment (to the post) was delayed because the vacant position was always occupied
*La promesa de una vida de ocio fue frustrada **al negarse** el Fisco a devolverle el dinero* (not *al Fisco negarse)	The promise of a life of leisure was frustrated when the Revenue Department refused to return the money to him
Se equivocó por no haber pensado antes	He made a mistake as a result of not thinking beforehand

37.3.2 Set phrases are not broken up

Set phrases, particularly set verbal phrases like *tener que* 'to have to', *llevar a cabo* 'carry out', *hacer público* 'make public', *surtir efecto* 'produce an effect', *tener lugar* 'take place', *darse cuenta de que* 'realize', should not be broken up by the insertion of other words:

Probablemente las obras se llevarán a cabo para febrero (not **se llevarán probablemente a cabo . . .*)	The work will probably be carried out by February
Por eso hacemos pública esta información (and not the typical English word order? *. . . hacemos esta información pública*)	This is why we are making this information public

37.3.3 No insertion of words between *haber* and participles

As a rule, words should not be inserted between *haber* and a participle, e.g. *siempre he dicho* or *he dicho siempre* 'I've always said', but not *he siempre dicho (students of French take note: *j'ai presque toujours pensé que* is *casi siempre he pensado que* or *he pensado casi siempre que*). This rule is occasionally broken with certain words; see 14.8.1 for discussion.

37.3.4 Unstressed object pronouns remain with their verb

Unstressed object pronouns (*me, te, se, la, lo, le, nos, os, los, las, les*) are never separated from their verb: *te lo diré luego* 'I'll tell you later', *sólo/solo te quiero a ti* 'I only love you'/'I love only you', etc. There are often optional positions when a finite verb governs an infinitive or gerund: *no debí decírtelo* or *no te lo debí decir*, *estoy haciéndolo* or *lo estoy haciendo* 'I'm doing it'. This is discussed at 11.14.4.

37.3.5 Adjectival phrases are kept close to the noun they modify

Spanish does not like to separate adjectival phrases from the noun they modify:

Regresó como a las seis y media con un ejemplar arrugado y manchado de huevo de las Últimas Noticias *del mediodía* (C. Fuentes, Mexico)	He returned around 6.30 with a crumpled and egg-stained copy of the midday *Últimas Noticias*

This sentence would sound awkward (at least in polished styles) if the adjectival phrase were put at the end: ? ... *con un ejemplar de las Últimas Noticias del mediodía arrugado y manchado de huevo.* However, compound nouns formed with *de* are not broken up. One says *un reloj de pared suizo* 'a Swiss wall-clock', not **un reloj suizo de pared.* There is no infallible way in this case of determining whether nouns connected by *de* are inseparable compounds or not. The subject is discussed further at 4.11.5.

37.3.6 Keep verbs close to their subject

Verb-Subject order is commonly used to avoid separating a subject from its verb. Spanish does not like to leave a verb dangling at the end of a clause or sentence far from its subject. Compare the English and Spanish versions of this sentence:

*El tratamiento debe repetirse durante toda la vida, salvo que **se realice** con éxito un trasplante de riñón (Ercilla, Chile, in Variedades, 220; rather than ... un trasplante de riñón se realice con éxito)*

The treatment must be repeated throughout [the patient's] life, unless a successful kidney transplant **is performed**

37.3.7 Numerals are usually avoided at the beginning of sentences: see note to 10.16 for discussion

37.3.8 Word order in apposition

When a noun is in apposition to a preceding noun, nothing should separate the two nouns: one says **había muerto** *J. M., leyenda de la música rock de los años sesenta* 'J.M., legend of sixties rock, had died', not ?*J.M. había muerto, leyenda de la música rock* ....

37.4 Position of adverbs and adverbial phrases

37.4.1 Adverbs and adverb phrases are kept close to the words they modify

Generally speaking, adverbials (i.e. adverbs, adverbial phrases and adverbial clauses) are placed either immediately before or, more usually, immediately after the word(s) that they modify. In this respect, *El País* (*Libro de estilo*, p. 134) specifically admonishes its journalists and editors against:

(a) separating adverbs from their verb: *el rey ha inaugurado hoy* ... 'the king today inaugurated ... ', not *hoy, el rey ha inaugurado* ... ;
(b) breaking up verbal phrases by inserting adverbs in them: *el presidente está dispuesto claramente a dimitir* 'the president is clearly prepared to resign', not *el presidente está claramente dispuesto a dimitir* (which is the usual English order and, despite *El País*, very common in Spanish);
(c) beginning articles with an adverb other than *sólo/solo* or *solamente*, on the grounds that since adverbs modify other phrases the latter should precede them. But this rule applies only to formal writing.

37.4.2 Adverbs are not left at the end of sentences

English differs from Spanish in that it regularly puts adverbs and adverb phrases at the end of the sentence: 'I saw that lady who lives next door to your grandmother **yesterday'**. For the reason given at 37.4.1, Spanish puts 'yesterday' close to 'saw': *vi ayer/ayer vi a esa señora que vive al lado de tu abuela*. If the *ayer* ended the sentence it would seem to modify *vive*. The Spanish requirement that adverbs should stay close to their verb therefore often produces the un-English order Verb-Adverbial-Object (adverbial in bold):

Besó **fervorosamente** la mano de su anfitriona	He kissed his hostess's hand fervently
El tribunal fijará **discrecionalmente** la duración de la fianza (Spanish legal dictionary)	The Court will fix the period of the bail bond at its discretion
Casi siempre **a la una** seguía en chanclas y bata (A. Mastretta, Mexico, dialogue; in Spain chanclas = zapatillas)	She was nearly always still in her slippers and dressing-gown/(US 'bathrobe') at one o'clock

Adverbials of time are very often put before adverbials of place: 'we went to grandma's house yesterday' = *ayer fuimos/fuimos ayer a casa de la abuela*.

Note particularly the position of the adverbials in bold in the following sentences (other orders are possible but are not shown here):

Fue inútil que los párrocos advirtieran **en los pueblos** a las mujeres que sus maridos las abandonarían si llegaba la ley del divorcio (*Cambio16*, Spain)	It was no use the parish priests in the villages warning women that their husbands would leave them if the divorce law was introduced
Parece que la habilidad más importante es la de memorizar información para **luego** escupirla en un examen (Spanish popular press)	It seems the most important skill is memorizing information in order to churn (lit. 'spit') it out later in an examination
Alguien dijo que uno de esos desventurados había huido a Mysore, donde había pintado **en un palacio** la figura del tigre (J. L. Borges, Argentina)	Someone said that one of those unfortunates had fled to Mysore, where he had painted the figure of the tiger in a palace
Me di cuenta de que había estado **antes** en aquel sitio	I realized I'd been in that place before
¿Sabes que el presidente Romeo Lucas sufrió **ayer** un atentado? Estaba en su coche parado en un semáforo cuando **desde una bicicleta** le arrojaron un diccionario (joke in *Cambio16*, Spain, about an illiterate Guatemalan dictator)	Do you know someone made an attempt on President Romeo Lucas's life yesterday? He was waiting in his car at some traffic lights when someone threw a dictionary at him from a bicycle

For further remarks about the position of adverbs see 37.2.6 and 31.3.8.

37.5 Word order not explainable by sentence structure

Even when all the foregoing more or less codifiable rules are taken into account, there are many cases in which word order is determined by less easily definable factors that reflect the informational content of the sentence. It is never easy to explain these factors in a grammar book, which is bound to quote fragments of language out of context. There are also important differences between written and spoken language with respect to word order. The following remarks by no means exhaust the subject and do not apply to questions or negative sentences.

37.5.1 The topic of a sentence may be put first

Utterances naturally consist of a 'topic' – someone or something we want to say something about – and a 'comment' – what we want to say about the topic. In simple declarative sentences (i.e. which are neither questions nor orders) the subject of the main verb is usually also the topic of the sentence: '**Mary** hates strawberry yoghurt' is a comment about Mary, '**polar bears** have amazingly thick fur' is a comment about polar bears, and the usual order in such sentences in both English and Spanish is topic + comment: *María odia el yogur de fresa*, *los osos polares tienen un pelaje extraordinariamente espeso*.

However, the topic need not necessarily be the subject of the verb. It may be some adverbial phrase, as in '**on Fridays** I usually play bridge' / *los viernes suelo jugar al bridge* or, less commonly, it may be the direct object of a transitive verb or the predicate of a verb like 'to be': '**pork** I'm not eating!' / *carne de cerdo no como*, '**stupid** she isn't' / *tonta no es*.

Since spoken Spanish makes less use of stress and intonation than English, this device of shifting topics to the head is quite common, and regularly produces 'un-English' word order, as in a sentence like *me gusta la miel* 'I like honey', *a María le encanta el yogur de fresa* 'Mary loves strawberry yoghurt', where I and Mary are the topics of the utterance but happen to be grammatical objects in Spanish. But more unusual shifts are also found, especially in emotive colloquial language, and much more commonly than in English, which usually relies on intonation and stress rather than shifts in word order. In the following sentences the speakers emphatically 'declare' the topic they wish to raise, and then add a comment afterwards:

¡De dinero no quiero volver a oír ni una palabra!	About *money* I don't want to hear another word!
Trabajo le costó a Maruja convencerlo de que no (G. García Márquez, Colombia)	It was really hard work for Maruja to convince him otherwise
Americano vino uno solamente (Cuban TV interview)	As for Americans, only one came
Como en la foto de la boda no creo que yo vuelva a estar	I don't think I'll be like I was in the wedding photo again
—Lléveme adentro de una de esas casas . . .	'Take me inside one of those houses . . . '
—Casas fueron antes, ahora son oficinas (M. Puig, Argentina, dialogue; Peninsular usage requires *dentro de . . .*)	'They used to be houses, now they're offices.'
Muchas cosas he leído, pocas he vivido (J. L. Borges, Argentina)	I've read many things but lived few

Notes

(i) When a direct object is placed before the verb, it is resumed or echoed by a pronoun: *al verano inglés debían llamarlo estación de las lluvias* 'the English summer ought to be called the rainy season', *estos/éstos los dejo aquí, los demás me los llevo* 'I'll leave these here; I'll take the others with me'. This rule is not applied to nouns that are not preceded by an article or demonstrative adjective, as in *carne no como* 'I don't eat *meat*'. See 11.16.1 for more details.

(ii) One of the functions of the passive with *ser* is to make the direct object of the equivalent active sentence into a topic by putting it at the head of the utterance: *Miguel fue atropellado por un coche* 'Miguel was run over by a car' is more likely than *?un coche atropelló a Miguel ?* 'a car ran over Miguel'. Informal Spanish generally avoids the passive with *ser*, so placing the direct object at the head of the sentence is a good way of producing the same effect as a passive: *a Miguel lo/le atropelló un coche*.

(iii) Latin-American headline writers exploit the fact that the topic of an utterance can come first. This produces an unusually high number of sentences in which a direct object, or the predicate of *ser* or *estar*, or sometimes a verb, is shifted to the head of the sentence for dramatic purposes: *a tres coches quemaron* (Colombian headline) 'three cars burnt', *ingeniero buscamos* (advertisement, Venezuela) 'engineer sought', **signada por muchos altibajos** *estuvo la actividad bursátil* (headline in *La Nación*, Argentina; *signada* = *caracterizada* in Spain) 'Stock Exchange Activity marked by many rises and falls', **gigantesco tiburón de una especie desconocida** *capturó un pesquero frente a las costas del Chuy* (*El País*, Uruguay) 'giant shark of unknown species caught by fishing boat off Chuy coast', **causa de deslizamiento** *verán expertos* (*El Comercio*, Lima) 'experts to investigate cause of landslide', **capturan** *la policía y el ejército a 23 miembros de Sendero Luminoso* (*UnomásUno*, Mexico) 'Police and Army capture 23 Members of "Shining Path"'.[5] This word order sounds strange to Spaniards.

(iv) The topic may be specifically identified by some phrase like *en cuanto a* 'as for', *con respecto a* 'with regard to', *en/por lo que se refiere a . . .* 'with reference to', 'as far as . . . is concerned', e.g. *por lo que se refiere a Pedro, no lo/le he visto* 'as far as Pedro's concerned, I haven't seen him'. Use of such phrases is normal in written language; informal language might say *a Pedro no lo/le he visto*.

37.5.2 *El profesor viene* or *Viene el profesor?*

This section discusses sentences consisting only of a subject and verb. The principle explained at 37.5.1 – that the topic of an utterance may precede the comment made about it – explains the difference between *Antonio viene* and *viene Antonio*, 'Antonio's coming', two sentences that can really only be differentiated by emphasis and intonation in English.

In a neutral statement, i.e. matter-of-fact declarations, the Subject and Topic normally coincide, so the Subject comes first (when none of the factors listed in 37.2–37.4 operates) : *el médico llega a las diez* 'the doctor arrives/is arriving at ten o'clock'. But the time could be the topic – *a las diez llega el médico* – and in some circumstances the verb is the topic, for example when the doctor's arrival is feared, unexpected or hoped for. In this case Verb-Subject order is appropriate: *¡llega el médico!* 'the doctor's coming!'

But this is an obvious example. In most cases departures from Subject-Verb order are also influenced by factors of style and rhythm that cannot easily be explained in abstract terms. When it is not clearly called for, Verb-Subject order may produce a heavily literary, even 'Academic' tone, cf. *recordará el lector que los complementos directos . . .* (Royal Academy, *Esbozo . . .* 3.7.3f) 'the reader will recall that direct objects . . .' where the order *el lector recordará que . . .* would have been less formal.

In the following examples, Subject-Verb order is preferred because the subject is also the topic:

Miguel *está leyendo* (answers the question 'what's Miguel doing?')	Miguel's reading
Bentley *se volvió*	Bentley turned round

In the following sentence, the verb is the topic; in other words, the sentences answer the question 'what happened?' rather than 'who did it?'

Ha muerto Franco (headline)	Franco is dead
Han vuelto a España ya muchos	Many have returned to Spain already
Se abrió la puerta y entró Juan	The door opened and John came in

37.5.3 Word order in sentences that include direct objects

A sentence consisting of a subject, verb and direct object can theoretically appear in Spanish in the following forms:

---

[5] A Peruvian left-wing guerilla organization.

(a) *Inés leyó el libro*	Subject-Verb-Direct Object
(b) *El libro lo leyó Inés*	Direct Object-(redundant pronoun)-Verb-Subject
(c) *El libro Inés lo leyó*	Direct Object-Subject-(redundant pronoun)-Verb
(d) *Inés el libro leyó*	Subject-Direct Object-Verb
(e) *Leyó Inés el libro*	Verb-Subject-Direct Object
(f) *Leyó el libro Inés*	Verb-Direct Object-Subject

Of these possibilities, only the first three are at all common in ordinary language: **(d)** is very unnatural and might occur in songs or comic verse, and **(e)** and **(f)** are only found in archaic or very flowery literary styles, unless they are questions.

(a) is a neutral word order corresponding to an English sentence spoken with equal stress on 'Inés' and 'book'. Since, in neutral sentences, the subject of the verb tends naturally to be the topic, Subject-Verb-Object order is normal.

(b) clearly makes the direct object, the book, into the topic of the sentence, and then adds the comment about what Inés did to it: 'as for the book, Inés read it'. It also may emphasize Inés: 'Inés (not someone else) read the book'. See 11.16.1 for the use of the redundant pronoun here.

(c) is not particularly common. It would only appear at the beginning of a sentence that has to be completed, and is likely to occur when the whole statement is the topic of a sentence, and some comment is added that refers to the fact that Inés read the book, as in *el libro Inés lo leyó antes que su hermana, lo cual hizo que las dos se pelearan* 'Inés read the book before her sisters, which (i.e. the fact she read it before her sister) made them quarrel.' Another example: *la moto la compró mi marido porque nos habían robado el coche* 'the motor bike was bought by my husband because they had stolen the car', literally, 'as for my husband's buying the motorbike, he did it because they'd stolen our car'.

38

Diminutive, augmentative and pejorative suffixes

38.1 General

There are numerous suffixes that add an emotional tone to a word, e.g. *-ito*, *-illo*, *-ón*, *-ote*, *-azo*, *-aco*, *-ejo*, etc. The effect of these suffixes is very unpredictable. Sometimes they simply create new words without any emotional colouring at all: compare *ventana* 'window', *ventanilla* 'window of a vehicle'/'box office', *la caja* 'box', *el cajón* 'drawer' (in furniture); these words are standard lexical items and must be learnt separately. But usually they add an emotional tone to a word or phrase, e.g. affection, endearment, contempt, irony, repugnance, and they may sound affected, effeminate, childish or too familiar if used inappropriately. Consequently foreign learners are advised not to experiment with them, since inexpert use may produce unfortunate effects: *estarías mejor con el pelo recogido* means 'you'd look better with your hair up'; *estarías mejor con el pelo recogidito* means the same, but sounds either painfully condescending or like an adult talking to a little child; ?*estarías mejor con el pelito recogidito* is ludicrous and would be said by no one.

In view of this and the fact that the forms and frequency of the suffixes differ widely from continent to continent and region to region, and also in some regions seem to be more common in women's speech than men's, the following account is very summary. For a detailed picture of Peninsular usage see Gooch (1970), from which some of the following examples are taken.

38.2 Diminutive suffixes

Diminutive suffixes have various uses, described at 38.2.1–38.2.5. Although it is not always the function of these suffixes, they often imply smallness, so a few words must be said about their relationship with the adjective *pequeño*.

The following remarks apply to spoken rather than to formal written Spanish. *Pequeño* means 'small', but it does not usually have the emotional overtones of the English word 'little'. It is most often found between an article, demonstrative or numeral and an abstract noun, in which case it means 'of little importance': *el/un pequeño problema* 'a small/slight problem', *la/una pequeña dificultad* 'a slight difficulty', *esas pequeñas complicaciones que mencionamos* 'those slight complications we mentioned', *España era una pequeña potencia* 'Spain was a small/unimportant power'.

In other cases the combination of *pequeño* + noun is, in spoken language, more idiomatically expressed by diminutive suffixes. One says not ?*el/un pequeño perro* but *el/un perrito* 'a little dog', not *?la/una pequeña casa* but *la/una casita* 'a little house': . . . *desde la primera vez que la vio leyendo bajo los árboles del* **parquecito** (G. García Márquez, Colombia) 'since the first time he had seen her reading under the trees in the little park', *conozco un barecito ahí en la calle del Pez* (J. Madrid, Spain, dialogue). 'I know a little bar nearby in Pez street'.

Due to the influence of English and French, use of *pequeño* with the nuances of 'little' is spreading in journalese, but literary and spoken usage still prefers to add a diminutive suffix to convey the overtones of 'little', French *petit/petite*. In formal usage diminutive suffixes are not used, and *pequeño* would be used, just as 'little' would be avoided in English: one would say, in formal styles, *cerca de la casa había un pequeño bosque/un bosque pequeño* 'near the house there was a small wood', rather than *un bosquecito*.

Pequeño follows the noun when it refers to size or age without affective overtones, e.g. *un árbol pequeño* 'a small tree', *un niño pequeño* 'a young child'. In Spain a little child is often affectionately called *el chiquitín, el nene, el pequeño* or even *el peque*.

Notes

(i) Sometimes abbreviations are used instead of suffixes, e.g. *mami* or *papi* for *mamá* or *papá*, which are in turn abbreviations for *madre* and *padre*; *cole* from *colegio* 'school', *tele* from *television*, *la peli* for *la película* 'film', etc.
(ii) Except where indicated, the remarks in this chapter apply to educated usage in Central Spain, but they should be checked against the speech habits of different Latin-American republics.

38.2.1 Formation of the diminutive

The following are found, *-ito* being the most common in Central Spain and *-illo* used especially in the South. *-ico, -iño* and *-ín* have a Northern flavour. The usual form is shown first, with variant forms in brackets:

-ito (-cito, -ecito, -ececito)	*-ete (-cete, -ecete)*
-illo (-cillo, -ecillo, -ececillo)	*-ín*
-ico (-cico, -ecico, -ececico)	*-iño*
-uelo (-zuelo, -ezuelo, -ecezuelo)	

All are marked for gender in the usual way: a final vowel is replaced by *-a; -ín* makes its feminine *-ina*.

Words of more than one syllable ending in *-n, -ol* or *-r*, and words ending in *-e* or having the diphthong *-ie* in their first syllable, usually take the form in *-c-*. The following formations were generated spontaneously by Peninsular informants, but not all are guaranteed to be in common use. It must be emphasized that diminutive suffixes are theoretically very productive and could conceivably be added to almost any noun:[1]

mujer woman: *mujercita*	*cajón* drawer: *cajoncito*	*puente* bridge: *puentecito*
mejor better: *mejorcito*	*madre* mother: *madrecita*	*nieto* grandson: *nietecito*
mayor bigger: *mayorcito*	*padre* father: *padrecito*	*piedra* stone: *piedrecita*
charlatán talkative:	*cofre* case/box: *cofrecito*	*sueño* sleep/dream:
charlatancito		*sueñecito*

---

[1] But suffixes are not usually added to nouns ending in *-d* like *habilidad* 'cleverness', *verdad* 'truth', *césped* 'lawn'.

But note *el café > cafelito* 'coffee'; *el cafecito* usually means 'a little café'. Also *el alfiler > alfilerito* 'pin', *la mano > la manita/la manecita* 'hand'.

Words of one syllable commonly take forms in *-ec-*:[2]

flor flower *florecita*	*rey* king *reyecito*	*voz* voice *vocecita*
pan bread *panecillo* bread roll	*tos* cough *tosecita/tosecilla*	*sol* sun *solecito/solito*
pez fish *pececito/pececillo*	*pie* foot *piececito* (?*piececillo* – rare)	

Words ending in an unaccented vowel or diphthong lose their final vowel, but if the vowel is accented it may be preserved and its accent transferred to the *i* of *-ito*:

armario wardrobe *armarito*	*estatua* statue *estatuilla*
silla chair *sillita*	*mamá* mummy *mamaíta* or *mamita*
papá daddy *papaíto* or *papito*	*tío/tía* uncle/aunt *tiíto/tiíta*

38.2.2 Uses of the diminutive suffix *-ito*

The main effects of this suffix are:

(a) To give a friendly tone to a statement:

This very common use of the diminutive may simply give a warm tone to a remark. In a bakery one might say *deme una barrita de pan* 'give me a loaf of bread', which is merely a cheery equivalent of *deme una barra de pan*. This use of the diminutive does not imply smallness but merely signals the speaker's attitude to the hearer:

Dame un paquetito por ahora	Give me just one packet for now
Me tiras el vaso con el codo. A ver si tenemos más cuidadito . . .	You're knocking my glass over with your elbow. Let's see if we can't have a little bit more care . . .
Voy a echar una siestecita	I'm going to have forty winks/a quick nap
Un momentito, por favor	Just a moment, please
Me lo contó un pajarito	A little birdie told me
¿Alguna cosita más? (often used in shops) (cf. *¿Alguna cosa más?* Anything else?)	Would you like anything else?
¿Te puedo coger una almendrita?	Can I have (just one) one of your almonds?

(b) To modify the meaning of adjectives and adverbs by adding a warm tone or, sometimes, by making them more precise – e.g. *ahora* 'now', *ahorita* (Mexican colloquial) 'right now':

cerquita de la catedral	just by the cathedral
Ahora mismito se lo sirvo	Don't worry, I'll bring it at once
Ya eres mayorcito	You're a big boy now
(*mayor* = grown up, older)	
Está gordito	He's put on a bit of weight
(*Está gordo*	He's fat)
¡tontito!	silly!
(*¡tonto!*	stupid!)

'Nice' or 'lovely' can be the English equivalent of some adjectival and adverbial diminutives in *-ito*:

---

[2] But note the following Latin-American forms: *tiene el vestido a florcitas verdes* (M. Puig, Argentina, dialogue) 'she's got the dress with green flowers', *y el solcito está lindo* (M. Benedetti, Uruguay, dialogue) 'and the sun's lovely'.

¿Un café calentito?	A nice cup of hot coffee?
Las empanadas están recientitas	The meat pies are lovely and fresh
Despacito	nice and easy/take it easy
¡Todo está tan verdecito!	Everything is so nice and green

(c) To denote endearment or affection: *hermanita* (lit. 'little sister') is often a term of endearment and does not necessarily imply that the sister is younger than the speaker. *Abuelita* 'grandma', for example, is merely an affectionate form for *abuela* 'grandmother':

Vamos, m'hijito (Latin-American; Spain: *vamos hijo mío*)	Come on, son
Se ha hecho daño en la patita	It's hurt its (little) paw
¡Pobrecito! ¿Te has caído?	Poor little thing! Did you fall down?

(d) To denote smallness:

el perro/el perrito dog/little dog/doggy	*la puerta/la puertecita* door/little door
el sillón/silloncito armchair/little armchair	*el coche/cochecito* car/little car/baby carriage

But sometimes the diminutive needs reinforcing, as in *¿tienes un sobrecito pequeño?* 'have you got a little envelope?' or —*¿quieres un poco? —Sólo/Solo un poquito. No tanto, un poquitín* '"Do you want a bit?" "Just a little bit. Not so much, just a tiny little bit."'

(e) Occasionally in an ironic way to emphasize largeness or grandeur: *¡menuda casita!* 'some house!' (looking at a vast mansion), *¡mira el cochecito ese!* 'nice little car!'(said about a gold-plated Rolls Royce).

Note

Occasionally there is a diminutive form of different gender: *la maleta* 'suitcase', but *el maletín* 'small hand case'; *la botella/la botellita* 'bottle' but *el botellín* (typically a small bottle of beer).

38.2.3 Diminutive suffix *-illo*

The suffix *-illo* is used:

(a) as a diminutive:

pan/panecillo	bread/bread roll
flor/florecilla	flower/little flower

(b) To downgrade the importance of something:

Falta una pesetilla	You're just one peseta short (cf. *falta una peseta* 'you're a peseta short')
Tengo unas cosillas que hacer	I've got a few little things to do
Ahora sólo/solo queda el jaleíllo de las entradas (*jaleo* = row, fuss)	All that's left is the business of the entrance tickets
Hacía un airecillo agradable	There was a pleasant breeze

(c) To soften a word that otherwise might sound too offensive:

mentirosillo	'fibber'
Es bastante dejadilla (*dejado* 'careless'/ 'sloppy')	She's pretty careless/She doesn't take a lot of care
Tú eres comiloncillo ¿eh?	You eat quite a lot!/You sure like your food!

(d) To give an affectionate tone:

Pero ¿qué haces, chiquilla? — But what **are** you doing, honey/darling? (addressed to a female)

He comprado un cachorrillo/cachorrito — I bought a little puppy

Diminutives in *-illo* are typical of Seville but they are also often used in central Spain.

(e) To give a specialized meaning to a word: compare English 'book'/'booklet'. In some of these cases the diminutive ending has no diminutive function:

el palo/palillo stick/toothpick
la caja/cajetilla box/cigarette pack, etc.
la vara/varilla rod/thin stick, spoke, wand (but *la varita mágica* 'magic wand')
la guerra/guerrilla war/guerilla warfare
el cigarro/cigarrillo cigar/cigarette
la cama/camilla bed/stretcher

la manzana/la manzanilla apple/camomile (also a type of dry sherry)
la masa/la masilla dough/putty
la ventana/la ventanilla window/vehicle window/ticket-window
la bomba/la bombilla bomb/light bulb
la parra/la parrilla vine/grill
el bolso/el bolsillo bag/pocket

(f) To denote a combination of diminutive and pejorative:

la cultura/culturilla — culture/'smattering of culture'
mujer/mujercilla — woman/unimportant woman

38.2.4 Diminutive suffix *-ín*

-ín is typical of Asturias, but it is used to express affection in many contexts in the rest of Spain:

¡Donde está el chiquitín? — Where's the little one?
¡chiquirriquitín! — my tiny little one!
¡mi (niña) chiquitina! (not *¡mi pequeña niña!*) — my little girl!

and also to form new words:

la espada/el espadín sword/dress sword
la tesis/la tesina thesis/dissertation

la peluca/el peluquín wig/small wig
el cerebro/un cerebrín brain/a brainy person

38.2.5 Diminutive suffixes *-uelo, -eto, -ete*

(a) *-uelo* can denote a combination of diminutive and pejorative:

la calleja/callejuela alley/narrow little alley
el arroyo/arroyuelo stream/trickle, rivulet

el rey/reyezuelo king/petty king/princeling
tonto/tontuelo stupid/dumbo (affectionate)

It may also be used to form new words: *el paño/pañuelo* 'cloth/handkerchief'.

(b) *-eto/a, -ete/a* may add a specialized meaning:

el avión/la avioneta aircraft/light aircraft
el camión/la camioneta truck/van (or light truck)

el caballo/el caballete horse/easel

(c) *-ete* may add a humorous tone:

amigo/amiguete friend/pal

gordo/regordete fat/chubby

38.2.6 Diminutive forms in Latin America

In many areas of Latin America, especially Central America and Mexico, diminutive forms pervade everyday speech to an extent that amuses Spaniards:

Viene ya merito (Mexico; i.e. *ahora mismo*)	He's coming right now
merito ayer no más (Mexico) (i.e. *ayer mismo*)	only yesterday
Ahorita lo voy a hacer (i.e. *ahora mismo/ahora mismito*)	I'll do it straight away (in practice it usually means 'when I can . . . ')
Clarito la recuerdo	I remember her vividly
Apártate tantito, que voy a saltar (Guatemalan, from Kany, 1970, 385)	Get out of the way a bit, I'm going to jump
Reciencito llegó . . . (see 31.7.2 for *recién*)	He arrived just a minute ago . . .
Las caras de los gringos son todititas igualitas (C. Fuentes, Mexico, dialogue)	Gringos' faces are all exactly the same

38.3 'Augmentative' suffixes

Typical, in order of frequency, are *-ón, -azo, -ote, -udo*.

(a) These are mainly used to denote intensity or large size, almost always with some associated pejorative idea of clumsiness, unpleasantness, awkwardness or excess:

rico/ricachón rich/stinking rich, 'loaded'	*la ginebra/un ginebrazo* gin/an enormous shot of gin
pedante/pedantón pedant/insufferable pedant	*el gringo/gringote* gringo/bloody gringo
el soltero/solterón bachelor/confirmed bachelor	*la palabra/la palabrota* word/swear word
contestón tending to answer back/cheeky	*el favor/favorzote* favour/'heck of a favour'
preguntón constantly asking questions	*El airón de la mañana había dejado el cielo azul* (A. Mastretta, Mexico, dialogue)
cursi/cursilón affected/incredibly affected	
fácil/facilón easy/facile	The gusts of breeze in the morning had left the sky blue
la broma/el bromazo joke/joke pushed too far	
el coche/cochazo car/'heck of a car'	
el libro/librazo book/tome	

However, *-azo* can in some contexts imply admiration, as in *debes ser un profesorazo* 'you must be one heck of a teacher':

(b) To form an entirely new word. The suffix may then have no connotations of size or awkwardness and may even imply smallness:

la rata/el ratón rat/mouse (animal or computer)	*la cintura/el cinturón* waist/belt
la caja/el cajón box/drawer	*el fuego/el fogón* fire/stove
la culebra/el culebrón grass-snake/soap opera (i.e. *telenovela*)	*la tela/el telón* cloth/theatre curtain
	la cuerda/el cordón string/shoelace

Note

-azo is much used to form nouns which denote a blow or flourish with some object: *el aldabón/aldabonazo* 'knocker'/'thump with a door knocker', 'blow on door', *el codo/codazo* 'elbow'/'dig with elbow', *la bayoneta/el bayonetazo* 'bayonet'/'bayonet thrust.'

38.4 Pejorative suffixes

These are not particularly frequent, especially now that graphic insults are often expressed by language once thought shocking. The words formed by them should be learnt as separate lexical items. Typical suffixes are *-aco, -arraco, -acho, -ajo, -astro, -uco, -ucho, -ejo* and a few others.

They variously denote ugliness, wretchedness, squalor, meanness, etc.

el pájaro/pajarraco bird/sinister bird
el poeta/poetastro poet/rhymer, poetaster
el pueblo/poblacho village/'dump', squalid village/dead-end town
el latín/latinajo Latin/Latin jargon, dog Latin

la casa/casucha house/pathetic little house
la palabra/palabreja word/horrible word word
el hotel/hotelucho hotel/dingy hotel

Some of these suffixes may be used affectionately:

¿Cómo va a poder estudiar con tres pequeñajas como ésas/esas?

How is she going to be able to study with three little terrors like them?

39

Spelling, accent rules, punctuation and word division

Index to chapter

In some cases, pronunciation is indicated by phonetic transcription. See footnote to 39.1.3 for an explanation of the signs used.

39.1 Spelling

39.1.1 The *Nuevas normas* and the alphabet

The spelling rules of modern Spanish are laid down by the Academy in the *Nuevas normas de prosodia y ortografía* which came into official use in January 1959. But even forty years later pre-1959 spelling is still commonly used by persons who are not connected with the world of publishing, and the *Nuevas normas* are still inconsistently applied in print. For further comments on the status of the *Nuevas normas* see 6.3 (demonstrative pronouns), 9.15 (*sólo/solo*) and 13.2.3 (spelling of *prohibir, aislar, reunir*).

The spelling – particularly the use of the accent – used in works published before 1959 will therefore differ in detail from this account. Among the more striking innovations were the removal of the accent from the words *fui, fue, dio, vio,* and its adoption in words like *búho, rehúso, reúne, ahínca, prohíbe, ahíto.*

39.1.2 The Spanish alphabet

Since April 1994, the Spanish alphabet has consisted of the following twenty-seven letters:

a *a*	h *hache*	ñ *eñe*	u *u*
b *be*	i *i*	o *o*	v *uve*
c *ce*	j *jota*	p *pe*	w *uve doble*
d *de*	k *ka*	q *cu*	x *equis*
e *e*	l *ele*	r *erre*[1]	y *i griega*
f *efe*	m *eme*	s *ese*	z *zeta*
g *ge*	n *ene*	t *te*	

---

[1] It can also be called *ere* according to the Academy.

Double *r* (*erre doble*) is a separate sound but it is not treated as a separate letter of the alphabet.

Before 1994, the signs *ch* and *ll* were treated as separate letters of the alphabet, so that in alphabetical lists words beginning with *ch* or *ll* followed words beginning with *c* or *l*: *mancha* followed *mancornas* and *collado* followed *colza*, etc. This was very inconvenient for computerized sorting and out of line with other languages that use Latin letters, so in April of that year the 10th Conference of Academies of the Spanish Language voted by a large majority to abolish *ch* and *ll* as separate items of the alphabet. The position of the separate letter *ñ* remains unchanged.

The Academy requires that accents should always be written on capital letters, a rule that is constantly ignored in print since it creates letters that are inconveniently tall.

Note

Letters of the alphabet are all feminine – *la cu, la uve* – and one says *la/una a, la/una hache*, despite the rule that singular feminine words beginning with a stressed *a* sound require the masculine article, cf. *el arma* (fem.) 'the weapon': see 3.1.2 for discussion.

39.1.3 Relationship between sounds and letters

Spanish spelling is not entirely rational, but it is much more logical than French or English. Basically one sound corresponds to one letter, so one merely needs to hear words like *colocar* [kolokár][2] 'to place', *chaleco* [chaléko] 'waistcoat'/(US 'vest'), *calenturiento* [kalenturyénto] 'feverish', to be able to spell them correctly. However, the rule of one sound for one letter is broken in numerous cases:

(a) *H* is always silent, except in some rural dialects, but it is common in writing, where it is merely a burden on the memory: *hacha* [ácha] 'axe'/(US 'ax'), *hombre* [ómbre] 'man', *Huesca* [wéska], *Honduras* [ondúras], *ahíto* [a-íto] 'gorged'/'satiated', etc. *H* had one useful function in the past: it showed that two adjacent vowels separated by *h* did not form a diphthong, as in words like *prohibe* [pro-íβe] 'prohibits', *buho* [bú-o] 'owl', *rehila* 'it quivers' [rre-íla], *la retahila* [larreta-íla] 'volley'/'string' (e.g. of insults). In its wisdom the Academy abolished this rule in 1959, so one must now write *prohíbe, búho, rehíla, la retahíla*, etc.

The sound [w] at the beginning of a syllable – i.e. when it is not preceded by a consonant – is spelt *hu*: *huele* [wéle] 'it smells', *ahuecar* [awekár] 'to hollow out', *Náhuatl* [ná-watl] 'the Nahuatl language (of Mexico)', etc.

(b) *Z* is pronounced [θ] (like the th of 'think') in standard European Spanish, like the s of 'sit' throughout Latin America and in Southern Spain and the Canary Islands. *Z* is written *c* before *i* or *e*: *cebra* [θéβra/séβra] 'zebra', *hacer* [aθér/asér] 'do', *nación* [naθyón/nasyón]] 'nation', etc. For this reason, a verb like *realizar* 'attain'/'achieve'/'bring about' undergoes spelling changes: *realizo, realice, realicé, realizó*, etc. See 13.5.3 for the effect of these and other spelling

---

[2] The transcription system used here deliberately departs from the International Phonetic alphabet to make it clearer for non-experts: χ = voiceless velar fricative, i.e. ch in 'loch' or *ch* in German *lachen*; β = bilabial voiced fricative (*v* pronounced with both lips); γ = voiced velar fricative (not found in English: g as in 'got' but without closure of the throat); θ = 'th' in 'think', ð = 'th' in 'this', ʎ = palatalized *l*, rr = rolled *r*. Stressed syllables are marked by an acute accent. Other signs should be given their usual Spanish pronunciation.

rules on the verb system. *Z* is written before *e* or *i* only in a handful of exceptional cases: *el eczema* (or *el eccema*) 'eczema', *la enzima* 'enzyme', *zeta* 'zed'/(US 'zee'), *Nueva Zelanda* (in Latin America *Nueva Zelandia*) 'New Zealand', *zigzag* (plural *zigzags*), *Zimbabue/Zimbabwe*, *zinc* (also *cinc*) 'zinc', *zipizape* 'rumpus'/'fuss'/'noisy quarrel'.

Spelling in Latin America and Andalusia is much more troublesome than in central Spain since *z*, *c(e)*, *c(i)* and *s* are all pronounced identically, so pairs of words like *caza* 'hunt' and *casa* 'house', *ves* 'you see' and *vez* 'time' (as in 'three times'), *Sena* 'the river Seine' and *cena* 'supper' sound the same.

(c) The sound of *c* in *cama* is written *qu* before *e* and *i*: *querer* [kerér] 'to want', *quiso* [kíso] 'wanted', *saque* [sáke] 'take out' (third-person present subjunctive of *sacar*), etc. The letter *k* is consequently not needed in Spanish and is found only in foreign words, for example measurements preceded by *kilo-*, or in *kantiano* 'Kantian', *krausismo*, 'Krausism', *el kiwi* [elkíβi] 'kiwi'/'kiwi fruit', *Kuwait* [kuβáyt] 'Kuwait', etc.

The sound [*kw*] is always written *cu*, e.g. *cuestión* [kwestyón] 'question',[3] *cuáquero* [kwákero] 'Quaker' (students of Portuguese and Italian take note!).

(d) The sound [χ] (like *ch* in 'loch') is always written *j* before *a*, *o* and *u*, and is usually written *g* before *e* and *i*: *general* [χenerál], *Gibraltar* [χiβraltár], *rige* [rríχe] 'he/she/it rules', *rugir* [rruχír] 'to roar', etc. There are numerous exceptions to the latter rule, e.g. the preterite of all verbs whose infinitive ends in *-ducir* (the preterite of *producir* 'to produce' is *produje*, *produjiste*, *produjo*, *produjimos*, *produjisteis*, *produjeron*), and many other words, e.g.

la bujía spark plug	*Jesús* Jesus
crujir to rustle/to crackle	*la jeta* thick lips/snout
dejé I left behind (from *dejar*)	*Jiménez* (a family name; also *Giménez*)
el equipaje luggage	*la jirafa* giraffe
el garaje garage	*el paisaje* landscape
la jeringa syringe	*tejer* to weave
el jersey jersey	*el traje* suit
el jesuita Jesuit	*el ultraje* outrage

(e) The sound of *g* in *hago* [áγo] is written *gu* before *e* and *i*: *ruegue* [rrwéγe] present subjunctive of *rogar* 'to request', *la guirnalda* [laγirnálda] 'wreath'/'garland'. The *u* is silent and simply shows that the *g* is not pronounced like Spanish *j* [χ].

The syllables pronounced [gwe] and [gwi], neither very common in Spanish, are written *güe* and *güi*, e.g. *lingüístico* [língwístiko], *el desagüe* [eldesáγwe] 'drainage'/'water outlet', *averigüe* [aβeríγwe] present subjunctive of *averiguar* 'to check', *nicaragüense* [nikaraγwénse] 'Nicaraguan', *el pingüino* [elpingwíno] 'penguin'. This is the only use of the dieresis in the modern language.

(f) *B* and *v* sound exactly the same and are most frequently pronounced as a voiced bilabial fricative [β], although they both sound like the English *b* after *n* or *m* or after a pause. The English sound [v] as in 'vat' does not exist in Spanish and English speakers of Spanish often make a false distinction between the pronunciation of the Spanish written signs *b* and *v*. For this reason they usually do not confuse these letters in writing.

---

[3] It means 'issue'/'problem'. Compare *la pregunta* 'question', i.e. something one asks.

Native speakers who are poor spellers make blunders like *ˣla uba* for *la uva* [la-úβa] 'grape', **Premio Novel* for *Premio Nobel* [prémyonoβél] 'Nobel Prize' – mistakes which are at least the sign of a normal pronunciation.

(g) In Spain, *x* (*equis*) is often pronounced like *s* before a consonant: *extender* = [estendér] 'extend', *el extracto*, = [elestrákto] 'extract', etc. Seco (1998), 459, rejects the pronunciation of *x* as [ks] in this position as affected, but Latin Americans insist on it and it is apparently becoming more common in Spain. For the pronunciation and spelling of the words *México, mexicano, Oaxaca*, see 4.8.1. note (iv)

X is pronounced [s] at the beginning of words: *la xenofobia* [lasenofóβya] 'xeno-phobia', *el xilófono* [elsilófono] (colloquially *el xilofón* [elsilofón]) 'xylophone'.

The pronunciation [ks] is normal between vowels and at the end of words: *el examen* [eleksámen] 'examination', *el taxi* 'taxi' [eltáksi], *Xerox* [séroks]. Learners should avoid popular pronunciations like [esámen], [tási], often heard in Spain.

(h) *N* is pronounced *m* before *b*, *v*, *p*: *en Barcelona* = [embarθelóna/embarselóna] 'in Barcelona', *invitar* = [imbitár] 'to invite', *en París* = [emparís] 'in Paris'.

(i) *R* and *rr* represent a flapped and a rolled *r* ([r] and [rr]) respectively, and in a few words they indicate a difference of meaning, e.g. *pero* [péro] 'but', *perro* [pérro] 'dog'; *caro* [káro] 'dear', *carro* [kárro] 'car'/'cart'; *enteró* [enteró] 'he informed', *enterró* [enterró] 'he buried'.

But *r* is pronounced like *rr* when it is the first letter in a word, e.g. *Roma* [rróma], *la ropa* [larrópa] 'clothes', or when it occurs after *l*, *n* or *s*: *Israel* [isrraél], *la sonrisa* [lasonrrísa] 'smile', *alrededor* [alrreðeðór] 'around'.

When a prefix ending in a vowel is added to a word beginning with *r*, the *r* is doubled in writing and is therefore rolled in speech: *infra + rojo = infrarrojo* 'infra-red', *contra + revolucionario = contrarrevolucionario* 'counter-revolutionary', *anti + republicano = antirrepublicano* 'anti-Republican'. Such words are not spelt with a hyphen in Spanish.

(j) *Ll* is properly a palatalized *l* [ʎ], but it is nowadays pronounced like the letter *y* by many speakers, to the dismay of many purists. Poor spellers sometimes make mistakes like **cullo* for *cuyo* 'whose', *la *balloneta* for *la bayoneta* 'bayonet'. It is much better to pronounce it *y* than to pronounce it like the *lli* of 'million', which is written *li* in Spanish. *Polio* [pólyo] 'polio' and *pollo* [póʎo] 'chicken' sound quite different in correct Spanish.

(k) *M* is often pronounced *n* at the end of words by many, though not by all speakers: *el álbum* = [elálβun/elálβum] 'album', *el referéndum* = [elrreferéndun] 'referendum', *el ultimátum* = [elultimátun] 'ultimatum'.

(l) The three initial groups of consonants *ps, mn* and *gn* are pronounced *s, n* and *n* respectively and may now, according to the Academy, be spelt this way. But many people cannot bring themselves to write *la sicología* for *la psicología* 'psy-chology' or *la siquiatría* for *la psiquiatría* 'psychiatry', and it is doubtful whether anyone would write *la nosis* or *nóstico* for *la gnosis, gnóstico* 'gnosis', 'gnostic'. The older spellings *ps-, gn-, mn-* are therefore still used – even by the Academy itself! *El seudónimo* 'pseudonym' is, however, universally used.

(m) The *p* in *septiembre* 'September' and *séptimo* 'seventh' is sometimes silent and may be dropped in writing according to the Academy. But many find the forms *setiembre, sétimo* repugnant and the forms with *p* are much more common.

(n) If the prefix *re-* is added to a word beginning with *e* one of the *es* may be dropped in writing: *re + emplazo > remplazo* or *reemplazo* 'replacement', *re + embolso > rembolso* or *reembolso* 'reimbursement', *reelige > relige* 're-elects'. The new spelling is frequently (but not universally) seen in Latin America, but the spelling with *ree-* is much more usual in Spain.

(o) The sound [y] (like the *y* in 'yacht') is always spelt *y* at the end of words: *Paraguay, convoy.*

39.1.4 *Trans-* or *-tras-*

Some uncertainty surrounds the spelling of words which begin with the prefix *trans-* or *tras-*. Educated usage seems to be:

Normally *trans-*	Usually *tras-*	Always *tras-*
transalpino	*trascendencia*	*trasfondo*
transatlántico	*trascendental*	*trashumancia*
transbordar	*trascendente*	*trashumante*
transbordo	*trascender*	*trasladar*
transcribir	*trasponer*	*traslado*
transcripción	*trasvasar*	*traslucir*
transcurrir		*trasluz*
transcurso		*trasnochar*
transferencia		*traspapelar*
transferir		*traspasar*
transformar		*traspaso*
transformación		*traspié*
transfusión		*trasplantar*
transgredir		*trasplante*
transgresión		*traspunte*
transgresor		*trasquilar*
transmediterráneo		*trastienda*
transmigración		*trastocar*
transmisión		*trastornar*
transmitir		*trastorno*
transparencia		*trastrocar*
transparentar		*trastrueque*
transparente		
transpiración		
transpirar		
transpirenaico		
transportar		
transporte		
transposición		
transversal		

Source: Seco (1998), 437. Seco notes that in the case of the first two columns the alternative spellings in *tras-* and *trans-* respectively are tolerated by the Academy but are not in general use.

39.1.5 Common non-Castilian forms

Words written in the other official languages of Spain are nowadays frequently seen in Spanish Castilian texts.

Latin-American spellings sometimes reflect the sounds of native American languages. In many of these languages, notably Maya and Nahuatl, *x* is pronounced sh. This affects some Mexican place names like Uxmal [ushmál], Tlaxcala [tlashkála], Xcaret [shkarét]. However, x is pronounced like Spanish j in some other Mexican place names, e.g. *México*, Oaxaca. See 4.8.1 note (iv).

Non-Castilian spellings	Pronounced as
j (Catalan, Galician)	s in 'pleasure'
j (Basque)	Spanish j
g before i, e (Catalan, Galician)	s in 'pleasure'
g (Basque)	g in English 'get'
h (Catalan, Galician, Basque)	silent, as in Spanish
tx (Basque, Catalan)	Spanish ch
ny (Catalan)	Spanish ñ
l·l (Catalan)	double l (not as Spanish ll)
x (Catalan, Galician, Basque)	sh
tz (Basque)	ts
-aig, -eig, -oig, -uig (Catalan)	-ach, -ech, -och, -uch
z (Catalan)	like English z
z (Basque)	like Spanish s

39.2 The written accent

The Academy and many grammarians call both the curly sign over an *ñ* and the acute accent (´) *una tilde*, a word which in everyday language usually refers only to the sign over *ñ*. *El acento* properly means 'stress' in linguistic usage, but in ordinary language it also means 'written accent'.

39.2.1 General rules

Native Spanish-speakers are rather careless about the use of the written accent in handwriting, but in printing and formal writing the rules must be observed.

The basic rule is: if a word is stressed regularly, no written accent is required. If a word is stressed irregularly, the position of the stress must be shown by an acute accent on the stressed vowel. Stress is regular:

(a) if the word ends in a consonant other than *n* or *s* and the stress falls on the last syllable;
(b) if the word ends in a vowel or *n* or *s* and the stress falls on the penultimate syllable.

The following words therefore have regular stress and require no written accent:

la calle street
la cama bed
contestad answer (*vosotros* imperative)
el coñac brandy
denle give him (*ustedes* imperative)
la imagen image
el jueves Thursday
Madrid

natural natural
(*el*) *Paraguay*
redondo round (adjective)
el reloj (pronounced *reló*) clock/watch
el sacacorchos corkscrew
la tribu tribe
la virgen virgin
volver return

The following are stressed irregularly and must have a written accent:

el álbum album	*las imágenes* images
alérgicamente allergically	*la nación* nation
contéstenles answer them (*ustedes* imperative)	*la química* chemistry
decídmelo tell me it (*vosotros* imperative)	*el récord* record (in sports, etc.)
difícil difficult	*el rehén* hostage
dirán they will say (from *decir*)	*la/las síntesis* synthesis/syntheses
fácil easy	*las vírgenes* virgins

Notes

(i) It follows from the rule that all Spanish words stressed more than two syllables from the end must be stressed irregularly, so they all have an accent: *díganmelo, teléfono, parasítico,* etc.

(ii) Words ending in two consonants of which the second is *s* (all of them foreign words) are regularly stressed on the last syllable: *Orleans, los complots* 'plots', *los cabarets* 'cabarets'. *El/los fórceps* 'forceps', *el/los bíceps* 'biceps', *el/los récords* are exceptions.

39.2.2 Diphthongs, triphthongs and the position of the stress accent

Spanish vowels are divided into two classes:

(1) Strong	**(2) Semi-vowels**
a, e, o	*i* when pronounced [y]
i when pronounced as in *ti*	*u* when pronounced [w]
u when pronounced as in *tú*	

Vowels may appear in combinations of two or three, e.g. *ea, au, uai, iai,* etc. An intervening *h* is disregarded, so that *au* and *ahu, eu* and *ehu, ai* and *ahi,* etc. are treated the same way (at least since the publication of the Academy's *Nuevas normas* in 1959).

When two or more **strong** vowels appear side by side, they are pronounced as separate syllables[4] and do not form diphthongs or triphthongs:

leo [lé-o] I read	*moho* [mó-o] rust/mildew
créamelo [kré-amelo] believe me	*Seoane* [se-o-á-ne] (a surname)
pasee [pasé-e] subjunctive of *pasear* 'to go for a walk'	*creí* [kre-í] I believed
	aún [a-ún] still/yet

A combination, in either order, of a **strong vowel** plus a **semi-vowel** creates a diphthong and is counted as a single vowel for the purpose of finding the position of the written accent. Therefore the following words are stressed predictably:

arduo [árðwo] arduous	*Francia* [fránθya/fránsya] France
continuo [kontínwo] continuous	*la historia* [laystórya] history/story
erais [érays] you were	*produjisteis* [proðuxísteys] you produced
la lengua [laléngwa] tongue/language	*hablabais* [aβláβays] you were speaking

and the following words have unpredictable stress and require a written accent:

---

[4] Adjacent strong vowels are in fact usually run together in rapid speech and pronounced as one syllable, a phenomenon known as syneresis when it occurs inside a word and synalepha when it occurs between words. Thus *león* is often pronounced [león] (one syllable) rather than [le-ón] and *la unión* is almost always pronounced [lawnyón] (two syllables); but this has no effect on spelling.

amáis [amáys] you love
debéis [deβéys] you owe
hacías [aθías/asías] you were doing

volvió [bolβyó] he/she returned
continúo [kontinú-o] I continue
ella respondía [eʎarrespondía] she was
  answering

If a semi-vowel is added to a diphthong, a triphthong is formed. Triphthongs are also counted as a single vowel for the purpose of determining where a written accent should appear:

continuáis [kontinwáys]
vieiras [byéyras]
cambiáis [kambyáys]

you continue (three syllables)
scallops (Spain only; two syllables)
you change (two syllables)

Note

Students of Portuguese should remember that Portuguese has very different rules and writes *colónia*, *história*, but *temia* (all stressed the same as Spanish *colonia*, *historia*, *temía*).

39.2.3 Written accent on stressed diphthongs and combinations of strong vowels

If one of a group of combined vowels is stressed, the written accent may or may not appear on it. There are three possibilities:

(a) If the combination is **strong vowel** and **semi-vowel** (in either order) the stress falls predictably on the strong vowel, so the following require no written accent:

vais [báys] you go (*vosotros* form)
el aire [eláyre] the air
veis [béys] you see (*vosotros* form)
el peine [elpéyne] comb
fui [fwí] I was
huido [wíðo] fled (past part. of *huir*
  'to flee'
la ruina [larrwína] ruin
tiene [tyéne] (s)he has (from *tener*)
luego [lwéɣo] then/later
cuenta [kwénta] (s)he counts

la causa [lakáwsa] cause
Palau [paláw] (personal surname)
Berneu [bernéw] (personal surname)
alcaloide [alkalóyðe] alkaloid
la tiara [latyára] tiara
acuoso [akwóso] watery
vio [byó] (s)he saw
dio [dyó] (s)he gave
el pie [elpyé] foot
la viuda [laβyúða] widow

and the following are exceptions:

el país [elpa-ís] country
el baúl [elβa-úl] trunk/car boot (US
  'car trunk')
aún [a-ún] still/yet (pronounced
  differently from *aun*, 'even')
reír [rre-ír] to laugh
reís [rre-ís] you (*vosotros*) laugh
el dúo [eldú-o] duet/duo
el búho [elβú-o] owl

frío [frí-o] cold
reúne [rre-úne] he reunites
prohíbe [pro-íβe] he prohibits
heroína [ero-ína] heroine/heroin
el arcaísmo [arka-ísmo] archaism
ahí [a-í] there
oís [o-ís] you (*vosotros*) hear
ríe [rrí-e] (s)he laughs (from *reír*)
se fía [sefí-a] (s)he trusts (from *fiarse*)

(b) If the combination is **strong vowel** + **strong vowel** the two vowels form separate syllables, so the following are stressed predictably:

los jacarandaes [losχakarandá-es]
  jacaranda trees (plural of *el jacarandá*)
los noes [losnó-es] noes (plural of 'no')

feo [fé-o] ugly
leen [lé-en] they read
la boa [laβó-a] boa (the snake may be *el boa*
  in Latin America)

el caos [elká-os] chaos
ahonda [a-ónda] (s)he deepens
el moho [elmó-o] rust/mildew

and the following are exceptions:

aéreo [a-éreo] air (adjective)   *el deán* [elde-án] dean (ecclesiastical)
el león [elle-ón] lion   *el rehén* [elrre-én] hostage

Notes

(i) *Huido, construido* and other words ending in *-uido* are stressed regularly (because the *ui* is a diphthong), whereas words like *creído* 'believed' (past participle of *creer*) and *reído* 'laughed' (past participle of *reír*) are written with an accent because they fall under the exceptions to **(a)** (the *i* is not pronounced like 'y').

(ii) Accented forms like *rió* [rri-ó] 'he laughed', *lió* [li-ó] 'he tied in a bundle', *huís* [u-ís] 'you (vosotros) flee', *huí* [u-í] 'I fled', etc., are apparent exceptions to rule that the strong vowel is predictably stressed in the combination semi-vowel + strong vowel: compare *fui* 'I was', *fue* '(s)he was', *vio* '(s)he saw', *dio* '(s)he gave'. Words like *rió, lió, fió* are given a written accent to show that the two vowels are pronounced separately, whereas *vio, dio, fui* and *fue* are pronounced as monosyllabic words [byó], [dyó], [fwí], [fwé]. Compare the pronunciation of *pie* 'foot' [pyé] with *pié* [pi-é], first-person preterite of *piar* 'to cheep' (like a bird: two syllables).

(iii) As mentioned in 39.2.2, a triphthong is treated like a single vowel for the purpose of determining the position of the stress, so that *continuáis* [kontinwáys] (from *continuar* 'to continue') is in fact an exception and must be written with the accent.

(iv) When, as sometimes happens in archaic or very flowery styles, an object pronoun is added to a finite verb form other than an imperative, an original written accent is retained: *acabó* + *se* = *acabóse* for *se acabó* 'it ended': see 11.14.1 note **(ii)** for a discussion of this construction. This spelling rule leads to the inconsistency of a normally stressed vowel bearing a written accent.

However, when a pronoun is added to an imperative the accent is not written if it becomes unnecessary, e.g. *dé* 'give' but *deme* 'give me', *detén* 'stop' but *detenlos* 'stop them'.

(v) If a word bearing a written accent is joined to another to form a compound, the original written accent is discarded: *tío* + *vivo* = *tiovivo* 'merry-go-round', *balón* + *cesto* = *baloncesto* 'basketball', etc.

39.2.4 Written accent: some common doubtful cases

The following forms are recommended (where *el/la* precedes the noun it may refer to a male or a female; when no accent is written the stressed vowel is shown in bold).

la acrobacia acrobatics
afrodisiaco aphrodisiac
amoniaco ammonia
austriaco Austrian
cardiaco cardiac
el/la chófer driver (see note i)
el cóctel cocktail
demoniaco or *demoníaco* demonic;
  likewise other words ending in
  -iaco/íaco, the unaccented form being
  more common
la dinamo dynamo (see note ii)
disponte familiar imperative of
  disponerse 'get ready' (see note iii)
el electrodo electrode
etíope Ethiopean

la exégesis or *la exegesis* exegesis
el fríjol bean (see note iv)
el fútbol soccer (see note v)
el géiser geyser (geological)
hipocondriaco hypochondriac (see
  demoniaco above)
ibero (less commonly *íbero*) Iberian
el láser laser
la metempsicosis metempsychosis
el meteoro meteor
el misil (less commonly *mísil*) missile
la olimpiada Olympiad
la orgía orgy
la ósmosis or *osmosis* osmosis
el pabilo wick (of a candle)
el parásito parasite

el/la pediatra paediatrician/(US pedia-
 trician)
el periodo or *período* period
el/la políglota polyglot
el/la psiquiatra psychiatrist
policiaco police (adjective; see *demoniaco*
 above)
la quiromancia palmistry/hand-reading
 (see note vi)
el rádar radar

el reptil reptile
el reuma rheumatism (everyday usage
 prefers *el reúma*)
el sánscrito Sanskrit
el termostato thermostat
la tortícolis stiff neck
la utopía utopia
el zodiaco zodiac (see *demoniaco* above)

Some 'mispronunciations' are usual in speech, e.g. *el soviet* 'Soviet', *el oceano* 'ocean' (written and correctly pronounced *el océano*).

Notes

(i) Written and pronounced *chofer* (i.e. [chofér]) in most countries of Latin America, including Mexico.
(ii) *El dínamo* in some Latin-American countries, including Argentina and Cuba.
(iii) Similarly *componte* 'compose yourself', *detente* 'stop'.
(iv) Stressed *el frijol* in Latin America.
(v) *El futbol* is heard in some Latin-American countries.
(vi) Likewise all words ending in *-mancia* that have the meaning 'divination'.

39.2.5 Accent on interrogative forms

In the case of some words, the interrogative form carries an accent. This indicates a fact of pronunciation: the interrogative form is stressed, as can be seen by contrasting the *que*s in *dice que* **qué** *pasa* 'he's asking what's happening' or the *cuando*s in *cuando llega* 'when he arrives . . . ' and *¿***cuándo** *llega?* 'when is he arriving?' These words are:

cómo how
cuál which
cuándo when
cuánto how much

dónde where
qué what/which (also *por qué* 'why')
quién who

See Chapter 24 for further details.

39.2.6 Accent used to distinguish homonyms

In the case of some two dozen common words, the written accent merely eliminates ambiguities:

	without accent	with accent
de/dé	of	present subjunctive of *dar*
el/él	the (definite Article)	he/it
éste/este	see 6.3	
ése/ese	see 6.3	
aquél/aquel	see 6.3	
mas/más	but (rare)	more
mi/mí	my	me (after prepositions)
se/sé	reflexive pronoun	(i) I know, (ii) *tú* imperative of *ser*

si/sí	if	(i) yes, (ii) prepositional form of *se*
sólo/solo (see 9.15)	alone	only (*solamente*)
te/té	object form of *tú*	tea
tu/tú	your	you

Notes

(i) *Dé* loses its accent if a pronoun is attached and the stress is regular: *denos*, 'give us', *deme* 'give me', etc. Spellings like *déme* are often seen, but the accent is unnecessary.

(ii) The Academy requires that *o* ('or') should take an accent when it appears between two numerals so as to avoid confusion with zero: *9 ó 5* '9 or 5'. However, the *Libro de estilo* of *El País* requires its journalists to ignore this rule and write *9 o 5*.

(iii) The following words do **not** have a written accent: *da* 'gives', *di* 'I gave', *fe* 'faith', *ti* prepositional form of *tú*, *vi* 'I saw', *ve* 'sees', *vio* '(s)he saw', *fui* 'I was', *fue* '(s)he was', *dio* '(s)he gave'.

(iv) *Aun* 'even' [áwn] and *aún* 'still/yet' [a-ún] are in fact pronounced differently in good Spanish.

39.3 Upper- and lower-case letters

39.3.1 Upper-case letters

These are used much less than in English. They are used:

(a) At the beginning of sentences, as in English.

(b) With proper nouns, but not with the adjectives derived from them: *Madrid*, *la vida madrileña* 'Madrid life'; *Colombia, la cocina colombiana* 'Colombian cooking'; *Shakespeare, el lenguaje shakespeariano* 'Shakespearean (or Shakespeare's) language'.

Adjectives that are part of an official name are capitalized, e.g. *Nueva Zeland(i)a* 'New Zealand', *el Reino Unido* 'the United Kingdom', *Los Estados Unidos* 'the United States', *El Partido Conservador* 'The Conservative Party', *Las Naciones Unidas* 'The United Nations', etc.

When a proper name includes the definite article, the latter is written with a capital letter *El Cairo* 'Cairo', *La Haya*. In the case of countries that appear with the definite article, the article is not part of the name so a lower-case letter is used: *la India* 'India', *la Argentina*. See 3.2.17 for discussion of this use of the article.

39.3.2 Lower-case letters

Lower-case letters are used for:

(a) Months, seasons and days of the week: *julio* 'July', *agosto* 'August', *verano* 'summer', *invierno* 'winter', *jueves* 'Thursday', *viernes* 'Friday', *martes* 'Tuesday', etc.

(b) Names of religions and their followers: *el cristianismo* 'Christianity', *el catolicismo* 'Catholicism', *el protestantismo* 'Protestantism', *el islam* 'Islam', *un testigo de Jehová* 'a Jehovah's witness', *los musulmanes* 'the Muslims', etc.

(c) Official titles, e.g. *el presidente de la República*, 'the President of the Republic', *la reina de Gran Bretaña* 'the Queen of Great Britain', *el papa Juan XXIII* 'Pope John XXIII', *los reyes de España* 'the King and Queen of Spain', *el señor García* 'Sr. Garcia', *el ministro de Obras Públicas* 'the Minister for Public Works', etc.

(d) Book and film titles: only the first letter is in upper case, as well as the first letter of any proper name that appears in the title: *Cien años de soledad (One*

Hundred Years of Solitude), *El otoño del patriarca* (*The Autumn of the Patriarch*), *El espía que surgió del frío* (*The Spy Who Came in From the Cold*), *Vida de Manuel Rosas* (*The Life of Manuel Rosas*), *La guerra de las galaxias* (*Star Wars*), etc.

However, the titles of newspapers and magazines are capitalized: *El País*, *La Nación*, *Ordenador Personal* (*Personal Computer*), etc.

(e) For points of the compass: *norte* 'North', *sur* 'South', *este* 'East', *oeste* 'West'. They are capitalized if they are part of a name: *América del Norte*, 'North America', etc.

39.4 Punctuation

These remarks refer only to major differences between Spanish and English. Readers who need a detailed account of Spanish punctuation should refer to specialized manuals.

39.4.1 Full stops/periods and commas

The full stop/(US 'period') (*el punto*) is used as in English, except that abbreviations are usually always written with a full stop:

English	Spanish
3000 ptas	*3000 ptas.*
Sr González	*Sr. González*

and a point is used in numbers where English uses a comma, and vice-versa: *1.567,50* = 1,567.50 and *1,005* (*uno coma cero cero cinco*) = 1.005 ('one point zero zero five'). However, Mexico, Puerto Rico and Central America use the system of Britain and the USA.

Commas (*la coma*) are used much as in English, except for writing decimals (see preceding paragraph). Commas are not written before the conjunction *y* in a series: *pumas, coyotes y monos* 'pumas, coyotes and monkeys'. Two clauses with different subjects are separated by a comma whereas in English the comma is nowadays often omitted: *Juan es uruguayo, y Marta es argentina* 'Juan is Uruguayan and Marta is Argentinian.'

39.4.2 Colons

Colons (*dos puntos*) are used as in English except that they appear after salutations in letters: *Muy Sr. mío:*[5] 'Dear Sir,' *Querida Ana:* 'Dear Ana'.

39.4.3 Semi-colons

Semi-colons (*punto y coma*) are used much as in English, and they are much used after a series of commas instead of a comma to denote a longer pause:

Tenía pan, huevos y vino; pero no tenía carne	He had bread, eggs and wine, but he had no meat
Miguel entró cansado, confuso; María le siguió, radiante y orgullosa.	Miguel came in, tired, confused. Maria followed him, radiant and proud

The semi-colon is also regularly used before connectors, e.g. *sin embargo/no obstante* 'nevertheless', *a pesar de esto* 'despite this', that are themselves followed by a comma:

---

[5] The formula used in the Southern Cone is *De mi consideración:*.

> *Le escribí más de una vez; sin embargo,*   I wrote to him more than once. However,
> *no me contestó*   he did not reply

39.4.4 Quotations and the representation of dialogue

There is no clear agreement over the use of *comillas* or inverted commas.

Chevrons (*comillas francesas* or *comillas angulares*, i.e. << >>) may be used (at least in Spain) like our inverted commas to indicate quotations or slang, dialect or other unusual forms, and occasionally to indicate dialogue within a paragraph:

> *Un inspector de bigotillo con acento <<pied noir>> acompañado de un gendarme de uniforme, va recorriendo las mesas pidiendo documentación: <<No pasa nada, es sólo una operación de rutina>>. Sin embargo, todo este impresionante montaje sorprende a todos.* (*Cambio16*, Spain)

A further quotation within << >> is indicated by " ".

However, the *Libro de estilo* of *El País* (11.31) explicitly forbids the use of << >> and requires use of " " for quoted material and ' ' for quotations within quotations. This convention is used in many publications.

Single quotation marks are much used to enclose isolated words: *la palabra 'esnob' viene del inglés* 'the word "snob" comes from English'.

There are three types of dash in Spanish:

el guión	hyphen	short -
el signo de menos	minus sign	medium length –
la raya	dash	double length —

In the representation of continuous dialogue inverted commas are not used, the words spoken being introduced by a *raya*.

A *raya* marks either the beginning of dialogue, a change of speaker or a resumption of dialogue after an interruption: *—Ahora váyase —dijo— no vuelva más hasta que yo le avise*. Dialogue is closed by a *raya* only if unspoken words follow it, as in *—¿Qué tal estás? —Angustias lo dice con una sonrisa.*

Punctuation in direct speech is disconcertingly placed after the *raya*: *—Aprovecha ahora que eres joven para sufrir todo lo que puedas —le decía—, que estas cosas no duran toda la vida*. (G. García Márquez, *El amor en los tiempos del cólera*). Example:

> *—¿Te parece que hablo de él con cierto rencor, con resentimiento? —Juanita hace un curioso mohín y veo que no pregunta por preguntar; es algo que debe preocuparla hace mucho tiempo.*
> *—No noté nada de eso —le digo—. He notado, sí, que evitas llamar a Mayta por su nombre. Siempre das un rodeo en vez de decir Mayta. ¿Es por lo de Jauja, porque estás segura que fue él quien empujó a Vallejos? —No estoy segura —niega Juanita—. Es posible que mi hermano tuviera también su parte de responsabilidad. Pero pese a que no quiero, me doy cuenta que le guardo un poco de rencor. No por lo de Jauja. Porque lo hizo dudar. Esa última vez que estuvimos juntos le pregunté: <<¿Te vas a volver un ateo como tu amigo Mayta, también te va a dar por eso?>> No me respondió lo que yo esperaba. Encogió los hombros y dijo:*
> *—A lo mejor, hermana, porque la revolución es lo primero.*

> (M. Vargas Llosa, *Historia de Mayta*, Seix Barral. Printed in Spain)

39.4.5 Question and exclamation marks

Spanish and Galician (*gallego*) are unique among the world's languages in that a question or exclamation must be introduced by an upside-down question or exclamation mark as well as being followed by normal question and exclamation marks.

The logic behind this is that it enables readers to start the appropriate intonation at the right moment, so words that are not included in the interrogatory or exclamatory intonation pattern lie outside the signs:

Oye, ¿quieres una cerveza?	Hey, d'you want a beer?
Hace calor, ¿verdad?	It's hot, isn't it?
Si te digo que no he gastado más que	If I tell you I've only spent 2000 ptas, will
dos mil pesetas, ¿me vas a creer?	you believe me?
Pero, ¡qué estupidez!	But what stupidity!
¡Lo voy a hacer! ¿Me oyes?	I'm going to do it! Do you hear me?

39.4.6 Hyphens

Hyphens (*guiones*) are used very sparingly, since compound words are usually written as a single word: *latinoamericano* (not **latino-americano*), *antisubmarino* 'anti-submarine', *hispanohablante* 'Spanish-speaking', *tercermundista* 'Third-World'.

They appear between compound adjectives in which each part represents separate things or people (not the case, for example, with *latinoamericano*). Only the second of two adjectives agrees in number and gender:

las guerras árabe-israelíes	the Arab-Israeli wars
negociaciones anglo-francesas	Anglo-French negotiations
el complejo militar-industrial	the military-industrial complex

In other cases the hyphen may be used to join two nouns:

misiles superficie-aire	surface-to-air missiles
la carretera Madrid-Barcelona	the Madrid-Barcelona road

Hyphens are sometimes printed between compound nouns of the sort *mujer policía* 'police-woman', *año luz* 'light year', but this does not conform either to the Academy's recommendation or to the best editorial practice.

39.5 Division of words at end of line

A thorough knowledge of the structure of Spanish syllables is necessary for a good pronunciation, and readers should consult manuals of phonology and phonetics for precise details. As far as word division at the end of a line is concerned, the following rules apply:

(a) The following combinations of written consonants are not divided: *ch, ll, rr, qu*, and the following combinations of consonants + *r* or *l*:

br	*cr*	*fr*	*gr*	*pr*	*dr*	*tr*
bl	*cl*	*fl*	*gl*	*pl*		

(b) Bearing in mind that the combinations listed under **(a)** count as one consonant, a single consonant is always grouped with the following vowel:

ha-ba	*ro-ca*	*nu-do*	*a-gua*	*pe-lo*	*ra-za*	*mar-ca*
ha-cha	*ca-lle*	*pe-rro*	*ca-bra*	*co-fre*	*o-tro*	*co-pla*

and no syllable begins with more than one consonant:

cal-do	*cos-ta*	*cuan-do*	*par-te*	*can-cha*
as-ma	*hem-bra*	*em-ble-ma*	*com-bi-nar*	*in-na-to*
ex-cla-mar	*con-lle-var*	*cons-truc-ción*	*al-co-hol*	*re-hén*
pa-guen	*se-quí-a*	*blan-den-gue*		

(c) Combinations of *i* or *u* with another vowel can be split only if an accent is written on the *i* or *u*. Thus:

viu-do	*cié-na-ga*	*fiel-tro*	*can-táis*	*a-ma-bais*
bue-no	*ha-cia*	*re-cien-te*		

but

ha-cí-a-mos	*de-cí-ais*	*con-ti-nú-as*

(d) Other combinations of vowels may be split: *pa-se-a-ban, lo-or, ne-er-lan-dés*. However, it is considered inelegant to begin a line with just one vowel, so *Ate-neo, aé-reo* are the preferred divisions, not *Atene-o, aére-o*.

(e) When a prefix ending with a vowel is added to a word beginning with *r-*, the latter consonant is doubled in writing: *contrarrevolucionario* 'counter-revolution-ary', *prorrogar* 'to adjourn'. If the prefix is divided from the word at the end of a line, the single *r* reappears: *contra-revolucionario, pro-rogar*.

Notes

(i) The above rules reflect the rules of Spanish pronunciation, but the Academy states that when a word is clearly divisible on etymological grounds it may be divided accordingly. An etymological division is preferred when the usual division does not reflect the correct pronunciation: *su-brogar* for *sub-rogar* 'to substitute' looks and sounds wrong:

Further examples: *de-sa-gra-da-ble* or *des-a-gra-da-ble* 'disagreeable', *sub-rep-ti-cio* (better than *su-brep-t-i-cio*) 'subreptitious', *sub-ru-ti-na* (better than *su-bru-ti-na*) 'subroutine', *sub-ra-yar* (better than *su-bra-yar*) 'to underline', *sud-a-me-ri-ca-no* or *su-da-me-ri-ca-no* 'South American', *vos-o-tros* or *vo-so-tros* 'you'.

(ii) Any of these rules is overridden to avoid a comic or shocking result. One does not write *sa-cerdote, cal-culo, al ser-vicio del gobierno*.

(iii) There is confusion over the combination *tl*. The rule is that it is optionally separable, except in the words *a-tlas, a-tle-ta* and any of their derivatives. It should also not be separated in Mexican place names of Nahuatl origin like Tenochtitlan, etc.

(iv) Foreign words should be divided according to the rules prevailing in the language of origin.

(v) Words containing the sequence *interr-* are divided thus: *in-ter-re-la-cio-na-do*).

Sources: Macpherson (n.d.), *Nuevas normas* (1959), Martínez de Sousa (1974), Seco (1998).

Bibliography and sources

The following general works are useful for serious students of Spanish:

Galimberti Jarman, B. and Russell, R., *The Oxford Spanish Dictionary*, 2nd edition (Oxford: Oxford University Press, 1998). Clear, accurate, comprehensive and rich in Latin-American examples.

Gerboin, P. and Leroy, C., *Grammaire d'usage de l'espagnol contemporain* (Paris: Hachette, 1991). A reference grammar useful for students who know French.

Moliner, M., *Diccionario de uso del español*, 2 vols, new edition (Madrid: Gredos, 1998). Unwieldy but invaluable for Peninsular usage.

El País, Libro de estilo, 14th edition (Madrid: Ediciones *El País*, 1998). Based on the house rules of this prestigious daily newspaper. A generally uncontroversial and reliable guide to good Peninsular written usage.

Ramsey, M. and Spaulding, J. K., *A Textbook of Modern Spanish* (New York, 1958; often reprinted). Composed by Ramsey in the 1880s and revised by Spaulding in the 1940s. Very thorough but dated.

Real Academia Española, *Gramática de la lengua española: Nueva edición* (Madrid, 1931, often reprinted). A useful but old-fashioned reference-point.

—— *Esbozo de una nueva gramática de la lengua española* (Madrid: Espasa Calpe, 1973).

Seco, M., *Diccionario de dudas y dificultades de la lengua española*, 10ª edición revisada y puesta al día (Madrid: Espasa Calpe, 1998). Increasingly indispensable amidst the flood of sometimes mutually contradictory guides to good usage now appearing in Spain.

Seco, M., Andrés, O., Ramos, G., *Diccionario del español actual*, 2 vols (Madrid: Aguilar Lexicografía, 1999). A new and up-to-date monolingual dictionary.

Smith, C., ed., *Collins Spanish–English English–Spanish Dictionary*, 6th edition (Glasgow and New York: HarperCollins, 2000). Rich in Latin-American usage and colloquial examples.

Mention must also be made of the two series *Problemas básicos del español* published by the Sociedad General Española de Librería of Madrid and *Problemas fundamentales del español*, published by the Colegio de España, Salamanca. Although uneven in quality, all these booklets contain important information for intermediate and advanced learners of Spanish.

The following works are mentioned in the text

Arjona Iglesias, M., *Estudios sintácticos sobre el español hablado de México* (Mexico: Universidad Autónoma, 1991)

Beinhauer, W., *El español coloquial* (Madrid: Gredos, 1964, reprinted)

Bello, A., [1847–64], *Gramática de la lengua castellana destinada al uso de los americanos* (a recent edition is Caracas, 1951)

Bolinger, D., 'The Subjunctive *-ra* and *-se*: Free Variation?', *Hispania* 39 (1956), 345–49, reprinted in *Essays on Spanish: Words and Grammar* (Newark, Delaware: Juan de la Cuesta, 1991), 274–82

Busquets, L. and Bonzi, L., *Ejercicios gramaticales* (Madrid: Sociedad General Española de Librería, 1983)

Carnicer, R. *Sobre el lenguaje de hoy* (Madrid: Prensa Española, 1969)

—— *Nuevas reflexiones sobre el lenguaje* (Madrid: Prensa Española, 1972)

The numerous articles of George DeMello of the University of Iowa, based on his statistical analyses of the Corpus of Educated Spoken Spanish from Eleven Cities, have been especially useful in determining the geographical range of certain constructions. The following are quoted in the text.

DeMello, G. (1992, 1) '*Se los* for *se lo* in the Spoken Cultured Spanish of Eleven Cities', *Hispanic Journal* 13:1 (1992), 165–79

—— (1992, 2) '*Le* for *Les* in the Spoken Educated Spanish of Eleven Cities', *Canadian Journal of Linguistics*, 37:4 (1992), 407–30

—— (1992, 3) 'El artículo definido con nombre propio de persona en el español hablado culto contemporáneo', *Studia Neophilologica* 64 (1992), 221–34

—— (1992, 4) 'Duplicación del pronombre relativo de objeto directo en el español hablado culto de once ciudades', *Lexis*, XVI:1 (1992), 23–52

—— (1992, 5) '*Cuyo* y reemplazos por *cuyo* en el español hablado contemporáneo', *Anuario de Lingüística Hispánica*, VIII (1992), 53–71

—— (1994, 1) 'Pretérito compuesto para indicar acción con límite en el pasado: *ayer he visto a Juan*', *Boletín de la Real Academia Española*, LXXIV:CCLXIII (1994), 611–33

—— (1994, 2) '*El cual* vs. *el que* en el español hablado culto: parte I: su empleo como objeto de preposición', *Hispanic Journal*, 15:1, (Iowa University Press, 1994), 89–110

—— (1994, 3) '*El cual* vs. *el que* en el español hablado culto: parte II: su empleo como sujeto u objeto de verbo, con sustantivo propio, con 'todo', con expresiones temporales', *Hispanic Journal*, 15:2, (Iowa University Press, 1994), 393–408

—— '*-Ra* vs *-Se* Subjunctive: a New Look at an Old Topic', *Hispania* (1993), 235–44

—— 'Concordancia entre el verbo pronominal de tercera persona y su sustantivo: *se venden flores* vs. *se vende flores*', *Anuario de letras de la Facultad de Filosofía y Letras: Centro de Lingüística Hispánica* XXXIII (Mexico: UNAM, 1995), 59–82

—— (1996, 1) [Pronombre 'sí'] vs [Pronombre no-reflexivo]: 'Juan lo compra *para sí*' vs 'Juan lo compra para *él mismo*', *Bulletin of Hispanic Studies* (Liverpool) LXXXIII:3 (1996), 297–310

—— (1996, 2) 'Indicativo por subjuntivo en cláusula regida por expresión de reacción personal', *Nueva Revista de Filología Hispánica* XLIV:2, (1996), 2, 365–86

—— (2000, 1) 'A acusativa con nombre propio geográfico', Hispania (forthcoming, 2000)

García, Yebra, V., Claudicauón en el uso de las preposiciones (Madrid: Gredos, 1988)

García, E., *The Role of Theory in Linguistic Analysis: The Spanish Pronoun System* (Amsterdam/Oxford: North-Holland, 1975)

Gili y Gaya, S., *Curso superior de sintaxis española*, 8ª edición (Barcelona: Biblograf, 1958; often reprinted)

—— *Estudios de lenguaje infantil* (Barcelona: Biblograf, 1972)

Gooch, A. L., *Diminutive, Pejorative and Augmentative Suffixes in Modern Spanish*, 2nd edition (Oxford: Pergamon, 1970)

Gutiérrez Araus, M. L., *Formas temporales del pasado en indicativo* (Madrid: Arco Libros, 1995)

Hammer, A. E., *German Grammar and Usage*, 1st edition (London: Edward Arnold, 1971)

Harmer, L. C. and Norton, F. J., *A Manual of Modern Spanish*, 2nd edition (London: University Tutorial Press, 1957; many reprints)

Ingamells, L. and Standish, P. , *Variedades del español actual* (London: Longman, 1975). A useful collection of texts from all over the Hispanic world.

Judge, A. and Healey F. G., *A Reference Grammar of Modern French* (London: Edward Arnold, 1983)

Kany, C. E., *Sintaxis hispanoamericana* (Madrid: Gredos, 1970, several reprints); English original published by University of Chicago (1945). A valuable guide to the variety of Latin-American syntax. It does not reliably mark register, so many examples may be substandard even on their own territory.

Lope Blanch, J. M., *Estudios sobre el español de México* (Mexico City: Universidad Nacional Autónoma, 1991)

Lorenzo, E., *El español de hoy: lengua en ebullición*, 3ª edición (Madrid: Gredos, 1980)

Luque Durán, J. de, *Las preposiciones* (Madrid: Sociedad General Española de Librería, 1978), 2 vols

Macpherson, I. R. *Spanish Phonology: Descriptive and Historical* (Manchester and New York: Manchester University Press, n.d.)

Marsá, F., *Diccionario normativo y guía práctica de la lengua española* (Barcelona: Ariel, 1986)

Martínez de Sousa, J., *Dudas y errores del lenguaje* (Barcelona: Bruguera, 1974)

Molina Redondo, J. A. de, *Usos de se* (Madrid: Sociedad General Española de Librería, 1974)

Moreira Rodríguez, A. and Butt, J. W., *Se de matización and the Semantics of Spanish Pronominal Verbs*, King's College London Hispanic Series II (London: KCL, 1996)

Navas Ruiz, R., *El subjuntivo castellano* (Salamanca: Colegio de España, 1986)

Quirk, R., Greenbaum, S., Leech, G. and Svartvik, J., *A Grammar of Contemporary English* (London: Longman, 1972)

Real Academia Española, *Nuevas normas de prosodia y ortografía. Nuevo texto definitivo* (Madrid, 1959)

Repiso Repiso, S., *Los posesivos* (Salamanca: Colegio de España, 1989)

Santamaría, A. et al., *Diccionario de incorrecciones, particularidades y curiosidades del lenguaje* , 5th edition (Madrid: Paraninfo, 1989)

Steel, B., *A Manual of Colloquial Spanish* (Madrid: Sociedad General Española de Librería, 1976)

Sources of examples

These are too numerous to be listed individually. Many of the examples are modified versions of extracts from printed or spoken sources; these are not attributed. Attributed quotations are often from sources chosen not for their literary qualities but because they exemplify the unadorned everyday Spanish that this grammar describes. Poetry and poetic prose have been excluded. The following authors and publications are quoted several times.

Argentina: Jorge Asís, Jorge Luis Borges, Julio Cortázar, *Gente*, *La Nación*, Abel Posse, Manuel Puig, Ernesto Sábato

Chile: Isabel Allende, José Donoso, Luis Sepúlveda, Sergio Vodanovic, *La Época*

Colombia: Gabriel García Márquez, *El Tiempo*, *El País*

Costa Rica: *La Nación*

Cuba: Reinaldo Arenas, Antón Arrufat, Pablo Armando Fernández, Guillermo Cabrera Infante (in exile), *Cuba Internacional*, *Granma* (official organ of the Communist Party of Cuba), Lisandro Otero, *Vindicación de Cuba* (the published transcript of a show trial)

Ecuador: *El Comercio, Hoy*

Mexico: Juan José Arreola, *Excelsior*, Carlos Fuentes, Sergio Galindo, Jorge Ibargüengoitia, *La Jornada*, Ángela Mastretta, *El Nacional*, Octavio Paz, Sergio Pitol, Elena Poniatowska, *La Reforma*, Luis Spota, *UnoMásUno*, Carlos Solórzano (born in Guatemala)

Panama: José de Jesús Martínez (born in Guatemala), *La Prensa*

Paraguay: *Abc Color*

Peru: Alfredo Bryce Echenique, *El Comercio*, Mario Vargas Llosa

Puerto Rico: Luis Rafael Sánchez

Spain: *Abc*, Ignacio Aldecoa, Josefina Aldecoa, Eloy Arenas, Carlos Barral, Antonio Buero Vallejo, *Cambio16*, Luis Carandel, Camilo José Cela, Miguel Delibes, *Diario16*, Manuel Fernández Álvarez, Antonio Gala, Federico García Pavón, Juan Goytisolo, Luis Goytisolo, Alfonso Grosso, José María Guelbenzu, Juan Madrid, Javier Marías, José Antonio Marina, Juan Marsé, Carmen Martín Gaite, Eduardo Mendoza, Terenci Moix, Rosa Montero, *El Mundo*, *El País*, Soledad Puértolas, Carmen Rico-Godoy, Alfonso Sastre, *La Vanguardia*, Maruja Torres, Manuel Vázquez Montalbán, Federico Umbral

Uruguay: *Hoy*, Mario Benedetti

Index of English words

The sign = should be read 'when it has the meaning of'. The word 'see' refers to items in the main index. English words not listed should be sought in the main index under their most obvious translation, e.g. 'to beat' under *pegar*.

'fear', see *temer*
'few', see *poco*
'find', see *encontrarse*
'first time', as in 'it's the first time I've
    seen it', 14.3.7
'for', see *para, por*; 'for *n* years, days', see
    Expressions of Time
'forget', see *olvidar(se)*
'former', 'the former . . . the latter', 6.4.2

'given that', 16.12.4d
'go', as in 'I'm going to do it', 14.6.4
'go around . . . -ing', 20.8.1
'greater', see *mayor*
'grow', see *crecer(se)*

'half', see *medio, mitad*, Fractions
'happy', see *feliz*
'hardly', see *apenas, nada más*
'have', see *tener, haber*
'hence the fact that . . .', 16.12.4c
'her', see *la*, Possessives
'here' 31.6.1
'him', see *le*, Possessives
'hope', see *esperar*
'how', see *como, cómo*, Neuter Pronouns
    (*lo*)
'however', 33.11.3a, 16.13.2, 16.13.4
'however much/little', 16.13.2
'hundred', see Numerals, *cien(to)*

'if', see *si*
'if only', 16.15.2
'improve', see *mejorar(se)*
'in' see *en*, also 3.2.27
'in case', see *por si*
'in front of', see *delante de, ante*
'in order to', 16.12.3
'in return for', 16.12.8a
'in spite of', see 'despite the fact that'
'in that case', see *entonces, pues*
'-ing' form of verbs in English, see
    Continuous Forms of Verb, Gerund,
    esp. 20.9; 'I saw her smoking', 18.2.5,
    20.6; used as noun, 18.6; 'talking
    doll'/'convincing argument', 19.4, 'a
    man speaking French', 20.3, 'while
    living in', 20.4.1; 'by working hard',
    20.4.2
'inside', see *dentro*
'it', see *lo*, Personal Pronouns, Object
'it's me', 'it's him', 11.6

'know', see *saber, conocer*

'less'/'least', see *menos*, Comparison,
    menor

'the less . . . the less', 5.11; 'less and less',
    5.12, translation problems, 5.14
'lest', 16.12.3b
'let', see *permitir*
'let's go'/'let's do', 17.5
'likewise', 2.3.4
'little' = 'not much', see *poco*; = *pequeño*,
    see *pequeño*
'look', see 'seem'
'lots', see 'many'
'love', 14.5.4, footnote

'many', see *mucho, la de*
'more'/'most', see *más*, Comparison; 'the
    more . . . the more', see *cuanto*, 'more
    and more . . .' 5.12; translation
    problems, 5.14
'moreover', 33.11.2
'much more/less', 5.10
'must' in suppositions, 21.3, 14.6.5, 14.7.2;
    see also *deber, haber que, tener que*

'neither', see *ni, tampoco*
'never', see *nunca*
'nevertheless', 33.11.3
'next', 32.10.6
'no', 'not', see *no*; = 'none of', see *ninguno*
'no one', see *nadie*
'none', see *ninguno*
'nor', see *ni*
'not even', see *ni*
'nothing', see *nada*

'of course' 33.11.11
'on', see *en, sobre*
'on condition that', 16.12.8
'on seeing/arriving', 18.3, 20.5
'on the contrary', 33.11.8a
'on the other hand', 33.11.9
'one' (impersonal pronoun), see *uno*,
    Impersonal *se*
'one another', 11.15b, 26.3
'only', see *sólo*
'or', see *o*
'order', see *mandar*
'other', see *otro*
'outside', see *fuera*
'own', see *propio*

'per cent', 10.7
'perhaps', 16.3.2
'play', see *jugar*
'possibly,' 16.3.2e
'probably', 16.3.2e
'provided that', 16.12.8a

'quickly', see *rápido*

Index of Spanish words and grammatical points

For the conjugation of individual verbs see 13.4 (irregular) and 13.5 (regular).

A preceding interrogation mark indicates a questionable form censured by grammarians, e.g. ?*contra más* . . ., ?*se los dije*.

a, main prepositional uses 34.1; Personal *a* Chapter 22; ?*problemas a resolver* 18.12; *a* used with certain verbs 18.2.3, 22.11; *a* + infinitive = 'if' 25.9e; use of *a* in adverbial phrases 31.3.2

a cambio de que 16.12.8a

a condición de que 16.12.8a

a despecho de que 16.12.9

a donde 24.9, 35.10 note (i)

a fin de que 16.12.3

a la . . . /*a lo* . . . (used to form adverbial phrases) 31.3.7

a lo mejor 16.3.2b

a menos que 16.12.8b, 25.9b

a modo de 3.3.12

a no ser que 16.12.8b

a personal, see Personal *a*

a pesar de que 16.12.9

a propósito 33.11.1

a que 16.12.3a

a solas 9.15 note (ii)

abajo 31.6.6

?*abajo de* (Lat. Am.) = *debajo de* 31.6.6

abolir 13.3.2

abrir(se) 26.7.1

aburrido 29.4.4

aburrirse de que . . . 26.4.2

acá 31.6.2

acabar with gerund 20.8.8; *acabo de hacerlo* or *lo acabo de hacer*? 11.14.4; compared with *acabarse* 26.7.2

acabáramos 16.15.3c

acaso = 'perhaps'16.3.2a; used to ask an ironic question 16.3.3

Accent (i.e. acute accent) 39.2; on diphthongs and triphthongs 39.2.2–3; doubtful cases 39.2.4; on demonstrative pronouns (*éste, ése, aquél*) 6.3; on *aislar, reunir, prohibir* 13.2.3; on question words 24.1; on adverbs in -*mente* 31.2.2; accent used to distinguish homonyms 39.2.6; for the dieresis (*ü*) see Dieresis

acercarse, pronouns with 11.8

-*aco* (suffix) 38.4

aconsejar 16.5.2c

acostumbrar 21.6, note (i), 16.5.2c

actuar, conjugation of 13.2.5

Acute Accent, see Accent

adelante 31.6.8

además 33.11.2

adentro 31.6.5

?*adentro de* (Lat. Am.) = *dentro de*, 31.6.5

Adjectival Participles (e.g. *andante*, *saliente*) 19.4

Adjectives Chapter 4; compared with nouns 4.1d, 3.3.11; forms of 4.2; adjectives ending in -*or* 4.2.1, especially note (i); adjectives ending in -*í* 4.2.2a; invariable adjectives 4.2.3, 4.4; invariable adjectives of colour 4.2.4; 'dark green/blue', etc. 4.3; *hirviendo* 4.4; compound adjectives 4.5; short forms of adjectives 4.6; agreement of adjectives, see Adjective Agreement; adjectives from countries 4.8.1; from towns 4.8.2; the suffix -*ísimo* 4.9; nouns used as adjectives 4.10; position of adjectives 4.11; position and change of meaning 4.11.8; adjectives found only before nouns 4.11.9; attributive adjectives 4.1c, 4.12; translating 'un-' 4.13. Comparison, see Comparison of Adjectives and Adverbs; *lo bueno/lo interesante* 7.2.1a; *lo guapa que es* 7.2.2; *ser* or *estar* with adjectives Chapter 29 *passim*; adjectives whose meaning is affected by use of *ser* or *estar* 29.4.4; adjectives used as adverbs 31.3.3;